D1478758

THE OTHER RENAISSANCE

THE OTHER RENAISSANCE

Italian Humanism between Hegel and Heidegger

ROCCO RUBINI

THE UNIVERSITY OF CHICAGO PRESS

CHICAGO AND LONDON

ROCCO RUBINI is assistant professor in the Department of Romance Languages and Literatures at the University of Chicago. He is the editor of *The Renaissance from an Italian Perspective: An Anthology of Essays, 1860–1968*.

The University of Chicago Press, Chicago 60637
The University of Chicago Press, Ltd., London
© 2014 by The University of Chicago
All rights reserved. Published 2014.
Printed in the United States of America

23 22 21 20 19 18 17 16 15 14   1 2 3 4 5

ISBN-13: 978-0-226-18613-9 (cloth)
ISBN-13: 978-0-226-18627-6 (e-book)
DOI: 10.7208/chicago/9780226186276.001.0001

Library of Congress Cataloging-in-Publication Data

Rubini, Rocco, author.
    The other Renaissance : Italian humanism between Hegel and Heidegger / Rocco Rubini.
        pages cm
    ISBN 978-0-226-18613-9 (cloth : alk. paper) — ISBN 978-0-226-18627-6 (e-book)
    1. Philosophy, Italian—20th century.   2. Philosophy, Italian—19th century.
    3. Humanism—Italy.   I. Title.
    B3601.R83 2014
    195—dc23

                                                          2014021324

♾ This paper meets the requirements of ANSI/NISO Z39.48-1992
(Permanence of Paper).

[L]a mente è come un terreno, che per quanto sia di fecondo ingegno, se tuttavia non s'ingrassa con la varia lettura, a capo di tempo si sterilisce.
—Giambattista Vico

[F]antasia concreta: l'attitudine a rivivere la vita degli altri, cosí come è realmente determinata, coi suoi bisogni, le sue esigenze, ecc., non per rappresentarla artisticamente, ma per comprenderla ed entrare in contatto intimo: anche per non far del male.
—Antonio Gramsci

CONTENTS

ACKNOWLEDGMENTS

M y greatest gratitude goes to a short list of mentors: Lucia Pietrosanti, for teaching me what culture and literature are all about; John Freccero, for reminding me, when necessary, that the study of Italian culture and literature is, indeed, a worthy and rewarding enterprise; Wolfgang Iser, for some very edifying walks around Lake Constance . . . and for those words; Giuseppe Mazzotta, for constant inspiration; and David Quint, for, among many other things, showing me the ropes of the profession. I am who I am, as an intellectual and scholar, thanks to the models they represent.

This book is in part about a recent past that would have been inaccessible to me were it not for long and repeated conversations with Michele Ciliberto, Brian P. Copenhaver, James Hankins, Ronald G. Witt, Enrico Castelli Gattinara, and Emilio Hidalgo-Serna. I thank all of them for generously sharing their recollections of and personal affection for the ever-influential men whose story is told in this book and who have become my mentors, too, in the process. Moreover, I have had the privilege of sharing my work and thoughts throughout the years with a number of engaged and congenial colleagues: Nancy S. Struever, Paul Richard Blum, Christopher S. Celenza, and Julius Kirshner. I am grateful for their support, their influence, and, most of all, their intellectual fellowship and willingness to allow our conversations to turn into lasting friendships. I also wish to acknowledge Wilhelm Büttemeyer and Elisabeth Blum for their useful comments on some portions of the final version of this book's manuscript.

For the details that have helped me bring this story to life, I owe a debt to the staff of Columbia University's Rare Book and Manuscript Library in New York, the Fondazione Giovanni Gentile in Rome, Archivi della Scuola Normale in Pisa, and Duke University's David M. Rubenstein

Rare Book and Manuscript Library in Durham. The writing of the book was supported generously by the Franke Institute for the Humanities in Chicago. Jen Paton, M. J. Devaney, and, especially, Catherine Skeen and Susan Tarcov have worked intensely to make this manuscript appealing to readers; among those readers are Arnold Davidson and Elizabeth Branch Dyson, whom I thank for believing in this project from the very moment they first heard about it.

This book was written in adverse circumstances and would never have been completed had it not been for the love of friends and family, especially Eleonora, my grandparents and uncles, and Mingo, Taniello, Nicola, Pietro, Spencer, Omri, Raffaello, Miguel, and Boris.

Last, my deepest and heartfelt love and gratitude go to my mother, a keen observer of the world and its inhabitants. I thank you for sharing with me every insight of yours regarding human beings and their ways . . . in short, for teaching me the true "humanism."

I dedicate this book to the memory of my father . . .

Some of the material in chapter 3 of this book was rehearsed in "Philology as Philosophy: The Sources of Ernesto Grassi's Postmodern Humanism," in *Humanisms, Posthumanisms, and Neohumanisms, Annali d'Italianistica* 26 (2008): 223–48, and "Humanism as *Philosophia (Perennis)*: Grassi's Platonic Rhetoric between Gadamer and Kristeller," *Philosophy and Rhetoric* 42, no. 3 (2009): 242–78, while a précis of this entire project appeared as "Humanism Is an Existentialism: Renaissance and Vichian Legacies in Italian Philosophy between Hegel and Heidegger," in *Italian Critical Theory, Annali d'Italianistica* 29 (2011): 431–58. All previously published material has been substantially revised and expanded in the present context. Unless otherwise noted, all translations are my own.

Works and archives frequently cited have been identified by the following abbreviations:

AEG   Archivio Eugenio Garin, Scuola Normale Superiore (Pisa).

AFGG   Archivio della Fondazione Giovanni Gentile per gli Studi Filosofici (Rome).

APEC   Archivio Privato Enrico Castelli (Rome).

CFI   Eugenio Garin, *Cronache di filosofia italiana*, 2 vols. (Rome: Laterza, 1997).

D   Enrico Castelli, *Diari*, ed. Enrico Castelli Gattinara Jr., 4 vols., *Archivio di filosofia* 65 (1997).

EG   Wilhelm Büttemeyer, *Ernesto Grassi: Humanismus zwischen Faschismus und Nationalsozialismus* (Freiburg: Karl Alber, 2009).

FKC   Brian P. Copenhaver and Rebecca Copenhaver, eds. and trans., *From Kant to Croce: Modern Philosophy in Italy, 1800–1950* (Toronto: University of Toronto Press, 2012).

FV   Enrico Castelli, *Filosofia della vita: Saggio di una critica dell'attualismo e di una teoria della pratica* (Rome: Angelo Signorelli, 1924).

GP   Eugenio Garin, *Giovanni Pico della Mirandola: Vita e dottrina* (Rome: Edizioni di Storia e Letteratura, 2011).

HBP   Hans Baron Papers, Duke University (Durham).

HIL   Francesco De Sanctis, *History of Italian Literature*, trans. Joan Redfern, 2 vols. (New York: Barnes and Noble, 1968).

HIP   Eugenio Garin, *History of Italian Philosophy*, ed. and trans. Giorgio Pinton, 2 vols. (Amsterdam-New York: Editions Rodopi, 2008).

IH   Eugenio Garin, *Italian Humanism: Philosophy and Civic Life in the
        Renaissance*, trans. Peter Munz (New York: Harper & Row, 1965).

IR   Eugenio Garin, *Interpretazioni del Rinascimento*, ed. Michele
        Ciliberto, 2 vols. (Rome: Edizioni di Storia e Letteratura), vol. 1.

MG   Ugo Spirito, *Machiavelli e Guicciardini* (Florence: Sansoni, 1968).

O   Bertrando Spaventa, *Opere*, ed. Francesco Valagussa (Milan: Bompiani,
        2008).

OF   Giovanni Gentile, *Opere filosofiche*, ed. Eugenio Garin (Milan:
        Garzanti, 1991).

PMF   Paul Oskar Kristeller, *The Philosophy of Marsilio Ficino*, trans.
        Virginia Conant (New York: Columbia University Press, 1943).

PMP   Ernesto Grassi, *Il problema della metafisica platonica* (Bari: Laterza,
        1932).

POKP   Paul Oskar Kristeller Papers, Columbia University (New York).

PS   Ernesto Grassi, *Primi scritti (1922–1946)*, ed. Ingrid Basso, Luca Bisin,
        and Massimo Marassi, 2 vols. (Naples: La Città del Sole, 2011), vol. 1.

RIP   *The Renaissance from an Italian Perspective: An Anthology of Essays,
        1860–1968*, ed. Rocco Rubini (Ravenna: Longo, 2014).

SFI   Giovanni Gentile, *Storia della filosofia italiana*, ed. Eugenio Garin,
        2 vols. (Florence: Sansoni, 1969).

SIP   Nicola Abbagnano, *Le sorgenti irrazionali del pensiero* (Genoa:
        Perrella, 1923).

SRTL   Paul Oskar Kristeller, *Studies in Renaissance Thought and Letters*,
        4 vols. (Rome: Edizioni di Storia e Letteratura, 1956–96).

SS   Vincenzo Cuoco, *Saggio storico sulla rivoluzione di Napoli*, ed.
        Antonino De Francesco (Manduria: Piero Lacaita, 1998).

UI   Eugenio Garin, *L'umanesimo italiano: Filosofia e vita civile nel
        Rinascimento* (Rome: Laterza, 1994).

VCR   Ugo Spirito, *La vita come ricerca* (Catanzaro: Rubbettino, 2007).

PREFACE

The Other Renaissance offers an introspective exploration of modern
Italian philosophy (1801–1947), an intellectual tradition, I argue, defined by a strenuous and longstanding confrontation with the legacy of
Italian Renaissance humanism, a confrontation informed by German
thought—mainly Hegel's idealism and Heidegger's 'existentialism'—as
it was apprehended and reworked in Italy. This project is rooted in what
was once a personal urge to reconnect (historically) and, possibly, reconcile (theoretically) the two core debates about 'humanism' which indel-
ibly informed the disciplinary frameworks I encountered as a student of
both comparative literature and Renaissance studies. I am referring to
two sets of long-distance quarrels or, rather, misunderstandings that simultaneously erupted in 1946/1947. One of these exchanges pitted (in
French reception) Jean-Paul Sartre's 'humanistic existentialism' against
Martin Heidegger's 'antihumanism,' with far-reaching consequences for
the reconfiguration of so-called Continental philosophy (and its American
derivative, 'theory') in the latter part of the twentieth century. The other
pitted Eugenio Garin (1909–2004) against Paul Oskar Kristeller (1905–99),
whose disagreement regarding the essence of fifteenth-century humanism
(was it philosophy or not?) would shape the postwar rebirth and professionalization of Renaissance studies on both sides of the Atlantic.

The story told in this book, about the emergence of a self-consciously
construed 'Italian' philosophical tradition enabled by combining nineteenth-century and interwar philosophy and Renaissance historiography,
will reveal that the displacement of Renaissance humanism in philosophical discourse is not just lamentable and, arguably, unwarranted, but
largely happenstance on historical grounds. At the same time, it is my am-

bition that a better grasp of the idiosyncrasies pertaining to Italian philosophical culture will inspire an attempt to challenge the 'Cartesian wall'
that still hampers productive dialogue among scholars currently seeking
to contextualize our modern (or postmodern) condition from the vantage
point of different disciplines (intellectual history, philosophy, Renaissance
scholarship, and Italian studies). In the aftermath of the postmodern moment, perhaps the defamiliarization that Italian philosophy affords in its
co-mingling of Continental and Renaissance thought will help prevent the
study of pre-Cartesian intellectual 'modernity' from becoming a form of
antiquarianism.

Recent international interest in Italian philosophy, which has been on
a notable upswing, provides some context for this study. A pioneering attempt to introduce the Anglo-American audience to Italian thought as the
'internal Other' in the body of Continental philosophy is *Recoding Metaphysics: The New Italian Philosophy*, a collection of contributions from a
roster of thinkers who have since become better known, translated, and
discussed by readers worldwide (Gianni Vattimo, Umberto Eco, Massimo
Cacciari, Emanuele Severino, and so on). In her introduction to this volume, Giovanna Borradori attributes the "perpetuation of a limited and dis-
continuous interest" in Italian philosophy to the provincializing consequences of the "Fascist dictatorial adventure," the limited diffusion of the
Italian language, and the "clear predominance in [Italian] exportation of
'visual' over 'verbal' messages."[1] These factors still complicate the daunt-
ing task outside Italy of attempting to reconstruct the complex "internal
horizon of referents in which the discourse" of modern Italian philosophy
has participated (and, it appears, still does)—a feat that requires a thorough "genealogical reconstruction."

Given the space constraints of an introductory essay, Borradori could
not, obviously, provide an exhaustive reconstruction, but she leaves us
with the insightful recommendation that the "essential incompatibil-
ity" of the Italian perspective with the Franco-German "hegemonic" discourse be traced back to Italian thinkers' realignment with Giambattista
Vico's anti-Cartesian stance at the outset of an enlightened modernity:
"Whereas France elected itself the land of rationalism, England the cradle of empiricism, and Germany the guardian of metaphysics, Italy, with
historicism, withdrew into an imaginary past, abandoning the role of cultural catalyzer that during the Renaissance had placed it as the center of

---

1. Giovanna Borradori, "Introduction," in *Recoding Metaphysics: The New Italian Philosophy*, ed. Giovanna Borradori (Evanston, IL: Northwestern University Press, 1988), 1–2.

the European *koinē*."[2] It was thus Vico who endowed Italian thought with
an "autochthonous" hermeneutical "matrix," an "anti-rationalist" bias, a
"'humanistic' *modus*" that would be cultivated, all the way down to Benedetto Croce, as a "hereditary given, ingrained in its genetic patrimony."

Additional collections eventually followed Borradori's, all equally invested in stressing, albeit with discrete emphases, the notion of an Italian philosophical 'difference.'[3] And a number of scattered initiatives and
publications are now helping to reconstruct the mosaic of the past and
future Italian intellectual horizon. Among these are translations of an
ever-widening pool of contemporary Italian thinkers; also noteworthy is
the "Series in Contemporary Italian Philosophy" from SUNY Press, which
is now, with its eighth volume under way, beginning to reach back to an
earlier generation of Italian thinkers; and the *Annali d'Italianistica* has
produced two special issues that seek to promote fruitful conversation between philosophy and Italian studies in the United States.[4] Yet what may
truly open the study of Italian philosophy to the previously uninitiated is
the publication of three indispensable reference books: the English translation of Eugenio Garin's massive *History of Italian Philosophy*, a work that
has been standard in its genre since its first edition in 1947; Brian P. Copenhaver and Rebecca Copenhaver's *From Kant to Croce: Modern Philosophy in Italy (1800–1950)*, an anthology of well-selected canonical texts of
nineteenth- and early twentieth-century Italian philosophy, with critical
introductions; and, most recently, Roberto Esposito's *Living Thought: The
Origins and Actuality of Italian Philosophy*, a work that aims to define a
specific "Italian theory" that is consistent with a philosophical canon that
includes, besides Renaissance humanists, Machiavelli, Giordano Bruno,
Vico, Vincenzo Cuoco, Bertrando Spaventa, Francesco De Sanctis, Croce,

2. Borradori, "Introduction," 5.

3. See Paolo Virno and Michael Hardt, eds., *Radical Thought in Italy: A Potential
Thought* (Minneapolis, MN: University of Minnesota Press, 1996); and Lorenzo Chiesa and
Alberto Toscano, eds., *The Italian Difference: Between Nihilism and Politics* (Melbourne,
Australia: Re-Press, 2009). See also Thomas Harrison and Peter Carravetta, eds., *Contempo-
rary Italian Philosophy: Critique of Ideology and Hermeneutics*, special issue of *Graduate
Faculty Philosophy Journal* 10 (1984).

4. See Massimo Lollini, ed., *Humanisms, Posthumanisms, and Neohumanisms*, *Annali d'Italianistica* 26 (2008); and Alessandro Carrera, ed., *Italian Critical Theory*, *Annali d'Italianistica* 29 (2011). Titles in the SUNY series, edited by Silvia Benso and Brian
Schroeder, include an introductory collection titled *Contemporary Italian Philosophy: Crossing the Borders of Ethics, Politics, and Religion* (2007), Carlo Sini's *Ethics of Writing* (2009),
Between Nihilism and Politics: The Hermeneutics of Gianni Vattimo (2010); and, at the time
of this writing, a translation of Luigi Pareyson, *Truth and Interpretation* (2013), a seminal
text (originally published in 1971) in the philosophical hermeneutics developed in Italy.

Giovanni Gentile, and Antonio Gramsci. According to Esposito, these are some of the more or less familiar names that an international audience must learn to approach *together* if it wishes to understand biopolitics—the theory propounded by Esposito, Giorgio Agamben, and Antonio Negri, to name a famous few—on its own terms.

The Other Renaissance, conceived and written as some of these texts were published, draws on, integrates, and expands this recent scholarship. It provides the Vichian genealogical reconstruction called for by Borradori, and it reintegrates Garin's *History* as a primary source, indeed, as the belated fruit of that genealogy, which began in the early nineteenth century, when Italian thinkers first set their sights on an intellectual history of their own as they embarked on a quest for national and spiritual unity. Some of the philosophical literature pertaining to this journey, which extends from Spaventa and De Sanctis to the competing twentieth-century intellectual alternatives of Gentile, Croce, and Gramsci, is usefully brought together in *From Kant to Croce*, a publication itself inspired by the realization that "Pico and Garin were both Italian philosophers" (*FKC*, ix). The present work, and any other work on this topic that follows, owes a debt to the editors of *From Kant to Croce*, for converting the convoluted lexicon in which Italian thought has expressed itself into an international language—the first necessary step in the 'cultural translation' of Italian philosophy differently, but complementarily, pursued in Roberto Esposito's *Living Thought* and in this study.

Writing two decades after Borradori, and with an eye to recent developments on U.S. campuses, Esposito feels justified in announcing an intellectual shift toward Italian theory. In support of such a shift he points to the difficulties encountered by both the analytic and the Continental brands of thought as they attempt, and fail, to renew their paradigms. This is a trend most prominent in French theory, once hegemonic, but now clearly in its death throes, having devolved into a "repetitive and even self-referential" discourse. Death by implosion was to be expected, claims Esposito, given the tendency of modern philosophy since Hegel—through the likes of Wittgenstein, Heidegger, and Rorty—to place "itself in the self-confuting framework of its own end, yielding to that attraction for the 'post' that dominates the entire semantics of late modernity."[5]

Generally speaking, according to Esposito, the anomalousness of Ital-

5. Roberto Esposito, *Living Thought: The Origins and Actuality of Italian Philosophy*, trans. Zakiya Hanafi (Stanford: Stanford University Press, 2012), 6. Esposito's book, which was written with a double audience in mind, American and Italian, was originally published in Italian in 2010.

ian thought can be attributed to geographical and historical conditions. Drawing on Gilles Deleuze's notion of "geophilosophy," Esposito focuses on the peculiar relationship between philosophy and territory in Italy, where "territory" and "nation" hardly ever coincided.[6] This point has merit: with Dante, Petrarch, Machiavelli, Bruno, and Vico, Italian thought developed in an institutional void, and may thus be termed essentially "deterritorialized." Nevertheless, it is difficult to agree with Esposito's assertion that there are absolutely no ties between Italian philosophy and the nation. Indeed, Esposito himself hoists the flag of his biopolitics firmly on a canon of Italian thinkers that was put together between the Risorgimento and Fascist periods in congruence with a national cause. It is the latter circumstance that until recently has kept contemporary Italian thinkers from branding their thought as distinctively 'Italian.' If it is possible now, it is because scholars in Italy have recently had some success in dismantling the purported 'provincialism' of Italian thought and at countering a longtime tendency to superimpose judgments of fascism on judgments of individual philosophers.

More fascinating is Esposito's claim that because of its supranational qualities (in the early modern period) Italian thought is out of step with respect to the beginning and unfolding of mainstream philosophical 'modernity.' Long before the advent of Cartesianism, Italian thought was established in its extroversion toward the historical and political world and openness to "the influences of people and the force of circumstance"; thus it partook only tangentially of the strict epistemological framework in which modern philosophy developed. Here Esposito draws on the work of Ernesto Grassi, a longtime collaborator of Heidegger and among the first to theorize an Italian philosophical eccentricity since the Renaissance, and the work of Garin, whose definition of Italian thought as a "civil philosophy" he co-opts for the sake of a new theoretical age able to overcome the "postmodern celebration of its own end" and "resume functioning in an affirmative mode."[7]

In *The Other Renaissance*, I focus closely on the collaborative efforts of Grassi and Garin to effect a postnationalist rehabilitation of Italian Renaissance and modern thought. I complement this by providing what Esposito does not in his thought-provoking, but strictly theoretical, redressing: namely, a detailed historical account of how Italian philosophy came

6. Esposito, *Living Thought*, 20. For the work that made the notion of 'geophilosophy' current in Italian philosophy, see Massimo Cacciari, *Geofilosofia dell'Europa* (Milan: Adelphi, 2003).

7. Esposito, *Living Thought*, 11.

to perceive itself as a distinct tradition. Such an account is necessary to
ensure that cultural determinations ('Italian') and their specifications ('difference') are not raised to the status of mental categories or seen as markers of incommensurability—which can happen despite the best intentions.
Most important, as French thinkers themselves bemoan the end of the
French philosophical "moment," we must resist the temptation to reinstate
Italian philosophy as the next stage in a renewed, albeit now open-ended,
dialectic of spirit.[8] To the contrary, we have before us the opportunity to
attempt something still largely untried and, possibly, more ambitious in
what it might achieve for our intellectual self-awareness: a comparative
(intercultural) approach to the study of the history of philosophy.

8. Alain Badiou discusses the French "moment" in philosophy, as one that followed
"Greek" and "German" moments, in *The Adventure of French Philosophy*, trans. and ed.
Bruno Bosteels (London: Verso, 2012), li. The waning of French cultural "exception" is also
discussed in Tony Chafer and Emmanuel Godin, eds., *The End of the French Exception?
Decline and Revival of the "French Model"* (New York: Palgrave, 2010); and Donald Morrison
and Antoine Compagnon, *The Death of French Culture* (Cambridge, UK: Polity Press, 2010).

How We Came to Be *Such As We Are and Not Otherwise*

If only Italy had lent an ear to Giambattista Vico, and if, as in the time of the Renaissance, she had served as Europe's guide, would not our intellectual destiny have been different?

When French historian Paul Hazard pointed to this unrealized possibility in intellectual history, in a work published posthumously in 1946, Europe was again anxiously anticipating a renaissance.[1] Busy printing presses testified to the fact that thought had not lain dormant in the wake of catastrophe. Established thinkers, having hastily cleared their consciences, jumped at what was possibly their last chance to renegotiate in person the terms of their philosophical legacies. At the same time, their erstwhile students, having matured into independent scholars, were keen on seeing the anticipated intellectual rebirth coincide with a generational renewal. What all thinkers had in common despite differing agendas was a need for self-affirmation, and so headlong confidence prevailed over caution, to the detriment of debate and genuine conversation.

Nowhere, arguably, is this trend more visible than in the history of that body of thought referred to as 'Continental,' whose rebirth Jean Beaufret promoted with a question, also in 1946: "How can we restore meaning to the word 'humanism'?" Beaufret's question is related to Hazard's, but differs in that it was not rhetorical. It sought an enlightened answer from a specific addressee: Martin Heidegger.[2]

1. Paul Hazard, *La pensée européenne au XVIIIe siècle: De Montesquieu à Lessing*, 3 vols. (Paris: Boivin, 1946), 1:46.
2. Martin Heidegger, "Letter on 'Humanism,'" in *Pathmarks*, ed. William McNeill, trans. Frank A. Capuzzi (Cambridge: Cambridge University Press, 1998), 241. Beaufret addressed this and other queries to Heidegger in a letter dated 10 November 1946.

The circumstances surrounding this exchange are well known, as are its consequences. Beaufret had hoped to facilitate a conversation between Heidegger and Jean-Paul Sartre, who had for some time, it was thought, been misappropriating the substance and thrust of Heidegger's philosophy, most recently in a controversial lecture, "Existentialism Is a Humanism," delivered on 29 October 1945 at the Club Maintenant in Paris.[3] In his response to Beaufret, the "Letter on 'Humanism,'" Heidegger confirmed these suspicions. He claimed that Sartre's proposition regarding the precedence of *existentia* over *essentia* could not undergird "existentialism," if by the label one meant a philosophy fit to obviate the strictures of "metaphysical subjectivism" and the consequent "oblivion of being."[4] Instead, in Heidegger's opinion, everything had to be rethought more radically, starting with the very notion of "humanism," itself the marker of an unquestioned presupposition, since Plato, regarding the true essence of man.

HUMANISM AS CARTESIANISM

Heidegger, after providing a brief survey of "humanism" in its different historical manifestations, including Greek *paideia*, Latin *humanitas*, and the Hellenism (*studium humanitatis*) of the "so-called Renaissance of the fourteenth and fifteenth centuries in Italy," famously concluded:

> Every humanism is either grounded in a metaphysics or is itself made to be the ground of one. Every determination of the essence of the human being that already presupposes an interpretation of beings without asking about the truth of being, whether knowingly or not, is metaphysical. The result is that what is peculiar to all metaphysics, specifically with respect to the way the essence of the human being is determined, is that it is "humanistic." Accordingly, every humanism

3. The lecture was published in 1946. See Jean-Paul Sartre, *Existentialism Is a Humanism*, trans. Carol Macomber (New Haven: Yale University Press, 2007). Insight into Beaufret's enduring conversation with Heidegger can be drawn from Jean Beaufret, *Dialogue avec Heidegger*, 4 vols. (Paris: Minuit, 1973–85). One of the volumes has an English translation: Jean Beaufret, *Dialogue with Heidegger: Greek Philosophy*, trans. Mark Sinclair (Bloomington: Indiana University Press, 2006). For an assessment of Beaufret's mediation of Heidegger's thought in France, see Pierre Jacerme, "The Thoughtful Dialogue between Martin Heidegger and Jean Beaufret: A New Way of Doing Philosophy," in *French Interpretations of Heidegger: An Exceptional Reception*, ed. David Pettigrew and François Raffoul (Albany: State University of New York Press, 2008), 59–72.
4. Heidegger, "Letter on 'Humanism,'" 250. For Sartre's famous claim, see *Existentialism Is a Humanism*, 22.

remains metaphysical. In defining the humanity of the human being, humanism not only does not ask about the relation of being to the essence of the human being; because of its metaphysical origin humanism even impedes the question by neither recognizing nor understanding it.[5]

The unity of metaphysics and 'humanism' that Heidegger perceived throughout Western thought was the impasse his philosophy would set out to "overcome" or attempt to "twist out" from.[6] Whether 'humanism' would be retained in the process depended on the ability to rethink the essential *humanitas* of *homo humanus* more "primordially," "restoring to the word . . . a historical sense that is older than its oldest meaning chronologically reckoned."[7]

The reception in France of this philosophical charter was dramatic and telling. If such was his intention, Heidegger indeed managed to momentarily divert attention away from his political allegiances. What was more surprising, perhaps even to him, was that he came to replace Sartre as the leading philosopher of France. And so French Heideggerianism was born, a movement identifying with the sentiment (for it was not properly a program) we call 'antihumanism,' which largely contributed to our historical self-consciousness as postmoderns.[8] If Heidegger called for 'humanism' to be circumvented (or, better, reinvented), however, it is not immediately clear why we should have felt the need to jettison 'modernity' in its entirety, as well.[9] And which 'modernity,' at that?

Recent reappraisals of the (mythic, never actual) confrontation between

5. Heidegger, "Letter on 'Humanism,'" 245.

6. Heidegger's stance toward the Western philosophical tradition lends itself to different interpretations depending on whether the stress is laid on his notion of *Überwindung* or *Verwindung*. On this point see Gianni Vattimo, *The End of Modernity*, trans. Jon Snyder (Baltimore: Johns Hopkins University Press, 1988), 40–41.

7. Heidegger, "Letter on 'Humanism,'" 262.

8. On Heidegger, French thought, and the postmodern moment, see Gregory Bruce Smith, *Nietzsche, Heidegger, and the Transition to Postmodernity* (Chicago: University of Chicago Press, 1996); and Stuart Sim, "Postmodernism and Philosophy," in *The Routledge Companion to Postmodernism* (New York: Routledge, 2011), 3–14.

9. Debate surrounding the correct interpretation of Heidegger's "Letter" is still alive today. See for instance the essays collected in Bruno Pinchard, ed., *Heidegger et la question de l'humanisme: Faits, concepts, débats* (Paris: Presses universitaires de France, 2005), and Stéphane Toussaint, *Humanismes, antihumanismes: De Ficin à Heidegger* (Paris: Les Belles Lettres, 2009). Heidegger's own misgivings regarding the possibility of transcending 'humanism' altogether are more clearly visible in the first draft of his letter, which was published in French translation as "Lettre à Jean Beaufret," *Fontaine* 63, no. 11 (1947): 786–804.

Sartre and Heidegger hint at a willingness, finally, to ask these questions, as philosophers currently stress the "paradox" of the encounter between the French rationalist and the German phenomenological traditions. Heidegger, they explain, provided the French with "the means of breaking out from a Cartesian-inspired reflexive philosophy, and of thinking the concrete situation of human beings in the world and in history."[10] This led French thought to attempt a complex intellectual emancipation over many decades, which eventually spawned the American brand of Continental philosophy (or theory).[11] With his aggregate of existentialism and humanism, Sartre had provided not much more, ultimately, than an *oxymoronic* "existential Cartesianism."

What I have sketched briefly in these few pages serves as an introduction, albeit provisional, to the critical misgivings that inspire the investigation pursued in this book. I write in response to an immense yet unexplored ambiguity inherent in the postwar Franco-German reflection on being-human: its complete disregard (with the exception of a passing reference by Heidegger) for the Renaissance and for the 'humanism' associated with it.[12] The neglect is baffling, not only because the French made notable contributions to that epoch and intellectual movement, but because Descartes premised his cogito-centered revolution in confrontation with the humanist alternative as he conceived it:

> But I thought I had already given enough time to languages and likewise to reading the works of the ancients, both their histories and their fables. For conversing with those of past centuries is much the same as travelling. It is good to know something of the customs of various peoples, so that we may judge our own more soundly and not think

10. Françoise Dastur, "The Reception and Nonreception of Heidegger in France," in Pettigrew and Raffoul, *French Interpretations of Heidegger*, 267.

11. For an interpretation of French theory as being, in the main, an American construct, see François Cusset, *French Theory*, trans. Jeff Fort (Minneapolis: University of Minnesota Press, 2008).

12. Interestingly, in presenting the "Letter on 'Humanism'" to the French public, Beaufret calls on Montaigne only to dismiss him: "Ce sera la méthode de Heidegger. Montaigne écrivait déjà: 'Toute science a ses principes présupposés par où le jugement humain est bridé de toutes parts.' Mais, dans ce phénomène de la 'présupposition,' Montaigne ne voyait encore qu'une occasion de scepticisme. Il faudra attendre l'époque contemporaine pour que l'implicite devienne le lieu privilégié de la recherche." Jean Beaufret, "Martin Heidegger et le problème de la vérité," *Fontaine* 63, no. 11 (1947): 760–61. For a sustained attempt to relate Montaigne and Heidegger, see Marc Foglia, "L'historicité de l'homme: Montaigne et Heidegger, un dialogue qui n'a pas eu lieu," in Pinchard, *Heidegger et la question de l'humanisme*, 107–33.

that everything contrary to our own ways is ridiculous and irrational, as those who have seen nothing of the world ordinarily do. But one who spends too much time travelling eventually becomes a stranger in his own country; and one who is too curious about the practices of past ages usually remains quite ignorant about those of the present. . . . [T]hose who regulate their conduct by examples drawn from these works are liable to fall into the excesses of the knights-errant in our tales of chivalry, and conceive plans beyond their powers.[13]

In the brisk, impatient account of his formative years that begins the *Discourse on the Method*, the "first modern philosopher" justified his dour, solitary, and book-bereft defection from the Renaissance enterprise by suggesting that the past was no longer of interest, nor were intercultural exchange and *con*-genial (transhistorical) recognition.

These facts call our attention to what a student of Renaissance thought, if not a philosopher, is bound to perceive as another oxymoronic contradiction: the conflation of Cartesianism and 'humanism.' In other words, if our postmodern efforts to recover man's situated consciousness have been directed at precipitating the bankruptcy of Cartesian subjectivism, it is to be lamented that French philosophers would not seek a historical precedent for their endeavors.[14] If they had sought such a precedent, Hazard seems to suggest, they possibly would have discerned their own as a Renaissance endeavor, that is, they would have identified their anti-Cartesianism as in fact a 'humanism' and, therefore, on historical grounds, as a pre- or early 'modern' ambition.

HUMANISM AS VICHIANISM

Though not himself a Renaissance scholar, Hazard's pioneering interest in a comparative evaluation of the Enlightenment led him to venture where philosophers seldom do. In Italy he encountered the work of Giambattista Vico, a thinker who appealed to Hazard, as to many others, for standing on his own in stark contrast to the self-contained whole of Cartesian mo-

13. René Descartes, *The Philosophical Writings of Descartes*, trans. John Cottingham, Robert Stoothoff, and Dugald Murdoch, 3 vols. (Cambridge: Cambridge University Press, 1984–91), 1:113–14.
14. On the French quest for an anti- or postsubjectivism via Heidegger, see Ethan Kleinberg, "The 'Letter on Humanism': Reading Heidegger in France," in *Situating Existentialism*, ed. Jonathan Judaken and Robert Bernasconi (New York: Columbia University Press, 2012), 386–413.

dernity. It is no surprise that, traditionally, historians, more than philosophers, have been drawn to this apparently solitary figure. Vico insisted, over and against Descartes, that the study of the past matters to philosophy, and not simply for erudition's sake. With his theory of the *ricorso*, the repetitive pattern of history, Vico set the past squarely against the horizon of our future expectations. It was ideas such as this, alongside his forcefully pursued reconnection of philology and philosophy and the preeminence he allotted to imagination over reason, that fueled the legend of Vico's *incomparable* genius. This same legend, however, is also what distracted most self-avowed Vichians from conducting a systematic inquiry into what was generally intuited regarding Vico's own sources and legacy: namely, Vico's connection to the Renaissance, or more specifically, the possibility of seeing his anti-Cartesianism, to some extent at least, as an attempted philosophical vindication of Renaissance humanism, and the extent to which Italians failed to capitalize on the Vichian alternative.

To understand the relevance of Hazard's comment (in hindsight, more akin to a provocation) in the context of the postwar debate on 'humanism,' it is necessary to reintegrate the Italian perspective. And this because, as this study will show, modern Italian philosophy developed as an increasingly confident Vichianism, invested in a Renaissance precedent that Italians trained themselves to enliven, reactivate, and improve upon, in order to advance or contrast their interlocking political ambitions: unity (Risorgimento), empire (Fascism), and democracy (Republicanism). To illustrate this, I will describe how, at the turn of the nineteenth century, Italian thinkers first turned programmatically to Vico in reaction to the 'revolutionary' standards of French thought and politics, but I will focus most closely on the outcome of this quest in 1946–47. It was in the latter period that a generation of Italian existentialists came together to produce, collaboratively, a philosophical interpretation of Renaissance humanism. This interpretation drew inspiration from both the Italian Vichian tradition and Heidegger, but despite its philosophical origins it was neglected by philosophers, and instead went on to steer a postwar reorientation of Renaissance scholarship.

By focusing on the Renaissance and on humanism, *The Other Renaissance* will certainly clarify the so-called Italian 'difference' vis-à-vis the main strands of Continental philosophy (French, German, and their American elaborations), and yet my chief aim points elsewhere: I seek to reintegrate what I see as a savvy, historicist Italian perspective on 'humanism' circa 1946 and by doing this to deepen our comprehension and refine our criticism of the foundational debate that emerged, to endure, at that time. Meanwhile, by bringing the Italian perspective into the conversation, I hope to enable a much needed rapprochement between students of Continental and Renaissance philosophy, something both parties appear to have been seeking in recent years as they engage in some public stock-taking. Just as a new generation of philosophers and intellectual historians feels, today, a need to probe the sources of our mistrust of our 'modern' heritage (i.e., our 'antihumanism'), for their part, students of Renaissance humanism are starting to see themselves as having safeguarded the pre-Cartesian origins of this heritage for too long in theoretical isolation.[15]

It is worth remarking from the outset that if Italian philosophical interest in the Renaissance had been motivated solely by fanatical, blind patriotism, as is often assumed, that perspective would be of little use to us now. Rather, what makes the phenomenon we might call the 'Italians' Renaissance' meaningful, particularly in relation to our disillusionment with a protracted antihumanism, is that patriotic Italians did not view the Renaissance unconditionally, that it was with much resistance, rather, that Italian thinkers came to appreciate the intellectual potential of pre-Cartesian strands of thought. When the Risorgimento, Italy's nineteenth-century unification movement, first elected the Renaissance as its antecedent, it did so negatively. The love of country that promoted the construal, a posteriori, of a continuous intellectual tradition was redirected internally *against* the Renaissance man—against those disengaged intellectuals of the Quattrocento and Cinquecento who were perceived as having pursued the cult of literary form to the detriment of the *patria*.

This study shows, then, that among philosophers Italian intellectual identity was founded on an original 'Renaissance shame' and the attempt to recover from it. This de facto antihumanism, although checked and diluted at various points, did not entirely dissipate until Quattrocento humanism's anti-Scholasticism, which had engendered its own (Vichian) tradition in Italy, was rediscovered as the plausible historical background of an alternative philosophical 'modernity' that could now be reclaimed for the antifoundational pursuits of mainstream European existential thought. Obversely (not contrary) to Sartre, who said that existentialism

15. See Stefanos Geroulanos, *An Atheism That Is Not Humanist Emerges in French Thought* (Stanford: Stanford University Press, 2010), for a work that investigates every nook and cranny of the 'humanism' debate in France. Interestingly for our purposes, it appears that there was no concern for Renaissance humanism in the matter. For an acute assessment of the current state of Renaissance scholarship, see Christopher S. Celenza, *The Lost Italian Renaissance: Humanists, Historians, and Latin's Legacy* (Baltimore: Johns Hopkins University Press, 2004).

is a humanism, Italians came to maintain that (Renaissance) humanism is an existentialism. This difference, a crucial one, reflects the historicist bent of Italian philosophy but ultimately prevented it from participating in the postmodern moment.

Being sidelined was not new. Italian philosophers never figured prominently, if at all, in the canon of Western thought, and to understand why we can look further back once again to the reception of the *counterinitiative* that emerged from Descartes's *poêle*. Jacob Brucker's *Historia critica philosophiae* (1742–44), arguably the prototype of all modern histories of philosophy, was written at the end of what was, perhaps, a period unconsciously attracted to Cartesianism.[16] Brucker's guiding assumptions in this work—whose last installment coincided with the publication of the definitive edition of Vico's *New Science*—are strictly epistemological and depend on the notion of a "system of philosophy." Brucker draws a line (but does not attempt to justify it) between what counts as philosophy and what doesn't, and what he admires in the true philosopher is the ability to emancipate himself from "hollow and impure tradition" through meditative withdrawal, in order to grasp truth by means of reason alone.[17]

As has been recently noted, Brucker defined the scope of 'philosophy' more narrowly than how people actually experienced it in antiquity and in the Renaissance (and in the present day), with the result that the history of philosophy was born abridged, riddled with awkward silences.[18] In philosophical historiography, the longest of these silences (periods allegedly marked by unphilosophical thought) occur between Hellenistic thought and Plotinus's Neoplatonism, and between Ockham and Descartes. In fact, at times one might wish that Rome and the Italian Renaissance were simply omitted, these periods providing moments of leisure for the historians, as they subject unnamed Quattrocento humanists and their philosophically weak heirs—from Pico della Mirandola and Marsilio Ficino to Giordano Bruno and Tommaso Campanella, just to name a preferred few—to a sound thrashing for their alleged superstitions, inconsistencies,

16. On the early history of Descartes's reception and his contemporaries' inability to notice that a revolution was in the making, see Daniel Garber, "Descartes, the Aristotelians, and the Revolution That Did Not Happen in 1637," *Monist* 71, no. 4 (1988): 471–86.

17. Leo Catana, "The Concept 'System of Philosophy': The Case of Jacob Brucker's Historiography of Philosophy," *History and Theory* 44, no. 1 (2005): 75.

18. Catana, "Concept 'System of Philosophy,'" 77. See also Christopher S. Celenza, "What Counted as Philosophy in the Italian Renaissance? The History of Philosophy, the History of Science, and Styles of Life," *Critical Inquiry* 39, no. 2 (2013): 367–401.

and trivialities. This became standard in the historiographical tradition that Brucker launched, from Wilhelm Gottlieb Tennemann to Wilhelm Windelband, and it is true of Hegel's *Vorlesungen* as well.[19]

Given the distinct Cartesian origins of this prejudicial neglect, it might be expected that Italians would react once Vico was thoroughly assimilated to the national cause. And they did, by beginning to articulate the *integrative* value of Italian philosophical difference and exception. For example, what was perhaps the first programmatic apology of Vichian philosophy, authored by Vincenzo Cuoco, took the form of a reprimand letter addressed (but perhaps never actually dispatched) to Joseph Marie de Gérando, who had overlooked the Italian thinker in his *Histoire comparée des systèmes de philosophie* (1804).[20] Similarly and perhaps more emblematically, Baldassarre Poli's first extensive history of Italian philosophy, published in 1836 as *Supplements*, was an addendum of 894 pages tacked on to the Italian translation of Tennemann's *Grundriss der Geschichte der Philosophie*. Tennemann, too, was faulted for having omitted the Italian Renaissance and, most egregiously, Vico.[21] This was a trend that would continue into the twentieth century as well. For example, Benedetto Croce dedicated *The Philosophy of Giambattista Vico* (1911), which finally and firmly put Vico on the map, to Windelband with the "expectation and hope" that the "gaps" in the latter's history be "filled."[22] In simple terms, Vico functioned as a kind of Trojan horse, a way to breach the heavily

19. To this day, the student of philosophy will see this trend reflected in university course offerings and reading lists, which are now, lamentably, pared down to a bare minimum. For Brucker's influence, see Leo Catana, *The Historiographical Concept 'System of Philosophy': Its Origin, Nature, Influence, and Legitimacy* (Leiden: E. J. Brill, 2008), chap. 6. A thorough, multivolume survey of the history of philosophical historiography through the centuries was launched under the direction of Giovanni Santinello. For the section concerning early modernity up until Brucker, see Gregorio Piaia and Giovanni Santinello, eds., *Models of the History of Philosophy*, 2 vols. (Dordrecht: Springer, 2011).

20. See Vincenzo Cuoco, "Abbozzi di lettere a Jean Marie De Gérando sulla filosofia vichiana," in *Epistolario (1790–1817)* (Rome: Laterza, 2007), 345–62.

21. See Baldassarre Poli, *Supplimenti al Manuale della storia della filosofia di Guglielmo Tennemann: Saggio storico* (Milan: Antonio Fontana, 1836). On Poli, see Gregorio Piaia, "Baldassarre Poli e l'eclettismo fra Italia e Francia," in *I filosofi e la genesi della coscienza culturale della 'nuova Italia' (1799–1900)* (Naples: Istituto Italiano per gli Studi Filosofici, 1997), 41–57; and Ilario Tolomio, *Italorum sapientia: L'idea di esperienza nella storiografia filosofica italiana dell'età moderna* (Catanzaro: Rubbettino, 1999), 159–71.

22. Benedetto Croce, *The Philosophy of Giambattista Vico*, trans. R. G. Collingwood (New York: Russell & Russell, 1964), viii. Windelband in fact briefly refers to Vico in relating Rousseau and Herder. See Wilhelm Windelband, A *History of Philosophy*, trans. James H. Tufts (New York: Macmillan, 1901), 526.

guarded citadel of the history of philosophy. The assumption was that if Vico could get 'in,' then the entire Italian intellectual legacy, Renaissance and modern, could be smuggled in with him.

If these preliminary observations on the historiographical trajectory of Vichianism allow us to point to 'exclusion' as defining the Italian experience of philosophy, then the question arises: what, exactly, deserved inclusion? A superficial answer to this question would point to a specific doctrine or to a roster of neglected Italian thinkers, but a better answer can be found by looking at Vico's most direct or 'personal' confrontation with Descartes, which occurred in a commissioned autobiography in 1725. Here, evidently reacting against what he perceived as the anti(Renaissance)-humanism displayed in the *Discourse on the Method*, Vico resurrected Descartes for a face-to-face bout:

> We shall not here feign what René Descartes craftily feigned as to the method of his studies simply in order to exalt his own philosophy and mathematics and degrade all the other studies included in divine and human erudition. Rather, with the candor proper to a *historian*, we shall narrate plainly and step by step the entire series of Vico's studies, in order that the proper and natural causes of his *particular development* [*tale e non altra riuscita*] as a man of letters may be known.[23]

And in a 1731 addendum to the same, he defended his decision to write an autobiography, commenting (again in the third person):

> [A]s may be seen, he wrote it as a philosopher, meditating the causes, natural and moral, and the occasions of fortune; why even from childhood he had felt an inclination for certain studies and an aversion from others; what opportunities and obstacles had advanced or retarded his progress; and lastly the effect of his own exertions in right directions, which were destined later to bear fruit in those reflections on which he built his final work, the *New Science*, which was to demonstrate that his intellectual life *was bound to have been such as it was and not otherwise* [*tale e non altra*].[24]

23. Giambattista Vico, *The Autobiography of Giambattista Vico*, trans. Max H. Fisch and Thomas G. Bergin (Ithaca, NY: Cornell University Press, 1944), 113. Emphasis added.
24. Vico, *Autobiography*, 182. Emphasis added.

Vico presents himself as a historian and a philosopher interchangeably. Moreover, in recounting his formative years he becomes convinced of the enduring legacy of the Renaissance, a legacy so strong that, as Vico saw it, Descartes could marginalize it only by "feigning" an amnestic philosophical catharsis.[25]

"Masked I advance" (*larvatus prodeo*), Descartes claimed in his early writings, and although Leibniz preceded Vico in wishing that the founder of modern philosophy had provided more details about his studies, it was Vico who saw in Descartes's dissimulations the opportunity to build anew on one of the forgotten cornerstones of humanist inquiry since Petrarch, namely, the idea that thought and life, that a derivative philosophy (Cartesianism) and the philosopher (Descartes) who originated it, should never be disengaged.[26] This is how the autobiographical dimension comes to occupy a central role in Vico. Moreover, this is why Vico's inquiry, at the level of both the personal (*Autobiography*) and the world historical (*New Science*), takes its cue from a question that embarrasses those thinkers who refuse to see themselves and their philosophies as the product of their intellectual formation. The question, of course, is: How do we come to be *tali e non altri*, such as we are and not otherwise?

This question, derived from looking at Vico's most intimate experience of anti-Cartesianism, points to the new philosophical deontology that Italian Vichianism made its own and adapted for national use. What needed to be integrated was life content, those very *cultural* elements (birth, language, readings, formative experiences) that Cartesian historiography dismissed as "hollow and impure tradition" but that, according to the Vichian perspective adopted by some Italian thinkers, allow for philosophy's situatedness and for the plurality of its modes of expression. To trace the historicist leanings of Italian thought back to Vico's autobiographical account is not far-fetched, if we consider that philosophical historiography in Italy is considered not as one form of knowledge among others but instead as "for the longest time the fundamental structure of national con-

25. A thorough introduction to Vico's motives and aspirations in writing an autobiography is in Donald P. Verene, *The New Art of Autobiography: An Essay on the* Life *of Giambattista Vico Written by Himself* (Oxford: Clarendon Press, 1991).

26. For an attempt to relate Vico's autobiographical anti-Cartesianism to Petrarch's equally autobiographical anti-Scholasticism, see Rocco Rubini, "How Did We Come to Be *Such as We Are and Not Otherwise?* Petrarch, Humanism, and the History of Philosophy," *Graduate Faculty Philosophy Journal* 33, no. 2 (2012): 403–36. For Leibniz's statement, see Verene, *New Art of Autobiography*, 62.

sciousness and civic life."[27] Philosophical historiography, then, came to be written as the "nation's autobiography," a collaboratively written life story that, inevitably, like other life stories, paid particular attention to its origins and youth—in this case, the Renaissance.

A PENINSULAR PHILOSOPHY

Even as pleas for inclusion and reintegration continuously characterized Italians' theoretical endeavors, the prospect of Italy's political unification neared in the mid-nineteenth century, and the search for a national philosophy intensified. If Italians chose to embrace Hegelianism as fulfilling this role, it was most certainly because of Hegel's apparent compatibility not only with Vico but also with the proto-idealism (as it was construed in hindsight) of late Renaissance thinkers such as Bruno and Campanella. Although imported, the Hegelian vantage point afforded Italian patriots a fully fledged legacy that they could initially reclaim as having originated with them and then, once they had gained greater intellectual confidence, could advance and modify according to their needs. This strategy bore fruitful consequences for spiritual unity, for although European thought, having lost interest in Hegel just as Italians took notice of him, would be deaf to these efforts, a prolonged naturalization of German idealism ensured that the Italian philosophical tradition would gain a solid internalist perspective on itself. Once honed, this perspective in turn placed other European philosophies in a supplementary role, providing material to bridge any gaps (and there were gaps!) in the line of worthy Italian thinkers between the age of the Renaissance and Vico and between Vico and the Risorgimento.

But what would define the Italian anomaly is that Italians could not turn philosophical history inside out overnight. Time dragged on, and what began as a projected cosmopolitan exchange between Italy and Germany gave way to a nefarious political axis. Once this occurred, the inheritance of Italian Hegelianism became a burden. In fact, it has long been a staple of debate among Italian thinkers, the so-called 'hegemony' of idealism in the earlier part of the twentieth century. Students of Italian philosophy have long been aware that idealism's preeminence was ephemeral and that it underwent a slow process of 'dissolution' in the interwar period, and yet they still struggle to shake off a dichotomous characterization of Italian thought, one that would split it neatly between a totally provincial out-

27. Michele Ciliberto, *Figure in chiaroscuro: Filosofia e storiografia nel Novecento* (Rome: Edizioni di Storia e Letteratura, 2001), 3.

look on philosophy until 1945, and an emancipatory 'deprovincialization' (*sprovincializzazione*) after this date.[28]

The year, of course, marks a watershed in European politics; at the same time it also closely follows the death of the nation's most prominent Hegelian, Giovanni Gentile. His career, together with Benedetto Croce's (but more so, as I shall argue), was principally responsible for the perception of a 'hegemony' in the first place. The problem is that Gentile, a self-avowed heir of the Risorgimento and a scholar whose long list of institutional achievements makes him, arguably, the closest approximation in history to the ideal of a 'philosopher king,' was also, by personal choice, the 'philosopher of fascism.' In the end, he rented out his brand of Hegelianism, the *attualismo* or 'actual idealism' he had formulated in more innocent times, in support of Mussolini's cause.

The overlapping of actualism and fascism was defining and perhaps inevitable, and like Mussolini, Gentile paid with his life for his actions (a year earlier, in 1944). The question today, after a delay of more than half a century, is whether, in transitioning to a new era, Italians threw out the baby with the bath water. Was there not something worth preserving of a philosophical movement that originated in the Risorgimento and whose contribution to the formation of an Italian intellectual identity was paramount and, ultimately, indelible, despite its late collaboration with the regime? Italians have only recently begun to ask this question, having now realized that the long era of deprovincialization (essentially an unconditional embrace of philosophical currents spawned by Heidegger in Germany and France) contributed little to strengthen the currency of Italian thinkers on the international market. By focusing on the intense, if short-lived, overlap of Italian and European concerns in the interwar period, my study contributes to and deepens this internal debate. My principal contribution is to recover the lost perspective of a generation caught in the middle, as it were, a group of early deprovincializers who were born in the first decade of the twentieth century, formed during the Fascist *ventennio*, and who came into full maturity in the immediate postwar period as, inevitably, a self-conscious group of "survivors" of Italy's second Renaissance (or Risorgimento).[29]

28. The Italian philosophical community first began to reckon with the legacy of its postwar activity in two conferences during the early 1980s. For the proceedings, see *La cultura filosofica italiana dal 1945 al 1980 nelle sue relazioni con altri campi del sapere* (Naples: Guida, 1982); and *La filosofia italiana dal dopoguerra a oggi* (Rome: Laterza, 1985).

29. For this eloquent characterization, see Enrico Castelli, "L'avventura filosofica italiana: l' 'Archivio di Filosofia,'" *Quaderni della "Biblioteca Filosofica di Torino"* 36 (1970): 3–4.

The members of this 'existential generation' differed from their better-known French counterparts in that unofficial censorship (the consequence of having a somewhat official national philosophy) forced them to cultivate their new philosophical passion in secret and to dissemble their criticism of idealism in apparently unobtrusive scholarly work.[30] In contact with Gentile's actual idealism, they re-formed German and French thought into a 'positive' or constructive (co)existentialism, and through this lens they took a fresh look at what they felt was a largely misconstrued Renaissance heritage. It was in Renaissance scholarship that a democratic and post-idealist age began to be dreamt of (or rehearsed) in the interwar period, as Quattrocento 'civic' humanists, reshaped into proto-existentialists, were made to speak otherwise unutterable antifascist or, better, anti-idealist sentiments. Only in 1946 were these young thinkers allowed to shed the 'Nicodemism' or 'honest dissimulation,' as they termed it, that had marked their early scholarly and philosophical endeavors, referring of course to the dissembling they had carried out by identifying with the predicaments of the late Renaissance man. When they came out, they came out boldly, immediately seeking to reorient philosophy around a long-awaited and plausible convergence of the Italian, French, and German perspectives.

These facts and observations enable us to make a preliminary characterization of Italy's philosophical *peninsularity* (not quite 'provincialism') between the Risorgimento and the Fascist *ventennio*. We see the emergence in this period of an intellectual identity marked by a Renaissance shame, which in Italy amounted to self-loathing, itself symptomatic of a philosophical complex that occasionally sent Italians over their borders in search of a philosophy that could counterbalance the relentless anti-humanism on which they thought their nation should be built. Throughout, Vico was the arbiter of this tension and a protean figure who, variously interpreted, depending on circumstances and agenda, allowed Italian thinkers to argue either that modern Western philosophical thought could be traced to all-Italian origins, or, conversely, as advanced by pre- and post-idealist thinkers, that the tradition of modern Western philosophy, in so far as this identifies with Cartesianism, was utterly incommensurable with Italian thought.

This study will trace these alternative interpretations over the course of a century and a half, into the immediate postwar period. However, some

---

30. The story of the French existentialists is provided in Ethan Kleinberg, *Generation Existential: Heidegger's Philosophy in France, 1927–1961* (Ithaca, NY: Cornell University Press, 2005).

familiarity with the Italian stance, and related initiatives around 1946, is necessary if we are to attain a full grasp of the context in which the Sartre-Heidegger exchange took place, and to comprehend completely the interconnected history of the postwar revival of philosophy and Renaissance scholarship.

SUPPLEMENTING A WELL-KNOWN STORY

In 1968, Jacques Derrida was invited to give a paper at conference in New York. The theme "imposed" on him—"Where is France as concerns man?"—allowed him to review the Sartre/Heidegger debate and to take a stance on it; the occasion also allowed him to explicate his position with respect to international philosophical conferences. In hindsight, Derrida's comments offer a useful gloss on the Italian program for a rebirth of philosophy in the postwar period and deserve to be cited at some length:

> At a given moment, in a given historical, political, and economic context, . . . national groups have judged it possible and necessary to organize international encounters, to present themselves, or to be represented in such encounters by their national identity (such, at least, as it is assumed by the organizers of the colloquium), and to determine in such encounters their proper difference, or to establish relations between their respective differences. Such an establishment of relations can be practiced, if at all, only in the extent to which national philosophical identities are assumed, whether they are defined in the order of doctrinal content, the order of a certain philosophical "style," or quite simply the order of language, that is, the unity of the academic institution, along with everything implied by language and institution. But the establishing of relations between differences is also the promised complicity of a common element: the colloquium can take place only in a medium, or rather in the representation that all the participants must make of a certain transparent ether, which here would be none other than what is called the universality of philosophical discourse.[31]

The internationalization of philosophy, which entails its prior nationalization, may run counter to the universalizing ambition of thought, says Der-

---

31. Jacques Derrida, "The Ends of Man," in *Margins of Philosophy*, trans. Alan Bass (Chicago: University of Chicago Press, 1982), 111–12. On the importance of this conference in Derrida's career, see Edward Baring, *The Young Derrida and French Philosophy, 1945–1968* (Cambridge: Cambridge University Press, 2011), 298ff.

rida, but may at some point be deemed necessary when the "transparent ether" of philosophy has come to naught. One such moment deserving of an "international encounter," at least from the Italian perspective, was in 1946. In fact, it is by asking "where was Italy with respect to man at that time?" that we learn that it was by mere chance that the Sartre/Heidegger debate did not take place in the context of an international gathering, a circumstance, perhaps, to be lamented.

On the 15th of November 1946, or exactly five days after Beaufret questioned Heidegger on the subject of 'humanism,' the first international philosophy congress of the postwar period was ceremoniously inaugurated in Rome. The occasion was a matter of great pride for Italian institutions, if only because in the buildup they had managed to outmaneuver a number of tenacious rivals intent on excluding defeated countries from a similar gathering.[32] Instead, the conference organizer, Catholic existentialist Enrico Castelli, along with his friend and collaborator Ernesto Grassi, a longtime associate of Heidegger, emulated what Pico della Mirandola had attempted (in planning a similar, yet thwarted, debate in Rome in 1487) and called for an immediate *pax philosophica* in which generations old and new, thinkers who had remained uninvolved as well as those who were compromised, could resume debate after a long period of forced mutual estrangement.

The event's location was itself a matter of debate, but when Rome was finally deemed an appropriate setting, owing to its classical heritage and proximity to the Vatican, the organizers briefly toyed with the idea of hosting the event at Palazzo Venezia. In the feverish months leading up to the congress, Grassi wrote to Castelli: "We are not competitive on the grounds of modernity. . . . [T]rust me, pick an *ancient* and *choreographic* site, otherwise we are headed toward a disastrous failure. Trust me, Palazzo Venezia makes for a genial idea. I know my foreigners!"[33] Authorities denied the organizers permission to use Mussolini's former headquarters, and so the

32. This was the case in the Netherlands, where philosophers and authorities opposed the attendance of an Italian delegation at their own international conference of 1948. In clear defiance of the Italian initiative, the opening remarks of the conference organizer, H. J. Pos, were: "I bid you welcome to this congress, that is the first to be held since the second world-war interrupted the tradition of international philosophical congresses that had been started in Paris in 1900." *Proceedings of the Tenth International Congress of Philosophy (Amsterdam, August 11–18, 1948)*, ed. E. W. Beth and H. J. Pos, 2 vols. (Amsterdam: North Holland Publishing Company, 1949), 1:3.

33. Grassi to Castelli, 12 September 1946, APEC. I wish to thank Marcello Simonetta for sharing with me his transcription of the voluminous exchange between Castelli and Grassi, which I cite throughout this book.

attendees—hundreds of Italian philosophers, secular and Catholic, and a conspicuous number of thinkers representing fourteen other countries— were greeted in the main chamber of a still inoperative Italian Senate.[34]

Published eyewitness accounts paint a striking picture.[35] The speaker's chair was occupied by Giovanni Calò, president of the Italian Philosophical Association. Next to him, on either side, sat Castelli and then minister of education Guido Gonella, who delivered messages from Enrico de Nicola and Alcide de Gasperi (the provisional head of state and the prime minister of the nascent Republic of Italy, respectively). Below this trinity, in the honorary box, sat representatives of the international delegations in front of a large audience of Europe's present and future intellects, while journalists with their shorthand machines occupied the first ring of benches above them. Still higher, perched on the topmost tiers, priests, monks, and leaders of Catholic seminars from Italy and abroad presided like archangels over what resembled an improvised Plato's Republic.

Castelli had summoned this cohort to Rome with the following words: "[To hold] an International Philosophy Congress even before peace is resolved among nations, goes to show that the efforts of the politicians to trace boundaries and limits between people is already called into question by the philosophers' doubts about the value of such boundaries."[36] Over the course of five days an eclectic group of philosophers was urged to discuss carefully selected topics: historical materialism (Castelli made sure that no reference was made to either 'Marxism' or 'Communism' in the advance flyers), existentialism, and the principles of science and language analysis. Throughout the conference, guests were entertained with trips to Roman ruins and other notable sites, but Castelli saved the best for

34. The fifteen countries represented were, in addition to Italy: France, Germany, Switzerland, Spain, Belgium, Ireland, Poland, Hungary, Sweden, the Czech Republic, Austria, Argentina, Peru, and the United States. As far as the United States is concerned, the question is a little thorny. While the proceedings list Mortimer J. Adler and George Santayana as representing the United States, a short cablegram signed by John Dewey, honorary president of the American Philosophical Association, attests that the United States was not, perhaps, officially involved: "The American Philosophical Association sends warmest greetings to philosophers assembled at the international Congress of Philosophy and best wishes for fruitful meeting. Regret American philosophers unable participate in person. We are with you in spirit. John Dewey Honorary President through Cornelius Kense Secretary." Enrico Castelli, ed., *Atti del Congresso Internazionale di Filosofia (Roma 15–20 Novembre 1946)*, 2 vols. (Milan: Castellani, 1947), 1:li.

35. For an exhaustive account, see Amedeo Rossi, "Il Congresso internazionale di filosofia (Roma, 15–20 novembre 1946)," *Divus Thomas* (1944–46): 321–70.

36. Enrico Castelli, "Programma," in Castelli, *Atti del Congresso Internazionale di Filosofia*, 1:xiii.

last. On the final day of the conference, a selected group from the foreign
delegations was led in full trim to the Vatican, where it was lectured by
a well-read Pope on the dangers posed by the existential notions of *Ge-
worfensein* and *délaissement*. Cued by Castelli, Pius XII accompanied his
apostolic benediction with a warning. "What is left of philosophy besides
desperation," he asked, "if it doesn't recover its solutions in God, in personal eternity and personal immortality?"[37] Castelli's staging of the event
was belabored and obvious but, perhaps, effective. Even Julien Benda, the
French intellectual of Jewish ancestry whose *The Betrayal of the Intellectuals* (1927) had compelled thinkers to do some soul-searching in the
interwar period, allegedly fell to his knees and hinted at the gesture of
crossing himself. Some would swear they heard him muttering: "Mon an-
ticléricalisme a fléchi."[38]

With this event, Castelli wished to remind his compatriots that Italy
could not aspire to either a military or an industrial mission and that its
mission was rather a moral and cultural one (*D*, 1:341). Toward this end,
however, Italy needed to forge an alliance with France and Germany if
European cultural and religious values were to stand a chance vis-à-vis the
looming threat posed by the American and Russian (godless) technocracies. Gabriel Marcel, the Christian existentialist and host of a célèbre philosophical salon, had been among the few to concur when Castelli sounded
people out about the conference during a trip to Paris the previous fall. Indeed, Castelli faced some resistance as he sought to bring his irenic plans
to fruition. During the same Paris trip he met with many of his longtime
correspondents, including René Le Senne, Georges Gurvitch, Jean Wahl,
and Vladimir Jankélévitch, who all expressed misgivings about Castelli's
desire to allow Germans to attend. After all, how could they be sure that
no Nazis would be involved? To put it more bluntly, the French delegation
would have withdrawn without hesitation had Castelli managed to secure
the presence of Heidegger. Sartre represented another thorny issue, but one
that immediately resolved itself. After Max-Pol Fouchet was persuaded to
reveal Sartre's whereabouts (he had gone into hiding after delivering his
controversial lecture), Castelli attempted to reach the coveted thinker, but
his insistent calls to a hotel in Rue Jacob were repeatedly met with the
preordained reply: "Monsieur Sartre n'existe pas" (*D*, 2:279).

Although Castelli was rebuffed there, his visit to Paris was more pleas-

37. Castelli, *Atti del Congresso Internazionale di Filosofia*, 1:lix.
38. Castelli to Grassi, 9 December 1946, APEC.

ant than the trip he had taken that spring with Grassi to Germany. This ambitious trip, which actually began in Basel with a quest for Erasmus's apparently displaced grave, included stops in Freiburg, Baden-Baden, Marburg, Hamburg, Frankfurt, Heidelberg, and Stuttgart. The plan was to hop from university to university, meeting, interviewing, and of course inviting to Rome every surviving genius mind. Though he had been forewarned by Grassi (a longtime resident of Germany), the desolation far exceeded Castelli's imagination, who in his travel journals noted repeatedly that he had not seen a single child either cry or laugh (*D*, 2:208). Romano Guardini, the Catholic intellectual, expressed his doubts regarding the possibility of a spiritual renewal. Karl Jaspers and other figures of early twentieth-century philosophy did the same. They were going about their affairs listlessly, lecturing to amputees, the blind, and widowers—to the dismay of the visiting Italians (210). Even as it became obvious that few, if any, of the top German thinkers would be able to make the trip to Rome (Heidegger himself, as we shall see, was found famished, in tatters and in despair in his hut in Todtnauberg), the trip served to fortify the Italians' belief in their enterprise. In the presence of international authorities at an official event in Marburg, they proceeded to describe—naïvely, to be sure—the importance of abating physical distance in pursuit of an international meeting of minds.

Evidently, each country, victorious or defeated, was facing its own set of problems, and Italy, which formally partook of both outcomes, was in an even more perplexed position. The first victim of Castelli's premature ideals of reconciliation was Castelli himself. Before failing to secure the attendance of either Sartre or Heidegger, he had failed to persuade Italy's own great surviving thinker, Benedetto Croce, to attend. Croce simply would not take part in an event organized by a clericalist and a Heideggerian under the aegis of a philosophical institution born under the Fascist regime. Croce's sentiments were widely shared, even by members of the interwar generation whose values Castelli and Grassi wanted to represent. In his closing statement to the conference, Castelli pushed his luck when he commemorated in a single breath Pilo Albertelli, an anti-Fascist thinker who had lost his life in a traumatic mass execution conducted by German troops in 1944, and Giovanni Gentile, "the great thinker who led idealism to its ultimate consequences and who militated in the adverse camp," who was killed some three weeks later on the doorstep of his home. "This congress," Castelli concluded, "was organized with the aim of reestablishing that kind of freedom which allows these thinkers to be commemorated together."[39] In the weeks and months following the congress, Italian thinkers took to the newspapers to apologize formally for not having taken offense at Castelli's remarks at the time. As Norberto Bobbio, a champion of secular and democratic values, wrote to Castelli a few years later during a time of reckoning: "[Y]ou have often prided yourself on that commemoration as an act of bravery (that I consider an act of arrogance); in the present moment, those acts of bravery (or of arrogance) are punished."[40]

It would be naïve, of course, not to take some of the details of Castelli's travel journal with a grain of salt. Nonetheless, what comes across is Castelli and Grassi's distinct approach to a postwar philosophical reorientation: they wished Europe to join them in a renaissance—not another intellectual revolution, but rather a humanist convergence, in conversation—of distinct traditions originating from a common source. They had in mind an ideal of ecumenism at odds with the embrace by modern philosophers of solipsism, scientism, and logical rigor, philosophical stances that they had already been self-consciously combating throughout the 1930s, in both Italy and Germany, with editions of Quattrocento and Cinquecento sources, with journals and institutions, and with any available tool at their disposal to spread the gospel of Italian Renaissance humanism. In view of this, far too little has been made of the fact that Heidegger—knowing Grassi's 'mission'—entrusted him with the definitive draft of his "Letter." Grassi, who as we shall see was actually instrumental in commissioning Heidegger's testament at the time of his German trip with Castelli, went on to publish it in 1947 alongside a previously commissioned work: Eugenio Garin's *Italian Humanism*, arguably the first philologically accurate and unapologetic defense of the philosophical merits of Italian Quattrocento thought.

RENAISSANCE SCHOLARSHIP AND
THE HISTORY OF PHILOSOPHY

We know at this point that Garin's work would not be read alongside Heidegger's, or Sartre's, for that matter. It did, however, become part of a parallel conversation that can be credited with the postwar reshaping of Renaissance studies. Garin's interlocutor was a German Jewish scholar, Paul Oskar Kristeller, a student of Heidegger who was at one point a pro-

39. *Atti del Congresso Internazionale di Filosofia*, 1:liv.
40. Norberto Bobbio to Enrico Castelli, 29 August 1948, APEC.

tégé of Gentile as well, having initially emigrated to Italy before settling in the United States. What seems to have begun as a conversation, however, soon descended into a transatlantic scuffle, marking, although the participants would sometimes deny it, a profound divide between Italian and Anglo-American students of Renaissance thought.

Kristeller and Garin brought a similar competence and philosophical background to their study of Quattrocento sources, but Kristeller interpreted those sources very differently. He felt that humanism was merely a phase in the history of rhetoric, and starting in 1946, he began insisting that this intellectual movement had no relevance to philosophy. Eventually, as the incommensurability of their approaches became evident in the postwar period, Kristeller no longer countenanced what he perceived as Garin's wish to have all strands of Renaissance thought (Platonism, Aristotelianism, and so on) be subsumed into the category of a loosely interpreted 'humanism.'[41] For his part, Garin emphasized ever more staunchly over the course of his career that the philological and rhetorical practices of Quattrocento humanists carried within them, to different degrees, a new approach to philosophy and man. He wrote: "Very far from and in opposition to the interpretation dear to Kristeller of a Renaissance humanism as a substantially grammatical fact . . . , I have tried to individuate its distinctiveness in the deep nexus of its multiple aspects, and above all in the conception of life, of man, and of man's activity."[42]

This debate, which I will unpack thoroughly, points to the common rebirth of Continental philosophy and Renaissance studies in a chiasmatically ordered series of publications: Sartre's 'humanistic existentialism' (1946), Kristeller's 'humanism as mere rhetoric' (1946), Heidegger's 'antihumanism' (1947), and Garin's (and Grassi's) 'existential humanism' (1947). From the point of view of the Renaissance scholar, it would seem that philosophical 'antihumanism' arrived at an untimely juncture: the

41. Paul Oskar Kristeller, "Changing Views of the Intellectual History of the Renaissance since Jacob Burckhardt," in *SRTL*, 2:10: "I have more serious reservations concerning Garin's conception of Renaissance humanism. He minimizes and sometimes even seems to forget the tremendous role that literary and scholarly pursuits played in the life and work of the humanists. On the other hand, he blurs the contribution of the humanists, even as far as their moral thought is concerned, by extending the term humanism to include all philosophers of the Renaissance period, not only Platonists like Ficino and Pico . . . , but even Aristotelians like Pomponazzi or natural philosophers like Patrizzi and Bruno." See also Kristeller, "Studies on Renaissance Humanism during the Last Twenty Years," in *SRTL*, 2:34–35. For Garin's reply on this point, see "Sull'uso della parola 'umanista,'" in *Giornale critico della filosofia italiana* 33 (1954): 127.

42. Eugenio Garin, *La filosofia come sapere storico* (Rome: Laterza, 1990), 146–47.

moment when a handful of competent scholars were making a first systematic study of Quattrocento thought and were intent, despite their differences, on weighing its philosophical import and recovering it from the
margins of intellectual history. The irony of the timing was compounded
by the fact that Garin and Kristeller, in particular, were applying their
philosophical and philological training to unplumbed sources in the hopes
of arresting the abuse of the term 'humanism' that, in their view, had been
uncritically perpetuated by misinformed philosophers in Europe and the
United States for far too long.

Informing their mission was a distinction, untranslatable in English
and German but made current in Italy by, among others, Gentile, between
historical (Renaissance) *umanesimo* and modern philosophical *umanismi*.
Kristeller objected to the way that every new philosophy appropriated the
qualification of 'humanism,' all the more so since humanism was no philosophy at all. For his part, Garin, true to his intentions, allowed for such
appropriation, as long as modern philosophical *umanismi* were informed
by Renaissance humanism per se. Understanding the clash between
Kristeller and Garin is therefore useful if we are to recover an original and,
if pursued to its end, incisive critique of some of the pillars of our intellectual and historical self-fashioning as antihumanists and postmoderns.
For what we can glean from a thorough philosophical contextualization of
their work is that both viewpoints may be ascribed to a historiographical
solecism.

Some might question whether the debate between Garin and Kristeller
has philosophical value, or indeed whether they qualify as philosophers
at all. Such doubts, however, stem from the hierarchy of disciplines that
informs our academic expectations. Most of the Renaissance 'scholars'
discussed in this book were trained and perceived themselves to be historians of philosophy, which, in the Italian and German academic culture in
which they were formed, meant that they were considered rightful, card-
carrying members of the philosophical community. Where they diverged
was in choosing to specialize in the Renaissance, a field that would not
have been seen (then as now, for that matter) as central or as deserving a
chair of its own. That this was so was due in no small part to the canon
formation attributable to Cartesian historiography; at the same time it re-
minds us that the professionalization of Renaissance scholarship has occurred only recently, and so we can appreciate the role played by these
thinkers—the scholar-philosophers Garin and Kristeller, of course, and
others such as the philosopher Grassi and the historian Hans Baron (who

would famously promote the interpretation of Quattrocento humanism as a 'civic' movement of momentous consequence in Western history)—in effecting a shift in the study of the Renaissance.

Before these men entered the field, Renaissance historiography had exhausted itself with debating the so-called problem of the Renaissance: namely, was there an Italian Renaissance? Paradoxically, this was the question engendered by the founding text in the field, Jacob Burckhardt's *The Civilization of the Renaissance in Italy*. This work, published in 1860, or, as is seldom remarked, on the eve of Italy's unification, had strongly (perhaps too strongly) affirmed the splendor and temporal autonomy of the Italian Renaissance.[43] But because it was written in reaction to Hegel's philosophy of history, it eschewed exploration of the epoch's philosophical contributions. And so, just as historians would labor in the following century to eliminate the chasm that Burckhardt had dug between the Renaissance and the medieval era before it, a handful of thinkers took it upon themselves to breathe some philosophy into the period.

Many scholarly fields make reference to a founding text of sorts, but few develop continuously on arguments pro or contra such a text. This is what we find in the case of Renaissance studies. In fact, at a nascent moment in the professionalization of the field, in 1948, a historical account was published with the stated aim of liberating the field from a perceived dependence on Burckhardt. The text in question, *The Renaissance in Historical Thought*, by Wallace K. Ferguson, is still standard, and its second half is devoted to Burckhardt, to the "Burckhardtian tradition" and "reaction against the Burckhardtian tradition," and, in a final chapter that considers recent developments, to the "revolt of the medievalists," who, with their plausible claims for continuity between the Middle Ages and the Renaissance, seemed, in the late interwar period, to be about to drive Renaissance scholarship out of business.[44] As was recently noted, it is unfortunate that the timing of Ferguson's work ensured that Baron, Kristeller, and Garin—three figures who were taking steps to steer the profession—were

43. Jacob Burckhardt, *The Civilization of the Renaissance in Italy*, trans. S. G. C. Middlemore, 2 vols. (New York: Harper and Row, 1958).

44. This seminal work was recently republished. See Wallace K. Ferguson, *The Renaissance in Historical Thought: Five Centuries of Interpretation* (Toronto: University of Toronto Press, 2006). For alternative introductions to the debate and useful appendixes, see also Cesare Vasoli, *Umanesimo e Rinascimento* (Palermo: Palumbo, 1969); and Michele Ciliberto, *Il Rinascimento: Storia di un dibattito* (Florence: La Nuova Italia, 1975). See also Jonathan Woolfson, ed., *Palgrave Advances in Renaissance Historiography* (New York: Palgrave Macmillan, 2005).

left out.[45] Indeed, from our vantage point, Ferguson's march through "five centuries of interpretation" of the Renaissance seems to end in medias res, just when the revolt of the medievalists is about to be countered by the well-armed forces of a revolutionary generation of Renaissance scholars.

In that it is largely dedicated to the figures whom Ferguson necessarily left out, one may view *The Other Renaissance* as supplementing that story. Yet the story I tell adopts the same temporal boundaries as the second half of Ferguson's work, providing a different genealogy altogether, an account of the Renaissance in 'philosophical' rather than 'historical' thought. This interpretive tradition originates in Italy with Bertrando Spaventa, in the same year, 1860, as the tradition initiated by Burckhardt. This conveniently allows us to track its formation as a tradition distinct from the mainstream German one that has informed, for better or worse, our view of the Renaissance so far. Ferguson did allot some space to the Renaissance of the philosophers (including Spaventa) but necessarily, from his historiographical angle, with notable brevity and miscomprehension. Besides Spaventa the influential philosophers were, among others, Gentile (exclusively but decisively in Italy) and Ernst Cassirer. Historical events kept Gentile and Cassirer apart (and lamentably this continues to be the case in scholarly work), but their Renaissance-informed thought, or *umanismi*, shared a common fate in losing out to Heidegger's irresistible magnetism.[46] They were European thinkers who combined Renaissance scholarship and a theoretical bent, the worthy interlocutors of a "Letter" they never got to read but that they left to their younger admirers, most self-consciously among them Garin and Kristeller, to answer.

Since the scope of this book does not extend beyond the immediate postwar development of Renaissance studies, it is worth noting the ways that the work of Garin and Kristeller continues to resonate. We see the strength of their legacy, for example, in the acknowledgment pages of virtually every recent collaborative anthology devoted to Renaissance philosophy. These remarks all stress that Garin and Kristeller were the first to highlight the pluralism of the Renaissance's philosophical perspective.

45. See Ronald G. Witt, "L'umanesimo civile di Eugenio Garin da una prospettiva americana," *Giornale critico della filosofia italiana* 84, no. 1 (2005): 40. In fact, Ferguson managed to sneak in only a cursory overview of Baron's early scholarship. See Ferguson, *Renaissance in Historical Thought*, 228–29.

46. On Cassirer's legacy and Heidegger, see Peter E. Gordon's comments in *Continental Divide: Heidegger, Cassirer, Davos* (Cambridge: Harvard University Press, 2010), xiii and 359ff.

The work of Garin and Kristeller also influences various current attempts in Anglo-American Renaissance studies to acknowledge the philosophical merits of Renaissance humanism, attempts that generally, on this side of the Atlantic, entail a 'Garinian shift' and, consequently, an apology or *pace* to Kristeller.[47] If disagreements persist as to humanism's role in the history of philosophy, however, students of the Renaissance do seem to agree that the philosophical pluralism that Garin and Kristeller saw in the Renaissance is the same philosophical pluralism that we know and accept today, after the archeological investigations of modern reason by the likes of Michel Foucault, Richard Rorty, Alasdair MacIntyre, and Stephen Toulmin, among the names best known. It would truly seem to be the case, in view of this affinity, that we may see ourselves in the Renaissance man, not least because we can "see the philosophers of the Renaissance as persons who have walked down paths we ourselves now travel and who can to some degree act as guides to unfamiliar country."[48]

What the Renaissance scholar sees so clearly, however, is not always clear to philosophers, who are rarely interested in the Renaissance. Toulmin is an exception; having discerned strong similarities between Montaigne and his teacher, Wittgenstein, he advanced a word to the wise that remains to be heeded and acted upon:

After the destructive work of Dewey, Heidegger, Wittgenstein, and Rorty, philosophy has limited options. These boil down to three possibilities: It can cling to the discredited research program of a purely theoretical (i.e., "modern") philosophy, which will end by driving it out of business; it can look for new and less exclusively theoretical ways of working, and develop the methods needed for a more practical ("*postmodern*") agenda; or it can return to its pre-17th-century traditions,

47. See, for example, *The Cambridge Companion to Renaissance Philosophy*, ed. James Hankins (Cambridge: Cambridge University Press, 2007); Paul R. Blum, ed., *Philosophers of the Renaissance*, trans. Brian McNeil (Washington, DC: Catholic University of America Press, 2010); and *Le filosofie del Rinascimento*, ed. Cesare Vasoli (Milan: B. Mondadori, 2002). Also notice that emphasis changes between volumes published in Italy and the United States. Recent attempts at investing 'humanism' with philosophical value are Timothy Kircher, *The Poet's Wisdom: The Humanists, the Church, and the Formation of Philosophy in the Early Renaissance* (Leiden: Brill, 2006), 14–15; Lodi Nauta, *In Defense of Common Sense: Lorenzo Valla's Humanist Critique of Scholastic Philosophy* (Cambridge, MA: Harvard University Press, 2009), ix; Gur Zack, *Petrarch's Humanism and the Care of the Self* (Cambridge: Cambridge University Press, 2010), 15.

48. James Hankins, "The Significance of Renaissance Philosophy," in Hankins, *Cambridge Companion to Renaissance Philosophy*, 341.

and try to recover the lost (*"pre*-modern"*) topics that were sidetracked
by Descartes, but can be usefully taken up for the future.[49]

By the time Toulmin was writing, in the late 1980s, philosophy had already embarked resolutely on the 'postmodern' path, so the challenge remains, now that the 'postmodern' path is no longer an option, to see how
Renaissance modernity may be reclaimed for its relevance to the present
and future. In this enterprise philosophers, if they are interested in pur-
suing it, may have it easier than Renaissance scholars; the latter may be
inhibited in their ambitions by a fear of tampering with the mode of disinterested competence that Garin and Kristeller are said to have brought to
bear on the study of fifteenth-century sources. And so, what if we were to
discover that, their claims to the contrary, there was nothing objective or
disinterested in the scholarship of either Garin or Kristeller? Would that
discovery make their example a blessing, an admonition, even, confirming that Renaissance thought should not remain *lettera morta*?

It has been a defining feature of Renaissance scholarship on humanism
in the new century, a transition that coincided with the death of an older
generation of scholars, to critically reappraise, in an act of soul-searching,
past interpretive paradigms. So far, these reappraisals have been piecemeal
and all too fainthearted—no doubt because of a resistance to push past the
limits of a particular discipline's comfort zone. In a reappraisal of Garin's
and Kristeller's scholarship, this might mean admitting that the interpretive paradigms that still dominate (in their general gist, if not on details)
and that we still routinely apply were not just vaguely informed by some
philosophy or other, as is often advanced; we might be forced to recognize
that in the mid-twentieth century Renaissance scholarship was reborn as
a philosophical discourse in its own right, one in which a remarkable plurality of post-Kantian streams of thought (Hegelianism, Neo-Kantianism;
phenomenology, existentialism, etc.) continued to vie for supremacy, without our notice, in the second half of the twentieth century.

As this introduction suggests, in *The Other Renaissance* I have taken
on the task of relating—for mutual enlightenment and irrespective of artificial disciplinary boundaries—some contrasting yet interlocking perspectives on the question of 'humanism' around 1946. If pursued to its end, this
rapprochement may reveal mid-twentieth-century Renaissance 'scholarship' as a forgotten chapter in the history of recent philosophy, one that,

---

49. Stephen Toulmin, *Cosmopolis: The Hidden Agenda of Modernity* (Chicago: University of Chicago Press, 1992), 11.

to an extent that may surprise, may alter and illuminate the larger narrative of twentieth-century intellectual history. Surely, if the *philosophical* history of Renaissance scholarship succeeds, it will also be because it includes the neglected perspective provided by Italian philosophy.

In chapter 1, I provide a sketch of nineteenth- and early twentieth-century Italian philosophy through texts selected and closely read for their . relevance to the Renaissance legacy. My aim is to introduce the reader to the dramatis personae of Italian philosophy, its lexicon, its conversations, and its conflicts, and ultimately to the shared mindframe that allowed for the emergence of an idealist hegemony in Italy between Spaventa and Gentile. I emphasize in particular those features of the era—its Vichianism, its ambivalence toward the Renaissance man—that would inform, in large part, the philosophical humanism of the existentialists.

In chapter 2 I turn to the existentialists, delineating the gradual demise of idealism in the interwar period, a moment in which three distinct generations of thinkers, each with its own agenda, momentarily overlapped, as a commixture of Gentilean idealism and Heideggerianism merged to create a self-consciously 'positive,' that is, constructive existentialism that, finding little outlet in philosophy per se, would immediately be channeled, fruitfully, into an original reading of Renaissance humanism. Following chapters depict Grassi, Garin, and Kristeller in their early years, demonstrating that their careers were grounded in the contest between Italian and German philosophies.

In chapter 3, I examine the career of Grassi, Heidegger's only Italian student in Germany, to determine why Heidegger would entrust the publication of "Plato's Doctrine of Truth" and, especially, his antihumanist manifesto, "Letter on 'Humanism,'" to a man who so staunchly promoted the philosophical merits of the *studia humanitatis*. Archival sources and a close reading of Grassi's work show that Heidegger's "Letter" was as much a response to Italian existentialists (and their revived Renaissance humanism), as it was, at Jean Beaufret's behest, a reply to Sartre. Indeed, Grassi at first hoped that the "Letter" would support his plan for a revival of Renaissance thought, a plan in which he had already involved his teacher. Grassi's confrontation with Heidegger, I will argue, elicits a new understanding of the origins of 'antihumanism' and, thus, of contemporary thought and theory.

Chapter 4 is devoted to an equally close reconstruction of the career of Garin, a self-conscious heir of Gentile's legacy. I detail his 'dissimulations' of antifascist sentiments in his groundbreaking work on Pico della Mirandola (1937), whose *Oration on the Dignity of Man* he read as a pacifist manifesto. Furthermore, I use archival sources to reconstruct the background of Garin's *Italian Humanism*, one of only three works that preeminently shaped postwar Renaissance studies. I reveal it to be a piece of existential scholarship based on the syncretic assimilation of Italian Hegelianism, Grassi's Heideggerianism, and, from a distance, Hans Baron's pioneering scholarship on the Italian Quattrocento, itself informed by the tradition of German *Historismus*. Furthermore, since Garin was among the first outspoken admirers of Gramsci, we gain in this chapter a new understanding of the role played by existential exigencies in the initial attraction to Gramscianism in postwar Italy.

Finally, in chapter 5, I explore the early career of Kristeller, the doyen of Renaissance studies in the United States. I examine Kristeller's relationship to Gentile and to the Italian scholarly community as well as his student career in Germany in order to understand his reasons for downgrading Renaissance humanism from the status of philosophy to that of mere rhetoric, and, concomitantly, his efforts to elevate Marsilio Ficino's Neoplatonism to the status of 'true' philosophy. Rather than tracing his motives to his life experience as a German Jewish émigré, as is often done, I show that Kristeller based his scholarly choices on his close adherence to the axiological approach of Kantian epistemology, which was advanced by his teacher Heinrich Rickert against the historicist and existential lines of thought embraced by Kristeller's interlocutors.

The contextualization offered in this study will prove that these debates were not so much the result of different temperaments as a restaging, in Renaissance scholarship, of the philosophical conflicts of interwar Europe—and, ultimately, as I argue in conclusion, they constituted a central episode in modern times of the perennial quarrel between rhetoric and philosophy.

A NOTE ON METHOD

The Other Renaissance is unapologetically narrative; it tells its story primarily through bibliographical narratives based on close readings of early publications and first books, which are mined for youthful aspirations with the aid of archival materials made available to scholars only recently. In so doing, I self-consciously advance the hermeneutics employed in reading the Renaissance humanists by those very scholars whose careers I study. As I shall argue, their interpretive approach was novel and, more important, inspirational, in that it was empathetic. It successfully managed to relate the Renaissance to twentieth-century philosophical concerns by turning to those discrepancies and contradictions that, in the past as in the present, make up a given thinker's bio-bibliography (outlines, reviews, polemics, letters) and that are often invisible in the definitive works on which scholars usually rely.

It is too often forgotten, to the detriment of historical knowledge, that diverging 'philosophies' or worldviews may equally explain the facts. Faced with this realization, we may either take the shortcut, instinctively siding with one option, or, as Raphael Demos noted, take the longer but more rewarding way of forcing ourselves into confronting those "minute considerations" which make up the pattern of our own and our interlocutor's persuasion:

> Often the reason why so much discussion among individuals is futile is that what one person realizes vividly, the other does not. Evocation is the process by which vividness is conveyed; it is the presentation of a viewpoint in such a manner that it becomes real for the public. It is said that argument is the way by which an individual experience is made common property; in fact, an argument has much less persuasive force than the vivid evocation of an experience. The enumeration of all the relevant points in favor of a theory and against its opposite can never be completed; far more effective is it to state a viewpoint in all its concreteness and in all its significant applications, and then stop; the arguments become relevant only after this stage has been completed.[50]

A "vivid evocation" of how the Renaissance was (re)experienced by some of its leading interpreters is what I want to provide for my readers, in the hopes that having a better sense of the stakes will allow them to make better arguments, for our day and age, pro or contra the *philosophical* merits of historical humanisms.

50. Raphael Demos, "On Persuasion," *Journal of Philosophy* 29 (1932): 229.

CHAPTER ONE

Philosophy and Revolution: Italian Vichianism and the 'Renaissance Shame'

Our revolution was a passive revolution, whose only chance of success rested in winning the people's interest to its cause. Yet the views of the patriots did not coincide with those of the people: they had different ideas, different customs, and even two different languages.
—Vincenzo Cuoco, *Saggio storico sulla rivoluzione di Napoli* (1801)

In the midst of darkness, I could make out two lights in the distance, and I felt enamored. I had the pleasurable feeling that they were one and the same sun. They appeared as two, because they were the same sun on two different points of the horizon. To unlock the metaphor: Italian Renaissance philosophy and German philosophy.
—Bertrando Spaventa, *Logica e metafisica* (1867)

We see two Italys before us—one old and the other new. There is the Italy of the ages, which is our glory but which is also our sad legacy, heavy on our shoulders and a burden to our spirits. It is a legacy that, we must candidly admit, is a disgrace from which we would be free— for which we must make amends. That great Italy of the ages, that has so large a place in the history of the world, that is recognized and studied and investigated by all civilized people, is the Italy whose history is not a particular history, but an epoch in universal history: the Renaissance.
—Giovanni Gentile, *Che cosa è il fascismo?* (1925)

INTRODUCTION

If Italy, to use Metternich's incisive words, was nothing more than a mere "geographical expression" until its unification into a nation-state in 1860–61, the fault, agreed a group of nineteenth- and twentieth-century Italian philosophers, was with the Renaissance man. This was the same Renaissance man, of course, whose 'individualism' Jacob Burckhardt had just recently been gushing over in his 1860 masterpiece, *The Civilization of the Renaissance in Italy*. By the time Burckhardt 'invented' the Renaissance, Italians had already pinpointed the self-absorption, vainglory, and narcissism of their modern forefathers as the principal cause of Italy's political fractiousness and centuries-long subjugation to foreign rule, drawing here more on personal experience than on systematic historiographical research. In other words, from an idiosyncratic Italian perspective Burckhardt's creation of the modern historiographical conception of the Renaissance serendipitously coincided with the end of it as a historical period in the country that he had conclusively identified as its birthplace.

Certainly, 1860 may seem awfully late to serve as an end date for the Renaissance, and yet the problem that the Renaissance posed for Italians would endure politically (the annexation of Rome occurred in 1870) and, most important, spiritually for many more decades. Between the founding of a unifying constitutional monarchy and the rise and demise of fascism, Italian thinkers searched for a national philosophy with which to fill the empty and brittle vessel of post-Renaissance political infrastructure. The fragility of that vessel was due in no small part to the fact that Italians had lagged behind historical events in a parallel and correlative effort to emancipate themselves from their Renaissance prototype. It is thus to this psychological projection—to the relation that the modern Italian intellectual entertained with himself as a Renaissance man, to his internalization of the 'Renaissance' as an existential category—that one needs to attend in order to grasp the etiological myth I call the 'Italians' Renaissance,' the very myth that, in turn, informed the ambition for an Italian national philosophy.

The emotional bond between modern Italians and their Renaissance is already implicit in the notion of the Risorgimento, a word that usually refers to the nineteenth-century movement for Italian unification, but that throughout the nineteenth century was also Italians' preferred term for the cultural flourishing that signaled their precocious entry into modernity—even after Jules Michelet and Burckhardt, respectively, had introduced and made current the word *Renaissance*.[1] On close inspection the notions of 'rebirth' and 'resurgence,' though related, are not identical. Eventually, at the turn of the twentieth century, Italians would also adopt the Italianized word *Rinascimento*, perhaps out of inertia. And yet the event points to a distinction, one that reflects the significant effort that Italians put into distancing themselves from their stilted modern origins, into rebounding or 'resurging' from the decline the Renaissance had ushered in in Italy. In the highly competitive atmosphere that characterized the European struggle for cultural ascendancy, the very idea that other countries might have reaped the fruits of a seed of modernity planted in Italy—whether it was via religious reform or centralized government efficiency—remained a central national embarrassment. This context helps us understand the sense of 'shame' that in Italy accompanied the Renaissance as a "mobilizer of patriotic action," or, to put it another way (more in keeping with the equally *intellectual* enterprise that was the Risorgimento), it was the Renaissance that 'shamed' Italian thinkers into conceiving a personal philosophy.[2] Moreover, since this feeling of shame would persist until the end of World War II, the 'Renaissance' functions as a perennial touchstone by which to measure the evolution of the Italian national self, diachronically, as the history of a collective "anxious ego" (as it was recently described) prone to producing "an extremely refined discourse about the anxiety of [Italian national culture's] own existence."[3]

Concomitant with the recent 150th anniversary celebration of Italy's unification, Risorgimento studies have witnessed a renaissance of their own. A 'cultural turn' has led scholars to start thinking about patriotism not just as an ideology, given and ready-made, but as a discursive practice.[4] In the process, they have recouped from the pre- and postunification histories found in heretofore marginalized literary genres an understand-

1. The seventh volume of Michelet's *History of France*, which was published in 1855, bore the title *Renaissance*. Given the topic of this chapter, it is worth noting that Michelet was a fervent Vichian and the translator of Vico's works in France. See Lucien Febvre, *Michelet et la Renaissance* (Paris: Flammarion, 1992); Joseph Mali, *The Legacy of Vico in Modern Cultural History: From Jules Michelet to Isaiah Berlin* (Cambridge: Cambridge University Press, 2012), chap. 1.

2. On the interplay of "shame" and "pride" in Italian nationalism, see Silvana Patriarca, "A Patriotic Emotion: Shame and the Risorgimento," in *The Risorgimento Revisited: Nationalism and Culture in Nineteenth-Century Italy*, ed. Silvana Patriarca and Lucy Riall (Basingstoke, UK: Palgrave, 2012), 134–51.

3. Suzanne Stewart-Steinberg, *The Pinocchio Effect: On Making Italians (1860–1920)*, (Chicago: University of Chicago Press, 2007), 4–5.

4. For an introduction to recent developments in Risorgimento scholarship, see Silvana

ing of the Risorgimento that is no longer strictly political.[5] This approach has had the effect of widening, perhaps infinitely, what has been called the "Risorgimento canon," a canon that is in any case best approached noncanonically, with greater emphasis on contributions by the young and other minorities—by those who experienced Italy's resurgence, not just those who brought the event to fruition.[6] Such an approach benefits our understanding of an epoch in which, its practical achievements notwithstanding, traditions were "invented" and communities "imagined" (as the prevailing scholarship on nationalism might phrase it).[7]

There were in fact many patriotic discourses in Italy in the nineteenth century, and it is to be lamented that the philosophical one continues to be neglected given that it was arguably the most finely tuned, certainly the most self-aware. By failing to take into account, for example, the work of Vincenzo Gioberti, arguably the Risorgimento's most representative philosopher, and Giovanni Gentile, the self-avowed philosopher of fascism, Risorgimento scholarship loses the opportunity to learn from how they intersect, as does the equally flourishing field of Anglo-American fascist studies. It is not that Gioberti and Gentile have been completely overlooked, but rather that the philosophical core of their varied intellectual enterprises has not been thoroughly explored and their careers understood as end terms, as providing the coordinates of a distinct, if not self-enclosed, philosophical patriotism that developed in the span they represent. This neglect owes something, perhaps, to the fact that Italy is unlike other countries in that the 'philosopher' does not cut a figure who clearly defines himself, professionally, apart from the larger group of intellectuals (writers, artists, political militants, etc.) whose works currently serve as scholarly sources.[8]

Patriarca and Lucy Riall, "Introduction: Revisiting the Risorgimento," in Patriarca and Riall, *Risorgimento Revisited*, 1–17.

5. Examples of this new approach are Albert Russell Ascoli and Krystyna Von Henneberg, eds., *Making and Remaking Italy: The Cultivation of National Identity around the Risorgimento* (Oxford: Berg, 2001); and Norma Bouchard, ed., *Risorgimento in Modern Italian Culture: Revisiting the Nineteenth-Century Past in History, Narrative, and Cinema* (Madison, NJ: Fairleigh Dickinson University Press, 2005).

6. These guiding lines for a cultural turn in Risorgimento scholarship were offered in Alberto M. Banti, *La nazione del Risorgimento: Parentela, santità e onore alle origini dell'Italia unita* (Turin: Einaudi, 2000).

7. I refer here to theories put forth in two classic studies of nationalism: Benedict Anderson, *Imagined Communities: Reflections on the Origin and Spread of Nationalism,* (London: Verso, 2006), and Eric Hobsbawm and Terence Ranger, eds., *The Invention of Tradition* (New York: Cambridge University Press, 2012).

8. On this point, see the remarks in *FKC*, 3–6.

Indeed, we could characterize the 'Italian' philosophy that began to emerge in the mid-nineteenth century as a kind of dare, a way to show that philosophy belonged to Italy as well. At the same time, the challenge was to make sure that philosophy in Italy would not be strictly academic. Aspirations for a *civic* philosophy were part and parcel of the mission to recover from the Renaissance. If genuine patriotism was not prevalent in the early modern period, then that was again the fault of the Quattrocento humanist, an intellectual figure prone to institutional intellectual segregation.

The predicament of the Risorgimento man may be reexperienced by present-day readers if asked to name a modern Italian 'philosopher,' in the sense in which that word is applied to Descartes, Locke, Spinoza, Kant, or Hegel, for example. Cheating a little, the mind might turn to pre-Cartesian thinkers such as Pico, Ficino, Bruno, and Campanella, none of whom, however, seems to meet the degree of philosophical rigor and influence required for eponymity (Pichianism, Ficinianism, etc.). Faced with later periods, one would be even more at a loss unless one could turn, as Italian patriots did, to that odd figure, Giambattista Vico (1668–1744). A peculiar thinker, Vico failed to win over science-enthralled Naples with his humanist inquiry, but precisely because of this (admittedly often exaggerated) egregious neglect, he lived on, a figure perpetually to be rediscovered and, as Goethe prognosticated during a trip to Italy in 1787, to be elevated into the *Altvater* of a not yet existing nation. Benedetto Croce, glossing Goethe, described Vico as a touchstone, providing an occasion "to hark back for a time in order to imbue modern philosophy with an Italian feeling [*italianità*], however cosmopolitan it may be in thought."[9] Perhaps Croce did not need to remind his compatriots that Vico was Italian when, in 1911, he leveraged his reputation and put his favorite thinker on the international map. By then, Vico had long and consistently resided in the consciousness of Italian thinkers, and, collectively, their brand of thought had already grown into a distinctive Vichianism.[10]

The Vico who held sway among early patriots, however, was less the author of the *New Science* (1744), which investigated the common origins of nations and was somewhat abstruse even for an Italian readership, than the author of works such as *On the Most Ancient Wisdom of the Italians* (1710), in which Vico, analyzing the ancient Latin language, first delin-

---

9. Benedetto Croce, *The Philosophy of Giambattista Vico*, trans. R. G. Collingwood (New York: Russell & Russell, 1964), viii.

10. For the most exhaustive (though often biased) survey of Italian and non-Italian Vichianism, see Benedetto Croce and Fausto Nicolini, *Bibliografia Vichiana*, 2 vols. (Naples: Ricciardi, 1947–48).

eated an etymological equation between *verum* and *factum*, an equation on which he construed the catchphrase of his new line of inquiry: "The True is the Made" (*verum ipsum factum*).[11] Vico self-consciously opposed his formulation to Descartes's own (*cogito ergo sum*), in order to ground man's knowledge in man-*made* products, that is, history, and to curb, in the process, the Cartesian philosopher's tendency to dawdle in the laws attending to the physical, natural, God-*begotten* realm. It is well known that Vico often structured his philosophy as a more or less overt confrontation with Descartes, yet, perhaps because he elaborated on some of the anti-French sentiments already present in Petrarch and Machiavelli, his philosophy soon acquired an identitarian if not a nationalist aura—or at least this is what his Risorgimento followers made of it.

Patriots could latch on to some of Vico's particular concerns, such as the so-called 'genius of language,' which he addressed in 1708, in the last of a long series of programmatic academic orations:

> While we Italians praise our orators for fluency, lucidity, and eloquence, the French praise theirs for reasoning truly. Whenever the French wish to designate the mental faculty by which we rapidly, aptly, and felicitously couple things which stand apart, they call it *esprit*, and are inclined to view as a naïve, simple trick what we consider as forceful power of combination; their minds, characterized by exceeding penetration, do not excel in synthetic power, but in piercing subtlety of reasoning. Consequently, if there is any truth in this statement, which is the theme of a famous debate, "genius is a product of language, not language of genius," we must recognize that the French are the only people who, thanks to the subtlety of their language, were able to invent the new philosophical criticism which seems so thoroughly intellectualistic, and analytical geometry, by which the subject matter of mathematics is, as far as possible, stripped of all concrete, figural elements, and reduced to pure rationality.[12]

Contributing here to a long-lasting quarrel between French and Italian intellectuals, Vico reverses the notion that national character precedes language, put forth by Dominique Bouhours in an attempt to argue for the

11. Giambattista Vico, *On the Most Ancient Wisdom of the Italians: Unearthed from the Origins of the Latin Language*, trans. L. M. Palmer (Ithaca, NY: Cornell University Press, 1988), 45–46.

12. Giambattista Vico, *On the Study Methods of Our Time*, trans. Elio Gianturco (Indianapolis: Bobbs-Merrill, 1965), 40.

universality of modern French.[13] To each their language, Vico rebuts, and
thus their genius, of which a plurality exists, each with its place in the
intellectual realm. From this perspective, Vico gladly conceded the "dull"
and "inert" things that are "abstract ideas" to the French, but proudly
claimed "comparative," "metaphorical," "emotional" talent for the Italians. These were the qualities that made the Italian mind one of the "keen-
est," a mind that put Italians in the forefront, if not of the sciences, then
certainly of the arts.

Vico, or so went the scholarly myth (and to indulge in myth was, and
is, instrumental to partake of the Vichian moment), had no clear and distinct ideas to offer, nor a well-polished methodology, yet his opposition to
rationalist epistemology did not stop at sterile invective—an accusation
often leveled at his Renaissance predecessors, from Petrarch to Valla and
Poliziano, and their opposition to medieval school philosophy. However,
he developed enough of a positive contribution to inspire a philosophical
attitude worthy of being acted upon and the outlines of a research program
or 'history' that, if Italians would get around to writing it, would allow
them to recover an intellectual identity heretofore lost. The history that
Vico inspired touched on the distinctions between reason and ingenuity,
"critical" and "topical philosophy"—in other words, the perennial quarrel
of rhetoric and philosophy that Vico saw himself and Descartes, perhaps,
embodying for modern times. Taking this cue, his followers raised it into
a national race between France and Italy in the aftermath of the French
Revolution. This was the emotional atmosphere, throughout the nineteenth century and beyond, of Italian Vichianism, making it a 'rhetoric
of alterity,' a philosophy 'announced' (but rarely elaborated) in subsequent
inaugural academic addresses, just as Vico himself had done, by several
generations of Italians who were intent on talking themselves, literally,
into intellectual difference.

Vico, it has been insightfully argued, could not serve as an exemplar,
nor did he wish to. Rather, he emerged as an "idiosyncratic authority." His
brand of inquiry or humanism is a practice that "must be internalized,
personalized," "becoming material for another practice, another memoir."
The humanism he inspired will survive, if it survives, in "iteration," that
is, in tradition-making, rather than in "emulation."[14] These stipulations

13. I draw here from Paola Gambarota, *Irresistible Signs: The Genius of Language and Italian National Identity* (Toronto: University of Toronto Press, 2011), 100ff.

14. Nancy Struever, "Rhetoric, Time, Memory, Memoir," in *A Companion to Rhetoric and Rhetorical Criticism*, ed. Walter Jost and Wendy Olmsted (Malden, MA: Blackwell, 2004), 430.

are necessary because scholars who look to Italian intellectual history for the stuff that philosophy is usually made of (stringency, cogency, etc.) will, in large part, be disappointed in their expectations. Scholars will not be disappointed, however, if they are open to a theory of collective authorship, to an agenda that, despite the varying contributions of its representatives, endures and is pursued in ongoing conversation. This conversation is what makes up the community of Italian philosophers, one that was 'imagined,' yes, but in the Vichian sense of wanting to possess the inside perspective on that which it wanted to know, in this case, its very own tradition—and this, too, was 'invented,' but in the Vichian or etymological sense of 'recovered' and 'recollected' for the sake of introspection and self-understanding.

The substantial chapter that follows relies on an understanding of the Renaissance to sketch the self-contained trajectory of a self-avowed 'Italian' philosophy that extends from Vico to Antonio Gramsci. These two are the best-known of Italian thinkers, perhaps; they are also two thinkers whose popularity, outside Italy, has obscured the (Vichian) tradition that connects them, to the detriment of our understanding of Vico and Gramsci themselves. We see a connection in terms of Italian intellectual identity, for example, when Gramsci, writing from prison to his sister-in law, Tania Schucht, in 1927 announces that he will dedicate himself to "a study of the formation of the public spirit in Italy during the past century; in other words, a study of Italian intellectuals, their origins, their groupings in accordance with cultural currents, and their various ways of thinking, etc., etc."[15] Gramsci, who was "obsessed" by the idea of doing something *für ewig*, that is, "disinterestedly," in order to "provide a center to [his] inner life," was also out to test the 'translatability' of the concerns of Italian intellectuals. They are a "literary coterie," he explains elsewhere, isolated by a private language that "makes it not only difficult to translate from Italian but also often difficult to understand an Italian in conversation. The 'finesse' seemingly required in such conversations is not a matter of normal intelligence, but of having to know the intellectual minutiae and attitudes of a 'jargon' peculiar to literati or indeed to specific groups of literati."[16]

The 'translated' intellectual sought by Gramsci was the same intellectual that Italian thinkers had been trying to become (Gramsci would say

15. Antonio Gramsci, *Letters from Prison*, ed. Frank Rosengarten, trans. Raymond Rosenthal, 2 vols. (New York: Columbia University Press, 2011), 1:83.

16. Antonio Gramsci, *Selections from Cultural Writings*, ed. David Forgacs and Geoffrey Nowell-Smith, trans. William Boelhower (Chicago: Haymarket Books, 1985), 297.

unsuccessfully) vis-à-vis the disengaged Renaissance man and with the aid of Vico. These thinkers included, among others, Vincenzo Cuoco, Vincenzo Gioberti, Bertrando Spaventa, Francesco De Sanctis, Gentile, and Croce, whose work, conversation, and intentions this introductory chapter relates as a single palimpsestic corpus and makes familiar as a whole, so that subsequent chapters can further increase our understanding of how we came to think of the Renaissance and its humanists as we did or, perhaps, as we still have not.

VINCENZO CUOCO AND ITALY'S "PASSIVE REVOLUTION"

When King Ferdinand IV retaliated in bloody fashion against supporters of the short-lived republic that Napoleon established in Naples in 1799, the life of a young lawyer named Vincenzo Cuoco (1770–1823) was spared.[17] On his way to a forced exile in France, he first began jotting down his thoughts on recent occurrences in order to "idle away the boredom of emigration," and, in the process, he rediscovered himself as a "man of letters" (SS, 217–18). Indeed, those notes grew into a work that would be vastly influential, the *Historical Essay on the Neapolitan Revolution* (1801). In the manuscript he rushed to press in Milan upon his almost immediate return to Italy, Cuoco mused on how an event that was "meant to form the happiness of a nation" would instead "produce its ruin, at least for the time being" (221). He noted that in the course of history "generations quietly come and go" until natural cataclysms or extraordinary political occurrences "endow us with a new life, as new objects are presented to our eyes." Believing himself to have experienced such an event, Cuoco went so far as to claim that it is only when nations seemingly rush to their doom that one is inclined to see clearly into "the character of those very same nations, their customs, and the origins of those laws that were earlier perceived in their application solely" (222). What manifested itself to Cuoco's mind was none other than the Italian nation or, to be more precise, given his firm belief that a nation is the product of a shared cultural heritage, the outline of an Italian people.

Cuoco was aware that he would not be able to deliver a finished product during his lifetime, yet he was arguably the "inventor" of Italy's na-

---

17. On Cuoco's life, see Antonino di Francesco, *Vincenzo Cuoco: Una vita politica* (Rome-Bari: Laterza, 1996). For a historical account of the Neapolitan revolution of 1799, see the essays collected in *Napoli 1799: Fra storia e storiografia*, ed. Anna Maria Rao (Naples: Vivarium, 2002); and John A. Davies, *Naples and Napoleon: Southern Italy and the European Revolutions (1780–1860)* (Oxford: Oxford University Press, 2006), chap. 4.

tional character in that he pinpointed the challenges inherent in any attempt to advance patriotic feelings in Italy.[18] In a journalistic piece from
1815, for example, he efficiently explained the predicament by asking his
readers to imagine the arrival of a horse-drawn carriage in any French city.
As the travelers are greeted with a "Voici des voyageurs" and speak in response, they are classified either as "étrangers," if their language is incomprehensible, or, if they communicate in dialect, as "Gascons" or "Proven-
çaux," that is to say, as "French."[19] Lamentably, something quite different
occurs in Italy, where no difference is drawn between a foreigner and a
mere "forestiero," someone who happens to be from a different, perhaps
even neighboring, city. Cuoco had no doubt that the "false notion" that
leads Italians not to mistake, say, a "Scandinavian for an Italian" but to
treat a fellow Italian as if he were a Scandinavian "is the malefic source
of any political perturbation, in the past as well as in the present." Nevertheless, he drew hope from the same emigration experience that seems
to have refined his genius for comparison.[20] Marshaling Petrarch, an illustrious fellow émigré (and probably elaborating on a similar comment
made by his intellectual hero, Giambattista Vico), Cuoco noted that when
abroad even the most provincial of Italians will be inclined to give up his
diffidence upon meeting another, as the appellation "forestiero" naturally
morphs into an enthusiastic and nostalgic cry of "fratello!" or "compatri-
otto!" or "paesano!"[21]

By 1799, Italians had grown accustomed to coexisting with occupying
forces; there was no reason to expect that the most recent invasion would
by itself foster that sense of belonging and mutual recognition needed to
dissolve the "political egotism of the different families that make up the
Italic nation." Rather, in his *Essay* Cuoco looked to a different challenge:
to convey what he, again as an attentive reader of Vico, could perceive as
a profound asynchrony between France's and his own nation's historical
development. The kind of epochal turmoil that France was prepared to ex-

18. Cuoco rightly has a central place in Giulio Bollati, *L'italiano: Il carattere nazionale come storia e come invenzione* (Turin: Einaudi, 2011), 64ff.
19. Vincenzo Cuoco, *Pagine giornalistiche*, ed. Fulvio Tessitore (Rome-Bari: Laterza, 2011), 889–90.
20. Exile was a defining experience for nineteenth-century Italian intellectuals and men of action. On the first generation of exiles, to which Cuoco belonged, see Anna Maria Rao, *Esuli: L'emigrazione politica italiana in Francia (1792–1802)* (Naples: Guida, 1992); on emigration in later periods, see Maurizio Isabella, *Risorgimento in Exile: Italian Émigrés and the Liberal International in the Post-Napoleonic Era* (Oxford: Oxford University Press, 2009); and Agostino Bistarelli, *Gli esuli del Risorgimento* (Bologna: Il Mulino, 2011).
21. Cuoco, *Pagine giornalistiche*, 890.

perience as an effective revolution (though Cuoco came to question French achievements, too) was in Italy an extrinsic imposition and, as such, a "passively" experienced one. Members of the Italian elite, well versed in imitating foreign customs, were able to delude themselves as to the degree of their participation, but no such self-deception characterized the masses, without whose support or, rather, initiative no revolution can occur. For this reason Cuoco emphasized the presence in Italy of "two peoples," a minority of haves and a majority of have-nots, on whose reconnection hinged the positive outcome of any reforming impulse (*SS*, 325).

As he explored more closely the effects and to a greater extent the causes attending to the fall of ancien régimes, the rise of nationalist sentiments, and the attempted transformation of values, Cuoco came to distrust the very notion of 'revolution.' History, he felt, shows that the "will to change everything, brings about the destruction of everything" and, consequently, lays the premises for restoration (*SS*, 224 and 516). The change he wished for Italy would instead follow upon renewed familiarization with (and painstaking reinstatement of) those qualities and merits that make up national cultures and that deserve safekeeping (518). He did not worry, moreover, about the risk of basking in reflected glory. For the toil required to recover objects of pride would be so onerous that each Italian would perceive Italy's common "home," once built from scratch, as a personal achievement. Cuoco's lucid account of the causes of Italy's failures was based on the Vichian idea that unlike "natural catastrophes," which are imponderable acts of God, "political catastrophes" are manmade (they "follow upon the irresistible impulses of the heart") and as such are knowable in detail and deserving of being relived in historical reconstruction, rather than being dismissed, as is often the case, in "praise" and "satire" (222).

Today Cuoco's work lends itself to disparate interpretations. Was he animated by the desire to disengage, for good, the course of Italian history from that of France? Or was he laboring, principally, to endow Italy with a rivaling intellectual autonomy? Recent scholarship emphasizes convincingly that an "aporia between Bonapartism and national exigencies" is essential to the work of Cuoco, whose concessions to France's supremacy in arms and civil organization were offset by what he came to see as Italy's intellectual difference.[22] What interests us now are not Cuoco's

22. Antonino De Francesco, "Leggere il 'Platone in Italia' agli inizi del secolo XXI," in *Platone in Italia*, by Vincenzo Cuoco (Rome: Laterza, 2006), xlix. See also Antonino De Fran-

specific claims (these tended to be relatively sober in their enthusiasm), but his ability to produce a discourse that could be recognized as specifically Italian, or, in the words of one of the earliest students of Cuoco's work, Paul Hazard, as a "philosophie de l'italianisme."[23] Unable to rely on a well-established historiographical tradition, Cuoco sought to devise a discourse that was 'Italian' in its *way*, in that it conformed to the *forma mentis* displayed—also in contrast to French hegemony—not only by Vico but to an equal degree by Machiavelli, whose historiographical realism and attention to the "effective truths of things" (*verità effettuale delle cose*), as opposed to imaginary truths, Cuoco wanted to make his own. In fact, Cuoco specifies, thought and action are conjoined so tightly in Italian thought (and, until Montesquieu, in French thought as well) that "anyone whose head was full of the ideas of Machiavelli, Gravina, and Vico could neither have faith in the premises nor applaud the activities of the French revolutionaries once they gave up on the idea of the constitutional monarchy"—that is, once political pragmatism gave way to conceptual utopias (*SS*, 185).

With his "philosophy of nothing but human things," an elaboration of what he defined as the "philosophy of erudition" of Vico and his eighteenth-century heirs, Cuoco was reacting to what he perceived as the "abstruse metaphysics" of Jacobin rationalism. This is most evident in the letters he wrote to fellow patriot Vincenzo Russo on the question of constitutionalism. Indeed, Cuoco saw that it is in the difficult process of drafting constitutions that the deficiencies of *l'esprit de système* are revealed, as the philosopher's natural penchant for immutable "excellence" (*ottimo*) clashes with the intent of providing for the necessarily provisional "good" (*bene*) of the people:

> Constitutions are to be made for men as they are, as they will eternally be: full of vices, full of errors. To believe that people will give up their customs, which I deem almost second nature, to follow our institutions, which I deem arbitrary and variable, is as reasonable as for a shoemaker to expect the customer to whom he has provided a short shoe to shorten his foot. (*SS*, 516)

cesco, "Il *Saggio storico* e la cultura politica italiana fra Otto e Novecento," in *Saggio storico sulla rivoluzione di Napoli*, by Vincenzo Cuoco (Manduria: Piero Lacaita, 1998), 9–197.

23. Paul Hazard, *La révolution française et les lettres italiennes (1789–1815)* (Paris: Hachette, 1910), 218ff. Hazard's work was critically reviewed by Giovanni Gentile in *Albori della nuova Italia: Varietà e documenti*, 2 vols. (Lanciano: Carabba, 1923), 1:82ff.

Here and elsewhere on this topic Cuoco uses a sartorial metaphor, emphasizing the need for constitutions to be drawn in man's likeness and, nation by nation, epoch by epoch, custom made. As further evidence, Cuoco
compares the U.S. bill of rights to the French declaration of the rights of
man, concluding that the latter amounts to the "algebraic formula" of the
former in its appeal to "reason" rather than "sentiments" (258).[24]

Cuoco's notion of a "passive revolution," his theory of "two peoples,"
and his emphasis on the historical uniqueness of any constitution reflect
the influence of one of Vico's central axioms: "The nature of institutions
[cose] is nothing but their coming into being at certain times and in certain
guises. Whenever the time and guise are thus and so, such and not otherwise are the institutions that come into being."[25] The challenge, therefore,
is to allow and nurture institutions' historical development without imposing forceful accelerations. "Anything may be achieved," says Cuoco;
"the difficulty is in knowing how to bring things about. With time, we can
achieve those ideas that it would be crazy to want to get to today. . . . The
secret is in knowing where to start from" (SS, 348). Cuoco is credited with
having bequeathed a liberal moderatism to the Italian nineteenth century,
and it seems evident that his political stance was related to his 'humanism,' his particular recognition of the past's bearings on the present: "Re-
formers refer to the audacity with which they attack hoary institutions
[sollennità antiche] as a spiritual strength; I call it the stupidity of a spirit
which is unable to reconcile past intuitions with new ones" (350).

As he realized that Italy's national identity would be formed only
over the long haul, Cuoco laid the foundations for a fruitful collaboration. He suggested a working plan in the "Program" he wrote for the Giornale italiano, a magazine established in 1804 with the goal of "creating"
(rather than "maintaining") the "public spirit" that Italy still lacked and
whose promotion depended on the cultivation of "self-esteem" and on
consensus-creating "debate" on what was useful and harmful for the country.[26] Self-esteem would not be a matter of telling Italians that they are

24. Cuoco's constitutional theory is discussed and contextualized in Vincenzo Ferrone,
The Politics of Enlightenment: Constitutionalism, Republicanism, and the Rights of Man in
Gaetano Filangieri, trans. Sophus A. Reinert (London: Anthem Press, 2012), chap. 9.

25. Giambattista Vico, New Science, trans. Thomas G. Bergin and Max H. Fisch (Ithaca,
NY: Cornell University Press, 1948), 4.

26. On Cuoco's activity as a journalist, see Maurizio Martirano, "Politica e cultura
negli scritti giornalistici di Vincenzo Cuoco (1801–1806), in Scritti giornalistici, by Vincenzo
Cuoco, 2 vols. (Naples: Fridericiana Editrice Universitaria, 1999), 1:xxiii–lxvii; and Domenico
Conte "'Un felice ingegno d'Italia': Vincenzo Cuoco giornalista a Napoli," in Scritti giornalistici, 2:xvii–lxix.

"great," as the English and French often told themselves in the columns of their newspapers, because, Cuoco wrote, there is no way of "persuading oneself of truths for which one is not prepared." Rather, one would turn the humble inhabitants of the provinces into citizens of an Italian state only by "showing them those things" by which they themselves could come to be persuaded of their worth. These "things" would include the "memories of times gone by," provided they could be presented without distortion for "what they really were." At the same time, consideration for the "cose nostre" had to be balanced by an ongoing interaction with other nations—whose aura, Cuoco ventured, often owes more to their being distant than to their being superior.

Cuoco's most striking note in his statement of purpose for the *Giornale italiano* was perhaps his censure of the "theoretical sciences, which may never be an object of popular instruction." In fact, while Italy abounded in resources for scholars and legislators, "there [was] still nothing in place for the instruction of the people." Perhaps this is why Cuoco came to conceive of a massive epistolary novel, *Plato in Italy* (1804–6), with the aim to "pleasantly involve" a larger majority:

> Barthélemy in France and Wieland in Germany have endowed history with a dramatic garb which renders it at once more pleasant and more instructive. For the same reason that people prefer fables to speeches, they prefer drama to fables, for they become fellow citizens of the protagonists of the story, and they are instructed almost as if witnessing and acting in first person, which is the easiest and most efficacious way to instruct oneself.[27]

Pseudohistorical novels such as Jean-Jacques Barthélemy's *Voyage du jeune Anacharsis en Grèce* (1788–89) were a means by which to form readers' virtues in the school of long-lost civilizations, and Cuoco's use of the genre presented an opportunity to introduce modern Italians to their forebears.

Passing his novel off as an Italian translation of a Greek manuscript so ancient as to make its title barely discernible, "ΠΛΑΤΩΝ . . . ΙΤΑΛ . . . ," Cuoco elaborated on Plato's alleged visit to southern Italy sometime in the mid-fourth century BC. In Cuoco's rendition, Plato and a young disciple named Cleobolo encounter a panoply of industrious communities whose clockwork organization, respect for hierarchies, and peaceful demeanor are to serve as an example to modern Italian municipalities; meanwhile,

27. Cuoco, *Pagine giornalistiche*, 652.

the looming threat posed by the Romans and their leveling power stands in, of course, for French interference. The Italic populations, the Sannites above all, represent advancement in many realms, from the emancipation of their female population to their agricultural techniques; individual achievements, however, are attributed to a secret Pythagorean wisdom reposing in the Italian ethos. "I venture to say," says Cuoco's Plato, "that Pythagoras never existed; he is rather an idea conjured up by people to denote a system of cognitions whose origins are very ancient, and that has been conserved and handed down through a board of wise men who were born and raised in Italy."[28]

Pythagoras is quite clearly a Vichian 'poetic character,' an 'impersonality' employed by Cuoco in order to bypass the heroic narratives of standard historiography and present a group-bound core of communal capacities and actions. In the last analysis, the wisdom attributed to Pythagoras is none other than a way of life, and thus admirable rather than explicable. Following the cue provided by Vico in *On the Most Ancient Wisdom of the Italians*, Cuoco has Plato recover the immediacy and efficacy of Italian thought in the languages of the inhabitants of southern Italy:

> In the language of these people *truth* [*il vero*] is nothing else than the *made* [*il fatto*], there is nothing more to truth than being; there is no other manifestation of it than action [*il fare*]. To *understand* [*intendere*] is to grasp something in all of its parts, to know how it formed itself, to know its *causes*, and its *effects*: thinking is less valuable than understanding, which amounts to gathering truths one by one and almost gropingly. Man thinks but he may not understand all truths, because it is not in his power to make everything. God comprehends everything, because He can make everything, He made everything, and contains everything within Himself. Divine ideas are orders [*voleri*], and His orders are His works. We Greeks admire Homer so much because he painted Jove's eyebrow, whose twitch moves all the elements, but what Homer has described, the Italians have imitated, and they have come up with a word to describe the Divinity which indicates precisely that motion by which He can all that He wants. They call Him 'Nume.' I would not know how to better render this word in Greek if not by: *He spoke and it was done.*[29]

28. Vincenzo Cuoco, *Platone in Italia* (Rome: Laterza, 2006), 101.

29. Cuoco, *Platone in Italia*, 102–3. Compare with Vico's tenets in *On the Most Ancient Wisdom of the Italians*, 45: "For the Latins, *verum* (the true) and *factum* (what is made) are interchangeable, or to use the customary language of the Schools, they are convertible. For

The creative, metaphoric language of the ancient Italians, in which the words are inseparable from deed and thing, betokens their corporeal imagination. Reflecting on the language and landscape of these people, Plato finally concedes Italy's superiority: "These nations that we deem barbaric have been cultured long before us."[30]

With *Plato in Italy*, Cuoco challenged Greek (= French) vainglory and restored Italy—in accordance with an erudite tendency in vogue since the Renaissance—to its *primato* or chronological and, it is implied, intellectual preeminence.[31] The pseudohistory to which Cuoco resorted may appear at odds with the solid historiographical talent he displayed in the *Essay*. But it does so only if one ignores the educative solution that Cuoco saw as being the one way to dissolve the mutual incomprehension (and thus lack of cooperation) between the ruling class and the masses:

> Just as any human operation requires force and mind [*idea*], so are great numbers [*il numero*] and leaders [*condottieri*] necessary to bring about a revolution. Leaders present people with those ideas that they only barely perceive as if by intuition, which they often follow with enthusiasm, and that they rarely know how to form by themselves. (*SS*, 315)[32]

In Cuoco's view, those Neapolitans who had not turned French by 1799 had, indeed, remained "savages," yet his allegiance was to them. Having learned from Vico to treat nations as metaphorically human, he wished that leaders (they being the ones most in need of education) could learn how to tap into the "common mind of nations" and thereby govern people, gradually and according to their level of understanding, with that

---

them, the verb *intelligere* is the same as 'to read perfectly' and 'to have plain knowledge.' In addition, their *cogitare* was the same as our vernacular 'to think' (*pensare*) and 'to gather' (*andar raccogliendo*)."

30. Cuoco, *Platone in Italia*, 103.

31. Cuoco dedicated his novel to the pioneering natural scientist Bernardino Telesio (1509–88): "Questo libro è dovuto a te, che io riconosco primo tra gl'investigatori dell'antichissima filosofia degl'Italiani. Per opera tua l'Europa vide succedere la prima volta alle idee dell'aristotelismo quelle di Parmenide; e, sebbene i tempi non ti permisero d'innalzare il nuovo edificio con felicità eguale a quella colla quale avevi distrutto l'antico, pure ti rimane sempre la non piccola gloria di aver il primo indicata la nuova via, per la quale tanti progressi han fatto coloro che sono venuti dopo di te" (Cuoco, *Platone in Italia*, 5). See Paolo Casini, *L'antica sapienza italica: Cronistoria di un mito* (Bologna: Il Mulino, 1998), 238–67. See also Annalisa Andreoni, *Omero Italico: Favole antiche e identità nazionale tra Vico e Cuoco* (Rome: Jouvence, 2003).

32. Cuoco is here paraphrasing one of Vico's most famous axioms: "Men at first feel without perceiving, then they perceive with a troubled and agitated mind, finally they reflect with a clear mind." Vico, *New Science*, 75.

Italic wisdom which they inadvertently safeguarded in their actions and temperament.[33]

It can be argued that Cuoco was the first to gain consciousness of a national philosophical tradition.[34] It can be argued only in retrospect, however, with the knowledge that the enthusiasm for the illusive and elusive *primato*, a quest, we shall see, that was pursued forcefully in the first half of the nineteenth century, slowly gave way to reason once Vico was introduced to his mature self, Hegel, after yet another traumatic upheaval, the Spring of Nations of 1848. The transition took place in the context of Italy's unification in 1860–61, and it led to the realization that the practical, realist bent of Italian philosophy could be more than surmised from dubious ancient sources: it could be observed in the nation's modern history since the Renaissance.[35] What is striking, and what ultimately lends his work an aura of prophecy in the eyes of his self-avowed heirs, is that Cuoco anticipated Italy's philosophical emancipation in one of his articles for the *Giornale italiano*:

> The affairs that pertain to philosophical sects are closely related to the political state of a given society, and it is much more important than commonly thought if a nation has or has not its own philosophy. We have been receiving philosophy for a long time now, first from France through Descartes, later from England through Locke; but until the fifteenth century we had been giving it to other people. Review the epochs of political greatness of all nations; they are coterminous with those of their philosophical greatness. One's first power is in the mind; and the arm of him who has none, or believes himself to have none, is always weak.[36]

Cuoco rightly foresaw that Italians would come face to face with the Renaissance as a consequence of their quest for a national philosophy. What he failed to see, however, was that on meeting their Renaissance selves,

---

33. I follow here the suggestions of Paolo Casini, "Cuoco, l'immagine del popolo e l'antica sapienza italica," in *L'Europa tra Illuminismo e Restaurazione: Scritti in onore di Furio Diaz*, ed. Paolo Alatri (Rome: Bulzoni, 1993), 277–89.

34. See Luciano Malusa, *L'idea di tradizione nazionale nella storiografia filosofica italiana dell'Ottocento* (Genoa: Tilgher, 1989), 14.

35. See Ilario Tolomio, *Italorum sapientia: L'idea di esperienza nella storiografia filosofica italiana dell'età moderna* (Catanzaro: Rubbettino, 1999), 7–8.

36. Cuoco, *Pagine giornalistiche*, 203–4.

Risorgimento Italians would, at first and for a long time after, recoil in horror.

This said, the various reflections (and initiatives) with which Cuoco attempted to jump-start Italy's national reawakening after the failed revolution of 1799 became a storehouse from which a significant number of Risorgimento thinkers drew as they attempted to articulate, relentlessly, the outlines of the Italian man and his nation. Cuoco's jejune attempt to identify philosophical with political prowess shows why there was a discrepancy between practical and spiritual achievements. Had Italian history in fact demonstrated a parallel anything like what Cuoco claimed, the race to set a historical precedent would not have been as antagonistic or as sectarian as it turned out to be. Everyone could agree with Cuoco regarding Italian intellectual wealth "until the fifteenth century." The problem was that this loose periodization pointed to a break between the Middle Ages and the Renaissance. The question then became, did Italy make its contribution to world history through its late medieval civic and religious institutions or through its Renaissance secularism and humanism?

Cuoco most probably meant the latter. But in arguing for the predominance of one or the other paradigm, always in mutual exclusion, his heirs turned the search for an Italian *primato* into an internal affair. 'Italian philosophy' (and the peculiar interpretation of the Renaissance that would eventually determine its final formulation) would be produced in the friction between Catholic and lay interests within Italy. Moreover, contrary to Cuoco's claims, the late Risorgimento man found no counterpart in the political arena for the cultural affluence of the Italian Renaissance. Rather, it became increasingly obvious that the Renaissance, from an Italian perspective, presented a paradox: what led to the country's political decline had somehow come about within that context of unparalleled cultural flourishing. And until a way to resolve that paradox could be found—without totally forsaking the positive heritage of the Renaissance—the medieval and religious outlook prevailed.

ITALIANS AS DISCIPLES OF GOD: VINCENZO GIOBERTI AND NEO-GUELPHISM

One need only compare the work of Cuoco to that of his exact contemporary, Hegel, to gauge the *philosophical* incommensurability between Italy and Germany. Yet it is undeniable that the French Revolution triggered a very similar set of considerations in both countries. If it can be said that after gazing across the Rhine at events whose modernity they were destined to experience vicariously, at best, Germans began to open a *Sonderweg*, attempting to furrow their own 'special pathway,' then it can be argued that Italians faced a predicament even more difficult. That is, they had no "radical pedigree," comprising the Protestant Reformation and advances in philosophy, on which to rely—a pedigree that gave Germans a reason for spiritual, if not political, pride by intimating that they had anticipated those events.[37] Lacking that "radical" background, and thus left alone with a seemingly unmanageable historical "misalignment," the thinkers of the Italian Risorgimento followed, even as they denied it, in the Germans' footsteps. By the middle of the nineteenth century they would declare themselves 'philosophers,' Hegelians, or better, idealists, of an Italian ilk. This feat, however, would not have been possible without the emergence of a thinker, an 'Italian Hegel,' who could bridge the gap between Vico and the present and show, using the only leverage available to him—Italian 'primordiality'—that Italy, while unable to aspire to be last and thus best, could be first and, as such, not least.

Born in Turin in the same year in which Cuoco's *Essay* was published, the Catholic thinker Vincenzo Gioberti (1801–52) delved deeper than anyone before or, for that matter, since into the origins of that primal Italian difference which Vico thought he had teased out with his conjectural etymologies, and which Cuoco had narrated so creatively and comprehensively. The fact that Gioberti's work itself bore the marks of Vichianism testifies to the success of efforts to popularize and canonize Vico by Cuoco's generation of Neapolitan émigrés in northern Italy.[38] Even as the divide between northern and southern Italy grew deeper and wider during the Risorgimento, Vico's *De Antiquissima*, and to a lesser extent his *New Science*, insisted on a shared ideological basis for reactivating a tradition whose origins Gioberti would attempt to trace back not simply to the Renaissance or the Middle Ages, but to God himself.

As we have seen, Cuoco's study of history and his personal experiences had persuaded him that Italian patriotism could be cultivated abroad only, and Gioberti's experience confirmed it. His own exuberant nationalism was honed in exile, into which he was forced after his flirtation with Mazzini's subversive Young Italy movement. In Paris and, later,

---

37. See Rebecca Comay, *Mourning Sickness: Hegel and the French Revolution* (Stanford: Stanford University Press, 2011), esp. the introduction and chap. 1.

38. While a detailed study on the topic is still to be attempted, a useful introduction to Gioberti's 'Vichianism' is in Giulio Bonafede, "Presenza di Vico in Gioberti," *Nuovi quaderni del meridione* 4 (1968): 206–37.

during an extremely prolific decade in Brussels, he had the chance to as-similate, critically, the lessons of like-minded "prophets of the past" such as Louis Bonald, de Maistre, and Lamennais, as well as to refine, philo-sophically, the anti-Gallicism that fiery playwright Vittorio Alfieri, a fig-ure idolized by Gioberti, had raised into a prerequisite sentiment for the creation of an Italian consciousness.[39] Undoubtedly, the successive actions of Charles VIII, Louis XIV, and Napoleon had thwarted Italy's already slow progress toward independence, and yet—and here again adhering closely to Vico—Gioberti was more concerned initially with the "servile habit of Gallic theorizing," or, as he saw it, Italian intellectual subservience to the thought of Descartes, "the principal corruptor of philosophy in the mod-ern era, the author of those false principles and the awful method that would bring philosophy to its ruin."[40]

Descartes offended by turning the order of creation on its head: he sug-gested that Being derived from existence, with the formulation *cogito ergo sum; sum, ergo Deus est*. Gioberti worried that in modern times the Car-tesian disease he called "psychological egotism" was dangerously wide-spread, having been raised to a metaphysical level by the German tradition of pantheism that culminates in Hegel, and having provided the basis for Scottish sensism. Both of these were hot imports in Italy in the earlier part of the nineteenth century. However, the fact that he also described Cartesianism as "Protestantism applied to philosophy" suggested an intent to prove that Italy was outside of the modern framework created by the double rupture of the religious Reformation and the rise of phil-osophical subjectivism. "God is, God creates me, therefore I exist," was Gioberti's response, and it was in the process of restoring the precedence of essence over existence that Italy would recover its true genius and intel-lectual legacy. This legacy, it goes without saying, was proudly and utterly unmodern.[41]

The key component of the reform that Gioberti envisioned was a "pro-tology" or first science. In what would be a drawn-out process, Gioberti

39. I take the qualification from J. Barbey d'Aurevilly, *Les prophètes du passé* (Paris: Sandre, 2006 [1851]). Vittorio Alfieri is the author of a miscellaneous satirical work entitled *Misogallo* (first published anonymously in 1799) inspired by the events of the French Revolu-tion. For Gioberti's assessment of Alfieri, see Vincenzo Gioberti, *Introduzione allo studio della filosofia*, ed. Enzo Bonaventura (Florence: Sansoni, 1926), 24ff.

40. I cite from Marcello Mustè, *La scienza ideale: Filosofia e politica in Vincenzo Gio-berti* (Catanzaro: Rubbettino, 2000), 110, which offers an informative contextualization of Gioberti's anti-Cartesianism.

41. Vincenzo Gioberti, *Della Protologia*, ed. Giuseppe Massari, 2 vols. (Turin: Eredi Botta, 1857), 1:113.

began to conceive of it following an enervating spiritual and philosophical conversion whose far-reaching consequences he discussed in a heartfelt letter to Giacomo Leopardi in 1830, five years after being ordained.[42]
The "truth of Christianity (and therefore of Catholicism, which is its only
invariable form)," Gioberti wrote to the poet, depended on acknowledging the absolute incommensurability of the supranatural realm, and, because of that incommensurability, the higher order could be known only
through that Revelation which Christianity, as a historical fact, represents.[43] Throughout his career, Gioberti would hold true to the intention
expressed in this letter to recover the point of contact between reason and
God and to demonstrate the mind's conformity to a divinely revealed dic-
tate, which he saw as the only way to vanquish the dualisms of naturalism
and theism (the latter having proved attractive to Gioberti in his youth), as
well as monistic pantheism.

Vico had admired primitive men for their proximity to the "Supreme
Being." A similar feeling motivates Gioberti's own marshaling of all
known nations, from the most civilized to the most savage, in his works.
However, he wanted to venture where Vico—whom Gioberti does not spare
from criticism—would not: to a moment of true correspondence between
thought and Being, the logical and the ontological.[44] In his *Introduction
to the Study of Philosophy*, published ten years after his youthful letter
to Leopardi, Gioberti was finally in a position to explicate man's foundational judgment, not as a product of mental activity, but rather as a mental
item grasped in non-sensory intuition. The most primitive intuition, he
claimed, cannot but be of Being, and it would be impossible "without recognizing that Being is: in the contrary case, to be would be nothing and
real Being would not be real, which is contradictory" (*FKC*, 294). But since
"nothing is not only unthinkable but also impossible in itself," Gioberti
wished to render this first intuition as "Being is necessarily," in the sense
that God "posits himself in the presence of our mind and says 'I am necessarily,'" and this truth is one to which mind bears witness "as an auditor
of a verdict it does not issue" (294).

---

42. On the relationship between Gioberti and Leopardi, see Marcello Mustè, "Gioberti e
Leopardi," *La cultura* 38, no. 1 (2000): 59–113.

43. Vincenzo Gioberti, *Epistolario*, ed. Giovanni Gentile and Gustavo Balsamo-Crivelli,
11 vols. (Florence: Vallecchi, 1927–37), 1:42. Leopardi was a fitting interlocutor, having
recently (in 1824) put forth considerations on the Italians' 'difference' from the French. See
Giacomo Leopardi, *Discorso sopra lo stato presente dei costumi degl'italiani* (Milan: Rizzoli,
1998).

44. See Bonafede, "Presenza di Vico in Gioberti," 211.

This intuition, of course, is nonverbal; speech ensues, however, as a "second revelation" mediating between divine intuition and human reflection:

> Repeating the divine and objective judgment in an act of reflection is the first link in philosophy as human artifice. But this link is joined with a divine judgment and draws all its power from it. It follows, then, that the basis of philosophy lies in revelation; that God is the first philosopher, in the strict sense of the word; and that human philosophy is the continuation and repetition of divine philosophy. Therefore, God is not only the object of science; he is also its first teacher, the teacher of the knowable because He is the Intelligible. The work of philosophy begins not in man but in God. It does not ascend from mind to Being but descends from Being to mind. This is the deep reason in an ontology that makes psychology absurd. Before philosophy is a human activity, it is a divine creation. Psychologists deprive philosophy of its foothold in the divine, detach it from Being, make it mere human artifice, condemn it to skepticism, and assign it *nothing* as its origin and end. (*FKC*, 295)

The statement "Being is necessarily" is only one of the three terms composing the "ideal formula" sought by Gioberti, the formula that would cover everything cognized by man and that would ideally and organically link the discovery of Being or first concept to the resulting or second act of human cognition.

Gioberti finds the term "exist" and its root meaning, "appear, come out of, emerge, and be shown," particularly apt for illustrating the derivative nature of man's mental activity. The particle *ex-* denotes causality and direction and illustrates the passage from potentiality to act. *Exist*, therefore, may not be used interchangeably with *be*, as most philosophers tend to use it, starting with Descartes, who, as Vico had already pointed out, naïvely spoke as a god when he said "I am" as opposed to "I exist" (*FKC*, 297).[45] Gioberti's distinction also makes clear the nature of Being as both first and efficient Cause and, in relation to its effects, as a creative act linking, without eliding, the two terms of the ideal formula's final rendering: "Being creates the existent." Gioberti clarifies:

> Thus, when the Formula that we assume to be true is reduced to its genuine meaning—that of an objective and ontological process—each

45. Vico, *On the Most Ancient Wisdom of the Italians*, 134–35.

of its terms represents an objective reality that actually subsists on its own, outside the mind. This reality is absolute and necessary in the first element, in Being, but in its last element, in the existent, it is relative and contingent. The link between these two elements is creation, an action that is real and positive but free. (303–4)

With his ideal formula, Gioberti believed he had found an appropriate synthesis that illustrated, in accordance with the logic of subject and predicate, the dynamic dualism of necessity and contingence, God and world.

Gioberti's ideal formula, on which he based his interpretation of every natural and human phenomenon, was also the cornerstone of the "ontologism" (a term that Gioberti may have coined) that he wished to pit against modern psychologism, with a view toward a religious or Catholic restoration.[46] What is more important for our concerns is that he saw it as the necessary first step toward resolving the political vicissitudes (in the sense that they were moral and spiritual) of nineteenth-century Italy. In order to see the connection between the objective truth contained in the statement "Being creates the existent" and Italy's unification cause, it is useful to note Gioberti's understanding of human earthly activity as a "second creative act," also explicable by a corollary formula: "The existent returns to Being." In the return cycle, man, "the first secondary agent in the world," "participates" (in the Platonic sense of *metexis*) as God's cooperator, or rather, "concreator," by means of his intellectual endeavors, his advancement of sciences, and, generally, his varied contributions to the inexorable progress of civilization.[47] Man, who is a "living and concrete dialecticism," thus "proceeds from God with the creative act, and returns to god with the palingenetic act."[48] The balance of the ideal and the real postulated in the formula is as perfect as it is fragile; its observance and fruition in the historical order of things are contingent on absolute respect for the hierarchical or complementarian framework that it suggests.

Having recovered and thoroughly defended this philosophical prime, Gioberti eventually embarked on a vast historiographical project inspired by what it postulated. This became *On the Civil and Moral Primacy*

46. Gioberti's 'ontologism' is more broadly contextualized in Bernard M. G. Reardon, *Religion in the Age of Romanticism: Studies in Early Nineteenth-Century Thought* (Cambridge: Cambridge University Press, 1985), chap. 6.

47. I cite from the selection in *Gioberti*, ed. Giuseppe Saitta (Milan: Garzanti, 1952), 94ff.

48. *Gioberti*, 102.

of the Italians (1843), a work that immediately rocketed to the status of manifesto of Risorgimento thought and aspirations despite its length and convolutedness.[49] Not unlike Vico's *New Science*, it took origins and pre-historic civility as its topic but did so differently from Vico's model, and as the title suggests, it expressed a fierce patriotism, something that Vico, if indeed he ever shared such sentiment, had definitively shed in his intellectual maturity. As we have seen, the topic of Italian primacy was already drawing Cuoco's interest. It was only by means of the ideal formula, however, that a mythically envisioned chronological precedence could be made synonymous, according to divine will and logic, with intellectual superiority.

And yet Gioberti's notion of "primato" is less transparent than it would first appear. As he deploys the term, he sees Italy's supremacy or preeminence as not simply to be posited, for history in fact shows the opposite. Rather, it is to be proven, relying on what may be described as an Italian right of preemption or *usucapio*, bringing Italy's inhabitants along with her, a right earned in the first place as a most ancient geographical or geological expression. While Gioberti's "rational ethnography" often verges on the chauvinistic and racist, the crux of his argument remains the Italian *genius loci*, justifying the nation's privileged status in the eyes of God as either happenstance or predetermined, depending on the vantage point.[50] Even as Gioberti attempted, with his ideal formula, to justify the Italian primacy according to the proximity of the country and its people to divine philosophy and the truth of creation, the importance of his *Primato* for the development of Italian philosophy resided elsewhere, in his ability to fluidify his first principle into a dialectical term opposed, through all of Western history, to the encroachment of what he saw as the dark powers of Eastern pantheism. Accordingly, in what he sees as the alternating predominance of monad and dyad, Gioberti diachronically refashions the myth of the *primato* into a tradition or, more specifically, a philosophical heritage that is born *Italic* and matures properly *Italian* in the course of

---

49. For an attempt to make sense of this contradiction, the discrepancy between Gioberti's success in his time and his total neglect in the present, see Bruce Haddock, "Political Union without Social Revolution: Vincenzo Gioberti's *Primato*," *Historical Journal* 41, no. 3 (1998): 705–23.

50. Mirella Pasini takes due notice of Gioberti's most disturbing beliefs in "Un Gioberti positivista o dell'invenzione della stirpe mediterranea," in *I filosofi e la genesi della coscienza culturale della "nuova Italia" (1799–1900)*, ed. Luciano Malusa (Naples: Istituto Italiano per gli Studi Filosofici, 1997), 343–51.

history. The sketch Gioberti provided was not, perhaps, the first attempt at outlining a history of Italian philosophy, yet it turned into a standard against which future models were formulated.

Gioberti traces the earliest origins to the Italic teaching of indigenous Pelasgians. Of the three "luminaries"—Pythagoras, Socrates, and Plato—who drew on this wisdom in an attempt to restore the "light of revelation," Pythagoras was the most ancient, as much Italian as he was Greek, and the founder of the most representative of Italian schools of thought, Pythagoreanism. The essence of Pythagorean thought is its "universality"; especially in the realm of culture and science, it looks for harmony rather than identity, and it is realistically inclined in theoretical and political pursuits. And political realism would indeed be prominent in the next stage of Italian theorizing, in the "Latin philosophy" that emerged as thought crossed back over into the Italian peninsula from Greece and settled enduringly in Rome. Latin wisdom, however, like Stoicism, was too practical, too focused on civic applications, and its "theoretical weakness" would lead to the demise of the Republic. Balance was restored by the Church Fathers, many of whom, while not Italian (Tertullian, Augustine, and Bernard), drew from Catholic Rome the "breath that gave life" to their philosophy. The fourth stage of Italian philosophy would arrive in the form of Scholasticism, but only the realist version (Anselm, Bonaventure, and Aquinas), nominalism being a prerogative of the French and English.

As Gioberti tells it, the pitfalls of modernity were predicted in what he describes as the intra-Scholastic war between Celtic-Germanic (nominalist) and Pelasgic-Italic (realist) wisdom. Moreover, the waning of realism coincided with the "demise of papal dictatorship" and the presence of "barbarians" on the Italian peninsula: "Because Italy and the Pontiff represent the Idea manifest as a people and a person, they cannot preserve their rule when the senses take the place of ideas, following the canons of nominalism" (*FKC*, 269). The fifth stage of Italian philosophy grew out of the fifteenth-century renewal of classical antiquity but faltered, despite the merits of such thinkers as Patrizi, Girolamo Cardano, Bernardino Telesio, Giordano Bruno, and Tommaso Campanella, whose lofty ideas held no sway in Italy where theory was again abandoned in favor of that scientism inaugurated by the likes of Machiavelli, Galileo, and Paolo Sarpi. Equally unfruitful was the renovation of theory inaugurated by Vico, who in Gioberti's narrative is made to represent a philosophical epoch of his own, albeit one that was overlooked, arriving as it did after the reforms of Luther and Descartes. In conclusion, Gioberti describes Vico's *New Science* as "a fertile land that God set in the ocean," one just beginning to be explored by Gioberti himself and his contemporaries, such that nineteenth-century Vichianism could be made to signal a seventh and final stage of Italian thought.

It should be evident that Gioberti did more than provide a canon for a nascent Italian philosophy. By subsuming the stages of Italian thought into a providentially understood history, Vico's "ideal eternal history," Gioberti's narrative endowed Italian thinkers with a hieratic aura. It bestowed a sort of prelacy on their wisdom, a religious duty or mission to which Italy could lay claim owing to its longtime coexistence with the true Church, itself the organ entrusted with the safekeeping of the orthodoxy of the original revelation. This proximity to Catholicism is what Gioberti calls Italy's "strange destiny," one that he urges Italians to accept, "returning like the prodigal son to its parent." Moreover, the country's prerogative as the cradle of Christian civilization reflects that common identity which Italians failed to recover elsewhere:

> Italy and the Holy See are certainly two and essentially distinct, and whoever would confound them would engage in an absurd and rather impious and sacrilegious effort. However, a coexistence of eighteen centuries has so strongly and fraternally connected the two that if others may be Catholics without being Italians . . . one could certainly not be perfectly Italian in every respect without being Catholic.[51]

This claim made many cringe even in Gioberti's time, but no secular paradigm could match its universal appeal.

At this point the question arises as to what kind of nation-state Gioberti thought Italy could become, exactly. As scholars often note, all of his chauvinism did not prevent Gioberti from dashing hopes that Italy might mature into a nation like any other European country.[52] Nothing in Italian history indicated that it could. What history showed, rather, was that the papacy's proximity throughout history repeatedly made up for Italy's deficiencies. Therefore it was only in renewing this marriage that Italy could aspire to supranational status and rediscover her God-willed cosmopolitan calling. A pithy rendering of the ideal formula and its corollary would be that just as Italy brought forth Christian Europe, so Gioberti now called for Europe's return to Italy. Doing so would be the salvation of Europe as a whole, in that it would draw it away from the modern *status deviationis*,

---

51. Cited in Giorgio Rumi, *Gioberti* (Bologna: Il Mulino, 1999), 28.
52. On this point see Mustè, *La scienza ideale*, 205ff.

or fallen state. Gioberti, in other words, understood Italy's *risorgimento*, 'resurgence,' as possibly a pan-European palingenesis in its true sense: an abiding recreation in God.

With his radically ontological Vichianism Gioberti successfully managed to reconcile revolutionary pathos with conservative principles and moderate political stances.[53] He stirred an unprecedented interest in 'philosophy' understood as connecting to culture in all of its facets: history, politics, social theory, religion, literature, and more. More important, he showed how religious restoration, philosophical renovation, and political resurgence were all interlinked—and he did not hesitate to provide concrete suggestions, if not a fully fledged program, for carrying these through. Despite the fact that Gioberti's legacy has turned out to be primarily a philosophical one, he was celebrated in his own time for the Guelph solution he articulated as a way to achieve unification. His plan called for a confederation of regional municipalities that would be governed by the Piedmontese government but united under the spiritual aegis of the pope. Gioberti and many others came to see in a renewed Guelphism the only solution that would enable the inalienable wealth of Italy's varied cultures to be retained and channeled toward a shared set of goals, the first goal being (at the time that he was writing) Italy's liberation from the Austrian occupation.[54]

Gioberti enjoyed a triumphal return to his *patria* in 1848. He was paraded through Italy as her intellectual liberator and was entrusted with major responsibilities in the government. But where was the pope in all this? When Gioberti first published the *Primato* he drew skepticism from even the most sympathetic readers because the pontifical throne was then occupied by the illiberal and reactionary Gregory XVI. By the same token, however, the election in 1846 of the reformist Giovanni Mastai Ferretti (Pius IX) was viewed as a godsend by those interested in achieving the reconciliation that Gioberti envisioned between Church and revolution. One of Pius IX's first actions was to grant amnesty to more than four hundred political detainees and to broach concrete reform of Vatican government. All of this helped produce the myth of a "liberal pope" deserving of being represented in effigy alongside Gioberti. At first, Pius IX was dragged into the war against the Austrians, but in a famous consistorial allocu-

53. On this point see Giampietro Berti, "I moderati e il neoguelfismo," in *Il movimento nazionale e il 1848*, ed. Giovanni Cherubini (Milan: Teti, 1986), 227–58.

54. See Franco della Peruta, "La federazione nel dibattito politico risorgimentale: 1814–1847," in *Federalismo, regionalismo, autonomismo: Esperienze e proposte a confronto*, ed. Ettore E. Albertoni and Massimo Ganci, 2 vols. (Palermo: Ediprint, 1989), 1:55–79.

tion delivered on 29 April 1848 he bowed out, adducing the *super partes* nature of his office. After all, Gioberti had failed to outline what, exactly, he expected the pope to do when faced with the prospect of war against the brethren. It would seem that the Holy See would not merge into a single body with Italy.

Once Pius IX had made his stance clear, there was no need to await the outcome of the 1848 upheavals to see that Gioberti's ideological construct was not the perfect war machine it was cracked up to be. Events would eventually compel Gioberti to revise his program with an emphasis on "renovation" rather than on a close to eschatological "resurgence," but it was his early admirer and critic Cesare Balbo (1789–1853) who would most efficiently check what he saw as the "exuberance" and "deficiency" of his colleague's work.[55] His "observations" on Gioberti's *Primato* grew into a set of "hopes" or concrete "expectations" that would be realized only if Italy were liberated from Austrian occupation. This was Balbo's single-minded obsession and a goal that Gioberti had given short shrift.[56]

In his *Compendium of Italian History* (1846), the standard text of so-called Neo-Guelph historiography, Balbo provided what he believed to be the first general history explicitly invested in the advancement of national causes—that is, a history *ad usum* of the ruling classes.[57] He hoped that, faced with a compendium of the "many lost chances" for independence and a fierce accounting of the country's failures, Italy could be shaken out of the state of denial that it expressed through the exaltation of past achievements. What is of interest to us here is that while Balbo, like others, begins his account with the Italic Pelasgians, he devotes more than half of the book to comparing what he labels the sixth and seventh ages

---

55. See Vincenzo Gioberti, *Del rinnovamento civile d'Italia*, ed. Widar Casarini Sforza, 3 vols. (1850; Bologna: Zanichelli, 1943). On Balbo's criticism of Gioberti, see Giovanni Battista Scaglia, *Cesare Balbo: Il Risorgimento nella prospettiva storica del "progresso cristiano"* (Rome: Edizioni Studium, 1975), chap. 13; and Berti, "I moderati e il neoguelfismo."

56. See Cesare Balbo, *Le speranze d'Italia*, ed. Achille Corbelli (1844; Turin: Utet, 1944).

57. Cesare Balbo, *Della storia d'Italia dalle origini fino ai nostri tempi: Sommario*, ed. Giuseppe Talamo (Milan: Giuffrè, 1962), xxx: "Fra i tanti vanti che siam larghi a noi stessi, noi ci diam veramente pur questo, d'aver una letteratura storica superiore a tutte l'altre moderne; ma lasciati i cinquecentisti, che sono grandi per cinquecentisti, la verità è che, dal Muratori in poi, nel secolo in cui ciascuna delle altre nazioni si procacciò non una, ma parecchie grandi storie patrie nazionali, niuna tale fu fatta d'Italia, da niuno scrittore italiano. Eppure questa opera d'una storia nazionale è forse, è certamente l'opera letteraria più necessaria di tutte a qualunque nazione; quella la cui mancanza si fa sentire più ed in tutte le colture, e nella politica pratica di qualunque nazione: quella, che sola può dar color nazionale, aiuti, soggetti innumerevoli ed opportuni a tutte le composizioni letterarie ed artistiche; quella, che sola può dar esempi, consigli, opportunità e forza agli uomini politici."

in Italian history, namely, the Middle Ages, or as Balbo puts it, the "age of the communes," and the age of "foreign preponderance," which dates from 1494 and the arrival of Charles VIII in Italy. In Balbo's periodization, which has endured over time, the latter event ushered in the Italian Renaissance, an epoch that still characterized the Italy in which Balbo wrote the book, in that it was still under foreign subjugation. It could be argued that Balbo staged a confrontation between epochs, and that the Italians' Renaissance was thus born alongside the sense of 'shame' that would become its most characteristic feature and that, from Balbo on, would accompany every attempt by Italians to come to terms with an epoch that had been either praised or debunked according to a *parti pris*, but was yet to be systematically studied.[58]

Balbo construed his historiographical project around interrelated notions of freedom and culture. If culture contributes to freedom, then the former does not exist without the latter. In the "age of the communes" he was able to perceive a rare balance between the two, which attracted Balbo to this era, even though freedom at that time was not tantamount to independence. By the same token, he was critical of the fact that many of the thinkers and achievements so celebrated as being products of the Renaissance were in his view the products of the previous age's momentum. He saw on one side Italy's "three crowns" (Dante, Petrarch, Boccaccio), Quattrocento humanism, and the cultural splendor of Medicean Florence, and on the other side, in the years from 1492 to 1559, and more specifically during the papacy of Leon X (1513–21), an egotistical and vain revelry of sorts in which culture was rented out to foreigners for their sundry religious reformations and for the attainment of the very independence they would deny to Italy. Seeing in this period a rift between politics and culture, Balbo famously and poignantly characterized the Cinquecento as "nothing more than a splendid and happy-go-lucky free fall."[59]

The first notable figure to be pilloried by Balbo was Machiavelli, prominent for selling out to a regime he did not support and for conceiving that "codex" of villainies which would inform Italian political practices for some time to come. Two years before the pope withdrew from the Italian revolution—an event interpreted by many as proving Machiavelli right about the Church's inhibiting role in the history of Italian politics—Balbo

58. On Balbo's 'Renaissance,' see Michele Ciliberto, "Interpretazioni del Rinascimento: Balbo e Romagnosi," in *Il Rinascimento nell'Ottocento in Italia e Germania—Die Renaissance im 19. Jahrhundert in Italien und Deutschland*, ed. August Buck and Cesare Vasoli (Bologna: Il Mulino, 1987), 65–91.

59. Balbo, *Sommario*, 306.

pointed to *The Prince* as "the most fatal book" ever to have been written on a nation's behalf.[60] Meanwhile in the realm of literature, Ludovico
Ariosto, and the best of the bunch of comediographers he inspired, was
transporting readers away from the hardship of reality to a "smiley imaginary world."[61]

Balbo was less iconoclastic toward Italy's artistic achievements, which
evidently he felt he could not debase in good conscience. Nevertheless, he
saw "picciol vanto," or little reason for pride, in a single primacy or individual achievement as well as, more generally, in any chronologically based
primato that has no counterpart in a broader and wholesome excellence.[62]
Any glory that is "disputable," Balbo claimed, cannot be a "true glory." In
words that would stick in the Italian consciousness until midway through
the twentieth century, he explained that the much-celebrated Renaissance

> was a most refined bacchanal of culture. A commixture of wicked-
> ness, sorrows, and amusements that allows us to compare Cinquecento
> Italy to Boccaccio's merry party of storytellers, singers, and lovers in
> the midst of the plague. Only that here the repeated foreign invasions,
> wars, plunders, massacres, betrayals, stabbing and poisonings added
> themselves to the plague. Just as all kinds of literature and publica-
> tions, paintings, sculptures, and architectures added themselves to the
> songs and novellas. [This epoch displays] all kinds of infamy, all kinds
> of elegance, every kind of contrast.[63]

What lurks behind this impressive slapdown is self-loathing. As Balbo put
it, the point is that "perhaps no other [epoch] resembled so closely our own
times."[64] The "golden" age of the Renaissance was really of "mud" when
it came to politics, and Balbo, despite his anti-Machiavellian sentiments,
eventually declared himself ready to give up on the "Dantes," "Michelan-
gelos," "Raffaellos," etc., for a single "captain," and this as the only means
to recover from the 'Renaissance shame.'[65]

60. Balbo, *Sommario*, 343.
61. Balbo, *Sommario*, 350.
62. Balbo, *Sommario*, 349.
63. Balbo, *Sommario*, 341.
64. Balbo, *Sommario*, 304.
65. Cesare Balbo, *Lettere di politica e letteratura, edite e inedite, precedute da un discorso sulle rivoluzioni* (Turin: UTET, 1859), 445: "Vogliamo noi rialzarci di tali abbassamenti,
di tali vergogne? Questa è la questione principale per la patria nostra. La vergogna, la decadenza nostra è a tale, che per sorgerne e lavarcene noi dovremmo desiderare una guerra qualunque, quando fosse indifferente a' nostri interessi; noi dovremmo desiderare un'occasione

The few (in)famous pages that Balbo devoted to Cinquecento culture almost singlehandedly forced Italians into a confrontation that—Balbo's hyperbole notwithstanding—would prove as disquieting and as inescapable as he would have wished. In effect, his words would compel Italian intellectuals to despise something they were still trying to learn to love. It is perhaps useful to remind ourselves that at the time of Balbo's critique, the Renaissance was not a distinct epoch, nor did it have a name. Yet, if name giving and periodization are markers of historiographical sensitivity, as well as an acknowledgment of one's present difference, then the absolute identification suggested by Balbo, together with the shame he defined, is the hallmark of the Italians' Renaissance. In drawing Italians out from under their antiquarianism, Balbo demanded that an important question, one that Gioberti had implied but had largely eschewed, be heard: namely, how can an Italian national consciousness be established on antimodernist principles when Italy contributed so overwhelmingly to the modernity that is opposed?

It could be said that Italy's subsequent philosophy, which was thoroughly secular, was forged in the attempt to answer this riddle. Along the way, not only were the Renaissance and the Risorgimento identified ever more closely but the chasm, clear-cut and wide, that Balbo dug between the Middle Ages and the Renaissance would become even wider, leaving lay intellectuals increasingly alone with a Renaissance self that it would take them a century to embrace fully. The strategies that they would employ were many and were built one on top of the other. First, a few select figures would be recovered, and eventually, in piecemeal fashion, more and more of their contemporaries would be recovered as well. This rescue mission, interestingly, would begin on the periphery, at the end of the Renaissance and in closer proximity to pan-European achievements, and eventually reach back until it comprehended the whole Cinquecento, then

---

qualunque, da mostrare altrui, da sperimentare noi stessi, se la civiltà, se la moralità, se i costumi progrediti in Italia, ci abbian rifatti capaci di esercitare il nostro coraggio nativo. In somma, per le nazioni come per gli uomini, il coraggio è la prima delle virtù, è la virtù virile per eccellenza. Non serve scienza, non lettere, non arti, non colture, non politica, non civiltà di niuna maniera senza il coraggio; senza coraggio si disprezzano i più colti, i più ingegnosi, i più fini uomini del mondo; e senza coraggio le più colte, le più civili, le più ingegnose, le più fini nazioni. Pogniamo che potessimo avere tre o quattro Volta, tre o quattro Alfieri o Manzoni, o anche Danti, od altrettanti Michelangeli o Raffaelli, senza contare i Rossini e Bellini; io li darei, e meco ogni viril cuore italiano li darebbe tutti quanti per un capitano che si traesse dietro dugentomila italiani, a vincere od anche a morire, a provare in qualunque modo, in qualsivoglia guerra, l'esistenza presente efficace del coraggio italiano. Ma quanto non debbe accrescersi il nostro desiderio, se, invece di una guerra qualsiasi, noi potessimo sperare una guerra d'indipendenza?"

the late Quattrocento, and ultimately, once the Renaissance shame was overcome (or at least dealt with), the humanism of the earlier part of the fifteenth century.

OVERCOMING THE 'RENAISSANCE SHAME': ITALIAN HEGELIANISM

Although the pope-centered federalist solution promoted by the Neo-Guelphs came to naught after 1848, Gioberti's "ideal formula" and philosophy of "primacy" retained a firm purchase in the mainstream academy. Meanwhile, a group of left-leaning Hegelians in Naples had been cultivating a semiclandestine mania for German idealism, as a way of boosting revolutionary spirit among the youth, and from this eventually grew a rival paradigm. As Bertrando Spaventa (1817–83), one of the group's leaders, eloquently recalled:

> [I]n Naples, starting in 1843, the Hegelian idea penetrated the mind of the young cultivators of science, who, uniting fraternally, took to advocating it in speech and in writing as if moved by saintly love. Neither the early suspicions of the police, stirred by ignorance and religious hypocrisy, nor their threats and persecutions could dampen the faith of these daring defenders of intellectual independence. The numerous students who deserted the old universities gathered in the great capital city from all the corners of the kingdom; they rushed in throngs to heed the new word. It was an irresistible and universal urge driving toward a new and wonderful future, toward an organic unity of the different branches of human knowledge. Students of medicine, natural scientists, law students, mathematicians, and students of literature participated in this general movement, and their main ambition was, as it was with the ancient Italians, to turn into philosophers. . . . It was a cult, an ideal religion, in which those young people demonstrated themselves worthy descendants of the miserable Bruno.[66]

The emphatic tone of this passage is undoubtedly a reaction to the harshness with which these young idealists were persecuted by royal officials during the restoration.[67] Editorial initiatives were censored; private

---

66. Bertrando Spaventa, "Studi sopra la filosofia di Hegel," in *Unificazione nazionale ed egemonia culturale*, by Spaventa, ed. Giuseppe Vacca (Bari: Laterza, 1969), 23.

67. The most thorough accounts of Italian Hegelianism are found in Guido Oldrini, *Napoli e i suoi filosofi: Protagonisti, prospettive, problemi del pensiero dell'Ottocento* (Milan:

schools like Spaventa's that were devoted to teaching "Hegel's principles" were shut down. Students were sentenced to death or, as was the case with political activist Silvio Spaventa (Bertrando's brother), to decades in prison.[68] Bertrando himself, not unlike Cuoco half a century earlier, fled north for his life, settling in Turin after a short stint in "yawning" Florence.

In exile, Spaventa's revolutionary instincts gave way to sustained contemplations on Hegel as he attempted to fashion a new, strictly philosophical, program in support of the unification cause. In the mid-nineteenth century, the feeling was that Italy presented a twofold inferiority: it could not boast the civic and centralized infrastructure achievements of France or England, nor had it reached the universally acknowledged pinnacle that Germany, a country otherwise still struggling politically, had managed to achieve in the realm of thought. At this time there was a shared European perception that in exhausting itself as science, Hegelian philosophy would survive by trickling down into the realm of practical activity and informing social struggle, and Spaventa may have imported this perception to Italy.[69] But his real mission, given that Italy was in need first and foremost of an "intellectual revolution," was to mend the philosophical rift, to endow Hegelianism with a second life qua philosophy. To this end, the first order of business was to tackle the problem that kept Italians from embracing Hegel in the first place—the idea that "our thought is incommensurable with European thought." It is in pondering this original Neo-Guelph "prejudice" that Spaventa began to perceive, at first at a distance, Italian Renaissance philosophy and German idealism as two glimmering lights and, after adjusting his focus, as two glaring "suns," or really one sun "on different points of a common horizon" (O, 1775).

In his early writings, Spaventa did not dispute that something went awry in Italy during the Renaissance, but he attributed the problem less to

Franco Angeli, 1990), and Guido Oldrini, *La cultura filosofica napoletana dell'Ottocento* (Rome-Bari: Laterza, 1973). Also useful are Oldrini's anthology of early Hegelian texts, *Il primo hegelismo italiano* (Florence: Vallecchi, 1969) and his survey of recent bibliography, *L'ottocento filosofico napoletano nella letteratura dell'ultimo decennio* (Naples: Bibliopolis, 1986). For alternative readings, see also Giustino Broccolini, "Vincenzo Finamore e le origini dello hegelismo in Italia," *De homine* 51, no. 2 (1975): 149–84; and the essays collected in *Gli hegeliani di Napoli e la costruzione dello stato unitario* (Rome: Libreria dello Stato, 1989).

68. On the activity of Silvio Spaventa see Elena Croce, *Silvio Spaventa* (Milan: Adelphi, 1969); and, for relevant documents, *Silvio Spaventa e i moti del Quarantotto: Articoli dal "Nazionale" e scritti dall'ergastolo di Santo Stefano* (Naples: La Scuola di Pitagora, 2006).

69. For the political relevance of Spaventa's philosophy, see Eugenio Garin, "Filosofia e politica in Bertrando Spaventa," in *La filosofia del Risorgimento: Le prolusioni di Bertrando Spaventa* (Naples: La Scuola di Pitagora, 2005), 13–42. More extensively, see Giuseppe Vacca, *Politica e filosofia in Bertrando Spaventa* (Bari: Laterza, 1967).

the forsaking of Christian beliefs than to the decadence of the epoch's individualism, which climaxed when "science, art, religion, and other spiritual activities came to serve personal interests, when these activities were turned into nothing more than a means to the particular goals of men's will." The martyrs of Italian thought, principally Bruno and Campanella, had fought for the *libertas philosophandi*, and the "shackles and tortures they had to endure," Spaventa emphasized, certainly "mark the beginning of our ruin." However, he deplored the notion of looking to a more remote past for solace, considering such a venture to be an embarrassing whitewash. As he famously stated:

> Italian philosophy was not smothered on the pyres of our philosophers; rather, it removed itself and went on to develop in a freer country and in freer minds. Thus, to look for it in its new fatherland is not to engage in a servile imitation of the German nationality. Rather it amounts to a reclamation of what belonged to us, of what, under different guises, has become a property of universal spirit, the essential condition of our civilization and of all people. It is not our philosophers of the last two centuries, but Spinoza, Kant, Fichte, Schelling, and Hegel who are the true disciples of Bruno, of Vanini, of Campanella, of Vico and other illustrious thinkers. (O, 1777)

Hegel had suggested a similar connection in his posthumously published *Lectures on the History of Philosophy* (1837). Yet a bias toward the Reformation had him downplay the continuity between some of those Italian thinkers and the German tradition. In Hegel's view, Bruno, Vanini, and Campanella were indeed possessed by a "burning desire" to chase "after the conscious knowledge of what is deepest and most concrete," but their "confusion of mind" was so great that they came to mark a self-contained "interval of transition and fall within the period of the Reformation."[70]

In Spaventa's view, to the contrary, the "fanciful" and "extravagant" southerners (in Hegel's terms) and the pantheist barbarians (as Neo-Guelphs generally viewed the Germans) shared a common intellectual destiny. As he saw it, German thought was not only the natural development of the philosophy that the Counter-Reformation had stifled in Italy; it was its afterlife, a new chapter in its history, to the potential benefit of both nations. If only one could bring about a homecoming, effect a "trans-

70. G. W. F. Hegel, *Lectures on the History of Philosophy*, trans. E. S. Haldane and Frances H. Simson, 3 vols. (Lincoln: University of Nebraska Press, 1995), 3:115–16.

lation" (by which Spaventa meant a 'naturalization') of Hegel in Italy, then Italy would come to participate finally in a modernity it had prepared but never enjoyed, while the spiritual reunification of present (Germany) and past (Italy) could inaugurate a new, at once nationally grounded and cosmopolitan, future.

Spaventa's insight regarding the "circulation" of Italian and European thought, although it bore an exciting novelty, presented several problems on historiographical grounds.[71] As Spaventa noted, the development of Italian philosophy had been "truncated, thwarted, and dogmatic"; one could perceive true "voids" between Bruno and Vico and between Vico and Gioberti (O, 1361). Vico, clearly, was the fulcrum, whose ties to the Renaissance would require as much attention as his role as the precursor of Kant and subsequent German thought. Italian philosophy could accomplish this, especially given the Vico frenzy that rose after 1799 and endured in Neapolitan culture; the true quandary was how to reintegrate the much despised "friar," Gioberti. In fact, a dialectical squaring of the circle and the vanquishing of Neo-Guelphism required that Gioberti be *aufgehoben*—negated in his errors yet recast and preserved as the "Italian Hegel"—and interpreted as the first harbinger of the Owl of Minerva's return to its Italian birth nest.

Spaventa seized the opportunity to lay out his program in two related academic inaugural addresses, delivered in 1860 and 1861, in effect reinventing Italian philosophy as dependent on a thriving study of the Renaissance. In the first talk, delivered in Bologna, titled "Character and Development of Italian Philosophy from the Sixteenth Century until Our Time," Spaventa called on his audience to "pick up again the sacred thread" of Italy's philosophical tradition from Bruno to Gioberti, to heed the word of Italy's "heroes of the mind," and, without stressing difference or primacy, to restore Italy's *equality* in "the community of nations." In Spaventa's speech, the myth of a *primato* was exploded by recasting interior/exterior dichotomies into an ancient/modern mutual exclusion:

> The character of our philosophy is just the same as that of all modern philosophy, essentially different from the character of ancient philosophy: it is the search for the first principle of everything not in absolute

71. Although the term "circulation" appears only once in Spaventa's corpus (at the very beginning of his 1860 address), the concept would, in time, become central to a characterization of his philosophy.

objectivity, material or ideal, but in absolute mind. Its development is the unfolding, the opposing, and ultimately the uniting of the two moments of the absolute mind, objectivity and infinite subjectivity, the living reality of nature, and the autonomy of human consciousness. (*FKC*, 367; *O*, 289)

This switch in emphasis, evidently, had the double advantage of reuniting Italians and Germans on the same side of the equation, leaving the medievalism and the ancient Italicism of the Neo-Guelphs on the other side.

Spaventa tackled the challenge of reintegrating Gioberti by suggesting that he had misunderstood his own philosophy. With his "ideal formula" Gioberti thought that he had restored a true ontologism. Yet, as in Greek philosophy, ontologism understands Being as "the absolute principle of existence and knowledge," a substance separated "from the world and human intellect that contemplates it." Gioberti's prejudices and convoluted prose had kept him from realizing that what he had achieved in fact was a pure spiritualism, a "more human kind of absolute" brought about by a continuous interpenetration of matter and idea in absolute "motion." This is evident for Spaventa in Gioberti's notion of the *One* as *Triune*, which allows Being to be grasped as "absolute Relation" and thus as a conscious force triggered by thought. In Gioberti the idea *"is* because it *thinks,"* and, in this mental action, real and ideal converge in a Being whose essence "is self-knowing and whose self-knowing is the root foundation" of its worldly manifestations, "of all being" (*FKC*, 347; *O*, 260–61). Thus does Gioberti come to conceive of Being as a creative act and God as a "self-aware personality," as a Creator "in the true sense of the term, as creative and re-creative activity." How would the author of the *Primato* have fared, Spaventa asked his public, had his ideas appeared in the sixteenth century? Would his destiny have differed from that of Bruno, whose philosophy Gioberti inadvertently fulfills?

Spaventa accordingly lists a number of sixteenth-century thinkers who pursued in the sciences that ideal which had been given up in the realm of politics. Telesio, Pietro Pomponazzi, Andrea Cesalpino, Alessandro Achillini, Cesare Cremonini, and Jacopo Zabarella all represent this aspect of the age, but the *Zeitgeist* was truly embodied, in all of its contradictions, by Bruno and Campanella. In Campanella, for example, the medieval man's subservience to the Church as universal monarchy survives alongside new reforming instincts to advance the human social condition. He contemplates nature as the work of God, but the world ultimately remains a vestige of the Creator, who is accordingly divested of any "humanity" and "worldliness." Ultimately, Campanella turned to skepticism, as his belief in man's divine powers was not solid enough. And although skepticism (wherein theologism is a result) presents some advance with respect to Scholastic dogmatism (wherein theologism is a beginning), Campanella is still considered "the least free of our free philosophers" and the "philosopher of the Catholic restoration after the Reformation" (*FKC*, 354; *O*, 271).

Campanella spent most of his life in prison; his compromises allowed him to die a free man. For Giordano Bruno, it was the reverse. The true protagonist (perhaps the only one) of Spaventa's Renaissance, Bruno traveled restlessly and widely around Europe only to be burnt at the stake upon his return to his homeland. Citing Hegel, and the paragraph from his *Lectures* that admires the "sacred frenzy" of this thinker, Spaventa goes on to describe Bruno as the daring mind who ventured past the self-imposed boundaries that would define Campanella to investigate the "incomprehensible source" that moves the universe. Bruno reduced this source to a monad, to "the tiniest little point that causes no torment for the human mind," for what this point conceals can be contemplated by the mind freely in the world. As such it is a revelation, a mirror reflection perhaps, but this is enough to turn God into a real infinity. Until Campanella, thinkers fell back on skepticism in order to justify the weakness of human thought; in Bruno, instead, skepticism was reduced "to a mere appearance." As Spaventa puts it, "Bruno does not believe because he is not skeptical enough" (*FKC*, 356; *O*, 273)

It is in his contentment with the manifestation of divinity in nature, "judging knowledge of God as nature to be the final and most complete level of knowledge," that Spaventa locates Bruno's thought. Yet Bruno committed a *philosophical* blasphemy with the notion that God may be known in revelation "finally" and "completely." This seems to suggest that God may not know himself, thus placing man above his Creator. And so, with skepticism dismissed, the only available option is to believe that God is more than substance and nature, that God is Spirit. Neither Bruno nor Campanella pushed this far, but, with them,

> the route that modern philosophy must follow is already set: in one direction, the autonomy of the Spirit as awareness of the self and of things, as intellect and sense; in the other, God, not as an empty name but as a real infinity living in the world. The Spirit has come so far that it no longer wants to know about a God—about a truth, in other words—of which one can say only that there is nothing to say. It wants

a truth that can not only be thought but also felt as an object of experience. (*FKC*, 357; *O*, 275)

Descartes, Locke, Spinoza, Vico, and German idealism (Kant, Fichte, Schel-
ling, and finally Hegel) would perfect the process that Bruno launched. As
Spaventa perceived, the problem that remained to be solved was that all
of these philosophies came to accompany the formation of nation-states
and in the process were nationalized themselves. This is why Italy needed
to reconquer its own tradition, however belatedly, for in doing so it would
complete the picture of a united states and philosophy of Europe.

Focusing on Gioberti, Spaventa Germanized Italian thought; focusing on the Renaissance, he Italicized (if not properly Latinized) German
thought more than Hegel would have accepted. But the interesting thing
to notice is the coincidence that makes 1860 an annus mirabilis for a Renaissance scholarship to be. In that same year, Jacob Burckhardt published
The Civilization of the Renaissance in Italy, a portrait so eloquent as to
engender singlehandedly the question or 'problem' that would raise Renaissance scholarship into a profession: Was the Italian Renaissance truly
the great and autonomous epoch that Burckhardt took it be? Burckhardt, a
working historian, kept a well-advertised distance from Hegel's thinking
about history and the state. Yet one cannot help but notice that his Renaissance, characterized as an epochal emancipation from the Middle Ages,
was substantially identical to the one that Spaventa created in embracing
Hegel wholeheartedly. The biggest difference, therefore, is in how these
paradigms fared. Burckhardt's, being self-contained, had to be unpacked if
it was to be *refuted*. Spaventa's, being a sketch or outline, had to be completed, integrated, and polished. It had to be *confirmed* before it could be
negated. The concurrence would allow for a conversation between Germans and Italians, at least. The differences, however, were what would
define the Italians' Renaissance.

In the second inaugural address, a sort of prequel to the first, Spaventa
spoke at the University of Naples, where he now held the chair in logic and
metaphysics (after his triumphant return in 1861). According to Spaventa,
this address was less a thought-out composition than a rushed retort to
another inaugural address (a farewell speech, as it turned out) delivered by
the then chair and staunch Giobertian, Luigi Palmieri (1807–96), a week
earlier (on 16 November 1861). Indeed, Palmieri's talk, an unctuous and
tongue-in-cheek harangue against idealist thought, begged for a response.

Palmieri had expressed himself overjoyed to see that, at long last, the
state and the academy had come to peaceful terms and that in the new Italy

"study is no longer synonymous with conspiracy, but a duty to accomplish, a right to experiment with."[72] (Meanwhile, back in 1847 he had secretly connived to have young idealists persecuted and Spaventa's private school closed.) Palmieri then expressed the wish that, after some initial coordination, the state would leave the academy in peace to develop autonomously. Moreover, the Italian state would prove that it had achieved full maturity when it gave up the ministry of education. The only problem for Palmieri was that Francesco De Sanctis was about to be appointed to such a post. And De Sanctis, a leading Hegelian, made it his first order of business to oust Giobertians, including Palmieri, from the University of Naples.[73]

Palmieri brought his ouster on himself when he articulated what were in his view the prerequisites for the advancement of the "predominance of thought, the autonomy of nations, and the redemption of the plebeians."[74] All three of these goals depended on a thorough nationalization of science and literature, one that would carry the "imprint" of Italy's "ethnographic nature" or "ethnologic subjectivity" over and against the servile imitation of foreign (say, German) thought.[75] To this end Palmieri discouraged the study or use of languages other than Italian, and he proposed a single canon in philosophy, one based on the tradition of the Italian Pythagoras: the "Italo-Greek" Plato, Augustine, Thomas Aquinas, Anselm, Bonaventure, Vico, and Gioberti. In conclusion, Palmieri voiced his confidence that things would turn out fine for Italy, if only because "the sweetness of our climate, the beauty of our sky, the fire of our volcanoes make our mind ready, intuitive, and alert, so that it often forges ahead solitarily and without a guide in the discovery of truth." It is unclear whether Palmieri, who managed the observatory at Mount Vesuvius and was an esteemed volcanologist, was aware that the much feared Hegel had in his *Lectures* blamed Italy's philosophical irresoluteness on the "volcanic" and "explosive" nature of its best representatives. In any case, Palmieri's speech provides a clear example of the xenophobic provincialism into which Neo-Guelph ontologism devolved (less than two decades after being formulated) in the hands of Gioberti's followers, or, as Spaventa called them, "Brahmins."[76]

72. Luigi Palmieri, *Nuovo indirizzo da dare alle università italiche* (Naples: Gargiulo, 1861), 3.

73. For a dramatized account of the restoration of Hegelians at the University of Naples, see Benedetto Croce, "La vita letteraria a Napoli dal 1860 al 1900," in *La filosofia del Risorgimento*, 147–91.

74. These were the three challenges for the century indicated by Gioberti in *Del rinnovamento civile d'Italia*, 1:107.

75. Palmieri, *Nuovo indirizzo*, 17–20.

76. Spaventa accused the Giobertians of being unable to conceive of distinct national-

By comparison, Spaventa's talk sounds like a radical act of deprovincialization. When Gioberti and his followers characterized Italy's primacy as "perennial," they meant it in the sense of enduring in a primordial and static condition of knowledge that is effortlessly accessed (provided one be Italian) and transmitted exoterically. Spaventa, by contrast, presents a dynamic understanding of national identity in which multiple modern philosophies proliferate in view of a long-lost and, as it were, pre-Babelian spiritual, if not properly linguistic, unity. Accordingly, Spaventa's stated goal in his second address is to recast "the relation between nationality and philosophy" by elaborating on the history of the ancient world, a history that was absent from his talk of a year earlier. In his review of ancient philosophy—Indian, Greek, and Roman—Gioberti borrows freely from Hegel to deliver a death blow against Scholasticism, a brand of thought whose 'objectivism' returns philosophy to the super-intelligible Being of Neoplatonism, the end of Greek thought, or, worse, to a vision of the object as empty and fantastic as the one represented by the Brahman of Hinduism (*RIP*, 56).

Needless to say, Spaventa's appraisal was unfair, but it was instrumental in foregrounding that gradual "renovation of the *heart*" in which all epochs participated (despite the Middle Ages) in their own way so that ultimately Descartes could proclaim the shared mental reign of man and God in a single breath: *cogito ergo sum, Deus cogitatur ergo est*. This freedom cry, however, was anticipated by the courageous and life-giving thinkers of the Italian Renaissance, such that Italian thought, which appears to be "nowhere," is actually to be found "everywhere." In Spaventa's final formulation:

Italy opens the doors to modern civilization with a phalanx of heroes of thought. Pomponazzi, Telesio, Bruno, Vanini, Campanella, Cesalpino: all seem to be the sons of many nations. They serve more or less as a

---

isms as part of a dynamic, multiple whole and, thus, quite perceptively saw their attitude as being conducive to hierarchization rather than equality of people: "Each nation, they [the 'Giobertians'] say, has its own particular philosophy, and each philosophy makes up a caste. And woe to those who confuse the castes! In Europe today one is born an *ontologist* or *psychologist*, pure or impure, theist or pantheist, just as in the valley of the Ganges one was born and is still today born Brahmin, Kshatriya, Vaishya, or Shudra. Naturally, we Italians are the Brahmins—the firstborn of Brahma; and there is no need to say who are the Shudras, or better the Chandalas, the impure, the rejects, the *outlaws*. If our new Brahmins were right, or if they had as much power as they have little justification, they would truly make of Italy a new Brahmanic India, and we would sleep peacefully on the ruins of the new Buddhism!" Spaventa, "Italian Philosophy in Relation to European Philosophy," in *RIP*, 63.

prelude to all of the following courses of thought that constitute the period of philosophy from Descartes to Kant. So Bacon and Locke have their precursors in Telesio and Campanella, Descartes in Campanella, as well; Spinoza in Bruno, and in Bruno himself one finds a bit of the monadism of Leibniz (who was the adversary of Spinoza). Finally, Vico discovers the new science; he anticipates the problem of *knowledge*, calling for a *new metaphysics that proceeds on the basis of human ideas*; he posits the true concept of the word and of myth, and so he founds philology; he intuits the idea of the spirit, and so he creates the history of philosophy. Vico is the true precursor of all of Germany. I said the precursor, but I ought to have said more, since Vico still waits to be fully discovered. (*RIP*, 59–60)

Modern philosophy no longer depends on a mere reconnection of German thought to its Italian origins. All countries play a role in an intricate game of cross-references between precursors and fulfillments, Italian suggestions and European elaborations. This is a philosophical Esperanto whose key to comprehension is Giambattista Vico, a thinker who had to be mastered if an Italian-declined Hegelianism were to be presented as a national philosophy.

Spaventa made the discovery of a 'new Vico' his goal in the ten lectures he delivered in Naples during the 1861–62 academic year. Before these lectures—in which Spaventa refined his interpretation of Gioberti, Bruno, and Campanella and beefed up his Renaissance canon with new names (Valla, Ficino, Pico, among others)—Vico had been a name bandied about rather than the subject of sustained study.[77] In the first of his lectures on Vico, Spaventa sets out to question Vico's paternity of the myth of the *primato*. It is true that in *On the Most Ancient Wisdom of the Italians*, an early work, Vico argued that an "inward learning" could be drawn from the study of ancient Italic languages. Yet Vico's more mature philosophy suggests that such a doctrine reflects the activity of the imagination, not of reason. It is not "philosophy" because it lacks that self-reflection which is the mark of mature science. To stick with what Vico calls the "fantastic universals" is to dawdle in the infancy of man. Spaventa does not believe

---

77. Alessandro Savorelli suggests that Spaventa's interpretation of Vico may have served his ultimate goal, the reintegration of Gioberti. See Savorelli, "*L'altro* Vico di Spaventa," in *L'aurea catena: Saggi sulla storiografia filosofica dell'idealismo italiano* (Florence: Le Lettere, 2003), 103–26. See also Luciano Malusa, "Bertrando Spaventa interprete della filosofia di G. B. Vico," in *Saggi e ricerche*, ed. Carlo Giacon (Padua: Antenore, 1971), 71–108.

Vico wanted to deduce national philosophy from language, but if he did, he would have been wrong. He would have had to argue that nations develop in some sort of "patriarchal isolation" or to presuppose (as Gioberti did) an original philosophy prior to language and thus prior to any kind of human interaction. Such a philosophy would not be Italic, let alone national; if anything, it would be pre-Adamite. There is no way around it, Spaventa insists: Pythagoras was Greek, Scholasticism universal, and only the philosophy that came out of the Renaissance can be called Italian (RIP, 72; O, 1231).

This, Spaventa argues, is why Italians must give up a "false notion of originality" and must look instead to the "natural, free, and self-conscious" development of German thought. On these terms, looking to German thought is as looking into a mirror, an introspective activity, and, Spaventa's lectures conclude, the only means by which Italians "will achieve in the realm of thought, as, recently, in the realm of politics, an enduring Italy: not an imaginary Italy—Pelasgic, Pythagorean, Scholastic, or whatnot—but a historical Italy" (O, 1362). In using the future tense Spaventa betrays, perhaps, his awareness that his 'Italy' is as yet no more 'historical' than Gioberti's. His task is to enable future generations to pursue a systematic investigation of the Italian intellectual tradition, and to do so according to the rules of thumb he has provided in a fledgling philosophical historiography. These assert that there was no Italy, beyond a mere "geographical expression," before the Renaissance; that philosophy, its universal aspirations notwithstanding, should be attributed to particular individuals operating in particular epochs; that the "character" of a philosophy cannot be disassociated from its "development"; and that philosophy, as a cultural product, forms an organic tradition that is relevant to national culture as well as to Western culture more generally.

Spaventa himself contributed little to his own project, laboring unsuccessfully to produce a first Italian monograph on Bruno.[78] But his method (or direction) was picked up by a host of thinkers who, fruitfully tempering Spaventa's idealism with a nascent positivism, made Renaissance culture their central scholarly concern. Among them was Francesco Fiorentino (1834–84), who wrote important studies of Pomponazzi and Telesio, and the first extensive (albeit unfinished) study of Renaissance philosophy to

78. For Spaventa's work on Bruno, see the texts collected in *Lettera sulla dottrina di Bruno: Scritti inediti, 1853–1854*, ed. Maria Rascaglia and Alessandro Savorelli (Naples: Bibliopolis, 2000).

extend to the Quattrocento; Felice Tocco (1845–1911), who provided what
Spaventa could not, the first Italian monograph on Bruno, alongside editions of his Latin writings; and, Pasquale Villari (1827–1917), whose books
on Machiavelli and Savonarola, rare models of Italian scholarship for the
period, went on to enjoy international success in English translation.[79]
Spaventa was thus the unifying mind defining the aims of what grew organically into Italy's *Grossforschung*, a vast and necessarily collaborative
study of the Renaissance that continued through the first half of the twentieth century and beyond, as Giovanni Gentile, we shall see, again came
to understand Spaventa's unfulfilled Renaissance as worthy of national
enterprise.

Despite these achievements, one might ask how much of the Renaissance was in Spaventa's work, really. It has been noted that Spaventa projects his Renaissance so far into the future that very little of it remains
as a concrete historical epoch, and that for Spaventa the Renaissance remains a "category" employed to advance the cause of the Risorgimento.[80]
Yet it cannot be denied that by articulating the Renaissance 'problem' in
strictly philosophical terms, Spaventa turns the Renaissance into an intellectual activity and Renaissance thinkers into potential conversation
partners. As Spaventa sees it, then, the burden of proof of the existence
of a Renaissance rests not on the historiographical activity of the scholar
(Burckhardt's self-contained portrait had been attacked on historiographical grounds), but on the ability of future thinkers to continue to behold the
Renaissance origins of modernity in the scope of *their* "horizon."

Ironically, Spaventa's insistence that the "character" of an epoch (philosophical or national) always be linked to its "development" made his Renaissance more dynamic but also potentially less enduring than, say, the
Burckhardtian utopia. In other words, the Renaissance, if defined as the
earliest part of modernity's thought cycle, could potentially peter out as
modernity itself peters out. This explains why Spaventa may have felt some
urgency in bending Hegel's perfectionist teleology into a Vichian, anti-

79. For a detailed account of the debt owed by late nineteenth-century thinkers to
Spaventa, see Luciano Malusa, *La storiografia filosofica italiana nella seconda metà
dell'Ottocento: Tra positivismo e neokantismo* (Milan: Marzorati, 1977). See also Fabiana
Cacciapuoti, "La 'scuola' di Bertrando Spaventa: Da Francesco Fiorentino ad Antonio Labriola," in *Gli hegeliani di Napoli*, 317–96; and, for Spaventa's influence on even later generations, Girolamo Cotroneo, "La scuola di Spaventa," in *Bertrando Spaventa: Dalla scienza
della logica alla logica della scienza*, ed. Raffaello Franchini (Naples: Pironti, 1986), 161–85.

80. These opinions are expressed and discussed in Fulvio Tessitore, "L'idea di Rinascimento nella cultura idealistica italiana tra '800 e '900," in *Contributi alla storia e storia della
cultura* (Bologna: Il Mulino, 1990), 89–123.

systemic circularity. And although there are no eschatological elements in his philosophy, one cannot help but wonder what Spaventa thought would happen if the circle were squared and German idealism tied to its Italian origins.

In Spaventa's motives and achievements we see a whole other set of problems, one that bears more closely on the period of Italy's unification. With his myth history, challenging the philosophical canon of the Giobertians, was Spaventa merely substituting one illustrious genealogy for another? When he reduced the *primato* to a mere chronological precedence, was he truly advocating an anti-*primato*, or did a sense of superiority linger in it?[81] After 1861, Spaventa attracted a cohort while continuing to be opposed by Giobertians; but clarification of these issues, if not a strong and integrative rewriting of his paradigm (and, for that matter, Burckhardt's), came from what may be considered an unexpected source: his fellow Hegelian, Francesco De Sanctis (1817–83).

Not only did Spaventa and De Sanctis share an exactly coterminous lifespan, but their lives had been moving in parallel since their early formative and teaching years in pre-1848 Naples. At that time De Sanctis earned celebrity status in one of the most prestigious private schools in Naples, notably in aesthetics and literary criticism.[82] Owing to this precocious academic success, more is known through De Sanctis of the hotchpotch of philosophical influences that eventually led his generation to Hegel in proximity to 1848. Particularly influential among them was Victor Cousin's brand of eclecticism and the method he developed to select and recompose the elements of truth of all philosophical systems against any form of exclusivism. This eclecticism informed the deprovincializing efforts of Neapolitan intellectuals who, predictably, traced Cousin's interplay of historical and psychological observation back to Vico, who had defined the relationships between the "true" and the "certain" (or, in more general terms, history and metaphysics, rationalism and empiricism) and was thus heralded as the founder of the modern school of eclecticism.

Gioberti was a formative influence on De Sanctis, too, although their

---

81. A negative assessment of Spaventa and Italian idealism can be found in Pietro Rossi, "Il mito della tradizione filosofica italiana e la sua dissoluzione," in *Antonio Corsano e la storiografia filosofica del Novecento (Atti del Convegno di Studi, Lecce-Taurisano 24–25 settembre 1999)*, ed. Giovanni Papuli (Galatina: Congedo, 1999), 19–41. For a reply, see Savorelli, *L'aurea catena*, 7–21.

82. For what follows I rely on Guido Oldrini, "L'apprendistato filosofico prequarantottesco di De Sanctis," in *Francesco De Sanctis nella storia della cultura*, ed. Carlo Muscetta, 2 vols. (Rome: Laterza, 1984), 1:3–34.

future rivalry would obscure this fact; his *Primato* had circumvented the censorship of the mid-forties Neapolitan government to stirring effect. In De Sanctis's own words, Gioberti's oeuvre "made a great impression. It finally appeared that there was such a thing as an Italian philosophy," and, more important, "one in which all oppositions seemed reconciled." Gioberti's philosophical patriotism should thus be counted as an important catalyzing force in forming the ideology that in 1848 drove young intellectuals, including De Sanctis and his students, to the barricades. After this revolution, and beset by remorse and despair over the death of his most beloved pupil, De Sanctis fled to Calabria only to be apprehended and consigned to a Neapolitan jail, where he spent three years (1850–53) studying and translating Hegel's *Logic*.

De Sanctis had a more fraught relationship with Hegel than Spaventa did. The source of his doubts was the "unnatural schematicism" of Hegel's logical apriorism or (in terms that De Sanctis drew from Gioberti) what he perceived as his "ontologism."[83] In every case, it seems, he contrasted Hegel to Vico. For example, the autonomy of religion and especially art could be guarded against Hegel's subsumption of them into philosophy by drawing on Vico's emphasis on the creative or poetic moment of the human mind. Similarly with Hegel's reservations concerning material reality and historical contingencies, which De Sanctis countered by reaffirming the temporal and corporeal compass of Vichian existence, and any form of teleologism, against which Vico's resolutely progressive and circularly open-ended historicism could be summoned as an alternative. De Sanctis's stance toward Hegel was an anti-intellectual stance, in that it sought—and here the influence of Cuoco's Vichian reaction against Jacobin rationalism is palpable—to recall philosophical pretensions to their "limits" both as intellectual pursuits and as political applications.[84]

When, eventually, the charges against him were dismissed, De Sanctis was placed on a steamship to America, but he disembarked in Malta, worked his way to Turin, and reconnected there with many fellow émi-

83. On De Sanctis's reading of Hegel, see Maria Teresa Lanza "De Sanctis e Hegel," in Muscetta, *Francesco De Sanctis*, 1:155–84.

84. Fulvio Tessitore, from whom I draw here, rightly insists on the importance of Cuoco's influence on De Sanctis's Vichianism in "La filosofia di De Sanctis," in Muscetta, *Francesco De Sanctis*, 237–76; and, more broadly in *Da Cuoco a De Sanctis: Studi sulla filosofia napoletana nel primo Ottocento* (Naples: Edizioni Scientifiche Italiane, 1988). On De Sanctis's notion of "limit," see also Francesco De Sanctis, "Il limite," in *I partiti e l'educazione della nuova italia* (Turin: Einaudi, 1970), 170–73.

grés.[85] Soon, however, he, too, grew impatient with what Spaventa described as the "scientific Middle Ages" of Italy's soon to be capital city, and he accepted a position at the University of Zurich. There he was greeted by the *Neue Zürcher Zeitung* as "certainly the reformer, if not the founder, of Italian literature"—a generous assessment at the time, but a prophetical one, considering the future developments of his career. And yet his correspondence shows him to be in low spirits during the four years that he spent abroad (1856–60). This, despite the fact that he led a stimulating life: on at least one occasion, he vocally accompanied a piano performance of Franz Liszt; he was also, rumor had it, Richard Wagner's rival in a love triangle. More important for his intellectual career, De Sanctis had the chance to interact with figures such as Friedrich T. Vischer, the aesthetician, and Burckhardt, while Theodor Mommsen's attempt to map Roman culture onto German culture still resonated. Both interlocutors failed the test. De Sanctis could not appreciate Vischer's dispassionate, cerebral approach to art, nor could he fail to notice that his colleagues' knowledge of modern Italian culture was dour and out of date. It was only upon the arrival of his Italian colleague, for example, that Burckhardt scrambled to familiarize himself with Giacomo Leopardi, previously unknown to him.

In short De Sanctis seems to have suffered culture shock in this disengaged and literal-minded intellectual community, which had him pining all along for his "volcanic Neapolitan disciples." Yet after returning to Italy and after lending a hand in the unification cause, De Sanctis matched the productivity he had admired in Vischer, and with his magnum opus, *History of Italian Literature* (1870–71), he took apart and reframed the Burckhardtian Renaissance. In his *History* he weaves the Renaissance into the vivid, thick fabric of Italian culture (in the sense of any manifestation of the human spirit), while the Cinquecento, albeit still something of a centerpiece, becomes the anticlimax of a glorious and too hastily ended medieval period. Meanwhile, he resists any form of facile, international, or future-oriented escapism such as is to be found in Spaventa's Renaissance. For De Sanctis, who on this point draws close to Balbo, the Renaissance is a moment in which an enduring problem, not yet resolved, originates for Italy's national consciousness, a problem so particular to Italy that it is for Italians alone to solve.

85. In what follows, I rely on Renato Martinoni, "Gli anni Zurighesi (1858–1860)," in Muscetta, *Francesco De Sanctis*, 1:89–110.

Since De Sanctis's Renaissance owes much of its appeal to its counter-intuitive interpretation of the period as the decadent outcome of a cultural crescendo, it is worth approaching his writing as he approached his goal: gradually and carefully. De Sanctis's narrative, or as his *History* is often aptly described, his *Bildungsroman*, of the making of Italian national con-sciousness begins with the "primitive," "direct," and "elementary" forms associated with the "spontaneous" and "popular" poets of the Sicilian school, whose "original sin" was to have failed to knead "national life" into the fantastic chivalrous world it acquired from abroad as a "ready-made product" (*HIL*, 1:12–13). Meanwhile the "cult of chivalry throve but poorly" in more refined and politically advanced Tuscany, where those materials were first recast in a new national language and eventually and forever discarded, together with "spontaneous and popular poetry" more generally, when they came into contact with the scholarly concerns that were developing in the university center of Bologna. Out of this encounter with the "scientific consciousness" of detached academics, says De Sanc-tis, the Florentine poets acquired a "purpose": to "proclaim truths . . . in a manner that could be understood by the people" (51). Ideal types of this "twofold man" who is both scientist and artist included Cavalcanti and especially Dante, whose career De Sanctis follows over several chapters in order to lay out the poet's efforts to harmonize the opposed exigencies of head and heart.

De Sanctis shows that in Dante's early prosimetrum, the *Vita Nuova*, verses are rudimentarily juxtaposed with prosaic self-commentary to en-sure that poetry's "innate value of being lovely and giving delight" is re-tained even when its meaning, glossed in prose, is beyond the reach of the common reader. By the end of the work, emancipation has occurred with Beatrice's death. A God-borne Beatrice is a symbol of "Truth" and, as in Dante's *Convivio*, transfigured into "Philosophy," that is to say the object of a love that is "no longer personal, but is the principle of divine and human life." De Sanctis's Dante is opposed to the empty abstraction of Scholastic speculation; to him love is a "moral feeling" and philosophy something that "seizes on the whole man, penetrating his life in its every aspect," actuating his will (*HIL*, 1:65).

Just as "love is made strong by [Beatrice's] death," philosophy acquires strength in its own demise, in "its conflict with life." A modern poet might throw his hands up in despair, but Dante combats the pain caused by the separation of "the ideal and the real" by making the recovery of "unity of life" his mission: "Philosopher and poet, [Dante] feels as if he had been given a mission, a kind of lay apostolate; and when he talks to the multitude from his rostrum, he does it with the sureness and authority of a man who possesses the truth." And yet while Dante has recovered his goal, he still struggles with the means. Words, unlike sculpture, can "express only a content that has defined limits," as De Sanctis puts it. The doctrinal and mystical contents of scientific Scholasticism can be expressed only in allegory, which, as Dante realizes, "adds a new difficulty to a content already so abstruse and scientific" (*HIL*, 1:68–69).

For a time it seemed that prose was the answer. Indeed, new municipal freedoms enabled a cultivated laity to emerge in the thirteenth century, and, like the poets, they aimed to popularize science, which had been the exclusive preserve of learned men. Yet they translated, compiled, and continued to allegorize with little, if any, creative success, in effect confirming the idea that "serious subjects had to be treated in Latin." Dante himself tried his hand at Latin scientific prose with *De Monarchia* and *De Vulgari Eloquentia*, only to come to the conclusion that he was a bad philosopher or no philosopher at all. His great achievement had been his Beatrice, symbolic of "the presentiment and lyrical accent of a world still enveloped in science, still outside life," and the Trecento would achieve new heights with the birth of a second Beatrice as "ideal unity, the love that joins together intellect and act, science and life" (*HIL*, 1:145). It is, of course, in Dante's *Divina Commedia* that agreement between the earthly and heavenly realms is achieved, not in "expounding" but in "realizing" "that realm of science or that Kingdom of God which everyone was seeking, by turning it into a living world" (156).

As De Sanctis sees it, what marks Dante's masterpiece is its ability to achieve reconciliations at different levels. First, the *Commedia* brings together highbrow and lowbrow literature on a theme that they hold in common, namely, the "mystery of the soul." In the interplay of literal and allegorical meaning, furthermore, the *Commedia* is perhaps the first literary work to address "every [social] class," as it attracts both the learned and the masses to an extent that is unprecedented. De Sanctis undoubtedly has Cuoco's theory of the "two peoples" in mind when he credits Dante with the insight that in order to popularize science, it is necessary to emphasize its moral scope. And this Dante achieved, specifically, by reuniting knowledge and desire, by showing that while beatitude may rest in the contemplation of God, the forward path must be desired: "Each of [Dante's] acts of knowing leads to an act of the will" (*HIL*, 1:169).

After Dante a new "century" (or "secolo," by which De Sanctis means a self-contained cycle) begins, compassing the Renaissance *at its end*. De Sanctis, like Burckhardt, characterizes the epoch of "transition" of the late Trecento and Quattrocento in terms of rediscovery of the classics, a renewed sense of patriotism, and, more important, a breaking loose from the collective institutions (family, class, Church, etc.) that had stifled subjectivity in the Middle Ages. But was this nascent individualism to be admired? De Sanctis does not think so, not wholeheartedly at least, and his reasons reflect specifically Italian concerns. Less than a decade before the publication of Nietzsche's *Human, All Too Human*, De Sanctis stresses that Renaissance individualism was not productive of new moral and social strength and that the fault lay with Petrarch. Petrarch may have Latinized his name but there was little Roman resoluteness and will power in his soul. Petrarch's was an "artificial consciousness," and for this naturally solitary and contemplative man the active life was a mere "diversion."

With Petrarch's introspection the "sphinx is unveiled: man is found," and while this is a mark of "progress" in some sense, it is also true that the man recovered by Petrarch is himself, a single protagonist at center stage, not a common, universal man, or even a civically engaged one. As De Sanctis analyzes the structure of the *Canzoniere*, a jumble of discrete, stylistically impeccable utterances, he finds that Petrarch has no "story," no way to work his way back to a unity, for no other reason than that he "is weak and his life is aimless" (*HIL*, 1:275). Petrarch confines himself to his dreams for fear of disillusionment, and while acknowledging that this reflects a fragility that is all too human, De Sanctis makes the point that a purely mental world ends up getting the better of its master:

> So the mind is worn away in imaginings and reflections, each as useless as the others. The poet is punished where he has sinned. He has wished to absorb the whole of life into himself, and now he finds at last that he is alone, and he feeds on himself, and becomes his own vulture. Weary, disheartened, disgusted by a reality to which he feels himself a stranger, he turns his back on the world and retires to the solitude of Vaucluse, as to a hermitage, and remains alone with himself—"alone and lost in thought," thinking, imagining, pursued by his inner vulture. (276–77)

The Renaissance individualism that De Sanctis identifies through Petrarch and others is as potent as, perhaps more potent than, what Burckhardt described and Nietzsche elaborated, and it troubles him. Petrarch, De Sanctis writes, failed to realize fully that his state of mind was a "disease"; consequently it was a disease that he passed on to that large and long posterity he often directly addressed. In Petrarch Italy found its "artist," a producer of perfectly balanced verse, but Petrarch also turned out to be the proto-type of another ideal-type: the "letterato," the man who elevates the cult of form to the detriment of man, fellow man, and, ultimately, *patria*.

As he moves from Petrarch to Boccaccio, De Sanctis finds his suspi-cions confirmed. With the arrival of Boccaccio no "evolution" or resistance is to be perceived, only "a cataclysm, . . . one of those sudden revolutions that from one day to another show us a changed world." In the context of a negative assessment of 'revolutions,' De Sanctis again reveals Cuoco's influence on his thinking about French culture and history. He describes Boccaccio as the "Voltaire of the fourteenth century" and the "carefree gai-ety" of his work as the "first step into [a] new world of matter or the flesh, the sinful, the cursed—with loud and jesting voice" (*HIL*, 1:304). Notably, it is while discussing Boccaccio that De Sanctis is finally able to pinpoint the Renaissance 'problem' as an Italian ought to perceive it. He notes that in just three decades Italians went from producing a "divine comedy" to putting forth its parody, the "human comedy"—an acceleration that is un-sustainable. Dante's work was a reform; he built on a firm foundation and made sure not to sweep anything away. Boccaccio's work, by contrast, was a revolution that knocked down the whole building.

For De Sanctis the Italian 'difference' depends on its Renaissance and its 'man.' In Italy, the reaction against the exalted spiritualism of the Middle Ages is not a gradual change as in other countries, especially in Germany with Luther's Reformation; it is not "constructive" but totally "destructive." The Italian Quattrocento literati who followed on the heels of Petrarch and Boccaccio disengaged from society, creating a "fissure" (*scissura*), never to be mended, between "two separate and distinct soci-eties, living side by side, and on the whole without bothering each other too much." It is here that De Sanctis locates the origin of that division between the "two peoples" which Cuoco perceived in Naples at the end of the eighteenth century. Presumably historicizing Cuoco's insight, how-ever, De Sanctis discards Cuoco's central idea that the Italians, unlike the French, experience revolutions of mind and politics only as something external. On the contrary, he suggests, the Renaissance man continually countered revolutions with other revolutions.

There was the friar Savonarola, for example, who at the end of the fif-teenth century believed he could arrest the progress of Italy's decadence by abruptly "decivilizing Italy" and destroying books, paintings, and fes-tivals. The "disease was in the consciousness," De Sanctis stresses, and it takes centuries to form as well as to destroy a "collective consciousness."

A rather rough wakeup call occurred at the dawn of the Cinquecento, at the time that Charles VIII first came into Italy:

> Italy in those happy years of peace and prosperity could still be interested in the fate of Cephalus and the loves of Ergasto and Corimbo. The academies, the festivals, the bands of cultured people, were a literary Arcadia, and the public, idle, heedless, and empty-headed, took an active share in it all. In Naples, in Florence, in Ferrara, they lived in a perpetual atmosphere of tales, romances, and eclogues; men who in the olden days would have taken a part in life as conspirators, orators, or patriots, slayers or victims, were languishing among nymphs and shepherds. . . . The negative side of this ideal was the comic; a licentious and gay and jesting sensuality, which caricatured Heaven in the name of the earth, and painted the superstitions, the malice, the easy-going temperament, the customs and speech, of the lower classes with all the ironical expressions of a higher culture. . . . One fine day, toward the end of the century, when Pontano was frolicking in Latin verses and Sannazaro was playing the flageolet, suddenly in the middle of that society of balls and festivals and songs and idylls and romances came the foreigner and shook it awake. And at the first clash with the foreigner the monarchy collapsed, like a thing that was rotten at the core. Charles VIII rode into Italy and conquered it "with chalk." (*HIL*, 1:424–26)

These lines from the first three paragraphs of De Sanctis's chapter on the Cinquecento convey a morose tone. Those same "barbarians" who had been the subject of perpetual jeering by the cultured classes conquered Italy effortlessly. More telling and traumatic was that Italy, with its superior intellect and all of its books, could do nothing about it. The sacking of Rome in 1527 would merely confirm that Italy was no longer its own.

One cannot fail to notice that De Sanctis draws his words from the Neo-Guelph literature associated with Balbo. And yet De Sanctis takes a stance that is not "moralistic" or even "pessimistic" but matter-of-fact.[86] He seems to be saying that from an Italian perspective, the greatness of the Renaissance poses a paradox or an enigma rather than a problem. But

---

86. See Vasoli, *Umanesimo e Rinascimento*, 163. On the 'moralistic' approach of Risorgimento thinkers to the Renaissance, see Carlo Dionisotti, "Rinascimento e Risorgimento: La questione morale," in Buck and Vasoli, *Il Rinascimento nell'Ottocento in Italia e Germania*, 157–69. Translated as "Renaissance and Risorgimento: The Moral Question," in *RIP*, 235–45.

this, too, is only an apparent paradox because, as he learned from Vico, a transition into decadence is the natural outcome of any civilization that has reached its apogee. Again, the 'difference' is Italy's unsustainable rate of cultural acceleration and the fatal force with which it hurtled into its decadence. The one source of hope, the one redemptive virtue that remained intact in this collision was the seriousness with which Italian men of letters took their "calling": "Here was the germ of life, and here also the germ of death: the greatness of the century and its weakness" (*HIL*, 1:433). In modern times, however, one could not return to Dante or rewrite Petrarch. Instead, two related yet opposite ideal types emerged at the beginning of the Renaissance. These were the 'man of Machiavelli' and the 'man of Guicciardini,' and De Sanctis wants modern Italians to look to these models as they near the end of the nineteenth century.

Tackling the positive model first, De Sanctis describes Machiavelli as a man who despite being raised under the Medicis' rule breathed that modicum of "independence, glory of the fatherland, and love of liberty" that was allowed in Italy. Like Dante, Machiavelli is a diamond in the rough; he draws away from the otherworldliness of thought, and this trait is reflected in his writings, in that he is "quite unconscious" of or even opposed to the cult of form, and for this reason he becomes the "master" of a form that "mirrors" consciousness and reflects "life," in whose texture speech and act are one and the same. De Sanctis sees Machiavelli, more importantly, as the man who gave a name, "corruttela," to Petrarchan moral disease. Unlike Boccaccio, he is not inclined to destroy; unlike Savonarola, he is not inclined to restore. Machiavelli sees "corruption" for what it is: "nothing else than the Middle Ages in putrefaction" (*HIL*, 2:542).

Accordingly, and unlike Savonarola, Machiavelli came to understand that "to renew the people of Italy it was first necessary to renew their consciousness," and in the process a new man is potentially born:

> Man, as Machiavelli conceived him, has not that ecstatic, contemplative face of the Middle Ages, not the tranquil, idyllic face of the Renaissance. He has the modern face, the face of the man of modern times, who has an aim in life and who works and produces around that aim. Every man on this earth had his mission, suited to his abilities. Life is not a game of the imagination, and is not contemplation. It is not theology nor art; life is a serious thing in itself, and its ends and its means are here on the earth. To make this life on earth the important thing that it once had been, to give it a purpose, and to bring back health to the inner stream of character, to restore seriousness and activity to

man—here is the vital motive that breathes in all the works of Machiavelli. (*HIL*, 2:543–45)

It is worth noting De Sanctis's use of periodization. Machiavelli's "man"
is "modern." He rejects both the "ought to be" of the mystical Middle
Ages and the idyll of the Renaissance and is endowed with a whole new
"purpose," perspective, and material—what Machiavelli summarized in
the formula "effectual truth of things" (*verità effettuale delle cose*) (545).

Perhaps De Sanctis realized that he had weighted down the Italian
Renaissance too much, making it impossible to find any kind of redemption within its boundaries. Machiavelli represents the beginning of a new,
modern cycle, one in which Italians still reside. In describing Machiavelli
as dismissing divine and artistic contemplation as notable digressions, De
Sanctis makes him the discoverer of the immortality, immutability, and
autonomy of the human spirit, the precursor of Vico's understanding of the
developmental pattern of nations, and the precursor, too, of the Hegelian
"philosophy of history" (*HIL*, 2:550). At the same time, De Sanctis makes
Machiavelli into a living contemporary and a lesson for modern Italians,
and he does so rather sharply. After remarking on the death blow that Machiavelli's observational method dealt to abstruse Scholastic science, De
Sanctis pauses to interpolate: "Even as I am writing these words the bells
are ringing far and wide, unceasingly, pronouncing that the Italians are in
Rome: the temporal power is falling, the people are shouting, 'Long live
the unity of Italy!' Let there be glory to Machiavelli!" (585). In other words,
on 20 September 1870, at the very time (if we are to believe him) that De
Sanctis was writing, the Risorgimento was fully realized when the Italian
army led by General Cadorna captured Rome, the last missing piece of a
completely united Italy. Now a post-Risorgimento era could begin, originating from the moral reform Machiavelli had called for and that a lack of
political unity had left untried in the post-Renaissance era.

But Machiavelli, like Dante, was an exception to the norm. Just as during the Renaissance people had succumbed to Petrarch's "disease," modern
Italians were attracted to another ideal type, personified by Guicciardini.
Like Machiavelli, Guicciardini hated the clergy and foreigners and wished
for a unified Italy, but "he only wishes for these things—he would not
have lifted a finger to realize them" (*HIL*, 2:588). De Sanctis's discussion of
Guicciardini in the *History* derives from a programmatic piece, "The Man
of Guicciardini," that he wrote hurriedly as a gut reaction to the publication of Guicciardini's *Ricordi*, which, De Sanctis insisted, had made him
understand the Italian Renaissance paradox, its greatness in its smallness.

The "man" of Guicciardini is the kind of "gentleman" that only the most advanced societies can produce. He is endowed with prudence, doctrine, experience, he is a sage, almost perfect man, and everything in him is discretion and discernment. This man does not believe in anything but his own "speculations," and he refashions himself into a serene and ironic god. And yet to what use are all of these qualities put? To no use other than what Guicciardini called his "particulare," his personal interest. The man of Guicciardini was the man modern Italians had grown into. At the end of the essay, De Sanctis sounds the alarm:

> The Italian race has not yet recovered from this moral weakness, and time has not yet erased that mark of duplicity and pretense which history has stamped on our forehead. The man of Guicciardini "vivit, imo in Senatum venit," and you run into him everywhere. This fatal man will always block our way unless we find the strength to kill him in our consciousness. (*RIP*, 125)

In his attempt to reach into the unconscious, repressed, and destructive libido of the Renaissance/Italian intellectual man, De Sanctis writes literary criticism that, were it not anachronistic to do so, one would almost call Freudian.

His *History*, originally intended to be a school textbook, was certainly therapeutic—shock therapy, that is. De Sanctis was out to slay the Renaissance man that had survived, and while this was certainly more effective than nineteenth-century suppression as a way of dealing with the Renaissance shame, it is still unclear what was supposed to happen in the aftermath. De Sanctis himself confronted this issue in his intellectual testament, an inaugural address titled "Science and Life" that he delivered at the University of Naples in 1872. De Sanctis begins by wishing that his will be the last academic address in Italian history; he says that after all the vileness and blame that have been heaped on academic science it makes sense that he is at a loss. He indirectly acknowledges that the moral of his *History* was that sciences accrue to the detriment of life, that science stands at the end of the course of people and nations, and that this can be seen in the example of Greece and Rome, not only in the Italian Renaissance. The only way out, he says, is to have recourse to the notion of "limit." The events of 1789 showed that revolutions are a "reaction of nature against society," of "freedom against boundaries," and science played a role in reuniting the fatherland and freedom. But in Italy, at least, did it create Italians? Not at all, says De Sanctis. "And what would Italy

be without Italians?" Italians will be created only in moderation, by making science, a restoration of the "limits of freedom," rather than "freedom
against the limit."[87] "Wild egotism" will unite with sacrifice, and duty
will come only from this restoration of the "limits in consciousness."

De Sanctis was fully aware that his was not an exciting speech for
an incoming class of young students. But he was probably addressing his
peers of old: they who had helped bring the Risorgimento to fruition, they
who had come of age and even grown old since the enthusiasm of 1848.
Since then Italian thinkers had gradually come to rediscover the Renaissance, to probe the problem that it poses and in the process to assimilate
that epoch to the Risorgimento. De Sanctis himself had achieved a perfect
identification with the Renaissance in his empathic reexperience of it. In
short, he had brought together and reconciled the concerns of his age. In
De Sanctis's purely 'Italians' Renaissance,' the Renaissance shame of the
Neo-Guelphs is reconciled with the budding Renaissance pride of Spaventa. It is with these achievements in mind that the Renaissance would be
picked up again in the twentieth century, by Giovanni Gentile especially,
who would draw from both De Sanctis and Spaventa to reformulate the
Renaissance problem, but also, finally, to offer a solution.

HUMANISM REBORN AND FULFILLED: FROM
POSITIVISM TO GIOVANNI GENTILE'S ACTUALISM

In the conclusion of his 1872 address, De Sanctis sounded a disheartened
note as he urged universities not to be factories for the production of pro-
fessionals (lawyers, doctors, etc.) but to recover their "mission," their duty
to action: to be relevant to the activity of the state and the advancement
of the nation and to promote forever a spiritual regeneration among the
youth. Indeed, the reform of higher education was one of the prickliest,
most pressing issues facing the newly formed centralized state in the postunitary period. The resulting establishment of research institutes was a
largely palliative response, one that could meet the needs of future ruling classes, when secondary-level reform of rote learning was harder to
accomplish.

The first among these experimental graduate schools was founded
in Florence in 1859. The Institute for Advanced Studies (Istituto di Studi

---

87. Francesco De Sanctis, "La scienza e la vita," in Lanza, *L'arte, la scienza e la vita*,
324ff.

Superiori) was introduced self-consciously as an heir to Florence's Studio Generale, which itself had been intended to rival the University of Bologna when plans were drawn up in 1321, just as Dante, the greatest of Florentine popular 'scientists,' according to De Sanctis, was dying in exile.[88] Despite attracting refugee scholars from the crumbling Byzantine Empire—and thus at the cutting edge of the teaching of Greek (to name an example from the humanities)—the Studio had failed to entice the great personalities of its time (such as Petrarch or Ficino). Thus the highest level of intellectual fervor had remained within the circle of private academies. Its modern manifestation, the Institute, experienced its share of vicissitudes but nonetheless became the primary destination for what is sometimes defined as the post-1861 Neapolitan diaspora, as Hegelians took chairs in every major university. Former Catholics and former Hegelians (some having served both causes) came together to make the Institute the center of 'positivism,' a new philosophical credo —and again an inaugural address served as the means of announcing it.

This address, "Positive Philosophy and Historical Method," was delivered by Pasquale Villari (1827–1917) just as Florence was designated, briefly, the nation's capital city in 1865. Villari shared a predicament that idealists had faced, namely, that positivism—like Spaventa's Hegel—might look like "foreign merchandise" (FKC, 371). If it was true that the names of Auguste Comte and John Stuart Mill linked positivism to France and England, then Villari hastened to reassure his audience that the movement had recently been embraced in congenial Germany as well. As Villari saw it, what made positivism the natural, even epochal, outcome of Hegelianism could be seen if one took the correlation drawn by Vico between the history of nations and human lives and applied it to the history of philosophy, which likewise shows a pattern of "action and reaction" (372).[89] Villari explained that just as humanity moves or matures from poetry to philosophy and, fed up with abstractions, returns to the regenerating powers of poetry, so has modern thought moved from the materialism of the eighteenth century to German pantheism to a general European cry of "Keine Metaphysik mehr" (374)!

In his address Villari spoke not for the natural sciences per se but rather

88. In what follows I draw from Eugenio Garin, La cultura italiana tra '800 e '900 (Bari: Laterza, 1962), chaps. 1 and 2.

89. Needless to say, Villari, too, will attempt to trace back to Vico the roots of the positivism he advocated. See Francesco De Aloysio, "Il Vichismo di Pasquale Villari: Un itinerario nelle regioni dello storicismo," Nuova rivista storica 62, nos. 1–2 (1978): 29–81.

for the kind of positivism through which philology and, more importantly, historiography could aspire to the status of science. He evidently saw this humanist positivism as a way to enforce those constraints on reason that De Sanctis had been calling for since his early years in Naples, when Villari was his student:

> The positive philosophy renounces, for now, absolute knowledge of mankind; indeed it renounces all absolute conclusions, but without denying the existence of what it does not know. It studies only facts and social and moral laws by patiently checking the inductions of psychology against history and finding the laws of the human spirit in the laws of history. Thus, it does not persist in studying an abstract human person, beyond space and time, composed only of pure categories and empty forms; instead, it studies a real living person, mutable in a thousand ways, stirred by a thousand passions, limited at every turn, and yet filled with boundless aspirations. (*FKC*, 395)[90]

The point was less to oust metaphysics for good than to rescue it from its many ambiguities, to "find a way to get from the *I* to what is outside the *I* by checking and testing the ideas that we find in ourselves" (386).

Villari was sincerely persuaded that a turn to the 'positive' could not fail to appeal to Italians; after all it was Galileo who had freed the natural sciences from their metaphysical grounding. Galileo was concerned with nature, but his insights were furthered by Vico, who, in Villari's account, can be understood as having applied the experimental method to the realm of man. From Vico's realization that "the laws of the world of nations are the same as the laws of the human spirit that created the social world," one arrives at the realization that "history somehow gives you the external world on which to experiment and verify the inductions of your psychology, [and] the psychology then becomes the torch that illuminates history. The laws of the one, if they are true, must be checked against the other, and vice versa" (*FKC*, 394). Perhaps a positivism with an Italian (Galilean-Vichian) ancestry could not—and did not want to—solve the great problems posed by philosophy (the existence of God, for example), but it could certainly promote a practical knowledge of the human heart. In other words, in a post-Risorgimento era, it could help Italians

---

90. On Villari's apprenticeship at the school of De Sanctis, see Mauro Moretti, "Alla scuola di Francesco De Sanctis: La formazione napoletana di Pasquale Villari (1844–1849)," *Giornale critico della filosofia italiana* 63, no. 2 (1984): 27–64.

reconfigure the role of the intellectual and the hoary institutions to which he attaches.

Villari's speech was received as a manifesto by fellow positivists, yet, despite making no antagonistic claims, it was not welcomed by older Hegelians. Eventually it elicited a disgruntled response, in the form of an open letter, from Spaventa, who reiterated his reading of Vico and his understanding of spirit as being "doubly positive" in that spirit always participates in—and never merely observes—phenomena from the outside. Spaventa, whose study of Hegel Villari had once tried to support financially by soliciting donations from fellow Hegelians, arrived, finally, at a disavowal of positivism (and thus of the generation his Hegelianism had begotten), calling it a "warmed up naturalism" (O, 458–60). This notion that Villari was responsible for a "betrayal" of Hegelianism would be reaffirmed brutally in the twentieth century. The truth, however, is that the first champion of positivism displayed a rare coherence in his antidogmatism.

Villari's intellectual testament from 1891, *Is History a Science?*, reflects his ongoing interest in the study of European post-Hegelian philosophy, and it consciously marks the end of the brief age of positivism that Villari himself had inaugurated a mere quarter century earlier. In essence it is a detailed review of the best works of European historicism (Henry T. Buckle, Bruno Gebhardt, Ernst Bernheim, Wilhelm von Humboldt, Leopold von Ranke, Michelet, Barthold Georg Niebuhr, Friedrich Carl von Savigny), which Villari sees culminating in Nietzsche's *Untimely Meditations* (1876), a text that he might have been the first to cite in Italy.[91] Less than two decades earlier Villari had asked scholars to devote themselves to the facts of history; now he joined Nietzsche in denouncing the modern excess of scientific historicity, the cause of a disturbing "disease." Humanist positivism had not turned out to be the balanced method he had called for. Instead, much like their German counterparts according to Nietzsche, Italians had indulged in amassing sources without endowing their evaluation with sentiments inspiring vital action. And Nietzsche had been onto something in identifying "antidotes" in the "unhistorical" (*das Unhistorische*) and the "suprahistorical" (*das Überhistorische*), by which he meant art and religion, the powers that lead us away from the "always mutable becoming" and direct our gaze to the infinite.[92] It is at this juncture, as we

91. On Villari's historicism, see Maria Atonino Rizzo, "Storia e storiografia nel pensiero di Pasquale Villari," *Nuovi quaderni del meridione* 6, nos 23–24 (1968): 348–83 and 451–65. Some of Villari's methodological studies are collected in *Teoria e filosofia della storia* (Rome: Editori Riuniti, 1999).

92. Pasquale Villari, *La storia è una scienza?* (Catanzaro: Rubbettino, 1999), 91.

shall see, that Villari committed the error that doomed his future reception: he asked Italian intellectuals to begin to open their hearts again to religious, namely, Catholic, faith.

Meanwhile, in the realm of historiography, Villari turned to Wilhelm von Humboldt's famous text "The Task of the Historian" (1821), which served as a de facto blueprint for future developments in German historicism, to ask historians to hone the talent that makes them akin to artists, the ability to unite scattered and fragmentary evidence into a coherent and meaningful whole. Villari's suggestions were not exactly new or cutting-edge; nevertheless we can appreciate his efforts to accelerate the course of Italian thought. There were reasons why Italian philosophy had tarried with Hegel, but at present there was no reason, positivism having quickly fulfilled its epochal task, not to take a step forward and join that new epoch of pluralist thinking in history that in Germany was marked by a long-lasting *Methodenstreit*. By the end of his career, Villari had enlarged the scope of Italian philosophy. He had resurrected personalities who had been overshadowed by Hegelianism (Telesio, Galileo), found new affinities to European thought (Bacon), and endowed Vico, finally, with an appropriate heritage that would endure—what was called by Mill the "moral sciences" or, in Germany, the *Geisteswissenschaften*.

Villari's text elicited many reactions, the most important for future Italian philosophy being Benedetto Croce's "History Brought under the General Concept of Art" (1893). Croce, who in retrospect deemed this, his first philosophical piece, to be a "revelation of myself to me," claimed that Villari and everyone before him had been focused exclusively on defining science rather than art, and Croce was determined to establish a new way of thinking about the relationship between rationalism and empiricism.[93] Most people, he states, would assert that the goal of art is pleasure, but in fact its goal is "producing the Beautiful," and the beautiful is not pleasure, nor should it be identified with the true or the good; rather it is a "highest ideality" that should be kept distinct, with no overlap with the worlds of theory and ethics (*FKC*, 487). As for the eternal problem of the role of history in art, Croce suggests that it may be resolved by showing how, unlike science—in which the particular is subsumed under a general concept—history aims at a "representation of reality," the mere reproduction of the particular "in its concreteness."

Croce's reply to Villari would perhaps have fallen on deaf ears had it

---

93. Benedetto Croce, *Contributo alla critica di me stesso* (Milan: Adelphi, 1999), 31.

not become the foundation for *Aesthetic as a Science of Expression and General Linguistic* (1902), the work that put Croce on the map as one of the leading European thinkers of his generation. In Italy, meanwhile, Croce's investigation of the beautiful represented the first installment of a massive project (comprising investigations of the true, the good, and the useful) whose aim is evident in the name Croce gave to it: "philosophy of the spirit." In this, his attempt to correlate the "highest idealities of the human spirit" horizontally and holistically, Croce made himself the heir of De Sanctis, whose work he saw as a first attempt to explode the ranking of those qualities in Hegel's work.

The neo-idealism that he advocated needed an institutional base, and Croce, who was not a university professor, founded *La critica* (1902), a successful journal that would become the mouthpiece for the rebirth of idealism. According to the journal's statement of purpose:

> The editor firmly believes that the disciplining of method and documentation in research is one of the most progressive moves undertaken in Italy in the last decades; therefore the journal is a loyal advocate of what is called the historical and philological method. But the editor is as strongly convinced that such a method does not meet all the demands of thought and therefore that it is necessary to promote a widespread reawakening of philosophical spirit. In this regard, literary criticism, historiography, and philosophy itself will profit from a judicious return to the tradition of thought that was unfortunately interrupted after the achievement of the Italian revolution, a tradition in which the idea of spiritual synthesis resounded—the very idea, that is, of *humanitas*.[94]

Neo-idealism was a neohumanism, or a humanism fulfilled, and the goal had to be pursued with a forceful refutation of positivism, to which, however, some merits should be granted. Joining Croce in this enterprise was a young Giovanni Gentile, who, in an ideal division of labor (though there was inevitably some overlap) would extend Spaventa's philosophical legacy at the same time that Croce, who was actually Spaventa's nephew, did the same for De Sanctis's literary legacy.

Born and raised in peripheral Sicily, Gentile came of age intellectually at the Scuola Normale Superiore in Pisa (1893–97) and at the Istituto di Studi Superiori in Florence (1897–99). He was thus a direct and active wit-

---

94. Benedetto Croce, "Programma," *La critica* 1, no. 1 (1903): 2–3.

ness, if not the living product, of the rough coexistence of positivism and idealism in fin-de-siècle Italian academic life. Although from the outset Gentile found his mentor in Donato Jaja (1839–1914), a defrocked priest who had been a student of Fiorentino (himself Spaventa's student), he incurred a lasting debt in Pisa to Alessandro D'Ancona (1835–1914), a pioneering scholar of Italy's theatrical tradition and a pugnacious spokesperson for philological rigor in approaching historical sources. It was D'Ancona who, after attempting in vain to rescue the promising student from the vile philosophical "chatter" of Jaja, endowed Gentile with the tools that would allow him to pursue influential and comprehensive historiographical research on Italian intellectual history, starting, it turned out, with the Renaissance. This collaboration between D'Ancona and Gentile thrived solely on the basis of their shared affinity for De Sanctis, the only Hegelian whose "genius" D'Ancona accorded respect.

Under D'Ancona's watch, Gentile began honing his skills with two essays dedicated, respectively, to *Rosmunda* by Giovanni Rucellai, a typical Sophoclean tragedy of the Cinquecento, and to the comedies of Anton Francesco Grazzini, one of the many epigones of Boccaccio on whom, in his *History*, De Sanctis had piled a barrage of epithets ("insipid," "gross," "careless"; *HIL*, 1:455) by way of illustrating Italian Renaissance decadence. In his treatment, which amounted to his first academic publication, Gentile, too, used Grazzini's work to produce a general statement, his first, on the Renaissance, and his words may give us a sense of déjà vu:

> On a given night a farce or a comedy would be performed. And look at all those literati running to it in order to observe the novelty of the plot and immediately claim it was banal: another haphazard mix of Plautus and Terence. On another night you could hear burlesque or nasty sonnets, in which erudite men were mocked for their great pedantry, while the prolific poet, who shirks any kind of erudition, would be teased for his vulgar ignorance. And everyone would take an interest in it, and the number of contenders would grow. So that between those meager passions and academic ambitions, the interests of the bookworms and the frequent merry gatherings, one would forget, or forget to mention, all that really matters. The Florentine literati were all imbued with this perennial lightheartedness, whose buoyancy and indolence they would transpose into rhymes. This peaceful life, which was promoted by the grand ducal family, made people forget about the famous siege and lose all sense of civil dignity. The brave-hearted would leave Flor-

ence: but most men would yield to that sweetly imposed servitude which flattered the literati in many respects.[95]

Whether it was to ingratiate himself with his teacher D'Ancona or, more probably, to pledge an early allegiance to a Hegelian stance, Gentile thoroughly assimilated the De Sanctis (and Neo-Guelph) view of the Renaissance as an epoch of "turbid ferment" (Gentile's expression). Furthermore, it was this publication that allowed Gentile to seek a first contact with an admired model, Croce, his senior by nine years. The approval that Gentile's missive elicited from Croce ("I find the conclusions you reach to be very exact [esattissime]") interestingly reveals that the most momentous intellectual partnership in modern Italian history was established on a shared concern for what the nineteenth century had come to identify, in various terms, as Italy's 'Renaissance shame.'[96]

Having already paid homage to the methodological requirements enforced by positivism, Gentile could move on to what was dearest to his heart: reviving the philosophical tradition of the Risorgimento that in his view had been left hanging in the age of positivism. His graduation thesis was directed by his beloved Jaja, the man who introduced him to Spaventa and infected him with the "daemon" of philosophy.[97] Titled *Rosmini and Gioberti: A Historical Essay on the Italian Philosophy of the Risorgimento*, it was first published in 1898, and in the preface to this edition, it is clear that a twenty-three-year-old Gentile had determined his life mission. He begins by lamenting that, medieval and Renaissance thinkers excepted (since they "belong more to European than to Italian" history), modern Italian philosophy, even Vico, has been written out of the many histories of philosophy produced in Germany. Foreigners, Gentile insists, are under the impression that nothing has been thought in Italy since Bruno and Campanella, and for this they are not to be faulted: "Have we ever actually tried hard enough to prove the importance of our philosophers for the history of thought? Do we have anything to match the rich literature that

95. Giovanni Gentile, "Delle commedie di Antonfrancesco Grazzini detto il Lasca," in *Frammenti di critica e di storia letteraria* (Florence: Le Lettere, 1996), 113.
96. Croce to Gentile (27 June 1896), in Benedetto Croce, *Lettere a Giovanni Gentile (1896–1924)*, ed. Alda Croce (Milan: Mondadori, 1981), 1.
97. On the momentous relationship between Gentile and Jaja, see Alessandro Savorelli, "Gentile e Jaja," *Giornale critico della filosofia italiana* 74 (1995): 42–64; and Francesca Rizzo Celona, *Da un secolo all'altro: Figure e problemi della filosofia italiana tra Otto e Novecento* (Catanzaro: Rubbettino, 1994), chap. 3.

hard-working foreigners have amassed on the major as well as minor philosophers of their respective countries?" (*SFI*, 1:695). Gentile places some
of the responsibility on Gioberti or, to be more specific, on the Giobertian
emphasis on an ancient Italic primacy. In his view, there is a path still
largely untrodden, extending from the idea of "the circulation of European
thought," perhaps the "most conspicuous outcome" of Italy's philosophical history.

Although Gentile does not mention him by name, Spaventa is the beacon leading the way in what turns out to be merely the first installment in
a historiographical project that will shed light on what Hegelians, including Spaventa, left in darkness. This, to be sure, was a large territory. This
time, Gentile's publication elicited a full-fledged review from Croce, who
commended Gentile's attempt to restore intellectual continuity in a country, Italy, in which "traditions never develop and exhaust themselves but,
rather, snap."[98] Furthermore, perhaps wanting to spare the young student
from the criticism to be expected from the positivists, Croce claimed that
Gentile was superior to Spaventa, endowed as he was with the philological
wherewithal for a reconstruction that was at once philosophical, historical, and social.

Gentile pocketed Croce's appreciation and moved on to the Institute for
Advanced Studies in Florence. This time his teachers were Felice Tocco, a
former student of Spaventa who had strong ties to the historical school of
D'Ancona, and, of course, Pasquale Villari. Both were reformed Hegelians
to different degrees and as such were viewed with suspicion by Gentile,
but at the same time they were also two of Italy's pioneering Renaissance
scholars, having produced the aforementioned first monograph studies and
editions of Bruno, Savonarola, and Machiavelli. In their classes Gentile
was introduced to the systematic study of philosophical historiography,
and under Tocco's supervision, Gentile pursued his Spaventian project in
a dissertation focusing on Antonio Genovesi (1712–69) and Pasquale Galluppi (1770–1846), who occupied, roughly, what Spaventa had perceived as
an unexplored "void" between the time of Vico and that of Gioberti.[99] On
the whole, his experiences in Florence gave Gentile the chance to define
his stance and his aversion to positivists or any type of reformed Hegelians; clearly defined enemies would be necessary if his and Croce's neo-
idealism was to acquire epochal momentum.

98. Cited in *HIP*, 1:683.

99. Giovanni Gentile, *Storia della filosofia italiana dal Genovesi al Galluppi*, collected
in *SFI*, 1:453ff.

It was not long after he left Florence that Gentile began to collaborate with Croce on *La critica*, and for more than a decade (from 1903 to 1914) Gentile produced pieces aimed at razing anything that had come between Spaventa and himself, temporally and philosophically. In *The Origins of Contemporary Italian Philosophy*, the volume collecting these essays, no one is spared from harsh criticism, including his former teachers.[100] Tocco, for example, is a "cold," even "frozen type" of Hegelian, "scientific," "deprived of any poetical afflatus," "weak," "spiritually indifferent," and unsupported by any "profound intuition of life" (*SFI*, 2:461). Furthermore Tocco is the author of an empty model for philosophical history, reduced to "pure philology." His base temperament is best illustrated, writes Gentile, by his comment on Bruno's allegedly disdainful reaction to the cross that was presented to him as he was burning at the stake. Whereas Hegelians of yore would have "exalted that supreme annoyance," Tocco instead insists that Bruno was rejecting only the attempt to impose with force a religion that deep in his heart he could not but accept as bearer of peace and forgiveness (461–62).

His other teacher, Villari, also came under fire. Gentile tended to hold Villari's original enthusiasm for Spaventa's Hegelianism against him. After all, was it not Villari who had written an encouraging letter to Spaventa in the late 1850s, stating: "To make Hegel accessible in Italy would amount to regenerating Italy" (*SFI*, 2:258)? Villari's flaw was his spineless, "enthusiastic," "naïve idealism" that made him turn coat at any chance; the same term employed in Italy to refer to cases of political opportunism, 'transformism,' could also be applied in the realm of ideas. It is certainly true that Villari in his career embraced each philosophical current with equal fervor (Giobertianism, Hegelianism, positivism), but also in his case what was unforgivable was the undampened Catholicism and, worse, Neo-Guelphism that emerged from his studies of Machiavelli and Savonarola. In other words, his religiosity was not the intimately experienced spirituality of the idealist, but that which fixates on religion as "Church, as institution, as historical fact, itself observable," like the weights that Galileo tossed from the leaning tower of Pisa (261). In his celebrated works on the Medicean Renaissance, this same moralistic religiosity had Villari doubting Machiavelli, whose genius he viewed "through the eyes of Savonarola." Villari, in the last analysis, was a representative of that group of neo

---

100. On Gentile's tormented relationship with the legacy of positivism, see Alessandro Savorelli, "Il gatto e il sorcio: Gentile e il positivismo nelle 'Origini,'" *Giornale critico della filosofia italiana* 78, nos. 1–2 (1999): 181–211.

"weepers" (from the name, *piagnoni*, given to Savonarola's followers) who thrived, with deleterious consequences, in nineteenth-century Florence, a phenomenon to which Gentile devoted another controversial work.[101]

There are interesting insights to be drawn from the *pars destruens* of a resurgent idealism. It is worth noting, for example, how Gentile brings the same tone with which De Sanctis disparaged the Renaissance literati to bear on the positivist culture of his age, and there is certainly some correspondence between the "man of Guicciardini" and Gentile's assessment of his contemporaries. More important for our concerns, however, might be the militant anticlericalism and anti-intellectualism that animated Gentile during the decade in which he (mainly) made his study of the Renaissance.

At the same time, we might wonder if Gentile, who at the turn of the century was beginning to abandon historiography for independent theoretical pursuits, would have even bothered with the Renaissance had it not been for a commission too good to refuse. On 12 July 1901, the prominent Milan-based editor Cecilio Vallardi contacted Gentile with an idea for a single-volume history of Italian philosophy. It "should serve not so much as a guide for studies at the secondary level," wrote Vallardi, "but rather as support for those who have the wherewithal and yearn to broaden the horizon of their cognitions."[102] Gentile's recent publications, Vallardi said, identified him as the perfect man for such an endeavor. Vallardi added that time was of the essence, for he wished the volume to be associated with the "dawn of the new century." Gentile responded affirmatively and with a touch of arrogance. He assured the editor that if he managed to bring to fruition what he had in mind, his history would be "a revelation for foreigners," for he had found the key that would endow Italian philosophy with the continuity it had always lacked. We now know that he saw the commission as a chance to bring Spaventa's project to fulfillment; moreover it is likely that he saw it as providing an opportunity to do

101. Giovanni Gentile, *Gino Capponi e la cultura toscana del secolo decimonono* (1922; Florence: Sansoni, 1942).

102. Cecilio Vallardi to Giovanni Gentile, 12 July 1901: "Volgendo al suo termine la *Storia Letteraria d'Italia* che Ella certamente conosce, ho pensato a una nuova pubblicazione che studi, in una serie di volumi, e separatamente, ciascun genere della nostra letteratura, sotto il titolo: *Storia dei generi letterari italiani.*

"Essa dovrebbe servire non già di guida per gli studi secondari, ma di sussidio per coloro che sanno ed amino allargare l'orizzonte delle proprie cognizioni.

"Avrei poi pensato a Lei per il volume riguardante: *La Storia della Filosofia*, soggetto da Lei degnamente coltivato e mi auguro che Ella voglia aderire al mio invito notificandomelo con cortese sollecitudine, volendo iniziare l'opera coll'alba del nuovo Secolo." AFGG.

what De Sanctis, also in a single work, had done for the history of Italian literature.

The only problem that Gentile had with the commission was one of time. If Vallardi was initially hoping for a submission as early as 1902, Gentile availed himself of the editor's leniency to alter the contract and commit to complete the work by 1903. In hindsight, Vallardi's initial insistence on timely submission seems laughable. Over the next forty years or so Gentile would produce a mere introduction spanning from Scholasticism to Lorenzo Valla. It is easy to understand why Gentile could not come up with the goods: the material continued to grow in his hands, especially as he delved into a largely unexplored Quattrocento humanism. Therefore, it is to Vallardi's credit that, decade after decade, as Gentile rose to the status of philosopher and minister of Mussolini's regime, Vallardi persistently hammered him with correspondence, using every means at the editor's disposal (threats, pleas, appeals) to elicit something from Gentile, who would in fact produce just enough to influence and direct the scholarly production of a future generation of Italian Renaissance scholars.[103]

Gentile's *History* begins with a seemingly external assertion: "The court of Frederick II of Sicily was the cradle of Italian lyrical poetry" (*SFI*, 1:13). It begins, in other words, where both Burckhardt and De Sanctis begin their own narrations, but Gentile diverges from their lukewarm assessment of Sicilian culture. Frederick was an admirable man, an unmatched cultural impresario who attracted all sorts of talented people to his court, including "cultivators of philosophy," and while scholars believe that Frederick's court was the center of "Arabic culture and religious indifference," the truth is that one could breathe there a certain "aura of skepticism, which is the mark of the beginnings of a new philosophical age, given that it is an established opinion that philosophy begins when doubt emerges, along with the need for a demonstration of that truth which faith merely presupposes—the very need of which science is made" (13).

One page in, and Gentile had set the direction for his reinterpretation of the Renaissance. His history would go on to narrate man's emancipa-

---

103. See, for example, Cecilio Vallardi to Giovanni Gentile, 30 July 1931: "Anche la mia raccomandata del 10 c.m. è rimasta senza risposta come le precedenti del 9 Marzo e del 10 aprile. La cosa mi rammarica sopratutto per una considerazione d'indole generale. Io, che sono più vecchio di Lei, pensavo che durasse ancora il principio per cui, non soltanto il dovere della correttezza, ma anche quello del reciproco riguardo e della cortesia fossero tanto più sentiti quanto più alta è la condizione sociale delle persone. Lei invece mi fa dubitare anche di questo principio. Visto quindi che Lei non degna di risposta le mie lettere, io mi limiterò a ricordare che fra Lei e me esiste un regolare contratto; e mi regolerò di conseguenza" (AFGG).

tion from institutionalized faith, the struggle for a purely spiritual, that is, confessionally unmediated, reconciliation between man and God, immanence and transcendence, subjectivity and objectivity, the very struggle by which human excellence and dignity accrues. Gentile would assert that Averroism was the philosophy of the age in that it was the first to check the Aristotelian criticism of Platonic transcendence with an awareness of the single universal intellect shared by all human beings. The first concrete sign of dissatisfaction with the limits of transcendentalism, Averroism was the "philosophy of the free thinkers," the philosophy of the "medieval Aufklärung" (SFI, 1:24). The problem inherited from ancient philosophy, from Plato and Aristotle, is the concept of transcendence, the negation of human autonomy, and although Christianity, "with its notion of a God-man as mediator between the divine and the human worlds, virtually contained the germ for a definitive solution," this solution is thwarted by Catholic institutions, by the Church and Scholasticism both. Gentile devotes the second chapter to Thomas Aquinas, whom he introduces as the philosopher of a "double truth" in which the power of reason is again potentially affirmed, while also remarking that he is "caught in the transcendental web of Scholasticism" (36).

As noted, Gentile is not out to deny religion any worth at all; he targets only its institutionalized form. Thus, in chapter 3, he introduces Francis of Assisi and the movement that he inspired as having the necessary but not sufficient conditions for a fledgling philosophy: the Franciscan movement is the first strong assertion of a spiritual renewal. At the same time, it also subscribes to an ascetic model, and although the Church has by this time secularized itself too much to support such a reform, the Franciscan spirit will inform the Ghibelline reaction against the "overexcessive mundanity of the Church," which is itself "contributing, indirectly, to that negation of transcendence, or, at least, to that redemption of reality from transcendence which will mark the end of the Middle Ages and the beginning of the modern epoch" (SFI, 1:54). But Gentile is also ready to grant the importance of mysticism for philosophy per se. Mysticism's negation of sensuality does not serve only religious or moral perfection; the "gathering of the spirit" it calls for is necessary to establish the "independence of spirit from nature" and thus the autonomy of mind and of the very science that Franciscans actively opposed.

The book's fourth chapter, too, shows the influence of De Sanctis, as Gentile reaffirms Dante's status as the first Italian philosopher. And as with De Sanctis, it matters to Gentile that Dante chose to express his philosophy in poetry rather than prose, in Italian, rather than Latin. The motive for his choice, writes Gentile, was "psychological" in that Dante was by nature a poet and his concern was with "form." The result is that anyone interested in the history of Italian thought must contend with the multiple generic guises taken by philosophy in Italy, more so than in other countries. The rich De Sanctian definition of "culture" allows Gentile to point to a philosophical tradition whose main idiosyncrasy is to have developed outside or, rather, against the grain of academia and irrespective of generic and linguistic boundaries. And yet his embrace of these 'literary' concerns here jars with the sharp counter-De Sanctis turn that the book takes in the next chapter, a turn that may in fact have been informed by De Sanctis's own suggestion in his *History* that whoever would eventually take it upon himself to write the history of Italian thought would interpret it as a history of "opposition" against the Church and academic philosophy.[104]

Adhering to what has been described as the rationale of nineteenth-century national historiography, which favors the vernacular over Latin, De Sanctis could describe only the Petrarch of the *Canzoniere*, and only the Quattrocento that came through the *Stanze* of Angelo Poliziano.[105] Humanism, in other words, is passed over in silence by De Sanctis, just as it was ignored by Spaventa. Gentile, by contrast, accounts for the Quattrocento exclusively through its Latin literature and makes no excuses for doing so. In the process he rescues from oblivion the philological enterprises of a panoply of figures: Luigi Marsili, Coluccio Salutati, Leonardo

---

104. *HIL*, 2:716 (emphasis added): "There were men of learning with the reaction too. The difference was in this. In the men of the reaction speculative vigour and intellectual activity were suspended; the whole work of the mind was turned on the forms and accidents rather than on the substance, which was also the case with the literati. But the men of the opposition were engaged in a serious intellectual progress, and were moved by faith and spurred by passionate feeling. The victory, of course, was entirely with the reaction; the whole of the forces of society were solidly behind it, whereas the others, chased as they were from the schools and academies and curbed by the Inquisition and the censor and prevented from expanding, were the tiniest minority, so small as to be barely noticeable in that vast social movement. So the reaction was deprived of the struggle that is necessary for the sharpening of intellect and the quickening of feeling, and remained Arcadian and stationary. Activity of intellect and ardour of faith were the privilege of the opposition. Whenever in the literature of that day we light on a movement of the intellect, we invariably find the opposition, in a greater or lesser degree, and often involuntary and barely realized by the writer himself. *A history of that Italian opposition has still to be worthily written. Yet there were our fathers, there was beating the heart of Italy, there were the germs of the new life. Italian life was dying from an empty consciousness, and the history of this Italian opposition is nothing else at bottom than the slow reconstruction of the national consciousness.*"

105. See Christopher S. Celenza, *The Lost Italian Renaissance: Humanists, Historians, and Latin's Legacy* (Baltimore: Johns Hopkins University Press, 2004), chap. 1.

Bruni, Niccolò Niccoli, Giannozzo Manetti, and more. What undoubtedly influenced Gentile's choice was a source that appeared just one year before Burckhardt's work, was subsequently overshadowed by its success, and to this day remains largely untapped. The source was Georg Voigt and his awkwardly titled work *The Revival of Classical Antiquity, or The First Century of Humanism* (1859). Yet if Voigt's work provided a source, it provided little in terms of spirit. In other words, throughout his work Voigt looked coldly at the humanists' devotion to antiquity, viewing their emulation as contributing little creatively and their efforts as formalistic: "The unabashed pursuit of antiquity turned its devotees in a certain sense into idealists and fanatics."[106] Voigt's opinion was matched and superseded by De Sanctis, but Gentile, relying on Spaventa's thoroughly philosophical Renaissance, could reevaluate humanism from a vantage point for which the future and glorious legacy of Quattrocento philology had cleared the way.

Gentile's (Latin) Petrarch is not so much an exemplar of a *letterato*-to-be as a fierce opponent of Scholasticism and of any values that attach to medieval science. This Petrarch is readily evident in the pamphlet *On His Own Ignorance and That of Many Others* (1367), in which Petrarch emblematically takes on four unnamed "friends" who are cult followers of a degenerate Aristotelianism. In a critique of their natural philosophy, which has been reduced, says Petrarch, to investigating the number of "hairs a lion has in its mane" or "how many feathers a hawk has in its tail," the 'father of humanism' most vehemently affirms the centrality and dignity of man as the ultimate object of scientific speculation.[107] Petrarch's view, Gentile writes, was a "negative position," but it was precisely the position required to affirm the "necessity of a superior science of which the Averroists have no inkling" (*SFI*, 1:132). Petrarch, to be sure, had little to offer by way of an alternative, but he did contribute three ingredients essential to dissolving Scholasticism: a solid skepticism ("Petrarch is the only true skeptic of his age"), which eradicates faith in the sciences while

106. I cite from Georg Voigt, "A New World in Italy," in *The Renaissance Debate*, trans. and ed. Denys Hay (New York: Holt, Rinehart, and Winston, 1965), 29. Voigt's pioneering study was translated into Italian, with the title *Il risorgimento dell'antichità classica*, in 1888. On Voigt, see Paul F. Grendler, "Georg Voigt, Historian of Humanism," in *Humanism and Creativity in the Renaissance: Essays in Honor of Ronald G. Witt*, ed. Christopher S. Celenza and Kenneth Gouwens (Leiden: E. J. Brill, 2006), 295–325; and Mario Todte, *Georg Voigt (1827–1891): Pionier der historischen Humanismusforschung* (Leipzig: Leipziger Universitätsverlag, 2004).

107. Francesco Petrarca, "On His Own Ignorance and That of Many Others," in *Invectives*, trans. and ed. David Marsh (Cambridge, MA: Harvard University Press, 2003), 239.

retaining some in religion, his purported "ignorance," that is, the attitude from which all philosophy takes its cue, and his constant "meditation on death," the element common to every true philosophy of life.

There is no reason to be ashamed of Petrarch, therefore, or of those great thinkers who in the first half of the fifteenth century elaborated on and formed a school around his precepts, completing the "revolution" (a term that Gentile does not hesitate to use) started by Dante and Petrarch together. In a dense chapter with the significant title of "Philology," Gentile investigates every nook and cranny, every merit of humanist erudition. The rediscovery of the classics, the controversies surrounding the relative merits of Italy's 'three crowns,' the translations from the Greek, the concurrent reevaluation of Greek ethics and political theory, and more generally all the means employed to shake off a dead scientific tradition for good—all of this contributes to an assessment that fundamentally rewrites De Sanctis:

> This humanism, which empties the souls and dampens the religious faith, which makes of philology a philosophy, and gives to Italy the enduring disease of the *letterato*, does not represent Italy's decadence, that decadence which consigned Italy to the hands of the French and the Spaniards, inflicting that shame derived from the harmful experience of servitude. Decadence, rather, is represented by that which was destined to fall under the blows of humanism: [the decadence] was in the medieval world, with all of its institutions and its ideologies. Humanism was a violent spiritual countercharge that was readied in the slow but profound social shift that began as early as the eleventh century and brought about the autonomous life of communal cities and the consequent ruin of the imperial notion and authority. Humanism produces the heretical Franciscan mysticism and the consequent annoyance with a hierarchical and theological Catholicism. Humanism restores new freshness to the soul and a new need for intimacy, for human restoration that achieves self-consciousness, as we have seen, in Francis Petrarch, and turns a cold shoulder to medieval science, art, religion, forms of a spirit that is no more. . . . Humanism frees man from deadly concerns, and prepares the freedom of spirit of modern times. (*SFI*, 1:159)

Humanism's merits lie in the philosophical legacy for which it "prepares" with its philology. The notion of "precorrimento," anticipation, that Spaventa employed to reevaluate Campanella and Bruno in view of their European influence is applied to the historical background of those very same philosophers. In fact the last chapter of Gentile's history is devoted to Lorenzo Valla (1407–57), the humanist who exposed the Donation of Constantine as a fraud and in whose hands the "disinterested philology" of the early humanists accrues "rebellious violence" against traditional culture and thus begins to acquire a philosophical purpose (199).

Gentile's interest in the Renaissance did not cease utterly. Throughout his career he would compose many programmatic portraits of figures that the nineteenth century had made canonical (Telesio, Bruno, Galileo, Campanella, etc.), and these portraits all owed something to the Quattrocento and to his general statements on what he took the epoch to be. Gentile expressed his principles most clearly, perhaps, in a piece from 1920 that bares a Spaventian title, "The Character of the Renaissance": "Humanism is the preparation for or, if you like, the beginning of the Renaissance" (RIP, 143). It is also a movement that has suffered from a "totally extrinsic consideration of historical facts" that wants to attribute its significance only to the rebirth of the classics that it brought about, while, in fact, "in regard to the concept of man," humanism is indistinguishable from the Renaissance. Furthermore, if a "spiritual transformation" may be observed between the humanist and the Renaissance man, the withdrawal of the former into himself and his sources to "celebrate what is distinctively human" is merely improved by the "gaze" that the latter "turns outside of man to embrace intellectually the totality of the world to which man belongs and in which he happens to live" (144). In this he is "natural" or cosmic, an "amplification" of the former:

> Therefore, beyond the philosophy of philosophers, there is the philosophy of nonphilosophers. That is, those who are not professional philosophers. They are not philosophers because they are not capable of instituting a critique of the systems of their time on the same level as those same systems, nor do they completely understand the language of professional philosophers. They have a reason for not wanting to know this language, however, and this reason of theirs already has a philosophical value; it is a critical position. (RIP, 151)

Humanism, in other words, is the unreflective stage of man's affirmation of himself as "a spiritual reality"; it is "the philosophy of the non-philosophers."

The transitional nature of humanism can be observed as well in the religiosity of its representatives. Neither pagans nor Christians, they are anticlerical but for this reason "more profoundly and progressively Christians" in their establishment of a mediated relationship with transcendence, the true aim of an original Christianity that wanted to have God descend to man in order to raise man to God. Prior to this, Gentile states elsewhere, during antiquity and the Middle Ages, "when the Christian wanted to contemplate his God, he thought more about God the father than God the son, and thus got caught in the web of Aristotelian metaphysics" (*SFI*, 1:244). In what is considered his manifesto on the Renaissance, "The Concept of Man in the Renaissance" (1916), Gentile highlights the celebration of human dignity, the concept of the "value which is man's own and of man's superiority to nature"—which was already acknowledged by Burckhardt as an "achievement that alone imposes on us the obligation to give eternal recognition to the men of the Renaissance." Yet neither Burckhardt, nor, to this day, anyone else, has "studied the philosophical form it assumed early on" (229).

Perhaps, had Gentile not been distracted by other ambitions, he would have told the complete story, the story of that Italian Renaissance philosophy which Spaventa had left unnamed but which Gentile sometimes wanted to call "umanismo" to keep it distinct from the philosophically insignificant "umanesimo" or *Humanismus* of the Germans. Gentile had written the first part of man's spiritual paean to himself in the modern period, the story of the making of that kingdom of man (*regnum hominis*) which owes nothing to God's grace but everything to the autonomous initiative of man: that "quidam mortalis deus" which Giannozzo Manetti was the first to celebrate consciously in his *De excellentia hominis*, and after him Giovanni Pico della Mirandola in *Oration on the Dignity of Man*. Later, Bruno and Campanella would do so, but their naturalism entails that the ultimate goal is still beyond man, with residues of transcendence remaining (*SFI*, 1:250). After these thinkers, as Spaventa, too, had believed, the struggle to seamlessly reconcile subjectivism and objectivism would be pursued outside Italy, and it would not be Gioberti, Hegel, or Spaventa who reconciled them, but Gentile himself.

Introducing the last edition of his collected writings on the Renaissance in 1939, Gentile stated plainly that it was not a book that as a young man he would have foisted on those "older brothers" whom he revered, those "thinkers who had infused my heart with light and warmth" and who had shaped his early formation.[108] It is worth noting that his Renaissance scholarship and his theoretical concerns had been running in paral-

---

108. Gentile, *Il pensiero italiano del Rinascimento* (Florence: Le Lettere, 2003), x.

lel from 1903—when his first installments for Vallardi's *History* appeared simultaneously with his first philosophical statement, "The Rebirth of Idealism"—to 1916, when his Renaissance research culminated in "The Concept of Man in the Renaissance," which appeared in the same year as *A General Theory of the Spirit as Pure Act*, the definitive statement of the neo-idealism that he had been formulating and that he dubbed 'attualismo' or actual idealism. By comparing and contrasting these concurrent streams of work we can see how Gentile's theoretical concerns grew and acquired clarity at the same time that he was gaining clearer consciousness, in his historiographical research, of the unfulfilled ambitions of his Renaissance "brothers."

Gentile delivered "The Rebirth of Idealism" in the temple of old Hegelianism, the University of Naples, with the intent of celebrating and reviving Spaventa's legacy, a legacy that Gentile believed had been passed on to him as a "sacred torch" from the hands of Jaja. Gentile did not offer much that was constructive at this point; his intent was simply to counter the "petty naturalism" of positivism and herald the coming "revenge" of idealism via not so much a perfectly achieved monism as a *coincidentia oppositorum* between subject and object (or immanence and transcendence). In a talk that he gave in Palermo in 1907, Gentile attributed the latter concept to the dualism that originated in Platonic-Aristotelian science:

> Such a science does not make itself, because it is ready made; it does not become, but rather is: it is, I mean, for itself. We discover it with the analysis of our ideas: we *remember*, Plato used to say mythically, what we had already seen in a previous life. Truth in a word (and this is the diehard Platonism) is in itself that which is; is in itself all that it is: *kosmos teleios*, a world per se perfect. All error is pinned on the forgetful man: truth is pure, nothing but truth and light. We stand against it; we see it or we do not; we are enlightened by it or we remain shrouded in darkness; in the latter case, shame on us. This does not concern truth, which is per se blissful. This is what the ancient objectivism that culminates in Plato amounts to, and which, I repeat, remains consecrated in Aristotle's logic for millennia. It remains, or rather, it was always in the consciousness of humankind, which feels the need to posit truth, and thus true justice, true freedom, everything for which it fights and for which it lives above and beyond errors and human wickedness. This objectivism is in fact a moment of truth. But, as with any moment, it is destined to be overcome. (*SFI*, 1:280)

These words were written at the same time that Gentile was composing the section of his *History* that was dedicated to Quattrocento philology and to the dignity of man recovered therein. And so all that follows upon the age of Aristotelian dominance is labeled "modernity," which itself is described as "amounting to the slow, gradual conquest of subjectivism: the slow and gradual identification of being and thought, of truth and man. It amounts to the foundation, so celebrated throughout the centuries, of the *regnum hominis*: the establishment of a true humanism" (280–81).

In a talk that Gentile gave in 1913, "The Method of Immanence," he elaborated on an etiological myth in which Vico's well-known anti-Cartesian polemic played a central role. In Gentile's view, it was in Descartes's *cogito* that one could grasp the connection between truth and the act of thought, and Vico—who had shed light on the connection between knowing and making—provided the vitality that Descartes lacked, having made a deadly, and rather Platonic, turn to an objectified *res cogitans*. Nevertheless, by 1914 ("Pure Experience and Historical Reality"), Vico's *verum-factum* principle had also come to seem too static to Gentile, whose favorite heuristic device was to fluidify any philosophical concept or noun with the goal of establishing a "living logic" (*logica vivente*) (SFI, 1:417). In his final word on actual idealism, in 1916, Gentile proffers a significant variation on the guiding Vichian motif of Italian philosophy. While continuing to vitalize Latin terminology (as a way of countering Scholasticism), Gentile alters Vico's *verum et factum convertuntur* into *verum et fieri convertuntur* or, even more trenchantly, *verum est factum quatenus fit* (475). Truth is never a fact, something made once and for all, but rather something perennially in the making: an act. As Gentile puts it: "The act [*atto*], so that it not be converted into a fact [*fatto*] and that it be grasped in its actual nature [*natura attuale*], as a pure act [*atto puro*], can only be conceived of as thought [*pensiero*]. . . . As soon as we descend from act to fact, we find ourselves outside of thought, in the realm of nature. There are not spiritual facts, just acts [of the mind]" (318). It appears that without Gentile's intervention, Vico's philosophy might have lapsed into sixteenth-century naturalism and its outward projections.

In a surprising turn that may be qualified as a 'Vichian Cartesianism,' Gentile grafts a newly vitalized Vico, his *verum ipsum factum*, back onto Descartes, his *cogito ergo sum*. In so doing, he identifies or rather assimilates life, history, reality, and, indeed, God to the eternal and all-encompassing act of a thinking subject, leaving no residues of a primitive dualism. This is the achievement that Gentile attributed to his *attualismo*,

which itself represented a new, perhaps final, stage in the development of
the human spirit. Actual idealism amounts to the idea that to eradicate
abstract objectivity, it is not enough to think *about* a thought, as when we
think of someone else's thought or our own past thoughts. Instead, this
kind of abstract thought (*pensiero pensato*) is turned into an absolute subjectivism in the concrete act of thinking (*pensiero pensante*), where such
thinking is my thinking, wholly actual and present as my own. In Gentile's words:

> The act of the *I* is consciousness in that it is self-consciousness: the
> object of the *I* is the *I* itself. Every cognitive process is an act of self-
> consciousness. This is not abstract identity and immobility but con-
> crete act. If it were something identical, inert, it would need another
> to be moved. But that would annihilate its freedom. Its movement is
> not a *posterius* in relation to its being; it coincides with the being. Self-
> consciousness is movement itself or process. (*FKC*, 692)

Only in pure thought in action, a gerundive "eternal process of thinking,"
in the process of "autoctisi," self-construction, is man free and thus properly Man.

Was Gentile's *attualismo* the "true humanism" first envisioned by Petrarch and his Quattrocento followers? Did Gentile manage to do what
Spaventa had envisioned, that is, squaring the circle of European thought,
reconciling Renaissance thought and Hegelianism? For some time, and as
Gentile became self-consciously the 'philosopher of fascism,' *attualismo*
did indeed rise to the status of national philosophy. Yet objections cropped
up immediately. The moniker of "purus philosophus," which an ever more
distant Croce would bestow on Gentile, ostensibly as a nod to his forsaken
philological and historicist talent, was perhaps well deserved by a thinker
who had overstepped all limits by equating philosophy to a perverted *re-
dire in se ipsum* (*OF*, 275) and man to a greedy giant who, unlike Tanta-
lus, was capable of devouring all the fruits of nature and of absorbing all
dimensions of reality into the infinite sphere of its conscience (249–50).
Gentile's "divinized" man was bound to appear, especially to younger generations, as a monstrous *Übermensch*.

As we shall see in the next chapter, in the interwar period charges of
mysticism and solipsism were leveled at a philosophy that appeared unable
to contemplate interaction with anything other than the self, neither God
nor, more dangerously, one's fellow man. Furthermore, a philosophy that

had originally aimed to transform man into an "actor" or maker of truth was perceived as having ended by staging a monologic one-man show—be it Gentile's own or Mussolini's. "Aut Caesar, aut nihil" (*OF*, 754). This is what the Renaissance man had failed to grasp fully when Gentile published "The Humanist Conception of the World" in 1931. At this time *attualismo* got caught in a crossfire that would spell its demise, the casualty of a renewed scholasticism, the defection of Gentile's onetime janissaries, and the disillusions of a younger existential generation.

CONCLUSION: A PROBLEM UNSOLVED

This chapter has reviewed and found interconnections among major phases in the emergence and development of a 'new' Italy and her philosophy, the contours of which were first traced with a sure hand by Cuoco. Certainly, Cuoco was instrumental in ensuring that Italian philosophy, whatever its form, would be under the aegis of Vico, who was increasingly seen as the *trait d'union* between it and a Renaissance whose legacy, it quickly became apparent, could not be taken for granted. Italians could reclaim some European philosophical and historiographical achievements as their own, provided they were deft about it. Moreover, by rejecting the notion of 'revolution' on the basis of its links to abstract thought, Cuoco set the stage for Italy's second rebirth, a 'renaissance' or, better, a *risorgimento* or 'resurgence' whose positive outcome depended on the Italians' ability to restrain and pace themselves (the slower the better). He was also setting standards for an Italian philosophy-to-be, a realistic 'humanism' capable of assimilating the past to the present, life to science, and of reuniting the concerns of the intelligentsia and the masses. When a competing triad of twentieth-century thinkers—Gentile, Croce, and Gramsci—turned to Cuoco, these were indeed the first principles, the aspirations, that they recovered. In Cuoco they instinctively identified a Petrarchan figure in whose company they, late Renaissance men opposed to the positivist literati or narrow-minded humanists of the postunitary period, could make a last attempt to tally up the intellectual legacy of the Risorgimento.

Gentile described Cuoco as the "first disciple" of Vico (himself the living "antithesis of the eighteenth century") and as the first "prophet of the Risorgimento."[109] Accordingly, Cuoco had provided Italians with a well-

---

109. Giovanni Gentile, "Vincenzo Cuoco nella storia d'Italia: Commemorazione," in *Vincenzo Cuoco: Studi e appunti*, by Giovanni Gentile (Florence: Sansoni, 1927), 88ff.

articulated program for a national awakening. He had spurred Italians to
"great actions" (*agire in grande*), for he understood that Italians were the
sum of their manual and intellectual labor. More to the point, Gentile saw
Cuoco as a link between Vico and Giuseppe Mazzini, for Mazzini would
translate thought into action and, together with Garibaldi and Cavour,
concretize the nation that Cuoco could only envision. In other words, Gentile refashioned Cuoco as the originator of the Risorgimento inasmuch as
it was a movement that fascism and actualism could be understood as continuing or fulfilling.[110]

In one of his first attempts to endow Fascism with a historical rationale, Gentile depicted Renaissance Italy as the "old Italy," an epoch of
unrestrained individualism against which the "new Italy" of the Risorgimento and Fascism was contrasted:

> In the Renaissance there is much light, yes, and there is much in it
> about which Italians may share national pride. But there is much
> darkness. For the Renaissance is also the age of individualism, which
> through the splendid visions of poetry and art brought the Italian na-
> tion to the indifference, skepticism, and distracted cynicism of those
> who have nothing to defend, not in their family, their fatherlands, or
> in the world where every human personality conscious of its own val-
> ues and personal dignity invests itself. The Italians of the period had
> nothing to defend because they did not believe in anything beyond the
> free and pleasurable play of their own creative fantasy. From thence
> came the frivolity of a pattern of behavior both decadent and corrupt.
> The behavior slowly extinguished the active sentiment of nationality
> and thereby enfeebled souls. . . . All of that is the culture of particular
> individuals who think of themselves and nothing more. An Italy not of
> Italians. Italians without faith and therefore absent. Is not this the old,
> decadent Italy?[111]

110. The first edition (1923) of a work collecting Gentile's thoughts on other "prophets
of the Risorgimento" (Mazzini, Gioberti, Mameli) was dedicated to Mussolini: "A Benito
Mussolini—italiano di razza, degno di ascoltare la voce dei profeti della nuova Italia." Now,
see Giovanni Gentile, *I profeti del Risorgimento italiano* (Florence: Le Lettere, 2004), vii. On
the many ways in which the Risorgimento legacy was appropriated to serve the cause of Fascism, see Massimo Baioni, *Risorgimento in camicia nera: Studi, istituzioni, musei nell'Italia
fascista* (Rome: Carocci, 2006).

111. These words were delivered in a speech to a Fascist audience in Florence on 8 March
1925. For the printed version (first published in 1926), see Giovanni Gentile, *Politica e cultura*
(Florence, 1990), 1:7–37. I cite from Giovanni Gentile, *Origins and Doctrine of Fascism: With*

It was recently advanced, half jokingly, that "if Gentile turned into a Fascist . . . it was the fault of Petrarch" and the *letterato* he spawned.[112] And yet perhaps Petrarch, and his lack of philosophy, can also be credited for Gentile's having become a philosopher in the first place. If the connection between the Renaissance and Fascism is asserted in the case of Gentile, it is only because Gentile contributed vastly to Renaissance scholarship (where he made Spaventa's project his own); the claim is less exaggerated when it comes to political rhetoric (in which case De Sanctis's, or a Neo-Guelph, assessment of the epoch prevailed).

Gentile's notion of "two Italys," old and new, may be compared usefully to Cuoco's notion of "two peoples," high and low. Both help us narrow down which features of Italian Renaissance scholarship grew out of the nationalist ambitions of modern Italy. In other words, Italian intellectuals had long experienced the dilemma, at least since Petrarch, of being unable to be at once men of letters and effective patriots. If Cuoco's anti-intellectualism was aimed at reconnecting the different strata of Italian society, then it is also true that, in his mind, this reconnection assumed the prior re-Italianization of the intelligentsia. That Italian intellectuals had lost themselves in this preliminary process without making any step toward an 'active' revolution would in due time emerge as the opinion of Gramsci, who famously portrayed Croce in his *Prison Notebooks* as the ultimate Renaissance man in De Sanctis's terms.[113] Needless to say, this was a portrayal that jarred with the perception that Croce had of himself.

Croce, too, himself a fierce custodian of the Italian historicist tradition, had framed the entire epochal shift between what he saw as an all-rationalist and antihistoricist eighteenth century and an all-historicist and humanist nineteenth century as hinging on Cuoco and his peers. Croce

---

Selections from Other Works, trans. A. James Gregor (New Brunswick, NJ: Transaction, 2002), 44–45.

112. See Gennaro Sasso, *Le due Italie di Giovanni Gentile* (Bologna: Il Mulino, 1998), 75. On how Gentile managed to have Cuoco himself co-opted by Fascist ideology, see Monica Galfré, "La fortuna di Vincenzo Cuoco nella scuola fascista," in *Vincenzo Cuoco nella cultura di due secoli*, ed. Luigi Biscardi and Antonino De Francesco (Rome-Bari: Laterza, 2002), 287–301.

113. It is assumed that Gramsci never read Cuoco but might have read the introduction that Croce wrote for an edition of Cuoco's *Saggio*. See Gianpasquale Santomassimo, "Rileggere il Risorgimento, rintracciare le origini del fascismo: L'opera di Cuoco nella riflessione di Antonio Gramsci," in Biscardi and De Francesco, *Vincenzo Cuoco nella cultura di due secoli*, 302–10; and Rosalinda Renda, "Vincenzo Cuoco: gli insegnamenti della 'rivoluzione passiva,'" in *Il nostro Gramsci: Antonio Gramsci a colloquio con i protagonisti della storia d'Italia*, ed. Angelo d'Orsi (Rome: Viella, 2011), 59–66.

acknowledged that in Italy this transition toward a new intellectual era
was initiated in subservience to foreign scholarly models, but he insisted
that the generation of Neapolitan émigrés forced to relocate to Milan at
the turn of the century were soon tapping into the original source (still
unknown to most) of that intellectual paradigm—Giambattista Vico—and
were doing so with accelerating and deepening consequences. A century
or more later their achievements might be taken for granted, but

> he who will transport himself to the times in which these principles
> were articulated—in the prisons of the Bourbons of '99 and on the ship
> that carried Cuoco and other exiled patriots to Marseille—cannot fail
> to see in them the first vigorous manifestation of Vichian thought,
> anti-abstract and historical, and the beginning of a new historiography
> founded on the organic notion of the people; and of a new politics, the
> politics of national liberalism, one which is at once revolutionary and
> moderate.[114]

Cuoco, "the most ingenious of these Vichian apostles," takes pride of place
among this group of patriots not only because he restored most forcefully
"moral and political sciences" to their Italian origins. He also originated
the image of Vico as the utterly isolated and premature soothsayer of a
century he did not live to see.

Non-Cuoco-like, however, was what Croce's critics, starting with
Gramsci, perceived as his attempt to circumnavigate some of the thorni-
est epochs in Italian history, most notably in his 1928 *History of Italy*.[115]
The temporal boundaries introduced in this work's subtitle, "from 1871 to
1915," would seem intended to rescue an epoch usually smothered between
the Risorgimento and the emergence of fascism, and to deny the continuity between them. Croce's justification sounded a pusillanimous note; at
best it was disengaged. On the one hand, he held fast to the principle that
the history of a nation should not be written before a country had formed
into a nation, properly speaking. On the other hand, he shrugged off fascism as a digression of sorts (*parentesi*), a sudden outbreak with no clear
etiology, and this is what placed him in a harsher light. As he famously
put it in 1944:

114. Benedetto Croce, *Storiografia italiana nel secolo decimonono*, 2 vols. (Bari: Laterza,
1921), 1:11–12.
115. Benedetto Croce, *Storia d'Italia dal 1871 al 1915* (Naples: Bibliopolis, 2004).

Italy [at the beginning of the twentieth century] enjoyed for about fifteen years a swift progress in every aspect of her life, until she was
forced, in 1915–18, to fight alongside her allies for the freedom of Europe. The hope of a freer and more vigorous Italian life was wrecked by
the invasions of the Hyksos. For this, I believe, is how the interregnum
of the Fascists is most conveniently described, with the solitary but
happy exception that the savageries of the Hyksos, who went so far as
to try to introduce foreign deities, lasted in Egypt for over two hundred
years, while the unwieldy truculence and inebriation of the Fascists
exhausted itself in little more than twenty years, and we Italians never
conformed to it.[116]

Oversimplifications such as these, which assured that Croce would become the butt of jokes among the most engaged philosophers of the postwar period, point, too, to Croce's rejection of linear determinism and casuistry in historiography.

Such was the stance that Croce brought to bear in an article of 1939, in
which he attempted to refute the Italian self-perception that the Risorgimento (and fascism) had created vis-à-vis the Renaissance. He argued that
in projecting its own aspirations onto the Renaissance, the Risorgimento
falsely came to believe itself to be a countermovement, while in fact the
"freedom" sought everywhere in more recent times was a sentiment almost absent in the Renaissance, a sentiment that only slowly developed
through the Renaissance achievements of the seventeenth century, the
period of Italy's so-called *decadenza* or decline. Therefore, "the Risorgimento was substantially a reawakening of the Renaissance, or, rather, a
reawakening of its rational and religious kernel. Thus, even the *hiatus* between these two periods, the intermediary age of decline, should not be
understood as marking a total detachment and decline" (*RIP*, 170).[117] This
is why, Croce explains, he focused his research, uncustomarily for an Italian, on the Baroque period. And yet at the same time this is how, from our

116. Cited in Gennaro Sasso, La *"Storia d'Italia"* di Benedetto Croce: Cinquant'anni
dopo (Naples: Bibliopolis, 1979), 83.
117. Benedetto Croce, "La crisi italiana del Cinquecento e il legame del Rinascimento
col Risorgimento," in *Poeti e scrittori del pieno e del tardo Rinascimento* (Bari: Laterza,
1945–52), 1:1–16. See also Croce's introduction to his *Storia dell'età barocca in Italia*, ed.
Giuseppe Galasso (Milan: Adelphi, 1993). On the topic, see Fulvio Tessitore, *Nuovi contributi alla storia e alla teoria dello storicismo* (Rome: Edizioni di Storia e Letteratura,
2002), chap. 17.

perspective, Croce subtracted himself from that debate which we call the Italians' Renaissance.

Unlike Croce and Gentile, who were working as the last heirs of the Risorgimento, Gramsci posed as the internal critic of that very same tradition. In fact, he came to extend the notion of a "passive revolution" (and Edgar Quinet's similar formula) to the entire epoch:

> One would say that both Quinet's "revolution-restoration" and Cuoco's "passive revolution" express the historical fact that popular initiative is missing from the development of Italian history, as well as the fact that "progress" occurs as the reaction of the dominant classes to the sporadic and incoherent rebelliousness of the popular masses—a reaction consisting of "restorations" that agree to some part of the popular demands and are therefore "progressive restorations," or "revolutions-restorations," or even "passive revolutions." Carrying this idea over . . . one might say that this is about "the revolutions of Guicciardini's man," in which dominant classes always looked after their *"particulare."*[118]

Gramsci, who presumably knew Cuoco only through Croce's mediation, nevertheless understood that Cuoco's emphasis on "passivity" was to serve as a 'word to the wise,' if not as a formal program, such that future ruling classes would encourage an energetic popular initiative. Cuoco called not for an utter abandonment of revolutionary ideals, as the Risorgimento seem to have thought, but rather for the blazing of a less fiery and tragic but also more conscious path, one free of illusions.

It is well known that one of Gramsci's major concerns in his *Prison Notebooks* is to figure out who—be it the pope, Croce, or Gentile—best represents contemporary Italian society from a theoretical and moral point of view. Throughout his work the title seems to be given over to Croce, but in a totally negative sense. Gramsci describes Croce as either a Guicciardini or, what is much the same thing, an Erasmus. "[Croce's] philosophy, especially in its less systematic manifestations[,] was a true intellectual and moral reform of the 'Renaissance' kind." That is, like Erasmus or Guicciardini, Croce "did not 'advance toward the people' he

118. Gramsci, *Prison Notebooks*, ed. and trans. Joseph A. Buttigieg, 3 vols. (New York: Columbia University Press, 2007), 3:252.

did not want to turn into a national element."[119] Gramsci sees in Croce's
historical writings the tendency typical of intellectuals to avoid committing to the real historical act (Erasmus's position with respect to the Reform); he sees the moments of struggle (revolutions) being written out to
present a history devoid of strife. By subtracting class conflicts from his
histories, Croce, in Gramsci's view, becomes a historian of abstract idea(l)
s, the greatest representative of a conservative ideology and, ultimately,
the promoter of an endless "passive revolution."

Clearly Gramsci means to cast a negative light on more than five centuries of Italian history by yoking Cuoco's theory of a "passive revolution"
to De Sanctis's notion of the "man of Guicciardini." Yet the enthusiasm
with which Gramsci's interpretation of Italy's history was received and
elaborated on in the immediate postwar period did not carry with it the
sense of 'shame' that persists in Gramsci's approach to the Renaissance, a
sentiment that he, too, had inherited from the Risorgimento. As we shall
see, a young interwar generation of thinkers emerged that shared many
of Gramsci's concerns. They, too, came to perceive fascism as the umpteenth failed revolution; they, too, came to distrust the practical applications of Croce's and Gentile's philosophy and the idealist reconstructions
of Italian philosophical history. Yet, unable to voice their dissent openly,
they resorted to historiography, and in so doing, they turned to the Italian
Quattrocento, rather than a thoroughly colonized Cinquecento, and what
they found there was, finally, a source for unreserved pride.

119. See Michele Ciliberto, *Figure in chiaroscuro: Filosofia e storiografia nel Novecento*
(Rome: Edizioni di Storia e Letteratura, 2001), 116.

CHAPTER TWO

The (Re)Generation of Italian Thought:
The Interwar Period

In order to achieve that serene humanism which in the '40s was still very much in the making one needed to experiment with existentialism, dispel its ambiguity, point to its significance. But in order to do this concretely—that is to say, historically—in Italy, in a well-defined cultural situation, it was necessary to link the vital stances of contemporary thought to what was still valid in our past culture. Recall the instruments this culture had offered and, most importantly, their enduring value for an industrious renovation of our critical consciousness.

—Eugenio Garin, *Cronache di filosofia italiana*

INTRODUCTION: PHILOSOPHIZING IN THE
TIME OF FASCISM AND BEYOND

In 1938, a year marked by the German-Austrian Anschluss, the Munich crisis, the Kristallnacht pogrom, and the enactment of anti-Jewish laws in Italy, Giovanni Gentile reprinted his summa of actual idealism, *A General Theory of Spirit as Pure Act*. In the preface to this edition, the last published in his lifetime, a disgruntled Gentile attacked the second generation of his disciples, once loyal, now "wretched Don Quixotes without a Sancho Panza," who in recent times had dared to run afoul of what Gentile had labored to present, persuasively, as the nation's official philosophy, his own. Gentile's bitter diatribe concluded with a plea to future generations: "Italian youth is much more pensive and serious than is usually acknowledged, and I have faith in them. For them I thus set out to republish with renewed care a book that was originally meant for them" (OF, 458).[1] As it happens, the generation Gentile so vehemently disowned was the last to partake of his actual idealism.

By this time, it had taken Gentile over three decades to erect a philosophical empire. His governance had been firm throughout, but his leadership did not go unchallenged. Indeed, it is through a careful scrutiny of Gentile's gradually waning influence (though not exclusively) that we may gain insight into Italian philosophy during the interwar period. Because Gentile was killed in 1944, a year that verged on a new beginning, it might be thought that he left no legacy. This assessment is, in part, true. It is also true, however, that Gentile continued to stir the course of postwar Italian philosophy, even in absentia. The fervent scholarly attention devoted to Gentile in the past few decades in Italy suggests that a rediscovery is overdue.[2] And yet his phantasmagoric presence cannot be assessed properly without first underlining what he had come to represent. For one thing, by labeling himself the "philosopher of Fascism," Gentile legitimized the identification between his actualism and Mussolini's regime.[3] In times prone to exorcisms, understandably, such identification presented a tempting opportunity to jettison the past, philosophical and political, wholesale.

In fact the opportunity proved to be irresistible. Postwar historiography promulgated the myth, destined to endure, that an idealist "hegemony" had existed until 1945 and that, like any hegemony, it was stifling and provincial. As would be acknowledged eventually, this assessment proved to be as feeble as it had been expedient in its immediate moment. One could

1. In *A General Theory of Spirit as Pure Act*, Gentile collected and rearranged his notes for a course taught at the University of Pisa in the 1915–16 academic year. The book underwent at least five editions during Gentile's lifetime (1916, 1917, 1920, 1924, and 1938) and was from the outset conceived as a sort of philosophical breviary for younger thinkers in the making. According to the first preface (1916): "Stampo dunque questo volumetto (e altri spero stamparne negli anni avvenire) per rimanere co' miei scolari anche dopo l'esame, ed esser pronto, se l'opera mia non andrà perduta, a ripeter loro da queste pagine la mia risposta o il mio stimolo a cercarsene una da sè, ogni volta che in loro risorgerà il bisogno,—spero non di rado,—di rispondere ai gravi problemi, così antichi e pur sempre nuovi, da me agitati in iscuola" (OF, 455).

2. Some seminal studies in the Gentile renaissance of recent years are Salvatore Natoli, *Giovanni Gentile filosofo europeo* (Turin: Bollati Boringhieri, 1989); and Augusto Del Noce, *Giovanni Gentile: Per una interpretazione filosofica della storia contemporanea* (Bologna: Il Mulino, 1990).

3. See Sergio Romano, *Giovanni Gentile: Un filosofo al potere negli anni del regime* (Milan: Rizzoli, 2004); and Alessandra Tarquini, *Il Gentile dei fascisti: Gentiliani e antigentiliani nel regime fascista* (Bologna: Il Mulino, 2009).

not overlook, for example, that idealism owed its hegemony as much to Benedetto Croce as to Gentile. Croce was at first Gentile's talent scout, then a partner-in-arms in idealism's rebirth, then a worthy philosophical competitor, and finally, when Croce came to represent the antifascist position, an alter ego of sorts. Unlike Gentile, however, Croce lived long enough in the postwar period to have an opportunity at first hand to renegotiate (albeit unsuccessfully) his legacy, and to witness the unearthing of Antonio Gramsci, who would posthumously bury both of them, nationally as well as internationally, to become perhaps the most read and translated Italian thinker of all time.[4] Croce's antifascism, then, did little to salvage idealism in retrospect, not least because his opposition, in comparison to that of Gramsci, had been too tolerated to fend off suspicion.[5] More to the point, Croce's legacy offered nothing to counter charges of intellectual provincialism, since Croce had resisted, possibly more than Gentile, opening out toward the world in a way that might have inspired questioning of the Italian intellectual *primato* or difference.

Saddled with this legacy and a difficult transition, the philosophical community in the postwar period found itself split between a majority of philosophers and a minority of 'Italian' philosophers. The split persists to this day. In the larger group were those seeking to deprovincialize thoroughly by thirstily lapping up phenomenology, neopositivism, philosophy of science—in short, everything that Italian idealism, believed to have stopped at Hegel, had withheld from Italian thinkers. In the smaller group were those who, having borne first-person witness to the Fascist ventennio or having been influenced by those years, thought it best, in the interest of moving forward, to produce new readings that made a serious attempt to come to terms with the immediate past. Most conspicuous among the doyens of this latter group are Eugenio Garin (1909–2004) and Norberto Bobbio (1909–2004), two towering intellectuals with coterminous life spans, whose year of birth, they often noted, placed them in the privileged

4. Croce, primarily owing to his work on aesthetics, enjoyed much more success than Gentile, who remains direly understudied outside Italy. It could be argued, however, that without Gentile one cannot know Croce, and without knowing both in their relationship cannot fully understand Gramsci, at least not in his Italian context. And yet both Croce and Gentile walk in the shadows of two thinkers they largely 'created,' Vico and Gramsci. On this point and for a review of the fortunes of Croce and Gentile, or lack thereof, in American scholarship, see David D. Roberts, *Historicism and Fascism in Modern Italy* (Toronto: University of Toronto Press, 2007), chap. 4.

5. On this thorny issue, see Fabio Rizi, *Benedetto Croce and Italian Fascism* (Toronto: University of Toronto Press, 2003).

position of being too young to participate in certain historical events—events that would nevertheless direct their entire careers. Because of their timing, it is not surprising that in their later years they were called on by their students and younger colleagues to serve as moral arbiters for a series of pioneering "bilanci," or appraisals, of post-1945 Italian philosophy. It amounted to a dismal assessment and, as even younger thinkers independently realized, an examination of consciousness that had long been avoided. In other words, postwar Italian thinkers had faced a "double problem of liberation," needing to liberate themselves from Fascism (and, it is implied, from Gentile) and from Croce, and were thus justified, perhaps, in their intellectual extroversion, but it could no longer be denied after four decades that ultimately it had had little positive effect. Neither unity nor originality nor direction was visible in contemporary Italian philosophy—only a haphazard and even frenzied "eclecticism."[6]

Bobbio and Garin, who did not see eye to eye on everything (most important, on whether a distinct "culture" emerged during the Fascist period), had to agree with this assessment, but they could also claim that they had tried to forewarn Italy's younger generation, having each produced in the same year, 1955, solitary yet insightful and astute works that differently sought a reckoning with Italy's endless Risorgimento.[7] As their work shows, they shared a skeptical view of the prevailing periodization that wanted to set 1945 as a viable terminus a quo. The histories of ideas and of facts, they insisted, though intersecting, do not run on a single "track." Idealism, especially Gentile's version, underwent an internal dissolution and was marked for death long before the end of World War II, wrote Bobbio. Conversely, wrote Garin, an "agonizing" idealism could be said to have survived, through institutions, textbooks, and the general frame of mind, well after the war.[8] They felt equally that it was willfully ignorant to describe the advent of "militant" philosophies as a postwar phenom-

6. See Carlo Augusto Viano, "Il carattere della filosofia italiana contemporanea," in *La cultura filosofica italiana dal 1945 al 1980 nelle sue relazioni con altri campi del sapere* (Naples: Guida, 1982), 9–56. See also the essays collected in Pietro Rossi and Carlo Augusto Viano, eds., *Filosofia italiana e filosofie straniere nel dopoguerra* (Bologna: Il Mulino, 1992).

7. The reference is to Norberto Bobbio, *Politica e cultura* (Turin: Einaudi, 2005); and Eugenio Garin, *Cronache di filosofia italiana*. The correspondence between Garin and Bobbio has recently been published together with an appendix of their respective reviews and articles on common topics. See Norberto Bobbio and Eugenio Garin, *"Della stessa leva": Lettere (1942–1999)*, ed. Tiziana Provvidera and Oreste Trabucco (Turin: Aragno, 2011).

8. Eugenio Garin, "Agonia e morte dell'idealismo italiano," in *La filosofia italiana dal dopoguerra a oggi* (Bari: Laterza, 1985), 3–29.

enon; they pointed to the case of existentialism, for example, which, contrary to the claims of a postwar generation, had yielded its best fruits during the Fascist ventennio.

It was true, as Bobbio put it, that "[f]ascism had forced us into abstinence and we had run the risk of dying of starvation." But it was also true that in the present day "the risk was of dying of indigestion."[9] Subsequent to these remarks, Bobbio, a cosmopolitan thinker if ever there was one, took a surprising turn, recalling with a tinge of regret the national character that Italian philosophy had acquired between Gioberti and Gentile, and even earlier starting with Vico. Of course it was not nationalism that he mourned but, especially as "Italy" seemed to retreat again to a mere "geographic expression," the "civic" and "pedagogic" role that philosophers, including Gentile, had once assumed. Garin sounded a sigh of his own when he reminded younger generations for the umpteenth time that there was something worth "treasuring" about that same philosophical experience.

Since the time of these early debates, the philosophical culture of the Fascist era has been put under the magnifying glass, resulting in solid historiographical and introspective gains, not least of which is the realization that Gentile had feet of clay, and yet the year 1945 continues to mark a divide. Scholars have resisted reintegrating the work and the initiatives of the generation of thinkers that Bobbio and Garin so assiduously tried to represent as integral to the story of interwar philosophy. As this chapter illustrates, it is by reviewing their work side by side with that of those whom they called their "fathers" that we may understand the lesson of idealism and its survival in Italian scholarship, most particularly (for the purposes of this study), Renaissance scholarship.[10] Central to the 'treasuring' of idealism, albeit altered beyond recognition, was existentialism, which was imported by a younger generation and which will prove instrumental, I argue, to a revision of idealist historiography and the portrait of the Renaissance that it contains. In the previous chapter we saw that the forefathers of Italian idealism, Spaventa and De Sanctis, bequeathed to modern Italians the quandary of a Renaissance legacy that could be rehabilitated only by overcoming it. A Renaissance shame with Neo-Guelph origins persisted in the neo-idealism of Gentile; Gentile's actualism, before it was lent out to Fascism, was the 'philosophy' that the Renaissance man had made possible without ever achieving. Gentile's career, in other

---

9. Norberto Bobbio, "Bilancio di un convegno," in *La cultura filosofica italiana*, 307.
10. See Norberto Bobbio, "La colpa dei padri," reprinted in *Della stessa leva*, 124–42.

words—and this is the central realization that can be derived from the work of Italy's existentialist generation—revealed the Renaissance shame to be, essentially, a philosophical complex.

This is perhaps what Croce had in mind when, in a pithy contribution to the 1930 issue of *La critica*, he wrote the following:

> The figure of the "Philosopher," of the pure, sublime "Philosopher," no longer lives in the soul of intelligent Italian men, the figure of him who, incurious about small things, is intent on resolving the great problem, the problem of Being: he no longer lives, because (if one is to speak the truth, even at the risk of being immodest) I have killed such a "Philosopher."[11]

De Sanctis, we may recall, held that the entire destiny of the Italian nation hinged on whether Italians could succeed in murdering the Renaissance man that they carried in their collective soul. Croce, who took to referring to Gentile as the "purus philosophus," perhaps meant by this label that Gentile had not offered a solution to the problem that De Sanctis had posed. And yet, if this were the case, it would be a curious remark to make, for Italy had never abounded in pure philosophers. In any case, it was not to Croce that the younger generation of Italian thinkers turned, in order to overcome the Renaissance shame and accompanying philosophical complex, but to an existentialism that allowed them to look at the abused figure of the humanist with fresh eyes. What follows is the history of idealism's dissolution during the interwar period, a declining parable that allowed for an alternation in Italian interest between Telesio, Campanella, and the frenzied Bruno in particular—that is, Spaventa and Gentile's heroes of thought—and another set of protagonists: the more modest, perhaps, but more effective community comprising Coluccio Salutati, Leonardo Bruni, and Leon Battista Alberti, among other Quattrocento humanists.

TWENTIETH-CENTURY HUMANISTS AND SCHOLASTICS

If, throughout his mature career, Gentile shared his influence over Italian culture with former friend and ally Benedetto Croce, at a less personal level, the predominance in philosophy of actual idealism was continuously and effectively opposed by Neothomism —an institutionalized movement

---

11. Benedetto Croce, "Il 'Filosofo,'" *La critica* 28 (1930): 238.

endorsed by the encyclical *Aeterni Patris* (1879) of Pope Leo XIII, who had normatively elected Thomas Aquinas as the ultimate standard of Catholic philosophy.[12] In the aftermath of World War I, scholastics held secular philosophies responsible for the dissolution of modern society and urged for a return to the spiritual values of the Catholic Middle Ages.[13] By 1919, when Italian Neothomist thinkers regrouped around Friar Agostino Gemelli (1878–1959)—a sworn enemy of Gentile who was thereafter their leader—actual idealism was finally identified as the poisoning trend to be combated. "The point," Gemelli stated, "is to defend our dualism against the idealistic monism."[14]

The concurrent rise of Fascism soon turned this philosophical dispute into a highly antagonistic race to purchase the regime's support. The entrenched battle in which these two institutional forces engaged during the interwar period may be considered the final defining act in the Italian dispute over an intellectual and historical *primato*, a concern bound to be renewed in an age of fevered nationalism. Accordingly, as late as 1926, Gemelli offered his bid to present Thomism as the ultimate Italic philosophy. He stated that "by fighting idealism, we engage in the purest and most ideal love of the *patria*, of our Italy, the Italy of Dante, of Thomas Aquinas, and Alessandro Manzoni[;] it is certainly not by importing the culture and thought of idealism from northern countries that one contributes to the making of an Italian consciousness [*Italianità*], because the doctrines defended and disseminated by a nation have to conform to its genius."[15] This was a well-beaten path

12. The pope's encyclical strengthened the position of a preexisting Neothomist movement. See Roger Aubert, "Die Enzyklika 'Aeterni Patris' und die weiteren päpstlichen Stellungnahmen zur christlichen Philosophie," in *Christliche Philosophie im katholischen Denken des 19. und 20. Jahrhunderts*, ed. Emerich Coreth SJ, Walter M. Neidl, and Georg Pfligersdorffer, vol. 2 (Graz: Styria, 1988), 310–32; and, in relation to the development of the neoscholastic movement in Italy, Luciano Malusa, "La rinascita del pensiero cattolico e il programma della neoscolastica," in *Storia della filosofia*, ed. Pietro Rossi and Carlo Augusto Viano (Bari: Laterza, 1997), 5:602–17.

13. The 1914 encyclical, *Ad Beatissimi Apostolorum*, of Pope Benedict XV, Leo XIII's successor, illustrates that postwar disillusionment was seized on as an opportunity to restore Christian values in modern society. (http://www.vatican.va/holy_father/benedict_xv/encyclicals).

14. Agostino Gemelli, "Per il programma del nostro lavoro," *Rivista di filosofia neoscolastica* 11 (1919): 3. In an early manifesto, his first, Gemelli's attack was instead launched against a vaguely defined "modern philosophy." See "Il nostro programma," *Rivista di filosofia neoscolastica* 1 (1909): 3–23. For a thorough introduction to Gemelli, see Maria Bocci, *Agostino Gemelli rettore e francescano: Chiesa, regime, democrazia* (Brescia: Morcelliana, 2003).

15. Agostino Gemelli, *Il mio contributo alla filosofia neoscolastica* (Milan: Vita e Pensiero, 1932), 8. For a useful contextualization of Gemelli's statement, see Italo Mancini, "La

and one that could lead the scholastic cause nowhere. Gemelli was aware that Italian idealists, from Spaventa to Gentile, could back their claims with an equally illustrious roster of names and that they had been working long, hard, and successfully to prove Hegel's congeniality to Italy.[16]

Gemelli had a stronger case when arguing—along with the Italian Hegelians—in favor of the rationality of reality, while pointing to an apparent contradiction in idealist historicism: "It appears to us that the very principle that establishes the rationality of history forbids the cutting of history in two halves and the condemnation of one half. As it is inconceivable to have history develop rationally only until the thirteenth century, it is just as inadmissible to have rationality begin with Descartes and the Italian Renaissance."[17] It should be noted that Gemelli's reproach, whose fairness needs to be carefully weighed, conceded victory to Gentile and at the same time attempted to pay him back with his own coin. In fact, in a review he had just reprinted of the work of Maurice De Wulf—an influential scholar of medieval philosophy at the flagship Catholic University of Leuven—Gentile had argued for the necessarily apologetic nature of Neothomist historiography.[18]

According to Gentile, a philosophy spurred by a pope's decree and aiming to enforce a historically untouched body of dogmas, albeit those of a lofty mind such as Thomas Aquinas, could hardly sell itself as "actual," that is to say, relevant in the here and now. Man's future, from such perspective, is in the past, and Thomism could not but boil down to some form of antiquarianism. Gemelli's much-vaunted 'medievalism' seemed to confirm this suspicion: "We are medievalists—this is our program. . . . We feel profoundly detached, enemies of so-called 'modern culture.' . . . It amounts to an artificial mosaic elaborated by an abnormal child [ragazzo anormale], who does not have a sense for colors and figures. . . . We feel infinitely superior to those who extol the greatness of modern culture."[19]

Neoscolastica durante gli anni del fascismo," in *Tendenze della filosofia italiana nell'età del fascismo*, ed. Ornella Pompeo Faracovi (Livorno: Belforte, 1985), 263–91.

16. All of Gemelli's early programmatic writings are imbued with a sense of belatedness with respect to the idealists' achievements. For this reason the Neothomist movement may be said to have been playing catch-up throughout the 1920s.

17. Gemelli, *Il mio contributo alla filosofia neoscolastica*, 9.

18. Italian Neothomists modeled their movement and institutions after the example of the University of Leuven and their best representatives. The Università Cattolica del Sacro Cuore and the journal *Rivista di filosofia neoscolastica*, which followed the standards of *Revue néoscolastique* (founded in 1894 and renamed *Revue néoscolastique de philosophie* in 1910) are clear examples of this.

19. Agostino Gemelli, "Medioevalismo," *Vita e pensiero* 1 (1914): 1–2.

It is evident that Gentile (the "abnormal child") and Gemelli were engaged in more than a genuine epistemological clash; theirs was a quarrel of ancients and moderns. Yet was Gentile's 'modernism' tantamount to 'Renaissancism,' as implied by Gemelli's criticism and medievalist stance? This point deserves further clarification.

As illustrated in the previous chapter, Gentile's interest in the Renaissance in historical research, like that of his predecessor Spaventa, overtly rested on the epoch's 'modern' and 'national' qualities—the Quattrocento had inaugurated an age to which twentieth-century man, at least in Italy, still belonged both philosophically and politically. In his review of De Wulf, Gentile affirmed that the epochal shift that occurred in the fifteenth century can be denied only by those who are unable to recover the philosophical "standpoint" (*Standpunkt*) of either age, let alone their relationship: "Anyone familiar with the history of philosophy is aware that in the fifteenth century Scholasticism was not put aside, just as anyone who knows history is aware that generally speaking the Renaissance is not the absolute negation but, rather, the continuation (but also, *in a certain sense* but only in a certain sense, the negation) of the Middle Ages."[20] The to-and-fro conveys Gentile's awareness that epochal transitions may be invisible to the naked eye. But Italians could rely on some hard empirical evidence that others lacked: what Gentile, elaborating on De Sanctis, defined as the "abyss" that separates Dante from Petrarch, two men with overlapping life spans who cannot be called contemporaries.[21] This transition, however, was not necessarily for the better. As Gentile specified elsewhere, "Petrarch heralds the spiritual movement that will make Italy great in modern history; but he also heralds the dissolution of that unity, so perfectly exemplified by Dante."[22] Spaventa and De Sanctis reconcile in Gentile, whose life mission was to personally bring the glimmering adumbrations of the first modern and Italian men to rational fruition.

The real problem lay elsewhere. Gentile the historian was more fair-minded than the philosopher he eventually became. The transition occurred during Gentile's tenure at the University of Palermo (1909–14),

20. Gentile's review of De Wulf's *Introduction à la philosophie néo-scolastique* (1904) dates to 1905 and was published in *La critica*, the then newly founded journal of Benedetto Croce. The text was reprinted in a collection of Gentile's early essays on religion in 1920. I cite from "I neoscolastici," in Giovanni Gentile, *Il modernismo e i rapporti fra religione e filosofia* (Florence: Sansoni, 1962), 131.

21. Gentile, "I neoscolastici," 126.

22. Giovanni Gentile, "Il carattere della filosofia italiana," in *I problemi della scolastica e il pensiero italiano* (Florence: Sansoni, 1963), 219. This is the printed version of a lecture presented in 1918.

a time he spent pondering the question of religion and its relationship to philosophy. Two years before reviewing De Wulf, he had published a short piece—"The Absolute Forms of the Spirit"—that outlined some of the presuppositions of the actual idealism he developed over the following decade. In this essay, Gentile set out to isolate the three moments that dialectically attend the unfolding of human consciousness: the I, the not-I, and their unity, or, otherwise stated, the subject, the object, and the subject-object unity. These forms or moments, according to Gentile, are conveniently separable only by "logic" and may not be "chronologically" juxtaposed, for in the act of thought they eternally coexist (OF, 434).

In a Hegelian fashion, the three categories of the spirit that are made to correspond to the triadic movement of spiritual activity are art, religion, and philosophy. According to this schema, religion is the opposite of art— the realm of subjective consciousness—insofar as it posits the absolute objectivity of God, to whom the saint's own subjectivity and freedom are sacrificed: "Religion is essentially mysticism, an affirmation of the Absolute as extrinsic to the activity [of thought] that affirms it; hence the negation of this very activity" (OF, 440). Gentile argued that aesthetic and religious expressions are by themselves incomplete and that they necessitate philosophical self-consciousness of their synthesis, so that "philosophy subtracts the spirit from the finitude of artistic consciousness as well as from the heteronomy of religious consciousness, therefore allowing spirit to realize infinity and liberty according to their true nature: that is, as a free infinity and infinite liberty" (441). In Gentile, philosophy emerges as a regulative discipline that solves the antithesis of art and religion by reuniting the two perspectives.

Gentile's peculiar take on Catholicism derived from these philosophical premises. Catholicism was a system that in relying on the dogmas of grace and the pope's infallibility comes to be established on oppositions in which God is posited as an ontologically independent reality from the activity of the human spirit. This is to show that Catholicism (as philosophy) partakes of the realism of old metaphysics, and that its efforts to reconcile human finitude with divine infinity through the mediation of ecclesiastical institutions (extrinsic syntheses) may never achieve the existential fullness brought about by spiritual *autoctisi* or self-construction (true synthesis). Catholicism (as an institution) thereby betrays its innermost aspirations, which for Gentile consisted in glamorizing man's partaking of the divine nature.[23]

23. See, for example, Gentile, "Bernardino Telesio," SFI, 1:281.

From the outset or, rather, essentially, Gentile related religion and philosophy hierarchically, and in pushing the point, his rigorously logical distinctions gave way to concrete chronological markers:

> The essential difference between religion and philosophy is revealed by
> the contrast between Catholicism and modern philosophy: *by which I
> mean the philosophy that begins with the Cartesian cogito and leads
> to the absolute idealism uncovered by Hegel*, which may be called the
> philosophy of immanence. Not so much because Catholicism is not a
> philosophy, or because philosophy of immanence is not a religion, but
> because Catholicism posits the immediacy of the object—that is, the
> subject of freedom and rationality—as a premise, as its very principle.
> (*OF*, 273)

This passage reveals the blasphemous quality, as it were, of actual idealism. The depiction of religion as a *philosophia inferior* implies, to a certain
extent, the construal of the philosophy of immanence as a *superior religion*. What matters here is that, after all, Gentile's 'modernism' was not a
Renaissancism, for only with Descartes does modernity become 'rational.'
According to Gentile's peculiar ecclesiology, rather, the Renaissance man
signals the advent of immanent philosophy by renouncing official reli-
gions and turning to the celebration of the human spirit, for those persecuted men of letters "whose books are banned" are "more Christian than
their persecutors": the literary man "shattered and cast away, with the
force of youth, that old philosophy that is the eternal and loyal ally of the
medieval Church, of today's Church and any future Church (for there will
always be a Middle Ages)" (*SFI*, 1:284). Unsurprisingly, then, on 20 June
1934 Gentile's works were put on the index of forbidden books, presumably with Gemelli's *placet*.[24]

---

24. For an exhaustive account of this inquisition, which also led to the ban on Croce's
works, see Guido Verucci, *Idealisti all'indice: Croce, Gentile e la condanna del Sant'Uffizio*
(Rome: Laterza, 2006). The recently published correspondence between Gentile and Gemelli
shows that their relationship was far less inimical than their public outings would suggest.
Gemelli was particularly grateful to Gentile for his 1923 school reform, which, as we shall
see, enabled the reintroduction of the teaching of religion in Italy's public school system.
In their letters, the two philosophers confronted each other mainly as pedagogues, almost
exclusively focusing on their concern for the spiritual amelioration of future generations of
Italian thinkers. In a letter dated 16 December 1925, Gemelli acknowledged Gentile's sway
over young religious thinkers and tried to win him over to the Catholic cause, while, in a letter dated 24 June 1929, Gemelli attempted to keep his distance when rumors of an impending
inquisition of Gentile's works began circulating. For a contextualization of this exchange,
see Luciano Pazzaglia, "Il carteggio Gemelli-Gentile nel contesto dei rapporti tra Univer-

It is difficult to determine who won this institutional conflict. On the one hand, Mussolini's ratification of the Lateran Accords of 1929, whereby the Italian government officially reconciled with the Vatican after the rupture of 1861, is sometimes interpreted as a personal defeat for Gentile, the staunchest promoter of a secular state. On the other hand, Gentile's philosophy remained the ultimate point of reference for the Italian philosophical community until actual idealism died a common death with Neothomism in the wake of World War II. In any case, this dispute offers a unique vantage point from which to grasp the aberrant framework in which Italian Renaissance scholarship was forced to develop during the interwar period. First, one should emphasize that by recasting their philosophical disagreement in terms of sovereignty and Church and state separation, Thomists and idealists hurled early twentieth-century intellectual life back into the Quattrocento. Five centuries earlier, Scholastics had been wronged by the humanists, and any amount of success gained in the present was experienced by the medievalists as a vindication. Indeed, on both ends, the degree of identification with their historical predecessors at times bordered on the insane.

This psychological derangement may be further illustrated by casting a glance at scholarly developments outside Italy. In 1927, for example, as Gemelli and Gentile were at each other's throats, American historian Charles Homer Haskins launched a rehabilitation of the Middle Ages with his vastly influential *The Renaissance of the Twelfth Century*. His goal was to modernize the Middle Ages by recovering many of those exceptional qualities that Burckhardt had attributed to the Italian Renaissance in (it should be emphasized) *pre-Scholastic* Europe—individualism, rationality, secularization, and so forth. The complaint that motivated Haskins's research is comparable to Gemelli's own: "The continuity of history rejects such sharp and violent contrast between successive periods, and . . . modern research shows us the Middle Ages less dark and less static, the Renaissance less bright and less sudden, than was once supposed."[25] While Gemelli's and Haskins's shared reliance on developments in French medieval scholarship of the time should be acknowledged, the coincidence is nevertheless striking: Burckhardt's and Spaventa's exactly coeval, but nonetheless autonomous, celebrations of the Renaissance lost their mo-

---

sità Cattolica e idealismo (1911–1929)," *Annali di storia dell'educazione e delle istituzioni scolastiche* 19 (2012), 117–60. See also Adriano Bausola, "Gemelli e Gentile," *Vita e pensiero* 88 (2000): 104–30.

25. Charles Homer Haskins, *The Renaissance of the Twelfth Century* (Cambridge, MA: Harvard University Press, 1971), v.

mentum just as synchronically and independently in the mid-twenties. But the analogies do not stop here. The belligerent and religious metaphors that scholars have used to describe Haskins's book—which they interpret colorfully as a climax in the *"revolt* of the medievalists" and an act of "heresy" with respect to the "established *orthodoxy"* of the Burckhardtian paradigm—are all too realistically applicable to the Italian scenario.[26] For at the outset, at least, Gentile's students tended to approach their mentor's (religious) philosophy as orthodox devotees.

A case in point is represented by Giuseppe Saitta (1881–1965), Gentile's oldest student in Palermo and eventually the foremost Renaissance scholar of idealist inspiration. Saitta, who was destined to priesthood in his youth, experienced his embrace of actual idealism as a spiritual conversion. This is evident from his late historical survey dedicated to the "problem of God" since Homer and Hesiod, which concludes with an act of Gentilean faith—"There is no other God than the one that is celebrated in the life of the human spirit whose history is the history of the divine itself" —as well as in his erudite historical accounts of Thomism's misfired attempts to combat the advent of modern philosophy.[27] Yet the most treacherous repercussions of a generation's devotional attraction to actual idealism are to be recovered in the field of Renaissance and philosophical historiography, where Gentile's principles were translated into methodological standards that disregarded the example set up by his historical research. According to Saitta, speaking as a historian,

> The historian who fixates [*si irrigidisce*] on the past is the bearer of decadence and death. The past is, in fact, mere content, objectivism, sundered from its form, that is to say, subjectivism. In order to revalue history's incitement to action and life we need to restore the intimate unity of subject and object . . . that very same unity of which development is made up, spurred by a potent yearning for novelty, and novelty is the only truth than can broaden our horizons [*dilatare il nostro respiro*]. All we need to do is to glance at the history of individuals

26. This characterization was first introduced in 1948 by Wallace K. Ferguson, *The Renaissance in Historical Thought: Five Centuries of Interpretation* (Toronto: University of Toronto Press, 2006), 329ff. On the fortune of Haskins's book and program, see Leidulf Melve, "'The Revolt of the Medievalists': Directions in Recent Research on the Twelfth-Century Renaissance," *Journal of Medieval History* 32, no. 3 (2006): 231–52 (emphasis added).

27. Giuseppe Saitta, *Il problema di Dio e la filosofia dell'immanenza* (Bologna: Cesare Zuffi, 1953), 202. See also Saitta, *Le origini del neo-tomismo nel secolo XIX* (Bari: Laterza, 1912), with a foreword by Gentile (vii–xi).

and people to persuade ourselves that they assert themselves and have value only inasmuch as they progressively alienate themselves from the parasitism of the past. We are not saying that the past may not be an incentive to action, but we want to underscore the fact that a criticism and thus a condemnation of the past is a necessary condition for that future to which, it cannot be denied, our present life tends.[28]

Catholic antimodernists had found in Saitta a worthy and equally intransigent opponent. His acute anticlerical feelings and ardent faith in idealist theism contributed to the amalgamation of the categories of 'transcendence,' 'religion,' 'Middle Ages,' and, more important, philosophical realism or 'objectivism' with the entire (pre-Renaissance) 'past.'

Naturally, when applied to the study of Renaissance thought, such an attitude was bound to upset the comparatively balanced frame that Gentile had so diligently constructed. In Saitta's Renaissance scholarship—whose vastness and influence make it a force to be reckoned with, as we shall see in following chapters—the rift between the Middle Ages and the Renaissance could not be sharper, and as the medieval man turns into an "uncouth, brutal, and violent" instrument in the Church's hands, the Renaissance man is saved from Gentile's own lukewarm appreciation.[29] In Saitta's massive magnum opus, *Italian Thought in the Age of Humanism and the Renaissance* (1949–51), Risorgimento misgivings over the Renaissance literary man all but dissolve as Petrarch emerges as the bearer of modern self-consciousness and as Lorenzo Valla (1407–57), the humanist grammarian who exposed the historical hoax of the Donation of Constantine, is unsurprisingly singled out as the possessor of that enlightened rationality that will ever after radiate over the rest of Europe.[30] If Saitta's philosophy has been described as an intensification of "absolute immanentism"—the exacerbation of actualism, a radical philosophy per

28. Giuseppe Saitta, *La libertà umana e l'esistenza* (Florence: Sansoni, 1940), 137.

29. Giuseppe Saitta, "Per l'intelligenza dell'umanesimo e del Rinascimento," in *Niccolò Cusano e l'Umanesimo italiano: Con altri saggi sul Rinascimento italiano* (Bologna: Tamari, 1957), 1:262.

30. Giuseppe Saitta, *Il pensiero italiano nell'Umanesimo e nel Rinascimento*, 3 vols. (Florence: Sansoni, 1961), 261. Interestingly, the current philosophical rehabilitation of the Italian Quattrocento also pivots on the work of Valla. For the recent Valla Renaissance, see Jill Kraye, "Lorenzo Valla and Changing Perceptions of Renaissance Humanism," *Comparative Criticism* 23 (2001): 37–55; the essays collected in the *Journal of the History of Ideas* 66, no. 4 (2005); Lodi Nauta, *In Defense of Common Sense: Lorenzo Valla's Humanist Critique of Scholastic Philosophy* (Cambridge, MA: Harvard University Press, 2009); and the proceedings *La diffusione europea del pensiero del Valla*, ed. Mariangela Regoliosi (Florence: Polistampa, 2013).

se—or as a form of proto-'existentialism,' Gentile's first student no doubt considered his own to be a (Renaissance) humanism: "For he who says philosophy says Humanism, and Humanism cannot but place man at the center of its investigation as its main concern. He who shifts this center does not know what he is talking about and aimlessly wanders in the obscurity of a transcendence that stifles and kills life itself, that is to say, essentially, freedom."[31] Saitta's scholarship indeed qualified, differently from Gentile's, as a 'Renaissancism'—one comparable in intensity to that of Nietzsche, Burckhardt's exalted student.

Saitta's philosophical outlook and Renaissance scholarship exemplify the pitfalls of a largely uncritical adherence to actual idealism—the very ones younger Gentileans and non-Gentileans alike trained themselves to avoid during the interwar period. Perhaps unsurprisingly, the representatives of that second generation of students who first attempted to unfetter themselves from the grip of Gentilean actualism are usually referred to as "heretics." For them, too, the battle was waged contemporaneously on epistemological as well as historiographical grounds. Despite its best representatives' efforts, Neothomist historiography ultimately proved unable to supply a qualitatively better scholarship than that of the idealists.[32] To the contrary, younger generations of Italian thinkers eventually resurfaced after World War II with a brand new philosophical attitude and an inspiring new Renaissance. This shift to a new historiography, which was enabled by the advent and rise in Italy of existentialism, drew sustenance from a rather dramatic forsaking of Gentile and the Risorgimento legacy.

31. See Gianfranco Morra, "L'immanentismo assoluto di Giuseppe Saitta," *Giornale critico della filosofia italiana* 33, no. 3 (1954): 392–400. Saitta firmly rejected any association with existentialism (which was suggested by Luigi Pareyson): "L'esistenzialismo è una antifilosofia, perché esso, sotto qualunque forma, si presenta come negazione della ragione, e trae alimento unicamente da uno stato d'animo disperato o patologico, dove s'avverte una strana ossessione, che confina colla pazzia, per una ideuzza troppo vecchia e troppo banale, che è quella del finito, e vi si avvolge con un sadismo ripugnante e spregevole, che fa pensare ad esseri invertiti. Ciò che, invece, io cerco, è la sanità spirituale, lontana dalle angosce spesso simulate degli esistenzialisti." *La teoria dello spirito come eticità* (Bologna: Zanichelli, 1948), ix.

32. For a critical comparison of idealist and Neothomist historiography, see the first two chapters in Paolo Rossi, *Storia e filosofia: Saggi sulla storiografia filosofica* (Turin: Einaudi, 1975). For Neothomism specifically, see Cesare Vasoli, "La neoscolastica in Italia," in *Gli studi di filosofia medievale fra Ottocento e Novecento*, ed. Ruedi Imbach and Alfonso Maierù (Rome: Edizioni di Storia e Letteratura, 1991), 167–89. For a representative work of Neothomist historiography, see Francesco Olgiati, *L'anima dell'Umanesimo e del Rinascimento: Saggio filosofico* (Milan: Vita e Pensiero, 1924).

PROBLEMATICISM AND DIALOGISM: UGO SPIRITO AND GUIDO CALOGERO

Though many of Gentile's second-generation followers would abandon him, the defection of Ugo Spirito (1896–1979), *nomen omen*, was certainly the most painful. Very much like Saitta, Spirito at first related to Gentile as a disciple to a prophet, and later, as a mature thinker, he earnestly attempted to remodel actual idealism and to rethink its contribution to the regime's plans for an epochal reshaping of society.[33] Thus wavering between an 'orthodox' and a supposedly 'heretic' stance within the combined cult of actualism and fascism, Spirito eventually tested the limits of his mentor's patience and overt interests in philosophical child rearing. The friction that emerged between Gentile and his onetime loyal student exemplifies the so-called "problem of actualism," which according to an insightful metaphor amounted to the realization that "one is not eternally young or, to put it another way, that our *body* in the long run refuses to keep up with" a philosophy defined by its exclusive concern for that ever-changing present on which it operates. In light of this challenge, Spirito's efforts to keep actualism on the move in its declining years may well be considered "euphoric and desperate."[34]

In the early 1930s, Spirito distinguished himself as a Gentilean activist or, in other words, an actualist interpreter of fascism. Animated by Gentile's idea regarding the identity of the individual and the state and by revolutionary socialism (Bolshevism), he was among the foremost advocates and ideologues of fascist corporativism at a time when the regime was fighting the critique of liberalism and legislating on national economy.[35]

---

33. Gentile's immediate legacy is commonly described as dividing into two schools and generations: the first generation of students in Palermo—including Saitta, Vito Fazio-Allmayer (1885–1958), Vladimiro Arangio-Ruiz (1887–1952), and Guido De Ruggiero (1888–1948)—and a second generation raised during his tenure at the University of Rome, including Ugo Spirito and Guido Calogero, whose works are discussed in the following pages. For this standard periodization, see Antimo Negri, *Giovanni Gentile: Sviluppi e incidenza dell'attualismo*, 2 vols. (Florence: La Nuova Italia, 1974), 2:37ff.

34. Pasquale Serra, "Ugo Spirito: Il problema dell'attualismo," in *Ugo Spirito tra attualismo e postmoderno*, ed. Hervé A. Cavallera and Francesco Saverio Festa (Rome: Fondazione Ugo Spirito, 2007), 72–73.

35. I follow here the lucid account in A. James Gregor, *Mussolini's Intellectuals: Fascist, Social, and Political Thought* (Princeton: Princeton University Press, 2005), chap. 6. Spirito's writings on corporativism are collected in Ugo Spirito, *Il corporativismo* (Florence: Sansoni, 1970). Also, for details of the connection between political activism and philosophy in Spirito, see A. Negri, *Dal corporativismo comunista all'umanesimo scientifico (itinerario teoretico di Ugo Spirito)* (Manduria: Lacaita, 1964).

When in the wake of the Great Depression Spirito's plans for an economic revolution went nowhere despite Mussolini's adherence to its rationale, Gentile's student resolutely turned his attention to what he perceived as the failing momentum of the philosophy that had inspired him. Under the banner of a "constructive actualism," he began fighting against the academic turn of Gentilean idealists, who, he rightly perceived, had grown ever more estranged from the political and economic arena.[36] Spirito reminded his peers that actualism was born of dissatisfaction with abstract rationalism and that, by the mid-1930s, it appeared to have gone full circle, removing itself from the rhythm of dialectical becoming and hardening into a new synthesis. History, then, was pushing actualism back into the number of past metaphysics, and at best it could now count as the latest form of intellectualism. The challenge was to "to bring contemplation back into action, without residue," and the first step in this "internal reform" had to be one's frank acknowledgment that actualism no longer knew how to inform lived experience.[37]

In 1937—as Italy's future *maître à penser*, Antonio Gramsci, was dying in a Roman hospital, shortly after his acquittal—Spirito finally backed down on behalf of actualism with a book entitled *Life as Research*, which amounted to that grandiose gesture of philosophical altruism and personal immolation expected of Gentile. Spirito's *livre à scandale*, in which its author self-consciously exploited his firstborn rights and official affiliations to legitimize philosophical dissent, was dedicated to that "youth" whose "life still develops at the margins of the world." The reference was to the traumatized offspring of a disastrous marriage between politics and philosophy to whom Spirito, certainly wracked by personal remorse, charitably offered protection and from whom alone he expected to elicit a sympathetic "answer" (*VCR*, 221).

Believing he had exhausted his 'constructive' suggestions, all Spirito could provide in the late 1930s was a Vichian clearing of the forest within which a new philosophical and civil society could plant its seed. The eloquent opening paragraph of *Life as Research*, which as a whole manifestly bears a Socratic ring, immediately returns philosophy to long forgotten principles:

> To think is to object. The ingenuous person listens and believes: he passively receives another person's words just as his eyes receive light. As

36. Ugo Spirito, "Attualismo costruttore," in *Scienza e filosofia* (Florence: Sansoni, 1950), 35–43. This essay was originally published in 1933 in Gentile's *Giornale critico*.

37. Ugo Spirito, *Dall'attualismo al problematicismo* (Florence: Sansoni, 1976), 22.

soon as the first doubt emerges from within man's soul and he slowly becomes aware of it, dogma gives way to the problem and thinking emerges. When this occurs man does not limit himself to listening; rather, he reacts and talks. The first word that endows his discourse with a life replete of his personality, the first word, certainly, by which one's personality distinguishes and affirms itself is a terrible monosyllable: "but." The thesis gives way to the antithesis, faith to doubt, conclusions to antinomies. This is how a conversation with others begins and with it the incessantly resurging problem of providing answers to objections that continuously engender new objections until, at some point, one stops either because disappointed at not having been able to reach a conclusion or because satisfied of the one so far achieved. Yet, in both cases, thinking has come to an end. The discussion is over when objections are exhausted. (VCR, 39)

Spirito, a disappointed devotee, raised his personal experience to an exemplary status. What is particularly conspicuous in this text is his rejection of those universal ideals to which human individuality had been sacrificed in support of fascism's promises of a higher quality of freedom. What had been for long peddled as the voice of providence was finally recognized by philosophers as a single man's dogma. For, at bottom, what hid behind this fundamental philosophical interjection ("but") was simply the wish to disagree with Giovanni Gentile.

Self-consciously writing a book dedicated to youth, but admittedly no longer young himself, Spirito evoked that original wonder that invests human beings when they are confronted by the absolute relativity and questionability of reality and, along with it, the recognition of their own insignificance vis-à-vis the incessant flow of history and its renewed cataclysms. But these discouraging realizations notwithstanding, Spirito maintained that one should not mistake the "unknown," which traditionally forces humankind into a skeptical *epoché*, for life's true mystery. Rather, according to Spirito's central tenet, the secret to life is represented by the essential "antinomy" of nature and thought that permanently keeps human beings on their toes and deprives them of any form of intellectual rest (VCR, 42), including what he described as the "loopholes" of skepticism or wise ignorance (48). "Objection" thus heralds novelty, while antinomy refers to the perpetual suspension between a problem and its solutions that Hegelian and Gentilean dialectics forsake, to the advantage of synthesis or conclusive dogmas. Finally, the ultimate resolution to all antinomies, or intellectual rest, is the exclusive privilege of a saintly reconnection with God to which Spirito, a self-avowed agnostic, makes no claim (46).

Spirito's book expressed a belated disillusion with Hegelianism and the numerous forms of modern philosophy that between Descartes and Gentile had repeatedly acknowledged the antinomic essence of nature only to infallibly cave into philosophical hubris and the myth of absolute truths. "Problematicism," the name that Spirito eventually gave his nonphilosophy, intended to explore the possibility or, rather, the opportunity for human beings to hold themselves within the confines of "research"—a "perennially critical attitude" (or "hypercriticism")—while retaining absolute confidence in future progress (*VCR*, 104).[38] Problematicism thus amounted to a pause for reflection within which to reckon with the epilogue of modern thought and the consequent conclusion of an age that Spirito qualified—exactly as did Gentile, but at this moment in time from an opposite perspective—as being obsessed with the "immanentization" of the divine and exaltation of the human subject. For, as Spirito eagerly pointed out, in the modern epoch of technology immanentism triumphs as Cartesianism gets transfigured into an egotism so crass that any consideration for the divine absolute therein implied—"cogito *ergo* sum, *ergo* Deus est"—melts into the air (58; emphasis added).

Undoubtedly, when perceived from the speculative altitudes achieved elsewhere—the contemporary development of phenomenology from Husserl to Heidegger, to name one—the degree-zero philosophy into which Spirito reduced Gentilean actualism is bound to appear somewhat sophomoric. Yet Spirito's unfeigned humility provided what no foreign thought could: that Trojan horse which could implode an isolated intellectual empire that mistook entrenchment for invincibility. Philosophical modesty was the strategy Spirito employed to dispel Gentile's illusions of having provided an ultimate identification of knowledge and action and thus a faultless philosophy of praxis. Instead, according to Spirito, actualism, too, had lost all revolutionary impetus by folding back into that "typically conservative attitude" that ensues when

the dynamic motive of creation is superseded by the static motive of philosophical knowledge and the motivations for action dissipate or, at

38. Spirito officially dubbed his philosophy "problematicismo" in 1948. See his *Il problematicismo* (Florence: Sansoni, 1948). Spirito's philosophical suggestions were interestingly taken up from a religious stance by his foremost interlocutor in the Neothomist camp. See Gustavo Bontadini, *Dall'attualismo al problematicismo* (1946; Milan: Vita e Pensiero, 1996), and *Dal problematicismo alla metafisica* (Milan: Marzorati, 1952).

least, weaken. After all, the very formula of dialectic, by which reality accrues upon itself—always overcoming itself without ever losing any part of its creation—makes one distrust any radical innovation that would require the sacrifice of anything that rests on a tradition. Tradition, which is internal to the dialectic of creation, reemerges as an exclusive concern, thereby thwarting creative development. Even more so, it gradually acquires the consistency of a myth—the myth of the past—to which a frightened present sacrifices itself lest history be lost in some indistinct future. This is how one explains the terror and confusion of the idealist philosopher when confronted by any event as well as any action plan that too glaringly compromises the social frame in which he comfortably operates. (*VCR*, 73)

According to Spirito, "tradition" negatively "takes center stage" as the idealist philosopher, just as much a "conformist and bourgeois" as the average man, dedicates all of his efforts to the maintenance of the status quo, the "preservation of history," and the upholding of the "bureaucratic ideals of good administration" (91).

While Spirito recovered the most "evident expression" of actualist incongruous conservatism in idealistic historiography—whose only overt goal was to weed out anything that would impede the historical fulfillment of immanentism—his focus rested on Gentile's practical efforts in the reorganization of culture (*VCR*, 88). Specifically, according to Spirito, actualism had failed in the school reform over which Gentile had toiled and that he had managed to enforce by 1923 as the most concrete and significant of the cultural applications of his philosophy. Gentile's theory of education, just like his actualism, was based on a triadic interpretation of spiritual formation modeled on the dialectic development of reality: subject (thesis), object (antithesis), and their unity (synthesis). The school curriculum was thus expected to pander to the lower levels of consciousness, with art (pure subjectivity) and religion (pure objectivity) relegated to primary school, while the study of philosophy, in which the nature of the spirit is fully realized, was to predominate at the secondary level wherein the future elite was educated. The humanities, the study of man's workings in history and of tradition, were to be elevated above the certainties of hard sciences, for in providing testimony of the activity of the spirit they at once offered a model and pointed the way to future development.[39]

39. For some orientation in the vast scholarship on Gentile's pedagogy, see Hervé A. Cavallera's bibliography in Giuseppe Spadafora, ed., *Giovanni Gentile: La pedagogia, la*

Spirito's criticism of Gentile's school reform was arguably the most humiliating blow a nascent problematicism struck against actualism and one that retains some of its shock value to this day:

> The school that may result from [Gentilean idealism] is indeed of the humanistic sort—one in which, beyond any possible specification, the attempt is made to spiritually form man in the totality of his aspects— yet it is that sort of historical and literary humanism that is reaffirmed as an untouchable and enduring model. That is, a man is formed who is not the man of the twentieth century defined by the grandiose multiplicity of his exigencies and the ever-accelerating rhythm of his life but, rather, the kind of man that can emerge only from the reconstruction of the past, according to the examples and works of those classics that are so hard not to approach coldly. . . . Once out of school, therefore, we cannot but perceive that our present is in the past, . . . that books were everything, that scholarship amounted to true action, and that man, in final analysis, identifies with the classics. . . . With much despair, finally, we realize the horrifying and inhumane action that one carries out in the name of humanism by alienating thousands upon thousands of young students from reality. (91–93)

One cannot fail to appreciate the anachronistic ring of a statement that appears to be drawn from some 1968 manifesto rather than from the considerations of an established representative of the interwar intellectual elite. To fully grasp Spirito's position, furthermore, one need only recall the De Sanctian and Risorgimento fixation with that perceived breach between philosophy and lived life that was believed to have continuously marred Italian culture since the Renaissance. In the final analysis, according to Spirito, twentieth-century idealism came up short in fulfilling the highest of post-Unitarian ideals, while its school reform reassured the reproduction of that Renaissance *letterato* long identified as the cause of Italy's backwardness.

Spirito's efforts to restore the engaged, constructive, and ultimately moral quality of actualism—for, after all, the Gentilean "pure act" was meant to be at once theoretical and practical—were matched by those of another heretic student of Gentile's, Guido Calogero (1904–86), the so-

scuola (Rome: Armando, 1997), 581–93. For a dated but still useful introduction in English, see Merritt Moore Thompson, *The Educational Philosophy of Giovanni Gentile* (Los Angeles: University of Southern California Press, 1934).

called philosopher of "absolute moralism."[40] His 1939 *The School of Man* focused almost exclusively on pedagogy as a prime locus of moral production, and again as with Spirito, the premises were borderline simplistic: "Any reasonable man [*uomo di buon senso*] knows that no conversation is to be had unless two are present and that in order to have an impact on a person's soul it is first of all indispensable that another person be present. One can then rest assured that [the reasonable man] will have nothing to object to the assertion that in order to have education it is necessary to have, on the one side, someone who educates, and, on the other side, someone who is educated."[41] Appealing to, we can assume, Gentile's own 'reason,' Calogero humbly pointed to the extremely formalistic and Scholastic terms into which actualism had forced itself with, for example, the idea that "education . . . is self-education; that is, that one never properly educates others but always, rather, oneself; that there is no difference [*alterità*] between an educator and him who is educated, for someone who assumes he is already educated and not still to be educated is not a real teacher, and there is no student that does not ultimately educate himself, for he feels that the work of his teacher is a moment of his own spiritual development."[42] These were the words with which Calogero quite accurately summarized the ethical and pedagogical ideal of an increasingly monologizing and solipsistic actualism.

Battling against an all-encompassing historicism in which everything happens for a reason beyond any concern for the fundamental human choices between good and evil, Spirito's problematicism and Calogero's so-called "dialogism" sought to recover the basic principles of that altruism, intersubjectively forged morality, and intellectual commitment necessary to the creation of a postfascist and presumably democratic society.[43] However, if Spirito and Calogero are now credited with having heralded a

40. Calogero's early career has recently received thorough attention. See Stefano Zappoli, *Guido Calogero (1923–1942)* (Pisa: Edizioni Della Normale, 2011); *Guido Calogero a Pisa fra la Sapienza e la Normale* (Bologna: Il Mulino, 1997); and, on Calogero's politics, Luigi Gallo, *Guido Calogero: Etica, politica, e filosofia estetica nel pensiero dell'esponente del "moralismo assoluto"* (Florence: Atheneum, 2000).

41. I cite the latest edition, Guido Calogero, *La scuola dell'uomo*, ed. Paolo Bagnoli (Reggio Emilia: Diabasis, 2003), 5. In this famous work, Calogero developed his criticism of idealism, both the Crocean and the Gentilean kind, which he had broached in earlier works (with suggestive titles). See Guido Calogero, *La filosofia e la vita* (Florence: La Nuova Italia, 1936), and *La conclusione della filosofia del conoscere* (Florence: Le Monnier, 1938).

42. Calogero, *La scuola dell'uomo*, 5.

43. Calogero refined his notion of "dialogism" in subsequent works. See Guido Calogero, *Logo e dialogo* (Milan: Edizioni di Comunità, 1950); and Guido Calogero, *Filosofia del dialogo* (Milan: Edizioni di Comunità, 1962).

postidealist era, it should be noted that in the late 1930s the intentionally vague terms in which their problematization of philosophy was couched were not well received.

The debate that followed in the wake of Spirito's book in the *Giornale critico della filosofia italiana*, the journal Gentile founded as mouthpiece of actualism in 1920 upon divorcing from Croce and renouncing their collaboration on *La critica*, is particularly helpful in illustrating the extent and reasons for this failure. It could be assumed that by having *Life as Research* immediately reviewed by one of the most promising intellectuals of a younger generation and a student of Saitta, Delio Cantimori (1904–66), Gentile complied with Spirito's explicit wish to be answered by Italian youth.[44] In an appended note, nevertheless, Gentile did not miss the chance to pan Spirito's "fundamentally mistaken" book that "is, however, significant as a very sincere document of a widespread state of mind among the most intelligent Italian philosophers, young and old"—"a state of mind," Gentile specified, "that has nothing to do, not even minimally, with philosophy, be it of the idealistic kind or not" (*VCR*, 248).[45]

This curt dismissal would have sufficed for Gentile had Spirito not demanded, in an open letter published in the same journal, that the father of actualism personally provide his book with that detailed review that his long-standing militancy in the ranks of Italy's official philosophy entitled him to. Eventually acquiescing with an open letter of his own, Gentile put forth a lesson in philosophical deontology at a time of crisis:

> Your book is mistaken because . . . it is not inspired by that virile resolve to see clearly into the crisis and to reaffirm the conquest of reality that is expected of a thinker—that is, a man . . . , who is at the same time a professor and socially responsible for his ideas, or at least for their communication, should have qualms about enhancing, or gratify-

44. In a letter to Guido Calogero (20 September 1937), Gentile reported that his journal had received a barrage of responses to Spirito's book and announced that he would publish Cantimori's because it was the most "balanced." In this letter, in fact, Gentile rejected Calogero's review—which was also written in the form of an "open letter"—because Calogero identified with Spirito's criticism to the point of half jokingly accusing him of plagiarism. Gentile asked Calogero not to publish the text because he did not want people to think two of his best students were defecting at once. Calogero's review of Spirito and Gentile's letter were only recently recovered and published. For these exchanges and some useful contextualization, see Gennaro Sasso, *Filosofia e idealismo: De Ruggiero, Calogero, Scaravelli* (Naples: Bibliopolis, 1997), 3:415–40.

45. Cantimori's and Gentile's responses to Spirito were published in the *Giornale critico* in 1937 and 1938, respectively, and are now reproduced in an appendix to *VCR*, from which I cite.

ingly describing, the confusion and panic that ensues from any crisis. At the very least, he should not, amid the general panic and stampede, shout at the top of his voice that there is no hope of seeing clearly and recovering one's path. (VCR, 251)

Gentile evidently took Spirito's generational concerns to heart as he proudly reasserted the impossibility that a traditionally intended philosophy may inhabit the gray zone between affirmation and negation (tra il si e il no) and reaffirmed its (virile) representative's proper humility in acknowledging that there is a time to talk (tempus loquendi) and a time for silence (tempus tacendi). Gentile added that history, for which Spirito showed little respect, also proves that past and future philosophies are interconnected as in a golden chain and that "revolutions" are one and the same as "true conservation." Unable to deny an epochal crisis, Gentile could only reaffirm the original aspirations of a progressively reconfigured and, for him, abused discipline such as philosophy.

If opposition was to be expected from the father of actualism, it is surprising that both Gentile and Spirito failed to engage with the perceptive scrutiny of Italian philosophical life that Cantimori had provided in his commissioned review of Life as Research. Commending Spirito for having written a "bitter and courageous" book, Cantimori, unlike Gentile, straightforwardly denied the universal value of Spirito's "state of mind" and "philosophical and moral perplexity" (VCR, 223–24). Rather, according to Cantimori, the narrow scope of Spirito's philosophical concerns marked him as a typically Italian (that is, idealist) philosopher, while his exclusive interests in juridical, economical, and social doctrines were representative of the "average cultured person in Italy." Also, from a generational stance, Spirito's awkward grasp of popular culture attested to his estrangement from the real concerns and interests of younger generations. Most strikingly, Cantimori discerned the exact aspirations of the age group to which he himself belonged, one that, as Spirito had rightly envisioned, was about to emerge as truly the first in a postidealistic era.

On the one hand, a young Cantimori dug a narrow path between Gentile and Spirito by pointing out that while the latter did well in condemning the prejudices built into idealist historiography, his work made no reference beyond the usual suspects of philosophical history (Descartes, Hume, Kant, Fichte, etc.). On the other hand, this time squarely siding with Gentile, he condemned Spirito's attack on history and its study: "The school's function is precisely that of liberating [disgelare] young people's souls from the rigid, barbarian residues that prevent them from fruitfully approaching the classics, the great examples of humanity. . . . A book is, indeed, just a book: dead letter . . . yet a classic is a man, a living and great man, and through contact with him one gets in touch with true great action, a teaching and comfort to one's own" (VCR, 241). Cantimori's unconcealed indignation at Spirito's iconoclasm is arguably the first statement of a new generational awareness, one that had long been in the making, to be published in an official organ.

Before we consider the various intellectual influences that inform the paradigmatic revisions and progressive conservatism of Cantimori's generation, it is worth taking a look at what Spirito himself thought about the Italian Renaissance (thoughts he eventually presented in 1944), not least because he illustrates that all Italian thinkers, even those not given to philosophical historiography, felt an obligation to ground their philosophical solutions in Renaissance sources.[46] His *Machiavelli and Guicciardini* is a book totally lacking in footnotes in which an investigation of the "true Machiavelli" is admittedly sacrificed to the necessity of recasting the Florentine secretary's relevance for a postfascist era.[47] From the outset, Cantimori's suspicions regarding Spirito's inability to detach himself from the paradigm established by idealist historiography are confirmed: Spirito, too, presented the transition between the Middle Ages and the Renaissance uncritically as an entrenched battle waged by the humanists in the name of immanence. For his own purposes, however, Spirito focused on the dualism of ethics and politics as the most concrete application of the metaphysical gap. From this perspective, Leon Battista Alberti (1404–72), "the founder of modern economy," originally emerged as a central figure in modern immanentism. According to Spirito, the concept of *masserizie* (thrift) that Alberti put forth in his dialogue *On the Family* is the source of the mundane reduction of ethics to economy that prefigured Machiavelli's own reduction of ethics to politics as well as what Spirito described as Guicciardini's radical utilitarianism (MG, 18).

Like any other strong reader of Machiavelli, Spirito wished to rephrase the Machiavellian problem. In contrast to those who interpreted the Flo-

46. It is not emphasized enough that second-generation actualists, Spirito especially, differed from first-generation ones, such as De Ruggiero and Saitta, and from Gentile himself in one significant respect: they did not cultivate philosophical historiography.

47. As will soon become evident, Spirito's interpretation differs greatly from the antidemocratic or fascist reading of Machiavelli—which climaxed in Mussolini's self-identification with the Prince—that emerged between World War I and the rise and affirmation of fascism in Italy. On the abuse of Machiavelli during Fascism, see Michele Ciliberto, "Il mito di Machiavelli dalla guerra al fascismo," in *Filosofia e politica nel Novecento italiano: Da Labriola a "Società"* (Bari: De Donato, 1982), 135–88.

rentine secretary as either immoral or amoral or as the founder of a new morality, Spirito understood Machiavelli to be quite simply posing the question "as to whether and to what extent it is possible to respect the moral imperative in political life" (*MG*, 57). This is a problem that Machiavelli introduced but did not solve. According to Spirito, Machiavelli's reliance on a dogmatically received (from antiquity) notion of *patria* and *stato*, the only entities to which one's own life should be sacrificed, symbolized a fall into a medieval dependence on universals. Spirito affirms that "if the fatherland is truly the universal through which all of life acquires significance and value, the demonstration of its absolute character should not have been posed in deceptive terms" (100). The presence of a nondescript state in Machiavelli is a sign of a "logical error," or, to put this in terms that are in keeping with philosophical parlance, it embodies one of those pseudo-universals on which faulty philosophical systems rest, for "the state or fatherland is left hanging between the universal and the particular," thus "impeding a rigorous overcoming of [medieval] dualism" (106). Yet Spirito's goal was not to condemn this kind of ambivalence but, rather, to learn how to accept it.

In Spirito's 'problematized' interpretation of the Renaissance, Guicciardini emerged as the corrector of the Machiavellian logic and the true alter ego of Spirito, a disillusioned but honest thinker. Spirito's personalization of the Renaissance is evident in his overt praise of Guicciardini's empiricism and exclusive concern for the *particulare*. If Machiavelli (like Gentile) attempted to overcome antinomy by relying on a metahistorical reality (the hypostatization of the state), Guicciardini (and Spirito) refused to hide behind the humanistic cult of a dead past and the support it can provide: "In the history of modern immanentism, Guicciardini's version is the first great attempt on behalf of the subject to reduce the world to one's own self" (*MG*, 109). With no possible recourse to ideals or universals, moral standards needed to be drawn from within one's own mundane comportment, which is why honesty becomes all important. Spirito was intent on proving that Guicciardinianism is a problematicism: "Machiavelli's honesty, . . . and even more so that of Guicciardini, establishes a dominion of men and things that necessitates an autonomous superintendence of the self and of the reality on which action operates." "This means," Spirito adds, "that the agnosticism on which" such honesty "is founded should not be confused with a negative form of skepticism but, rather, should support more profound research [*ricerca*] and a concrete faith in the possibility of bringing forth a truly constructive activity" (139). Interestingly, here Spirito seems to be renewing De Sanctis's criticism of

Italian society but to base it on the rehabilitation rather than the condemnation of Guicciardini.

Machiavelli and Guicciardini mirrored Spirito's personal spiritual crisis as well as the historico-political catastrophe of the 1930s and 1940s to
which a misunderstanding of the essentially antinomic nature of Renaissance thought had contributed. "The Renaissance," Spirito adds in conclusion, "is the epoch best suited to describe the internal antinomy to the
concept of Fatherland, for as an epoch it marks a transition between the
exigencies of universal and national states" (*MG*, 105). Thus the inevitable
question was, at the war's conclusion, would the world resolutely turn to
cosmopolitanism or would it insist on the value of nation-states despite
the failed revolutions of various fascisms? Spirito's answer to this question is willfully left open. What is clear, however, is that a reinterpretation of the Renaissance could once again be instrumental to the creation
of a new world. If this was indeed to be the case in Italy, it would come
about only after thinkers had achieved that *philosophical* cosmopolitanism that Spirito, a chip off the old Gentilean block, evidently lacked. After
all, at the onset of World War II, Hegel was still the last thinker imported
by mainstream Italian philosophy, and Spirito's problematicism amounted
to a reform of Gentile's reform of Hegelian dialectic—one of little consequence for a *radical* rethinking of the Renaissance and its legacy in contemporary Italy.

PHILOSOPHERS IN THE MIDDLE: THE "OUTSIDERS"

It should be clear by now that the matter of overhauling an ego-centered
Italian philosophy was not a mere academic question. Rather, the make-
over of a still Risorgimento-inspired national ethos depended on it. The
younger group of thinkers who eventually met this challenge is often
misdescribed as the first generation to have come of age in the postwar
period. In truth, Italy's philosophical regeneration was already well on
its way at the time Spirito and Calogero catalyzed an implosion of actual idealism, and it was led by 'outsiders' who shared a downright anti-
idealistic upbringing at the hands of some of the most conspicuous,
albeit isolated, heterodox voices in Italian philosophical thought. In comparison with their (at some point) 'orthodox' Gentilean contemporaries,
they were all equally provided with a head start that spared them from
a personal and laborious disengagement from actual idealism. Their careers confirm this. On reaching full maturity in 1945, they could boast
an impressive number of daring initiatives on which they would seek to

capitalize as soon as the war eventually swept away many of the obstacles, including Gentile and Croce themselves, that were thwarting a free and speedy intellectual emancipation.[48] The problem, in retrospect, is that the stature they attained after the war also eclipsed their notable prewar achievements.

Admittedly, the elements that contribute to the making of outsiders—their disavowal of a single tutelary deity or sacred book and their rejection, for that matter, of an official school or movement invested in a well-defined alternative—complicate their identification. In any case, a means of selecting these elements may be drawn, in hindsight, from Cantimori's criticism of Spirito, which called for a qualified cosmopolitanism in philosophy and a thorough revision of the link that idealist historiography had established between Renaissance immanentism and actual idealism. Following this cue, the rest of this chapter begins to introduce and correlate a host of apparently dissimilar scholar-philosophers whose shared fascination with the French and German philosophical avant-garde—in a word, existentialism—went hand in hand with a resolutely Italian belief in the enduring relevance of the Renaissance and Quattrocento humanism.

A notable group of such existential outsiders, from whose perspective the history of Italian philosophy during the interwar period deserves to be retold, were assembled in an autobiographical account by Eugenio Garin, who was perhaps the most self-conscious representative of his generation. He wrote:

Between 1943 and 1944, I often conversed about the Italian Quattrocento with Ernesto Grassi, with whom I would read fifteenth- and sixteenth-century texts while discussing the image of humanism he was attempting to create in confrontation with Heidegger, whom he knew well. In those very same years, Enrico Castelli was planning for *later* times—indeed, in case any *later* times would come to pass—an edition of Italian philosophers about which he would often come to talk to me in Florence, as I spent my spare time working on my *History of Italian Philosophy* that was published in 1947. . . .

If Grassi argued with Heidegger about humanism, and Castelli originally revisited existential itineraries in his own way, the profound crisis of culture and the perception of the world's tragedy were given

48. For a heartfelt survey of the many phases of Croce's reception in Italy, see Norberto Bobbio, "Il nostro Croce," in *Filosofia e cultura: Per Eugenio Garin*, ed. Michele Ciliberto and Cesare Vasoli, 2 vols. (Rome: Editori Riuniti, 1991), 1:789–805.

voice in a multiplicity of languages against the backdrop of a varied existentialism. Despite the superficiality of many debates, up to the 1943 debate on Bottai's *Primato*, the problems that began to call into question the meaning and function of philosophy and its possibility of survival in view of political urgencies and religious concerns . . . emerged in the context of a general dissatisfaction with idealistic certainties.[49]

The wide spectrum of a generation's idiosyncratic contribution to an overcoming of idealism can be viewed through the compact filter of this memoir. In 1943 Garin was poised to become at once Italy's foremost Renaissance scholar and its foremost intellectual historian of nineteenth- and twentieth-century Italy. His close collaboration with Enrico Castelli (1900–1977), his generation's most unconventional Christian existentialist and cultural promoter, and Ernesto Grassi (1902–91), Heidegger's only Italian student and staunch defender of the *studia humanitatis*, to produce an alternative route to philosophical renewal for the epoch still goes largely underestimated. Completing the list of the members of this inconspicuous team, Garin obliquely identifies the chief representative of Italian secular existentialism, Nicola Abbagnano (1901–90), who in 1943 was forced into an ultimate showdown with the remnants of old-school philosophizing, including Gentile, in a journal, directed by former Fascist minister of education Giuseppe Bottai (1895–1959), that bore a title (*Primato*) reminiscent of Risorgimento concerns.

The account should begin with the opening acts of Castelli and Grassi's lifelong partnership. Their correspondence significantly antedates the origins of idealism's dissolution and allows one to grasp the exact contours of a younger generation's philosophical discontents. On 9 November 1925, following a first encounter in Rome, a twenty-three-year-old Grassi resumed contact from Milan with a slightly older Castelli:

> We are today faced with a well-defined state of things: Italian culture is by now completely in the hands of absolute idealism, which, like any other school, dogmatically regiments all the powers that contribute to its development. However, numerous younger thinkers—despite their acknowledgment of idealism's great merits—are dissatisfied by this enclosed unity for multiple, theoretical as well as practical, reasons,

---

49. Eugenio Garin, "Sessanta anni dopo," in *La filosofia come sapere storico: Con un saggio autobiografico* (Rome: Laterza, 1990), 141.

etc. In other words, there is a whole movement that perceives idealism as a profound spiritual and cultural crisis. Therefore, if perhaps in no other European country would it make sense to conceive of a journal dedicated to overcoming a specific systematic direction by means of a negative union and collaboration, I believe this may be legitimate in Italy. (APEC)

With hardly any publications to his name, Grassi was already outlining the shared destiny and goals of his generation's contribution to philosophical thought. Particularly striking is Grassi's awareness of Italy's exceptionality in the realm of philosophy, which could justify in principle a purely critical (or negative) confrontation with idealism even in advance of a clear and systematic elaboration of a counterphilosophy. For the time being, Grassi stated, some sort of "eclecticism" would have to do.

In fact, Grassi appeared to be prematurely downgrading his generation to the role of intermediary between epochs. Further along in the same letter, he specified:

This younger generation would thus gather around a journal in order to determine the shape and outline of that "life" they feel meandering [serpeggiare] around and the yearning for it that one encounters in isolated thinkers in the most disparate [philosophical] realms. True, the crisis that torments this generation cannot be solved by a movement, but only by a *single* thinker who will overcome those needs and those issues that idealism has forever conquered with respect to ancient Platonic transcendence. Anyhow, we cannot fail to acknowledge that a movement always carries along a particular contribution to the overcoming of a given historical condition, while admitting that the fulfillment of such a request is expected of a single thinker.

A younger Grassi at once identified the most urgent need with a return to "life" while sticking to a rather backward belief in the contribution of master thinkers to the dialectical progression of thought. To be sure, a restless Italian youth could not rest idle, yet Grassi was either gravely shortsighted or naïve and neither accurately assessed the epoch's academic small-mindedness nor foresaw the escalation of terror that would take place in those very same months. As for academic pettiness, just two weeks after dispatching his programmatic letter, Grassi contacted Castelli again to call off the project. The famously cantankerous Friar Agostino Gemelli had dissuaded Grassi and other viable candidates from their undertaking with the threat of banning them from the newly founded Catholic University of Milan, of which Gemelli was chancellor.[50]

Grassi and Castelli soon realized that Gemelli's injunction was symptomatic of a graver malady. A year earlier (on 21 April 1925), following the first 'Fascist culture conference,' Gentile had rallied some Italian thinkers with the publication of his notorious "Manifesto of Fascist Intellectuals," which Croce famously rebuked, supported by a host of opposite-minded thinkers, with a countermanifesto originally entitled "A Reply from Italian Writers, Professors, Journalists."[51] This double publication took the census of the dichotomized world of the Italian intelligentsia and was a prelude to the so-called *leggi fascistissime* (most fascist laws) in 1926. The fascistization of every sector of Italian culture came to bear on the philosophical community during the sixth conference of national philosophy (March 1926), at which Grassi and Castelli had arranged to meet for a second time. As Garin would comment many years later, the conferences of those years plainly displayed the epoch's philosophical decadence and the "the human even more than doctrinal breaches in Italian philosophical life," as so-called "philosophers" in different camps began unleashing the police against one another (*CFI*, 2:447). The traumatic impact of the following events on bright-eyed students of philosophy should thus be properly assessed.[52]

Castelli's mentor, Bernardino Varisco (1850–1933), the president of the Italian Philosophical Association, had put religious thinker Piero Martinetti (1872–1943), Grassi's own teacher at the time, in charge of the Milanese conference. Though Martinetti is sometimes singled out as the "third crown" of early twentieth-century philosophy (after Croce and Gentile), he

50. Grassi to Castelli, 28 November 1925, APEC.
51. Both manifestos were recently published in English translation. See "Manifesto of the Fascist Intellectuals," in *FKC*, 706–12; and "A Reply by Italian Authors, Professors, and Journalists to the 'Manifesto' of the Fascist Intellectuals," in *FKC*, 713–16.
52. In what follows, I gather some detailed but scattered accounts of the 1926 event to retell its importance from the perspective of younger generations. Particularly useful are Bobbio, "La cultura e il fascismo," in *Fascismo e società italiana*, ed. Guido Quazza (Turin: Einaudi, 1973), 211–13; Daniela Visintin, "Martinetti e Gallarati Scotti: Un volto inedito del Congresso del '26," *Rivista di storia della filosofia* 55, no. 1 (2000): 79–97; Enrico I. Rambaldi, "Eventi della Facoltà di Lettere di Milano negli anni di trapasso dall'Accademia all'Università," *Rivista di storia della filosofia* 52, no. 3 (1997): 517–62; Giorgio Chiosso, "Libertà e religione nel Congresso di filosofia di Milano (1926)," *Annali di storia dell'educazione e delle istituzioni scolastiche* 3 (1996): 237–64; Barbara Riva, "Il congresso della società filosofica italiana del 1926," *Bollettino della Società filosofica Italiana* 157 (1996): 19–32.

was arguably the major cause of the entrenched war between Neothomism and actualism, both of whose tenets he combated. Martinetti had been a longtime promoter of religious renovation by means of a critical revision of dogmatic stances via scientific rationalism.[53] His scholarly career began with a dissertation on ancient Indian philosophy, from which he retained a lifelong belief in the incommensurability between higher and lower spheres of reality—roughly speaking, matter and spirit. His early interests merged with the Western tradition, especially Platonism and Neoplatonism, and crystallized in his unshakeable faith in that transcendence to which human beings constantly strive. The determination of the exact content of humankind's achievements in the ladder of being was the enduring interest of his particular brand of "religious philosophy" or "lay metaphysics," which remained unwaveringly above any religious confession.

Regrettably forgotten as a philosopher, Martinetti, a partisan of a 'third way,' takes pride of place in twentieth-century Italian intellectual history as a champion of civic morality. Together with another eleven or so (out of a total of twelve hundred!), Martinetti refused to swear by the oath that in 1931 the regime imposed on academics who wished to retain their chair ("I swear . . . to form industrious citizens, upright and devoted to the fatherland and the fascist regime").[54] The same spirit that led Martinetti to this courageous and symbolic action equally animated, a few years earlier, his painstaking organization of a conference that signaled in Italy the temporary suspension of the *libertas philosophandi*. While Martinetti perhaps could not be fully prescient about what was to take place, the resistant forces he marshaled ensured that philosophical freedom would go out with a memorable fight.

If, indeed, Varisco's choice of Martinetti was a provocation in and of

53. I rely here on the succinct introduction of Gianfranco Bosio, "L'idealismo 'trascendente' di Piero Martinetti," in *Idealismo e anti-idealismo nella filosofia italiana del Novecento*, ed. Piero Di Giovanni (Milan: FrancoAngeli, 2005), 95–107; and Bosio, "L'uomo e l'assoluto nel pensiero di P. Martinetti," in *Filosofie "minoritarie" in Italia tra le due guerre*, ed. Pietro Ciaravolo (Rome: Editoriale B.M. Italiana, 1982), 35–45.

54. This formula just slightly altered the oath that had been enforced since 1924: "Giuro di essere fedele al Re e ai successori del Re, di osservare lealmente lo statuto e le leggi, di osservare i doveri accademici e di educare dei cittadini operosi, leali e fedeli alla patria." The oath may have been conceived by Gentile as retaliation against Croce's anti-Fascist manifesto. For the words with which Martinetti justified his dissension to Fascist minister Balbino Giuliano, see Norberto Bobbio, *Italia civile: Ritratti e testimonianze* (Florence: Passigli, 1986), 98–99. The story of the twelve dissidents is told in Giorgio Boatti, *Preferirei di no: Le storie dei dodici professori che si opposero a Mussolini* (Turin: Einaudi, 2001).

itself, Martinetti made sure to overstep the boundary. He unhappily acceded to the presence of Neothomist thinkers, for whom he had close to no esteem, but in order to give space to some persecuted voices in the renovation of Italian religious life and thought, he extended an invitation to Ernesto Buonaiuti (1881–1946), the leading representative in Italy of that universal movement of Catholic reform that goes under the name of "Modernism."[55] To state that Buonaiuti was persona non grata devalues the problem of his participation in the conference. On 25 January 1926, Martinetti's guest had finally received an irreversible ecclesiastical excommunication that had marked him in Neothomist circles as "vitando"—expressly to be avoided.[56] As a consequence of his announced presence, the Catholics officially withdrew from the conference on 2 March and rode the wave of a smear campaign against Martinetti, who had been recently accused of having publicly scorned the holy Eucharist—with the words "God-eaters are simply inconceivable"—during his latest course on the topic of Christology.[57]

On the opening day of the conference, a disillusioned and fatigued Martinetti lamented the rise of a "sort of philosophical schism" among philosophers who by definition should be "citizens of a world without persecutions and excommunications." Exceptionally "disgraceful," in his view, was the current alliance between politics and philosophy. When philosophy stoops to politics, it asks for "a kind of protection or privilege in compensation, and as a result, that unpleasant thing which one calls official philosophy is bound to emerge." Demanding that he never be called on again for the organization of a similar event, Martinetti urged *everyone* to "search their soul."[58] The conference proceeded unhampered for two days, with presentations by, among others, Croce, who is said to have attended reluctantly.[59] By the third day, however, another of Martinetti's

55. Buonaiuti was another of the twelve who refused to swear by the Fascist oath.

56. Buonaiuti is introduced in Lorenzo Bedeschi, *Il modernismo italiano: Voci e volti* (Cinisello Balsamo: San Paolo, 1995).

57. On this slanderous campaign, see Barbara Riva, "La stampa e il congresso del 1926,' *Rivista di storia della filosofia* 51 (1996): 357–81.

58. Martinetti's opening statement was published posthumously with an ad hoc title: Piero Martinetti, "I congressi filosofici e la funzione sociale e religiosa della filosofia," *Rivista di filosofia* 35 (1944): 101–8.

59. The list of presenters was published in the journal that Martinetti edited: Bernardino Varisco, "Le funzioni dello stato"; Benedetto Croce, "La filosofia italiana nel secolo del Barocco: Dal Campanella al Vico"; Emilio Chiocchetti, "La filosofia unita"; Francesco de Sarlo, "L'alta coltura e la libertà"; Adelchi Baratono, "Il pensiero come attività estetica"; Ernesto Buonaiuti, "La religione nel mondo dello spirito"; Giovanni Antonio Borgese, "Figurazione

special guests, Francesco De Sarlo (1864–1937), Garin's own teacher, made sure to address the elephant in the room: fascism.[60]

In a speech previously agreed on with Martinetti, one that had been rehearsed a few months earlier in aftermath of a sanguinary raid of Florence conducted by the Blackshirt squads, De Sarlo singlehandedly defied the regime's meddling in cultural and academic life:

> Science will never alter its nature and turn into a political institution, an administrative appendix, a hierarchical organization, or a government-directed office. . . . Professors have the right to consider superfluous any law aimed at instructing them in regard to that order, convenience, and decorum which are implicit to their very profession. . . . It is still to be seen whether the new orientation and the new vision have a right to the triumphal praise some want to grant them and whether they contain those germs of spiritual elevation for the individual and society proclaimed by the same.[61]

This talk raised the ire of Armando Carlini, the only representative of a notable group of absentees, the actualists. Before the conference could turn into an antifascist demonstration, it was cut short *manu militari*— even before, it should be noted, Buonaiuti could take center stage.

In his extemporaneous farewell, Martinetti stated: "For the first time in the history of civilization a gathering uniquely intended to advance the purest of sciences was boycotted. In any case, let us hold onto our shared values, for we will harvest in due time. The little that we could achieve will set a standard for many poor [read 'young'] souls."[62] In a few short days, Carlini reported back to Gentile, noting that "those

---

e trasfigurazione dell'arte"; Giuseppe Tarozzi, "L'insegnamento propedeutico della filosofia nelle scuole secondarie." See *Rivista di filosofia* 17 (1926): 111.

60. Bernardino Varisco, Abbagnano's teacher, had already praised fascism in his speech, apparently with no consequences. Varisco's address was immediately published as "Idea dello stato," in *Discorsi politici* (Rome: De Alberti, 1926), 9–39.

61. Francesco De Sarlo, "L'alta cultura e la libertà," in *Francesco De Sarlo*, ed. Giuseppe Cacciatore, Ciro Senofonte, and Angela Costabile (Potenza: Ermes, 1994), 90–91. De Sarlo is known to have modeled his speech after a famous academic address, "L'università e la libertà della scienza," that Marxist thinker Antonio Labriola delivered in 1896 at the University of Rome. Fearing repercussions, De Sarlo had proposed an alternative speech, but Martinetti insisted that he present his antifascist statement. Garin recalls the Fascists' violence and De Sarlo's speech in "Ricordi di scuola," *Annali di storia dell'educazione e delle istituzioni scolastiche* 3 (1996): 267–68.

62. Cited in Rambaldi, "Eventi della Facoltà di Lettere di Milano," 541.

individuals should not get away with it."[63] Gentile rushed to put forth a barrage of slurs against the "dimwitted" (*imbecilli*), "disoriented," and "disbanded" representatives of Italian philosophy.[64] In the following year the Italian Philosophical Association was dissolved and replaced by a Fascist-controlled institution. Disciplinary actions were immediately taken against Martinetti and De Sarlo, while, as a period of martyrdom ensued and Martinetti allegedly began packing a gun to class, a host of other dissidents were either imprisoned, as was the case with Gramsci, or brutally lost their lives, as was the case with liberal thinker Piero Gobetti, to the squadrists.[65]

While future conferences would prove that the 1926 double sabotage on behalf of the Neothomists and idealists succeeded in eliminating the outsiders of an older generation, what significance did experiences such as the one just recounted have for that younger generation whose allegiance all involved parties were competing for?[66] Both dejection and stubborn resolution can be detected in the testimonies of a generation that was forced into growing up fast and, ultimately, very much on its own. According to Garin's late recollection:

> That younger generation sincerely felt the need . . . to find a new path, to see things clearly. . . . They had not questioned the idealists because, as they eventually asserted, they already knew their answers; but they should have stated more exactly that those were the answers they wished to avoid without yet knowing how to. For idealism was the school in which they were formed and that could be overcome only from within, critically, and not by means of a downright rejection. . . . On the one hand, they were born into fascism and had to live their lives within it, and, on the other hand, they waged a justified but unjust rebellion, hence fruitless, against that idealism of which they rep-

63. Cited in Gennaro Sasso, *Per invigilare me stesso: I taccuini di lavoro di Benedetto Croce* (Bologna: Il Mulino, 1989), 136.

64. Giovanni Gentile, "Il congresso filosofico di Milano," in *Politica e cultura* (Florence: Le Lettere, 1990), 1:293–97.

65. As Grassi rushed to report to Castelli (12 April 1926): "Ti scrivo oggi in seguito a una notizia che forse ti può interessare, che forse tu conosci già. Ho appreso oggi che la sospensione di Martinetti è in corso, come pure quella di De Sarlo, e pure quella di Mondolfo, Villa e altri due. Tu che vivi tra i magnati dirigenti, ne sarai già informato ma a buoni conti te ne avverto" (APEC).

66. The following national congress of philosophy took place in Rome on 26–29 May 1929. Fascism was no longer in question as actualists and Neothomists were given full rein to fight their isolated battle. For the proceedings, see *Atti del VII Congresso nazionale di filosofia: Roma, 26–29 maggio 1929* (Milan: Bestetti e Tumminelli, 1929).

resented the unsatisfied and rebellious children: those were the boundaries of a prison-house they still did not know how to escape. (*CFI*, 2:467–68)

As for Grassi and Castelli, their correspondence confirms a generation's will to forge ahead despite the poor example posed by those aging teachers. The diary entry that Castelli dedicated to describing the conference—which demonstrates his exclusive concern for its philosophical contents—is particularly striking for its curtness: "I have had the opportunity to meet many Italian philosophers in these days . . . no seriousness; too much oversimplification" (*D*, 1:11). Was this an expression of youthful overconfidence? Not quite. Unlike most of his peers, by 1926 Castelli could already boast a very incisively argued criticism of Gentile's actual idealism.

REHEARSING DEPROVINCIALIZATION: ENRICO CASTELLI AND NICOLA ABBAGNANO

The events described above capture the atmosphere in which Italian philosophical culture found itself stuck during a crucial period as, elsewhere in Europe, thinkers were capitalizing on the intellectual upheavals of the late nineteenth and early twentieth centuries. In France, for example, there had been Henri Bergson's "vitalism"; in Germany, Wilhelm Dilthey's legitimization of the *Geisteswissenschaften*; in Spain, Miguel de Unamuno's emphasis on the "tragic sense of life" and on the *íntima biografía* of the philosophers. All of these were 'philosophies of life' that had more or less successfully managed to disengage the philosophical task from sterile competition with the empirical sciences, while at the same time avoiding a relapse into abstract intellectualism. These were just a few of the transitional but formative (in their impact on younger students) philosophies that, it is generally agreed, prepared the way for existentialism in the interwar period.

In Italy, the practice of philosophy was affected by fascism, and so this transition took place surreptitiously, for the most part. This is not to say that life philosophies received no attention from the establishment; on the contrary, what would happen was that Gentile or Croce might write a review so curt and dismissive that it had a censorship-like quality. Thus the interest and engagement of younger generations with these sources became an almost clandestine activity. In their dissertations and earliest work, these younger scholars imported proto-existentialist philosophies, not only for personal consumption and edification but as a way to test

Gentile's actualism, and they did this in full consciousness—and here is the Italian anomaly—that actualism, born of a dissatisfaction with positivism and abstract rationalism, could in fact count as Italy's own philosophy of life. Among these scholars were Enrico Castelli and Nicola Abbagnano, who, profiting from the relative protection afforded by their teachers, the organizers of the 1926 conference, and by their youth, made a precocious attempt to deprovincialize Italian philosophy, just before culture became fascisized. Their early work gives us a sense of which existential exigencies found their way to Italy, which is significant because they would later produce some of the most self-consciously 'Italian' reformulations of existentialism (Abbagnano especially).

The title of Castelli's 1924 debut book—*Philosophy of Life: A Criticism of Actual Idealism and a Theory of Practice*—openly reveals the original sources supporting his criticism of Gentile: the French "philosophy of action" of Lucien Laberthonnière (1860–1932) and, mainly, of Maurice Blondel (1861–1949), whose 1893 *Action: Essay on a Critique of Life and a Science of Practice* had recently, in 1921, begun circulating in Italian translation.[67] "Yes or no, does human life make sense, and does man have a destiny?" From this question Blondel set out to reveal "the idealist illusion"—to say nothing of the disillusions of practical nihilism—regarding a disembodied mind's purported self-sufficiency and the self-validating philosophical discourse that supports it.[68] Consideration for human pathos and "truth conceived as an *adaequatio mentis et vitae* rather than as an *adaequatio intellectus et rei*" were for Blondel indispensable to the positive revaluation of life's concreteness.[69]

67. Castelli began corresponding with Laberthonnière sometime around the publication of his first book. In 1927 he produced a short introduction to the French philosopher whose works, as is well known, had been consigned to the Index because they were erroneously considered sympathetic to the current of religious reform that the encyclical *Pascendi Dominici grecis* (1907) disparaged as "modernism." In his introduction, Castelli took pains to distinguish Laberthonnière's philosophy from the work of modernists such as Alfred Loisy (1857–1940) and Eduard Le Roy (1870–1954), and in the concluding chapters he defended Laberthonnière's philosophy from Gentile's recent attacks. Though scholarship on Castelli is surprisingly scant, a few attempts to tackle his life and work comprehensively have been made recently. See Raffaele Pettenuzzo, *Enrico Castelli: Senso comune e filosofia dell'esistenza*, 2 vols. (Rome: Leonardo Da Vinci, 2001); and Gianfilippo Giustozzi, *Enrico Castelli filosofia della vita ed ermeneutica della tecnica* (Naples: Edizioni Scientifiche Italiane, 2002).

68. The reference is to Blondel's famous attack on any form of "intellectualism" entitled "L'illusion idéaliste." See Maurice Blondel, "The Idealist Illusion," in *The Idealist Illusion and Other Essays*, trans. Fiachra Long (Dordrecht: Kluwer, 2000), 75–94.

69. Oliva Blanchette, *Maurice Blondel: A Philosophical Life* (Grand Rapids, MI: William B. Eerdmans, 2010), 49.

Introducing his famous book, Blondel urges intellectual modesty and radical commitment on the part of thinkers to their purported object of study—'man':

Amusing people, all these theoreticians of practice who observe, deduce, discuss, legislate on what they do not do. The chemist makes no claim to produce water without hydrogen and oxygen. I will not claim to know myself and to test myself, to acquire certitude or to appreciate the destiny of man, without having thrown into the crucible all the man I bear in myself. The organism of flesh, of appetites, of desires, of thoughts whose obscure workings I feel perpetually is a living laboratory. That is where my science of life must first be performed.[70]

From within the "living laboratory" that human beings represent, Blondel attempted to construct "a philosophy which by the logic of its rational movement, would lead spontaneously to Christianity and, without imposing faith, would inevitably pose the Christian problem."[71]

Castelli will make this task his own, at first by producing an Italian edition of Blondel's important short piece "The Elementary Principle of a Logic of the Moral Life," and, later—throughout the 1930s—by backing Blondel's involvement in the fiery religious debates that raged in France over the possibility of a Christian philosophy.[72] Against the rationalists Émile Bréhier (1876–1952), Léon Brunschvicg (1869–1944), and Fernand Van Steenberghen (1904–93), who had differently condemned the paradox of reason and faith's coexistence, Blondel—together with Étienne Gilson (1884–1978) and Jacques Maritain (1882–1973), among others—had conversely pointed to the insufficiency of any stance unable to entertain all of life's exigencies and the sway of the supernatural.[73]

In his contribution to the debate, Castelli identified Christian philos-

70. Maurice Blondel, *Action (1893): Essay on a Critique of Life and a Science of Practice*, trans. Oliva Blanchette (Notre Dame, IN: University of Notre Dame Press, 1984), 6.

71. Henry Bouillard cited in Adam C. English, *The Possibility of Christian Philosophy: Maurice Blondel at the Intersection of Theology and Philosophy* (New York: Routledge, 2007), 1.

72. This was a talk Blondel had presented in 1900 (published 1903). Maurice Blondel, *Principio di una logica della vita morale* (Rome: Signorelli, 1924). For the English translation, see Blondel, *Idealist Illusion*, 95–113.

73. Some of the materials relevant to these French debates—which were carried out in three phases (1931, 1932–1933, and 1933–1936)—are now available in English translation with a thorough introduction. See Gregory B. Sadler, ed. and trans., *Reason Fulfilled by Revelation: The 1930s Christian Philosophy Debates in France* (Washington, DC: Catholic University of America Press, 2011).

ophy with Blondel's Augustinian restlessness.[74] For Castelli, too, life determines itself in action, and only those who operate with "faith," "arrogance," and "impetus" in the face of vicissitudes will succeed and emerge as "deserving" human beings (FV, 60). If indeed an unwavering commitment to life is the "greatest benefit bestowed upon man by his religious faith," then Blondel, Castelli argued, is to be credited for having realized that (divine) determinism is a "liberating authority" or condition for freedom. Rather than limiting our action from the outset, God's offer *orients* human beings toward a nondesultory goal (95).

Castelli's elaboration rested on the belief that only within a Christian framework is every action ultimately an "act of faith." "A man," he states, "cannot orient himself in life without some belief, some certainty. Even the man who doubts believes in something by the very fact that he doubts. . . . If it is true, then, that an action is impossible without a belief that is ultimately an act of faith, we can state that action is conditioned by faith in the same way as thought is conditioned by action; faith, therefore—far from resisting the process of logic—represents its very condition" (FV, 107). Castelli will insist on forsaking the path cleared by abstract logic in favor of the wider trail of "deontological necessity" blazed by the divine workings in man: the only course on which, in what could be considered as Blondel's premature refutation of Sartre's atheist existentialism (founded on the idea that "existence precedes essence"), existence (or action) neither precedes nor follows but, rather, identifies with being.

French philosophy of action alerted Castelli to the ruthless teleological, as opposed to ontological, configuration of man's existence. The divine pull or transcendence intervenes in life by bestowing on human actions a meaning that supersedes their circumstances and agency, which has the effect of dignifying what traditional philosophy (and Gentile's was no exception in Castelli's view) all too easily dismissed as relative and ephemeral.[75] Castelli was thus inspired to retrieve the ethical/practical (or deontological) dimension of philosophy vis-à-vis the exclusively epistemological concerns of Italian idealism, which, in his view, had proven unable to yield a full-fledged moral philosophy apt to supersede the an-

74. Sadler, *Reason Fulfilled*, 194.
75. In the preface to his edition of "The Elementary Principle," Castelli reproduced a letter he had received from Blondel on 8 December 1924. In this letter Blondel stated: "Ma préoccupation constante a été de montrer que, au sein même du relatif et du passager où semblent plonger nos pensées et nos volontés, il y a déjà du permanent et du consistant qui donne à ce relatif même une solidité certaine, et qui justifie l'application faite à notre vie, si défaillante qu'elle paraisse, d'un jugement absolu et éternel" (*Principio di una logica*, 9).

tinomy between theoretical and practical pursuits.[76] In his first book, Castelli brought to bear Blondel's cardinal themes—well captured as "the necessity of action," the impossibility of "nihilism" or discouragement, and the acknowledgment of the "divine source" of human volition—on Gentile's actualism and, rather prematurely, on the *political* embodiment this philosophy was just then undergoing.[77] All of this, it should be noted, to Blondel's bemused curiosity.[78]

In fact, the boldness and breadth of Castelli's 1924 frontal attack would be lost without some consideration of Gentile's sudden heart-and-soul investment in the Fascist cause. Central to this 'actualization' of fascism was the theorization of the 'ethical state,' first broached by Gentile in a 1923 public speech entitled "My Liberalism." From the perspective Castelli had acquired, Gentile's program was bound to sound like a Blackshirt Blondelianism. The ethical state, Gentile wrote,

> is not external to the individual; it is, rather, the very essence of his individuality. This [individuality] manifests itself in no other way than

---

76. In the same letter/preface: "Mon premier dessein a été d'assouplir et d'étendre la logique; sans en atténuer en rien la rigueur; j'ai voulu en manifester tout le rôle, toute la portée. . . . La dialectique des faits, des sentiments et des actes, fussent-ils en conflit avec ce que nous estimerions la logique idéale, comporte une implacable précision. Il y a une *logique* dans l'illogisme même: il n'y a rien d'*alogique*. Et c'est cette logique même du désordre apparent ou réel qu'il s'agit d'instituer" (*Principio di una logica*, 5–6).

77. English, *Possibility of Christian Philosophy*, 10.

78. The correspondence between Blondel and Castelli shows that the Frenchman could only vaguely grasp the anti-Gentilean purpose his philosophy was serving. Upon receiving a copy of Castelli's book, for example, Blondel responded (24 July 1924): "Je voudrais avoir une connaissance plus complète de la langue italienne pour apprécier, avec toute la précision désirable, votre pensée qui me paraît généreuse, pleine de sève, et promettant beaucoup pour l'avenir spirituel de l'Italie qui m'est très cher. L'activité Philosophique y est en grand progrès. Et nul doute que vous ne soyez un des bons ouvriers, un des maîtres de cette Renaissance—ou de cette promotion de ce que vous nommez l'idéalisme, d'inspiration spiritualiste et chrétienne, et qui, en un autre sens du mot, est aussi une expression du réalisme le plus intégral et le plus soucieux de la hiérarchie des valeurs." Cited in Annarita Meoli, "La corrispondenza Castelli-Blondel e la traduzione del *Principe élémentaire*," in *Logica della morale: Maurice Blondel e la sua ricezione in Italia*, ed. Simone D'Agostino (Rome: Istituto della Enciclopedia Italiana, 2006), 199. On another occasion (28 January 1925), Blondel specifically requested "some clarifications" on actual idealism (*Logica della morale*, 207). Blondel's obliviousness is particularly interesting when we consider that in a 1909 essay treating religious modernism, Gentile had shown interest in Blondel's notion of immanence. As we shall see in the next chapter, Blondel would in due time be instructed in Gentile's actual idealism by Castelli's friend Ernesto Grassi. For Gentile's criticism of Blondel, see Giovanni Gentile, "La filosofia dell'azione del Laberthonnière," in *La religione* (Florence: Sansoni, 1965), chaps. 2 and 3. On Gentile's take on Blondel and Catholic modernism, see the essays of Mauro Visentin, Antonio Russo, and Daniela Floriduz in *Logica della morale*.

as volition aiming at universality, without limits and obstacles that it
cannot surmount. . . . For this reason man brings his nature into action
inasmuch as he makes himself into the state, and he feels in the most
intimate part of his consciousness the incessant throbbing of a morality that transcends the confines of his abstract personality singularly
taken.[79]

The ethical state and the superior ideal it embodied, Gentile argued, requires "subordination" and the "sacrifice" of one's own interest, almost
a "holocaust of the self." "Political life," he persisted, "is by definition
a life of abnegation and disinterest, a religion of the fatherland [*religione
di patria*]; a flame that consumes the by-products of man's crass egotism,
and purifies him in the cult of an ideal."[80] A state so conceived, Gentile
believed, would contribute to the development of an energetic sense of religiosity and morality, unify the Italian people in a common cause, and,
we can add, cure them once and for all of the disease contracted during the
Renaissance: extreme individualism.[81]

Though, as we shall see, Castelli was a fervent *cultural* patriot, he re-
coiled at the idea of the impersonal and utilitarian 'religiosity' Gentile
promoted. Taking the stance of the average religious man, rather, Castelli
pointed to the unresolved antinomy between politics and religion and their
incommensurable aims.[82] The ethical state, from a religious worldview,
can hardly be life-fulfilling. In a convoluted sentence that perhaps betrays
some fear of repercussions, Castelli stated that "the religious interest,
in relation to the political one, is not that of impeding the realization of
particular goals—the only ones recognized by a controlling body—rather,
[religion's] interest is to make sense of the abstract conception predicated
by such an official organ . . . ; not to suppress the organ that in fact has a
value, but to clarify some new and different vital exigencies that are conducive to a life lived in full awareness, that is, a religious or universal life"
(*FV*, 14). Recalling the persecution affecting the newly converted during
the Roman Empire, Castelli points to the dire consequences that a sup-

79. Gentile, "Il mio liberalismo," in *Politica e cultura*, 1:115.
80. Gentile, "Il mio liberalismo," *Politica e cultura*, 1:115.
81. Castelli continued to attack Gentile's participation in Fascist institutions at later
times in his life. See Enrico Castelli, "Polemica obbligata: A proposito del Senatore Gentile
e di una polemica dell'Istituto Nazionale Fascista di Cultura," *Archivio di filosofia* 1, no. 4
(1931): 91–93; and Enrico Castelli, "Individuo e Stato: Nota critica," *Archivio di filosofia* 2,
no. 2 (1932): 121–23.
82. Castelli's state of mind at the time of his critique is well captured in his diary entries.
See, for example, *D*, 1:4.

posedly ethical and mundane dictatorship could have on a traditionally Catholic collectivity such as represented by Italians. In what way, then, can a true Christian philosophy usefully amend the assumptions of actual idealism?

By answering this question, Castelli believed that the "absolute immanentism" on which actual idealism proudly rested could be shaken once and for all. For, in his view, by neglecting the mysterious workings of transcendence in human experience, actual idealism was not only deeply flawed in its overt aims—that is, as a theory of human amelioration—but also naturally unlikely to promote social solidarity. The jettisoning of transcendence implies the ousting of anything that is 'Other,' including one's fellow man. This is the crux of the matter: "Actual idealism cannot but be an immanentistic conception of philosophy, of an absolute kind. . . . Beyond myself, which in Gentile's philosophy is the only possible real self, there cannot be any other person in an absolute way" (FV, 89).

In Castelli's final analysis, actual idealism was a new "Protagorism" and a "solipsism" that by giving up on transcendence was ultimately oblivious to the very principles of sociability in humankind:

> Action indissolubly ties man to the goal he wishes to attain. For this reason the man who believes he can live irrespective of the society he lives in cannot, in truth, even claim to know himself. In moving toward a particular goal, from which the work that completes him emerges, man wants to perceive the intimate spirituality of cooperation, and in every action of his, he wishes to find the action of his fellow man. (FV, 131)

A twenty-four-year-old Castelli could not have more firmly rejected an epoch, its values, and its constitutive philosophy. Indeed, nation, family, and society are life's greatest values, yet only when grasped from within the framework of that truly universal (or divine) "methexis" or participation the state cannot provide.

Castelli's invalidation of actual idealism was matched, albeit from a resolutely lay perspective, by the other *enfant prodige* of the existential generation to which they both eventually came to belong. A 1923 book entitled *The Irrational Sources of Thought* marks the first appearance of Nicola Abbagnano, the thinker who in the next twenty years or so would singlehandedly define the existential experience in Italian academic terms and who, unlike a rather neglected Castelli, would immediately emerge as the official and most inconvenient 'outsider' of his generation. Abbagnano's own critique, which, admittedly, was not as insightful as that of Castelli, rested on a source even more unfamiliar in Italy than Blondel, pragmatism, and therefore his study represents another exemplary case of early deprovincialization.[83] Animated by a sort of Nietzschean icono-clasm, Abbagnano provided a critical survey of Western intellectualism from Plato to Gentile and, as has been rightly argued, a Rorty-like refuta-tion of the correspondence theory of truth on which this philosophical canon relies.[84]

In very broad strokes, according to Abbagnano the first phase of West-ern rationalism—from Plato to Aquinas—is characterized at once by the awareness of reality's essential unrelatedness to thought and the "naïve certainty that" somehow "the objects of nature are directly accessible to spirit in their full reality" (*SIP*, 8). Only starting with Descartes is this primitive faith lost and certainty sought within man's own conscious-ness, though not unreservedly enough. Philosophy, after Descartes, is still caught in the same contradiction whereby, as in Leibniz's case, "an abyss is dug, on the one side, between thought and being, ideas and reality, spirit and body; while, on the other side, [rationalism] tiredly attempts to reestablish that unity for which it yearns in order to satisfy its realistic in-stinct and salvage the absolute and certain nature of knowledge" (16). Ac-cording to Abbagnano—and here lies one of the novelties of his venture in Italy—the problem posed by the ontological dualism of thought and being is more accurately broached in the tradition of English empiricism, start-ing with Locke, whose philosophy affirms that knowledge begins and ends in the world of ideas, through Berkeley, in whose philosophy the doctrine of correspondence is "repudiated for the first time," and finally coming to rest with Hume, who posits "a total opposition between our senses and reason" (26).

According to Abbagnano, the achievements of empiricism, though not complete, had created the premise for an epochal turning point in the history of philosophy: its representatives had, albeit dejectedly, acknowl-edged the irrationality or arbitrariness of our commonsense belief in the correspondence theory. Nevertheless, the skepticism that ensued did not achieve its ultimate consequences, since

83. Interestingly, a rare survey (mostly negative) of pragmatism had been produced by Spirito. See Ugo Spirito, *Il pragmatismo nella filosofia contemporanea* (Florence: Vallecchi, 1921). See also Henry S. Harris, "Ugo Spirito and Pragmatism," in *Il pensiero di Ugo Spirito*, 2 vols. (Rome: Treccani, 1990), 1:51–59.

84. Nino Langiulli, *Possibility, Necessity, and Existence: Abbagnano and His Predeces-sors* (Philadelphia: Temple University Press, 1992), 32–34.

the course of man's life never seals itself off and completely concen-
trates in the realm of thought. . . . The idea of a world independent
from our mind emerges only from the *experience of action*. When we
feel that the outpouring of our activities is stifled and stinted, when
our movement hits an obstacle or our impulses knock on some form
of resistance, we get the idea of a reality opposed to our volition and,
therefore, independent from it. The opposition of subject and world is
the product of a fundamentally alogical experience; it is the symbolic
and ideal transcription of the sense of resistance and of the effort indis-
solubly connected with action. . . . The fact that the idea of an action
presupposes logically that of an external reality does not invalidate the
original priority of one's own *experience of action*. (*SIP*, 32–33)

Philosophy, its history reveals, was far from ready to reach these conclusions, as Kant ushered in a third and last phase of rationalism that set
philosophy again on the hunt for the "universal and necessary value of
truth" (36). While we cannot here follow through his meticulous review
of idealism's history, the point is that Abbagnano, Italy's future leading
historian of philosophy, ended his survey of intellectualism with Gentile's
actualism.

Like Castelli, Abbagnano also displayed a newly found conviction that
with Gentile, Italy had provided philosophy not with a new beginning but,
rather, with a glorious second ending. Their stance or age notwithstanding, Italian thinkers were all deeply aware that Gentile's efforts were spent
on overcoming the many dualisms of philosophical tradition. If Castelli,
through Blondel, had focused on the two-worlds dualism—the supernatural and natural—Abbagnano focused his attention on Gentile's attempt
to overcome the subject/object distinction. Actual idealists believed they
surpassed old-fashioned rationalism by means of absolute immanentism,
whereby truth is found no longer in an objectification of thought, but
rather in a thought that continuously and infinitely thinks and thus reintegrates all of reality within the sphere of its incessant and eternally present act (of thought). This way spirit can never become the object of its own
meditation without, by this very abstraction, ceasing to be spirit. A young
Abbagnano added:

The very effort [*atto*] to contract all of reality and all of life within
thought goes topsy-turvy: the act of celebrating thought's utmost
power, its absolute spontaneity, irremediably removes reality, life, and
truth outside its [thought's] abstract circle. When nothing seems to fall

outside of the pure activity of a thought that develops eternally, here is when we behold an incredible and paradoxical fact: real thought can never become the object of itself, it can never be thought! Well then? Well, the reduction [of everything] to thought was not possible unless thought was not real thought but something different and opposite. That is, a creative energy outside and beyond thought—the irrational life of spirit. Believing himself to have affirmed thought, Gentile has in fact affirmed this obscure vital power. (*SIP*, 90)

If these, Gentile's own, were the meager results to which the Italian philosophical tradition had come, where to start from? Again, here, Abbagnano pointed to the Anglo-American tradition—specifically, pragmatism—which by reconnecting with Hume "rigorously affirms the importance of the irrational and practical exigencies within the field of theoretical pursuits" (92). With Charles S. Peirce (1939–14), F. C. S. Schiller (1863–1937), William James (1842–1910), and Abbagnano's beloved John Dewey (1859–1952), the passionate nature of humankind reenters as an "active factor" in the production of knowledge: human beings are ultimately the creators of all truth within the field of action (94).

A close survey of Castelli's and Abbagnano's germinal books reveals some crucial considerations regarding the resolute transition that will soon take place among a number of younger Italian thinkers between the recognition of actualism's illusions and a sudden but also immediately reformative embrace of French and German existentialism. First, Castelli and Abbagnano's earliest efforts illustrate Grassi's claim regarding a shared demand for "life" among younger intellectuals as well as the as yet purely negative or critical features of their proposals. In pre-existentialist times, both works claimed that actual idealism led to the oblivion of lived life and its pathos. Though Gentile had defined his philosophy as an "absolute immanentism," he appeared to have failed in his stated goal of providing ideas with arms and legs.

Also, each work in its own way ultimately realized that the crux of the matter lay in the need to formulate a new kind of personal commitment and to abolish the unnecessary reliance on overarching political structure. From a strictly Italian perspective, furthermore, the striking convergence between the 'internal' overcoming of actualism provided by 'heretics' such as Spirito and Calogero and the deprovincializing approach of 'outsiders' like Castelli and Abbagnano cannot go unnoticed: both groups insisted on actualism's ethical and historiographical failures. Yet the point that is too often neglected is that the outsiders' efforts precede that of the heretics by some fifteen years. Very important years at that, for they almost perfectly coincide with the Fascist dictatorship.

The absolute anachronism that premature thinkers like Castelli and Abbagnano represented is definitely confirmed by the review article Spirito dedicated to Abbagnano's first book in 1923. According to Spirito, who by his own later confession was at this time still writing from the perspective of an "orthodox actualism" and inspired by an almost "fanatic" faith in its promoter, Abbagnano had proved to be "more of an idealist than all idealisms."[85] Abbagnano, specifically, had failed to distinguish between idealism conceived as "theory"—and thus a philosophy among many philosophies, just another form of intellectualism—and idealism as "ideal" whereby "the intimate and concrete of our finite creative freedom amounts to the need we feel to act, to work, to fulfill, to apply all of our powers and all of our time to endow our lives with the greatest possible value: the joy of acting, building, and creating."[86] Evidently, at the time of his review Spirito was a whole two steps behind—he still believed in actualism's "constructive" potential and did not realize that in 1937, when he finally believed he had caught up with a younger generation, Martin Heidegger's *Being and Time* had been circulating for well over a decade. The youth he eventually came to address, in other words, had long stopped looking for answers in Italian philosophy *exclusively*.

POSITIVE EXISTENTIALISM

Existentialism, an intellectual mood or 'family' of thinkers rather than a well-defined academic current or 'school,' is a 'philosophy' that, in reappraisal, naturally lends itself to a (trans)national contextualization.[87] Russian novelists (Dostoevsky and Tolstoy, above all) earn their place in the canon of existentialism, as do philosophers like Kierkegaard and Nietzsche, forefathers of an existentialism that in Germany, with Jaspers and Heidegger, countered philosophical essentialism and scientism and in France, mainly with Sartre, acquired a popular, even sensational, quality that made it exportable beyond the continent, to American campuses, to

---

85. Ugo Spirito, *L'idealismo italiano e i suoi critici* (Florence: Le Monnier, 1930), 114. Spirito admits his fanatism in *Giovanni Gentile* (Florence: Sansoni, 1969), 8.

86. Spirito, *L'idealismo italiano*, 116.

87. See the first three essays collected in Steven Crowell, ed., *The Cambridge Companion to Existentialism* (Cambridge: Cambridge University Press, 2012).

British theaters, or to Spain, where it offered an occasion to reflect on an enduring Quixotism.[88] The fact that, mainly by contagion, existentialism may be found in virtually every philosophical and literary culture alerts us to its transitional as well as its transnational qualities. That is to say, for all of its elusiveness, a quality that makes it easier to describe in context than to define, existentialism in any of its manifestations may be credited with a concrete function: it favored a settling of accounts with entrenched and obsolete practices and frames of mind. The transmutational pertinence of existentialism is clearly observed in Italy, where a very self-consciously distinct form of existentialism emerged that, although it sought primarily a constructive exoneration of Gentilean idealism and thus was primarily an internal affair, deserves attention now, if only because it made a significant contribution to a fresh understanding of historical, Renaissance humanism.

Owing to their long training in Gentilean and foreign life philosophies, younger Italian thinkers seemed to be overly primed for the advent of *Existenz-philosophie*. In fact, it could be argued that besides the comfort to be found in sharing a pan-European philosophical disquiet, its catchy name, and its formal dressing or style, German existentialism had little to contribute toward the solutions yearned for by a younger generation of philosophers. Italy's convulsive reception of Heidegger—and less so of Sartre—testifies to the Italians' hunger for an alternative as well as to their premature overcoming of this formative philosophical experience. Between 1930, when Ernesto Grassi first introduced Heidegger to an Italian readership, and 1944, when Norberto Bobbio apologetically dedicated one more book to this philosophical "fad," Italy's vast bibliography on existentialism was mostly composed of criticisms or critical adaptations.[89]

In *The Philosophy of Decadentism*, Bobbio identified existentialism as the "mode of philosophizing" or, rather, the "philosophical vogue" of an epoch that "at once attracted and repelled Italians": a "'philosophy of crisis' which needed to be rejected just as soon as it was experienced."[90] Bobbio was disturbed by the teenage quality or dilettantism into which

88. Existentialism is informatively broached in its Russian, German, French, American, British, and Spanish contexts in Jonathan Judaken and Robert Bernasconi, eds., *Situating Existentialism* (New York: Columbia University Press, 2012).

89. A bibliography published in 1946 collects more than 700 entries. See Vito A. Bellezza, "Studi italiani sull'esistenzialismo," *Archivio di filosofia* 1–2 (1946): 161–217. For a thorough account of existentialism in Italy, see Antonio Santucci, *Esistenzialismo e filosofia italiana* (Bologna: Il Mulino, 1959).

90. Norberto Bobbio, *The Philosophy of Decadentism: A Study in Existentialism* (Oxford: Blackwell, 1948), viii.

this popular "mental dimension" had degenerated, especially, he observed, in France, thus making it easy to dismiss. This is why Italian existentialism was all the more seriously construed, according to rigid academic standards, the more it was scoffed at by the senior mentors of Italian philosophy. When Bobbio returned to the existential experience ex post facto, he could be relieved of his embarrassment, for in his assessment Abbagnano had managed to live up to the most intransigent expectations of the examiners.

In Bobbio's own incisive words, Abbagnano's 1939 *The Structure of Existence*—the manifesto of Italian existentialism—appeared like a "meteorite fallen from the sky," as a "work of rupture" that had been long in the making and that surprised mostly for its stylistic and linguistic "Unheimlichkeit."[91] Among younger generations, Abbagnano's existentialism instantly made works like those of Ugo Spirito obsolete. Unfamiliar though it may have seemed at a first reading, Abbagnano's philosophy has traditional qualities, as his students have recently pointed out, being quite consciously construed as a "national philosophy suited to substitute for Gentilean idealism."[92] This point cannot be stressed enough. In Abbagnano as in all of the best of Italian existentialism, Heidegger did *not* replace Gentile; rather, he provided the leverage needed for a final removal, through revision, of actual idealism. Furthermore, since Gentile and Heidegger never looked for contact, Italian existentialism represents a rare attempt at their reconnection, something they were both aware of.

More concretely, it may be said that Italians confronted Heidegger's 1927 *Being and Time* as a 'German philosophy,' the last act of a tradition they had been 'translating,' that is, naturalizing, for the benefit of the nation's cause since Spaventa. This consideration allows one to draw a parallel between the reform of Hegelian dialectics pursued between the Risorgimento and Gentile and Abbagnano's reform of Heidegger's existential analytic. In both cases, the overt aim was to rekindle what appeared to be a conservative or bookish potential that would have a visible effect on society. German existentialism, instrumental empiricism, and American pragmatism joined forces in Abbagnano against the teleological triumphalism of what he called "Romantic philosophy," which accepted no errors in history and interpreted humankind as a manifestation of "Pure

91. Norberto Bobbio, "Discorso su Nicola Abbagnano," in Nicola Abbagnano, *Scritti scelti*, ed. Giovanni De Crescenzo and Pietro Laveglia (Turin: Taylor, 1967), 14–15.
92. Pietro Rossi and Carlo Augusto Viano, "Premessa," in *Nicola Abbagnano: Un itinerario filosofico*, ed. Bruno Miglio (Bologna: Il Mulino, 2002), 7.

Act" or "Infinite Spirit."[93] To this end, Abbagnano immediately embraced the German notion of man's "thrownness" into the world; however, he emphasized *possibility* as the norm and supreme category of existentialist thought against the defeatism in which German philosophy resulted.

The prologue to Abbagnano's groundbreaking book, which begins with a citation drawn from Karl Jaspers, is a manifestation of an epochal, generational, and personal turning point: "Wir haben die Naivitaet verloren." It is rarely acknowledged that in Abbagnano the loss of philosophical naïveté is further developed in a plan clearly intended to challenge Spirito's problematicism. He states: "Philosophy [with existentialism] sheds its early naïveté and presents itself as the fulfillment of human existence according to its very nature. . . . The movement that, from the constitutive problematicity [*problematicità*] of life, leads to the *foundations* of such problematicity . . . is acknowledged as the movement that situates man squarely in his finitude, while death emerges as the supreme condition of his freedom. Man's true destiny, his authentic constitution in *history*, depends on his *allegiance to death* [*fedeltà alla morte*], his acknowledgment and realization of the fundamental risks of existence."[94] In Abbagnano, Italian problematicism and German existentialism complement each other in rescuing the centrality of human existence; yet either they too easily postpone the possibility of a constructive resolution to humankind's existence, as with Spirito (who goes uncited in the text), or they entirely give up on it, as in what Abbagnano goes on to describe as Jaspers's and Heidegger's prospectively divergent—but conclusively convergent—ontologies.

Considering the struggle toward being "from its starting point," where "existence appears to be an existence from nothingness," Heidegger, according to Abbagnano, nullified possibility in accepting only death—a necessity. Similarly, Jaspers, who considered the struggle toward being with respect "to its final [or limit] situation" and placed being "beyond the effort that moves toward it," sanctioned the inevitable *Scheitern*, *scacco*, or 'shipwreck,' to which human search is destined. Either option offers human beings no criteria by which to distinguish between possibilities and leaves in its trail only suffering, unhappiness, or death:

The two fundamental directions within which the problem of being moves about in its existential form amount to two *limits* that have

93. Nicola Abbagnano, "Existentialism in Italy," in *Critical Existentialism*, trans. and ed. Nino Langiulli (New York: Anchor, 1969), 8.

94. Nicola Abbagnano, "La struttura dell'esistenza," in *Scritti esistenzialisti*, by Nicola Abbagnano, ed. Bruno Maiorca (Turin: Utet, 1988), 60.

a demolishing effect on the significance and the very essence of existential philosophy. In Heidegger's metaphysic, the effort toward being
turns into *anguish*—that is, *an existence for nothing(ness)*—while in
Jaspers's metaphysics it turns into the *fulfillment of one's own impossibility*. In both cases, the essence of philosophy as existence brings
about its own destruction. The effort toward being becomes the effort
toward the impossibility of such struggle or a *struggle toward nothingness*: either stalemate [or failure] or anguish [or dread].[95]

Instead, in Abbagnano's reconfiguration, existentialism would emerge, in
its Italian fashion, as a philosophy of (plausible) success and hope.

The criticism that Abbagnano leveled against Jaspers and Heidegger
and, in due time, against French existentialism(s)—both the Sartrian and
the theistic brand of Gabriel Marcel, Louis Lavelle, and René Le Senne—
concerns the paradox of a commonly posited *equivalence* of the constitutive possibilities of existence.[96] Such *equivalence*, in Abbagnano's view,
amounts to a covert determinism or indifference to lived life that repli-
cates the idealistic contradictions that existentialism intends to fight. In a
late clarification of his thought, he wrote:

95. Abbagnano, "La struttura dell'esistenza," 69.
96. On Sartre, Abbagnano wrote: "The first response that is presented to these questions
is the acknowledgment of the absolute *equivalence* of all human possibilities, an acknowledgment that implies that every choice, by the very fact of being such, is justified; and that
man is essentially free, that is, indifferent, before all the possibilities that are proposed to
him. This is the response of the latest French brand of existentialism (Sartre, Camus). This
is undoubtedly the most obvious answer, but also the most paralyzing. A choice that is not
supported by the faith in the value of what one chooses is not possible since the acknowledgment of equivalence *is* already the renunciation of choice. That acknowledgment is equivalent, therefore, to the nullification and the loss of all possibilities indiscriminately, and
hence, to the negation of existence as such." Nicola Abbagnano, "Existentialism Is a Positive
Philosophy," in *Critical Existentialism*, 43–44. Similarly, on French theistic existentialism:
"Whether God is conceived as a *Mystery* who gives Himself to man in love rather than in
rational speculation (Marcel); whether He is conceived as *Being* totally present to interior
experience (Lavelle); or whether He is conceived as the supreme *Value* who gives Himself in
the moral experience (Le Senne), the result of these interpretations is, in each case, that of
offering man the guarantee that the possibilities of his existence are realized in the best of
ways. The guarantee resides in the fact that existence is, in each case, a relation with a being
(God) who has, by definition—or better who *is*, by definition—the possibility of fulfillment
of all the highest human possibilities. The human possibilities are, in other words, already,
from this point of view, *realized* possibilities inasmuch as they have been given or conceded
to man by Being Himself, who contains them all in their full realization. Time then ceases
to be a threat of destruction, and becomes a condition of realization. The success of human
undertakings is guaranteed from the outset since, as Lavelle says, every possibility is destined
to be realized" (*Critical Existentialism*, 46).

The existential possibilities have been, in fact, clarified and described in their negative and nullifying sense, as if the exclusive prospect were the radical impossibility of all that man can be and can do. . . . Aggressively intent on destroying the illusion of certitude—an important task and rich in positive implications—these philosophies have taken no interest in that which is probable for man. They have ended by neglecting the sources from which man draws the means and the techniques of his positive expectations: nature and society.[97]

Italian existentialism—though sharing in the struggle against past idealisms—would not sacrifice values to the analytic of existence. Its distinguishing feature is visible, rather, in a coherent use of the category of possibility, supported by a particularly strong-willed "attitude" or "stance" (*atteggiamento*) and a truer "commitment to one's own finitude" (*impegno nella propria finitudine*).

In order to rescue existentialism and restore it as a positive ontology, Abbagnano introduced a third or "privileged alternative" in which "the final situation of the effort toward being achieves its essential unity with the initial situation."[98] This recapitulatory unity is what Abbagnano described as that "structure" of existence which is never preordered but, rather, appears as a "possibility to be achieved." While human beings may never reach full possession of Being, which by its very nature is "pure possibility," they can nevertheless participate in its vitality by exercising their freedom to choose between the many possibilities they are offered. Inevitably struggling against instability and personal dissipation, in a life certainly replete with errors and defeats, human beings are nevertheless capable of construing a coherent existence as long as they learn how to choose that single "destiny" that is their own. One's identity, the unity of one's personality, is built into the unwavering commitment to one's choices and manifested in the perseverance of a particular, well-defined goal. Man "can, *therefore he should*. . . . This reasonable faith is all that can constitute his dignity and his value as man."[99] The possibility of choice was for Abbagnano a norm or an obligation to exercise one's freedom, and the duty of achieving one's own structure is a duty owed to society as well. Faith in human dignity and self-realization is ultimately

97. Abbagnano, "Existentialism in Italy," 7.
98. Abbagnano, "La struttura dell'esistenza," 69.
99. Abbagnano, "Existentialism Is a Positive Philosophy," 51.

what sustains the "positive," if not resolutely optimistic, and 'civic' brand of Italian existentialism.

In the wake of World War II, the kind of "commitment" and positive "attitude" sponsored by Abbagnano attracted the interest of those Fascist party elders concerned by a disillusioned Italian youth—soldiers and intellectuals alike. Among them, Giuseppe Bottai, Mussolini's onetime minister of national education, was a notable revisionist of Fascist cultural policy. Firmly convinced of Italy's role as defender and guardian of civilization and of the failings of propaganda in bringing about new cultural orders, Bottai relentlessly pushed for the regime's engagement with younger intellectuals and for their cultural militancy at an international level.[100] *Primato*, a short-lived journal published between 1 March 1940 and 15 August 1943, was the most notable among his late efforts to marshal Italy's intellectual forces in view of a common goal. To this effect, the journal was intended as a "laboratory of culture" and hosted a number of debates (*inchieste*) intended to review and sanction the radical changes that had occurred in the past twenty years of Italian history.[101] In due time, Bottai urged Abbagnano to initiate a debate on existentialism, described in the editorial as a philosophy worthy of attention because, in its Italian form, it was "aimed at a constructive and positive vision of reality."[102]

In hindsight, this final debate, dedicated to philosophy, is particularly symbolic, for it took place between 1 January and 1 June 1943, a few months before the fall of the Fascist regime (25 July), heralding the inevitable dissolution of the journal and the opening of a new era in political and philosophical life. The roster of participants—representing Neothomists, actualists, first- and second-generation 'heretics,' as well as second-generation 'outsiders'—provided *in nuce* the whole history of early twentieth-century Italian philosophy. Among them, an increasingly isolated Giovanni Gentile unwillingly yielded to the pressure of the journal's editors to confront a philosophical community that, by this time, had resolutely overcome

100. See Giordano Bruno Guerri, *Giuseppe Bottai: Un Fascista critico* (Milan: Feltrinelli, 1976); and Alexander J. De Grand, *Bottai e la cultura fascista* (Rome: Laterza, 1978). Needless to say, all of Bottai's efforts in the cultural realm were tainted by his fascist and racist beliefs. See Stefanella Spagnolo, *La patria sbagliata di Giuseppe Bottai: Dal razzismo coloniale alle leggi razziali (1935–1939)* (Rome: Aracne, 2012).

101. See Vito Zagarrio, *Arte, cultura, cinema del Fascismo attraverso una rivista esemplare* (Rome: Edizioni di Storia e Letteratura, 2007), chap. 2.

102. See Abbagnano's recollections in *Ricordi di un filosofo*, ed. Marcello Staglieno (Milan: Rizzoli, 1990), 52–57.

him.[103] In his opening and closing statements, Abbagnano was given the chance to present his positive existentialism as that long-awaited counter-philosophy that former actualists had failed to provide. His programmatic manifesto emphasized "coexistence"—the acknowledgment that "*my own* existence is not *all* of existence, . . . which means the acknowledgment of the dignity and importance of the existence of *others* vis-à-vis *my own*"— and a correlated revision of idealist historicism: "Man *is not* history: he has to *make* himself history . . . by moving toward the future with the resolution to reconnect the future to the past and thus recover in the past his own true self and the true form of his coexistence with others. This kind of faith we call destiny."[104] In sum, an existential revision of idealist historiography was instrumental to a resolute overcoming of Gentile's solipsistic epistemology.

Abbagnano's philosophy, which is sometimes referred to as a 'humanistic existentialism' owing to its overt secularism, was in effect a Renaissance 'humanism' because of a link Abbagnano wished to draw between his concerns and the achievements of the Italian Quattrocento. This Renaissance connection still goes largely unrecognized despite the thorough investigation recently conducted into Abbagnano's intellectual sources and his philosophical lexicon, which clearly amounts to an updated variation on the *homo faber* theme and the related topics, all so dear to the Italian humanist tradition, of *dignitas hominis*, *libero arbitrio*, and *virtù*'s mastery of *fortuna*.[105] The Renaissance qualities of Abbagnano's positive existentialism may best be unearthed through a closer consideration of the historiographical premises that support his systematic thought. In fact, the debate that took place in *Primato* had been rehearsed a few years earlier in Pisa (1940–42), where at least six out of its twelve participants— including Abbagnano, Spirito, and Gentile—had gathered for a series of seminars dedicated to "the problem of history." The paper Abbagnano de-

103. In his paper Gentile openly claimed that he no longer wanted to converse, and that, ultimately, existentialism repeated in foreign words what Italians had long been saying. See Bruno Maiorca, ed., *L'esistenzialismo in Italia: I testi integrali dell'inchiesta su "Primato" nel 1943 e la discussione sulla filosofia dell'esistenza fino ai nostri giorni* (Turin: Paravia, 1993), 140. Interestingly, some loyal Gentileans would eventually argue that actualism was already an existentialism and of course a better, 'positive' one. See, most notably, Vito A. Bellezza, *L'esistenzialismo positivo di Giovanni Gentile* (Florence: Sansoni, 1954). For a dispassionate comparison of Abbagnano and Gentile, see Giovanni Fornero, "Abbagnano e Gentile," in *L'esistenzialismo in Italia*, 491–509.

104. See Maiorca, *L'esistenzialismo in Italia*, 93–94.

105. On the sources of Abbagnano's positive existentialism, see Silvio Paolini Merlo, *Abbagnano a Napoli: Gli anni della formazione e le radici dell'esistenzialismo positivo* (Naples: Guida, 2003).

livered at this conference, together with his inaugural lecture to a class taught in 1939—which he later introduced as an appendix to the first edition of his *The Structure of Existence*—deserves special attention, for they reveal Abbagnano's contribution to an existentialist reappraisal of Renaissance humanism.

Abbagnano noted that in its most mature form historicism's "claim regarding the identity of reality and rationality, the chronological order with an ideal order," excludes the possibility of investigating humankind according to its temporal nature and as a self-reflexive agent and investigator of history.[106] In Abbagnano, the historian emerges as the quintessential man, for in his genuine "commitment" to historical reevocation he is granted the possibility of reconnecting the structural coherence of his individual existence with that of history as a whole: "The problem of history is not a problem regarding a given historical reality, or the problem of historical evaluation, but the problem regarding the *existence* of a being [*ente*] that raises itself to history owing to its very temporal nature and authentically recovers its structure in history: such a being is man."[107] From this existential vantage point, in which human existence takes precedence and (in)forms historiographical research, human freedom is no longer curtailed by historical determinism. This claim requires a better grasp of that objectivity and impartiality required of historical research: "Its objectivity consists in that total commitment by which the subject recovers his unity, while its impartiality is tantamount to the attempt man makes to free himself from his particular and dispersive interests in order to affirm himself through that unique and fundamental interest that is his own."[108] Historical research, thus, consolidates and realizes the personality of him who commits to it as "life's true mission."

Another concern of Abbagnano's was the "coexistential solidarity" fostered by historical research. Historians may all too often fail in their intended goal to meet the past on genuine historical grounds, but the risk is always worth taking: "In coming into his own as unity, man fully attains his personality and brings about a historical situation that transcends contingency by establishing the possibility for comprehension among men and their common participation in universal values."[109] On this point, Abba-

106. Nicola Abbagnano, "La ricerca storica," in *Il problema della storia* (Milan: Fratelli Bocca, 1944), 14

107. Abbagnano, "La ricerca storica," 20.

108. Abbagnano, "La ricerca storica," 27.

109. Nicola Abbagnano, "La storicità della filosofia," in *La struttura dell'esistenza* (Turin: Paravia, 1939), 195.

gnano seemed to agree with Cantimori's criticism of Spirito: humankind's engagement with historical documents amounts to an effective exchange with past personalities in view of a common historical destiny. However, Abbagnano wished to specify that man's "acknowledgment of the past as his very own past" occurs in phases, starting with the "philological moment." A revaluation of philology intended as a fundamental step in restoring the past according to its very nature is the ultimate requirement for overcoming the ingrained prejudices and philosophical presumptions of idealist historiography and their repercussions on the Italians' assessment of the Renaissance.

Just two years after the publication of *The Structure of Existence*, in 1941, Abbagnano put forth two volumes in the field of Renaissance scholarship—a monographic work on Bernardino Telesio (1509–88), the pioneering Italian natural scientist, and an overview of the epoch deceptively entitled *Bernardino Telesio and the Philosophy of the Renaissance*.[110] In the latter, Abbagnano provided a strikingly novel interpretation of the period. He began by addressing some moot problems in Renaissance scholarship: First was the traditionally maintained opposition between the Middle Ages (transcendence) and the Renaissance (immanence), which he rapidly dismissed with reference to updated bibliography. Second, and more important to him, was the opposition supported by idealist historiography between humanism—understood as an epoch of transition between Petrarch and the Neoplatonist Marsilio Ficino—in which medieval transcendence is not resolutely overcome and the Renaissance proper of the sixteenth century in which "the value of man's individuality and of the truth of scientific research is defended."[111]

If this contrast has had the benefit of endowing humanism with that philosophical relevance the Risorgimento had denied it, it nevertheless continues to undervalue the universal contribution of Quattrocento thought for all epochs, as well as the essential unity (for the two were never truly reconciled by the idealist) of 'humanism,' which continued to be identified with the Quattrocento, and 'Renaissance,' which was synonymous with the Cinquecento. In other words, and as future scholarship

110. Nicola Abbagnano, *Bernardino Telesio* (Milan: Bocca, 1941). Interestingly, this book was caustically reviewed by Eugenio Garin, whose interpretation of the Renaissance and historiographical principles, as we shall see in chapter 4, are akin to Abbagnano's. Garin's review is in *Giornale critico della filosofia italiana* 25 (1944–46): 180–83.

111. Nicola Abbagnano, *Bernardino Telesio e la filosofia del Rinascimento* (Milan: Garazanti, 1941), 4.

would confirm, in the early 1940s, an "interpretation of the true *historicity* of the Renaissance" and its humanism was still lacking. This problem, Abbagnano argued, may be broached and resolved by means of a firm grasp of humanism's supposed "cultism" with respect to antiquity from, expectedly, the perspective afforded by his positive existentialism.

Abbagnano pointed out that in the Quattrocento, antiquity is reborn neither as mere "repetition" nor in a new form, as something distinctively modern. Rather, the Renaissance "aims at uncovering what antiquity truly and authentically is qua antiquity": "Humanism's love for classical culture is precisely directed at this culture in its proper and specific form, in its historical authenticity. . . . In the Renaissance, for the first time, the history of man historicizes itself and establishes and justifies a historiographical attitude. *Humanism is this kind of historicization.*"[112] In Abbagnano, humanism is seen no longer as an epoch, the Quattrocento, but as that quintessential existential act, or movement, defined by a new "philological exigency" and "historiographical attitude" (*atteggiamento storiografico*). The discovery of individuality attributed to the Renaissance thus depends on a humanism that amounts to

> the discovery of man's individuality and personality, that is, his freedom as independence vis-à-vis nature, fate, fortune, and any force directed to bend his will; all of those attitudes and values, that is, that refer to individuality find their center and justification in humanism, inasmuch as dignity, freedom, and independence may be grasped only as attributes of an individuality. . . . Yet individuality is such only by means of the very act by which it defines itself vis-à-vis other individualities and thus vis-à-vis its very own past. The importance that Renaissance individuality acquired is a byproduct of the humanistic attitude; for we know ourselves only after having recognized others in their own specificity, only after having determined other personalities in their own genuine historicity.[113]

Here Abbagnano personalized the Renaissance by affirming that the "historiographical attitude" that strengthens and supports man's structural coherence was a firm conquest of the Renaissance. Paraphrasing the title of Sartre's well-known 1946 existential pamphlet *Existentialism Is a*

---

112. Abbagnano, *Bernardino Telesio e la filosofia del Rinascimento*, 8.
113. Abbagnano, *Bernardino Telesio e la filosofia del Rinascimento*, 13.

Humanism, Abbagnano may be said to have supported the idea, one that would gain large currency among some of his Italian peers, that (Italian or positive) existentialism is an (Italian Renaissance) humanism.

CONCLUSION

Even though Abbagnano's philosophy represented the most systematic renegotiation of the Gentilean theory/praxis nexus, it was uncertain at the time whether it could amount to anything more than a rigorous intellectual exercise. The revisionism advocated by positive existentialism was relegated to the field of philosophical historiography and therefore remained a strictly academic matter unable to bridge that gap between life and science denounced by De Sanctis. In the conclusion to a 1944 self-portrait, Abbagnano himself admitted to the practical inadequacy of his thought by pledging to work hard in the future at concretely applying in society his theorization of humankind's commitment to "existential finitude" and "coexistential freedom" in view of a philosophical and political rebirth.[114]

In Eugenio Garin's assessment, philosophical solipsism, intellectual egotism, and moral egoism were in fact still standing in the way of a "humanistically" conceived society at the time of Italy's positive transfiguration of German existentialism:

> In Italy, philosophical debate of the nonacademic and nonevasive type was starved of a full-bodied, mundane, and truly human experience. It was hungry for things, for humanly carried out works that were tangible, beyond a worn-out rhetoric. It was hungry for freedom, a freedom not preached but experienced according to its rightful boundaries, a freedom that was defended against constant acts of negation and cultural and political tyranny. It was hungry for a society of men, beyond the modifications of the master/servant nexus, according to a collaborative coexistence. Some would say that what was needed was a humanism. (*CFI*, 2:470)

Was the socialization of philosophy at all possible during the conjoined 'dictatorship' of actual idealism and Fascist politics? Was there a conversa-

---

114. Nicola Abbagnano, "Metafisica ed esistenza," in *Filosofi italiani contemporanei*, ed. M. F. Sciacca (Como: Marzorati, 1944), 24–25. The collection includes midlife testaments by, among others, Castelli and Spirito.

tion to be had, moreover, between France, Germany, and Italy in the inter-war period in spite of the solitary monologues of master thinkers; or was it necessarily to be postponed until after World War II?

The staggering proliferation of philosophies notwithstanding, cultural initiatives aimed at fostering some sense of professional and civil solidarity continued to be direly yearned for in the lower (that is, younger) tiers of the philosophical establishment. The belief was that through their aggregation, existentialism and (Renaissance) humanism could be saved from their bookish retreat and restored to a sense of duty to action. This goal was adamantly pursued by itinerant philosopher Ernesto Grassi, whose life and practical initiatives, moreover, offer a unique vantage point from which to assess the predisposition of European thinkers to transnational and interdisciplinary exchange.

CHAPTER THREE

Averting the End of Tradition:
Ernesto Grassi

This past, to which our lectures are seeking access, is nothing detached from us, lying far away. On the contrary, we are this past itself. . . . To understand history cannot mean anything else than to understand ourselves—not in the sense that we might establish various things about ourselves, but that we experience what we *ought* to be. To appropriate a past means to come to know oneself as indebted to that past. The authentic possibility to *be* history itself resides in this, that philosophy discover it is guilty of an omission, a neglect, if it believes it can begin anew, make things easy for itself, and let itself be stirred by just any random philosopher.
—Martin Heidegger

INTRODUCTION

When a disillusioned and novelty-craving Ernesto Grassi (1902–91) took off for two edifying tours of France and Germany in 1927 (a year after the Fascist sabotage of the Milan conference), he could not have anticipated that a chance turn of events would have prevented him from ever settling back in his native country.[1] Grassi, who was the first Ital-

---

1. Grassi's forays into Germany were certainly facilitated by his being born of a German mother and raised bilingual. For a thorough account of Grassi's youth, see *EG*, chap. 1. This important recent book has unearthed a prodigious amount of information regarding Grassi's activities up until ca. 1946. I was pleased to note that Büttemeyer's thorough contextualization supports my own accounts of Grassi's philosophical development, also based on a close reading of Grassi's early works, which resulted in two publications (2008 and 2009). In refining my interpretation of Grassi in this chapter, I am also indebted to other, though sometimes botched,

170

ian to be attracted to what Hannah Arendt qualified as the "rumor of the Hidden King," followed Heidegger to Freiburg in 1928 and, throughout the 1930s, went on to establish himself, unofficially, as a cultural attaché to Germany. Eventually, in 1945, he took shelter in Switzerland, where he doggedly resumed his teaching and editorial activities before returning to Germany in 1948, where he held an honorary chair at the University of Munich, to found one of the first international cultural institutions of the postwar period, the still standing Italian Center for Humanist and Philosophical Studies.[2] Eventually growing unhappy with his position in Germany and with the Italian academy's neglect of his achievements, he accepted the challenge to 'evangelize' the *studia humanitatis* in faraway Chile (1951–55); then, following a rather fortuitous encounter with editor Ernst Rowohlt (1887–1960), he again settled in Germany to direct a number of series of low-priced scientific pocketbooks intended for mass consumption: "Rowohlts deutsche Enzyklopädie" (1955–78), "Rowohlts Klassiker der Literatur und der Wissenschaft" (1957–78), and the "rororo studium series" (1970–78).[3] After retiring from his long tenure at the University of

---

attempts at a comprehensive grasp of Grassi's life and work. See Eberhard Bons, *Der Philosoph Ernesto Grassi: Integratives Denken, Antirationalismus, Vico-Interpretation* (Munich: Wilhelm Fink, 1990); Luigi Russo, ed., *Un filosofo europeo: Ernesto Grassi* (Palermo: Centro Internazionale Studi di Estetica, 1996); Emilio Hidalgo-Serna and Massimo Marassi, eds., *Studi in memoria di Ernesto Grassi*, 2 vols. (Naples: La Città del Sole, 1996); Robert J. Kozljanič, *Kunst und Mythos: Lebensphilosophische Untersuchungen zu Ernesto Grassis Begriff der Urwirklichkeit* (Oldenburg: Igel Verlag, 2001); Robert J. Kozljanič, *Ernesto Grassi: Leben und Denken* (Munich: Fink, 2003); and Rita Messori, *Le forme dell'apparire: Estetica, ermeneutica e umanesimo nel pensiero di Ernesto Grassi* (Palermo: Centro Internazionale Studi di Estetica, 2001).

2. This center is still associated with the University of Munich and has since been renamed "Seminar für Geistesgeschichte und Philosophie der Renaissance." Keßler notes that according to the original plan, the center also meant to make up for the loss of the Warburg Institute and its famous library, which was forced to relocate to London in the 1930s. See Eckhard Keßler, "L'attività di Ernesto Grassi all'Università di Monaco di Baviera dal 1948 al 1974," in Hidalgo-Serna and Marassi, *Studi in memoria*, 1:229. See also Keßler "Ernesto Grassi e il 'Seminario di storia delle idee e di filosofia dell'umanesimo' (1948–1974)," *Il Protagora* 35 (2007): 315–31; and Marta N. D. von Schwerin, "Gli anni di fondazione e la prima attività promossa dal 'Centro Italiano di Studi Umanistici e Filosofici' di Monaco: Un Ricordo," in *Studi in memoria*, 1:211–23.

3. See Joaquín Barceló, "Ernesto Grassi e la sua esperienza sudamericana," in Hidalgo-Serna and Marassi, *Studi in memoria*, 1:241–54. Grassi also produced a fascinating philosophical travelogue of his South American experience. See Ernesto Grassi, *Reisen ohne anzukommen: Südamerikanische Meditationen* (Hamburg: Rowohlt, 1955). For Grassi's editorial activity in postwar Germany, see Michael Neher, "Ernesto Grassi curatore della *rowohlts deutsche enzyclopädie*: Radici critico-culturali, programmi e primi inizi," in *Studi in memoria*, 1:255–87. Grassi accidently met prominent editor Ernst Rowohlt during a stormy night on a German highway. Rowohlt's car had stalled and Grassi rushed to offer his assistance. During the storm, the two discussed the spiritual rehabilitation of German culture and

Munich in 1973, he launched the experimental "Zürcher Gespräche" (Zurich conversations), a cycle of privately funded international discussions across the humanities/science divide, and finally landed on U.S. soil where he went on to enrich rhetorical and Vico, albeit regrettably not so much Heidegger and Renaissance, studies.[4]

In light of the self-enclosed identity of Italian philosophy described so far, Grassi's thoroughly international curriculum is bound to stand out. He, too, however, was at first an Italian thinker of his time, that is, an 'importer.' To be sure, Grassi removed himself from Italy in order to satisfy his curiosity as well as to forage for new material in an attempt to update Italy's obsolete records. A position as foreign correspondent was a fascinating way for a young thinker to make a name for himself, despite the suspicion it could give rise to with, for example, such eminent figures as Jaspers, Heidegger, or even Hans Deichmann, who viewed Grassi as "the master of disguise."[5] Yet, if Grassi greatly benefited from a refreshing international exposure, his incursions into classrooms and distinguished philosophers' offices soon led him to realize how little was known abroad

people. By the end of their conversation, Rowohlt was convinced he had found a worthy editor for his press. As for the then demoralized Grassi, this was a lifesaving encounter. See his dedication in Ernesto Grassi, *Die Theorie des Schönen in der Antike* (Cologne: M. DuMont Schauberg, 1962), 7: "Dem unvergeßlichen Freund ERNST ROWOHLT zum Gedächtnis in der Erinnerung an einen Winterspaziergang bei dem er mir das Leben rettete." I am indebted to Emilio Hidalgo-Serna for this anecdote and reference.

4. See Donald P. Verene, "A Note on the *Zürcher Gespräche* (Zurich discourses): Zurich, Switzerland, 1976–1980," *Philosophy and Rhetoric* 14 (1981): 66–68; Vittorio Mathieu, "I temi di Grassi nei 'Colloqui Zurighesi,'" in Hidalgo-Serna and Marassi, *Studi in memoria*, 1:305–14; and Hugo Schmale, "Lo spirito dei 'Colloqui Zurighesi,'" in *Studi in memoria*, 1: 315–23. The proceedings from some of these encounters are published. See Ernesto Grassi and Hugo Schmale, eds., *Das Gespräch als Ereignis: Ein semiotisches Problem* (Munich: Wilhelm Fink, 1982); Ernesto Grassi and Hugo Schmale, eds., *Anspruch und Widerspruch* (Munich: Wilhelm Fink, 1987); and Ernesto Grassi and Hugo Schmale, eds., *Arbeit und Gelassenheit: Zwei Grundformen des Umgangs mit Natur* (Munich: Wilhelm Fink, 1994). Grassi made a name for himself in the United States principally through translations of his German works on Renaissance humanism, his interpretation of Vico, and his long-standing collaboration with the journal *Philosophy and Rhetoric*. See Donald P. Verene, "Grassi in America," in *Studi in memoria*, 1:289–303.

5. See *EG*, 367. After meeting Grassi, Heidegger voiced his qualms in a letter to Jaspers (10 February 1928): "Herr Dr. Grassi machte im ersten Augenblick durch seine Intensität und ein gewisses Verständnis Eindruck. Ich bin aber zweifelhaft geworden, wie weit das nicht eine im Grunde journalistische Natur ist, die nach dem dernier cri fahndet." Martin Heidegger and Karl Jaspers, *Briefwechsel 1920–1963*, ed. Walter Biemel and Hans Saner (Frankfurt: Klostermann, 1990), 86. To which Jaspers responded (12 February 1928): "Dr. Grassi hat mir in der Folge denselben Eindruck gemacht wie Ihnen. Gibt man ihm den kleinen Finger, will er einen gleich ganz auffressen. Aber es bleibt erstaunlich, wie geradezu er philosophische Dinge auffaßt. Er ist ein glänzender Interviewer" (*Briefwechsel*, 88–89).

of the Italian philosophical ferment, old and new. The international community's neglect of Italy immediately spurred Grassi to refashion himself into a pioneering 'exporter' of Italian culture as well, and to this day he remains unmatched in that enterprise. This is evident as early as his stay in Aix-en-Provence, the first leg in his 1927 journey, where he went to meet with Maurice Blondel, whose 'philosophy of action,' as we have seen, Grassi's recently befriended and soon-to-be collaborator Enrico Castelli had employed to deprovincialize Italian philosophy.[6] At that time, he had hoped to urge the French thinker into a sustained confrontation with Gentile, but Blondel's ignorance of contemporary Italian philosophy forced Grassi to spend his time tutoring him in actual idealism.[7]

A more telling anecdote Grassi often related in the attempt to account for his uncharacteristic formation concerns one of his preliminary incursions into Germany.[8] One of his top priorities was to score a hearing with an aging Edmund Husserl (1859–1938), by whom he was received after being carefully vetted by the philosopher's wife. The Italian must have favorably impressed the German philosopher, who, as Grassi recalls, concluded the meeting with a flattering remark: "Young man, as an Italian you are already predestined to philosophy. Work peacefully, without haste, and you will reach the goal." Urged to elaborate, he added that the reason for this preordained success was that "Italians, unlike Germans, do not start out from abstract and a priori assumptions and do not rely on historical schemata; rather with your philosophical sense for the concrete

6. Grassi announced his trip to Castelli and asked him for recommendations in a letter dated 3 March 1927: "Il 25 marzo avrei intenzione di partire per Aix. Sono molto inquieto anche a questo riguardo: non vi conosco nessuno, non so se potrò essere in contatto con Blondel, non so se questo viaggio sarà veramente fruttifero. Cosa credi? Senti ti pregherei *caldamente* di farmi avere una lettera proprio un po' speciale per potermi presentare a Blondel e in cui si dica che desidero frequentare le sue lezioni ed essere un po' in contatto con lui e volermi accogliere con benevolenza e come giovane che non desidera altro che studiare. Se quindi fosse anche possibile facilitarmi l'uso delle biblioteche di Aix e la conoscenza di qualsiasi professore che ha attinenza coi nostri studi" (APEC).

7. In a letter (27 April 1927) to Paul Archambault, another philosopher that Grassi was eager to meet, Blondel recommended the young Italian with the following words: "J'ai en ce moment à Aix un jeune professeur italien, Ernesto Grassi, Docteur de l'Université C[atholique] de Milan qui vient étudier la philosophie de l'Action pour la différencier de la doctrine de Gentile et l'actualisme italien qui nous exploitent illégitimement et dangereusement. Il ira ensuite à Paris où il désire vous voir. Je le recommande à votre accueil car il me paraît vraiment intelligent et il peut rendre à notre cause catholique de très précieux services" (cited in *EG*, 80n34). See also Blondel's letter (10 May 1927) to Joannès Wehrlé (cited in *EG*, 81n40).

8. Büttemeyer notes that Grassi's encounter with Husserl may not be precisely dated (*EG*, 78). Nevertheless, it is certain that Grassi participated in Husserl's last seminar in Freiburg—"Phänomenologie der Einfühlung"—during the winter semester of 1928–29 (*EG*, 120).

you get straight to the phenomena." When the baffled Grassi informed his interlocutor that Italians were in fact diehard Hegelians—rather than, it could be added, natural or protophenomenologists—Husserl quipped: "Son, if indeed you have been raised in such a context, then you are lost and have no hope."[9] This encounter could be expected to strongly resonate with a self-conscious representative of a generation whose goal was to return philosophy to lived life. Earlier than Abbagnano, Grassi realized that Italy's escape from the Hegelian prison house could be facilitated by German means—phenomenology and existentialism, above all—a cognizance that he rushed to disseminate by composing one of the first assessments of Heidegger in Italy, which Gentile accepted for publication in his *Giornale critico della filosofia italiana* in 1930.[10]

Equally important, eventually, was to instruct Europeans regarding Italian thought, starting with its strongest currency—the Renaissance. To this end, Grassi honed his entrepreneurial ability, as the popularization of a foreign legacy in Nazi Germany could be achieved only by means of a skillfully planned and apparently unobtrusive complex of editions, translations, and ad hoc venues for debate and exchange. Grassi's crowning achievement in this respect was the foundation of the Italian institute "Studia Humanitatis" in Berlin, which may have marked the height of the cultural collaboration between the Italian and German regimes.[11] In fact,

9. Ernesto Grassi, *Einführung in philosophische Probleme des Humanismus* (Darmstadt: Wissenschaftliche Buchgesellschaft, 1986), 3–4. The same story is told in different words in Ernesto Grassi, *Rhetoric as Philosophy: The Humanist Tradition*, trans. J. M. Krois and A. Azodi (University Park: Pennsylvania State University Press, 1980), 2–3.

10. See Ernesto Grassi, "Il problema della metafisica immanente di M. Heidegger," in *PS*, 203–28. The only precedent to Grassi's sustained interest in introducing Heidegger and existentialism in Italy is Giulio Grasselli, "La fenomenologia di Husserl e l'ontologia di Martin Heidegger," *Rivista di filosofia* 19 (1928): 330–47. A year earlier, Grassi had already published two survey articles dedicated to the latest developments in German philosophy. See Ernesto Grassi, "Empirismo e naturalismo nella filosofia tedesca contemporanea (*PS*, 63–179); and "Sviluppo e significato della scuola fenomenologica tedesca contemporanea" (*PS*, 181–202). Grassi finally reworked his early essays on German philosophy in a more comprehensive book. See Ernesto Grassi, *Dell'apparire e dell'essere: Seguito da Linee della filosofia tedesca contemporanea* (Florence: La Nuova Italia, 1933). This book interestingly compares with contemporaneous attempts to make sense of Heidegger in France. See, for example, Georges Gurvitch, *Les tendances actuelles de la philosophie allemande: E. Husserl, M. Scheler, E. Lask, M. Heidegger* (Paris: J. Vrin, 1930). For a thorough survey of the use and abuse of Heidegger's *Being and Time* in Italy during the interwar period, see Roberto Tommasi, *"Essere e Tempo" di Martin Heidegger in Italia (1928–1948)* (Rome: Pontificio Seminario Lombardo, 1993).

11. See *EG*, 296–337. See also Marcello Simonetta, "Filosofia e potere: Su Ernesto Grassi," *Intersezioni* 15 (1995): 463–71; Romke Visser, "Da Atene a Roma, da Roma a Berlino: L'Istituto di Studi Romani, il culto fascista della romanitas e la 'difesa dell'umanesimo' di Giuseppe Bottai (1936–1943)," in *Antike und Altertumswissenschaft in der Zeit von Faschismus und*

this feat of *Kulturpolitik*, which Grassi, together with his friend Castelli, undertook to ensure some degree of autonomy for Italian culture in Nazi Germany, came at the price of a compromise with ministers Giuseppe Bottai and Bernhard Rust. Presented with the project to create a venue for the study of the Italian Renaissance legacy in Germany's capital city, Mussolini himself allegedly commented, "But how can this be accomplished?!"[12] Impractical as it may have been, the institute was dutifully inaugurated (without official headquarters) on 7 December 1942, on the threshold of an epochal catastrophe. After the war, all that Grassi was left with was the unwavering conviction of the enduring worth of Italian Renaissance humanism for modernity. By then, he had come to appreciate the validity of Husserl's offhanded evaluation, for he had acquired the wherewithal to personally guarantee that the Italian way of philosophizing was not 'German' in any Hegelian sense.

This brief survey of Grassi's accomplishments and aspirations, which entailed the building of a global network, begins to explain how he alone with Castelli could succeed in putting together an international conference at very short notice in the immediate postwar period. More important, it alerts one to the conceivable, though as yet disregarded, implications of Heidegger's resolution to entrust his "Letter on 'Humanism'" to the foremost advocate for the Italian humanist legacy in Germany. The general neglect of Grassi's work in Heidegger studies is certainly due to the reliance of most scholars on the readily available works of his late career, which make for a skewed perspective.[13] By focusing on the interpretation of humanism Grassi put forth in the 1980s, scholars create the perception that, though intriguing, his work may have been an idiosyncratic

---

Nationalsozialismus, ed. Beat Näf (Mandelbachtal: Edition Cicero, 2001), 111–23; Domenico Pietropaolo, "Giuseppe Bottai e la fondazione dell'*Istituto Studia Humanitatis*," in Hidalgo-Serna and Marassi, *Studi in memoria*, 1:193–210; Michela Dongu, "La difesa della tradizione umanistica: L'Istituto 'Studia Humanitatis,'" *Giornale critico della filosofia italiana* 87 (2008): 307–31. For corrections to the previous, see Wilhelm Büttemeyer, "Rettifiche: Laurea, libera docenza e 'Studia Humanitatis' di Ernesto Grassi," *Giornale critico della filosofia italiana* 89 (2010): 148–76; and Frank-Rutger Hausmann, "Italienischer und deutscher Humanismus im Widerstreit: Zur Gründung des Berliner Instituts 'Studia Humanitatis' im Jahr 1942," in *Spiele um Grenzen: Germanistik zwischen Weimarer und Berliner Republik*, ed. Gerhard Kaiser and Jens Saadhoff (Heidelberg: Synchron, 2009), 109–47.

12. Giuseppe Bottai, *Diario 1935–1944* (Milan: Rizzoli, 1982), 284.

13. In particular, *Rhetoric as Philosophy: Heidegger and the Question of Renaissance Humanism—Four Studies*, trans. U. Hemel and J. M. Krois (Binghamton, NY: Center for Medieval and Early Renaissance Studies, 1983); *Renaissance Humanism: Studies in Philosophy and Poetics*, trans. W. F. Veit (Binghamton, NY: Center for Medieval and Early Renaissance Studies, 1988); and *Vico and Humanism: Essays on Vico, Heidegger and Rhetoric* (New York: Peter Lang, 1990).

reaction to the antihumanism developed by Heidegger and in Heidegger's French reception. To the contrary, as Grassi took pains to explain in his introductions, his late works harkened back with renewed conviction to the conclusions he had reached in the 1940s *in collaboration*, or so he believed, with his mentor.

A case in point is a book Grassi published in the immediate postwar period, significantly titled *Defense of Individual Life: Studia Humanitatis as Philosophical Tradition* (1946), in which he definitively reworked his scattered thoughts on the Renaissance.[14] This study, to whose contents we shall have to return in detail, appeared in a series—"Überlieferung und Auftrag" (Tradition and Mission)—that Grassi edited in Switzerland together with Heidegger's onetime preferred student, Jewish-Hungarian philosopher Wilhelm Szilasi (1889–1966).[15] These publications embodied the at once theoretical and practical understanding of 'humanism' that Grassi had acquired by the end of the war. According to the aims and scope of the series,

> A living tradition clarifies the present by means of a worthwhile inter-pretation of the past and of "Bildung" according to its precise sense as humanism, which attends to the education [*Erziehung*] of man in his totality. Accordingly, antiquity as well as the Renaissance can again in a lively and fruitful way come to the rescue of the present spiritual collapse of the European world. What is at stake is that philosophical and historical consciousness which, through a critical confrontation [*Auseinandersetzung*] with antiquity, has time and again shaped Euro-pean spiritual life.

Grassi elaborated on his editorial intentions in the preface to the first work to appear in the series in 1945. He traced the present Western mal-aise back to the Enlightenment, a period in which, in his view, the claims to "objectivity" of the natural sciences (*Naturwissenschaften*) first gained predominance over the formative qualities of the humanities (*Geisteswis-senschaften*), with grave results for the appreciation of Quattrocento hu-

14. Ernesto Grassi, *Verteidigung des individuellen Lebens : Studia Humanitatis als philosophische Überlieferung* (Bern: A. Francke, 1946).

15. According to Grassi's account, Heidegger cherished Szilasi as one of his most sym-pathetic students until his turn to Nazism. See Grassi's heartfelt dedication to Szilasi in *Macht des Bildes: Ohnmacht der rationale Sprache. Zur Rettung des Rhetorischen* (Cologne: DuMont Schauberg, 1970), 9–12.

manism—ever since misunderstood as a solitarily conducted and sterile admiration and imitation of classical antiquity.

With the publications he sponsored, Grassi sought to challenge such a nefarious devaluation of tradition and both to refurbish the humanities' claim to objective knowledge and to emphasize their constructive or "future-oriented task."[16] Grassi maintained that interpretation or hermeneutics also has a claim to "objective unity" when, in a genuinely Renaissance fashion, one is trained to approach the text divested of linguistic or conceptual presuppositions: "To read means first of all to learn how to keep silent before a text, to avoid concealing it with our feelings and thoughts."[17] To read a text with such "feelings and thoughts" amounts to "dilettantism" and a "spiritual barbarism," and, in Grassi's view, mid-twentieth-century Europe direly needed to reexperience the Renaissance, and not in any figurative sense.

It should be noted at this point that Grassi's interpretation of humanism as a vivifying hermeneutical practice originally owed more to his Heideggerian training than to the study of Renaissance sources. Even though it was his reading of *Being and Time*—which was published in 1927, a year before their acquaintance in Marburg—that induced Grassi to seek out Heidegger, it was only once he attended one of Heidegger's famously inspiring seminars that he was convinced he had found a teacher worth sticking with and, in due time, a Renaissance humanism redivivus.[18] In fact, when corresponding with his friends and mentors, Grassi was first and foremost keen to relate that he had found a teacher whose reading method allowed for a novel understanding of ancient philosophy.[19]

16. Ernesto Grassi, "Geleitwort zum Ersten Band," in Romano Guardini, *Der Tod des Sokrates: Eine Interpretation der Platonischen Schriften Euthyphron, Apologie, Kriton und Phaidon* (Bern: A. Francke, 1945), 7. Grassi elaborates here on what he had just recently published in a collaborative volume. See Thure von Uexküll and Ernesto Grassi, *Wirklichkeit als Geheimnis und Auftrag* (Bern: A. Francke, 1945).

17. Grassi, "Geleitwort zum Ersten Band," 9.

18. Jaspers had originally recommended Grassi to Heidegger as a well-versed reader of *Being and Time* (14 January 1928): "Der Überbringer dieses Briefes, Dr. Grassi aus Mailand, möchte Sie gern persönlich sprechen. Er studiert deutsche Philosophie, hat Ihr Buch gelesen und weiß darin überraschend Bescheid—natürlich mit Mißverständnissen durch die Tradition, aber zugleich mit erstaunlicher Nähe. Ich glaube, Sie werden Freude haben an dem lebendigen Interesse, und an den klaren Fragen, die er stellt." Heidegger and Jaspers, *Briefwechsel*, 85.

19. See, for example, Grassi to Castelli (18 November 1928): "Mi sono fissato a Friburgo, perché durante le mie peregrinazioni germaniche nell'anno scorso ho trovato in M. Heidegger uno dei più interessanti pensatori contemporanei. Proveniente dal cattolicesimo, che oggi ha però abbandonato, riassume quanto di fecondo e interessante c'è nella storia della fil[osofia]

Therefore, even though his path intersected Heidegger's career just as the "rumor" concerning a pedagogue was transforming into a lasting fame, Grassi may be numbered among "Heidegger's children"—those early students who enjoyed the "privileged proximity" and esoteric initiation afforded by the seminars and who, after the Nazi affair, "sought to philosophize *with Heidegger against Heidegger.*"[20]

In dealing with his teacher's powerful legacy, however, Grassi faced a predicament and a set of prejudices that were wholly different from those faced by his Jewish colleagues. The so-called *Kehre*, or turn, that Heidegger's philosophy is said to have taken with the "Letter on 'Humanism'" amounted to a personal disavowal of what had become Grassi's mission— the philosophical rehabilitation of Italian Renaissance humanism. In his recollections, Grassi noted that his teacher's radical philhellenism and correlated anti-Romanitas bias had bothered him since his first years as a lecturer in Freiburg, when he often traced this Heideggerian prejudice back to Hegel's own in discussion with other concerned "Latin" students, such as José Ortega y Gasset (1883–1955) and José Xavier Zubiri (1898– 1983).[21] Among the notable representatives of this generation of firsthand Heideggerians, nevertheless, Grassi best compares to Hans-Georg Gadamer (1900–2002). In an assessment of Gadamer's philosophy, Vico scholar Donald P. Verene pointed out that besides Ernst Cassirer, "Gadamer is the only thinker of the first order in twentieth-century German philosophy to involve Vico as part of the basis of his thought." And if, as Verene claims, "to study Vico is to study humanism and to study what humanism is,"

---

tedesca degli ultimo 40 anni e sviluppando criticamente la fenomenologia di Husserl e il problema della comprensione storica di Dilthey ha elaborato un pensiero immanentistico dei più interessanti. . . . Sono felice di essere qui, perché ho in lui uno splendido maestro: i suoi seminari su Aristotele, Kant, ecc. sono una scuola e insegnano un metodo di lavoro critico interessantissimo e fecondissimo" (APEC).

20. Richard Wolin, *Heidegger's Children: Hannah Arendt, Karl Löwith, Hans Jonas, and Herbert Marcuse* (Princeton: Princeton University Press, 2001), 8.

21. Ernesto Grassi, "L'antiumanesimo e il nazionalsocialismo di Heidegger: A proposito del libro di Farías," *Intersezioni* 8, no. 2 (1988): 347. In another autobiographical account, Grassi specified: "Heidegger, ad esempio, nel suo giudizio su Cicerone rimaneva fermo agli schemi tradizionali, prevalentemente dominati dalla interpretazione hegeliana che, di fatto, si riduceva ad un giudizio radicalmente negativo, anzi polemico. Se l'occasione si presentava, Heidegger non mancava di formulare giudizi sprezzanti sull'incapacità speculativa del mondo latino, sempre da lui visto in funzione dei problemi del pensiero greco. Riecheggiavano in lui i giudizi di Hegel dei quali ricordo solo il seguente su Cicerone; il suo pensiero appartiene alla 'filosofia' popolare, cioè egli è incapace di elevarsi dal particolare all'universale." Ernesto Grassi, "Politica e religione: La riscoperta della tradizione latina," *Archivio di filosofia* 57 (1978): 33–43.

Gadamer may count among the few Continental philosophers not to have shared in Heidegger's unwarranted antihumanism.[22] Similarly, Jean Grondin, Gadamer's biographer, maintains that the question concerning "humanism" is a test to determine "why and at what point a Heideggerian such as a Gadamer ceases to be a Heideggerian." According to Grondin, Gadamer's 1960 *Truth and Method* should certainly be read as a rejoinder to Heidegger's "Letter on 'Humanism.'" "To put the thesis bluntly," he writes, "Gadamer is a humanist and Heidegger isn't."[23]

A careful analysis of Grassi's early philosophical development—which, as we shall see, unfurled side by side with Gadamer's for some time—substantiates as well as complicates the assumption that the question of 'humanism' may function as some sort of litmus test to determine the degree of one's Heideggerianism. As is already evident from his postwar editorial activities, which displayed a premature grasp of what in the 1960s became associated with the Gadamerian notion of the "fusion of horizons" (*Horizontverschmelzung*), Grassi was instead convinced (as Gadamer may have been at that time) that Heidegger's hermeneutics were through and through a (Renaissance) 'humanism.'

This chapter explores the Italian, French, and German sources of Grassi's formation in an attempt to show how in the immediate postwar period he could come to sponsor continuity, if not straightforward identification, between Italian Quattrocento and Heideggerian hermeneutical ventures. Insight into Grassi's work and intentions sheds new light on the forces at play in the "Letter on 'Humanism,'" which was handed to Grassi and, as Heidegger could very well have expected, went on to be published in 1947 in the same series Germany's mastermind had largely inspired with his seminars and in which Grassi himself had just put forth his pioneering philosophical apology for Renaissance humanism. Despite some warning signs, Heidegger's resolutely anti- or, better, posthumanist turn of 1947 certainly sent a shock down Grassi's spine, who also rushed to publish, in the same series and in the same year, a long overdue and philologically unimpeachable account of Italian Quattrocento thought: Eugenio Garin's *Italian Humanism*. Thus framed between Grassi's and Garin's endeavors (which are explored in the next chapter), Heidegger's mani-

22. Donald P. Verene, "Gadamer and Vico on Sensus Communis and the Tradition of Human Knowledge," in *The Philosophy of Hans-Georg Gadamer*, ed. Lewis E. Hahn (Chicago: Open Court, 1997), 138.

23. Jean Grondin, "Gadamer on Humanism," in Hahn, *Philosophy of Hans-Georg Gadamer*, 157. See also Gadamer's reply to Grondin (171–72).

festo may be read beyond its overt addressees: Jean Beaufret and, through him, the French philosophical community headed by Sartre. The Italian-oriented contextualization proposed here allows for a closer assessment of Heidegger's instrumental role in supporting a younger generation's overcoming of Gentile's actual idealism, as already outlined in the discussion of Abbagnano, as well as his responsibilities in at once encouraging and debunking, via Grassi specifically, original scholarship on Italian Renaissance humanism.

BETWEEN ITALY AND FRANCE:
A CHRISTIAN THINKER'S DISCONTENTS

Grassi's student days and early professional career afford a survey of interwar Italian philosophy. Born and raised in Milan, which a newly founded Catholic University turned into the stronghold of Neothomism in the early 1920s, Grassi studied with and for a short period adhered to the cause of Agostino Gemelli, Gentile's nemesis, and that of less radical scholastics. He was then attracted when he was in Milan to the *super partes* outsider Piero Martinetti, the organizer of the infamous 1926 philosophical conference, and, like most of his generation of thinkers, he engaged (mostly from afar) in a love-hate relationship with the neo-idealism of Croce and especially Gentile, whose actualism Grassi, too, like Abbagnano, came to admire as a challenging conclusion to Western philosophy. Throughout an intense decade of philosophical experimentation, Grassi was after a reconciliation of philosophy and religion, immanence and transcendence—one that he eventually attained in successively subsuming Gentile, Blondel, and Heidegger (three anti-Platonists) under the banner of the unconventional Platonism he developed in his first book published in 1932. Given that Grassi came to identify his brand of Platonism with (Renaissance) humanism, the twists and turns attending this early philosophical revelation deserve some introduction.

In one of his earliest scholarly endeavors from 1923—"Scholasticism and History: Regarding Two Articles of G. Saitta"—Grassi provided a first display of philosophical partisanship. He came to the rescue of Neothomism against, ironically, the attacks of Giuseppe Saitta, Gentile's uncompromising crony, whose glorification of Renaissance humanism only Grassi, in the history of Italian philosophy, would come to match, albeit from a different perspective. In keeping with the idealists' usual refrain, Saitta had argued that a return to past philosophies (to already established truths) makes any further thinking futile and deprives philosophy of its constitutive feature: freedom (*PS*, 50).[24] Intent on clarifying the role and aims of Thomism's view of history, Grassi responded by affirming that only when maintaining a correlated set of distinctions between different planes of reality—immanence and transcendence, history and divine providence—is philosophy allowed historical development:

> The history of philosophy is not a compound of cold and dead systematizations of reality but the lively coming into being of problems, whose solution—given that truth is not immanent—will always leave residual elements which present themselves as a new series of problems. These problems cannot be solved by the philosophical position that engendered them, because they are born of the insufficiency of the solution itself: therefore, a new solution is generated, a new system, which will in turn generate more problems. (53)

In a young Grassi's view, belief in a transcendence that we forever strive for but never attain qualifies Scholasticism as an *integrative* philosophy: a true *perennis philosophia* that is more akin, in Grassi's own metaphor, to an ever adapting "organism" than to "a book whose last page is never written" (52).

On close inspection, in effect, Grassi was less keen to validate any form of idolatrous 'medievalism' than to argue that, owing to its teleological conceit, actual idealism had removed itself from the process of dialectical becoming and solidified into a self-serving dogmatism. Taking the stance of Neothomism, Grassi stated, "This understanding of history reveals the abyss that separates us from the idealists: while for them all that 'is' is true, for us all that 'is' is an instrument of truth, even if it is *false*: if a philosophy represents a moment in the dialectical conquest of truth, this does not imply that only that given moment [of philosophy] is true" (*PS*, 53). In the near future, to put it differently, actualism, too, will be numbered—as, Grassi avowed, had been the case for Thomism—among past, and thus false, philosophies, for such overcoming is inevitable.

In an essay from the same year, discussing the notion of tragedy in Greek and Christian thought, Grassi elaborated on his religious take on and understanding of "reason." He maintained that tragedy, as notion and form, allows one to grasp the ways in which human beings have grappled with the irrational element of reality: "Philosophy, life, and drama, are

---

24. For the two articles Grassi was reacting to, see Giuseppe Saitta, "Medievalismo e idealismo: Risposta ad un neoscolastico," *L'Arduo* 2, no. 2 (30 April 1922): 81–85; and Giuseppe Saitta, "Pensiero moderno e neoscolastica," *L'Arduo* 2, no. 3 (30 June 1922): 121–24.

expressions of a single activity, the manifestation of a rationality which is not yet explicitly posed" (*PS*, 27). In Grassi's view so-called irrationality is in fact a misnomer:

> If by *irrational* we mean the reality that *man* is incapable of subjugating and grasping for his present purposes [*attualmente*], either because (as is the case with the ancient transcendental school) it transcends *human intellect*, or (as with the modern school of immanence) because spirit does not yet fully possess itself, the term 'irrational' is improper. We assert, instead, that reality is always rational but sometimes it presents itself *implicitly*, that is, not yet totally comprehensibly, and other times explicitly or totally comprehensibly. Moreover, what appears irrational to us today will become explicit tomorrow. (29)

Through tragedy Grassi recovered two ways in which human beings come to terms with irrationality or the not yet rational. In Greek antiquity, the age of objectivism, human life was at the mercy of superior powers (gods, fate, etc.), while in modernity the individual copes with the irrational with no recourse to such forces. Yet, "in both understandings [ancient and modern]," Grassi adds, "life intended as an obligation toward a solution of reality that is unattainable appears to us as immensely tragic" (37).

The notion of Christian redemption offers a solution to both views:

> If, on the one hand, Christianity denies that which is individual, negates earthly life by turning it into a vain shadow, . . . on the other hand, it endows our immanent nature with value, for the earth is necessary to reach the sky—because, as in ancient Judaism, pain and struggle are expiation, but in Christianity they are essentially *redemption*: that is, the eternal concretized in historical "becoming," transcendence which finds value in immanence, God in man, the Savior. (37)

Christianity amounts to a *via media* beyond the radical transcendence of Greek thought and the equally radical immanence of modern philosophy by offering a synthesis in which, through the ultimate tragedy of Christ's death, "immanence is intimately and organically tied to transcendence," so that, from the perspective of the believer, life's pain becomes tolerable, that is, no longer "tragic."[25]

---

25. On the topic of human pathos and philosophy, see also Ernesto Grassi, "La dialettica dell'amore: Il dolore del Tristano," in *PS*, 89–128. Grassi's first essays were published in

These early essays, in which Grassi displayed some unease over impos-ing clear-cut caesurae on the Western philosophical tradition, also demon-strate that, at this time in his career, he seems to have been oblivious to the possibility of recovering a philosophical alternative tucked away be-tween the waning of the Middle Ages and the emergence of Cartesianism. Nevertheless, the Renaissance and its humanism did make a brief appear-ance in Grassi's early corpus. In a politically charged piece from 1924—"Machiavelli's Thought and the Origins of the Notion of the State"—a young Grassi, like many others, employed Machiavelli to take a swipe at Renaissance scholarship. Presumably relying on Spaventa and Gentile, Grassi described the epochal shift heralded by the Renaissance as a "nega-tion of transcendence" (PS, 61). At the same time, he retained from Burck-hardt a mixed feeling toward the indomitable individualism of humanism, which he described in Gentilean terms as the "cold ashes under which lie the brazing coals of the modern spirit" (62). On the other hand, De Sanc-tis and Villari alerted him to Machiavelli's role as a transitioning figure between humanism and the Renaissance proper, and finally—perhaps through Croce—he arrived at the original view that Machiavelli's notion of "effective truth" (verità effettuale) stands midway between humanism's "tragic" "affirmation of empirical individuality" and Vico's notion of the "ipsum verum factum," whereby history is finally conceived as the ratio-nal creation of humankind (66).[26]

Just like Spirito, but a full twenty years earlier, Grassi lamented the missed opportunity Machiavelli represented. If the Florentine secretary was to be commended for having been the first to overcome the "negative principle" imposed by humanist individualism, he also did not go far (or high) enough in establishing a new overarching principle that could re-store rationality to history. Obliquely refuting the Gentilean notion of the ethical state—the identity of individual and state—Grassi (like Castelli) condemned Machiavelli's and, in the reading of the time, Gentile's and Fascism's divinization of nation and fatherland. The philosopher's task, a young Grassi concluded, would thus be to return to Machiavelli's Re-

---

Rassegna nazionale. For Grassi's collaboration with this journal, see EG, 40–56; and A. Gian-nuzzi, "Ernesto Grassi e la 'Rassegna Nazionale' (1922–1925)," Il Protagora 35 (2007): 295–313.

26. This may be Grassi's first mention of Vico. It is unclear whether the Machiavelli-Vico connection was inspired by Croce (who goes unmentioned at this point in a heavily annotated essay), who that same year (1924) put forth a very influential and often reprinted essay en-titled "Machiavelli and Vico." For the English translation, see Benedetto Croce, "Machiavelli and Vico: Politics and Ethics," in Politics and Morals, trans. Salvatore J. Castiglione (New York: Philosophical Library, 1945), 44–50.

naissance in order to retrieve a higher, supranational principle in which humankind's immanent life and eternal values would once again coexist. For, of course, in history as in philosophy the last word had not yet and would never be spoken.

Before meeting Blondel and Heidegger, Grassi had introduced himself to the academic world as a Catholic thinker, as a moderate Neothomist beleaguered by the predicament of at once retaining transcendence and exalting the philosophical relevance of human pathos and irrationality. He also, from a political perspective, presented himself as an antifascist and, given the movement's ties to Gentilean idealism and, in turn, the latter's foundation in Renaissance thought, as a suspicious, though fascinated, spectator of Italy's early modernity.

Upon resuming his scholarly activity from abroad, Grassi appeared instantly rejuvenated. In 1928 he published a survey article titled "The Most Recent Developments of French Philosophy of Action." With the support of unpublished work, a flurry of personal letters, and snippets of private conversations, Grassi closely related the works of Léon Ollé-Laprune (1839–1898), Lucien Laberthonnière (1860–1932), Paul Archambault (1883–1950), and Blondel in an effort to present French philosophy of action as the best spiritual reaction in Europe to nineteenth-century positivism and materialism. To clearly frame the merits that he was willing to attribute to the movement that climaxed in Blondel, Grassi referred to Pope Leo XIII's famous encyclical *Aeterni Patris*, a document that, in his view, had been instrumental in inspiring a strict Thomism *as well as* a moderate strain in religious philosophy whose goal was "to prove that only by maintaining oneself *within the boundaries of lived life* and by keeping *in touch with the tradition of modern philosophy* would it be possible to effectively legitimize the religious stance" (*PS*, 138; emphasis added). Grassi's reference was to Catholic Modernism, and half a decade after his defense of Neothomism, he believed he could recover in Blondel a superior form of religious thinking that could be relevant to the present. Noting that at the time of his survey Blondel was very much engaged in refining his theories, Grassi also admitted to being unaware of any better solution.

Grassi, it is clear, was looking for a new, fully fledged philosophical paradigm, one that, given his talent for keeping abreast of philosophical novelties, he immediately found in Heidegger's *Being and Time*. In the two surveys of German contemporary philosophy Grassi provided in 1929, he had already introduced Heidegger as a "critic of Husserl's phenomenology" (*PS*, 187) and, as the author of *Duns Scotus's Theory of the*

Categories and of Meaning, a theologically savvy thinker. From a strictly German perspective, Grassi avowed, Heidegger no doubt represented the latest thing in the wake of Hegelianism's demise: after and in connection with Dilthey, Neo-Kantianism, Husserlian phenomenology, and so forth. Yet, in communicating his 'discovery' to Gentile, Grassi also described Heidegger as the promoter of a new metaphysics that fruitfully advanced the immanentist ambitions of Italian actualism.[27] Specifically, as Grassi revealed to the Italian philosophical community in an essay from 1930— "On M. Heidegger's Immanent Metaphysics"—the Heideggerian notion of *Dasein* turned philosophy into a metaphysics of actual existence and overcame the objectification of the self typical in the natural sciences, where "man is an object; that is, a being which is studied, classified, observed among others without his essence ever being probed."[28] To the contrary, in *Being and Time* the "problem of man" is finally analyzed uniquely according to its existential nature:

> [E]xistence conceived as a personal action, as a being which always co-
> incides with myself, is essentially an existential anxiety (*Besorgtheit*),
> a constant pointing to and struggle (*Sorge*) vis-à-vis the insufficiency of
> every given moment. Such transcendental insufficiency (*Bedürftigkeit*)
> corresponds to the fundamental finitude (*Endlichkeit*) that existence
> carries within itself in its own self-realization. (215)

Heidegger's metaphysics, a self-contained ontology, had divested modern philosophy of its epistemological straitjacket: thought and action were again on a par.

Therefore, at this point in the development of his philosophy, Grassi believed that Heidegger had not only advanced Gentile's cause but also beaten Blondel to the punch:

27. When submitting the article to Gentile (29 March 1930), Grassi wrote: "Heidegger domina oggi . . . tutta la filosofia tedesca . . . portandola molto vicina alle conclusioni e alle ricerche della nostra filosofia italiana immanentistica. [Heidegger è] il pensatore tedesco contemporaneo più importante e che più si avvicina all'indirizzo delle nostre ricerche. . . . Data anche la linea teoretica immanentistica dell'articolo, e dato che vorrei con esso richiamare l'attenzione su Heidegger, le sarei molto riconoscente se volesse accettarlo" (*EG*, 131n46).

28. I translate here "Il problema della metafisica immanente di M. Heidegger" (literally: "The Problem of M. Heidegger's Immanent Metaphyics") as "On M. Heidegger's [etc.]" because in Italian usage "problem" does not carry any negative connotation. The same goes for the next work introduced below, *Il problema della metafisica platonica*, which I choose to translate as *On Plato's Metaphysics*.

What is the unity of being? Blondel developed this problem in an orthodox manner by conceiving reality as a "living anxiety"—like Heidegger's "Sorge"—as a process that points upward, to a transcendental
goal. . . . How does Heidegger conceive of this absolute goal within
the process of the self-realization of existence? Is this a transcendental
goal or, rather, does it coincide with the development of existence itself? Is it a process of spiritual ascension or self-realization? Heidegger
undoubtedly solves this problem according to immanence, by realizing that the absolute significance of the process of existence cannot be
some sort of goal—that is, some object procrastinated in time—but the
process of self-realization in and of itself. (PS, 216)[29]

Heidegger, in Grassi's view, had liberated philosophy of any teleological obsession, be it Hegelian or religious. He had provided a philosophy that no
longer relied on negative or opposite paradigms—be they past or present—
against which to define one's own stance. Grassi enthusiastically realized
that from this perspective, tradition was no longer a problem but rather
should be made contemporaneous, that is, part of the solution. In communicating his transition to a new, yet to be defined, stance to Castelli
(18 November 1928), Grassi stated: "I was led to philosophy by the desire to
rethink Catholic thought. . . . Today, I am aiming for a possible higher synthesis built on a serious and mature historical work. . . . I hope to achieve
new horizons through the study of the classics" (APEC). The classic that
Grassi turned to, under Heidegger's supervision, was none other than
Plato, a beleaguered philosopher at that time, in Italy and elsewhere.

HEIDEGGERIANISM IS A PLATONISM

Grassi's first book, a *Habilitation* thesis entitled *On Platonic Metaphysics*,
is a lamentably forgotten close reading of Plato's *Meno*, whose publication
in 1932 was sponsored by Benedetto Croce despite its dedication to Heideg-

29. Grassi to Castelli (Spring 1927): "[Blondel] è un uomo veramente superiore e il
contatto personale ne dà tutta la coscienza: la sua bontà profonda, la umiltà viva fa sì che il
suo spirito è pronto ad accettare qualsiasi preoccupazione e penetrare in posizioni lontante
dalla sua. Vado precisamente esponendogli e discutendo il pensiero di Gentile e mostrando
che esso non è affatto quel pensiero nozionale e astrattista che egli credeva: il punto per me
grave è l'insufficienza formale, la realtà come atto concreto, quale è affermata dal Blondel.
Non solo per l'impossibilità di trascendere l'atto concreto che viene così ad essere assoluto
e a costituire l'unità dell'esperienza, ma perché non vedo nemmeno quale concreto valore
intimamente rimanga alla nostra attività creativa, se l'inquietudine che la genera è trascendente" (APEC).

ger, a philosopher who by the following year (at the time of the *Rektorats-rede*) the Italian mandarin would publicly scorn.[30] At first glance, Grassi's interpretation seems to be unrelated to the question of 'humanism.' His overt goal was to obviate the risks implied in the traditional interpretation of Plato as the chief representative of an outmoded abstract rationalism (*PMP*, 7). For Grassi, who believed instead that Plato himself taught that philosophy is essentially "aporetic," a process of open-ended questioning, the condescending Hegelian belief that the present stands in a position of speculative superiority to the past was both useless and reprehensible.

In the first paragraph of his book, Grassi states that the notion of Plato's irrelevance for the present is "particularly common among us, for, more than any other current in modern thought, Italian philosophy [read 'actualism'] has continuously defined itself against the insufficiencies of abstract logic and of objectivist metaphysics" (*PMP*, 7). Indeed, Gentile's prejudice against the purported "realism" of past philosophies, taking Plato's as the prototype, had helped all but bury the study of the Greeks in Italy. Yet Grassi could not be persuaded that "Plato actually relied on a rationalist objectivism." By foregrounding the questing or Socratic aspect of Plato's philosophy, Grassi wished to "tease out the speculative conclusions that are *implicitly* given in dialogue," which is not a mere literary ornament (11). The *Meno*, in Grassi's view, was particularly representative for its metaphilosophical qualities; within it Plato's metaphysics are revealed *in practice* as a perpetually incomplete striving toward the manifestation of reality.

The task of eliciting the philosophical content of Plato's dialogism is challenging, Grassi realizes, as it demands compliance with the liveliness and abiding power of the Greek language:

Only by keeping open the meaning of any term relating to Platonic metaphysics—starting with the fundamental one, the Platonic "eidos"—will we by means of our questioning disclose, step by step, their determination. We should mention that the more we succeed in keeping the meaning of the terms that we encounter in the text open and problematic, the more we will be able to delve into the sense of Platonic metaphysics and recast previous interpretations. In truth, achieving

30. Croce's reaction to Heidegger's *Die Selbstbehauptung der deutschen Universitäten* was swift, curt, and crushing. See *La critica* 32 (1934): 69. Croce also privately vented his feelings about Heidegger in his correspondence with Vossler. See Benedetto Croce and Karl Vossler, *Carteggio 1899–1949* (Rome: Laterza, 1951), 340–44.

a new and more profound understanding of a text amounts to having managed to ask new questions when others failed to do so, and in this way, to enable a more profound research. (*PMP*, 9–10)

The imprint of Heidegger's unconventional approach to Greek philosophy is clearly discernible. Together with *Plato's Dialectical Ethics*—the *Habilitationsschrift* Gadamer also had written under Heidegger's supervision (completed in 1928) and published one year earlier, in 1931—Grassi's work should be understood as one of the earliest applications of Heideggerian *Destruktion*, an activity that Gadamer at some point qualified as a "hermeneutical task" whose "purpose is to take concepts that have become rigid and lifeless and fill them again with meaning."[31]

Moreover, the *Meno* dramatizes the confrontation between opposite worldviews: Meno's sophistic "false certainty" and Socrates's properly philosophical "fecund insufficiency." The dialogue stages this conflict in a way that reveals philosophy's dependence on the exchange between question and answer: a dialogue or conversation that always occurs in the 'here' and 'now' and that lends Platonic philosophy its concreteness:

> Just so, through Plato, we are led to absolute and radical questioning, and in that act Plato comes back to life in all of his concreteness; so that he is not outside or beyond us but within our own philosophizing. Through Plato our questioning is no longer determined by a simple text and our research is not mere science ("history" in the positivistic sense of the word); rather we are led instead to unearth truth within ourselves and in so doing to turn ourselves into philosophers. In this sense, the problem regarding the objectivity of an interpretation and the problem regarding the essence of philosophy are intimately connected. (*PMP*, 23–24)

The power of Socrates's philosophizing is irresistible, forcing the interpreter into participation. What needs to be emphasized is Grassi's idea that the recovery of the original essence of philosophical texts such as the *Meno* involves readers in the interpretive process that we today associate with Gadamerian hermeneutics but that could just as fairly be named Grassian. "The interpretive act," Grassi states, "is the stirring act par ex-

31. Hans-Georg Gadamer, "Letter to Dallmayr," in *Dialogue and Deconstruction: The Gadamer-Derrida Encounter*, ed. Diane P. Michelfelder and Richard E. Palmer (Albany: State University of New York Press, 1989), 99.

cellence, one that educates us to actively implement the process of knowledge" (223).

In a later passage, Grassi explicitly refers to the assumption by the interpreter of the Socratic "aporetic attitude" (*atteggiamento aporetico*)—the lack of knowledge that forces one to ask questions—and its relevance for the attempt to re-present the tradition of Western philosophy as a whole:

> Therefore we are always obliged to conquer the manifestation of that single being, and such effort is closely related to our historical judgment, precisely because Being and its revelation—which are never given but are always a task to be fulfilled—carry within themselves the possibility of their decadence, of the oblivion of what we once conquered; by realizing that this can happen philosophy is endowed with all of its weight and its ethical character. . . . On the one hand, it follows that the concept of a living tradition is never something that we can consider acquired and achieved for all times by forgetting the toil that led us to such conquest; on the other hand, we realize why the philosophies of truly great philosophers always coincide. *It is thus possible now to give up the speculative contrast between ancient and modern philosophies.* (PMP, 172–73; emphasis added)

Grassi appropriated Heidegger's convictions to approach the Greeks in a way that questioned Gentile's dismissive attitude. Philosophical questioning, unlike scientific questioning, necessitates continuous confrontation with tradition. Moreover, such an approach should eschew a sterile doxographic listing of past views and instead reach over (or pierce through) the sedimentation of interpretive traditions to recover the original stance.

The young Grassi and Gadamer were not oblivious to one another's endeavors and strong affinity. In an essay from 1933, responding to a negative review of his book in Italy, Grassi went as far as to name Gadamer as the main representative of those "outstanding achievements" (still unknown to the Italians) reaped by the new German approach to Greek philosophy (see PS, 334). For his part, Gadamer, in that very same year, expressed his support for Grassi's endeavor in a detailed review of the latter's book. According to him, Grassi "shakes up . . . the consolidated dogmatism in the interpretation of Platonic ontology, achieving a new perspective [*ein neues Auge*] in establishing the present relevance of Greek philosophy."[32] Both

---

32. Hans-Georg Gadamer, *Griechische Philosophie I*, in *Gesammelte Werke* (Tübingen: Mohr Siebeck, 1985), 5: 306. Gadamer closely followed Grassi's work. In the same volume of

Grassi and Gadamer had fallen under the spell of Heidegger's hermeneutics and undertook to reinvent antiquity with the firm conviction that,
in Gadamer's words, "philosophical and philological inquiry cannot be
divorced."[33] Similarly, for Grassi only the Greek language

> in its grammatical structure, in the formation of its substantives, ad-
> jectives, in its vitality and resilience that always offer us clear and dis-
> tinct images, has the power to force us to reexperience from within
> ourselves its originary explicative power. From here we get the inti-
> mate relationship that can occur between philology and philosophy
> and that endows the former with a particular educative significance.
> (*PMP*, 214–15)

Here, for the first time, Grassi makes that particular connection between
philology and philosophy that, as we shall see, he would use to establish,
through Vico, his rehabilitation of Renaissance humanism *as philosophy*.
Before we turn to this application, some considerations are in order to
show how Grassi's *On Platonic Metaphysics* was in fact simultaneously
reacting to the main strands of Italian, French, and, in some distinct way,
German philosophy.

Grassi's book did not fare well in Italy. Gentile had it reviewed in the
Giornale critico by his most competent student (soon to turn 'heretic') in
classical philology, Guido Calogero. Given that Grassi had undeservedly
styled himself as a classicist, Calogero had an easy task of refuting him on
linguistic minutiae. More strikingly, however, Calogero denied any possibility of modernizing Plato, resolving Platonism into actualism by col-
lapsing Gentile's "absolute immanentism" into what Grassi interpreted
as Plato's "absolute aporeticism" (*aporetismo assoluto*). Calogero, who
had himself been forced to relocate to Germany (where he had befriended
Grassi) to pursue his classical studies, lamented the German fixation on
Plato, "who generates more books each year than Aeneas's prolific sow.
We wish that Grassi would not be influenced by this almost pathological
milieu and that he would not learn from his teacher, Heidegger, to gently

---

the *Gesammelte Werke* (5:310–15, 357–63), he reprinted two other reviews of his Italian col-
league's work: *Vom Vorrang des Logos* (1939) and *Geistige Überlieferung: Ein Jahrbuch* (1940).
See also Giuseppe Civati, *Un dialogo sull'umanesimo: Hans-Georg Gadamer e Ernesto
Grassi* (Aosta: L'Eubage, 2003).

33. This statement is drawn from an autobiographical blurb Gadamer appended to his
Habilitation thesis, cited in Jean Grondin, *Hans-Georg Gadamer: A Biography*, trans. Joel
Weinsheimer (New Haven: Yale University Press, 2003), 118.

question the texts [*solliciter doucement les textes*] in service of his own speculative constructions."[34]

Calogero concluded by urging Grassi either to dedicate himself exclusively to the exposition of Heidegger's philosophy, for which he demonstrated true competence, or, if he wished to pursue his study in ancient thought, to follow in the footsteps of real philologists such as Werner Jaeger, Julius Stenzel, and Ernst Hoffmann.[35] Calogero, we shall see shortly, had already taken a stance—as, he realized, had Grassi—with respect to an important debate in Germany on the relative merits of philology, philosophy, and their intersection. As for Gentile himself, a thank-you note he addressed to Calogero shows just how adamant he was about stifling Grassi's line of criticism: "Thank you for the review of Grassi's book, who deserves this lesson. . . . I hope he will benefit from it, for he is a little overweening. Otherwise, he would not have given birth to this monstrosity [*aborto*]."[36] Gentile went on to deny Grassi the honor of compiling the entry on Heidegger for the *Italian Encyclopedia*. That entry, as well as those on Socrates and Plato, went to Calogero instead.

Again here, it is possible in hindsight—as was the case with Spirito's review of Abbagnano's first work in 1923—to see how particularly striking Calogero's lack of sympathy for Grassi's ultimate aim is. For, as we have seen in the previous chapter, when Calogero himself went rogue in the late 1930s and early 1940s he did so by conceiving of a philosophical attitude named "dialogism," the very same attitude that Grassi was attempting to recover in his reading of the *Meno*. Indeed, Grassi's first book should be appreciated for prematurely adumbrating most of the concerns of later deprovincializing reforms of actualism: besides Calogero's insistence on the ethical and educative relevance of exploratory dialogue and dialectical interchange, there was also Spirito's "problematicism," that is, the ability to hold oneself suspended within open-ended research, and the concern everyone shared for a revision of the idealist historiographical paradigm— one that Grassi, like Abbagnano, would promote through an existential understanding of the 'philological moment.' Be that as it may, Grassi was forced to come to terms with the fact that, in 1932, the time was not ripe for a thorough overhaul of actualism.

34. I cite from a later and titled reprint. See Guido Calogero, "Platone fra soggettivismo e oggettivismo?" in *Scritti minori di filosofia antica* (Naples: Bibliopolis, 1984), 347–48.

35. For an account of Calogero's German years, see Stefano Zappoli, *Guido Calogero (1923–1942)* (Pisa: Edizioni della Normale, 2011), chap. 5.

36. Giovanni Gentile and Guido Calogero, *Carteggio (1926–1942)* (Florence: Le Lettere, 1998), 43.

If, somewhat more humbly, Grassi had hoped to jump-start a renaissance of Plato studies in Italy, at a more personal level he also had to formally take leave of his past as a Christian thinker, a firm promoter of transcendence, and supporter of Blondel's philosophy of action. This closure was achieved in one of the two essays he appended to *On Platonic Metaphysics* titled "On Transcendence and Platonism in an Interpretation of Augustine." The object of Grassi's concern was an essay Blondel published in 1930 on the occasion of the fifteenth centenary of Augustine's death, in which he had attempted to offer a new hermeneutical approach to the corpus of the saint's writings.[37] Blondel had opposed the tendency to extrapolate haphazardly definitive doctrines from Augustine's many writings and instead focused relentlessly on the "internal coherence" between apparently opposing statements as well as on the inseparability of life and doctrine in the saint's works. Augustine's philosophy, according to Blondel, was one of "retractions" in which doctrines are never *conceptualized* once and for all but, rather, *realized* or fulfilled through a constant sympathy between philosophy (*via veritatis et scientiae*) and religion (*via salutis et beatitudinis*) (*PMP*, 190).

Grassi's objective was to show that Blondel had, indeed, managed to prove the nondoctrinal essence of Augustine's theory of ideas and God: "According to Blondel, Augustine's awareness of his own deficiency and poverty cannot be distinguished from the philosophical act inasmuch as it is such a realization that compelled Augustine to always try to keep his own experience open-ended" (*PMP*, 188–89). Yet, according to the vantage point afforded by his reading of Plato, Grassi concluded that rather than distinguishing Augustine's (Christian) metaphysics from Plato's— for Blondel, too, held fast to a traditional view of the Greek philosopher— Blondel had actually proven their affinities, if not their identity (197ff.).

The following passage shows just how far Grassi had come from his early concerns and convictions:

> It is correct to say that our ideas are true in function of the irradiation and of the enlightenment bestowed upon them from something transcendental (which Blondel and his Augustine would have coincide with the God of some revelation), *but we do not see the ideas in God, we don't have divine thoughts, absolute truth*, precisely because our

---

37. See Maurice Blondel, "Pour le quinzième centenaire de la mort de saint Augustin (28 aôut 430): L'unité originale et la vie permanente de sa doctrine philosophique," *Revue de métaphysique et de morale* 37, no. 4 (1930): 427.

vision of transcendence is always grounded and develops within the realization of our insufficiency, of the finitude of our thoughts. . . . In the
realization of our insufficiency we do not thus enter into truth, but are
always already within it; a truth reveals itself as a process, a dialectical
act. (*PMP*, 193–94; emphasis added)

By 1932, Grassi had fulfilled his stated goal of rethinking religious philosophy through the exposure to Greek thought afforded to him by Heidegger's seminars. It seems likely that he could no longer consider himself a
Christian or Catholic thinker, perhaps even surprising himself.

   With Italy and France closed to him, it remains to be seen what kind of
contribution Grassi believed he could make to contemporary German philosophy. Certainly, from his standpoint at that time, Grassi conceived his
Plato study as an application of Heideggerian hermeneutics to a thinker
on whom Heidegger himself—who was admired by his students mainly as
a reader of Aristotle—had yet to pass a conclusive judgment.[38] However,
from our present vantage point, Grassi's Heideggerian Platonism acquires
outstanding significance. That is, there is no sign in Grassi's work of his
awareness that Heidegger was, or was about to become, the most influential anti-Platonist in the tradition of modern Western philosophy. For
Gentile's direct engagement with Plato was scant and instrumental, while
Blondel's feelings toward the Greek philosopher were determined by his
Christian outlook.

   Heidegger *suddenly* revealed his anti-Platonic turn, which we now
know to have actually been long in the making, in a famous text entitled
"Plato's Doctrine of Truth." This was the only taste of his pedagogy and
reading of Plato that he chose to publish during that time: Heidegger offered his own translation and a close exegesis, extrapolated from the larger
context of the *Republic*, of Plato's allegory of the cave. In Heidegger's view,
as is well known, the Platonic allegory pointed to "a transformation in
the essence of 'truth'" that had ever since—until Heidegger, that is—neg-

---

38. This was certainly the case for Gadamer. In the preface to the published version of his
Habilitation thesis he stated: "What I owe to the teaching and research of Martin Heidegger
is revealed by many references, both explicit and tacit, to his book *Sein und Zeit* (*Being and
Time*) and still more by the whole methodological attitude of my work, which *tries to extend
what I have learned from Heidegger and above all to make it fruitful by practicing it in a
new way*." Hans-Georg Gadamer, *Plato's Dialectical Ethics: Phenomenological Interpretations Relating to the* Philebus, trans. Robert M. Wallace (New Haven: Yale University Press,
1991), xxvi (emphasis added). Similarly, in the preface to the 1967 edition: "My intention in
writing it was really only to apply the art of phenomenological description, which I had just
learned, to a Platonic dialogue" (xxix).

atively affected Western thinking.[39] If "truth" had originally been *experienced*—for "education" (*paideia*) and truth were linked in "an essential unity"—as unconcealment (*aletheia*), with and after Plato, "truth" instead had been *thought of* as "correctness," as describing "the agreement of the representation in thought with the thing itself: *adaequatio intellectus et rei*."[40] Within this new order of things, Heidegger avows, a genuine questioning of the meaning of truth and Being was blocked. What concerns us here is that Heidegger's anti-Platonic turn was closely related to Grassi and his work and not only for the obvious reason that it amounted to a refutation of Grassi's identification of Heidegger and Plato.

A precise dating of "Plato's Doctrine of Truth" has proved problematic. Based on Heidegger's assertions, scholars have long traced its conception back to a 1930–31 lecture course—to a time, that is, that coincides perfectly with the publication of Grassi's and Gadamer's dissertations.[41] Based on Heidegger's recently published lectures, however, it has recently been argued that in the form in which it was published Heidegger could not have conceived of it before 1940, when a "radical change" in his understanding of *paideia* occurred.[42] Among the reasons adduced for this sudden turn is Heidegger's attempt to distance himself from classicist Werner Jaeger (1888–1961), whose work, as we shall see in more detail, had influentially suggested a *positive* identification of Platonic *paideia*, *Bildung*, and humanism. Thus, the argument is that the affirmation concluding "Plato's Doctrine of Truth" ("The beginning of metaphysics in the thought of Plato is at the same time the beginning of 'humanism'"), which previews the contents of the "Letter on 'Humanism,'" should be read as an anti-Jaegerian statement.[43]

The assumption regarding a decisive contention between Heidegger and Jaeger, though fundamentally correct, may not be fully grasped without consideration of Grassi's own activities and philosophical development after the publication of *On Platonic Metaphysics*. Suffice it to say for now that Heidegger himself directly acknowledged his students' involvement in his philosophical turn by entrusting the publication of "Plato's Doc-

39. Martin Heidegger, "Plato's Doctrine of Truth," trans. Thomas Sheehan, in *Pathmarks*, ed. William McNeill (Cambridge: Cambridge University Press, 1998), 167.

40. Heidegger, "Plato's Doctrine of Truth," 168.

41. For the earliest dating, see Robert J. Dostal, "Beyond Being: Heidegger's Plato," in *Martin Heidegger: Critical Assessments*, ed. Christopher E. Macann, 4 vols. (New York: Routledge, 1992), 2:61.

42. Francisco J. Gonzalez, *Plato and Heidegger: A Question of Dialogue* (University Park: Pennsylvania State University Press, 2009), 150ff.

43. Gonzalez, *Plato and Heidegger*, 181.

trine of Truth" to Grassi in 1942.[44] Looking ahead, moreover, we can say that while Heidegger's manifesto did assimilate Western "metaphysics," "Platonism," and "humanism," the latter term was at this time still used as a loose cognate for the Greek notion of "anthropology," with no reference to its accepted Renaissance meaning.[45] In briefly accounting for how "the characterization of the essence of truth . . . becomes normative for the whole of Western thinking," Heidegger refers to "medieval Scholasticism" (Thomas Aquinas), the "beginning of modern times" (Descartes), and "the age when the modern era enters its fulfillment" (Nietzsche).[46] It is only beginning with the "Letter" that Heidegger expands his grasp of Western thought to include "Rome," where "we encounter the first humanism," the "so-called Renaissance of the fourteenth and fifteenth centuries in Italy," and displays a sensitivity to the notion of humanism as "a studium humanitatis, which in a certain way reached back to the ancients and thus also becomes a revival of Greek civilization."[47]

How are Heidegger's efforts to include some reference to the Italian legacy—which, given his total lack of interest in it, seems a forced interpolation—to be explained? Between 1942 and 1947, when Heidegger also entrusted Grassi with the publication of the "Letter on 'Humanism,'" which he appended to a second revised edition of "Plato's Doctrine of Truth," Grassi had at once more closely involved his teacher in an anti-Jaegerian campaign and employed his brand of 'Heideggerian Platonism' to reveal the philosophical import of Italian Renaissance humanism.[48] It would seem that throughout the 1930s and 1940s, Heidegger followed in Grassi's footsteps with the purpose of erasing his traces.

HEIDEGGERIAN PLATONISM MAY OR MAY NOT BE A (NIETZSCHEAN) TRUE HUMANISM

Insofar as their dissertations prematurely challenged their teacher's future programmatic anti-Platonism, Grassi and Gadamer were certainly Heidegger's twin children. However, Grassi might be even more suited than his

44. Martin Heidegger, "Platons Lehre von der Wahrheit," in *Geistige Überlieferung: Das zweite Jahrbuch*, ed. Ernesto Grassi with Walter F. Otto and Karl Reinhardt (Berlin: Helmut Küpper, 1942), 96–124.
45. Heidegger, "Plato's Doctrine of Truth," 181.
46. Heidegger, "Plato's Doctrine of Truth," 178–79.
47. Martin Heidegger, "Letter on 'Humanism,'" in *Pathmarks*, ed. William McNeill, trans. Frank A. Capuzzi (Cambridge: Cambridge University Press, 1998), 244.
48. Martin Heidegger, *Platons Lehre von der Wahrheit: Mit einem Brief über den "Humanismus"* (Bern: A. Francke, 1947).

German colleague—who is often exclusively called on in such cases—to the task of supporting current attempts to dispute Heidegger's (mis)understanding of Plato and to argue for the actual affinities of their philosophical stances.[49] At the outset of his *Plato's Dialectical Ethics*, which also offers a close reading of a single dialogue, the *Philebus*, Gadamer states:

> Aristotle projected Plato onto the plane of conceptual explication. The Plato who presents himself in this explication is the object of Aristotle's critique. What makes this critique problematic is that this projection cannot also catch the inner tension and energy of Plato's philosophizing as they speak to us, with such incomparable convincingness, in his dialogues. . . . The gain in unambiguous comprehensibility and repeatable certainty is matched by a loss in stimulating multiplicity of meaning.[50]

This passage shows that for Gadamer, just as for Grassi, Platonic truth is a *happening* emerging in intellectual exchange and open-ended questioning. Plato is not the dogmatist Aristotle made him out to be, and the incommensurability of their forms of philosophizing needs to be acknowledged. Yet in a far less quoted passage that immediately follows, Gadamer also states that

> just as all reflection on the relation between concepts and what is living can itself be grasped only in concepts, so the Platonic existence of

49. For criticisms of Heidegger's reading of Plato, see, among many others, Robert J. Dostal, "Gadamer's Continuous Challenge: Heidegger's Plato Interpretation," in Hahn, *Philosophy of Hans-Georg Gadamer*, 289–308; Francisco J. Gonzalez, "Dialectic as 'Philosophical Embarrassment': Heidegger's Critique of Plato's Method," *Journal of the History of Philosophy* 40, no. 3 (2002): 361–89; Francisco J. Gonzalez, "Confronting Heidegger on Logos and Being in Plato's *Sophist*," in *Platon und Aristoteles, sub ratione veritatis: Festschrift für Wolfgang Wieland zum 70. Geburtstag*, ed. G. Damschen, R. Enskat, and A. G. Vigo (Göttingen: Vandenhoeck & Ruprecht, 2003), 102–33; Otto Pöggeler, "Ein Streit um Platon: Heidegger und Gadamer," in *Platon in der abendländischen Geistesgeschichte: Neue Forschungen zum Platonismus*, ed. T. Kobush and M. Burkhard (Darmstadt: Wissenschaftliche Buchgesellschaft, 1997), 241–54; Catalin Partenie and Tom Rockmore, eds., *Heidegger and Plato: Toward Dialogue* (Evanston, IL: Northwestern University Press, 2005); Catherine H. Zuckert, *Postmodern Platos: Nietzsche, Heidegger, Gadamer, Strauss, Derrida* (Chicago: University of Chicago Press, 1996). On Gadamer's early work specifically, see François Renaud, *Die Resokratisierung Platons: Die platonische Hermeneutik Hans-Georg Gadamers* (Sankt Augustin: Academia Verlag, 1999); and Christopher Gill and François Renaud, eds., *Hermeneutic Philosophy and Plato: Gadamer's Response to the* Philebus (Sankt Augustin: Academia Verlag, 2010).
50. Gadamer, *Plato's Dialectical Ethics*, 7.

philosophy can be grasped *philosophically* only if one repeats, oneself, the same kind of projection onto the conceptual plane that Aristotle undertakes. All scientific philosophy is Aristotelianism insofar as it is conceptual work, and thus if *one wants to interpret Plato's philosophy philosophically*, one must necessarily interpret it via Aristotle.[51]

Surprisingly adhering in principle to more conventional philosophical standards, Gadamer maintained that Aristotelian theory should ultimately be preferred over Platonic ambiguities, fascinating and stimulating though they may be.

Gadamer certainly derived this momentary philosophical conservatism from his teacher. The winter semester 1924–25 lectures on the *Sophist*—one of Heidegger's most sustained confrontations with Plato—begins with the assertion: "What Aristotle said is what Plato placed at his disposal, only it is said more radically and developed more scientifically."[52] Following the hermeneutical principle according to which "interpretation should proceed from the clear into the obscure" and believing that "Aristotle was not followed by anyone greater," Heidegger turned Plato's most distinguished follower into an indispensable entry point into Greek philosophy. This may explain why Gadamer ingratiatingly qualified his own first work as an "Aristotle book that never got off the ground," a gesture that was certainly appreciated by Heidegger, who evaluated Gadamer's thesis accordingly, as a token of a loyal schoolman: "The present work is of great value not only as an interpretation of a Platonic dialogue but just as much in relation to the author's intended project of penetrating more thoroughly the main problems of Aristotle's works on ethics."[53] It is unfortunately impossible to precisely determine what Heidegger might have thought of Grassi's coeval and uncompromising apology for Plato. What is certain, however, is that Grassi was no Aristotelian in the making. Unlike Gadamer, he could not have been privy to his teacher's lectures on the *Sophist*, and he repeatedly expressed his wish to extend his research to other Platonic dialogues.[54]

---

51. Gadamer, *Plato's Dialectical Ethics*, 8 (emphases added).

52. Martin Heidegger, *Plato's* Sophist, trans. R. Rojcewicz and A. Schuwer (Bloomington: Indiana University Press, 1997), 8.

53. Grondin, *Hans-Georg Gadamer*, 138.

54. While Grassi's career turned out to be less Plato-oriented than expected, he again focused on a Platonic dialogue (the *Theaetetus*) in his second book. See Ernesto Grassi, *Vom Vorrang des Logos: Das Problem der Antike in der Auseinandersetzung zwischen italienischer und deutscher Philosophie* (Munich: Beck, 1939), 69ff.

For all of their similarities, therefore, a lot can be learned from exploring how Grassi and Gadamer differed in their exploitation of the Heideggerian momentum. First, it should be noted that while Grassi considered
himself a philosopher through and through, Gadamer was a philologist by
profession (if not by vocation).[55] Academic affiliations matter because, then
and now, they inform graduate students' strategies in relating to the larger
scholarly community. What is of interest for us here is that in attempting
to jumpstart their careers, both Grassi and Gadamer (again in tandem!)
felt the urge to take a stance with respect to Jaeger, at that time one of
the leading "academic crusaders for cultural conservatism" and the true
"prophet" of a movement known as "third humanism."[56] Between 1914
and the end of the Weimar Republic, Jaeger wrote a series of articles—
culminating in a celebrated work on Greek education (*paideia*)—aimed at
founding a "new humanism" on an exclusive and unmediated engagement
with the normative and timeless values of Greek antiquity.[57] Therefore, in
comparison with Heidegger, whose seminars had been blurring disciplinary lines, Jaeger was presumably *the* conservative, at least in the eyes of a
younger generation of Heideggerians. Gadamer's and Grassi's handling of
the matter bespeaks a rivalry between Heidegger and Jaeger on the question of 'humanism,' a notion that philosophers and philologists could both
claim as their own, that was certainly more acutely experienced in the
classroom than the parties involved would make us believe.[58]

Gadamer's story is better known. He gained a reputation as a classicist
early on, in 1927, with a daring essay challenging Jaeger's well-established

55. See Grondin, *Hans-Georg Gadamer*, 117.

56. Donald O. White, "Werner Jaeger's 'Third Humanism' and the Crisis of Conservative Cultural Politics in Weimar Germany," in *Werner Jaeger Reconsidered*, ed. William M.
Calder III (Atlanta: Scholars Press, 1992), 269.

57. Jaeger's programmatic articles—"Der Humanismus als Tradition und Erlebnis" (1919),
"Antike und Humanismus" (1925), "Platos Stellung im Aufbau der griechischen Bildung"
(1927), etc.—to which Grassi refers in his work were first collected in 1937. See now Werner
Jaeger, *Humanistische Reden und Vorträge* (Berlin: De Gruyter, 1960). The first volume of
Jaeger's *Paideia* appeared in German in 1933. For the English edition, see Werner Jaeger,
Paideia: The Ideals of Greek Culture, trans. Gilbert Highet, 3 vols. (New York: Oxford Uni-
versity Press, 1965–71). For an interesting collection of essays centered on the German debate
on 'humanism,' see also Hans Oppermann, ed., *Humanismus* (Darmstadt: Wissenschaftliche
Buchgesellschaft, 1977).

58. Contact between Heidegger and Jaeger was scant, though by no means nonexistent.
See Frank H. Edler, "Heidegger and Werner Jaeger on the Eve of 1933: A Possible Rapprochement?" *Research in Phenomenology* 27 (1997): 122–49. For Heidegger's relationship with
another representative of "third humanism," Julius Stenzel, see Antonio Cimino, "Neou-
manesimo, Ontologia, Platonismo: Il confronto di Martin Heidegger con Julius Stenzel,"
Rinascimento 44, no. 2 (2004): 77–114.

evolutionary or chronological paradigm in approaching Aristotle's corpus.[59] As noted by his biographer, "Gadamer liked to use his philological work as a calling card for purposes of his own advancement" and thus, throughout his early career, sought to establish a collegial relationship with Jaeger despite his true feelings toward him, which he revealed only at a later (and, surely, safer) time.[60] Gadamer recounted his first meeting with Jaeger in a letter to Heidegger (2 October 1928): "[Jaeger] started talking about your book. It was clear that he was content with the observation that antiquity is only *one* element among others in the formation of your philosophy and thus [that your philosophy is] no 'humanism.'"[61]

Jaeger's fear of a possible encroachment by Heidegger was perhaps well founded. Two years later, in 1930, Heidegger turned down a job offer at the University of Berlin, one that Jaeger, as a member of the search committee, may or may not have obstructed. In commenting on this offer in a letter to Jaspers (17 May 1930), Heidegger personally dropped another hint: "But—the dimwits! This is not the first time that I've had doubts about whether such cowards are the right people to try to get a new humanism on its feet." Frank Edler notes that this remark shows that Heidegger was not only aware of Jaeger's 'third humanism' but "also aware, at least to a certain extent, of the political problems which may be involved in getting a movement 'on its feet.'"[62] In truth, by this time, the "Gesellschaft für antike Kultur," founded by Jaeger in 1924, and its mouthpiece journal *Die Antike* had already turned this movement into a well-established institutional force. Moreover, in 1930, Jaeger hosted a celebrated event in Naumburg, dedicated to the "problem of the classical," in which the "new credo" of a new generation of philologists was announced in a series of programmatic essays.[63] Therefore, if Heidegger seriously entertained any humanist ambition, he must have been frustrated by the impossibility at that point of infiltrating the movement and dethroning its established leader.

59. Hans-Georg Gadamer, "Der aristotelische 'Protreptikos' und die entwicklungsgeschichtliche Betrachtung der aristotelischen Ethik," in *Griechische Philosophie I*, 164–86. For the object of Gadamer's criticism, see Werner Jaeger, *Aristotle: Fundamentals of the History of His Development*, trans. Richard Robinson (London: Oxford University Press, 1962).

60. Grondin, *Hans-Georg Gadamer*, 123.

61. Grondin, *Hans-Georg Gadamer*, 416.

62. Edler, "Heidegger and Werner Jaeger on the Eve of 1933," 126.

63. See Manfred Landfester, "Die Naumburger Tagung 'Das Problem des Klassischen und die Antike' (1930): Der Klassikbegriff Werner Jaegers, seine Voraussetzung und seine Wirkung," in *Altertumswissenschaft in den 20er Jahren: Neue Fragen und Impulse*, ed. Hellmut Flashar (Stuttgart: Franz Steiner, 1995), 11–40.

Grassi, who at this point may be said to have modeled his career after that of Gadamer, differed in his approach by engaging in a frontal and, for him, intellectually defining assault on the philologist, starting with the second appendix to his *On Platonic Metaphysics*: "The Educative [*pai-deutico*] Significance of Platonic Thought and of the Interpretive Act." For Grassi, who was clearly fighting an ideological battle on behalf of his teacher, Jaeger epitomized the hypostatization of abstract models and the mere repetition of the *unquestioned* merits of classical antiquity. Grassi stressed that a new humanism needed to be informed by a critical, that is to say, *philosophical* return to the past—to be sure, by an implementation of Heideggerian hermeneutics.

In an article also published in 1932, Grassi succinctly connected the interpretive or hermeneutical efforts of his book to both a condemnation and an overcoming of Jaeger's program. The following passage is particularly interesting in that it may provide insight into the conversations Heidegger's students may have had in or after class:

> Jaeger tells us that the humanistic program consists in holding fast to the fundamental explication of our "true human nature" or in educating man "toward what constitutes his essence, as it is objectively prescribed by nature." But we feel that an objectivistic concept infiltrates these affirmations: this so-called essence of human nature is a philosophical problem and does not exist as nor can it be conceived as something predetermined. Therefore, humanism cannot have its foundations in that general affirmation but only in rigorous philosophical research. A true living humanism has to be a philosophy. This is true not only from a speculative point of view but also historically: that is, for example, when we want to refer to Plato as the founder of the humanist concept. (*PS*, 258)

Just after having recovered in Heidegger a method and line of inquiry that allowed for overcoming the Italian/Hegelian quarrel between the ancients and the moderns, Grassi adamantly fought against a relapse into what he must have perceived as an inverted teleology or—mindful of the contemporaneous 'medievalism' of Italian scholastics—as a purblind antiquarianism.

In Grassi's view, Jaeger had accepted his criticism in a personal letter that Grassi often published with evident self-satisfaction. Jaeger wrote to Grassi (20 October 1932):

I am aware that any such *renovatio*, if it is to amount to more than the hypostatization of a segment of history and mere scholarly reinstatement of the past, must emerge from within the depths of the problem of human existence [*Existenz des Menschen*]. By so doing, it no longer constitutes a mere philological concern but an immediate philosophical problem. Every living humanism has always recovered its philosophy, and even today such a philosophy is charged with the task of grounding and justifying its existential necessity [*existentielle Notwendigkeit*] by means of a return to the Greeks and their educational ideal. Without the aid of philosophy, humanism cannot develop and accrue strength.[64]

"Existenz des Menschen," "existentielle Notwendigkeit": was Jaeger slyly indicating his approval of Heidegger through a third party? That may be. In any case, if the philologist was willing to admit that any living humanism had to recover its own philosophy, Grassi was prepared to go further and to take on the actual task of recovering it himself. The time, however, was not yet ripe for such a daring struggle. One should be reminded that Grassi was at this point a thirty-year-old untenured lecturer in Italian with a single and, as he was then just about to learn, unappreciated book to his name. Moreover, the "existential humanism" he eventually conceived was still unformulated. In fact, there is still no evidence at this time of Grassi's sustained engagement with Renaissance sources.

It took Grassi several years to realize that his reaction to Jaeger's programmatic 'third humanism' was not just a consequence of his Heideggerian upbringing but also owed to a central feature of his formation. Between 1932 and 1939—when he accepted an honorary professorship at the University of Berlin and published his second book, *On the Priority of Logos*—the rise of National Socialism gave Grassi time to ponder and, as it were, personalize the problem of humanism. After all, the German ideologues of academic and political renovation, starting with philosopher and psychologist Eduard Spranger (1882–1963), had themselves qualified their brand of 'humanism' as coming in 'third' in a long line that originated in the Italian Renaissance.[65] It could be argued that, henceforth, Grassi's in-

---

64. In Grassi, *Vom Vorrang des Logos*, 25–26.

65. Spranger coined the term "dritter Humanismus" in a talk delivered in 1921. The second 'humanism' was also German and more or less coincides with the Goethezeit.

tellectual career was defined by an attempt to make sense of this uncritically established affiliation.

In a series of articles published in the late 1930s, Grassi insistently returned to the question of humanism through a threefold *Auseinandersetzung* (a key term in these works): a critical confrontation between Italian and German nineteenth- and twentieth-century philosophies, the respective relationship of these philosophies to antiquity (and to the notion of tradition more generally), and the quarrel between philology and philosophy. As for Italy's debt to German philosophy, Grassi of course was forced to focus on the 1840–70 period, a time when, as we have seen, opposing forces had clashed as to which direction to impress on Italian thought. Grassi hailed the idealist victory over the ultranationalist and orthodox Catholic quest for the primordial and uncertain origins of Italian or, better, Italic thought. And this because he agreed with Spaventa that "the problem concerning origins may be resolved only by determining the essence of tradition, and not the other way around," as Gioberti and the cultivators of the *primato* were wont to.[66]

Such an essential core, as Spaventa was right to say, had to be recovered in the Renaissance. Nevertheless, Grassi noted that the forefathers of modern Italian philosophy failed to notice that Hegelian future-oriented dialectics is at its core irreconcilable with a legacy such as the Italian— made up of Christian Scholasticism and Renaissance and Vichian humanism—which recurrently established itself through a problematic, to say the least, relationship with both its immediate and its distant past. Admittedly, through Hegel, Italian thinkers learned how to approach the past from a philosophical perspective; however, in the process they detrimentally accepted the notion regarding the "preeminence of reason," a notion that, developing according to an unbendable linearity, naturally demotes the Renaissance to the role of *precorrimento*, *Vorahnung*, or anticipation of 'modern,' be it Cartesian or idealist, thought.

At this juncture, Grassi's thorough knowledge of German philosophical vicissitudes came in handy. It could not have escaped his notice that by the time Hegelianism began to be employed to shape the Italian consciousness, it already had expired in Germany. With this realization Grassi

---

66. Grassi returned to this subject, in Italian and German, many times. I am summarizing from "Beziehungen zwischen deutscher und italienischer Philosophie" (1939; *PS*, 437–61); "Deutsche Philosophie, italienische Philosophie und die Antike: Das Problem einer philosophischen Überlieferung" (1940; *PS*, 537–51); "La filosofia tedesca e la tradizione speculative italiana" (1940; *PS*, 553–75); and "Die Auseinandersetzung mit der deutschen Philosophie in Italien" (1941; *PS*, 583–99).

added a new name to his long roster of German competences and interests, one through whom he could finally reconnect his appraisal of the
relative merits of Italian and German philosophies to his antiphilological
campaign: Nietzsche. His sustained interest in this philosopher, whom he
had barely mentioned before, was occasioned by Karl Löwith's *Nietzsche's
Philosophy of the Eternal Recurrence of the Same* (1935), to which Grassi
dedicated an enthusiastic review article in 1936.[67] Grassi found an ally in
Löwith because, just as Grassi had done with Plato's work, Löwith qualified the literary (aphoristic) element of Nietzsche's thought as an explicit
move to counter systematic pretensions in philosophy—in Nietzsche's
case those of Hegel.

Also, Löwith reconnected Nietzsche's anti-Hegelianism to his antiphilological campaign during his early years in Basel. Indeed, the young
Nietzsche had already established what Grassi, through Heidegger, had
been working hard at reconquering: "Philosophy as philology, as renewed
love for the ancient word, as a new relationship with classical thought."
For all of Löwith's merits, however, Grassi criticized him for not going the
whole stretch. Löwith did not see that behind Nietzsche's thesis regarding the death of God lay a fully fledged historiographical paradigm. Grassi
states:

> If, as Hegel affirms, Christianity does not fulfill ancient thought, a re-
> turn to ancient thought is a return to the originary and free resources
> of man, so that the history of philosophy is characterized neither by
> progress nor by regress but by an eternal return. This is why Nietzsche
> offers a new and truly organic conception of the history of philosophy,
> perhaps the only one that can be set side by side with Hegel's. (*PS*, 416)

In presenting Löwith's refurbished Nietzsche to an Italian readership,
Grassi stressed the, as it were, Vichian elements of his philosophy: historiographical circularity and philological philosophy. Nevertheless, Grassi's
interests were now in Germany, and one needed to capitalize on a certain
connection: Nietzsche had also been the nemesis of the greatest Hellenist
of his time, Ulrich von Wilamowitz-Moellendorff (1848–1931), Jaeger's
teacher and predecessor at the University of Berlin. Perhaps it was at this
point that Grassi began entertaining the ambition of refashioning himself
into a Nietzschean figure in the history of Italian Hegelianism.

---

67. Karl Löwith, *Nietzsche's Philosophy of the Eternal Recurrence of the Same*, trans.
J. Harvey Lomax (Berkeley: University of California Press, 1997).

The epoch-making struggle between Wilamowitz and Nietzsche is well known. Its occasion was the 1872 publication of *The Birth of Tragedy*. Nietzsche's book, which had defied all standards of scholarship by being bereft of footnotes, had in fact elicited little interest among the scholarly community, and it was Wilamowitz's retort that ultimately endowed it with its enduring power as an antiphilological manifesto. In his scathing critique entitled "Future Philology!" Wilamowitz famously writes:

> But one demand I make. Let Herr Nietzsche keep to his word. Let him take up his thyrsos. Let him journey from India to Greece. But let him descend from the lecture-platform from which he is supposed to be teaching *Wissenschaft*. Let him gather tigers and panthers at his knees but not the philological youth of Germany, who are to learn in the asceticism of self-denying work, to seek everywhere truth alone, through willing submission to be freed of prejudice.[68]

Nietzsche would indeed leave the academic lectern. However, as Grassi would notice throughout the 1930s, his voice did not go unheard.

The feud between Nietzsche and Wilamowitz had been kept alive by "a group of talented, self-admiring aesthetes, [who] interpreted Nietzsche as John the Baptist, forerunner of a Messiah."[69] One such figure was legendary lyric poet Stefan George (1868–1933), who during his lifetime was indeed nothing short of a prophet and whose works circulated among an ever-widening circle of inspired devotees. Recent scholarship is piercing the veil of secrecy that, by his own choice, surrounded George's doings and goals and those of his circle of initiates.[70] Specifically, scholars are beginning to restore George, long forgotten and disregarded, to his rightful place in the development of German *Wissenschaft* and to explore the determining role of his movement as an opposing or competing force to Jaeger's 'third humanism': George's 'humanism' should not be simply catalogued as a literary and artistic variant but rather appreciated for shaping a scholarly alternative that had an interdisciplinary or even holistic breadth.[71]

In his late attempt to grapple with George's influence on German

---

68. William M. Calder III, "The Wilamowitz-Nietzsche Struggle: New Documents and Reappraisals," *Nietzsche-Studien* 12 (1983): 233.

69. Calder, "Wilamowitz-Nietzsche Struggle," 233

70. See, for example, Robert E. Norton, *Secret Germany: Stefan George and His Circle* (Ithaca, NY: Cornell University Press, 2002).

71. Barbara Stiewe, *Der 'Dritte Humanismus': Aspekte Deutscher Griechenrezeption vom George-Kreis bis zum Nationalsozialismus* (Marburg: De Gruyter, 2001), 13.

scholarship, Gadamer, who also was strongly attracted to the poet, recalls the notion of *Gestalt* that the George circle turned into a "catchword" pointing to a comprehensive and life-bound style of scholarship.[72] Gadamer points in his recollections to outstanding unconventional classicists— such as Paul Friedländer, W. F. Otto, and Karl Reinhardt—who in the ear-lier part of the century and in various degrees were forced into an existen-tial choice between different ways of conceiving scholarship: Wilamowitz or Nietzsche?[73] Even Heidegger, Gadamer avows, "was ever more at home with George's poetry."[74] George's great influence on Plato studies specifi-cally certainly derived from a connection drawn at that time between Plato's Academy, the George circle, and Heidegger's fabled seminars.

By 1940, Grassi was ready to complement his relentless tirades against Jaeger with a brief remark on a nascent antiphilological movement com-prising the same group of thinkers recalled by Gadamer many years later:

> This second approach—once freed from the last philological attempts of neohumanism, which had unsuccessfully attempted to defend the classical world (a clear example are Jaeger's writings)—takes its cue from a clear awareness of the need for a radical revision of the tradi-tional frameworks by which we usually approach ancient thought. This clearly antiphilological approach is nothing more than the continua-tion of that movement Nietzsche had begun in the nineteenth century in his early works at Basel. So, too, the current interest in Hölderlin's thought should be grasped within this line of inquiry and should start with the acknowledgment that the German tradition is pursuing very particular goals. Specifically within the world of classical philology, the names of W. F. Otto and K. Reinhardt are very significant, and we should not forget that Heidegger also gave new impetus to the interpre-tation of Aristotle in a blatantly antitraditional sense. (*PS*, 574)

Three things should be emphasized in this passage: Grassi's reference to the 'third humanism' in the past tense, for Jaeger had relocated to the United States in 1936, making room for dissent; the reference to Hölder-

---

72. Hans-Georg Gadamer, "Stefan George (1868–1933)," in *Die Wirkung Stefan Georges auf die Wissenschaft: Ein Symposium*, ed. Hans-Joachim Zimmerman (Heidelberg: Carl Winter, 1985), 43.

73. On the formation of this "credo," see William M. Calder III, "The Credo of a New Generation: Paul Friedländer to Ulrich von Wilamowitz-Moellendorf," *Antike und Abend-land* 26 (1980): 92.

74. Gadamer, "Stefan George," 42.

lin, which points to the reintegration of poetic and artistic concerns in the struggle against scientism; and Grassi's insistence that Heidegger, certainly a thinker connected to this Nietzschean group, is however to be considered a student of Aristotle (i.e., not Plato), and thus as slightly out of step with the aforementioned group.

What is striking in this essay is not only that Grassi affiliates himself with such a group of renowned classicists as Reinhardt, Otto, Heidegger, and the young Gadamer (to whom Grassi refers with a footnote to *Plato's Dialectical Ethics*) but that they are also described by him as composing a "movement" (*movimento, indirizzo*) united by a threefold purpose: namely, "the problematization of ancient thought outside the framework we inherited from [Quattrocento] humanism and the Renaissance; the clarification of humanism's essence beyond the traditional, generically historico-cultural evaluations proper to the nineteenth century; and, finally, a revaluation of those trends that already in the nineteenth century, and for the first time in Germany, attempted to achieve a new vision of ancient thought and of the relevance of humanism" (*PS*, 574–75). On what authority did Grassi make such a programmatic statement? As we shall see, the scholarly disregard of Grassi in matters concerning German classical scholarship and George is surprising, for he emerged, albeit for a short period, as the legitimate leader of a posthumous George-inspired intrigue.

The occasion was given to Grassi upon his arrival in Berlin in 1938, where he immediately befriended Helmut Küpper (1904–56), also an affiliate of the George circle. Küpper had long been employed in the firm of Georg Bondi (1865–1935), an editor who had won George's trust after a chance meeting in 1898 in the Roman apartment of painter Ludwig von Hofmann and thereafter became one of his closest collaborators.[75] In 1935, after the consecutive deaths of George and Bondi, Küpper took over the firm—eventually renamed "Helmut Küpper vormals Georg Bondi"—and thus became responsible for the poet's legacy, which was at that point on the wane. The plan for revitalization was drawn up by Grassi, who persuaded the penniless editor that the question of 'humanism' was still a worthwhile pursuit in Nazi Germany. Grassi conceived of a series dedicated to publishing the works of George- or Nietzsche-inspired classicists (Schriften für die geistige Überlieferung), a parallel series of relevant pri-

75. On Bondi, see Norton, *Secret Germany*, 219–21. On Küpper, Bondi, and Grassi, see Peter Pawlowsky, *Helmut Küpper vormals Georg Bondi (1895–1970)* (Düsseldorf: Verlag Helmut Küpper vormals Georg Bondi, 1970).

mary sources (Quellen der geistigen Überlieferung), and, most significantly, a *Yearbook for the Spiritual Tradition* (Jahrbuch der geistigen Überlieferung), which was to function as the mouthpiece for the movement.

By the end of 1940, all three enterprises had yielded fruit. Grassi took a
leading role in the yearbook as sole editor, with Otto and Reinhardt listed
as collaborators, and also composed the introductory piece, in the form of
an open letter to Otto, dedicated to the "definition of the task." Grassi was
frenzied:

> We take our cue from the conviction that in our day and age the bound-
> aries between different academic disciplines are problematic. Neither
> philology nor archeology alone can solve the problem concerning the
> relationship with antiquity and its importance. These disciplines,
> taken individually, are founded on the premises that antiquity has a
> historical relevance, and nowadays such historical importance, which
> was once unquestioned, is not only doubted, but revoked and uprooted
> for different scientific as well as nonscientific reasons. The day that
> Nietzsche prophesied for the philologist has come: the one when phi-
> lologists are asked to account for the reason they endow antiquity with
> so much value, the day when they are asked to justify their science but
> will not know how to defend their stance toward the past. This day—I
> am tempted to say, thanks be unto God—has finally come.[76]

While Grassi does not mention George here (or elsewhere for that matter),
the tribute is all too clear. When George finally persuaded himself to go
public, he conceived of a *Yearbook for the Spiritual Movement* (Jahrbuch
der geistige Bewegung), whose first issue came out in 1910 with an opening attack on Wilamowitz penned by Kurt Hildebrandt.[77] Grassi's project
was the same in form, if not in content, only that now the enemy was Jaeger and his 'third humanism.'

Before the enterprise was cut short in 1942, Grassi had managed to collect at least three exceptional contributions. The second and last installment of the yearbook presented a manifesto written at Grassi's behest and
not originally intended for circulation: Karl Reinhardt's "Classical Philology and the Classical." Taking his cue from the Naumberg event organized
by Jaeger in 1930, a notoriously reserved Reinhardt mustered the courage

76. Ernesto Grassi, "Die Frage der geistigen Überlieferung," in *Geistige Überlieferung:
Ein Jahrbuch*, ed. Ernesto Grassi with Walter F. Otto and Karl Reinhardt (Berlin: Verlag
Helmut Küpper, 1940), 11–12.

77. On George's *Yearbook*, see Norton, *Secret Germany*, 428ff.

to voice his stance with respect to Nietzsche, George, Wilamowitz, and Jaeger. In reference to the latter, he states: "In contrast to the revivalist tendencies of the George circle, Jaeger's humanism did not stem from a revelation [*Offenbarung*]."[78] A second document, also not intended for circulation, was none other than Heidegger's "Plato's Doctrine of Truth," which may now be read in light of the heavily construed context in which it was published. That is, Jaeger's role in shaping Heidegger's anti-Platonism no longer needs to be surmised. We are also now in a position to make sense of Grassi's reference to Heidegger's Aristotelianism, a philosophical allegiance that made him an oddball in this group of Platonists. Moreover, if Plato was the alpha of the metaphysics Heidegger wanted to reject, it is equally important in this context to note that Nietzsche, the other muse of this movement, represented the omega.

Enlightening on this point is a recollection Grassi provided in his late years regarding a visit to Heidegger, which presumably took place in the late 1930s:

It happened during an evening in his former house on the Rotebuck-weg, an electrical storm had gathered; his study—looking towards the hills—was in half darkness, and lightning flashed over the Black Forest. To start, I asked him how he was. He answered: "Bad." I asked him whether the reason lay in his recent bad relationship with the Party. His answer was: "Certainly, but not only because of that. Rather it is because I have been removed as member of the advisory committee of the Nietzsche archive." Whereupon I congratulated him, for to my knowledge Reinhardt and W. F. Otto had shortly before been expelled also. His verbatim response was: "No, matters are not simple. Because of what has happened I have taken revenge on posterity." When I asked what he meant by the enigmatic phrase "taking revenge on posterity," he told me: Today I have destroyed a new arrangement of Nietzsche's *Will to Power* which contradicts the one made by his sister Elisabeth Förster and on which I have worked for a long time.[79]

<hr/>

78. Karl Reinhardt, "Die klassische Philologie und das Klassische," in *Geistige Überlieferung: Das zweite Jahrbuch*, 50. In a disclaimer at the beginning of the essay, Reinhardt states: "Zum Abdruck hier ein Vortrag, der in diesem Frühjahr auf Einladung des Herrn Grassi vor einem kleinen Kreis geladener Zuhörer gehalten wurde, mit jenen Zufälligkeiten und Willkürlichkeiten, die man einem Gespräch allenfalls zugute hält; eine Umschrift in Essay-Form ist auf Wunsch des Veranstalters unterblieben. Ohne aufgefordert zu sein, würde ich kaum zu diesem Thema mich geäussert haben."

79. Grassi, *Renaissance Humanism*, xvi.

Heidegger, a self-avowed anti-Platonist, had also tampered with Nietzsche's legacy. Why, then, would Grassi, a Heideggerian-Nietzschean Platonist, not take exception to his teacher's stance but instead work ever more assiduously to involve Heidegger in his project? In fact, at this time, Grassi's interests and competence, among a group of specialists he could not equal, lay elsewhere—namely, in the Italian Renaissance.

ITALIAN RENAISSANCE HUMANISM
IS ALSO A HUMANISM

In light of the fact that Jaeger was long gone and far removed at the time the yearbook was being published, Grassi's theoretical and editorial efforts were certainly an overdue epilogue to what Fritz K. Ringer describes as the decline of German academic "mandarinism."[80] Grassi's venture was in fact destined to fail at the hands of another (assumed) foe in 1942, when Goebbels and the ministry for propaganda took exception to Heidegger's vague and all-encompassing—that is, not strictly political and Hellenistic—use of the term 'humanism.' The Nazis had rightly perceived that Grassi's publications provided elbowroom for the Roman legacy and thus for more modern humanisms such as the Italian.[81] In effect, the *Yearbook* presented a suspiciously miscellaneous array of contents. The scholarly pieces of Reinhardt, Otto, Heidegger, Hugo Friedrich, and others were followed by an illustrative section of primary sources intended to "place the reader in immediate contact" with the experience of antiquity in past epochs.[82] The problem was that such experiences, presented under the title "Varia," were exclusively Italian: for example, excerpted passages (in German translation) from leading civic humanist Leonardo Bruni (1370–1444), an anonymous fragment on the life of proto-revolutionary Cola di Rienzo (1313–54), and, in the second installment, samples of the new art of biography inaugurated by fifteenth-century Florentine chroniclers Filippo Villani and Vespasiano da Bisticci.

As baffling as it might have appeared at first sight, the coexistence of a Heidegger and, for example, a Bruni was made possible by the interpretation of humanism Grassi put forth with unprecedented clarity in his own contributions to the yearbook: starting with an essay titled "The Begin-

---

80. Fritz K. Ringer qualifies Jaeger as a "single-minded humanist" in *The Decline of the German Mandarins: The German Academic Community (1890–1933)* (Hanover, NH: University Press of New England, 1990), 291.

81. See *EG*, 286ff.

82. Grassi, "Vorbemerkung," in *Geistige Überlieferung: Ein Jahrbuch*, 215.

ning of Modern Thought: On the Passion and Experience of the Primordial" that Grassi described in hindsight as a blueprint for all of his future
work.[83] As will become immediately evident, Grassi's interpretations are
noteworthy not only in that they accommodate Heidegger's thought in an
apparently extraneous tradition but also because his nascent Renaissance
scholarship was informed and inspired by the equally embryonic poetics
and theory of language of the *second* Heidegger.

Grassi's essay starts off with a legitimate consideration: "Modern
thought is said to begin with Descartes. Yet it is undeniable that the modern worldview emerges in the epoch of Italian humanism and the Renaissance. Are these two theses in contradiction?" (*RIP*, 171). Grassi noted
that from Hegel's *Lectures* to Ernst Cassirer's *Das Erkenntnisproblem* the
idea that the Renaissance may have been *independently* philosophical had
never been given serious thought and, as a consequence, Quattrocento
humanism had been investigated uniquely for its historical relevance. In
contrast, Grassi schematically presupposed that (1) modern thought, as distinct from medieval thought, was indeed born in the Italian Renaissance
and that (2) the beginning of modern thought may be traced to Descartes
only when philosophy is identified with the question concerning the "preeminence of the problem of knowledge" (*RIP*, 172).

Grassi was unconcerned with periodization per se; rather he engaged
in providing a precise qualification of that "other orientation of modern
thought" that Renaissance humanism represents, on a par with Cartesian
rationalism. To be precise, Grassi avowed that Italian Renaissance humanism was mostly committed to the "overcoming" of philosophical rationalism. If we keep in mind that for Grassi, unlike Heidegger, Greek thought
was by no means 'rational,' then by a process of elimination we can say
that his paradigm rested on the assumption that Renaissance humanism
could be interpreted as a form of anti-Cartesianism. This apparent anachronism is readily explained by the fact that Grassi's interpretive paradigm,
as was the case with Spaventa and Gentile, hinged on the ingrained Vichianism of Italian philosophy.

Contemporaneously with and more forcefully than Abbagnano (and,
as we shall see in the next chapter, alongside Eugenio Garin), Grassi came

---

83. Grassi's essay was the first to appear in the 1940 yearbook after an introductory
exchange between Grassi and Otto. See Grassi, "Der Beginn des modernen Denkens: Von
der Leidenschaft und der Erfahrung des Ursprünglichen," in *Geistige Überlieferung: Ein
Jahrbuch*, 36–84 (*PS*, 495–536). I cite from the translation in *RIP*, 171–99. Grassi later described
this essay as "my first still rather tentative outline of the problem of Humanism." Grassi,
Renaissance Humanism, xviii.

to view Vichian inquiry as a philosophical fulfillment of Renaissance humanism and thus—given Vico's defining quarrel with Descartes—as anti-Cartesianism through and through. This circular or, as it were, recapitulatory view yielded by the assimilation of Vico to Renaissance humanism affords a thoroughly internalist approach to the history of philosophical humanism, one that, by allowing for a pluralistic understanding of philosophy, makes it possible to unconventionally, and heuristically, see Descartes and early Cartesianism as themselves a mere alternative sandwiched between the Italian Renaissance and Vichian legacy. This explains why Grassi's essay begins with a preamble on Descartes aimed at specifying what humanism is not. Though undeniably instrumental, Grassi's interpretation of the French thinker should not be skipped over, for, on a close inspection, it appears to have been modeled after Heidegger's "Plato's Doctrine of Truth," a text that, one should be reminded, was published in the yearbook a year or so *after* Grassi's own contribution.

Grassi's stated goal is to understand what "the essence of philosophy" may consist of from a Cartesian view. He begins by proposing an unconventional interpretation of Descartes's methodical doubt to illustrate how "the character of modern philosophy" came to be "predetermined" through and after him (*RIP*, 173). In Grassi's hypothesis, Descartes was not originally an objectivist; his turn to rationalism occurred instead somewhere between the second and third meditations. In fact, according to Grassi, at the outset of his *Meditations on First Philosophy*, Descartes's "methodical doubt" is not tantamount to a suspension of judgment (*epoché*), nor are "clarity" and "distinction" the qualities of a "truth" interpreted and established (as we do now through a *conventional* interpretation of Platonic ideas) on an "objectivated rational ground." Grassi therefore denies that the cogito may be properly grasped as a rational object of *inspectio* or, in clear reference to Husserl, as the object of a "phenomenological observation," for Descartes certainly *experiences* the cogito and doubt as an open-ended act: the cogito points to an "existential necessity" that is not an "object" but an "act in its enactment" (*RIP*, 174). Moreover, Descartes's famous queries in the second meditation ("What then am I? A thing that thinks. What is that? A thing that doubts, understands, affirms, denies, is willing, is unwilling, and also imagines and has sensory perception") illustrate that Descartes's understanding of the cogito was wide and inclusive of emotions and pathos.[84]

---

84. René Descartes, *Meditations on First Philosophy*, trans. John Cottingham (Cambridge: Cambridge University Press, 1986), 19.

Holding fast to these premises, Grassi concludes with an extrapolation
from Descartes's so-called "wax argument," the moment in which a turn
begins to take place as Descartes's trust in senses gives way to his sole
reliance on *inspectio* and visible examination. While Grassi is willing to
acknowledge that even at this point Descartes puts up a fight against an
objectification and universalization of the cogito, by the third meditation
the French thinker is fully the rationalist we take him to be. Abruptly,
without elaborating further, Grassi comments that at some point in Descartes's *Meditations*,

> the metaphysical problem is *no longer* left *open* as a question relating
> to the Being of beings but is posed as a question relating to the knowl-
> edge of Being. In other words, the metaphysical problem is no longer
> *open* as if we were looking for the foundation of the self-showing of be-
> ings. Rather, *the form of the self-showing is already identified* and thus
> predetermined by one of its forms, that of knowledge. This is already
> the case with Descartes, and it impinges on the idealistic identifica-
> tion of *seeing* and *knowledge* or, to be more precise, logical knowledge.
> (*RIP*, 176)

The affinities (in content, form, and language) between Grassi's "The Beginning of Modern Thought" and Heidegger's "Plato's Doctrine of Truth"
are striking. In what appears to have been a preemptive move, Grassi relo-
cates the shift from an *experienced* understanding of truth as self-showing
and revelation to a rationalist view of truth as "correctness" (as Heidegger
would have it) in modern rather than in ancient times: in Descartes's wax
argument rather than in Plato's allegory of the cave.[85] In so doing, Grassi
implies that plurality of philosophies—good and bad, ancient and modern—may be retained against Heidegger's reduction of Western tradition
to a single, selfsame, and nefarious kind of metaphysics. Also, for Grassi's
purposes, this shift opened up new possibilities for endowing Heideg-

---

85. Given the esoteric nature of the publications, one should not forgo the idea that
Grassi's paraphrase might have been intended as some sort of inside joke. Unfortunately, the
tag game in which Grassi appears to have involved Heidegger is not helpful in precisely dating
"Plato's Doctrine of Truth." Grassi's characterization of Descartes is in fact a verbatim repro-
duction of what he had already stated in an essay from 1933, "Dell'apparire e dell'essere" (see
PS, 293ff.). If I am correct in assuming that Grassi's interpretation of Descartes amounted to
an application of Heidegger's reading of Plato, then the 1931/32 version of "Plato's Doctrine of
Truth" may have been more definitive than was recently maintained. 1931/32 is also the date
Grassi gives for this text when he published it again, together with the "Letter on 'Humanism,'" in 1947.

gerian "immanent metaphysics" with that historical and philosophical precedent (humanism) which Heidegger, Grassi would soon discover, so adamantly shunned.

Perhaps confident that Heidegger would eventually give in to his requests to go public with his anti-Platonic statement, Grassi indeed began philosophizing with the second Heidegger against the second Heidegger by showing that the superior poetic humanism his teacher was just then recovering in Hölderlin was in fact a Renaissance humanism. It is thus that Grassi first came up with the programmatic interpretation of Renaissance humanism as the source of an alternative tradition developed in Italy:

> [T]he essence of the Italian tradition—different from the tradition that stems from Descartes and from the problem of truth and the ground of knowledge—lies in the nonpredetermination of the metaphysical problem in an epistemological sense. Starting with the *problem of the Word*, we no longer predetermine the form in which reality manifests itself. This nonpredetermination of the metaphysical problem is essential to the ancient speculative tradition and was forgotten for far too long. (*PS*, 562; emphasis added)[86]

Here Grassi affirms the affinities between Renaissance humanism and ancient, Greek, thought. Both traditions concern themselves with the "problem of the word," one that may be tackled only through incessant questioning, "passionately" or "pathetically."

At this early stage, Grassi set out to illustrate the existence of such an alternative in the *longue durée*, relying exclusively on three consummate Italian humanists and a handful of their texts: Leonardo Bruni (*The Study of Literature*), Giordano Bruno (*On the Heroic Frenzies* and *Cause, Principle, and Unity*), and Vico (*On the Study Methods of Our Time* and *On the Most Ancient Wisdom of the Italians*).[87] At first glance Bruni's *The Study*

---

86. Grassi's 1940 "La filosofia tedesca e la tradizione speculativa italiana," from which this citation is drawn, was written in response to Benedetto Croce's review of Grassi's second book, *Vom Vorrang des Logos*. Croce had taken exception to Grassi's attempt to attribute a particular essence to Italian thought. For Croce's review, see *La critica* 38 (1940): 39–41.

87. All of these texts are readily available in English translation. See Leonardo Bruni, "The Study of Literature," in *Humanist Educational Treatises*, ed. and trans. Craig W. Kallendorf (Cambridge, MA: Harvard University Press, 2002), 93–125; Giordano Bruno, *On the Heroic Frenzies*, trans. Ingrid D. Rowland (Toronto: University of Toronto Press, 2013); Giordano Bruno, *Cause, Principle and Unity: And Essays on Magic*, trans. Robert de Lucca (Cambridge: Cambridge University Press, 1998); Giambattista Vico, *On the Study Methods of Our Time*, trans. Elio Gianturco (Ithaca, NY: Cornell University Press, 1990); Giambattista Vico, *On the*

of Literature, a letter addressed to Lady Battista Malatesta of Montefeltro for the education of a gifted woman, seems to be irrelevant to philosophy. Its overt goal is in fact pedagogical: "the education of man" (*RIP*, 182). Bruni's neglected contribution to philosophy is to have realized that what is human (*das Menschliche*) is not predetermined but needs to be developed and attended to with care and self-denial. An appreciation of Bruni hinges on the unrecognized philosophical core of his concept of *eruditio*, which the humanist qualifies as *legitima* and *ingenua* rather than as *vulgaris* and *perturbata*, which is how the medieval viewed it. Such erudition is something that the pedagogue awakens in the youth through the two activities that compose the *studia humanitatis*: namely, *peritia litterarum* and *scientia rerum*, the former of which should not be seen as sponsoring some form of haughty elitism. Grassi explicitly held present and past philologists responsible for perverting the universal ideals of philology and the original meaning of *humanitas*: "If indeed the 'litterae' were the exclusive responsibility of a few . . . , then education through the 'litterae' would not be essential to man as such, but only to a particular clique." Indeed, "philologists themselves are principally responsible for this misunderstanding of the humanities, and not just since the nineteenth century" (*RIP*, 183).

Peritia litterarum is not merely 'literary' exercise because, Grassi avows, "through [the classics] different worlds are disclosed to us." If assimilated with *diligentia* ("commitment," "care," "love," and "abnegation"), this multifarious manifestation of reality results in that "self-sufficient wholeness" by which human beings are made "eloquent," *vari*, and *ornati*. *Scientia rerum* complements the study of literature by making sure that nothing be alien to man. Knowledge of divine things and knowledge of things necessary "ad bene vivendum" (for an appropriate way of life), such as philosophy, history, poetry, and oratory, all fall under the competences of the *studia humanitatis* (*RIP*, 184).

Starting with history, Grassi asserts that in Bruni the past is not raised and objectified against our being but rather employed as a source for experiences otherwise precluded to us. At its core, the new historiography that first emerged in the Quattrocento attempts to occasion a sympathetic identification (*Einfühlung*) with the past. As for oratory's contribution to the formation of human beings, it recognizes that they "suffer" or "bear" the "objective other" to which they are subjected and that reveals itself to them only though the word, and in copious speech these stifled emotions

Most Ancient Wisdom of the Italians: Unearthed from the Origins of the Latin Language, trans. L. M. Palmer (Ithaca, NY: Cornell University Press, 1988).

are made to surface again. As for poetry, finally, Grassi notes that Bruni distinguishes between a poetry *per studio et disciplina* (Dante's) and another form of poetry that, instead, originates in "astrazione et furore di mente," that is, from an intimately perceived commotion (*Ergriffenheit*), *furore*, or enthusiasm that "has nothing to do with knowledge." A close reading of Bruni, Grassi concludes, shows that the *studia humanitatis*, in its double aspect as *peritia litterarum* and *scientia rerum*, is concerned with the "development of man, the unfolding of his faculties and passions" (*RIP*, 185). Bruni's *eruditus* is thus a far cry from the academic philologist.

At this point Grassi takes leave of Bruni and turns to Vico, for it was Vico who realized that in imposing his method, Descartes had willingly given up and demoted the *studia humanitatis*. Vico's major accomplishments are to have more closely identified philology and philosophy, to have realized that the knowledge that we derive from the natural sciences is by no means related to truth, and to have restored philosophical dignity to the "verisimilar" alongside the primacy of logical truth (*RIP*, 187). Just like Bruni's, Vico's humanism is also conveyed through pedagogy: "[For Vico] the word is the expression not only of a logical experience but also of a poetic experience that has its autonomy in the image," a poetic experience more suited to the formation of youth (*RIP*, 188; *PS*, 518). Vico's understanding of the *studia humanitatis*, finally, also finds its application in everyday life, in cases concerning action, which are directed not by truth but by *prudentia*. In Vico's own words, "Discretion [*prudentia*] takes guidance from the countless particularities of events; as a consequence any attempt to grasp those detailed aspects, no matter how inclusive, is always insufficient" (*RIP*, 189).[88] Just how, then, Grassi asked with implicit reference to Gentile and Croce and their nineteenth-century forefathers, could Renaissance and Vichian humanism be turned into the precursor of German idealism?

Grassi concludes his essay with a final qualification of philology, which, starting with Bruni, he claims had the responsibility of unlocking reality in its multifarious manifestations. A philology thus understood necessarily calls for a new understanding of objectivity and subjectivity, as well as for a novel grasp of their relationship. Starting with the former, Grassi notes that no single word is endowed with a universal meaning per se; rather a word's significance is teased out from within the limits and unity of an ever widening context: a single sentence, passage, book, writer, and idiom:

88. Vico, *On the Study Methods of Our Time*, 46.

This is why the question of objectivity is posed anew: how do we achieve such objectivity, and where does it come from? In fact, we need to form and shape ourselves in attending to the object, that very same object that introduces us to the world of differences. Therefore, the question regarding philology needs to be raised to an essential level. To question something on the basis of something, to turn something into an object of investigation, actualizes *science*. We move from the general philosophical considerations of the Middle Ages on the question of essence—on being, becoming, matter, form, and so forth—to the problem of reality as it is to be known *from within well-defined boundaries*. The emergence of scientific thought from philosophy occurs, then, for the first time, *not* at the level of the natural sciences—as is usually maintained—but from within philology, where the boundaries of investigation are determined according to well-defined principles. (*RIP*, 192)

Philology, as love of the word, as something that brings humankind into its own, is thus not a science among others but rather "achieves the rank of philosophy and has as its object the essence of man. From this we arrive at the expression 'studia humanitatis,' because the word is here understood to be the defining moment of man, *zoon logon echon*, and to have, therefore, an eminent role" (*RIP*, 194). The connection that Grassi wanted to draw in this essay between Renaissance humanism and the unconventional purposes of his yearbooks is evident from his concluding remark, which makes Nietzsche's creed in *The Birth of Tragedy* his own: "Philosophia facta est quae philologia fuit" (*RIP*, 199).

In this first programmatic essay, Grassi mentions Giordano Bruno last and mainly as the thinker who most forcefully reacted to the erosion of the philosophical import of early humanist philology. Bruno's dialogues are a word to the wise for those who wish to engage in epochal battles against academic pedantry, and Grassi surely drew a connection between the pernicious pedants of the sixteenth century mocked by Bruno and Jaeger's crew. However, while Grassi only hinted at Bruno's heroic frenzy (*eroico furore*) in his essay, this notion became all important in a second programmatic piece published in the yearbook of 1942 ("On the Word and Individual Life") and in *Defense of Individual Life*, the book Grassi worked on during the war years and published in 1946 on resuming his activities in Switzerland.

Just as with his interpretation of Plato, Bruni, and Descartes, Grassi's analysis of Bruno's *On the Heroic Frenzies* is aimed at countering received opinions. This time, Grassi was intent on dispelling the Burckhardtian as well as idealist idea that Italian Renaissance humanism is the birthplace of 'individualism,' especially if by that term one intends self-centeredness, egotism, and an exaltation of the human subject. Grassi's presuppositions in this case are the following:

1. In the Italian tradition, the safeguarding and defense of the "individual life," of the "personal" (*des Persönlichen*), is intimately related to the problem of the word.

2. Such individual life has absolutely nothing to do with individualism; rather, it constitutes the basis for the theory of heroism, which brings to fulfillment the overcoming of any individualistic view (*Anschauung*) and leads to a fundamental explication of what is "objective."

3. The determination of the essence of the individual life, of the "personal," leads to the fundamental question regarding the essence of what is "common" (*des Gemeinsamen*).[89]

In Grassi's terms, humanism is explained by showing the interrelation between what he calls "individual life," the problem of the word, and (Bruno's) poetic heroism. These three elements, furthermore, underscore the particular relationship in humanist metaphysics between the single empirical "subject" and the "objective." Bruno is all-important because through his notion of heroism we are led to realize that what we deem "objective" is never "something at hand or something that lies in front," as already extant. Rather, the "objective" is something experienced; "it comes *into* human beings and, to be sure, only to a few, from a sovereign power." Bruno's hero is thus the "announcer of the objective, a mediator between gods and man who passionately experiences the primordial" (*PS*, 621).

According to Grassi a passage from *Heroic Frenzies* that Bruno dedicates to the path taken by heroic love and intellect toward its proper object, the supreme good and primary truth, in the tale of Actaeon's hunt for ideas illustrates in what way the "hero" may be said to "experience the objective":

---

89. Grassi, *Über das Problem des Wortes und des individuellen Lebens: Erwägungen aus der italienischen Überlieferung, PS*, 616.

He saw her: he understood as much as was possible; *and the hunter turned to prey*: he set out to hunt and became the hunted, this young man who hunts by the operation of the intellect, through which he converts the things he perceives into himself. . . . Thus, Actaeon with those thoughts—those dogs—who sought outside himself for goodness, wisdom beauty—the wild creatures—arrived into the presence of that prey, and was enraptured outside himself by such beauty. He became prey himself, and saw himself converted into what he sought. He realized then that he himself had turned into the longed-for prey of his own dogs, of his own thoughts, because once he had contracted divinity into himself, he no longer needed to seek it outside himself. . . . See then how Actaeon, preyed upon by his own dogs, persecuted by his own thoughts, runs, and *sought to bend / His lightened step towards denser forest depths*; he has been renewed in order to proceed divinely and more lightly, that is, with greater ease and with more effective energy *towards denser forest depths*, to the deserted places, to the region of things incomprehensible. He may once have been a common and ordinary man, but he has now become rare and heroic; he has uncommon actions and thoughts, and leads an extraordinary life.[90]

When confronting the objective the hero enters into an ecstasy or *furore*, which "reconnects him to the primordial" in ways unknown to traditional philosophy. The philosophers *see* the objective in what physically lies before their eyes, but the humanist and the *interpres* instead *perceive* and *endure* it in contact with a transcendence that is located above and beyond the sensual world. Furthermore, Bruno provides a more distinctive and original understanding of the "subject": he who is literally "sub-jected" and thrown under superior powers. In some cases, empirical individuality is redeemed by an exceptional destiny. How can it be, then, Grassi asks, that the Renaissance man has been viewed as being independently creative? In the Renaissance "individual life" or individualism is instead experienced as a "liberation from the subjective" (*PS*, 628).

Starting with the second issue of the yearbook of 1942 and into his *Defense of Individual Life*, Grassi's interpretation of humanism was clearly informed by Heidegger's turn to poetry and his notion of the heroistic founding of truth. Yet Grassi was in a position to reveal his sources of inspiration only many years later. In a brief memoir he lingered over the lectures his teacher delivered on Hölderlin in 1941, dwelled on how the bar

90. Bruno, *On the Heroic Frenzies*, 109–11.

was raised when Heidegger pointed to the German poet as the possessor of a higher humanism, and, finally, on the mysterious workings of poetry, wherein subjectivity is at once subject to and exalted by the word, for language is the "house of Being." Grassi refers on this point to Heidegger's interpretation of Stefan George's *Das Wort*, by whose closing line they were all impressed: "Where words break off no thing may be."[91]

Grassi's early career can be said to have been devoted to checking his teacher's received opinions, for in Grassi's view, Heidegger's talent for original thought and interpretation was matched by his inability to penetrate the rich abundance or *copia* of philosophical tradition(s). Heidegger no doubt played along. He clearly allowed Grassi to involve him in a tug of war that continued into the postwar period. As he eventually entrusted his Platonic student with his anti-Platonic statement, he again entrusted his Italian student with his antihumanist manifesto, the "Letter on 'Humanism,'" just as Grassi had completed his illustration of the "studia humanitatis as philosophical tradition." In conclusion to this chapter, we turn to the circumstances attending this momentous exchange.

CONCLUSION—STARTING FROM
SCRATCH (MORE OR LESS)

In the winter of 1945, Grassi began reconnecting with Castelli from Lugano. Grassi reported he had been smuggled into Switzerland from northern Italy by the National Liberation Committee, following a close encounter with a group of neofascists who sought retaliation for his support of pro-Allied troops. In a short span of time, he had already traveled the highways and byways of this "museum" of a country and was delighted to relate that colleagues and authorities had welcomed the idea of establishing four distinct Swiss divisions (in Basel, Bern, Zurich, and Fribourg) of the short-lived institute "Studia Humanitatis," which he and Castelli had inaugurated in Berlin on the eve of World War II. Moreover, one of the most illustrious presses in the country, the Bern-based Verlag A. Francke, had expressed its wish to resume the publication of his "Geistige Überlieferung" series albeit with a new title: "Sammlung Überlieferung und Auftrag." The collection was now projected to comprise books in three complementary series: "Texts" (Reihe Texte), "Writings" (Reihe Schriften), and "Problems and Interpretations" (Reihe Probleme und Hinweise).

Eager to capitalize on these favorable circumstances, Grassi pressed

91. Grassi, *Rhetoric as Philosophy*, 12.

Castelli to provide him with documentation from Italian authorities clearing his name of any association with Fascism. Equally important was his instruction to urge their Italian colleagues to get to work on previously commissioned editions of Renaissance and modern Italian classics. Heidegger's Italian student was particularly keen to put out translations of works by some of his favorites—Guicciardini, Vico, and Leopardi—as well as of Dante's *Monarchy* and Giannozzo Manetti's humanist manifesto *On the Dignity of Man*. Grassi observed that even though the Swiss seemed particularly impervious to philosophical considerations, they could hardly conceal their interest in humanism and the Renaissance. Conveying his determination to Castelli (19 October 1945), he stated: "Significance and international repute may accrue to our wretched country only through a rehabilitation of our [humanist] legacy" (APEC).

Castelli did not have to be asked twice. He set out to provide Grassi with the support needed to represent Italy in Switzerland and, in a few months time, rushed to meet his friend in the small frontier town of Cannobio. According to Castelli's diary entry from 15 October 1945: "I get to the Swiss border at 1:45 pm. . . . At the two ends of the bridge the usual barriers. In the middle, Grassi is already waiting for me in the neutral area. . . . He had tears in his eyes. . . . After half an hour we had come to agreements regarding our initiatives in Switzerland. Credentials delivered" (*D*, 2:94–95). Grassi could now resume his work, which he did with a gesture that for him symbolized freedom: the publication of Romano Guardini's *The Death of Socrates*. In this book, the Italian-born Catholic thinker closely examines the dialogues Plato dedicated to his teacher's trial and execution (*Euthyphro*, *Apology*, *Crito*, and *Phaedo*) without critical apparatus and according to the goals of the new *Platoforschung*: "These texts are queried for Socrates's vision of death, how he perceived his life in the presence of death, and how he endured his end."[92] Guardini's self-identification with Socrates is evident. In 1939, he had been forced into an internal exile after losing his chair in 'Catholic *Weltanschauung*' at the University of Berlin. Despite this censure, Grassi had made sure to have Guardini's book printed in Florence, in the shop of editor Vallecchi, which, with the connivance of the German consul in Florence and Helmut Küpper (two George circle affiliates), he then smuggled into Berlin and published in a limited but successful edition in 1943.[93] Socrates may very

92. Romano Guardini, *Der Tod des Sokrates*, 19.
93. The book was published in a series edited by Grassi and connected to the institute "Studia Humanitatis." A note on the last pages of this edition specifies: "GEDRUCKT IM

well have been the first martyr of philosophical freedom, but he was not the only one. Another emblematic figure was Giordano Bruno, a selection from whose *Heroic Frenzies* and other works Grassi also published in 1945, presumably in Guardini's own, though uncredited, translation.[94]

According to the editorial project, Guardini's and Bruno's manifestos would be followed by Grassi's *Defense of Individual Life*, other studies of Plato by notable George- or Heidegger-inspired interpreters such as Wilhelm Szilasi and Emil Staiger, and a short anthology of Francesco Guicciardini's *Ricordi*. Of course, at that time, Grassi could not expect that his collection would almost immediately come to host one of the most influential texts of the postwar period—Heidegger's "Letter on 'Humanism.'" By closely following Grassi and Castelli through their 1946 trip through Germany, one comes to the realization that their reception of the manuscript might not have been incidental. Rather, some evidence supports the idea that the (in)famous letter was in fact commissioned by Castelli as much as it was by Beaufret.

Castelli finally managed to cross over into Switzerland and reconnect with Grassi in Basel on the evening of 6 June 1946, after having planned for an international conference in Rome. The trip he undertook to Germany allowed him to pursue two goals: rallying German philosophers for the Roman event and participating in the discussions surrounding the denazification and reform of German universities that U.S. officer Edward Yarnall Hartshorne (1912–46) singlehandedly spearheaded in Marburg during that summer.[95] Castelli and Hartshorne were kindred spirits; they both wished for a swift rehabilitation of the German intelligentsia and cultural institutions, and they pursued this goal very much on their own initiative, impatient as they were with the sluggishness of the bureaucratic appara-

---

AUGUST 1943 VON DER GRAPHISCHEN ANSTALT VALLECCHI IN FLORENZ." I owe this information to Frank-Rutger Hausmann.

94. See Hanna-Barbara Gerl, *Romano Guardini: Leben und Werk* (Mainz: Matthias-Grünewald, 1985), 324. Gerl, who was a student of Grassi, refers to a letter sent to Grassi (31 October 1944), in which Guardini, before agreeing to translate Bruno, would have turned down the invitation to translate selections from Vico. It is unclear, however, why Guardini would not be credited, since the book appeared after World War II. See Giordano Bruno, *Heroische Leidenschaften und individuelles Leben*, ed. Ernesto Grassi (Bern: A. Francke, 1947).

95. Hartshorne's diary entries and correspondence from this period are collected in James F. Tent, ed., *Academic Proconsul: Harvard Sociologist Edward Y. Hartshorne and the Reopening of German Universities, 1945–1946. His Personal Account* (Trier: Wissenschaftlicher Verlag, 1998). For a thorough account of academic denazification, see James F. Tent, *Mission on the Rhine: Reeducation and Denazification in American-Occupied Germany* (Chicago: University of Chicago Press, 1982).

tus. Indeed, the *Hochschulgespräche* that took place in Marburg revolved around topics that had long been at the center of Castelli's professional and intellectual interest, such as "Science and Science Reform," "Academia and Politics," and especially "School and Christianity" and "International [Academic] Relations." The rather fortuitous presence of Grassi and Castelli in Marburg at that time ensured that Italy, though perhaps uninvited, would be represented at the winner's table.

Exactly why a rehabilitation of German academia was of paramount concern for Castelli can be gleaned from the speech Grassi delivered in German on behalf of his friend on 14 June:

> Italy and Germany share a common interest in resuming a deeper cultural exchange. However, we should not vaguely call for a reconnection. Rather, we should engage in an exchange of scholars and academic contributions as well as in establishing the sorts of academic chairs that may be apt to revalue tradition: as for example a chair in Roman law, on the one hand, and a chair in humanist literature, on the other, the former in recognition of the sources of any law, the latter in recognition of the principle of collaborative exchange. To this day, unfortunately, no Italian publication has made it to Germany. This isolation needs to be avoided. . . . I assure you that all efforts will be made to gratuitously send Italy's most significant publications to German universities and libraries. (*D*, 2:212)

First and foremost, Castelli feared that in the postwar period the spiritual progress of the West would be determined by American or Russian technocracies. His appeal to tradition, to the values of Christianity and the Italian Renaissance, was an anxious attempt to salvage hoary "wisdom" from the threats of scientism. Again, in addressing the delegations, he stated that "this wisdom [*sapienza*] became a common possession of our continent at the end of the Middle Ages thanks to Christian civilization, and such wisdom is what ties the new world to the old continent. We wish to remind you of this because such wisdom provides a common ground for winners and vanquished; it is a wisdom that replaces victory [*vincere*] with con-viction [*con-vincere*]" (212). Seizing the occasion, Castelli and Grassi concluded by inviting all the bystanders to their philosophical conference in Rome, for "a congress eschews all definitive conclusions and aims only at physically bringing together dissenting men, and we know that personal acquaintance and the possibility of staring in each other's eyes abates all conflicts. . . . The invitation we address to the representatives of German culture to participate in the conference is an invitation to return to tradition—that is, a return to human contact" (213).

No doubt, Castelli was keen on beating everyone to the punch. Despite the evident rhetorical overtones of his initiative, he was determined to have the rebirth of Europe take place in Rome and on his watch. To this end, Castelli set out to assemble traveling permits for a German delegation that, according to his original checklist, was supposed to have included Julius Ebbinghaus, Karl Jaspers, Gerhard Krüger, Hans Deichmann, Alfred Weber, Max Schreiber, and Willy Hartner (American zone); Thure von Uexküll, Mario De Rosa, and Nicolai Hartmann (English zone); and Robert Heiss, Romano Guardini, and Martin Heidegger (French zone) (D, 2:217).[96] The latter was the most emblematic figure and Castelli's most coveted prey. In fact, on 9 June—a week before the beginning of Hartshorne's seminars—Grassi and Castelli had already participated in what Gadamer called the "postwar international pilgrimage to Todtnauberg" by presenting themselves at the doorstep of Heidegger's ski hut.[97]

This encounter is described in Castelli's diaries, and it provides a rare account of Heidegger's rustification:

> Tod[t]nauberg, twenty houses in all. On the hilltop, an isolated wooden shack. This is Martin Heidegger's home. A short man with ripped pants and holes in his shoes. The wooden shack is made up of four tiny rooms: a main entrance room with a table, three minuscule double-paned windows, up high a shelf laden with cheap plates. They have no cutlery. It was stolen a few days before. In the next room three makeshift beds, and the following one is Heidegger's study room with a makeshift bed and a table, scattered papers, and a bookshelf, and two small windows overlooking the Black Forest. The space is not bigger than 1.5 meters in width and length. The fourth room is a kitchen of equal size. In the entrance room a small corner cupboard with some wildflowers, an old-fashioned clock on the wall with a large dried thistle over it. The drawing of a farmer friend of the philosopher.
>
> They gave us a cold welcome. The wife was a tough Prussian, daughter of a high-ranking military official. We talked about our children.

96. Among them, only Ebbinghaus and Deichmann eventually made it to Rome, while a paper by Jaspers was read in absentia. Unflustered, Castelli beefed up the German delegation with German scholars residing in Italy, among them Gustav Gundlach, Alois Naber, and Erik Peterson.

97. Hans-Georg Gadamer, *Philosophical Apprenticeships*, trans. Robert R. Sullivan (Cambridge, MA: MIT Press, 1985, 45.

Jörg Heidegger, Camp n. 276 in Jaroslawl (Volga).

Hermann Heidegger, Camp n. 399.

"We have no more news since December 1945," Mrs. Heidegger tells me in the Tod[t]nauberg shack. The two sons of Martin Heidegger, who are prisoners of the Russians, have not been in touch for six months. "Two Russians have taken some interest in the case, because my husband has some admirers in Russia, but so far to no avail."

I don't doubt it. But it must be a silent admiration, because they cannot possibly talk about it.

It's 2 p.m. The Heideggers don't eat, because they are afraid that they might have to offer us some soup. We set our food supplies on the table. "Bitte . . ." Heidegger would gladly accept a meat sandwich, but his wife shoots him a cold stare. Heidegger pulls his hand away from the table.

—Food?

—Vegetables and fruit?

—None of this can be found here.

It's a whispered conversation. The denazification process takes its toll on Heidegger's existence. (*D*, 2:205–6)

In his late recollections, Grassi mistakenly referred to this meeting in early June as the time in which the "Letter on 'Humanism'"—which was actually written in the following winter—was handed over. While, unfortunately, neither Castelli's diaries nor his dense correspondence with Grassi clarifies this mistake, it may be assumed that Grassi received the letter in his subsequent visits to Heidegger, which he also undertook at Castelli's behest with a specific goal in mind.

As already evident from the passages cited so far, the diary entries that Castelli dedicated to his German trip afford an intimate look at Germany during its 'zero hour.' Castelli was particularly impressed by what he perceived as German resignation, a recalcitrance toward starting new things that clearly troubled him. His meetings with prominent German editors such as Herder, Insel, Klostermann, and Grassi's onetime collaborator Helmut Küpper were particularly revealing to him of the Germans' intolerable state of mind. Indeed, in Bad Godesberg, where he reached Küpper and presented him with a barrage of editorial plans, Castelli's hopes for a speedy recovery of an Italo-German cultural axis began to fade. Küpper seemed dazed and fit merely to recount the story of his near escape from Berlin. He told his visitors that while fleeing from Charlottenburg in the midst of fires and explosions he was suddenly seized by the arm. To his dismay, he realized that he had been apprehended by a large primate ("an orangutan") that had fled the city's zoo. When the frightened animal laid its head on his shoulder and accompanied him for a bit along the Kurfürstendamm, one of Berlin's central avenues, Küpper was struck by a deep sense of shame on behalf of humankind. When Castelli, who clearly could not take a hint, again pressed the editor for his collaboration, Küpper finally served it straight to his "restless" and "overexcited" visitors.[98] Referring to the present state of German presses and the English censorship, he reported the case of a recently planned edition of the children's tale *Little Red Riding Hood*. Allowed at first, the publication was subsequently forbidden because, "at a closer look," the "barbarous killing of the wolf" could instigate German youth to violence (*D*, 2:220). Küpper's message was clear: Castelli and Grassi were kindly asked to take a step back and leave the German people in peace, at least for the time being.

Some appreciation of Castelli's emotions during his trip is needed to understand how he came to conceive of a documentary account of what he was experiencing. At first he drew up an outline for a book in which he would provide a series of portraits dedicated to German professors and intellectuals—those "wretched men alienated from the world"—including chapters on "the Black Forest wild boar," that is, Heidegger, and "the venerable old man of Heidelberg," Jaspers (*D*, 2:229). But shortly after meeting with Küpper and finding him not up to task, he resolved to edit a volume, *Letters from Germany*, comprising "open letters" written personally by German professors, in the present charged with the spiritual reform of their country and of the West. Allegedly, Jaspers immediately signed on (*D*, 2:225), then, in fast succession, Walter Eucken, Gustav Radbruch, Walter Hallstein, Uexküll, and Guardini. Finally, in a diary entry dated 29 June 1946, Castelli took note that following a second visit from Grassi and "after a long discussion, [Heidegger] appears to be persuaded to submit a letter for my volume" (232).

This is how Grassi, upon the French veto of Heidegger's participation in the Roman conference, came to be charged with an impossible mission. By the following winter Castelli expected his friend to provide him with two important documents: an open letter from Heidegger as well as Heidegger's approval of and signature on a short communication Castelli

98. In a letter to Edgar Salin (27 June 1946), Küpper stated: "Provai grande gioia quando lo incontrai e lo vidi di nuovo, ciò nonostante mi sembra che Grassi faccia andare il suo motore a regime altissimo, si percepisce talvolta una certa irrequietezza e sovraeccitazione e così spero tanto che riesca a realizzare i suoi progetti per il prossimo futuro" (Neher, "Ernesto Grassi curatore della *Rowohlts*," 259–60).

had written for him, one in which Heidegger was asked to lament his state of quasi-abduction at the hands of the French, concluding with his best wishes for the Roman conference.[99] Castelli vented his frustration to Hugo Friedrich: "If Heidegger doesn't muster the guts to produce an open letter with his thoughts of the present moment, he is then a man who deserves no esteem; he is finished and he has only his name as a weapon. The resonance of his voice abroad is a powerful weapon; if he doesn't take advantage of it, he is a man who does not deserve to be defended" (D, 2:232).

Grassi could not deliver. In the following September he was forced to flee Germany empty-handed on account of some rumors that may have involved him in the denazification process. The Roman conference, then, was inaugurated without Heidegger's communication. Just five days earlier Beaufret had addressed his famous query to Heidegger: "How can some sense be restored to the word 'humanism'?" In reference to Castelli's comment, it can be said that Heidegger was far too aware of the "weapons at his disposal." It has often and convincingly been argued that Heidegger deliberately and successfully took advantage of Beaufret's commission to replace Sartre as the leading philosopher of France. However, after having reintegrated the Italian involvement in the production of this testament, we can now appreciate Heidegger's talent in also stifling the nascent philosophical pretensions of the Italians. In one blow, Heidegger's letter forestalled any attempt to reduce his philosophical stance to a 'humanism,' be it Sartre's 'existentialism as humanism,' the Italian 'humanism as existentialism' of an Abbagnano or Grassi, or, through Grassi's initiatives in Germany, the anti-Jaegerian, Georgian, or Heideggerian humanism into which, we can now say in hindsight, Heidegger was unwillingly drawn.

From Spaventa to Gentile and further into a brand-new generation of thinkers, Italian philosophy had accrued confidence through a painstaking rehabilitation of its Renaissance legacy. The last step in this journey, a long-awaited appreciation of the alternative (to Cartesianism) philosophi-

99. The recommended communication read: "Sono spiacente che le autorità francesi occupanti non mi permettano di uscire dalla Germania e da questa Selva Nera dove sono relegato, dopo che mi è stata tolta la cattedra all'Università di Friburgo e l'abitazione, e la biblioteca occupata da un sergente dell'esercito francese con la sua famiglia. Credevo che uno stato liberale e democratico della libertà avesse un altro concetto. . . . La mia comunicazione, che la posta liberale non trasmetterebbe, consegno in mani amiche; l'abilità per raggiungere un fine è un dovere per chi crede di dover chiarire un idea e contribuire ad un'intesa sul terreno dei valori spirituali. Che la constatazione di un disastro sociale possa essere punto di orientamento per una collaborazione più viva tra i dotti, ai fini di una seria ricostruzione, questo è il mio augurio." In conclusion to his letter, Castelli asked: "Firmerà Heidegger? A te la cura. Nulla ha da perdere." Castelli to Grassi, 20 August 1946, APEC.

cal import of a much beleaguered Quattrocento humanism, was just then taking place. Thwarted by Heidegger's letter, Grassi was now left with the task of recovering from his censure. At a loss for strategies, his first reaction was to buy time. A significant blurb from Emil Staiger's review of Heidegger's text, originally published in the *Neue Zürcher Zeitung* on 20 December 1947, was reproduced in the final pages of the volumes that, in Grassi's series, followed Heidegger's "Letter." Via Steiger, Grassi stated: "In this work a thinker rises to speak, who is determined to question the Western philosophical legacy in its entirety and to resume thinking from the very point where pre-Socratic thought left off. Whether this task is heroic, conceited, titanic, grandiose, or deluded, this is a question of secondary importance that no single individual may dare to decide at this point." For all of their organizational and philosophical shrewdness, Grassi and Castelli were in dire need of assistance: a scholar equipped with the philological skills (they evidently lacked) necessary to substantiate their interpretation of Renaissance humanism as philosophy. The scholar-philosopher whom they had already turned to for a sound exegesis of primary sources and for a reliable *italienische Humanismus* was none other than Eugenio Garin.

CHAPTER FOUR

Holding It Together: Eugenio Garin

Just as we fully agree with Giuseppe Saitta's idea that "our" Renaissance philosophy—resolutely understood as a "humanism"—definitely
heralded something "new," this same lesson amounts to an invitation
to peruse those texts again, not only to establish a profound continuity
between us and them, but to seize the living person that stood behind
those texts: to seize *their own* word whose present relevance is due to
the fact that it is *one* and the *same* as well as *different*, very *different*
from our own, and for this very reason still apt to enrich us. Moreover,
the only living *maestri* of Italian thought are those who remain loyal
to that human interpretation of philosophy which was energetically
proclaimed in the Renaissance, *this* Renaissance: an interpretation of
philosophy that remains, ever since, the most significant gain of the
modern world.
—Eugenio Garin

INTRODUCTION

E ugenio Garin (1909–2004) was a thinker who strove to stand on the
shoulders of Renaissance giants and, therefore, a "maestro" of Italian thought in his own right—indeed, the very last. Garin's philosophical
scholarship does not easily lend itself to cultural translation, as it may
not be grasped from the outside in. Rather, his groundbreaking work on
the history of Italian philosophy, Renaissance and modern, must be understood from an internal perspective. The catch is that such a perspective
derives in large part from Garin's own historiographical work, on whose
coordinates this study, too, necessarily relied in developing its narrative.

This said, the epigraph above, which concludes a 1952 review of Giuseppe Saitta's monumental *Italian Thought in the Age of Humanism and the Renaissance* (1949–51), allows us to apprehend a few salient features of Garin's mature scholarly agenda just as they were being formulated.[1] Garin rightly characterizes Saitta's study as a posthumous testament, penned by its sole survivor, of a recent and too easily dismissed era. It could be added that in the postwar period Saitta's book went largely unread precisely because it epitomized the instrumentalization of the Renaissance typical of that brand of idealist historiography inaugurated by Spaventa, advanced by Gentile, and, later and in partial chronological overlap with Saitta's radicalization, reformed for a new epoch by Garin.

In chapter 2 of this study, Saitta was introduced as the oldest and most faithful among the first generation of Gentile's students and as the spokesperson of a 'Renaissancism' comparable in intensity to Nietzsche's. In his review, Garin specifies that Saitta's 'loyalty' to the Renaissance was founded on an uncompromising acceptance of 'humanism' as philosophy or, more correctly, on an understanding of all 'true' philosophy, including Gentilean actualism, as a (Renaissance) humanism. This was a conviction, Garin realized, that in and of itself amounted to a drastic, and seldom appreciated, break with the central assumption that, from the Risorgimento to (and *including*) Gentile, had informed what we call the Italians' 'Renaissance shame,' namely, the idea that Quattrocento humanists were at bottom faint-hearted and disengaged aesthetes, their scholarly and artistic achievements notwithstanding. Thus Garin agreed with Saitta that the humanists were neither the mere literati to whom the Risorgimento imputed the ruin of Italy nor the weak precursors of a modern immanentism perfected by Gentile; yet he believed that they could best be reclaimed for the present by restoring the distance that Italian idealism had progressively chewed up in its incessant 'actualization' of history.

It may be impossible for him to claim a direct identification, yet Garin sees a special affinity between modern Italians and their Renaissance ancestors ("'our' Renaissance"), given that modern Italian philosophy always labored to reconnect with and advance, often in fruitful misconstrual, the humanist cause. Precisely because Italian philosophy is eternally imbricated with its interpretive tradition of the Renaissance, the thoroughly historicized view of the epoch ("'this' Renaissance") that Garin announced and began to work on for a postnationalist era was bound to look different

---

1. Eugenio Garin, review of *Il pensiero italiano nell'Umanesimo e nel Rinascimento*, by Giuseppe Saitta, *Belfagor* 7 (1952): 481–82.

from the Renaissance created between the Risorgimento and the rise (and demise) of Fascism. This review gave Garin the chance to state unambiguously his ambitions as a Renaissance scholar: the *reaffirmation* of the Renaissance as a modern epoch and its humanism's enduring *philosophical* relevance, all while relying—and this was the challenge—on nothing but a sound exegesis of primary sources.[2]

Unambiguously and from the outset, Garin thus presented his scholarship as involving a critical subsumption of the major gains of idealist historiography. The fact that Garin never concealed the debt that he owed Gentile and his school is arguably the central hallmark of his intellectual activity. In the immediate postwar period, at a time when Gentile's name was unutterable and when many went along with the suggestion, attributed to Croce, to dismiss the Fascist ventennio as a mere interlude in Italian history, Garin repeatedly and variously called for a catharsis based on a thorough confrontation with and acceptance of the recent past, rather than its uncritical rejection and suppression. This is evident in Garin's attempts to avoid losing the idealists' 'Renaissance' in the wholesale jettisoning of actualism, for example—upon Gentile's assassination, Garin rushed to celebrate him as the "most profound scholar of the Renaissance in Italy" —as well as in his employment of new philosophical inspirations.[3] A case in point is Garin's espousal of Gramscianism, a philosophy that many in the postwar period embraced as a new credo and as a vehicle for escapism but that Garin, instead, immediately 'deposthumized' by presenting Gramsci as what he was: an 'other voice,' maybe, but still a contemporary of Croce and Gentile and thus an ideal interlocutor with whom to pursue an otherwise untenable deconstruction of early twentieth-century philosophical culture.

The heightened consciousness that Garin had of himself as a man in the middle, as a witness to both ends of the twentieth century, needs to be reckoned with in these preliminary remarks since it explains the metascholarly flair of his work. That is, there is hardly a line in Garin's corpus, especially in his early production, that may be taken at face value, as merely an informed and competent observation on the subject treated. Rather, more or less openly, Garin's scholarship self-consciously and ob-

2. On the achievements Italian academia attributes to Garin, see Michele Ciliberto, "Umanesimo e Rinascimento nella storiografia filosofica dell'ultimo cinquantennio," in *Figure in chiaroscuro: Filosofia e storiografia nel Novecento*, by Michele Ciliberto (Rome: Edizioni di Storia e Letteratura, 2001), 123–24.

3. Eugenio Garin, "Giovanni Gentile interprete del Rinascimento," *La Rinascita* 7 (1944): 63. Compare with "Giovani Gentile interprete del Rinascimento," *Giornale critico della filosofia italiana* 26 (1947): 117–28.

sessively draws attention to the specific circumstances of its production.[4] This aspect of his work makes Garin a tricky subject for intellectual history, a discipline that often intervenes in and reconstructs the unspoken premises attending a thinker's recorded utterances. For what is left to say or to uncover if Garin's autobiographical scholarship itself explains all, and often transparently and *bona fide*?

The fact is that Garin, relying on some emblematic publications, characterized his scholarship and that of his peers in the interwar period as a dissembling of sorts. In 1928, at the height of Fascism's reign, Croce rescued from oblivion a little-known pamphlet published in 1641, Torquato Accetto's *On Honest Dissimulation*. This short treatise was presented by Croce as "a meditation of a resplendent soul and full of love, who from this very light and love draws the intent (a moral intent) for caution and dissimulation."[5] With the message that not all dissimulation is hypocrisy, this work seemed to have been written for the very purpose of absolving and comforting the unquiet consciences of a generation too young to raise its voice against the regime. Then, a decade later, in 1939, that same generation saw its own vicissitudes reflected in that particular form of dissimulation called "Nicodemism," practiced by the representatives of the Italian heretical movement that Delio Cantimori depicted, in dissembling style of course, in a pioneering study on the subject.[6] The Nicodemism condemned by Calvin himself, Cantimori comments, was for the persecuted less a "specific doctrine than a moral attitude" on which to rely until fear of martyrdom was dispelled.[7]

Garin, a venerated figure in some circles, has not always been taken at his word when, referring to these publications, he asked that his early scholarship be read between the lines, for until 1946–47, he repeatedly stated, "the tragedy of the present was reflected onto the past; it helped us—or so we believed—to *see* the past."[8] Far from wanting to invalidate

4. In a pioneering essay on Garin, Dante Della Terza qualifies Garin's discourse as "mimetic," often developed through the words of others. See Dante Della Terza, "Eugenio Garin, critico della cultura italiana contemporanea," *Belfagor* 36 (1981): 395.

5. Torquato Accetto, *Della dissimulazione onesta*, ed. Benedetto Croce (Bari: Laterza, 1928), 12.

6. For a thoroughly introduced edition, see Delio Cantimori, *Eretici italiani del Cinquecento e Prospettive di storia ereticale del Cinquecento*, ed. Adriano Prosperi (Turin: Einaudi, 2002).

7. Delio Cantimori, "'Nicodemismo' e speranze conciliari nel Cinquecento italiano," in *Studi di Storia* (Turin: Einaudi, 1959), 519.

8. Eugenio Garin, "Sessanta anni dopo," in *La filosofia come sapere storico: Con un saggio autobiografico* (Rome: Laterza, 1990), 140.

his investigations, Garin asserted the belief that the endurance and appeal of his generation's interpretive paradigms were due to their *empathic* understanding of an equally turbulent epoch, the Quattrocento. Garin returned to this point ever more confidently during the postwar period, when the Renaissance began to be approached dispassionately, indeed more objectively, but, as he realized bitterly, with no intimate repercussions on a new generation of scholars and their society. At some point, reflecting on Cantimori's career, Garin went so far as to recall nostalgically the typical "enthusiasm" and "fecund pathos" that attended younger scholars' initiation into Renaissance scholarship in the school of Saitta. In hindsight, and safely emancipated from the distortion promoted by the idealists' "actualization of history" (his generation, said Garin, eventually realized that when attacking Thomas Aquinas Saitta was really after Agostino Gemelli), Garin could claim that, all things considered, he and his peers continued to use the Renaissance to "reconquer everything," to question every enduring value anew and thus, like and against their "fathers," reclaim their rightful place in history and society.[9] Certainly, plain scholarship, "erudite curiosity," could not by itself have inspired such lasting drive.

It should be emphasized that Garin articulated these recollections around 1968, in the wake of a new revolution brought about by a systematic liquidation of past values rather than their revaluation. For this reason, at this juncture in history, Garin felt that his generation had outlived its historical purpose. But had it really? In the field of Renaissance scholarship, at least, these interpretations have retained their inspirational appeal to this day. This fact in turn points to a failure that is epochal (as it involves several generations): a failure to repersonalize the Renaissance as we now reckon belatedly with the legacy not of our 'fathers' but, for the younger among us, of our grandfathers, indeed, great-grandfathers. Garin's message to the present is clear: our affection for his generation's Renaissance(s) can be attributed to our unwitting participation in a pathos kindled in the Risorgimento, rekindled in the interwar period, and safeguarded from snuffing by a first generation of postidealists, if not properly antifascists. And thus it is critical that current reappraisals of Garin and his epoch—on both sides of the Atlantic—not avoid confronting the most chauvinistic phases in the making of the Italians' Renaissance, for, as Garin never tired to emphasize, the Renaissance of his traumatized generation was not, nor

9. Eugenio Garin, "Delio Cantimori e gli studi dell'età del Rinascimento," *Annali della Scuola normale superiore di Pisa: Classe di lettere e filosofia* 37 (1968): 223ff.

it could be, a clear-cut deliverance from the past, but rather was marked by incorporations and introjections.

In his recent edition of Garin's early and lesser-known essays, Michele Ciliberto rightly notes that a proper contextualization of this corpus demands a broader investigation into a generation of intellectuals formed under Fascism (*IR*, 1:vii). While this work remains to be done, the following chapter attempts to restore Garin—who too often, implies Ciliberto, is treated as a thinker sui generis—to his rightful place within a generation of positive existentialists. The selection of those to discuss in this study was based on Garin's own suggestion in a central passage of his autobiography: Abbagnano, Castelli, and Grassi, among others. We shall see that like his fellow outsiders, Garin also initially engaged in philosophical deprovincialization, not to dismiss actual idealism, but to revive it in contact with comparable European experiences.

This ambition of Garin is more clearly visible in the *History of Philosophy* that was commissioned from him by editor Enrico Vallecchi, in 1943, "for a truer and wider acculturation of [the Italian] people."[10] Garin's history, which begins with the pre-Socratics, presents a double ending. The penultimate section, "Italian Philosophy," concludes with Garin's only recorded appreciation in his early works of Gentile's actual idealism: "The greatest merits and the profound efficacy of Gentilean philosophy lie in its consuming exaltation of the concreteness of the spiritual act, in its dissolution of solidified abstractions in the lively crucible of thought thinking [*pensiero pensante*], and in its profound awareness of the spiritual life."[11] Garin juxtaposed this assessment with that in a final section, "Contemporary Thinkers," dedicated to existentialism, both the German version (Jaspers and Heidegger) and his preferred French spiritual version (Le Senne and Lavelle). In describing existentialism as the latest manifestation of an ever-recurring dissatisfaction with systematic philosophy (since Saint Augustine), Garin pointed to this nonphilosophy's "adherence to living reality," its emphasis on the impossibility of "reducing thought to pure logic and intellectual processes" as man's "centrality" is recovered in his "finitude":

In the varied multiplicity of its manifestations, existentialism has restored philosophical reflection to the urgency of human problematicity

---

10. Eugenio Garin, *Storia della filosofia* (1945; Rome: Edizioni di Storia e Letteratura, 2011), v.

11. Garin, *Storia della filosofia*, 586.

that intellectual abstraction tended to overshadow: the deepest revelation of being is queried with an appeal to pain, suffering, and death. The harsh experiences of these bitter years have shattered idealistic optimism, emphasizing the tragic aspect of life. Yet conscience is not good or bad only; sin may not be detached from virtue; pain coexists with joy. If met with serenity, the downfall becomes a sublime sacrifice that saves man and paves the way to God. If the philosophy of yore was guilty of excessive faith, today's thinking is guilty of excessive discomfort.[12]

Garin himself, not unlike Abbagnano, resorted to a positively rearticulated existentialism to reexperience lived life, as his expectations of actual idealism dwindled owing to its increasing intellectualization and crystallization into a rigid, acritical, and thus naïvely optimistic faith in its own revolutionary powers.

If, given his penchant for the French *philosophie de l'esprit*, Garin's early philosophical stance may be defined in terms of a "religious existentialism," as Ciliberto has it, it is also true that such existentialism was characteristically 'positive' and cooperative. Unable to appeal to their compromised seniors, Garin, Abbagnano, Grassi, and Castelli all turned to existentialism, critically, for edification, and to rehearse a dream of a new collaborative society. Citing Louis Lavelle at the very end of his work, Garin states: "*Contradiction* is not the fundamental experience, rather, *participation* is."[13] In a period of intellectual isolation, they sought participation in the past, in a tradition that, without immediate intervention, was destined to bear the blame for present-day mistakes.

PICHIAN EXISTENTIALISM

As is well-known, Italian philosophy and the Renaissance were not Garin's trade from the outset. He began his career as a scholar of Joseph Butler and the English Enlightenment after having studied with Francesco De Sarlo (one of the heroes of the 1926 conference and the proponent of a reconciliation between philosophical and scientific methods) and, more closely, with Ludovico Limentani (a late representative of the positivist school against which Croce and Gentile hurled their anathema), who bestowed upon his student a particular approach to philosophy and history, one to which

12. Garin, *Storia delle filosofia*, 606–7.
13. Garin, *Storia della filosofia*, 605.

Garin "strove to remain faithful" throughout his life.[14] Garin recalls that at the University of Florence, from which he graduated in 1929 (the year in which the Lateran Accords shook Gentile's philosophical hegemony), the sound standards of historical research of pioneering Renaissance scholars such as Felice Tocco, Pasquale Villari, and Francesco Fiorentino were self-consciously safeguarded against the "idealist wave" that engulfed Italian academia in the first decades of the twentieth century.

At that time, the perception was that philosophical historiography could either tarry in inconsequential minutiae, as the philosophers said of their perceived antagonists, or, as the philologists rebuked, perpetrate "a violent and falsifying reconstruction of the 'true' author, or of the author's 'truth,' that is, of all that could be reintegrated in the prefabricated schemes of a progressively conquered truth, *de claritate in claritatem*— from Thales to Hegel, or beyond to Gentile and Neothomism."[15] Aligned with the 'erudites' by affiliation, Garin nevertheless endeavored to blaze a middle path. In his view, the more concrete studies of the idealists were not rubbish. Nor were the philologists' studies inconsequential for philosophy:

> To a dispassionate onlooker, that positivism of ours, that rigorous humanism was something very serious, and very close to that other form of rigorous humanism represented by absolute idealism, with whom positivism fought proudly but with whom, however, it shared many profound exigencies. At the end of the nineteenth century, this affinity had already been perceived by Fiorentino and Spaventa; and, diversely, in the twentieth century, by Gentile. . . . Positivists and idealists shared an aversion for the abstract aspirations toward a disembodied spiritualism; the same, radically human, inspiration; the same plan to counter arbitrary presuppositions and easy evasions. Both currents called for a meditation committed to formulate and solve problems that were concretely human, in terms that were exclusively human: in life, for life.[16]

---

14. Garin, "Sessanta anni dopo," 128. The influence on Garin of what he describes as De Sarlo's peculiar form of "psychologism" and "spiritualism" would deserve further exploration. See Eugenio Garin, "Lo spiritualismo di Francesco De Sarlo," *Archivio di storia della filosofia* 7 (1938), 298–316; and the collected essays in Liliana Albertazzi et al., eds., *Francesco De Sarlo e il laboratorio di psicologia di Firenze* (Rome: Laterza: 1996).

15. Garin, "Sessanta anni dopo," 133.

16. Eugenio Garin, "Ricordo di Ludovico Limentani," in *Ludovico Limentani a Eugenio Garin: Lettere di Ludovico, Adele Limentani e altri a Eugenio e Maria Garin*, ed. Maurizio Torrini (Naples: Bibliopolis, 2007), 163–64. Much of Garin's historiographical work on the nineteenth and twentieth centuries was dedicated to an exploration and assessment of Italian

Garin's attempt to renegotiate the terms of the coexistence of philology (positivism) and philosophy (idealism), though acknowledged as the trademark of his mature career, still goes largely unappreciated as the defining concern that may be said to have occasioned what he himself sometimes defined as his "conversion" to the Renaissance in the first place. Certainly, he was attracted to what he perceived as the period's distinctive insouciance for a unilateral definition of the philosopher's task. Standing in the wake of long-quarreling positivists and idealists, Garin, too, relying on Vico's mediation, came to conceive of humanism as, primarily, a form of 'philosophical philology.'

Limentani's work was a constant reminder that 'philosophy'—a term that Garin often set off in scare quotes—is inevitably the product of personal and social conflicts. Inspired by his teacher, Garin developed a reading method that is as easy to postulate in theory as it is hard to maintain in practice over the long term:

> I was persuaded that studying an author meant *reading him*, reading everything that he has bequeathed to us; to read every page of his, every fragment, so as to make manifest every shadow of meaning, every internal tension, every negligible variation of tone, every echo of his reading, conversations, polemics, contrasts. For this method, it seemed fundamental to me to parse out through time texts that appeared compact, to emphasize the variants of the sense of a term, recovering oscillations, uncertainties, conflicts.[17]

With this kind of scrutiny, one that favors process over end, man and his doing over product, Garin was after moral coherence, goodwill, rather than doctrinal consistency. In fact, Garin felt indebted toward Limentani (himself engaged in moral philosophy, an underpracticed field in Italian philosophy), less for methodology than for a deontology that he found to be epitomized "in the evangelical warning not to judge." In his student's assessment, Limentani argued "for the plurality of moral standards, in so far as any life, and thus any man, has his own standards, and to act morally is to act according to such standard; all stances are to be respected."[18] Thus, morality *is* first and foremost sincerity, "loyalty to one's cause," while evil is to be recovered in the rift between one's truest convictions and one's

positivism. On this particular concern of Garin's, see Alessandro Savorelli, "L'eredità del positivismo," *Giornale critico della filosofia italiana* 88, no. 2 (2009): 247–73.

17. Garin, "Sessanta anni dopo," 130.

18. Garin, "Ricordo di Ludovico Limentani," 169.

actions. Limentani's so-called "anarchic morality" and Kant's emphasis in
What Is Enlightenment? on the public use of one's reason ("that use which
anyone may make of it *as a man of learning* addressing the entire *reading
public*") coalesce in Garin's appreciation of intransigent thinkers, from
Pico della Mirandola to Gentile, Saitta, and, eventually, Gramsci.[19]

Reference to Kant's enlightened man—emancipated by his daring to
know ("Sapere aude!")—is not haphazard; for the young Garin, the century
of Kant, Hume, Rousseau, and Vico bore a close resemblance to an epoch,
the Renaissance, that concluded with Tommaso Campanella's battle cry:
"Think, man, think!"[20] As Garin often recalled, the French *philosophes*
themselves pointed to their Renaissance affiliation, as in d'Alembert's
Discours préliminaire to *L'Encyclopédie*; while Voltaire went so far as
to describe Cartesianism as a renewed scholasticism thwarting research
into the concrete manifestations of the human spirit.[21] More to the point,
Garin came to appreciate the pan-European influence of Florentine Platonism through a chance recovery of Pico in Thomas Stanley's 1655 *History of Philosophy* and, subsequently, through its influence on the Cambridge Platonists, Shaftesbury, Samuel Clarke, and others. Limentani, the
author of studies on Adam Smith and Giordano Bruno, had alerted Garin
to the connection between the humanism*s* of the Renaissance and the
Enlightenment, a connection that Garin could not resist elaborating on
once his teacher recommended the works of Ernst Cassirer, *The Individual and the Cosmos in Renaissance Philosophy* (1927) and *The Philosophy
of the Enlightenment* (1932).[22] That a young Garin engaged in a profound
conversation with this German philosopher is evident from the title and
subject matter of his first two books: *Giovanni Pico della Mirandola: Life
and Doctrine* (completed in 1934 and published in 1937) and *The English
Enlightenment: The Moralists* (1942), which collected and revised articles
published between 1929 and 1938.

19. Immanuel Kant, "An Answer to the Question: 'What is Enlightenment?,'" in *Political Writings*, ed. Hans Reiss (Cambridge: Cambridge University Press, 1991), 55.

20. Eugenio Garin, *L'illuminismo inglese: I moralisti* (Milan: Bocca, 1942), 12.

21. Garin, *L'illuminismo inglese*, 2.

22. Other contemporaneous works that fell within Garin's purview are Cassirer's *The Platonic Renaissance in England* (1932) and his essay from the same year, "The Question of Jean-Jacques Rousseau." Relevant works by Limentani include *La morale dell simpatia: Saggio sopra l'etica di Adamo Smith nella storia del pensiero inglese* (Genoa: A. F. Formiggini, 1914); and *La morale di Giordano Bruno* (Florence: Istituto di Studi Superiori Pratici, 1924). For an assessment of Limentani's Renaissance scholarship and its connection to nineteenth-century historiography, see Simonetta Bassi, "Bruno secondo Bruno: Le ricerche di Ludovico Limentani," *Rivista di storia della filosofia* 50 (1995): 617–44.

By the time Garin composed the introduction to his collection of early studies on the English Enlightenment, in 1941, his conversion to the Renaissance had already taken place. Like their Renaissance counterparts, the "minor" English moralists or humanists (Shaftesbury, Hutcheson, Clarke, Mandeville, Butler, etc.) are presented as having been written out of the history of philosophy owing to the "antisystematic nature" of their thought. "Enemies of all systems," it would seem, walk a parallel path to the "main street" (*strada regia*) of philosophical speculation, and "for this very reason they are penalized for what was perhaps their greatest merit: their studied eschewal of the subordination of moral problems to systematic constructions, in order to center philosophical research around ethics, the drama of good and evil, of man's destiny."[23] The "guiding idea of a human system created and nourished by love, the ultimate frontier on which morality and religion are satisfied"; their perception of the "multiple unity represented by men"; their faith in a "religion of humanity"; their vision of God "as an ideal limit to which a suffering humanity yearns" and that it strives to achieve in "brotherly collaboration"; and, moreover, their "divine sense of humanity," their emphasis on "concrete experience," and their negation of the "apriori": "these are the themes through which this kind of thought could affirm itself as a worthy and not degenerate heir of the truth of [Renaissance] humanism."[24] In conclusion to his first book, Garin notes that any "resurgent humanism" (*umanismo risorgente*) that wishes to emphasize the "liberating exigencies of spirit" will always turn with "profound sympathy" to the "vivacious form of polemical humanism of the Enlightenment" and, by implication, of the Renaissance.[25]

One cannot fail to notice that by drawing a connection between Renaissance and Enlightenment humanisms, Garin participated in the early philosophical deprovincialization advocated, in their first works, by other representatives of the existentialist generation to which he belonged.[26] Plato (Grassi), Blondel (Castelli), Anglo-American pragmatism (Abbagnano), and the British moralists (Garin), just to mention what has been

23. Garin, *L'illuminismo inglese*, 1.
24. Garin, *L'illuminismo inglese*, 5.
25. Garin, *L'illuminismo inglese*, 267.
26. Garin was perfectly aware that the attention he reserved for the Enlightenment amounted to a critical gesture. Many years later, commenting on the choices routinely made by Gentile and idealist historiography, he stated: "Una storia [that of the idealists], si è detto, fatta di scelte consapevoli, fra cui, forse, la più vistosa è la condanna dell'illuminismo a favore del romanticismo, il *sì* a Rosmini e il *no* a Cattaneo. Ma, va aggiunto, scelte operate sempre con grande finezza, si tratti di Bruno o di Vico, di Alfieri o di Leopardi, di Spaventa o di De Sanctis." Introduction, in *SFI*, 1:li.

covered in this book, were some of the many casualties of the highly ex-
clusivist (all-modern and Italo-Germanic) philosophy of the idealists. And
as with his contemporaries, Garin's approach to Renaissance humanism—
also in his case, an approach marked by circumspection—allows us to pinpoint some of the guiding assumptions in his early scholarship.

For one, it needs to be specified that Garin did not wish to turn Renaissance humanists into *forerunners*, in the teleological style of idealist historiography, of a future, better-defined philosophy. Rather, he posited only
a degree of "contiguity" or "affinity," what in later times he described as
"constancy of rhythm," the "permanence of problems and perspectives,"
"the persistence, intertwining, and transformation of certain 'ideas'" expressed in a "common language, itself owing to shared 'authors.'" Such
ideas are abiding, but at times they reemerge as "novel," never identical,
but recurring nonetheless in their "circulation."[27] Second, Garin was from
the outset concerned not so much with historical epochs as with particular individuals, taken singularly or in a group, who repeatedly vouched
in history for the possibility of a different philosophy, a moral philosophy that concerns human beings personally; this unspecified philosophy
is what Garin wishes to call 'humanism.' Third is his expectation that
a 'humanism' so understood, just like any other philosophy, be taken as
perennial, that it not be attributed to any given epoch.

Given these presuppositions, then, Garin's lifelong research on Renaissance humanism is as much a contribution to a particular field of study as
it is a meditation on the very nature of 'philosophy,' its boundaries (or lack
thereof), tasks, inspirations, and possible reactivations. In fact, by taking
a narrower, that is, strictly scholarly perspective, we are bound to come
across discordant assessments of his groundbreaking monograph on Pico
(1937). When the focus is on its method, comprehensive contextualization,
and sound reading of sources (including Kabbalah), Garin's study may be
exalted as "one of the most representative texts in the renovation of Italian scholarship on the Renaissance," as it rescued Pico from his role as
precursor of Italian idealism.[28] Conversely, when the focus is on Garin's
celebratory (surely, often excessively resounding!) statements and conclusions, the same book (*despite* its emphasis on Kabbalah) may be seen as

27. Eugenio Garin, *Dal Rinascimento all'Illuminismo: Studi e ricerche* (Florence: Le Lettere, 1993), 11–12. See also Maurizio Torrini, "Dall'Illuminismo al Rinascimento: Gli esordi
storiografici di Eugenio Garin (1937–1947)," *Historia Philosophica: An International Journal*
4 (2006), 124.

28. Cesare Vasoli, "Gli studi di Eugenio Garin su Giovanni Pico Della Mirandola," republished as an introduction to *GP*, vii.

advancing, albeit in new form, the ideologized Pico depicted by Gentile in his famous 1916 essay on the dignity of man.[29] Both views, which indeed may be maintained with equal right, equally fail to account for Garin's ambitions as a young scholar.[30]

Empathically recalling on one occasion the "Nicodemism" or "honest dissimulation" of his generation, Garin stated that

> the subject matter and the emphases of many of those studies were not founded, or at least were not uniquely founded, on historiographical documentation; the accent was purposely placed on those values that appeared to face a mortal risk, the very ones on which our civilization is founded. Those who will not keep in mind the conditions of Italy and of Europe in those years will not understand the motives behind certain accentuations and certain emphases; neither will they grasp the quality of a certain "absorption" [appassionamenti] in historiographical work.[31]

He added elsewhere, in direct reference to his work, that in Italy "one would engage in antifascism by rethinking [for example] Socrates or Pico della Mirandola."[32] Nicodemism and the "tendentious readings" such an attitude inspired were indeed, as Garin had the chance to observe repeatedly, a widespread phenomenon in European academia. For example, Garin singles out the study Augustin Renaudet dedicated in 1942 to Machiavelli—on whom the scholar "cast the long shadow of the European tragedy"—and the first works of Hans Baron, who read "into Republican Florence and his

29. I am indebted to Brian P. Copenhaver for sharing with me the manuscript of his very informative *Magic and the Dignity of Man: Pico and His* Oration *in Modern Memory* in advance of publication. See also Brian P. Copenhaver, "Magic and the Dignity of Man: De-Kanting Pico's *Oration*," in *The Italian Renaissance in the Twentieth Century: Acts of an International Conference. Florence, Villa I Tatti, June 9–11, 1999*, ed. Allen J. Grieco et al. (Florence: Leo S. Olschki, 2002), 295–320. Garin's interpretation of Pico—"a highly imaginative" "inaccurate," and "misconceived" reconstruction—has come under attack, together with those of Saitta and Cassirer, in William G. Craven, *Giovanni Pico della Mirandola, Symbol of His Age: Modern Interpretations of a Renaissance Philosopher* (Geneva: Librairie Droz, 1981). For Garin's reaction, following the Italian edition of Craven's book, see Eugenio Garin, "Un nuovo libro su Giovanni Pico della Mirandola," *Belfagor* 40 (1985): 343–52.

30. For a take on Garin's Pico that includes references to Garin's Enlightenment studies and intentions, see Maurizio Torrini, "Garin e gli studi pichiani," in *Giovanni Pico della Mirandola e le* Disputationes *contro l'astrologia divinatoria*, ed. Marco Bertozzi (Florence: Olschki, 2008), 19–29.

31. Eugenio Garin, *Il Rinascimento italiano* (Bologna: Cappelli, 1980), 7–8.

32. Eugenio Garin, *Intervista sull'intellettuale*, ed. Mario Ajello (Rome: Laterza, 1997), 34–39.

Bruni a utopian dream that never came to fruition in modern times."[33] For a philosophical and religious idealist such as Garin, however, the prize went to a particular feat of scholarship, Marcel Bataillon's massive *Érasme et l'Espagne*, also from 1937, to which he dedicated one of his very first book reviews.[34] The *humanitas erasmiana* and the religious irenicism extolled in that famous book for the comfort of a belligerent twentieth century were in fact a good match for the philosophical peace and intellectual concord that Garin had just called for through Pico.

That Garin's Nicodemism would rely on Pico, a restless thinker, rather than on a Machiavelli or Guicciardini, say, or on proto-Republicans fighting against tyranny, illustrates his generation's typical recourse to philosophy for a dissimulation of their antifascism.[35] Garin's Pico is, first and foremost, an existentialist deprovincializer who resisted the temptation to embrace wholeheartedly the official philosophy of his time, namely, the Neoplatonism of a Medici-groomed Marsilio Ficino.[36] Pico, the "last thinker of the 1400s," a man "tormented" by his dissatisfaction with the century to which he belonged and "troubled" by the one to come, "theorized a mental state" when he produced his "hymn to the unsatisfied infinity of man," his *Oration* on the dignity of man. His untimely death consigned Pico to an everlasting youth; that is, it preempted the possibility that he, too, would turn into a pure philosopher with systematic ambitions. In conclusion to his Pico study, Garin states:

33. Eugenio Garin, "Machiavelli e Polibio," reprinted in *IR*, 2:356. For Renaudet's own profession of 'Nicodemism,' see the preface to the second edition of his work, Augustin Renaudet, *Machiavel* (Paris: Gallimard, 1956), 9–10.

34. Eugenio Garin, review of *Érasme et l'Espagne*, by Marcel Bataillon, *La Rinascita* 2 (1939): 179–83. Bataillon's magnum opus can also be read in a recent edition. See Marcel Bataillon, *Érasme et l'Espagne*, 3 vols. (Geneva: Droz, 1991). On Bataillon's intellectual engagement, see Claude Bataillon, *Marcel Bataillon: Hispanisme et engagement* (Toulouse: Presses Universitaires du Mirail, 2009); and Charles Amiel et al., eds., *Autour de Marcel Bataillon: L'œuvre, le savant, l'homme* (Paris: Édition-Diffusion, 2004).

35. Philosophical dissimulation is perhaps the true reason behind Garin's unsurprisingly scant production on Machiavelli and Guicciardini, and on political theorists in general. This goes unacknowledged in recent scholarship on Garin, though, interestingly, it is pointed out that Garin's view of Guicciardini may have been influenced by the problematized Renaissance that Ugo Spirito put forth in 1941 in *Machiavelli and Guicciardini* (discussed in chapter 2 of this book). See Francesco Bausi, "Tra politica e storia: Machiavelli e Guicciardini nella riflessione di Garin," in *Eugenio Garin: Dal Rinascimento all'Illuminismo*, ed. Olivia Catanorchi and Valentina Lepri (Rome: Edizioni di Storia e Letteratura, 2011), 132ff.

36. Garin's anti-Ficinian sentiments are broached in a recent article that, however, fails to reconnect them, as I shall attempt in the following pages, to Garin's personal experience in the fragmented world of twentieth-century Italian academia. See Rita Sturlese, "Dall'umanista letterato al filosofo mago: Immagini di Ficino in Garin," in Catanorchi and Lepri, *Eugenio Garin: Dal Rinascimento all'Illuminismo*, 76–81.

> That Pico is still close to us and strangely appealing among his con-
> temporaries is due to his having avoided building a system; his having
> limited himself to outlining rather than resolving problems; his hav-
> ing probed [cercato]; his having talked not about the goals he did not
> achieve but about his attempts to get there [cercare]; his having been,
> even more than a rhetorician and a man of letters, a poet of the soul:
> his having theoretically justified the essential problematicity [proble-
> maticità] of human research, and at the same time the certainty on
> which such research is founded; all of this moves us to consent. At
> the same time, his love for the boldest attempts to bring light to every
> field, by every means, as much as his enthusiasm and the passionate
> lyricism that he brought to all of his investigations, truly seems to em-
> body and express the aspirations of the scholars [ricercatori] of a new
> epoch [tempi nuovi]. (GP, 224)

Whose epoch: Pico's or Garin's? The ambiguity is deliberate or, at least,
indicative of Garin's folding of the twentieth century into the Quattrocento and his personal identification with this representative Renaissance
thinker.

We have seen that a generation of positive existentialists had already
been after open-ended research and philosophical problematicity before
Ugo Spirito's *Life as Research*, which was incidentally published the same
year as Garin's monograph. Grassi had recovered philosophical indetermi-
nacy in his reformed Platonism, Garin, in his recast Pichianism (which,
however, was itself imbued with that "perennial Platonism" recently attributed to Garin's early scholarship).[37] In what may be considered his
first programmatic statement on the philosophy of the humanists, a long
introduction to an anthology of fifteenth-century thinkers provocatively
titled *Italian Philosophers of the Quattrocento*, published in 1942, Garin
explained the transhistorical appeal of Platonism, in particular for himself and his Pico:

> Just as Aristotle was the school philosopher, the philosopher of the de-
> fined precision of concepts, Plato was the teacher of those unsatisfied
> with mundane things, of the explorers [ricercatori] who were aware of
> the greatness of unending investigation, because the goal is at once

---

37. Claudio Cesa, "Momenti della formazione di uno storico della filosofia (1929–1947),"
in *Eugenio Garin: Il percorso storiografico di un maestro del Novecento*, ed. Felicita Audisio
and Alessandro Savorelli (Florence: Le Lettere, 2003), 22.

everywhere and nowhere. Plato was a beacon for those unquiet souls who saw their own unrest mirrored in him; those souls whose thirst was unquenchable. The dissidents of any accepted culture, of any oppressing authority, starving for a god that was no pure concept, are those who always found comfort in Plato. . . . Platonism amounted thus to a dissatisfaction with systems, it amounted to the realization that the goal always lies ahead just as it is continuously conquered, always possessed and working within us; Platonism amounted to the realization that the answer to the eternal questions is coterminous with the positing of those very same questions.[38]

The Heideggerian Platonism or "immanent metaphysics" of a Grassi, whose intellectual career had momentously crossed paths with Garin's just as these words were written, goes unmentioned here. However, beyond the determination of direct influences (highly probable in this case, as we shall see), what needs to be stressed is a generation's profound spiritual kinship.

At a closer look, in fact, we see that generational concerns, Garin's *and* Pico's, play a major role in Garin's redefinition of Pichian philosophy. We may recall that Gentile's manifesto, "The Concept of Man in the Renaissance," placed Pico in an ideal line of notable celebrators of human dignity: Giannozzo Manetti (1396–1459), the author of *On the Dignity and Excellence of Man*, Ficino (1433–99), and, after Pico (1463–94), Giordano Bruno (1548–1600) and Tommaso Campanella (1568–1639). This ideal lineup is abandoned by Garin, of course. While retaining Bruno, in passing, as a terminus ad quem, Garin mentions Manetti once, and only to distinguish his "celebration" from those of his purported successors (*GP*, 199). As for Ficino, it is seldom noted that one of Garin's primary concerns was to dispel the myth of his association with the younger thinker: "The Florentine men of letters and philosophers . . . have been far less decisively influential [on Pico] than too many presuppose; by depicting Pico from the outset of his philosophical training as clearly oriented toward Ficinian Platonism one precludes any possibility of understanding his stance" (7; see also 21, 41, 75, 78–79).

The reasons that Garin adduces to disengage Pico from his older interlocutor are many and erudite (different evaluations of Averroism, of Plato and Aristotle, and astrology), but the point seems to be as much about con-

---

38. Eugenio Garin, introduction, in *Filosofi italiani del Quattrocento* (Florence: Le Monnier, 1942), 22.

tent as about different spirit and temperament. "The synthesis dreamt up by Ficino," Garin states, "tended, on the one hand, to reduce itself to a leveling of various thinkers; more than resolving various peculiarities in higher unities, the features of a system were neglected in favor of the recovery of some common element. On the other hand, Ficino fought Averroes, he devalued Aristotle, limiting himself to gather thinkers sprouted on Platonic soil" (*GP*, 66).

Given Garin's own instructions on how to read his early works, it is hard not to take his appraisal of Ficino as a criticism leveled against the janissaries of idealist historiography, who were often accused of the same self-serving use of philosophical sources.[39] Pico, on the other hand, is depicted as the conciliator of all philosophical strands, a thinker who, even "when approaching Plato and Plotinus, did not rush to embrace Platonism like a 'deserter' [*transfuga*]" but rather dared to take on the challenge pursued throughout the history of Western thought: the conciliation of Plato and Aristotle (*GP*, 66).[40] Pico, thus, "overcame Platonizing humanism and ideally connected among themselves Padua [Aristotelianism] and Florence [humanism, Platonism], Rome [Catholicism], and Paris [Scholasticism]," and in so doing, far from being a "pedestrian imitator" of Ficino, he turned into an "uncompromising" and, surely, uncompromised thinker (70). Clearly, Garin's frequent use of urban surrogates was a tongue-in-cheek admonition to an Italian community that had not yet given up philosophical parochialism, as Milan (Neothomism), Rome (Gentilean idealism), Florence (positivism), Naples (Crocean idealism), and so forth, came to clash at philosophical conferences throughout the 1920s and 1930s.[41]

Garin depicts Ficino and Pico as distant in almost every respect; another divergence he particularly insists upon is in their respective *experience* of religion. Again, on this point, Ficino is described as the unflustered

39. See, for example, Norberto Bobbio's criticism of Guido De Ruggiero's historiographical work, cited approvingly by Garin in "Guido De Ruggiero," *Intellettuali italiani del XX secolo* (Rome: Editori Riuniti, 1987), 106.

40. Garin's phrasing is a play on Pico's own words in a famous letter he sent to Ermolao Barbaro (December 1484) after his arrival in Florence from Paris, at which time he switched his studies from Aristotle to Plato: "Diverti nuper ab Aristotele in Academiam, sed non transfuga ut inquit ille, verum explorator." Cited in Paul Oskar Kristeller, "Giovanni Pico della Mirandola and His Sources," in *SRTL*, 3: 237.

41. For this geographical self-consciousness, see Eugenio Garin, "L'Istituto di Studi Superiori di Firenze (cento anni dopo), in *La cultura italiana tra '800 e '900* (Bari: Laterza, 1962), 29–66; Michele Ciliberto, "Gli studi di storia della filosofia in Toscana (1930–1960)," in *Figure in chiaroscuro*, 19–59; and for its endurance in the latter part of the twentieth century, Pietro Rossi and Carlo Augusto Viano, eds., *Le città filosofiche: Per una geografia della cultura filosofica italiana del Novecento* (Bologna: Il Mulino, 2004).

amalgamator of "Plato, Plotinus, and Christ," while, in contrast, Pico, who experienced the "religious problem" dramatically, could not bring himself to accommodate his notion of God as "the justification of any experience of thought" to Catholic orthodoxy (*GP*, 71; see also 58 for Pico's "hereticism"). As a result, Garin continually emphasized a relationship that in his view tended to be largely underestimated, the one that tied Pico to the Dominican friar Girolamo Savonarola (1452–98):

> For all of the differences in their temperament, they [Pico and Savonarola] could understand each other: they both moved in a state of mind that, deep down, was far removed from that of the literati, the "grammarians," their contemporaries. Spiritual problems were not for them just curiosities to be quenched in the abstract world of the wise; rather, they amounted to vital questions [*questioni di vita*]. Thought was the means by which to reconnect the soul to the absolute; existence appeared to both as a task, a mission. In their eyes, the eternal values were not just elegant objects of dispute; the world of spirit did not detach from concrete life, which it had to permeate, fill, and transform. (8)

For Garin there is no exaggerating the spiritual kinship between Pico and Savonarola, derived from their aversion to "traditional religious formulas" and the useless quibbles of the basest humanists. They are brothers in arms in their rebellion as they "meet" on a common ground "descending from the quiet world of theoretical discussion, in order to fight the good fight of those who want to bend the world to their principles rather than deserting their post in order to take shelter, with fainthearted compromises, in the safe haven of abstract meditations" (9).[42] Perhaps inspired by De Sanctis's abiding admonition to reconnect *scienza* and *vita*, science and life, Garin claims that whether in books, as with Pico, or in the square, as with Savonarola, the fight is the same.

The quality of Savonarola's (political) and Pico's (intellectual) commit-

42. Compare to Garin's description of the walks Ficino had with Pico: "Con lui passeggia per i colli fiorentini, sognando di fantastiche dimore di filosofi, lontano dagli affanni delle contese terrene, mentre il giovane amico, stanco di tante prove, si piegava, almeno per qualche momento, a desiderare la pace, magari un po' atona, di chi cerca rifugio nel mondo dei fantasmi" (*GP*, 41). On Garin's interpretation of Savonarola beyond his 1937 study, see Gian Carlo Garfagnini, "'Perché d'uno tanto uomo se ne debba parlare con riverenza': Savonarola dall'esortazione retorica all'orazione politica," in Catanorchi and Lepri, *Eugenio Garin: Dal Rinascimento all'Illuminismo*, 103–16.

ment or engagement, which Garin defines as a "truer humanism" (un più verace umanesimo) (GP, 46), manifests itself in their resistance not just to the temptation of a dissembling Ficinian Platonism but also, at least in Pico, to another form of late and deleterious humanism, that of the literati: "One of the elements that is better suited to situate Pico's stance is precisely [his] contemptuous defense of philosophy against rhetoric, his defense of the concreteness of thought against the empty grammatical elegances, his defense of every doctrine independently of the gentleness of style" (60). In this context, after Ficino and Savonarola, Garin introduces Ermolao Barbaro (1454–93), an Aristotelian humanist and admired translator of Themistius, as Pico's third major interlocutor. Just as Pico would remain one of the few cornerstones in Garin's lifelong qualification of 'humanism,' so was the momentous epistolary exchange that took place between Pico and Ermolao in 1485 a preferred locus from which to derive the ultimate ambitions of a movement that, it should be emphasized, Garin was at this time still struggling to define via negativa or indirectly, for what it was not.

In his flowery missive, Ermolao advises his younger student to steer away from those "coarse, crude, and uncultured barbarians," the very Scholastics whom, in his response, Pico admits to having studied for years on end.[43] Indeed, if Pico is to procure for himself "immortal reputation," then he had better realize that lasting fame is achieved with a "shining and elegant style." With his letter, Ermolao drew Pico into the age-old dispute over the relationship of rhetoric and philosophy, between the "Parisian style" of the Scholastics and the Ciceronian style of the "degenerate" humanists, whose elegances, Garin comments, were intended to "dilute the speculative torment of any research" (GP, 61). In his reply "on the type of discourse appropriate to the philosophers," the Garinian Pico engages in a solitary battle against a century that, in its waning, appeared to have gotten its priorities all wrong. Moreover, forging his defense of the Scholastics, of veritas, in elegant Latin style, Pico displays his ability to disengage himself from futile squabbles and adumbrates his ambition for philosophical peace (64).

It is well known that Pico's major step toward the promotion of such

---

43. The exchange is available in English translation in the appendix to Quirinus Breen, "Giovanni Pico della Mirandola on the Conflict of Philosophy and Rhetoric," Journal of the History of Ideas 13, no. 3 (1952): 392–412. For a recent assessment and bibliographical information on the scholarly debate provoked by this exchange, see Jill Kraye, "Pico on the Relationship of Rhetoric and Philosophy," in Pico della Mirandola: New Essays, ed. M. V. Dougherty (Cambridge: Cambridge University Press, 2008), 13–36.

an intellectual armistice was the international conference he planned to take place in Rome in 1487, a plan thwarted by the intervention of the Roman pontiff. The undelivered oration Pico composed to preface the nine hundred theses (*Conclusiones*) he had gleaned for discussion from numerous authorities, irrespective of place and time, was also for Garin, in line with a well-established historiographical tradition, a sort of manifesto of Renaissance thought. However, the title by which this text eventually came to be known, *Oration on the Dignity of Man*, was one that Garin found fitting only with the proviso that human "dignity" be understood in light of the title that Pico had originally envisioned for it: "Carmen de Pace," or hymn to peace.

In a programmatic statement from 1942, Garin explains more clearly that Pico's manifesto "fully accounted for humanism intended as an abiding attitude of the human spirit"; in it, "humanism revealed all of its generously practical character, its ambition for human fraternity and for an earthly city worthy of the celestial one." And, again, in opposition to Ficino—who was occupied in lavishing "elegant praises" on the kings, princes, pontiffs, and cardinals of Europe—Pico, "lord of concord," dictated his "program, forging ahead like a new prophet whose words are endowed with the intransigence and the warmth of a prophecy." It is to Pico's credit, Garin insists, to have taught us why "human dignity" depends on philosophical peace: "Because humanity is fully revealed in human concordance, in the unanimous celebration of that which is truly worthy [*degno*] in humankind. In fights and struggles human spirit dies out, truth is annulled, God is cursed. Man is man when he feels human, that is, tied to and coexisting with his fellow man . . . ; peace is the goal to which all efforts tend."[44] Again here, Garin was voicing his discontent with Gentile's entrenched solipsism.

Finally, just as Ficino's partisan syncretism was for Garin representative of or conducive to bad historiography, we realize that for Garin personally, Pico's lesson in philosophical toleration inspired a new and, we can add, nonidealist kind of historical research: "Pico is thus not on the quest for a predetermined system, say, or for an accepted cult; rather he is motivated by the desire to extract from any stance, from all confessions, that unique truth that dimly shines in varied forms; the fundamental principle of *coincidentia oppositorum* is fully applied in that progressive and in-depth examination of one's consciousness of reality that is pursued in philosophical historiography" (*GP*, 58). Indeed, Pico's doctrine came to

---

44. Garin, introduction, in *Filosofi italiani del Quattrocento*, 13.

fruition in Garin's scholarship, most evidently in the aforementioned *History of Philosophy* he was invited to compose, in 1943, for the spiritual regeneration of the Italian people. This history, which Garin later defined as his staunchest "statement of antifascist belief" (*professione di fede antifascista*), was introduced by an eloquent citation and statement of purpose:

> While drafting this book, the author kept the words of a *maestro* of thought and life, Piero Martinetti, constantly in mind: "the faithful and exact determination of the individuality of every philosopher is in and of itself a value for historical research, and such value is enough to justify the toil that is dedicated to such activity. Yet, from a human point of view, it is more important to clearly establish the concealed agreement on fundamental matters that lies underneath divergences, since such divergences are due most of all to different historical conditions and languages." This profound harmony that, beyond historical epochs, circumstances, and quarrels, pacifies men of goodwill who intend to know themselves and live according to achieved wisdom, this philosophical peace that symbolized the unity of truth and of the spirit which seeks it, wants to be the premise and the conclusion of this modest work.[45]

Surely, these words amounted for Garin to a Pichian appeal, as Martinetti—himself a Platonist, the organizer in 1926 of a conference censored by Church (Neothomist) and state (idealist) philosophies, a symbol of integrity with his refusal to swear by the Fascist oath—had recently died in the exiled isolation into which he was forced by his brave struggle against the regime.

Was Garin's Pico the 'true' Pico? In 1963, Garin composed a sort of rule sheet for any aspiring Pico scholar. Given Pico's emblematic nature, he cautioned that his interpretation be pursued at the intersection of *Entstehungs-* and *Rezeptionsgeschichte*, genetic and reception history, for past and future cannot be divorced when the author is at once the reformer and the originator of a tradition. A given author's legacy, the more so in the case of a legendary one, belongs by right to his corpus. Most of all, Garin prompted interpreters never to forget that Pico's "activity was brief" and that his "writings are those of a young man, between the age of twenty and thirty," and for this reason achievements are fewer than ambitions.[46] To study Pico is to re-

45. Garin, *Storia della filosofia*, 8.
46. Eugenio Garin, "Le interpretazioni del pensiero di Giovanni Pico," in *L'opera e il pensiero di Giovanni Pico della Mirandola nella storia dell'Umanesimo: Convegno internazionale, Mirandola, 15–18 settembre 1963* (Mirandola: Comitato per le celebrazioni centenarie in onore di Giovanni Pico, 1963), 5.

cover the "dialectical tension" that never resolves itself in a solution, as the "problem of the many ways into philosophy" remains his central concern. Garin, who composed his work in his early twenties—surely, he realized, at about the same age as Pico when he wrote his oration—was keen to foreground *this* truth about his preferred Renaissance thinker, one that cannot be denied despite the evident presentism by which it was inspired.

In the 1930s, 1940s, and beyond, the dissemination of Pico's gospel, his message of intellectual peace, became one of Garin's main concerns. He teamed up with Enrico Castelli, a fellow religious existentialist and director of a newly established series for the publication of the classics of Italian thought (Edizione Nazionale dei Classici del Pensiero Italiano), in order to put forth Pico's *opera omnia* in Italian translation. The first volume, which included the *Oration on the Dignity of Man*, was published in 1942, the same year as *The English Enlightenment* and the anthology *Italian Philosophers of the Quattrocento*.[47]

CASSIRER, GENTILE, AND THE *HISTORY OF ITALIAN PHILOSOPHY*

With his Pico study Garin could be said to have converted into a Renaissance scholar, but in Italy, it meant equally that he had matured into a philosopher worthy of conversing with some of the leading thinkers of his time—among them, Ernst Cassirer and Giovanni Gentile. To both, he sent a copy of his book by express mail. Cassirer replied from his exile in Göteborg on 3 June 1938, even before having read through the entire volume. He claimed to have already recovered in the first two chapters "many valuable validations for his own basic view of Pico, but also many suggestions for its broadening and new stimulations. . . . Should the chance present itself to take up again my studies on the Italian Renaissance, I will profit greatly from your results."[48] In fact, such an opportunity seems to

47. Giovanni Pico della Mirandola, *De hominis dignitate, Heptaplus, De ente et uno e scritti vari*, ed. Eugenio Garin (Florence: Vallecchi, 1942). This volume was followed by an edition of the *Disputationes adversus astrologiam divinatricem* (books 1–4, published in 1946, and books 5–12 in 1952).

48. Cassirer's letter is published as an appendix to Saverio Ricci, "Garin lettore di Cassirer," *Giornale critico della filosofia italiana* 88, no. 2 (2009): 476. In the following pages I rely on Ricci to illustrate the relationship between Cassirer and the Italians. See also Saverio Ricci, "Garin lettore di Cassirer: Umanesimo, Rinascimento, Illuminismo," in Catanorchi and Lepri, *Eugenio Garin: Dal Rinascimento all'Illuminismo*, 391–442. A useful review of Cassirer's activity in Sweden is in Jonas Hansson and Svante Nordin, *Ernst Cassirer: The Swedish Years* (Bern: Peter Lang, 2006).

have presented itself immediately as Cassirer rushed to compose a long essay on Pico in the summer of that year (though it was not published until
1942), in which Garin was praised, on the one hand, for having dispelled,
through Pico, the "evil connotations the word 'syncretism' bears" and was
reprimanded, on the other hand, for having downplayed Pico's indebtedness to Cusanus (Cassirer's hero), even as he provided additional evidence
for their connection.[49] By this time, it would seem that Cassirer had read
Garin's book in its entirety and had come upon Garin's remark in the concluding pages that in *The Individual and the Cosmos* he had been "a little
too concerned to have all of the Renaissance derive" from this German
thinker (*GP*, 236).

It is well known that Cassirer largely conceived his influential work
of 1927 as a philosophical "integration" of Burckhardt's "great portrayal
of the Renaissance," itself programmatically unconcerned with this particular facet of the epoch.[50] Cassirer, however, had also realized that such
integration had been broached by Italian philosophers—most recently,
Cassirer noted, referencing a collection of essays republished in 1923, by
Gentile, who avoided any mention of Cusanus. Cassirer attributed this
neglect to those nationalistic sentiments against which Fiorentino, Spaventa's student, had raised his voice by urging Italians to acknowledge
that in the Renaissance "a new branch had been grafted upon the old Italo-
Greek trunk: namely, German thought." Yet the Italian scholar's work
"remained a fragment," and Cassirer found it "incumbent upon objective
historiography at least to heed Fiorentino's methodological exhortation
and warning."[51] By his own admission, then, Cassirer's plan was at least

49. Ernst Cassirer, "Giovanni Pico della Mirandola: A Study in the History of Renaissance Ideas," *Journal of the History of Ideas* 3 (1942): 129, 140.

50. Ernst Cassirer, *The Individual and the Cosmos in Renaissance Philosophy*, trans.
Mario Domandi (Chicago: University of Chicago Press, 2010), 3. The young Garin sympathized with Cassirer's philosophical reevaluation of the Renaissance vis-à-vis Burckhardt,
but he eventually came to voice his qualms: "Burckhardt, scrive Cassirer, trascurò il pensiero
filosofico! In realtà seguì la linea dei suoi autori che opponevano alla vecchia filosofia
teologizzante il loro nuovo tipo d'esperienze e di indagini. E fu, in questo, ben più fedele al
Rinascimento del Cassirer, che andò escogitando posizioni inesistenti, e venne attribuendo
alla mentalità rinascimentale dottrine da essa alienissime quali quella di Cusano. Solo che
Burckhardt, legato anch'egli a forme filosofiche diverse, non si rese contro che proprio tanta
parte di quella 'letteratura,' e retorica e poetica, era una nuova filosofia nascente, che non si
poneva accanto, ma che combatteva molto sul serio, ed intendeva sostituire la vecchia 'teolo-
gia'" ("Il 'Rinascimento' del Burckhardt," in Jacob Burckhardt, *La civiltà del Rinascimento in
Italia* (Florence: Sansoni, 2000), xxiv–xxv.

51. Cassirer, *Individual and the Cosmos*, 47. For a recent assessment of Cusanus's fortunes in Italian and German historiography, see Rita Sturlese, "Cusano tra Germania e Italia
e il ritorno di un noto dibattito," *Giornale critico della filosofia italiana* 84 (2005): 158–71.

in part a Germanization of the Italians' philosophical Renaissance, even though his remarks display an insufficient grasp of the Hegelian reform to which this interpretation of the Renaissance amounted. Indeed, an under-estimation of the German philosophical tradition is the sole charge that may not be leveled against the Italians in good conscience. Their struggle to carve out and safeguard a corner of philosophical history for themselves was an ambition that Garin, despite his deprovincializing tendencies, would not forgo.

If Garin can be said to have employed Gentile to doctor Cassirer's Renaissance, raising Pico, over against Ficino or Cusanus, to an emblem of the Quattrocento, then it can also be said he attempted to improve Gentile's methodology by combining it with Cassirer's more cosmopolitan notion of philosophy as a composite phenomenon, an all-around culture fact. Cassirer's dedication of *The Individual and the Cosmos* to Aby Warburg attracted Garin to the research pursued by the Warburg circle in Hamburg and London, a type of scholarship with which, he lamented, Italy, to its detriment, was and "remained fundamentally unfamiliar."[52] The negative criticism that Croce and other idealists had directed at Cassirer amounted to a preemptive censorship, as the German thinker continued to be known in Italy as a "historian," chiefly, as opposed to a "philosopher."[53] Gentile, who was often inclined to indulge the curiosities of his younger collaborators (recall Grassi's introduction of Heidegger in Italy in 1930), eventually yielded in 1934 to Calogero's request to have Cassirer's philosophical ideas illustrated in the *Giornale critico*. The piece was written by a German-Jewish refugee, Heinrich Levy, who labored to present a Cassirer congenial to the Italians: not so much the epistemologist of *Das Erkenntnisproblem* (1906–7), but the author of *The Philosophy of Symbolic Forms* (1923–29), a total theory of consciousness and culture. In conclusion to his essay, Levy alerted his Italian readership to Cassirer's Vichianism and predicted a fruitful confrontation between the German philosopher and Croce and Gentile.[54]

Although this presentation, orchestrated by younger idealists, failed to

52. Eugenio Garin, introduction, in Fritz Saxl, *La storia delle immagini* (Rome: Laterza, 1965), xi.

53. Benedetto Croce's criticism is in "Pretesa rivendicazione del Settecento," *La critica* 33 (1935): 316. For a review of Italian scholarship on Cassirer, see Beatrice Centi, "Die Cassirer-Forschung in Italien," in *Symbolische Formen mögliche Welten: Ernst Cassirer*, ed. E. Rudolph and H. J. Sandkühler, special issue, *Dialektik* 1 (1995): 145–54; and Riccardo Lazzari, "Cinquant'anni di studi su Cassirer," *Rivista di storia della filosofia* 4 (1995): 889–921.

54. Heinrich Levy, "La filosofia di Ernst Cassirer," *Giornale critico della filosofia italiana* 15 (1934): 247–80, especially 280.

jumpstart a Cassirer frenzy in Italy, it succeeded in abetting the only genuine rapprochement between the Jewish-German scholar and Gentile. In
1936, after having assured himself that his gesture would not be politically
instrumentalized, Gentile submitted a contribution to the Festschrift edited by Raymond Klibansky in England and presented to Cassirer on his
sixtieth birthday.[55] For his part, Garin found a way to chip in by preparing
a translation of Charles de Bovelles's *Liber de Sapiente*, a text that Cassirer had appended to *The Individual and the Cosmos* but that was excised
from the Italian edition of the book (and from the English translation, too,
for that matter). Garin's contribution was clearly meant as a tribute to
Cassirer's teaching, a tribute that Cassirer never, perhaps, had the chance
to appreciate as he relocated to the United States in 1941, a year before
Garin's edition was published.[56]

Meanwhile, Gentile had acknowledged Garin's gift of a desk copy of
the Pico monograph with encouraging remarks of his own (11 November
1937): "It was a great joy for me to see a book so seriously prepared and
so lucidly pondered on a subject so often and for so long mistreated . . . .
Please keep in mind that my *Giornale critico* welcomes your studies"
(AFGG). While a first contact between Gentile and Garin had already occurred in the early 1930s (when Garin submitted to the *Giornale critico* an
essay on Joseph Butler), the two had recently come together for an event
that Garin would later describe as epiphanic for his professional vocation.
In the morning of 18 April 1937, Italian-Jewish editor Leo S. Olschki inaugurated a "humanist exhibition" that amounted to a "profession of faith
in the values of human culture." Ten manuscripts and ninety incunabula
were revealed to an admiring public in Florence as Gentile took to the lectern to discuss those texts and in his speech "recovered all of his sincerest
humanity."[57] Gentile's words struck a chord with the young scholar:

> It will take time for man to gain full consciousness of his essence as
> essence of everything; but the seed of this process of which the history
> of modern man is replete is in humanism. And whoever is unable to
> perceive in this seed the fruit that time—that is, the spiritual labor and

55. Giovanni Gentile, "The Transcending of Time in History," in *Philosophy and History: Essays Presented to Ernst Cassirer*, ed. Raymond Klibansky and H. J. Paton (1936; New
York: Harper Torchbooks, 1963), 91–105.

56. See Charles de Bovelles, *Il sapiente*, ed. Eugenio Garin (Turin: Einaudi, 1943). See also
Garin's preface, vii–xv (vii–xxxiv in the second edition [1987]).

57. Eugenio Garin, "La scomparsa di Aldo Olschki," in Stefano de Rosa, *Olschki 1866–
1986: Un secolo di editoria (1886–1986)*, 2 vols. (Florence: Leo S. Olschki, 1986), 2:169.

the toil of European generations educated at the school of the humanists—derived from it voluntarily makes himself a bastard that ignores
his parents because he does not take pains to look for them.[58]

We have seen that Garin's chief concern in his Pico monograph (which
was in press at the time of this event) had been to send out a subliminal
condemnation of the partisan and mutually uncomprehending factions of
Italian academia, whose animosity Gentile often fomented. Yet no other
school of thought could match that of the idealists in its ability to promote
a sense of entitlement, of a personal and truly familiar share in Italy's Renaissance heritage. Intent on advancing such fellowship, Garin took up
Gentile's invitation to publish in his journal, albeit on topics strictly Gentilean (such as Ficino and Pico), reserving his best—that is, revisionist—
work for journals adverse to the idealist agenda.[59]

One such revisionist article, "Dignitas hominis and Patristic literature" (1938), openly checked Burckhardt's and Gentile's celebration of
the Renaissance man by referring to Konrad Burdach, whose *Reformation, Renaissance, Humanism* (1926) had recently been translated into
Italian (1935) in a deprovincializing effort by Cantimori. The novelty of
Burdach's philological program was explicit even in his preliminary statement, "What does Renaissance mean?" Burdach wrote. "Finally, in order
to answer this historiographical question, historians too . . . have posed a
purely philological query: Whence does the word Renaissance originate?
What does it signify?"[60] Like Cassirer's book, Burdach's was poised as a
corrective to Burckhardt in that it aimed to replace a vertical and static
"cross-section" of the Renaissance with a "longitudinal" view of the epoch, playing up "genetic processes" and the "concrete multiplicity and di-

58. Cited in Garin, "Giovanni Gentile interprete del Rinascimento" (1947), 17.

59. For his contributions to the *Giornale critico*, see Eugenio Garin, "Il commento
ai Salmi di G. Pico della Mirandola (Frammenti inediti)," *Giornale critico della filosofia
italiana* 5 (1937): 165–72; Garin, "Recenti interpretazioni di Marsilio Ficino," *Giornale critico
della filosofia italiana* 8 (1940): 299–318 (reprinted in *IR*, 55–73). It should be noted that
between 1934, when he completed his work on Pico, and 1937, when it was finally published,
Garin cautiously refrained from putting out any scholarship on the Renaissance. For recent
attempts to grapple with Garin's relationship to Gentile (none of which mention the momentous encounter of 1937), see Claudio Cesa, "Eugenio Garin tra Croce e Gentile," *Giornale
critico della filosofia italiana* 88, no. 2 (2009): 299–328; and Simonetta Bassi, "Immagini di
Gentile interprete del Rinascimento," in Catanorchi and Lepri, *Eugenio Garin: Dal Rinascimento all'Illuminismo*, 365–89.

60. Konrad Burdach, *Reformation, Renaissance, Humanismus: Zwei Abhandlungen über
die Grundlage moderner Bildung und Sprachkunst* (Darmstadt: Wissenschaftliche Buchgesellschaft, 1970), 2.

vergences of its creative forces."[61] Burdach was the first to show that many
metaphors associated with the concepts of Renaissance and the Middle
Ages, such as those of "light" and "darkness," could not simply be attributed to modern historiography but were already immanent in the rhetoric
of the humanists' own polemics.[62]

Among the continuities emphasized by Burdach were those concerning "religious inspiration." Aligning himself with Burdach, Garin argued
that the humanists' celebration of man was founded on a renewed engagement with "the letter and spirit of the Church Fathers," more than on a
revival of classical antiquity (*IR*, 1:1). In Giannozzo Manetti's *De dignitate
et excellentia hominis*, in Ficino's Platonism, and in Pico's *Oratio*, it is
possible to detect a yearning for a primitive unity, promoting a fusion of
docta religio and *pia philosophia* aimed at overcoming the late Scholastic divide between philosophy and religion, Aristotle and the Bible. Adam
and Jesus are better suited than Prometheus to underscore the motives and
sources behind the humanists' celebration of man:

> The Man-God motif, in which Cusanus's thought also culminates,
> paves the way for that humanly mediated conversion from the earth to
> the sky, which amounts to the profound relevance of the humanist cel-
> ebration: as it evolves from the traditional concept of man's in-between
> nature to a full appreciation of the human spirit's universal value, whose
> free activity is able to produce a world superior to that of nature. (7)

"Conversion," "incarnation," "redemption," and "expiation" are just some
of the Christian notions Garin employs against a revival of a Greek philosophy that, at its best, had lost any concern for history and the dramatic
nature of man's existence. Furthermore, the "cosmic function of man" so
perfectly symbolized by the mystery of Christ goes a long way toward illustrating human dignity beyond the "Ciceronian enumeration of human
talents" (9), the materialistic notion of man as microcosm, and any other
theory unable to grasp man as a *sacrosanctum animal* (15)—the only crea-
ture in which existence precedes being (*esse sequitur operari*), as Garin,
following Pico, claims. According to Garin, a refurbished Christian humanism lies at the heart of fifteenth-century elaborations on the ancient
notion of *humanitas* (17).

---

61. Burdach, *Reformation, Renaissance, Humanismus*, viii–ix.
62. Eugenio Garin, "Età buie e rinascita: Un problema di confine," in *Rinascite e Rivoluzioni: Movimenti culturali dal XIV and XVIII secolo* (Rome: Laterza, 2007), 5–47.

Again, it is worth noting that Garin's qualification of 'humanism' is attempted empathetically and from a distance. After the Enlightenment (overtly), after Italy's interwar period (covertly), it is the Hellenistic period, not the Hellenic, that he invokes as a parallel of the ferment typical of the Quattrocento.[63] Subsequent to his characterization of the fifteenth century and, correspondingly, humanism as a spiritual or religious epoch, Garin attempted in a pair of simultaneous essays to soften, if not outright reject, the sharp contrasts posited by both Burckhardt and Gentile in their comparisons of the Middle Ages and the Renaissance.

In light of the aims and gains of Garin's early Renaissance scholarship, it is unclear why Gentile would go out of his way to win this young outsider to his side. Again —as it had with Cassirer and with Leo S. Olschki— the Jewish question played a role in their relationship, for when Rodolfo Mondolfo was forced by anti-Semitism to relocate to Argentina, Gentile asked Garin to lend his name to Mondolfo's edition of Descartes's *Discourse on Method* (1940).[64] Moreover, in that same year, Gentile steered Garin's career with an offer that could not be refused: he asked or, rather, he elected Garin to complete the *History of Italian Philosophy* that had been commissioned from him by Vallardi four decades earlier. When detailing the vicissitudes of this long-standing project to Gentile's heirs in 1944, a new generation of Vallardis claimed that Gentile "designated Garin for the continuation of his work, telling us that he would not consent to any other name appearing side by side with his."[65] And so, as Gentile committed for one last time to complete the first volume of the *History* (on the Renaissance), Garin was charged with writing a second volume on Italian philosophy through the 1800s.

Gentile's confidence in Garin remains baffling for a number of reasons. For one, it is unclear why Gentile would select a young scholar affiliated with the positivist school. Furthermore, modern Italian philosophy— the subject that Garin was originally asked to cover—was not ostensibly familiar material for the young scholar. Finally, records confirm that Gentile's confidence in Garin did not derive from personal association, as the

63. Andrea Orsucci, "Il 'Nominalismo storico' di Konrad Burdach nella prospettiva di Eugenio Garin," in Catanorchi and Lepri, *Eugenio Garin: Dal Rinascimento all'Illuminismo*, 330. Orsucci's article reviews Garin's indebtedness to Burdach throughout his career.

64. Eugenio Garin ed., *Discorso sul metodo* (Florence: Sansoni, 1940). Mondolfo's name was restored in later reprints, starting in 1946.

65. For the original letter (G. Vallardi to F. Gentile, 29 May 1944), see Rocco Rubini, "The Last Italian Philosopher: Eugenio Garin (with an Appendix of Documents)," *Intellectual History Review* 21, no. 2 (2011): 225.

assignment itself was handled through an intermediary. Garin was befuddled as much as he was flattered:

> Your Excellence, I was very pleased by the offer, which was made to me on your behalf, to complete the Philosophy of Vallardi; if the project comes to fruition I will get to work with true joy, though aware of the responsibility that is made all the more great by my consciousness of the part that you so masterfully began. But even if contingent circumstances should intervene for a different outcome, it is important for me to let you know how grateful I am for your kind trust and how proud I am that you would think of me to complete a work begun by you. (AFGG)[66]

Garin's letters to Gentile during this time, letters that seem to have gone unanswered, illustrate his uneasiness. He continuously sought Gentile's validation and encouragement: "I am very anxious to receive your opinion, which would serve as a criterion and suggestion, regarding the way I am proceeding."[67] But Gentile had not hired Garin to be his ghostwriter, and his silence can be interpreted as either accord or disinterest.

As the war drew to a close, Garin dutifully attended to his part, while Gentile again failed to complete his review of Renaissance thought. On 18 April 1944, only three days after Gentile's assassination and as Garin rushed to celebrate Gentile as one of the most profound students of the Renaissance in Italy, the Vallardis contacted Garin again to ask that he complete the Renaissance section that Gentile had left unfinished.[68] A year later, on 29 June 1945, Garin was contacted yet again—this time, with a request to take on the whole project. This outcome, of course, amounted to a painstaking farewell to Gentile and the epoch he represented as Garin became the sole author of a history that Italians had been writing in piecemeal fashion for well over a century.

The Renaissance that Garin depicted in his *History* and in the essays that he published in the 1940s differs considerably from his previous ver-

66. This letter, dated 1 June, is presumably from 1941. In another letter (Florence, 29 December [1941]), similarly: "Eccellenza, aspetto ancora un biglietto Vostro che l'inviato della Casa Vallardi, venendo da me, dimenticò di portare e promise poi di spedirmi. Ad ogni modo me ne riferì, credo, il contenuto e prese accordi definitivi per la *Filosofia italiana*. Ed io sono ben lieto di concretare il lavoro, preoccupato tuttavia di non deludere troppo la vostra fiducia. Continuare, sia pure *degenere conditione et adulterata* un lavoro iniziato da Lei è, insieme, un bel compito e una bella responsabilità" (AFGG).

67. Garin to Gentile, 28 April [1942], AFGG.

68. Rubini, "Last Italian Philosopher," 223–24.

sion. Without ever losing sight of the heavenly Jerusalem, his attention at this time gradually turns to the earthly activity on which humanity founds its aspirations. As Garin makes this shift to the mundane, Pico and Savonarola begin to give way to Coluccio Salutati, Leonardo Bruni, and Leon Battista Alberti, whom he appreciates for their handling of concepts of time and death. These early humanists—like Pico, but more so—fought against the idea of philosophy as an ascetic "bios theoretikos," divested of any concern for country, society, and human interaction (*IR*, 1:107). In this period, Garin derives his motto from Salutati: "standum in acie." Salutati's call to stay the course inaugurates a century that will conclude in Pico's opposite yet, for Garin, correlative "evolemus ad Patrem." Garin charged that the best humanists founded their epoch's ideals on a new understanding of philology—based on its literal meaning, a "love of the word"—that has little to do with erudition. To this end, the young Garin never tired of repeating Bruni's claim, derived from Salutati, regarding the original emancipative ideal of the *litterae humanae* ("propterea humanitatis studia nuncupantur, quod hominem perficiant"). From Salutati to Pico—through Bruni, Filelfo, Bracciolini, Alberti, Ficino, and many others—the word ("velut cum ipsis rebus nata") is the key to comprehending the "secret of the spirit pronouncing it" (201). The "word" reveals reality once it is grasped, beyond common *consuetudo*, for its original *intentio*: language is a means to man's perennial quest for a new spiritual liberty rather than an end in itself (125).

In the early 1940s, after beating around the bush and taking many mediated approaches, Garin finally began confronting the humanists head on, and in the process he drew closer to Gentile. The object of his interest was now Gentile's "philosophy of the nonphilosophers," and in elaborating on Vico, he saw the originality of this kind of thought in its philosophical understanding of philology. Whether this rapprochement was due to Gentile's remarkable investment in Garin is hard to say. More evident is Garin's indebtedness to Grassi (his understanding of philology) and Hans Baron (his understanding of engagement), whose 'existential' and 'civic' humanisms he appropriated and elaborated in his most celebrated work, *Italian Humanism*.

THE MAKING OF THE ITALIAN PARADIGM: GARIN, GRASSI, AND CASTELLI

Italian Humanism was very much the product of a collaborative endeavor stemming from those heated conversations Garin had with Grassi and

Castelli during the war years, a time he spent completing the recently commissioned *History of Italian Philosophy*. Between 1943 and 1944, Garin and Grassi repeatedly sat together in Florence to explore unpublished Quattrocento sources (Garin recalled: Salutati, Bruni, Rinuccini, Valla, and so on) and to argue about their present relevance (*attualità*) in light of the 'humanism' Grassi was just then concocting vis-à-vis Jaeger and Heidegger. At the same time and just as frequently, Garin consulted with Castelli to determine the order in which they would edit and publish those same sources in case the world did not come to an end.[69]

In fact, conversations were turned into actions even before the cease-fire was announced. On 30 March 1945, Castelli wrote to Garin to inform him that Grassi had landed safely in Switzerland and that, all things considered, he was doing exceptionally well: "[Grassi] is full of enthusiasm in his attempt to resume the diffusion of Italy's high culture abroad" (AEG). More important, Castelli was keen to communicate that their friend had secured a deal with the Swiss editor A. Franke, who ("without subsidies!") was willing to take on editorial projects and translations. He concluded: "I rely on your extraordinary working stamina to prepare another volume of Coluccio Salutati or, if you think, the unpublished works of Marsilio Ficino you mentioned to me during our conversation in Florence a year ago." As had been the case with their 1942 collection of Pico's major works, Garin and Castelli finally settled for the most *relevant* author. Coluccio Salutati (1331–1406), the first chancellor of Florence and forefather of what Garin (elaborating on Hans Baron) had also begun conceiving of as a 'civic' brand of humanism, was certainly a more inspirational figure for an incipient democratic age than the Neoplatonist and unengaged Ficino.[70]

69. Garin, "Sessanta anni dopo," 141. I cite the relevant passage in chapter 2. Garin also recollects the sources discussed in conversation with Grassi in *UI*, xii–xiii.

70. Coluccio Salutati, *De nobilitate legum et medicinae: De verecundia*, ed. Eugenio Garin (Florence: Vallecchi, 1947). In the introduction, Garin writes: "Nel Salutati, veramente, le *litterae* sono *humanitas*, e sociale convivenza, e forma di vita integra e piena. Egli, il 'letterato,' può essere politico, perché la sua forza morale è così grande, e sincera, e concreta, che scende da sola a sgominare le armi e i soldati. Come i contemporanei chiaramente sentirono quando andarono attribuendo al Visconti il detto celebre, esser più pericolosa una lettera di Coluccio che mille cavalieri fiorentini. Egli non scendeva in campo a far deridere il teorico incapace di comandare una colonna d'uomini armati, perché la sua arma era un'altra, ma era così tecnicamente perfetta che giungeva al suo scopo; ed era così duramente concreta che non doveva cercare altrove sussidi" (xx–xxi). For the other volume of Salutati mentioned by Castelli, see Eugenio Garin, *I trattati morali di Coluccio Salutati* (Florence: Le Monnier, 1944). As for possible translations for a foreign public, Garin suggested that Landino would be better suited than Ficino: "Mi dici della svizzera e della pubblicazione di un volume umanistico. Sconsiglierei il Ficino che ha un interesse esclusivamente erudito, ma per se non ha alcun

For his part, Grassi made headway with his editorial activities before resuming contact with Garin on 26 October. He explained that with his new series, directed in collaboration with Wilhelm Szilasi, another former student of Heidegger, he was in effect resuming—albeit under a different title, "Tradition and Mission"—the publications he had sponsored with Helmut Küpper in Germany between 1940 and 1942. "The first three volumes have already appeared recently," Grassi wrote to Garin. "I immediately thought of you and your history of Renaissance philosophy, which—as you might recall—I have been wanting to have translated [into German] for some time now."[71] Grassi was referring to the Renaissance section of Garin's *History*, whose manuscript he had read a year or so earlier and had evidently thought of putting to an international use. Garin, however, had some reservations regarding the commission. Rather than extrapolating from his previous work, he wished to write from scratch. In the aftermath of World War II, after Gentile's assassination, and having completed his work on the *History*, Garin must have realized that the time was ripe to disengage the Italian Renaissance from its purported idealist legacy.

A tentative agreement regarding what would become *Italian Humanism* was finally reached on 12 November 1945, when Grassi—who was pressed for time—reluctantly gave in to his colleague's request to rewrite, albeit with provisions regarding content and form:

> Great as far as your work is concerned. Given that printing here costs an arm and a leg, I entreat you to be succinct, especially where the general introductory parts are concerned, reducing them to central ideas. Second, do not be too concerned with philosophizing but rather with providing a clear idea of the material treated by each individual author. A chapter on aesthetic theories would be particularly important. Arrange your work so as to truly, for the first time, provide a history in which the content of the main works of each individual author is accounted for. Why do you merely want to allude to Campanella? Please write on him comprehensively. The same goes for the political theory of the Quattrocento and lesser-known authors, leaving Machiavelli aside, who would need a book of his own. . . . I am not sure I am making myself clear: the main concern is to introduce little-known works.[72]

---

valore speculativo. Perché non un volume Landiniano. Ho qui le nitide fotografie dell'unico codice esistente del *De nobilitate*" (Garin to Castelli, 15 April 1945, Florence [APEC]).

71. For the original letter, see Rubini, "Last Italian Philosopher," 225–26.

72. Rubini, "Last Italian Philosopher," 226–27.

This exchange points to a tension between Garin and Grassi as to the boundaries of their collaboration. In fact, throughout 1946, they continued to arm-wrestle over which of them was entitled to philosophize. Grassi, clearly, was after some sort of reference book that could support his theories, and he eventually had his way: to its author's chagrin, *Der italienische Humanismus* was published with no introduction or conclusion. Garin, nevertheless, had the upper hand as to the book's scope: for example, Tommaso Campanella was not treated "comprehensively." Garin mentioned him only in the last pages of the book under the subtitle "new problems" (*IH*, 215–18; *UI*, 245–49).

Throughout his late career, Garin entertained a conflicted relationship with the work of his formative years during the interwar period. For example, he never allowed his monograph on Pico to be reedited, nor did he wish to recirculate *The English Enlightenment*. As for *Italian Humanism*, which he considered to have marked an end-point rather than a new beginning in his intellectual career, Garin all but disowned it with a string of increasingly longer "Avvertenze" or precautionary warnings with which he prefaced each new reprint of the work (1952, 1964, 1986, 1994). In later years, Garin insisted that the book was meant not for specialists but for a broader readership, that formally it was representative of an outmoded "genre" or scholarly style, and that as a whole it could only be taken as a "document" of a long-gone epoch. In his efforts to qualify *Italian Humanism* as some sort of *pièce d'occasion*, Garin even took to citing and glossing passages from his correspondence with Grassi. In one such instance, he wrote: "In more ways than one, those were still very difficult days, but, in spite of everything, one felt reborn. Grassi wrote to me: 'Do you remember those sad times? I am not saying that things are much better now, but at least life is starting again.' *Life is starting again*: our work was animated by a sense of rebirth" (*UI*, xi). They agreed that the humanists' return to the ancients could not be reduced to a mere "literary" or "rhetorical" event, for in the Quattrocento a new "way of philosophizing emerged just as the *very notion* of philosophy was changing" (xv). Yet Garin wished to specify that this kind of philosophy, though novel, "was certainly not Heidegger's" (xvi). Garin was disengaging himself not only from Grassi, but to a greater extent from the German thinker, who he claimed was never among his "favorite authors" despite admitting that he had "strongly attracted [his] curiosity in the 1940s and '50s." Grassi was aware of this, Garin insisted, but nonetheless continued "to serve himself for his own purposes with regard to authors and texts whose importance I would draw to his attention" (xvi).

In light of the much clearer idea we now have of his early existentialism, it should be evident that Garin's disclaimers were for the most part
retractions, attempts at covering up the traces of his former existential inclinations. Moreover, two reviews that Garin dedicated to his colleague's
work and cultural activities in 1943, which together amount to a rare (if
not unique) appreciation of Grassi in Italy, support the assumption that
the two scholars' aims were not that irreconcilable. Garin's first paean
was elicited by a Festschrift (published by Küpper) for the inauguration of
the institute "Studia Humanitatis" that Grassi and Castelli had managed
to establish in Berlin in 1942. In his review, Garin began by relating the
"extremely important" aims of the institute ("defining the relationship of
antiquity to modern times," specifically since the Italian Renaissance) to
Grassi's "outstanding" yearbooks, which as a whole sponsored "a humanist or Vichian," that is, philosophical, understanding of philology.[73] More
specifically, Garin felt that Grassi had moved appropriately to disengage
the Italian from the German philosophical tradition; for indeed "the universal value of thought is celebrated not by means of abstract generalizations and by positing mortifying and leveling uniformities, but rather by
keeping true to oneself, respectful of individual and concrete manifestations of thought."[74] In so doing, Garin avowed, Grassi had inaugurated a
"radical revision"—one worthy of being pursued through a closer analysis of nineteenth-century sources—of that historiographical paradigm in
vogue since Spaventa.

With regard to the Renaissance, Garin claimed that Grassi's notion
of *studia humanitatis* as the "essence of the Italian spiritual tradition"
was on the mark, to the extent that the Italian tradition "was always concerned with the formation of the concrete man in his totality," as Grassi
also maintained.[75] Garin concludes:

> If, as Giovanni Papini recently stressed, we today want to turn to the
> Renaissance motivated by an essential interest rather than by an er-
> udite curiosity, we cannot but wish the best to an institution whose

73. Eugenio Garin, review of *Studia humanitatis: Festschrift zur Eröffnung des Insti-
tutes* in *La Rinascita* 6 (1943): 416. It should be noted that Garin clearly understood that
Grassi's philosophical philology was an Italian (that is, Renaissance and Vichian) and not
German (Nietzschean, Georgian, Heideggerian) product.

74. Garin, review of *Studia humanitatis*, 416.

75. Garin's reference is to Grassi's inaugural address printed in the Festschrift alongside the addresses of Giuseppe Bottai and Salvatore Riccobono, which was read in Latin. See
Ernesto Grassi, "Studia Humanitatis als Wesen der geistigen Tradition Italiens," in *Studia
humanitatis*, 19–32. Reprinted in *PS*, 655–60.

aim—as is the case with our own Florentine one—is to recover within
the brightest moment in Italian spiritual history a guide to salvaging,
in this current terrible crisis, those sacred values of man, who is *magnum miraculum*, syllable of God, made in God's image, in whose flesh
God has suffered for the salvation of all of his children.[76]

At least this once, a notoriously composed Garin had let himself get carried away. Unfortunately, to his disappointment, the National Center
for Renaissance Studies (Centro Nazionale di Studi sul Rinacimento),
whose first director was Giovanni Papini, and its mouthpiece journal *La
Rinascita*, in which the review was published, eventually folded, as did
Grassi's institute "Studia Humanitatis" for the same reason: it had been
established (in 1937) under the aegis of former Fascist minister for education Giuseppe Bottai.[77] Yet Grassi was not just a model of cultural entre-
preneurship. The lengthy companion review that Garin dedicated to his
colleague's pioneering essay "The Beginning of Modern Thought" shows
just how inspiring he could be in matters of interpretation as well. Indeed,
Grassi's exposition deserves to be rehearsed again through Garin's gloss,
for undoubtedly what may be qualified as the postwar Italian paradigm of
Renaissance interpretation, 'humanism as philosophy,' was created in the
encounter of the two.

   Again, Garin was impressed by Grassi's ability to revise Spaventa's vision of Italian philosophy as a weak prequel to idealist epistemology and
to recover "the specific features . . . of that humanist current that, from
Salutati to Vico, situated 'humanitas' at the center of its concerns, nour-
ishing its investigation with an appeal to antiquity."[78] Garin agreed that
a return to "the inexhaustible pedagogical source that antiquity represents," a return that the humanist carried out against Scholasticism, was
again relevant in the present attempt to free oneself of the "theologizing
tradition of idealism." Furthermore, Grassi had insightfully observed that
Descartes, by not allowing himself to linger in doubt, inaugurated the attitude common in modern philosophy of approaching reality according to
a definitive and presupposed stance: "a violence by which logical thought

76. Garin, review of *Studia humanitatis*, 419.

77. On the history of this center under Fascism, see Giulia Calvi, "Rinascimento e Fascismo a Firenze," *Storica* 19 (2001): 7–73, starting at p. 37 for Garin's involvement.

78. Eugenio Garin, review of "Der Beginn des modernen Denkens: Von der Leidenschaft
und der Erfahrung des Ursprünglichen," by Ernesto Grassi, *Giornale critico della filosofia
italiana* 24 (1943): 204.

[*logicità*] turns itself into a centralizing and exclusive" option.[79] In contrast to this (Cartesian) "unilateral tyranny of knowledge," Italian humanism is qualified by its "humble" "openness" toward the manifestations of reality, which it lets live and holds in their "underivable and insoluble purity." This is particularly evident in Bruni, whose philological attitude Grassi "penetratingly" and "insightfully" describes as promoting the "need to understand the value of words in their proper context—be it poetic, political or logical—without forcing nature [*non sforzando natura*]," in words that Garin borrowed from Cristoforo Landino.[80]

Corroborating Grassi's thesis with citations from humanists Grassi himself was unconcerned with, Garin glosses:

> The revelation, the appearance of what is originary, occurs through the word; every man is a man inasmuch as he speaks, and the word, we would say, is an incarnation of spirit. To let oneself be carried away, or almost dominated by the word, means, therefore, to let that reality manifest itself in its autonomous and originary form. . . . Reality manifests itself in its originary nature in the word only when that word is allowed to speak, to speak, that is, with all the value of which it is replete. Only in such a case does the word educate us—that is, when in yielding to it, we allow it to become our own word as well. The words of a poet that are not ravished but understood, "suffered," become our own, and we conquer the "humanitas" that is expressed in them. This is precisely why Bruni could affirm that the letters are "studia humanitatis" *quod hominem perficiant.*[81]

In Garin's view, however, Grassi had tapped into the potential of humanism without acknowledging the movement's failure to live up to its own standards. In translating Aristotle, for example, Bruni often imposed his language on the text, relapsing in his concrete work into that "predetermination" of reality for which Descartes stands accused in the realm of

---

79. Interestingly, Garin, in stark contrast to Grassi, eventually presented Descartes as a humanist through and through in an attempt to show continuity between Quattrocento thinkers and Vico. See Eugenio Garin, "Cartesio e l'Italia," *Giornale critico della filosofia italiana* 29 (1950): 385–405; and, for a review of Garin's Cartesian studies, Carlo Borghero, "Cartesio e la cultura filosofica del seicento," in Catanorchi and Lepri, *Eugenio Garin: Dal Rinascimento all'Illuminismo,* 203–27.

80. Garin, review of "Der Beginn des modernen Denkens," 204.

81. Garin, review of "Der Beginn des modernen Denkens," 205.

knowledge; the Cartesian attitude is more often than not matched by the humanists' own aesthetic and rhetorical "closure."

According to Garin, the major works of mid- and late Quattrocento humanists that Grassi skips over—for example, Valla's *De Voluptate*, Ficino's *Theologia Platonica*, and Pico's *De Homininis Dignitate*—need to be valued, "positively or negatively," according to the "philological" standards recovered in Bruni. This is especially the case since Grassi shows himself to be aware of the humanists' "implicit tendency" to "rhetorical closure" when he turns to Bruno's "reaction" with an interpretation that is "subtly ingenious"—despite its narrow contextualization—in its elucidation of how man is possessed by primordial forms whose objectivity he "suffers and is subjected to." Garin concludes:

> It should be evident that Grassi's suggestive interpretation of the qualities that are proper to Italian humanism, while retaining all of its wealth of suggestion, calls for a deeper and more narrowly determined exploration of the brand of thought that is examined. This would be not for the sake of erudite curiosity but precisely in order to avoid relapsing into that "barbaric" historiography that too easily appropriates authors, without proper contextualization, for one's own purposes and designs. In any case, this essay provides, for now, a general outline and some suggestions that, as far as Bruni and some attitudes of the early Quattrocento are concerned, are inspiring and possibly very fecund. One would wish that this investigation be extended in order to comprehensively confront and specify the peculiar human wealth of our philosophical tradition.[82]

In hindsight, these words strike us as predicting the two scholars' future collaboration—four years later, Grassi's commission allowed Garin to furnish his colleague's insights with the contextualization they needed and deserved.

In fact, turning to *Italian Humanism* with this review in mind, one realizes that Garin's account in his most celebrated work amounted in many ways to an elaboration of Grassi's interpretation. Garin's humanism is also a movement that extends from Bruni to Bruno—from the former's philosophical philology to the latter's "heroic frenzies." Recent scholarship on Garin's interpretation of Bruno notes that it relied almost exclusively on two texts (*Spaccio de la bestia trionfante* and *Eroici fuori*), and

82. Garin, review of "Der Beginn des modernen Denkens," 207.

that it underwent a shift sometime in the 1940s, to focus on the philosopher's "religious afflatus" and concern for passionately experienced reconnection with truth and the overcoming of the limits imposed on the individual.[83] Yet this scholarship fails to notice that Garin's emphasis on Bruno's heroism was influenced by Grassi, who was, in turn, influenced by the poetic heroism Heidegger recovered in Hölderlin. If, admittedly, Garin's Bruni is more a 'civic' than a 'philosopher' humanist (owing to what I shall describe as Garin's momentous assimilation of Baron's paradigm), then Garin's Bruno is almost identical to Grassi's.

This connection was almost verbatim and it was lost in translation, as it were. It is most palpable in the last subsection—titled "Heroic Passions" ("Die heroische Leidenschaft")—before the introduction of Campanella's "new problems," where Garin, like Grassi, has the entire humanist movement end in the *Heroic Frenzies* and in one's coming into "consciousness of one's self and one's shortcomings, as well as the knowledge of what it means to be a man, and one's vocations":

> The main problem was concerned with an attempt to discover how the passivity of every finite being, subject to fate, contains another kind of passivity or suffering which is in reality an activity with God in God. This was the very problem expressed by Bruno in another form, in the myth of Actaeon. He said that Actaeon, chasing the naked Diana, was transformed from hunter into prey. He represents the human intellect which, in the presence of the divine, "is moved beyond itself by so much beauty." Thus he becomes the prey and is transformed into the very thing he sought. Actaeon noticed that he ended up becoming the prey of his own dogs, i.e., of his own thoughts. For as he had already grasped the deity, there was no need for him to seek the deity outside himself. The myth demonstrated that the internal and the external coincide, even as the many and the One coincide as soon as man turns away from the crowd and begins to see his Diana—no longer through windows, but "with eyes wide open to the whole of the horizon." (*IH*, 214; *UI*, 245)

Italian Renaissance humanism climaxes not only with Bruno, but specifically in the Actaeon myth, which, as we have seen in the previous chapter, Grassi took as the central metaphor illustrating the nature of humanism

---

83. Nicoletta Tirinnanzi, "Garin e Bruno," in Catanorchi and Lepri, *Eugenio Garin: Dal Rinascimento all'Illuminismo*, 160ff.

as a sacrifice of one's self for the sake of something Other, be it a particular text or author, the past in general, one's fellow man, or God and the absolute objective.

These textual correspondences and public displays of support allow for a closer qualification of Garin's existentialism as well as for a clearer understanding of the connection between his *Italian Humanism* and Heidegger's "Letter on 'Humanism.'" When Grassi acceded to Garin's wish to make *Italian Humanism* a totally original book in the winter of 1945, his letter concluded with a different demand:

> I wish to enter into negotiations with a truly reliable Italian press for the publication of a series that would substantially derive from the one I direct here. Among the authors are R[omano] Guardini, [K]arl Reinhardt—one of the few professors who resigned his post as university professor in 1933—W[ilhelm] Szilasi, Husserl's main pupil, W. F. Otto, the two Uexkülls, Jaspers, etc. Ideologically, as you know, all of these authors come from a confrontation with Heidegger's existential philosophy, and one need only compare them to Sartre, G[abriel] Marcel, or other so-called "existentialists" in Italy to appreciate their originality, due to their ability to free themselves from the fetters of Heideggerian terminology and their having pursued a clear, profound, and philosophical determination of the most relevant problems in the natural sciences as well. The problem concerning one's relationship to antiquity, and thus the humanist tradition, is central to these publications. While I have experienced the fact that in Italy our relationship to antiquity is primarily a matter of philological and erudite studies, the need here to defend spiritual values has led to an original examination and revaluation of the humanist tradition. . . . *If I were asked to summarize this new inclination in a word, I would call it an "existential humanism* [umanesimo esistenziale]."[84]

This may have been Grassi's only attempt to enlist an outsider. To be clear, after resuming his German series ("Geistige Überlieferung") in Switzerland under a new name ("Überlieferung und Auftrag"), Grassi was eager to make those very same works, including Garin's, available in translation to an Italian readership in a parallel series that, had the project come to fruition, he would have entitled, "Umanesimo Esistenziale." In his gloss of this passage, Garin conceded that his convergence with Grassi hinged

84. Rocco Rubini, "Last Italian Philosopher," 227 (emphasis added).

"on a rejection *avant la lettre*" of the "unhappy" and false (as far as Quattrocento culture was concerned) contrast between the humanities and the natural sciences, but he remained silent as to his complicity with an originally George-inspired and, by the time of the commission, projected Heideggerian/existentialist movement (*UI*, xiii–xiv).

Throughout 1946, Grassi continued to keep Garin abreast of his plans for his existential series, and by the end of that year, he was ready to announce that he had come close to sealing a deal with Sansoni, the Italian press once owned by Gentile and now directed by his heirs. Evidently considering his colleague to be an involved party, he asked Garin to please see the matter through by announcing his publication plans to the editors. According to Grassi's well-defined proposal the series would have begun with "the complete text of Heidegger's interpretation of the cave myth, unknown to most but very important," followed by a work co-authored by Uexküll and Grassi, *The Death of Socrates* by Guardini, and fourth, "the volume you [Garin] are preparing" (AEG). These instructions reveal that on 9 November 1946, when this letter was written, Grassi still believed that Heidegger's "Plato's Doctrine of Truth" (the "interpretation of the cave myth") could stand as a manifesto for an existential or Heideggerian (Renaissance) 'humanism.' In retrospect, the coincidence is formidable: Jean Beaufret's own letter containing the query "How can we restore meaning to the word 'humanism'?" was addressed to Heidegger one day later, on 10 November. We know that in his letter to Garin, Grassi mentioned "a recent trip to Germany," and we can assume that during that trip (or even earlier) Grassi asked his former teacher for permission to translate and include his "Plato's Doctrine of Truth" in a series entitled "Existential Humanism," and at the same time, as we have seen in the previous chapter, he beseeched him for an open letter to include in Castelli's volume (*Letters from Germany*). Considering all this, we would be justified in concluding that while composing his *Brief* Heidegger was necessarily as concerned about humanistic and existential miscomprehensions of his thought in Italy as in France.

On his return to Germany in 1947, Grassi's plans for an existential/humanist series were shattered. Along with his "interpretation of the cave myth," Heidegger handed over the "Letter on 'Humanism'"—two related texts that Grassi went on to publish together in his more loosely defined Swiss series. As planned, a German-language edition of Garin's *Italian Humanism* immediately followed, but necessarily, at this juncture, as a corrective countermanifesto. When read side by side with Heidegger's letter, Garin's *Italian Humanism* amounted to a philologically accurate description of Quattrocento humanism that appeared aimed at disproving Heidegger's claims about the Italian Renaissance just as they were being formulated. Or conversely, if Heidegger's call for a truer or more "primordial" humanism was to be taken seriously (in Heidegger's words: "the possibility of restoring to the word 'humanism' a historical sense that is older than its oldest meaning chronologically reckoned"), then Garin had provided evidence of it *in* rather than *beyond* recorded history.

Turning back to the question of how involved Garin was in the existential movement Grassi promoted, it is worth recalling that this whirlwind of momentous epistolary exchanges between France, Italy, Switzerland, and Germany occurred just as Grassi and Castelli were about to inaugurate their international philosophical conference in Rome (on 15 November 1946). A letter written by Castelli to Garin in the previous August allows us to define Garin's own brand of existential humanism more narrowly and to distinguish it more clearly from Grassi's. In this missive, Castelli regretfully informed Garin that the title Garin had suggested for his presentation, "Existentialism and Humanism," had already been submitted by Luigi Pareyson, another prominent Italian existentialist; Castelli hoped that Garin would not mind changing his title to "Existentialism and the Spirit of Humanist Thought."[85] In the end, Garin did not present—or, at least, his paper was not included in the proceedings and never published elsewhere. Thus we are left wondering, what would have been his take on this coveted subject?

A plausible answer may be drawn from the innumerable reviews Garin published in 1946, many of them relating to the matters at hand. One in particular, dedicated to recent existentialist literature outside Italy, suggests that, for such an occasion, Garin, like Heidegger, would have fashioned his paper partly as a response to Sartre's *Existentialism Is a Humanism*. In this review, Garin positively evaluates the recent work of one of his favorite spiritual existentialists—Jean Wahl's *Human Existence and Transcendence*—and then turns furiously to Sartre's atheist manifesto:

> I have no comment to make on certain arguments: for example, the idea that historical humanism is Fascism. I will put this to rest next to the idea, maintained in Italy, that existentialism is Nazism. All I wish to say, however, is that this [Sartre's] take on man, as something in the making rather than an essence, is far from being new and original, and it entails the problem of transcendence that Sartre so easily

85. Castelli to Garin, 28 August 1946, AEG.

dismisses. . . . Sometimes, knowledge of history could come in handy and the reading of any reference book could have prevented easy inferences. . . . For all of these reasons, Sartre's text is bound to stir a curious irritation: a mixed feeling of aversion and regret due to the fact that hoary and enlightened truths may be so strangely perverted by our lack of humility, an attitude that a certain humanist would have deemed barbaric.[86]

Holding true to his Pichian—and also, it is implied, Vichian—'existentialism,' Garin lamented Sartre's display of ignorance despite his valuable insight. He claimed that if the gain of existentialism consisted of bringing about an inversion between *operari sequitur esse* and *esse sequitur operari*—"existence precedes essence," as Sartre would have it —then, for those familiar with the history of philosophy and Pico's contribution to it, historical humanism was already an existentialism and not the other way around. Garin's reaction to Sartre mirrored Grassi's premature rejoinder to Heidegger's "Letter." The idea implied in that text that humanism is equivalent to Western metaphysics because it allegedly failed to understand that language is "the house of Being"—arguably, in Grassi's more than in Garin's view, the central achievement of Quattrocento humanism—was equally the product of philosophical arrogance and historical unawareness.

Garin postponed a sustained engagement with Heidegger's letter until 1968, when he was asked to provide an opening piece for a special issue of the *Revue Internationale de Philosophie* dedicated to "la crise de l'humanisme." The first thing he noted was that until 1954, Heidegger always placed the word 'humanism' between inverted commas, something that Garin commended given that the use that is made of such an ambiguous *word* is coterminous with the problem of 'humanism' as a *concept* open to interpretation. Also, Heidegger had clearly asserted that "humanism" had to do with the essence of man, his humanity, but had rightly realized that disagreement centered on the question of what, in metaphysical terms, constitutes man's essence, "'the humanity of the human'— which is understood in many different ways: from the Greek-Roman *paideia-humanitas* to the Christian notion of the 'children of God,' from

86. Eugenio Garin, "Esistenzialismo," *Leonardo* 15 (1946): 189. Garin published more than fifty reviews and review articles in 1946 alone, presumably on the books he read through the war years. See *Bibliografia degli scritti di Eugenio Garin (1929–1999)* (Rome: Laterza, 1999), 32–40. The most relevant ones to the argument developed here are nos. 105, 107, 108, 109, 111, 116, 120, 122, 126, 128, 132, 133, 142, 143, 151.

the Renaissance dignity of man to the natural needs of Marx's social man" (*RIP*, 225).[87] Thus, in Garin's view the great merits of Heidegger's text lay in "emphasizing the overuse of the term humanism ("this word has lost meaning""), and for having clearly indicated that the distinction between 'historical' humanism (Renaissance and post-Renaissance) and 'theoretical' humanisms cannot be reduced to the distinction between nonphilosophy and philosophy, between speculative positions and philological, historical, pedagogical, or rhetorical stances (227).

These appreciative remarks by one of the greatest champions of Renaissance humanism's merits should not surprise. They alert us, rather, to a perspective lost in our contemporary readings of Heidegger's letter, which, in light of French Heideggerianism, we interpret as an anthumanist manifesto. Instead, from the post-Hegelian perspective that Garin and Grassi had been moving toward, the "Letter" was the first text by a philosophical mastermind to state, unambiguously and uncompromisingly, that humanism (including its Italian Renaissance form) is genuine philosophy. To this extent, at least, Garin, Grassi, Sartre, and Heidegger were in agreement. The problem, rather ironically, was that Heidegger had gone too far too soon. He had equated humanism with traditional philosophy *tout court* without consideration for its peculiarities. Garin clarifies:

> On the one hand, we have a humanism in which man constructs himself through a 'historical' reference, that is, a cultural comparison. On the other hand, we are dealing with positions where nothing similar is traceable, with a discussion that hinges on an 'immutable' essence or nature of man. As such it is clear, and worth repeating, that both types of humanism imply a general notion of 'metaphysics,' even if Heidegger's indications in this regard are disputable. In any case, the distinctive trait that 'historical' humanisms have in common is amply characterized: in all of them human 'nature' defines itself and, as Vico would have said, "celebrates itself" in a critical and conscious relation among different cultural times, among different cultures, between modern and ancient. Man's 'nature' is none other than his culture, for which the relation with other cultures is integral: diversity through relation [*diversità nella relazione*]. (*RIP*, 226–27)

87. Eugenio Garin, "Quale Umanesimo? (Divagazioni storiche)," *Giornale critico della filosofia italiana* 84 (2005): 16–17. The essay was originally published in French translation as "Quel 'humanisme'? (Variations historiques)," *Revue internationale de philosophie* 22 (1968): 76–89.

Historical humanisms are philosophies created in confrontation; they amount to "projects to be carried out" for man's and society's sake in the future. Historical humanisms amount to "anxiety and labor, struggle and conflict," and they eschew exactly what Heidegger seemed to be after: a "return to the paternal home" or "origins," and a "peace" achieved in identification with Being (233).

We are now in a position to appreciate that *Italian Humanism* was a piece of existential scholarship through and through, its idiosyncrasies and composite nature notwithstanding. This original framework faded into the background in later years when Garin came into his own as one of the greatest Renaissance scholars of his generation and in the process began reclaiming the Grassian/existential work for his own purposes and a new epoch. When, in 1952, Garin eventually yielded to the pressure to publish the original Italian manuscript of *Italian Humanism*, he was finally given the chance to compose the introduction and epilogue that Grassi had denied him. Garin writes:

> *The people who condemn humanistic philosophy lament precisely the thing which the humanists wanted to destroy, that is the grand "cathedrals of ideas," the great logico-theological systematisations.* The humanists disliked the idea of a philosophy which deals with every problem under the sun and with all theological researches and which organizes and delimits every possibility within the pattern of *a preestablished order.* The age of humanism considered that philosophy vain and useless and substituted for it a programme of concrete researches, precise and defined in two senses: one in the direction of the moral sciences (ethics, politics, economics, aesthetics, logic, and rhetoric), and one in the direction of the natural sciences which were to be cultivated *iuxta propria principia,* free of all chains and all *auctoritas,* and which have on every level that bloom of which an honest but obtuse scholastic knew nothing. (*IH*, 3–4; *UI*, 10; emphases added)

Italian humanists wielded their mundane philosophy against the Scholastics, relying on a novel understanding of "philology," which, Garin notes, "was well understood" by "a historiography which is today only too easily despised" and which should not, "as someone believes, be considered side by side with traditional philosophy, as a secondary aspect of the Civilization of the Renaissance" but as an "effective philosophical method" (*IH*, 4; *UI*, 11). The historiographical tradition that had produced a proper interpretation was that of the Italian idealists; while the "someone" to whom the complaint was addressed was not Heidegger but, as the footnote reveals, he who had become Garin's main competitor in Renaissance scholarship, Paul Oskar Kristeller.

By the time the original Italian manuscript of *Italian Humanism* was published in 1952, it was no longer a *pièce d'occasion*: neither a reference book intended to support Grassi's theoretical humanism, nor an erudite piece of scholarship that fortuitously came to challenge Heidegger's claims. Rather, it was now readdressed to stand as a countermanifesto to Kristeller's 1946 classic essay "Humanism and Scholasticism in the Italian Renaissance," and in the process, as we shall investigate in the next chapter, postwar Europe had acquired another momentous, and perhaps rivaling, exchange on the question of 'humanism.'

THE ITALIAN PARADIGM CONTINUED: BARON'S "CIVIC HUMANISM" IS ALSO AN EXISTENTIALISM

An ad hoc 'Introduction' and 'Epilogue' were not the only means by which Garin attempted to re(ad)dress his *Italian Humanism*. The Italian edition of this work also bore *for the first time* an eloquent subtitle—"Philosophy and Civic Life in the Renaissance"—which underscored the book's central chapter ("La vita civile" [Das bürgerliche Leben]) and pointed to another influence on the making of Garin's interpretive paradigm: Hans Baron's notion of *Bürgerhumanismus* or "civic humanism."[88] It was recently noted that there has been a long-lasting quarrel as to the origin of this term and concept—an unnecessary quarrel given Garin's repeated acknowledgments in his footnotes of the debt owed to Baron's early papers, along with a claim that his use of the term was not identical.[89] Garin explained that the discrepancy in usage was owing to the "iron laws of chronology," which did not allow him to profit from (let alone adhere to) the more precise description of the phenomenon that Baron put forth in *The Crisis of the Early Italian Renaissance* (1955), a book that was exceedingly long in the making and ended up appearing years after *Italian Humanism*.[90]

It is well known that in this study, arguably the most influential mono-

---

88. For some inexplicable reason, the subtitle "Philosophie und bürgerliches Leben in der Renaissance" is everywhere cited as being present in the original German version, which is not the case. Grassi thought it best to suppress the subtitle for the German edition.

89. Ciliberto, "Una meditazione sulla condizione umana," in Garin, *IR*, xxxviii–xxxix.

90. Eugenio Garin, *Science and Civic Life in the Italian Renaissance*, trans. Peter Munz (New York: Anchor, 1969), xi n5. See also *UI*, xvii–xviii n10.

graph in Renaissance history written in the second half of the twentieth century (and thus the subject of constant and searching critique), Baron depicted an idealized Florentine Renaissance populated by engaged scholars consciously reviving ideals of public service, popular government, and patriotism drawn from ancient Greece and the Roman republic. Central to Baron's so-called 'thesis' stipulating a shift from a monarchic and contemplative fourteenth century to an active and ideological fifteenth century was the outcome of the Florentine-Milanese war, in which the year 1402 served as a turning point, as Florence risked capture, thereby catalyzing reflection on democratic values and peaceful coexistence that would mark the beginning of modern republicanism.

In order to compare Garin and Baron, it should be observed preliminarily that if in his major work Baron's 'civic humanists' are a self-contained group of early Quattrocento *Florentine* intellectuals and statesmen, Garin's humanists are an *Italian* crowd of Quattrocento *and* Cinquecento thinkers, whom he credits with enabling an epistemic shift and with safeguarding, over time, the option of a philosophical attitude that eschews any form of contemplative evasion (the "Aristotelian *bios theoretikos*," "Stoic asceticism," "monastic existence," and so on). From Bruni to Alberti, and far beyond into Vico, philosophy was for the *truer* humanists essentially a social affair: "culture is *humanitas* and therefore community" (*IH*, 41; *UI*, 51). As a self-contained group of protorepublicans, moreover, Baron's Florentine humanists are threatened by the expansionist ambitions of the Visconti dukes and other princes or tyrants; meanwhile, as emancipated intellectuals, Garin's humanists create their own evil. They are vulnerable, that is, to the inveterate habits of intellectual withdrawal sponsored by "official culture": the "temptation," in keeping with the Quattrocento, to reinstate a contemplative Platonism, for example, or the inability by many to resist philology's "degeneration" into a bookish or purely literary performance.

Though they are convergent, Garin's notion of 'humanism' overlaps with Baron's (and even then only partially) only when a causal nexus is drawn between political tyranny and foundationalist or contemplative models of philosophical inquiry. Such a connection was drawn by Garin in an essay that bears a Baronian title, "Humanism and Civic Life," in 1947, at a time when 'dissimulation' was no longer required:

> Before the stake on which John Huss was burned, Poggio is unable to hide his deep emotion and admiration. Before the stake of Savonarola, Ficino, a steady client of the Medici, is unable to hold back from dis-

pensing insults and calumny. Letters like those of Marsilio or Ermolao
are eloquent mirrors, not only of two men of immense learning but
utterly lacking in character, but of a fatal disease that penetrated deep
into the academic culture of Italy at the time. The highest praise for
living men perceived to be useful and dangerous; insults for the dead,
and groveling before the newly powerful.

But this was not humanism; it was the end of humanism. (*RIP*,
213–14)

With his anti-Ficinianism, and relying on Risorgimento feelings, Garin
wished to stress that the Quattrocento went "from a full comprehension
of human works, of human society, of knowledge as awareness of human
collaboration, to a Platonic escape to the heavens of pure knowledge, amid
the clash of changed life conditions, in the wreckage of Italian freedom."

In what may have been the only sustained consideration of his colleague's work, a review of the 1965 English edition of *Italian Humanism*,
Baron himself noted that Garin's book is conspicuously bereft of political
contextualization:

> There is, in Garin's canvass, a trace of a not fully resolved contradiction
> between his stress on passions, material goods, and civic life—Aristote-
> lian tenets—and his inclination to evaluate the rise of the *quattrocento*
> thought as a triumph of Christian, in particular Franciscan, attitudes
> over Scholastic Aristotelianism. In subsequent publications, he was to
> work out a more precise notion of a civic-minded type of Aristotelian-
> ism, representative of early *quattrocento* humanists. . . . A historian
> will in the early work miss clear indications that an exceptional place
> was occupied by Florence during the period analyzed in the longest
> chapter, "*La vita civile.*" No effort is made to trace the growth of cer-
> tain ideas to the impact of "civic society," the city-state, or any other
> specific environment, either in Florence or elsewhere. Rather, we find
> in this chapter discussions not only of Florentine citizen-humanists,
> but also of the new "philology" of the Valla and Poliziano, of the begin-
> nings of humanistic Epicureanism, of humanists in Rome and at the
> *Curia* and even at the Neapolitan court—of everything Garin wants to
> tell us about the early *quattrocento*.[91]

91. Hans Baron, review of Eugenio Garin, *Italian Humanism: Philosophy and Civic Life
in the Renaissance, American Historical Review* 72 (1966–67): 632.

As for what strikes Baron as an incongruity, we have seen that for the early Garin there was in effect no contradiction in a simultaneous concern for the earthly and heavenly cities. Rather, from his religious perspective, the celebration of the active life was the product of a properly experienced Christianity. Also, writing in the late 1960s, Baron was right to point to a mundane shift in his colleague's mature scholarship. As we shall see, however, this shift owed more to Garin's postwar espousal of Gramsci, by which his religious ambitions were tamed, than to a more orthodox Baronianism. Finally, Garin's geographical and temporal inclusiveness in his approach to humanism—in a word, his *philosophical* stance—unsurprisingly could not live up to the more concrete exigencies of the 'historian' Baron. Elsewhere, Baron states unequivocally and correctly that the "idea of 'civic humanism' and of the cause of Florence's primacy in culture and politics" was his own; he credits Garin with "the vital discovery" that elements of this Florentine *Weltanschauung* were "widely circulated" in the late Quattrocento and Cinquecento.

A contemporaneous piece that Garin composed for a Festschrift in honor of his German colleague shows just how deep-seated his philosophical (mis)appropriation of Baron's *Bürgerhumanismus* was. Garin conceived his contribution as a sort of apology for Baron's interpretive paradigm, whose viability had often come under attack.[92] Garin took the chance to admit unabashedly to the "lofty ideal pathos" (*alto pathos ideale*) that permeated Baron's as much as his own early scholarly production. In the interwar period, "liberty and tyranny, human dignity and humanism, Middle Ages and the Renaissance and the origins of the modern world" were not "neutral topics" into which to pour oneself in isolation or to approach motivated only by erudite curiosity. Emphasizing Baron's references to Hitler and Mussolini and the connection Baron evidently drew between twentieth-century fascisms and Renaissance tyrannies, Garin pointed to the beneficial intersection of past and present in the historian's inquiry: "one could perhaps even go so far as to maintain that the degree of one's grasp of the past is directly proportional to the degree of one's openness to the present."[93]

92. For a review of the criticisms made of Baron's 'thesis,' see James Hankins, "The Baron Thesis after Forty Years," *Journal of the History of Ideas* 56 (1995): 309–38. See also, most recently, the essays collected in James Hankins, ed., *Renaissance Civic Humanism: Reappraisals and Reflections* (Cambridge: Cambridge University Press, 2000).

93. Eugenio Garin, "Le prime richerche di Hans Baron sul Quattrocento e la loro influenza fra le due guerre," in *Renaissance Studies in Honor of Hans Baron*, ed. Anthony Molho and John A. Tedeschi (Florence: Sansoni, 1971), lxii.

In Garin's view, it was Baron's 'presentism' that allowed him to emerge as an exception at a time in which Renaissance scholarship tended to dwell on "general ideas" or vague "formulas" and on moments of disengaged philosophy. In contrast to, for example, Gentile, Cassirer, and Kristeller—grouped by Garin as being variously concerned with late Quattrocento *philosophy*—Baron had realized that an "indissoluble nexus subsists between culture and politics" and gone on to inaugurate a scholarship qualified by "precisely defined" questions, focused on particular, short segments of Renaissance culture.

In sum, Garin gave Baron credit for having shown that the "philosophy" of the humanists amounted to their "vision of social life [*vita associata*], moral and political." Moreover, Baron had realized that a profound transformation of culture and education "is unconceivable without a new vision of the world and of society." In conclusion, evidently folding Baron's notion into his own, Garin cautioned that

> "civic humanism" should not be taken as a formula or, worse, as some sort of political and cultural schema: one that should be either accepted or rejected programmatically. Rather it points to the realization of that tight connection, in the Quattrocento, between some theoretical stances and specific political circumstances. It amounts to an invitation to refrain from disengaging political commitment from literary as well as philosophical ventures. That is, it amounts to an invitation to give up interpreting humanism as merely a literary or courtly event, or as a scholarly episode.[94]

Simply stated, as we shall see in the following chapter, Baron's scholarship allows one to read the Renaissance in a thoroughly non-Kristellerian way.[95] What Garin failed to grasp is that Baron's work was not, like his own, an 'interpretation' of the Renaissance but an empirically demonstrable 'thesis.' That is, Baron had set the standard for an either/or reception of his work through his obsession with revisionary chronologies and for

94. Garin, "Le prime ricerche di Hans Baron," lxviii. Garin rightly notes that the reference to Mussolini, which appeared only in the first edition of *The Crisis*, was made in discussion of Ephraim Emerton's *Humanism and Tyranny* (1925), in which Fascist dictatorship was already used "to explain, by analogy, the situation in 1400." See Hans Baron, *The Crisis of the Early Italian Renaissance: Civic Humanism and Republican Liberty in an Age of Classicism and Tyranny*, 2 vols. (Princeton: Princeton University Press, 1955), 2:504.

95. Garin's appraisal of Baron is indeed replete with sly references to Kristeller. Baron's relationship to Kristeller is discussed in the following chapter.

what he calls the "interplay of ideas and events," for which he strove to recover irrefutable textual evidence.[96]

Into his late career, Garin continued to rely on the first impression or intuition of 'civic humanism' he had garnered from his colleague's early works. Baron's heartfelt response, written in English (on 20 March 1971), to Garin's unsolicited apology tangibly conveys the mixed feelings attending their association:

> You are probably the only one who, although a little younger yourself, can still conjure up from own experience the climate and the meaning of those years, and that you have done so and so masterly and with an eye for all the forces of the mind and of the sentiment toward life of which I am conscious myself, this is the happy and unexpected surprise for which I thank you so much. During the first two decades after the Second World War, it was one of my greatest delights and reassurances to find that your and my ways had been originally very close to each other. In later years, you travelled along so many other roads which I deeply admired but could not follow with work of my own, given the rooting of my interests and gifts in a narrow field, that we did not have much exchange with each other any more; but, when reading your pages, I look back upon those far-away beginnings also through your eyes. And your last words "[Baron's work] rests on the idea that a profound transformation of culture and education is not conceivable beyond a profound transformation in the vision of the world and of society" make me hope that there will be among us more than a little of common interest in the future as well. (AEG)

Baron points to a more strongly felt sodality in the immediate postwar period, one fraught with fruitful *malentendus*, that is key to comprehending how Garin could eventually come to reconcile Baron's 'civic' and Grassi's 'existential' humanisms.

For a start, it may come as a surprise that Garin and Baron met only once (and, it appears, unsatisfactorily). As Garin noted, their relationship developed through a "long and dense correspondence" that Baron initiated

---

96. See chap. 4, "The Interplay of Ideas and Events," in the second revised edition of Hans Baron, *The Crisis of the Early Italian Renaissance* (Princeton: Princeton University Press, 1966), 81–93. On this aspect of Baron's method, see Ronald G. Witt, "The *Crisis* after Forty Years," *American Historical Review* 101, no. 1 (1996): 110–18; and John Najemy, "Baron's Machiavelli and Renaissance Republicanism," *American Historical Review* 101, no. 1 (1996): 128.

in 1950 with a dispatch of offprints. Garin was delighted; in his response
(24 November 1950) he wrote, "I've benefited from [your work] since my
first steps in research, when I first met you as a student of Pico. (But I later
discovered the student of Bruni and Palmieri, of Quattrocento 'civic humanism [*umanesimo civile*]' and since then your works have been for me
enlightening)" (HBP). Garin, in fact, had initially "met" Baron through the
two essays the latter published in Italian journals, including *La Rinascita*,
as a follow-up to his short and unhappy stint in Italy in the 1930s.[97] However, we may believe Garin did not immediately espouse 'civic humanism':
it seems that in a letter to Papini, Garin described his own first contribution to *La Rinascita*—"*Dignitas hominis* and Patristic Literature"—as a
much more polemical and, thus, stimulating interpretation than the one
recently offered in the same journal by Baron.[98] Garin began citing his
German colleague approvingly only in 1941, and, interestingly, his original use of 'civic humanism' was rigorously Baronian: that is, it lacked the
philosophical spin that, as we shall see, accrued during the war years.[99]

It should be noted at this point that, despite his ubiquitous disclaimers, aimed at presenting himself as a 'historian' rather than as a 'philosopher,' Baron was in fact among the first to suggest that early Quattrocento
humanism may have had *philosophical* relevance. He did so most firmly
in the introduction to a collection of Leonardo Bruni's most representative
works, daringly titled *Humanistisch-philosophische Schriften*, which he
edited in 1928. This book, it is too often forgotten, was a major source of
inspiration for fledgling Renaissance scholars in the 1930s—among them,
certainly, Garin and Grassi—and its relevance to the making of the Italian
interpretive paradigm deserves to be acknowledged.[100] In the correspondence of Baron and Garin, reference to this anthology occurs early on, in
1952, when Garin sent Baron a copy of his own collection of humanist

97. For Baron's Italian publications, see Hans Baron, "La rinascita dell'etica statale
romana nell'umanesimo Fiorentino del Quattrocento," *Civiltà moderna* 7 (1935): 5–20; and
Hans Baron, "Lo sfondo storico del Rinascimento Fiorentino," *La Rinascita* 1 (1938): 50–72.
Garin was collaborating with both journals at the time of these publications. However, there
seems to be no trace of Baron's early paper on Pico in Garin's early publications. See Hans
Baron, "Willensfreiheit und Astrologie bei Marsilio Ficino und Pico della Mirandola," in
Kultur- und Universalgeschichte: Walter Goetz zu seinem 60. Geburtstag (Leipzig: B. G.
Teubner, 1927), 145–70.

98. See Calvi, "Rinascimento e Fascismo," 37.

99. See Eugenio Garin, "Noterelle di filosofia del Rinascimento," *La Rinascita* 4 (1941):
409–21.

100. Leonardo Bruni, *Humanistisch-philosophische Schriften*, ed. and introd. Hans Baron
(Berlin: Teubner, 1928).

writings entitled *Latin Prose Writers of the Quattrocento.*[101] This gift gave Baron the chance to report that he would have published a similar work in 1933, were it not for Nazi censorship. Baron was particularly grateful to his colleague for having referred to his Bruni collection as an "excellent volume" in his footnotes—a "praise" that he gladly collected as a "balm for an old wound."[102] The objects of his grievance were the two scathing critiques of his early scholarship (also cited by Garin) that a "grey eminence" (the qualification is Kristeller's) in Renaissance philology, Ludwig Bertalot (1884–1960), had written out of personal loathing, thought Baron, with the intention of crushing his career in Germany.[103] In his response, Garin comforted Baron with a citation from fifteenth-century humanist Angelo Poliziano: "It is time for us to truly feed ourselves on these authors whom we have sought out with so much effort." Joining Baron in his lamentations, Garin professed his revulsion for certain narrow-minded "philologists" and reasserted that their services to society were to the benefit of those who strive to tap into the "profound meaning" (*senso profondo*) of the humanists' works. For his part, Garin avowed that he would always be grateful to Baron's *Bruni*, "by all means a precious instrument of work."[104]

This exchange allows us to pinpoint the true common ground between the two scholars, which, more than in a similar interpretation of the Quattrocento, rested in a professional kinship that had the dissemination and, even, in Garin's (and Grassi's) case, the 'popularization' of humanist literature as a central concern. On this point, it is noteworthy that Baron seems to have been unaware of a very similar collection of humanist writings that Garin had published as early as 1942, a work whose own daring title amounted to a tribute to Baron's 1928 enterprise: *Italian Philosophers of the Quattrocento.* Not only were the Bruni selections in this anthology lifted out of Baron's collection, but, as we have mentioned, its introduction amounted to Garin's first programmatic statement regarding the humanists' philosophical relevance. In this, too, a parallel can be drawn

101. *Prosatori Latini del Quattrocento*, ed. Eugenio Garin (Milan-Naples: Ricciardi, 1952)

102. Baron to Garin, 2 June 1952, AEG.

103. For these critiques see Ludwig Bertalot's reviews of Baron's collection in *Archivum Romanicum* 15 (1931): 284–323; and *Historische Vierteljahrschrift* 29 (1934): 385–400. They were later reprinted in a collection of Bertalot's writings edited by Kristeller. For a detailed discussion of the *affaire* Bertalot and its long-lasting effect on the relationship between Baron and Kristeller, see Rocco Rubini, "A 'Crisis' in the Making: The Hans Baron-P. O. Kristeller Correspondence," forthcoming.

104. Garin to Baron, 8 June 1952, HBP.

with Baron's *Bruni*, whose introduction was Baron's own first attempt at conceptualizing the "bürgerliche Humanismus."[105] In fact, in their early and ubiquitous citations of the Bruni anthology, Grassi and Garin often emphasized that Baron had not only collected but, as the title page specified, "elucidated" Bruni's works.

As is well known, this collection of Bruni's works appeared as the first volume in a projected series dedicated to publishing the lost Latin literature of the Middle Ages and the Renaissance ("Quellen zur Geistesgeschichte des Mittelalters und der Renaissance"), directed by Walter Goetz, the teacher Baron singled out as having had the greatest influence on his intellectual development as a Renaissance scholar.[106] It is less known, however, that the young Baron was expected to carry the series on his shoulders with editorial responsibilities for all of the first five volumes (and perhaps as many as eight of the first set of ten), with editions, in addition to the one dedicated to Bruni, of the works of Giannozzo Manetti, Francesco da Fiano, and Marsilio Ficino. The pioneering quality of this series is reflected in a brief prologue that Goetz wrote, justifying the text selections made by his students (mainly Baron) under his supervision. He begins by admitting that "so much of the work of the humanists of the fourteenth and fifteenth centuries amounts to a great extent only to a repetition of ancient thought that one could limit oneself to printing those parts in which these men offer their very own." He adds that the series should print only that which indeed matters and is truly original, which, in the case of most of the "long-winded humanist literature"—although Bruni and Manetti may be exceptions—means just the prefaces to their works. His conclusion is practically a disclaimer:

> In any case, it needs to be determined conscientiously from case to case what can be dispensed with without harming scholarship. A consistent system for these editions cannot be established owing to the

105. Baron had coined the term "civic humanism" (*Bürgerhumanismus*) in 1925, in a review of F. Engel Jànosi's *Soziale Probleme der Renaissance*. For a useful bibliography of Baron's works, see Molho and Tedeschi, *Renaissance Studies in Honor of Hans Baron*, lxxiii–lxxxvii.

106. For Baron's career in Germany, see Riccardo Fubini, "Renaissance Historian: The Career of Hans Baron," *Journal of Modern History* 64 (1992): 541–74; for the later development of Baron's thought, see Kay Schiller, "Hans Baron's Humanism," *Storia della storiografia* 34 (1998): 51–99; and, with an emphasis on Baron's American emigration, Anthony Mohlo, "Hans Baron's Crisis," in *Florence and Beyond: Culture, Society, and Politics in Renaissance Italy*, ed. D. S. Peterson and D. E. Bornstein (Toronto: Center for Reformation and Renaissance Studies, 2008), 61–90.

always varying context of printed and unprinted, of original and repeated, of essential and inessential material. I have given the editors of
this collection full freedom to establish the rationale for each issue and
to make it known in their introductions.[107]

Goetz's comments may be glossed with Philippe Monnier's famous dismissal of the humanists—"Having nothing to say, they said it intermi-
nably"—though, perhaps owing to Baron's insistence, he was willing to
give them a chance.[108] These are the enduring prejudices that Baron (and
eventually Garin, Grassi, and Castelli with him) was among the first to
fight *testi alla mano*, in direct engagement with humanist literature.

Responding to such pressure, no doubt, Baron went out of his way in
his introduction to ascertain that his selection provided material of intrinsic interest for the history of philosophy (*geistes- und philosophiege-
schichtlichen Interesse*). In the process, he came to describe Bruni, if not
properly as a philosopher, then certainly as a thinker with philosophical
inclinations (*als philosophischer Denker*). "As a Quattrocento humanist,"
Baron avowed, "Bruni was congenial to a philosophy with a humane afflatus that accords with man's natural emotional life as well, not just with
his abstract reason."[109] In his introduction, Baron defended Bruni against
miscomprehension by, among others, a beloved thinker such as Wilhelm
Dilthey. And in advancing his theories he came to describe his favorite
Quattrocento humanist in terms that would later be congenial to the
Italians.

Baron's future influence on Grassi specifically is apparent in his treatment of Bruni's *The Study of Literature*, a work whose importance was
attributed by Baron not only to "the poignancy of its assertions or its practical usefulness . . . [but also to its] vivid and unmediated focusing of all
single pedagogical requirements on a new conception of what is 'natural'
and 'humane' in the spirit of mankind and, therefore, in every educational
resource." Baron adds,

> The notion of *litterae* as education [*Bildung*] in the modern sense led
> Bruni to equate their cultivation with cultural flourishing. If culture
> demands not only the thriving of scholarly sciences, but also the culti-

107. Walter Goetz, "Zur Einführung," in Bruni, *Humanistisch-philosophische
Schriften*, viii.

108. Philippe Monnier, *Le Quattrocento: Essai sur l'histoire littéraire du XVe siècle
italien*, 2 vols. (Paris: Perrin, 1924), 1:228.

109. Baron, "Einleitung," in Bruni, *Humanistisch-philosophische Schriften*, xxi.

vation of the free and "human" arts (the *artes liberales et ingenuae* and the *studia humanitatis*) by men who, while being engrossed by practical life, have enough leisure and inner strength to intellectually transcend the demands of material existence [*Daseins*], then cultural blossoming cannot be separated from the power and independence of the commonwealth and from the entire condition of political life: without political freedom humanities lack the appropriate human material.[110]

From the perspective of this study, these words are bound to sound Grassian, but the opposite is true: it is Grassi's interpretation that amounted to a hyperbolic version of Baron's.

In the previous chapter we saw that, if possible, Grassi's interpretation of humanism was even more *exclusively* founded on Bruni, a humanist who in Baron's 'elucidation' could perfectly serve his anti-Jaegerian purposes. In keeping with Grassi, moreover, we cannot fail to notice that Heidegger's *Being and Time* predated Baron's collection by just one year and that, undoubtedly, Grassi was among the few equipped to appreciate both books with equal delight. This is evident in his material juxtaposition of Heidegger and Bruni in his yearbooks as well as in his theoretical advancements. Grassi's programmatic essay "The Beginning of Modern Thought" in effect transformed Bruni—his philosophical philology, his notion of the *studia humanitatis* as science of man—into the most distant predecessor in modernity of Heidegger's pedagogy and hermeneutics. This was one of the central and far-reaching—some would surely say far-fetched—connections on which Grassian 'humanism' was originally formulated. But if Grassi's Heideggerization of (Baron's) Bruni is apparent, what can be seen as Garin's existentialization of 'civic humanism' requires more evidence.

Again, Garin's 1946 reviews of existentialist literature provide insight into his philosophical concerns at a time when he was composing *Italian Humanism*.[111] The name that recurs most often in these reviews is that of Christian existentialist Nikolai Berdyaev (1874–1948), a major influence on the spiritual brand of French existentialism to which Garin was always attracted. Garin had already devoted the last paragraph of his 1945 *History of Philosophy* to this Russian thinker, whom he had then singled out among a roster of prominent modern existentialists (Karl Barth, Karl Jaspers, Heidegger, Gabriel Marcel, and Le Senne) as the only one to have con-

---

110. Baron, "Einleitung," in Bruni, *Humanistisch-philosophische Schriften*, xvii.

111. In what follows, I summarize the contents of two reviews Garin published with the title "Existentialism" in *Leonardo* 15 (1946): 61–62, 187–89.

cerned himself with the individual's "relationship to others, the problem of social life."[112] After the war, Garin introduced the same thinker as the spokesperson of a "personalist socialism" (or "existentialist personalism") whose aim, after the double failure of Christianity and the socialist revolutions, was to mediate between the Russian penchant for "collectivism" and the "individualistic passivity" typical of the Western man.

Garin's fascination with Berdyaev rested in the latter's attempt to reconcile Christian truths with the new social exigencies that emerge in the creation of a "new man" as well as a new, classless society. Finally, Garin agreed with Berdyaev that in the mid-twentieth century, an effective revolution could be expected to take place only *in interiore homine*. Berdyaev's "man," Garin added, is thus not the "abstract" individual of the Enlightenment but, rather, a concrete "person" grasped in the "lively moments of his human interactions"; this is why, for Berdyaev, "human dignity should not be sought for elsewhere but in civic life [*consorzio civile*]." For Garin, Berdyaev's attempts to redescribe human subjectivity on "plural grounds" and existentialism's renewed appreciation for "the tragic sense of life," against any form of idealistic optimism, are proof that this philosophical current is "much older than the present war." What Garin meant is that the best kind of existentialism, an at once religiously and socially inclined one, had a precedent in the best kind of Quattrocento humanism.

In 1947, Garin also returned for one last time to Grassi's initiatives with a review of the series "Tradition and Mission," which he knew would shortly come to host *Italian Humanism* and with whose replication in Italy, in a projected series entitled "Existential Humanism," he had been involved. Garin's concluding remarks are particularly relevant, for they commented approvingly on the reformed existentialism or Heideggerianism that the editors of this series, Grassi and Szilasi, had presented recently at the Roman conference organized by Castelli. The conference, one should recall, revolved around two prevalent themes, existentialism (that is Heideggerianism) and historical materialism (Marxism), and the presentations of Grassi and Szilasi were notable because they alone attempted a reconciliation between the two currents. For his part, Szilasi had asked: "What is [man's] place in the world, in his association with others [*Miteinandersein*] and in his historical determination?" He maintained that Heidegger's existential ontology is by no means irreconcilable with historical materialism, for both strive after the determination of man in his totality, be it in his "projection" (*Entwurf*) or his "historical development" (*ge-*

<hr>

112. Garin, *Storia della filosofia*, 286.

schichtlichen Ablaufs).[113] In his own contribution, titled "Existentialism and Marxism," Grassi elaborated on Szilasi's attempted reconciliation by pointing to Marx's knowledge of and possible application of Vichian tenets. Just as Marx had salvaged the autonomy of the social sphere from Hegelian dialectics, Vico, who was himself advancing Machiavelli's and Guicciardini's intuitions, had realized that the forms in which human and social reality manifest themselves may not be logically derived from first causes but rather need to be dealt with by man's innate ability to seize on particular and ever-changing events.[114] Garin, who evidently was himself ready to take a step to integrate his existentialism with social concerns, applauded this comingling of Marx, Heidegger, and Renaissance 'civic' humanism.[115]

Christian existentialism, Berdyaev's personalism, Grassi's reformed Heideggerianism, and Baron's 'civic humanism' coalesce in Garin's interpretation of humanism around 1947. As Garin stated in the conclusion of an essay published that same year ("Humanism and Civic Life"), Quattrocento humanism had *successfully* inaugurated the modern world with that same reconciliation between man, the social world, and God which modern philosophy was again after:

> I believe that it is the concept itself of humanism, all that humanism upholds which is eternally valid, namely, its concept of what constitutes a complete person, which continues to be incorporated into its earthly manifestation, which is civil society, and to manifest itself in language, understood broadly as communication. Earthly humanity, which, in spite of everything, as Quattrocento humanism asserts in opposition to classical humanism, is in fact earthly humility, but also ardent pursuit, and the unrelenting drive to transcend, to challenge, to go beyond. Because humanity lies, precisely, not in being, but in action, industry, motion, and eager pursuit: a richness that constant want, its implacable dissatisfaction, makes miserable. And in this thirst the humanists find God incarnate and a living appeal to that great beyond which is One. Through a strange paradox, with its ever-present absence, the divine seems to give flavor and meaning to the great here-and-now, to our rigorous and humble and absolute faith in this world. (*RIP*, 214)

113. Wilhelm Szilasi, "Die Aufgabe einer existentiellen Analyse der materialistischen Dialektik," in *Atti del Congresso internazionale di Filosofia*, 2:139–40.

114. Ernesto Grassi, "Esistenzialismo e Marxismo," in *Atti del Congresso internazionale di Filosofia*, 1:321.

115. Eugenio Garin, review of "Tradizione e Missione," *Leonardo* 16 (1947): 63.

A year after these considerations, *Italian Humanism* was published concurrently with Antonio Gramsci's *Letters from Prison*, a book that Garin promptly reviewed alongside Berdyaev's *The Destiny of Man* and Kristeller's *The Philosophy of Marsilio Ficino*, among many others.

CONCLUSION: HISTORICIZING THE PRESENT THROUGH GRAMSCI'S "HUMANISM"

Past, present, and future coexist in Garin's publications from 1947: *Der italienische Humanismus* (the book that finally dissolved the Italians' 'Renaissance shame'), the first edition of *History of Italian Philosophy* (which realized the long-standing Risorgimento aspiration for a national intellectual biography), and two thick collections of humanist texts in translation (part of an ongoing effort to popularize Latin Renaissance literature) appeared simultaneously; more important, all were commissioned works.[116] In that same year appeared essays commemorating his teachers and mentors (Limentani, De Sarlo, Gentile) and about thirty book reviews covering the palingenesis efforts of the West (Sartre, Unamuno, Berdyaev, Aldous Huxley, Maritain, John Maynard, and so forth). At the age of thirty-eight, Garin was an overwhelmingly accomplished scholar but was also, for that very reason, at a loss for a new challenge, a first self-commissioned task. It is in view of this internal struggle to come into his own, *without* maturing into a complacent erudite or philosopher, that Garin's epiphanic encounter with Gramsci is best understood.

Evidently, Garin saw in Gramsci a mirror image of the Pico he had created or self-projected in order to dissimulate personal and generational ambitions. In his gut reaction to *Letters from Prison*, Garin describes the forever young Gramsci as, principally, a thinker who "preferred death to any compromise" and, in subsequent reviews, as the spokesman of an alternative Italy broached in innumerable unfinished projects.[117] Indeed, at first glance, Gramsci did resemble Garin's Pico in many respects: Gramsci, too, was a dissenting voice among his older peers (Croce and Gentile); his, too, was an "integral humanism," a true "absolute historicism," forged *with* and *against* similar humanisms (or historicisms) variously conjoined

---

116. In addition to a collection of Salutati's works, in the immediate postwar period Garin edited *La disputa delle arti nel Quattrocento: Testi editi ed inediti di Giovanni Baldi, Leonardo Bruni, Poggio Bracciolini, Giovanni D'Arezzo, Bernardo Ilicino, Niccoletto Vernia, Antonio De' Ferrariis detto il Galateo* (Florence: Vallecchi, 1947).

117. Eugenio Garin, "Le 'Lettere dal carcere,'" reprinted in *Con Gramsci*, by Eugenio Garin (Rome: Editori Riuniti, 1997), 127.

with tyranny (actualism, Croceanism). Most important, however, Gramsci was animated by what Garin perceived as an untried irenic mission: a
radical rethinking of Italian intellectual history starting from a national
"translation" of cosmopolitan stirrings and conducive to the foregrounding of unrealized possibilities, as vanquished men and their thoughts—in
other words, all intellectual strands—were reintegrated into the narratives
of the victors.

Furthermore, it could not have eluded Garin that Gramsci's intellectuals were created in identification with the Renaissance. In his role as
eradicator of the Renaissance shame, however, Garin could not counte-
nance Gramsci's interpretation of the epoch as essentially "reactionary"
(which Garin rightly attributed to the influence on Gramsci of "De Sanctis's moralistic devaluation of the Renaissance"); yet he found the Gramscian Machiavelli to be "truly original and suggestive."[118] Garin noted that
by reconnecting the Florentine secretary to Savonarola (the same sparring
partner Garin had chosen for his Pico), Gramsci realized that Machiavelli's
doctrine "was not bookish in nature, the monopoly of isolated thinkers."
Rather, *The Prince* and Machiavelli's other writings were a "manifesto"
goading to action. According to the well-known Gramscian passage that
Garin singles out,

> The Savonarola-Machiavelli opposition is not the opposition between
> what is and what ought to be but between two different notions of
> "ought to be": Savonarola's, which is abstract and nebulous, and Ma-
> chiavelli's, which is realistic—realistic, even though it did not become
> direct reality, for one cannot expect an individual or a book to change
> reality but only to interpret it and to indicate a line of action. Machia-
> velli had no thought or intention of changing reality; he only wanted
> to show concretely how the concrete historical forces ought to have
> acted to change existing reality in a concrete and historically signifi-
> cant manner.[119]

In this passage, Gramsci's Machiavelli and Garin's Pico coincide, as do—
to an extent—*The Prince* and *Oration on the Dignity of Man*. For this reason, Garin probably perceived that he and Gramsci had been working on
the same project. However, from the vantage point of prison and through

---

118. Eugenio Garin, "Gramsci nella cultura italiana," republished in *Con Gramsci*, 61
119. Antonio Gramsci, *Prison Notebooks*, trans. Joseph A. Buttigieg, 3 vols. (New York:
Columbia University Press, 2011), 3:283.

Machiavelli, a thinker Garin largely avoided, Gramsci had clearly identified his negative counterparts: Gentile and, especially, Croce. The latter, as we have seen, served as Gramsci's modern-day model of a Guicciardinian, Erasmian, detached or traditional intellectual. But Croce was also notably absent from Garin's intellectual career until the early 1950s, when Garin set about bringing Gramsci's project of a history of Italian intellectuals to fruition.

Garin had sent a copy of his Pico monograph to Croce in 1937, but to no avail. In subsequent years, the two met on several occasions, but Garin's only "indelible memory" is not flattering: Croce dozing off in an armchair at a common friend's home one evening in 1940, as his hosts and their guests, including Garin, huddled in agony around the radio to follow the news of Germany's assault on Norway and Denmark. Admittedly, the Olympian scholar had dispensed a few feeble encouragements upon receiving *Der italienische Humanismus* in 1948, but his interest was stirred only in 1951 upon hearing that Garin was working on a history of twentieth-century Italian philosophy. At Croce's request, Garin "anxiously" forwarded the published portions of his work along with his latest collection of Pico's writings, and soon after, on 6 November 1952, he received the verdict of the only living protagonist of his new story:

> I've received your new gifts, and as the sequel to Pico's works has found its place next to the previous volumes, I've turned to your pamphlets, among which I am particularly attracted to the recent history of actualist philosophy. You see, when Gentile began his teaching career, he was generally praised as a well-trained professor of the history of philosophy. I remained silent and did not complain, but to myself I thought that a student of the history of philosophy, especially one of Italian philosophy, needs to be an erudite explorer of philosophy. This Gentile was not, because he did not forgo vague and general notions. You are to be credited for being the first to peruse Italian philosophy from one end to the other and on living sources.[120]

An aging Croce, who was by then only a few months from dying, may finally have realized that his legacy, too, was in the hands of the insa-

---

120. Eugenio Garin, "Conversando con Benedetto Croce," *Belfagor* 50 (1995): 654. In this article, Garin published the few letters and postcards he received from Croce between 1948 and 1952. The exchange is discussed from another angle in Fulvio Tessitore, "Garin, Croce e lo storicismo," in Catanorchi and Lepri, *Eugenio Garin: Dal Rinascimento all'Illuminismo*, 341–64.

tiable Pico scholar. Perhaps recovering through Garin some of his erudite historicism, and ignoring Garin's known indebtedness to his onetime foe, Croce ventured to reaffirm his idea of Gentile as a "purus philosopher" and, thus, it is implied, as a lesser or 'impure' Italian philosopher. It was not an assessment with which Garin could agree. Indeed, he had recently, and repeatedly, exalted Gentile's merits as an erudite (and not just insightful) Renaissance scholar, and focusing on Gentile's early career, he would soon praise him as an indispensable intellectual historian of the Italian nineteenth century as well.

Between 1951 and 1953, just as the piecemeal publication of Gramsci's *Prison Notebooks* was completed (1948–51), Garin composed and published much of the material that he would gather in his history of Italian twentieth-century intellectuals, *Chronicles of Italian Philosophy*. This, his most celebrated and disputed work in Italy, appeared in 1955 just as Garin turned forty-six—Gramsci's age at the time of his death in 1937, the same year that Garin published his Pico monograph. It is worth noting these bio-bibliographical serendipities because Garin himself continued to qualify his empathetic scholarship in generational terms. If, as Garin believed, his youthful restlessness had been instrumental in conveying Pico's own, it was through Gramsci that he found the opportunity to experience a second youth divested of any dissimulation or Nicodemism. "It is not by chance," writes Garin in the prologue to *Chronicles*, "that these pages were written at the end of the Second World War, as a sort of soul-searching activity on behalf of someone who began his university studies at the beginning of the second quarter of the century, while the first quarter was still alive in the men, in the scholarship, in the unsilenced echo of the circumstances, in those very first confused cultural experiences." Garin is adamant on this point: he has provided a "document," not a "history," for those who, in writing a true history, "will want to take into account the various feelings and reactions vis-à-vis those men who from the lectern, in the academies and in books, presented themselves in Italy as teachers of truth and wisdom between the beginning of the century and the end of the Second World War" (*CFI*, 1:xi–xii)—that is to say, the "feelings and reactions" of those who in 1922 were still "youngsters" (*ragazzi*) and therefore innocent witnesses to a moral degeneration they would be left to puzzle out.

Palmiro Togliatti, Gramsci's successor as the head of the Italian Communist Party and the custodian of his intellectual legacy, described *Chronicles* as "the first scientific book in Italy, not written by a Marxist, in which philosophical stances are not taken as expressions of a purely ideal movement."[121] In the keynote speech that Togliatti invited him to deliver at the first Gramsci conference in 1958, Garin labored to cast the Marxist thinker as a founder of Italian discursivity, an ally in his effort to bring about a "settling of accounts" with Croce's historicism which, in its larger aims, failed to remain grounded. Paraphrasing Gramsci, Garin states:

> Croce is not the historian of revolutionary moments; Croce is the historian of the institutes and of "forms" to be conserved, not of the real [as opposed to "ideal"] liberties that are to be conquered. Gramsci . . . instead expressed the sharpest intransigent morality in the realm of culture, the staunchest imperative for the struggle for liberty, even at the cost of losing one's soul . . . : because humanity is served with a firm volition to build a common world. . . . And this common truth, one that is not oracular and not above time, but is rather built into history and is exhausted in history, entirely human, of men for men, is the one for which Gramsci seeks and fights: for this reason he is among those who in Italy attempted to work together, beyond partisanship, on precise problems (on "the small things") with simplicity and in the company of as many of his fellows as possible.[122]

Garin understood that the Gramscian critical operation that goes by the name of "Anti-Croce" was not goaded by resentment, but was intended as soul-searching activity. Garin accompanied Gramsci in his return to Croce in order to see more clearly where several generations of thinkers had come from and, in the process, recover the precise terms of their inheritance.

Believing that historical accounts were in no need of theoretical grounding, Garin engaged in historiographical theory only in a series of academic debates and speeches, which were collected, together with his 1958 Gramsci talk, in an eloquently titled volume, *Philosophy as Histori-*

121. Interestingly, Togliatti, criticized Garin's work for being too unconcerned with actual politics. Garin had received the same criticism from Baron for his *Italian Humanism*. See Palmiro Togliatti (Roderigo di Castiglia), "Cronache di filosofia italiana," *Rinascita* 12 (1955): 430. For some useful considerations of Garin's ties to Togliatti and the Communist Party, see Michele Ciliberto, *Eugenio Garin: Un intellettuale del Novecento* (Rome: Laterza, 2011), 116ff.

122. Eugenio Garin, "Gramsci nella cultura italiana," 61.

cal Knowledge (1959). Owing to the persistent belief in Italy and abroad in standards of "unity" in philosophy, in the late 1950s Garin could still address the issue as a fresh post-Hegelian. More than Gentile and Croce (at this point, perhaps, two vanquished idealists in Italy), Garin was troubled by the suspect reintroduction of notions that appeared to be willing to eliminate history from ideas; examples he mentions are Robert Curtius's "topoi," Etienne Gilson's philosophical "essences," and Arthur Lovejoy's "unit ideas." Philosophers, not philosophy, were his stated object of study:

> The historian, connecting ideas and doctrines to the occurrences, recovering their relationship, will reveal that "philosophies"—even the most bizarre ones—sprang from and gave voice to real exigencies, and amounted to answers to real exigencies; they helped men achieve self-knowledge, freeing them from illusions; they endowed them with ideals, means for coexistence, and helped them in creating for themselves more adequate tools for research and every sort of activity. By throwing light on nonobvious connections, evaluating the answers, unearthing all that lies hidden, pointing to inexhaustible possibilities at times when possibilities seemed exhausted, not only will the historian assist in conquering the memory of the past, but he will assist the reorientation of the future—truly, thought as action.[123]

For his 'reduction' of philosophy to historical researches, Garin was charged with antiphilosophical sentiments. In response, he reiterated his ideal of a sort of philosophy of scholarly praxis, for "there is no knowing without doing." It is in theorizing about reason and the purported essence of history and sciences that one really subtracts oneself from the "toil" of thinking *with* others. This, Garin's traumatized reaction to a protracted Hegelianism, may have protected Italian scholarship from relapsing into an *esprit de système*, but it also prevented Garin, who was among the few up to the task, from addressing the work of peers who in those same years were confronting the problem of the relationship of history and truth on theoretical grounds (Paul Ricoeur and Gadamer, just to name a few that Garin seems to have followed closely). But Garin was interested in the relationship between history and morality, and his only demand, formulated

123. Eugenio Garin, "Filosofia e antifilosofia (Una discussione con Enzo Paci)," in *La filosofia come sapere storico*, 27–28.

on behalf of his school of thought, was: "At the very least, let us work in peace!"[124]

It makes sense, then, that Garin dedicated his later career to ever-deepening investigations, which often led to recantations of his previous interpretations, or, as time went by, to additions, supplements, reckonings, and accretions of all sorts. Among them was a lengthy appendix to *Chronicles* that brought the book's coverage up to 1960, and an epilogue to *History of Italian Philosophy* accounting for the "rebirth and decline of idealism." In this definitive edition, from 1966, Garin's *History* materially illustrates what could be called the Italian 'difference' in philosophy or 'special path' to modernity.[125] In fact, it is remarkable that a venture inspired by mid-nineteenth-century revolutionary pathos and itself firmly founded on a belated Hegelianism could make its way, revised but unscathed, into so-called postmodernity, an area or state of mind with which Garin did not wish to get involved. Garin attached a premature 'farewell' (unbeknownst to him, he was then just midway through his scholarly career!) to the last paragraph of this work:

> The past, in order to return to be present in the historical reconstruction, must be enough removed so as to become subjected to an adequate prospective collocation. It must allow the determination of profound connections and junctions, in the silence of controversies and immediate reactions. As it used to be said, history is not about the events too close to us. The discourse in the last decades after World War II could begin with the announcement that the specters have returned; too many "philosophers" have also returned, not without advantages, to the enthralling castle to fight among the shadows, and to discuss the shadows of things. Philosophers, in the best hypothesis, are mistaking information for elaboration of thought. A discourse of this kind, which would be fine elsewhere, would risk substituting controversy with history. (*HIP*, 2:1065–66)

Garin was a resolute survivor of controversy, and he bit the bullet so as not to betray himself by engaging in a critique of the postmodern world. His last words, so to speak, were a commission to "new students," whom he

124. Eugenio Garin, "Osservazioni preliminari a una storia della filosofia," in *La filosofia come sapere storico*, 86.

125. Garin's *History* underwent a third edition in 1978, but additions, though substantial, were made only to the bibliography.

advised to follow Gramsci, "to trace the history of a national philosophy that Italy does not yet possess." Garin went on to collect and edit Gentile's scattered writings on virtually every aspect and figure of Italian philosophy, using the same title as his own history, *Storia della filosofia italiana* (1969). This time, he must have felt he had gone full circle; he stepped to the side as the history of Italian philosophy merged seamlessly with his life and career.

CHAPTER FIVE

A Philosopher's Humanism:
Paul Oskar Kristeller

Dear Kristeller, [T]o resume contact with distant friends, after these horrific years, is one of the few comforts that we are left with. . . . May your family, your studies, the students, and the friendly surroundings help you overcome the pain that fatally falls on those who have left dear people behind in this hell! It is in a brotherly spirit that I tell you this. . . . Since August of last year, I carefully avoid looking into the Arno, and I think that, if possible, I will avoid leaving Florence for a long time. Eventually we will accustom ourselves to different cities from those that time and love made sacred for us. But I am afraid that those of our generation, who have witnessed those things in first person, will never grow accustomed to it. . . . As for me, I tried to work until 1943; after that, I got distracted by the bombings, the loss of our home, the failure of all certainties, and troubles of all sorts. Today I would like to get started again, or at least try to. And sometimes my mind nostalgically goes back to the times when we worked as if side by side, but I knew then that we had to go through fire, as the Psalm says. Let's now just hope that real peace lies behind the fire.
—Eugenio Garin to Paul Oskar Kristeller (Florence, 10 July 1945)

Dear Garin, . . . I too am very pleased to resume contact with you and with the other friends I often thought about during these terrible years. The war that for me lasted twelve years is now over, and if the terrible toll we had to pay does not allow us too much happiness, we nevertheless have the right and the duty to hope. . . . I sympathize with your pain for the destruction of Florence and other places. But Florence will always be the most beautiful city in the world. It would benefit you to leave your isolation and look at the changed place. It is better to face the present. The past will always remain alive in your memory. I hope, moreover, that you will soon resume your work, which according to my experience is always the best comfort. Your beautiful book on Pico is a promise that you need to keep to yourself, to your friends, and to the world, despite everything. Our commonality of ideas and ideals, moreover, will allow us to work again together, even when we are far from one another.

—Paul Oskar Kristeller to Eugenio Garin (New York, 24 August 1945)

INTRODUCTION: THE ITALIAN(S') RENAISSANCE BEYOND ITALY

The exchange in the epigraphs bespeaks a personal, scholarly, and generational sodality whose mutation reshaped Renaissance scholarship in the latter part of the twentieth century, on both sides of the Atlantic.[1] The works of Eugenio Garin (1909–2004) and Paul Oskar Kristeller (1905–99) have come to represent polarities of a wide range of scholarly dispositions, priorities, methodologies, and agendas that went for a long time uncontested (in each camp) and are now being subjected, in a self-defining effort, to comparison and critical reappraisal by students of Italian humanism. Unsurprisingly, much of the recent stocktaking in the field has directed itself toward intelligibly articulating the terms of a disagreement that played out chiefly in footnotes and asides for the length of two perfectly (and uncannily!) coterminous careers (1929–99).[2] In fact, "brotherly spirit" gave way to antagonism within months of their reconnection, as Garin and Kristeller, both relying on a reassessment of Quattrocento humanism, simultaneously went public with apparently irreconcilable Renaissances.

1. For this exchange and a few more letters, see the appendix to James Hankins, "Garin and Paul Oskar Kristeller: Existentialism, Neo-Kantianism, and the Post-war Interpretation of Renaissance Humanism," in Olivia Catanorchi and Valentina Lepri, eds., *Eugenio Garin: Dal Rinascimento all'Illuminismo* (Rome: Edizioni di Storia e Letteratura, 2011), 497–99. The complete correspondence of Garin and Kristeller is forthcoming. I am grateful to the editors, James Hankins and Patrick Baker, for allowing me to read and cite these documents in advance of publication.

2. Compare Thomas Gilbhard, ed., *Bibliographia Kristelleriana: A Bibliography of the Publications of Paul Oskar Kristeller (1929–1999)* (Rome: Edizioni di Storia e Letteratura, 2006) and *Bibliografia degli scritti di Eugenio Garin, 1929–1999* (Rome: Laterza, 1999). The recent addenda to Garin's bibliography do not alter this stunning collimation, as most of Garin's publications after 1999 are either reprints or brief commemorative pieces. See "Aggiunte e correzioni alla *Bibliografia degli scritti di Eugenio Garin (1929–1999)*," in *Giornale critico della filosofia italiana* 88 (2009): 499–507.

Kristeller's "Humanism and Scholasticism in the Italian Renaissance," a programmatic essay published in 1946, immediately preceded
Garin's *Italian Humanism*.[3] After arriving in the United States in 1939,
Kristeller sympathized with the "legitimate objections" of the American
medievalists and with their "'revolt'" against the "cult" of the Renaissance. He therefore accepted the notion of an "Italian Renaissance" with
the proviso that this epoch be pitted against the "modest tradition of medieval Italy" rather than the "equally rich civilization of medieval France"
(*SRTL*, 1:556).[4] As for humanism, the period's "most widespread and characteristic intellectual trend," it surely amounted to a phase in the history
of rhetoric rather than philosophy: humanists are the professional "heirs
and successors" to the medieval teachers of grammar and rhetoric, the so-
called *dictatores*. Indeed, sources confirmed that *humanista* was a term
coined by university students in the late fifteenth century after the labels
their teachers gave to their field of learning, *studia humanitatis* or *studia humaniora*, which were in themselves resonant terms that "covered a
content that had existed long before," namely, grammar, rhetoric, poetry,
history, and moral philosophy (573).

In his classic piece, Kristeller set out to audit the Renaissance man's
own "illusion" regarding his epoch-making merits: "Several famous humanists, such as Petrarch, Valla, Erasmus, and Vives, were violent critics of medieval learning," but, in the main, the humanists' polemic was
often unsubstantiated, "a noisy advertisement" intended to "impose their
standards upon the other fields of learning and of science, including philosophy" (*SRTL*, 1:563). In modern times, says Kristeller (referring to the
Italian idealists), the controversy has been taken at face value, and even
exaggerated, leading to an "ambitious" but "unsound" interpretation of
humanism "as the new philosophy of the Renaissance" (560–61). Equally
deluded, however, are those who in defending the Scholastics are apt to
argue for humanism's weakness as philosophy. The point for Kristeller is
that humanism and Scholasticism developed side by side in the Renais-

3. Monfasani noted that according to the copyright date of the 1944–45 issue of *Byzantion* (the journal in which Kristeller's classic essay first appeared), the publication actually
occurred in 1946. See John Monfasani, "Kristeller and Manuscripts," in *Kristeller Reconsidered: Essays on His Life and Scholarship*, ed. Monfasani (New York: Italica Press, 2006), 183.
For an even closer determination of the date of publication, see Kristeller to Garin (10 April
1946): "Ho poi un articolo su umanesimo e scolastica nel rinascimento italiano che uscirà su
Byzantion" (AEG).
4. Kristeller discusses his sympathies for the activities of the Medieval Academy of
America in *Renaissance Thought and Its Sources*, ed. Michael Mooney (New York: Columbia
University Press, 1979), 3.

sance, and "their controversy . . . is merely a phase in the battle of the arts, not a struggle for existence," for, as he famously stated,

> most of the works of the humanists have nothing to do with philoso-
> phy even in the vaguest possible sense of the term. Even their trea-
> tises on philosophical subjects, if we care to read them, appear in most
> cases rather superficial and inconclusive if compared with the works
> of ancient or medieval philosophers, a fact that may be indifferent to
> a general historian, but which cannot be overlooked by a historian of
> philosophy. . . . I should like to suggest that the Italian humanists on
> the whole were neither good nor bad philosophers, but no philosophers
> at all. (561)

Kristeller identifies the peddlers of philosophical humanism in his footnotes: Cassirer, Gentile, and the idealist historiographer Guido De Ruggiero. By the time this essay was reprinted in 1956, Saitta, as author of *Italian Thought in the Age of Humanism and the Renaissance*, and Garin, as
author of *Der italienische Humanismus*, had been added to this roster.

We have seen that, starting with the introduction to the 1952 edition
of *Italian Humanism* —and, later, in his defense of Hans Baron—Garin
had already accused his colleague of a similar scholarly connivance: he
claimed that Kristeller, as a foremost authority on Marsilio Ficino, had
tarried (together with Gentile, Cassirer, and Saitta) in the late Quattrocento, seeking out systematic philosophies rather than picking up and
elaborating on Gentile's own insight regarding the philosophical import
of humanist philology or acknowledging, with Baron, the indissoluble link
between culture and politics in the early fifteenth century. It is unclear,
then, what to make of Kristeller's counteraccusation. Had he reinterpreted
Garin in the postwar period (their correspondence was interrupted in 1940)
as advancing the claims of idealist historiography?

If so, it is a baffling association for Kristeller to make, especially considering who he was: a German Jew who had emigrated in 1934 to Italy,
where he was groomed by Gentile as the next rising star in Renaissance
scholarship (until his second emigration to the United States five years
later). In other words, Kristeller could not have failed to grasp that the
story of the Italians' Renaissance had in effect been a history of emancipation from humanism: that for Gentile, still, humanism was a nonphilosophy (or, at most, a movement heralding a spiritual/religious rejuvenation),
and that even Saitta's contraposition of humanism and Scholasticism was
less philosophical than religious and institutional, as the Renaissance and

the Middle Ages (really, Gentile and Agostino Gemelli) clashed finally and decisively in the 1920s and 1930s. Taking the same internalist perspective that allows Garin's unreserved exaltation of 'humanism as philosophy' to be characterized as the first decisive break (Saitta excepted) with the Italians' 'Renaissance shame,' we can argue (this, indeed, seems to be Garin's point) that Kristeller was the true inheritor of the Italian brand of antihumanism.

In their postwar correspondence Garin and Kristeller immediately turned to the subject of the recently assassinated Gentile, their common guardian. Kristeller, like Garin and most of their peers, was perplexed by Gentile's unwavering loyalty to fascism, even in its demise, and lamented the betrayal and tongue-lashing to which he was subjected post mortem: "It is tragic that in the present day no distinction is drawn between the political element and the personal and philosophical element; this is shameful on behalf of those who have taken advantage of [Gentile's] support."[5] In this context, Kristeller thanked Garin for his "bravery," evident in his frequent citations of Kristeller and other Jewish scholars after 1938, and commended him for the "very noteworthy" assessment he had put forth of Gentile's Renaissance scholarship upon his death, in 1944. Furthermore, having read his colleague's latest production all at once, Kristeller noted that Garin had marshaled Gentile's insights without being guilty of some of his exaggerations or, worse, "falling for the arbitrary absurdities" of the Italian medievalists. All in all, Kristeller felt that he and Garin were of the same scholarly attitude: "I like the balanced interpretation you give of the relationship between medieval and humanist thought. . . . On this point, as on many others, I feel very close to your views."[6]

For Kristeller, too, had been grappling with the challenge of salvaging Gentile's Renaissance from the idealist agenda. In a 1941 bibliographical essay, co-authored with John H. Randall, he confronted, head on, the "crying need for the further study of Renaissance philosophies," by American

5. Hankins, "Garin and Paul Oskar Kristeller," 501. See also Paul Oskar Kristeller, review of *Opere Complete*, vol. 11: *Il pensiero italiano del Rinascimento*, by Giovanni Gentile, *Philosophic Abstracts* 3 (1940): 19.

6. Kristeller to Garin, 18 March 1946, AEG. In this letter Kristeller actually refers to Giuseppe Toffanin (1891–1980), who was neither a medievalist nor a Neothomist but, rather, the author of a controversial interpretation of humanism as an intrinsically religious movement. See Giuseppe Toffanin, *History of Humanism* (New York: Las Americas, 1954). Yet, in a bibliographical essay, Kristeller dismisses Toffanin's work together with that of Olgiati and other representatives of Neothomist historiography. See Paul Oskar Kristeller and John H. Randall Jr., "The Study of the Philosophies of the Renaissance," *Journal of the History of Ideas* 2, no. 4 (1941): 454–55.

scholars in particular. And in presenting all available sources (primary and secondary), he took great pains to point out Gentile's "great ingenuity in interpreting the 'Renaissance conception of man'" in order to alert readers to his motives (immanentism, antischolastic sentiments, etc.), but also to distinguish Gentile's Renaissance decisively from that of his followers (Saitta) and opponents (Neothomists), in whose work Renaissance thinkers were made indistinguishable, robbed of historical context, and never treated "for their own sake." While on the one hand Kristeller was skeptical of the scholar's ability, especially outside Italy, to orient himself within Gentile's varied corpus, on the other hand he could not in good conscience dismiss Gentile's—or, for that matter, Cassirer's—presentist efforts. The charter document with which Kristeller steered a rebirth of Renaissance studies in the American academy concludes with a plea that reveals his partaking of a shared dilemma:

> The closer we can get to the problems of the Renaissance itself, and the farther we can get away from viewing them in terms of problems of later incidence, the more likely we are to arrive at a genuine understanding. But even those who have clearly imported the issues of a later day into the field, like Cassirer or Gentile, have had instruments with which to ask questions. And they both have in the course of their use of these contemporary problems been led much nearer to the problems of the Renaissance. May we too be given an equal capacity to learn![7]

As a scholar of the Renaissance, and in his loyalties, his concerns, his models, and, mainly, in his aspirations, Kristeller belonged squarely to the generation of Italian scholars raised during the Fascist ventennio. And so the question immediately arises: how knowledgeable was he of Italian nineteenth- and twentieth-century philosophical aspirations, beyond the quarrels of actualism and Neothomism?

Of interest on this point are Kristeller's insistent demands that he be provided with a copy of *History of Italian Philosophy*, the only work that Garin seemed reluctant to put before him: "Your kindness toward my Italian 'Philosophy' is moving; I'll be very pleased if you will read it and provide me with your opinion; but do not feel obliged to bother yourself with a review."[8] But Kristeller did so anyway, describing Garin's "monumental history" as "designed primarily as a work of reference," indispens-

7. Kristeller and Randall, "Study of the Philosophies of the Renaissance," 496.
8. Garin to Kristeller, 11 October 1948, POKP.

able for its bibliographies, especially those pertaining to sixteenth-century thought, and its name indexes. Noting Garin's "keen effort toward an independent interpretation" (independent, presumably, from Gentile, whom Kristeller dutifully mentions as the original designated author of the work) and choosing to refrain from criticism of "details of judgment and emphasis," Kristeller recommended the book as "indispensable to philosophers and historians interested in any phase of Italian thought" and as especially useful in elucidating the French, English, and German influences on its development.[9] Kristeller's review says little about his own understanding of the phenomenon of 'Italian philosophy' or about his opinion regarding the possibility of presenting philosophy as culturally grounded. In any case, it may be surmised that in the immediate postwar period Kristeller was tinkering with the idea of representing, or at least mediating, knowledge of Italian philosophy in the United States.

Some odd entries in his bibliography from the 1940s show that Kristeller could be expected to engage with Italy beyond the Renaissance and that his cognizance of Italian twentieth-century philosophical anomalies was sharp: he published two (neutral) reviews of Sofia Vanni Rovighi's work, itself instrumental in the belated introduction of Husserlian phenomenology in Italy (we should remind ourselves that Italians had transitioned effortlessly from actualism to existentialism), as well as reviews of an important book by Augusto Guzzo, part of the second generation of Gentileans who, like Spirito, would eventually seek an 'internalist' reform of actualism.[10] Even more interestingly, Kristeller was called on to appraise the first translation in English of a work by Vico (the *Autobiography*), which was published with a comprehensive introduction, by Max H. Fisch, destined to become a cornerstone in American scholarship on the Italian philosopher.[11] In this review, Kristeller seems fully invested, and his command is that of a seasoned Italian thinker: Vico, for some the "greatest Italian philosopher of the 18th century," is perhaps the precursor of the Romantic movement and of the historiographical school of Herder and He-

9. Paul Oskar Kristeller, review of *La Filosofia*, by Eugenio Garin, *Journal of Philosophy* 46 (1949): 160–61.

10. Paul Oskar Kristeller, review of *La filosofia di Edmund Husserl*, by Sofia Vanni Rovighi, *Journal of Philosophy* 37 (1940): 587; Paul Oskar Kristeller, review of *Introduzione all studio di Kant*, by Sofia Vanni Rovighi, *Journal of Philosophy* 46 (1949): 875; Paul Oskar Kristeller, review of *Sic vos non vobis*, vol. 1, by Augusto Guzzo, *Philosophic Abstracts* 1 (1939–40): 19; Paul Oskar Kristeller, review of *Sic vos non vobis*, vol. 2, by Augusto Guzzo, *Philosophic Abstracts* 3 (1940): 19–20.

11. Paul Oskar Kristeller, review of *The Autobiography of Giambattista Vico*, trans. Max H. Fisch and Thomas G. Bergin, *Philosophical Review* 54 (1945): 428–31.

gel. Kristeller finds Fisch's exploration of Vico's sources (Bacon, Descartes, Galileo, Pufendorf, etc.) thorough in all but one respect: in accounting for the genesis of Vico's historical thought, Fisch fails to foreground the "strong influence" of the Renaissance humanists, a neglect that Kristeller attributes to the long-standing custom of dismissing humanist historiography as "empty rhetoric" and their philology as "barren erudition."

Kristeller, who through the first half of the review appears to be sponsoring a genuine Italian Vichianism, clarifies, or qualifies, his assessment when he lists the reasons why Vico, in his mind, is "the direct successor of the humanists": his attempt to recover jurisprudence, classical literature, and rhetoric in opposition to the "neglect of these subjects" by Descartes, "his attempt to obtain the position of chancellor" in Naples, and, most important, his role as professor of rhetoric at the university of that city.[12] In other words, the factors that make Vico a humanist disqualify him as a philosopher in Kristellerian terms: his recovery of nonphilosophical subjects, his extracurricular activities and political ambitions, and his professional affiliation. In this review, fascinatingly, Kristeller seems to exploit Vico's connection to the Renaissance, a touchstone in the Italians' philosophical recovery of humanism, to advance his cause. It is worth noting Kristeller's ingenuity here, for although a connection between Vico and the Renaissance had always existed in Italian philosophy, and had even been explicitly advanced by Gentile, it had not yet gained solidity in 1945, when this review was published. Instead, this new, Renaissance Vichianism was affirmed by the same generation of positive existentialists who had emphasized Gentile's philosophical understanding of philology as a way of overcoming idealist historiography and, in the process, rediscovering the Renaissance. Among them were Abbagnano, Grassi, and, principally, Garin, who on this point may be said to have been beaten to the punch by Kristeller: Garin's own resolute affirmation of Vico as heir of the Renaissance humanists—which as we shall see marked a turning point in Italian Vico studies—first appeared in *History of Italian Philosophy*, two years after Kristeller's review.

Kristeller was thus conversant with Italian philosophy as a specific 'tradition' relying on, but not fulfilled in, an eternally improvable and thus reclaimable Renaissance humanism, itself a movement invested in recovery. The (often neglected) premises of his 1946 manifesto bear witness to his grasp (unmatched for its synoptic terseness by his peers in Italy) of the Italian 'difference' or, in our terms, intellectual peninsularity:

12. Kristeller, review of *The Autobiography of Giambattista Vico*, 430.

The center of medieval civilization was undoubtedly France, and all other countries of Western Europe followed the leadership of that country. . . . Italy certainly was no exception to that rule; but whereas the other countries, especially England, Germany, and the Low Countries, took an active part in the major cultural pursuits of the period and followed the same general development, Italy occupied a somewhat peculiar position. This may be observed in architecture and music, in the religious drama as well as in Latin and vernacular poetry in general, in scholastic philosophy and theology, and even, contrary to common opinion, in classical studies. On the other hand, Italy had a narrow but persistent tradition of her own which went back to ancient Roman times and which found its expression in certain branches of the arts and of poetry, in lay education and in legal customs, and in the study of grammar and of rhetoric. . . . Influences from France became more powerful only with the thirteenth century, when their traces appeared in architecture and music, in Latin and vernacular poetry, in philosophy and theology, and in the field of classical studies. Many typical products of the Italian Renaissance may thus be understood as a result of belated medieval influences received from France, but grafted upon, and assimilated by, a more narrow, but stubborn and different native tradition. This may be said of Dante's *Divine Comedy*, of the religious drama which flourished in fifteenth-century Florence, and of the chivalric poetry of Ariosto and of Tasso. (*SRTL*, 1:554–56)

Considerations that could easily have been employed in nineteenth-century Italy to argue for an Italian intellectual *primato* are retained here by Kristeller to suggest some sort of idiosyncrasy. The question is whether things go awry ("narrow," "stubborn") in contact with Italy, or whether they turn to gold (Dante, Ariosto, Tasso). After articulating these premises, Kristeller treats humanism as also a "typical" Italian product, one so significant as to momentarily "wrest from France her cultural leadership in Western Europe," implying that if any primacy is to be granted, it will always and uniquely reside in letters and not in philosophy, a discipline, Kristeller's hurries to specify, traditionally neglected in Italian medieval universities. Equally striking is Kristeller's emphasis on "importation," and if one reads carefully through this oft-cited article one realizes that he is sifting the subjects originally indicated as germane to Italy: all that is left, in the end, are "style" and "elegance."

It has recently been suggested that Kristeller's *prise de position* smacks of the same anti-Romanitas sentiments—Latin literature as "weak in philosophy"—as run from Hegel to Heidegger (Kristeller's one-time teacher), the same sentiments that Italians, from Spaventa to Grassi, tried to counter, less in defiance of Greco-German affinity than in an attempt to combine it with the Romano-Italic tradition.[13] This may be the case, yet one may feel uncomfortable attributing a straightforward bias to Kristeller, whose field of study was, after all, Italian intellectual history. As we track the specific philosophical origins of Kristeller's stance, we should note what is perhaps the most baffling aspect of his attempted definition of humanism: the marginalization of the greatest humanists, whom he qualifies as "exceptions," in favor of a nameless "vast majority" (*SRTL*, 1:563). This, Kristeller's approach to humanism from the base, as it were, is what Italians find "disconcerting." In the words of Riccardo Fubini: "We have grammar, rhetoric, and philosophy; what we no longer have are names and last names, the grammarians, the orators, the philosophers. [Kristeller's] is a history of abstract forms, individuals are reduced to phantasms—though these phantasms are Petrarch, Lorenzo Valla, Erasmus. Would we want them all to be 'professional rhetoricians,' or, in any case, associated with some school discipline, really?"[14] What appears to be an indiscriminate approach to humanism on Kristeller's part is perfectly unintelligible from an Italian perspective, where it has more often resulted in defensive or dismissive evaluations than in critical confrontation. This is not the case in the U.S. academy, where Kristeller's stance has been embraced as an epoch-making turning point and frequently advanced with the ardor befitting a scholarly mission.

In his recent assessment of the relative merits of Garin and Kristeller, for example, James Hankins relies on a distinction Kristeller drew in his 1946 essay between a denotative sense of "humanism" as a "literary and educational tradition within Western culture" and a connotative sense of it as a "philosophy of man."[15] "Philosophical humanism," Hankins elaborates, emerged in the wake of the Enlightenment as a reaction to the "dechristianization" of culture, which set thinkers on a quest for new ethical standards independent of metaphysics or religious authority. Ever since, from Feuerbach to Gramsci and Sartre, philosophical human-

13. Christopher S. Celenza, *The Lost Italian Renaissance: Humanists, Historians, and Latin's Legacy* (Baltimore: Johns Hopkins University Press, 2004), 51.

14. Riccardo Fubini, *L'Umanesimo italiano e i suoi storici: Origini rinascimentali, critica moderna* (Milan: FrancoAngeli, 2001), 333–34. Similar charges, albeit in a less polemical tone, are now leveled at Kristeller by scholars operating in the United States.

15. James Hankins, "Two Twentieth-Century Interpreters of Renaissance Humanism: Eugenio Garin and Paul Oskar Kristeller," *Comparative Criticism* 23 (2001): 3.

ism has grown increasingly "more radical, more anti-metaphysical, more historicist, more insistent on the radical freedom of human beings."[16] According to this narrative, the identity of contemporary Renaissance historians depends in large part on whether they are inclined to stress a "genetic connection" or "emphasize the discontinuities" between these two humanisms: they can be identified, albeit imperfectly, as "lumpers" or "splitters."

A "lumper" is someone drawn to some form of presentism, to the Whiggish tendency "to trace elements of modern thought to Renaissance roots."[17] This trend, so widespread in nineteenth- and twentieth-century Renaissance scholarship, constitutes what may be called the "modern paradigm," which can be stated as "X, a constitutive element of modern thought or culture, has its origins or preconditions in the Renaissance."[18] In the case of a scholar like Garin, a representative "lumper" who, according to Hankins, remained very much rooted in the Italian idealist tradition, this tendency translated into an attempt to reinterpret Renaissance humanism according to the Gramscianism he so enthusiastically espoused:

> Garin's humanists are still united by a common philosophical outlook; they are Gramscian intellectuals, perhaps, but they are also still forerunners of the Enlightenment *philosophe*. Garin strips away the apparatus of Hegelian dialectic and the overt nationalist bias of previous Italian scholarship on the Renaissance, and he has contributed in a salutary way to the post-war emphasis within Renaissance studies on accurate documentation. But his Renaissance is still very clearly part of a modernist narrative of increasing rationalism and secularization.[19]

Garin remained "within the channels dug by the modern paradigm," while his Gramscianism prompted him to assimilate and advance Baron's notion of "civic humanism."

Meanwhile, according to Hankins, a notable reshaping of the paradigm can be attributed to Grassi, who, unlike most students of the Renaissance, regarded not Kant and Hegel but Heidegger as "the yardstick against which

16. Hankins, "Two Twentieth-Century Interpreters," 5.

17. Hankins, "Two Twentieth-Century Interpreters," 14.

18. James Hankins, "Renaissance Philosophy between God and the Devil," in *The Renaissance in the Twentieth Century: Acts of an International Conference, Florence, Villa I Tatti, June 9–11, 1999*, ed. Allen J. Grieco et al. (Florence: Olschki, 2002), 274.

19. Hankins, "Renaissance Philosophy between God and the Devil," 286.

to measure the Italian humanists."[20] From this vantage point, Grassi argued that Renaissance thinkers, their rhetoric and poetics, did not foreshadow the Enlightenment and rationalist metaphysics, but rather anticipated Heidegger's critique of this very tradition. Yet a "radical break" with the paradigm could occur only with an unconditional repudiation of any anthropological interpretation of humanism and of any kind of "Whiggish tendency" and "value judgment." This is the revolution associated with the name of Kristeller, whose role consisted in turning the study of humanism into a *Wissenschaft*, a science "completely independent of contemporary history" and consequently conducive to a historicized and impartial description of the Renaissance movement. Kristeller is a resolute "splitter," and though his work was "resisted by Baron and Garin, it led to a series of historicizing assaults on the Modern Paradigm backed by masses of empirical research."[21]

Hankins's pioneering attempt to grapple with this central debate is useful for understanding Kristeller's motives, aims, responsibilities, and self-perception—at least, in his postwar career as a Renaissance scholar in the United States. This perspective enables Hankins to emphasize particular contexts invisible to European scholars. For example, he observes that Kristeller's "historicizing penchant" was surely catalyzed by the muscular U.S. tradition of philosophical 'humanism'—extending from Ralph Waldo Emerson to Corliss Lamont, John Dewey (whose pragmatism was seen also as a 'humanism' by his disciples), J. E. Woodbridge, and John H. Randall, many of whom were associated with the philosophy department of Columbia University, which Kristeller joined almost immediately upon his arrival in the United States.[22] Nonetheless, debates are matters of perspective, and the 'Kristellerian' one that emerged in the postwar period in the United States is just one of many. In fact, there are as many perspectives on Renaissance humanism as there are combinations of terms: temporal (pre- and postwar), geographical (Italian, German, U.S.), disciplinary (scholarly, philosophical), and generational (at least four generations now, and counting). While attempting to integrate as many of these elements as possible, this chapter will foreground the Italian contribution, philosophical and scholarly, to the development of Kristeller's interpretive paradigm, all in relation to his German formation as a philosopher.[23] First, though, it

20. Hankins, "Renaissance Philosophy between God and the Devil," 287.
21. Hankins, "Renaissance Philosophy between God and the Devil," 290.
22. Hankins, "Two Twentieth-Century Interpreters," 12.
23. To my knowledge, the only account to emphasize the role of Italy's academic culture in Kristeller's formation is Warren Boutcher, "The Making of the Humane Philosopher: Paul

may be necessary to recapitulate the argument of this study thus far, especially since Kristeller's current reputation was significantly shaped by his purported quarrels with the Italians.

I have already suggested that a refined understanding of the Italians' Renaissance may reveal certain hidden affinities between the Risorgimento's negative appraisal of the Renaissance *letterato* and Kristeller's own lukewarm feelings toward that figure. This affinity does not make Kristeller more of a "lumper" than Garin; rather, it points to the fact that the Italians' participation in the modern paradigm may be less than commonly maintained. In chapter 1, we have seen that in the latter part of the nineteenth century the prevailing Italian belief was that the Italian Renaissance represented a glorious beginning of modernity for every major European nation except, paradoxically, Italy. De Sanctis's interpretation of the Renaissance as an intrinsically flawed epoch was only partially checked, or redeemed, by what Spaventa had been able to articulate on philosophical grounds, via Hegel. Meanwhile, these two Italys, these two Renaissances, coexisted in Gentile.

In chapter 2 of this study, I attempted to recover the idiosyncratic philosophical stance of a generation that, while fascinated by Gentile's actualism, felt the urge to appeal to existentialism in order to loosen the strictures of a consolidated idealism, most notably the epistemological solipsism and teleological historiography it had come to promote. Positive existentialism or co-existentialism, the product of that generational effort, was variously employed to call attention to dialectical tensions within corpora of distinct thinkers as much as in the history of philosophy more generally. Most important, Italian existentialism would eventually promote a dialogical recuperation of the early Renaissance, perceived no longer as the source and origin of idealist certainties but as a source of unrealized possibilities. It could be argued that by surmounting neo-Hegelian and actualist historiography in this way, Italians spilled out of the modern paradigm, not as "splitters" but as "lumpers" of a very different sort.

Specifically, we have seen that the connection Garin drew between the Renaissance and the Enlightenment was not progressive, nor, for that matter, was it aimed at promoting rationalism or secularism. Garin's Enlightenment, to be sure, was less the *siècle des Lumières* than it was the century of the British moralists, who, in Garin's description, unsystematically supported a collective, even collaborative, participation in the di-

Oskar Kristeller and Twentieth-Century Intellectual History," in Monfasani, *Kristeller Reconsidered*, 39–70.

vine. Most importantly (and, perhaps, most interestingly), careful attention to the transition between the prewar and postwar periods reveals that
Garin's 'humanists' owed nothing, initially, to Gramsci's 'intellectuals.'
They were created, rather, when Baron's 'civic' humanists and Grassi's
'existential' humanists comingled in his work in reaction to a set of interlocutors—Croce, Gentile, and Risorgimento thinkers—that younger
Italians shared with Gramsci. These details matter, and they point to the
resourcefulness of Renaissance scholarship, which has often relied on but
sometimes superseded its philosophical inspirations. At least, this is the
case with both Garin and Grassi, whose shared paradigm, 'humanism as
philosophical tradition,' was also in place before Heidegger's antihumanist
"Letter." In 1947, when Gramsci's writings began to emerge and Heidegger produced his "Letter on 'Humanism,'" Garin had the good fortune to
recover an unexpected and very powerful comrade-in-arms, while Grassi
found himself betrayed by his own pieties.

That Italian scholars of humanism are 'presentists' of some sort is undeniable. Nevertheless, in their presentism they were often seeking successors, not precursors, reactivation, not Whiggish anticipation (for tradition
is a work in progress and is never fulfilled).[24] Dismayed by the acritical and
acquiescent optimism of the idealists, they reacted by viewing the Renaissance in relation not so much to the present as to a still unrealized potential: X, a constitutive element or value of Renaissance thought, deserves
to be regained for the sake of the future. Kristeller fully shared in this
ambition, albeit with his own set of priorities and standards. When we assess the contribution of these scholars to Renaissance studies, their merits
in disengaging from the past should not be overestimated, just as their
importance as philosophers should not be underestimated. Their work
transformed the so-called problem of the Renaissance—really the problem
of Burckhardt's definition of the epoch—into a 'humanism problem,' the
very *philosophical* question that defined the terms by which the destiny of
Western culture was renegotiated around 1946. Perhaps, antagonism could
once again give way to that "brotherly spirit" mentioned by Garin in his

---

24. On the issue of 'presentism' in Renaissance scholarship, see Nancy S. Struever,
Theory as Practice: Ethical Inquiry in the Renaissance (Chicago: University of Chicago Press,
1992), ix–xiii, 231. For a Kristellerian response, see Donald R. Kelley's trenchant review of
Struever's work in *Renaissance Quarterly* 46, no. 3 (1993): 567–69. See also Marion L. Kuntz,
"Truth in History: Waswo's Ideological Relativism versus Kristeller's Empirical Objectiv-
ism," *Bibliothèque d'Humanisme et Renaissance* 44, no. 3 (1982): 645–48; and Richard
Waswo's reply, "Learning to Love Relative Truths," *Bibliothèque d'Humanisme et Renaissance* 44, no. 3 (1982): 657–60.

letter to Kristeller, if emphasis is given to their common achievement: the transformation of Renaissance scholarship into a genuine philosophical discourse.

ITALY IN THE INTERIM: BETWEEN GENTILE AND SAITTA

Kristeller's career began with the publication, in 1929, of a heavily revised version of his dissertation on Plotinus directed by classicist Ernst Hoffmann (1880–1952), Kristeller's mentor since high school in Berlin and a onetime collaborator of Cassirer.[25] Having followed Hoffmann to the University of Heidelberg, Kristeller studied with the Neo-Kantian philosopher Heinrich Rickert (1863–1936)—whose influence on Kristeller's historiography we shall return to in detail —and with Karl Jaspers and (during a stint in Marburg) Martin Heidegger.[26] Kristeller would avow later that his readings of Plotinus and Ficino were informed by these early encounters with a nascent 'existentialism.' The lessons he retained from Jaspers, Heidegger, and his own reading of Kierkegaard translated into an attention to the philosopher's "internal experience" ("which is not irrational, but is an excess of, is beyond sense perception, and beyond the reasoning in science and logic") and the recognition of the methodological viability of the so-called hermeneutic circle.[27]

It could be said that Kristeller retained what he, like other students, perceived to be the "profound and convincing method of Heidegger's interpretation" in order to tease out a systematic reading of philosophies presented in less than systematic sources (be they the *Enneads* or Ficino's varied corpus), while employing the notion of "interior awareness" or "metaphysical consciousness" to draw his own connection between Renaissance and

25. Paul Oskar Kristeller, *Der Begriff der Seele in der Ethik des Plotin* (Tübingen: Mohr, 1929). This text, which does not coincide with what Kristeller submitted as his dissertation, was published in a series Hoffmann edited in collaboration with Heinrich Rickert ("Heidelberger Abhandlungen zur Philosophie und ihrer Geschichte"). Hoffmann also collaborated with Cassirer, by whom he was induced to take an interest in Cusanus, on a textbook history of ancient philosophy published in 1925. As had been the case with Limentani and Garin, Kristeller was directed toward Cassirer by his teacher, who was formally invested in a different field. For Kristeller's relationship to Hoffmann, I rely on Paul Richard Blum, "The Young Paul Oskar Kristeller as a Philosopher," in Monfasani, *Kristeller Reconsidered*, 21ff; James Hankins, "Kristeller and Ancient Philosophy," in *Kristeller Reconsidered*, 131–33; and Hankins, "Garin and Paul Oskar Kristeller," 490–91.

26. Kristeller first met Heidegger during the summer semester of 1926 in Marburg, where he attended the seminar now published with the title *Die Grundbegriffe der antiken Philosophie*.

27. See Blum, "Young Paul Oskar Kristeller," 21.

contemporary philosophies.[28] In a relevant section of his book on Ficino, in
fact, he describes "internal experience" as an antiquated cognate for what
contemporary philosophy calls "existence"—a state of mind grounded
in the feelings of "suffering," "sorrow," "grief," and "melancholia," but
equally a "positive" stimulus, a "continual unrest" or "state of dissatisfaction" by which "all men without exception are driven to a truer life and
toward the higher end destined to them" (*PMF*, 211).

Like the existentialism of his Italian counterparts, then, Kristeller's
manifested itself as a restless Platonism, pointing to a positive resolution
of the age-old philosophical problem of dualism: subject/object, I/world.
And like other scholars of his generation Kristeller entrusted the moral of
his story (in other words, the relevance of his selected philosophy for the
present) to the concluding remarks of his first book:

> Two opposite trends, alternately taking power at different times, may
> be traced in the entire development of the Western spirit. One of them
> is exclusively concerned with the knowledge of reality and tries to
> grasp the world as it is, relying on definite principles without conced-
> ing validity to another—metaphysical—truth. The other trend, on the
> contrary, gets to metaphysics from internal human experiences and
> takes an indifferent or even inimical stand toward the outer world.
> The first trend is embodied by science, the second by religion. In the
> course of its history, philosophy has followed either of these trends at
> different times, placing the power of reason at the service of the given
> conviction. Only at particular times did philosophy endorse its proper
> task of uniting and reconciling the different realms of internal experi-
> ence with outside reality by intellectual perception. In the long epoch
> between Plato and Kant, it is to Plotinus's credit, above all, to have
> clearly acknowledged this task and to have pursued it with unwavering
> consequence. Therefore, he is among the few thinkers to have voiced
> the very essence of philosophy beyond the quarrels of schools and cre-
> dos, however strange and peculiar his doctrine may appear to us in its
> outer form.[29]

28. See Kristeller's opening remarks to his Plotinus volume: "Dem Interpreten eines philosophischen Textes ist besondere Vorsicht geboten, da er mit dem Philosophen sein Werkzeug
gemeinsam hat: den Gedanken. So darf er hinter jenem nicht zurückbleiben. Von der Deutung zum Text muß der Weg ebenso sicher führen wie vom Text zur Deutung" (Kristeller, *Der
Begriff der Seele*, 1).
29. Kristeller, *Der Begriff der Seele*, 107–8.

Kristeller shared in his generation's wish to bring about a long overdue refamiliarization with a misconceived or mismanaged philosophical heritage. Heidegger's pedagogy, even more than his existentialism, had again inspired a reappraisal of the Platonic tradition, one that played up the subject's mediation and mastery of reality. Most important, just like Garin's Pico, Plotinus had encouraged thinkers to seek peace among quarreling minds (past and present) even at the cost (a higher cost, evidently, for the older Kristeller than for his younger self) of projecting modern concerns onto the past.[30]

Upon receiving a less than excellent grade for his doctoral dissertation and fearing for his academic career, Kristeller, not unlike Gadamer (whom he befriended in those years) and Grassi (to an extent), began to prepare for a career in classical philology by moving to Berlin in pursuit of a degree that would allow him to teach Greek and Latin at the Gymnasium. In Germany's capital city, between 1928 and 1931, Kristeller's formation underwent a second major phase when he studied with no less than Ulrich von Wilamowitz-Moellendorf, Eduard Norden, and Werner Jaeger.[31] Again, as was the case with Grassi and Gadamer, his movements point to the fruitful exchange between philologists and philosophers in German academia, yet we are left guessing as to Kristeller's participation in the debate, fomented by his peers, between Jaeger and Heidegger. In fact, in his writings and recollections, Kristeller remained silent on many topics relevant to his early and mature career—among them, Jaeger's 'third humanism,' Stefan George, and the new *Platoforschung* in which younger students honed their interpretive skills. All that Kristeller cared to reveal was that the self-assigned review he attempted of the history of philosophy in those years (from the pre-Socratics to Husserl) included Nietzsche, the *trait d'union* between the two camps, whom he "never appreciated" (*SRTL*, 4:572).

But philosophy was Kristeller's first choice, and in 1931 he returned south to seek a sponsor for his *Habilitation* thesis. After being ditched by Hoffmann, who had already committed to mentor another Jewish scholar (Raymond Klibansky), he was eventually taken on by Heidegger for a project on Renaissance Platonist Marsilio Ficino. Although Kristeller

30. Reviewers criticized Kristeller for his modernizing reading of Plotinus. See Blum, "Young Paul Oskar Kristeller," 23–25.

31. On Kristeller's student years in Berlin, see Luigi Lehnus "L'antichistica berlinese nella formazione di P. O. Kristeller," in *Gli studi umanistici e l'opera di Paul Oskar Kristeller* (Milan: Istituto Lombardo di Scienze e Lettere, 2003), 17–29.

recalls that he and Heidegger met repeatedly to discuss his work, their correspondence suggests that Heidegger never had the chance to read more than early drafts of it, if anything at all.[32] In the spring of 1933, while on a research trip in Rome, Kristeller learned about the expulsion of Jewish scholars from German universities and resolved to emigrate to Italy, which he did the following year after having hurriedly composed the first half of his new book—which would prove necessary, he rightly predicted, as an entry card into Italy. *The Philosophy of Marsilio Ficino* was completed in 1937, translated into Italian in 1938 (though publication was delayed until 1953), first published in English translation in 1943, and finally released in its German original in 1972.[33] It was only at this later date that Kristeller, planning for a trip to Germany, forwarded his book to Heidegger in the hope that some sections of it would remind him of their conversations four decades earlier.[34] One of the two chapters that Kristeller flagged for his onetime teacher, "Unity of the World" (the other was "Internal Experience"), suggests that their conversations may have centered on the (anti-) Platonism Heidegger began developing, esoterically, in the early 1930s with the first drafts of "Plato's Doctrine of Truth."

Kristeller, in fact, dedicates this chapter to the role of philosophical metaphor in the illustration of the relation between image and idea—a use of allegories, associated with Ficino, that echoes "the famous metaphor of the cave in the *Republic*" and that serves "not only a literary but also a philosophical purpose." He adds:

> For Plato, as well as for Plotinus, the metaphor's primary task serves as a means of making abstract ideas evident to intuition, and since the relation of the image to the idea is produced by an arbitrary act of thinking, the metaphor can claim validity only for our thought, with-

32. Heidegger to Kristeller, 1933, POKP.

33. Kristeller provides a detailed, chapter-by-chapter account of his progress on the Ficino monograph in the preface to the German edition of the work. See Paul Oskar Kristeller, *Die Philosophie des Marsilio Ficino* (Frankfurt: Vittorio Klostermann, 1972), vii. It should be noted that the English translation was based not on the German original but on the Italian version Kristeller had prepared with the help of Alessandro Perosa in 1938. In this it followed the pattern of Garin's *Italian Humanism* and Baron's *The Crisis*, whereby the translations of these works were really considered as different editions, often significantly modified depending on the intended audience.

34. Kristeller to Heidegger, 9 April 1973: "Ich freue mich zu wissen, dass Sie mein Ficinobuch erhalten und hineingesehen haben. Vielleicht wird Einiges darin Sie an unsere Gespraeche in Freiburg erinnern. Wenn Sie etwas darin lesen wollen, so erlaube ich mir, Ihnen das 5. Kapitel des Ersten Teiles und das 1. Kapitel des zweiten Teiles zu empfehlen" (POKP).

out stating anything definite about real entities. For Ficino, on the contrary, the relation of image to idea is not merely suggested by thinking but also corresponds to a real relationship among objects. (*PMF*, 93)

The physical movements (mirrored in the soul in Ficino) and the progressive stages that, in Heidegger's reading, Plato had forsaken in his turn against *paideia* are all retained in Ficino's "dynamic" conception of the unity of the world. In the latter, the corporeal being is raised to the sphere of the intellectual being—a unity that amounts to a "lively community of action and movement"—according to a mediated "procedure" couched in allegory. Kristeller, it may be argued, was out to prove Ficino's eccentricity with respect to the rationalism whose origins Heidegger had pinned on Plato.

It has been noted that Kristeller's Ficino book, the second and last monographic study in an otherwise prolific career, can be seen as "a material extension of his identity as a German-Jewish émigré."[35] The Italian edition was dedicated to his parents and to all human and material victims of Nazism: "To the memory of my parents, Heinrich and Alice Kristeller, and to the memory of the men, women, and children, of the homes, cities, and monuments, of the books, thoughts, and feeling that perished under the reign of evil in Europe 1933–1945." Kristeller had spent the latter half of this period in the "undeserved and almost shameful tranquility" of his American exile (as he put it in a letter to Garin), while the first half was spent in an apparently congenial and welcoming Italy.[36] Though armed with letters of reference from Heidegger and Cassirer, Kristeller self-recommended himself to Italian academics with his Ficino project, parts of which he entrusted to Richard Walzer (already resident in Italy), who passed the material on to Leonardo Olschki (the son of famed Florentine editor Leo), who in turn passed it on to Giovanni Gentile.[37] Under the latter's patronage, Kristeller continued his extensive archival research throughout Italy, published an important anthology of Ficino's minor works, and was appointed lecturer in German at the Scuola

35. See Warren Boutcher, "From Germany to Italy to America: The Migratory Significance of Kristeller's Ficino in the 1930s," in *Weltoffener Humanismus: Philosophie, Philologie und Geschichte in der deutsch-jüdischen Emigration*, ed. Gerald Hartung and Kay Schiller (Bielefeld: Transcript, 2006), 133–53.

36. See Kristeller to Garin, 24 August 1945, cited in Hankins, "Garin and Paul Oskar Kristeller," 498.

37. For Leonardo Olschki, see Anke Dörner, "Europas geistige Emanzipation: Die italienische Renaissance in den amerikanischen Publikationen Leonardo Olschkis," in Hartung and Schiller, *Weltoffener Humanismus*, 155–70.

Normale di Pisa (despite the complaints of German authorities, who supported qualified 'Aryan' candidates). Kristeller recalls that while at Pisa he "made many friends and became part of the Italian academic scene," but this is an understatement (*SRTL*, 4:575). What is seldom acknowledged is that Gentile plainly elected Kristeller as his successor in the field of Renaissance studies and thus attempted to make him a conspicuous part of his intellectual legacy.

If we are to make sense of the extraordinary affection, protection, and expectations that the philosopher heaped onto the young German scholar, it helps to understand Gentile's status in Italy around the time of Kristeller's arrival. In the 1930s, Gentile, once the doyen of a most powerful and pervasive school of thought in Italy, was in fact scrambling to salvage his legacy. We have seen that after the Lateran Accords of 1929 he was forced to share his turf with the Neoscholastics, who would eventually, in 1934, place his works on the Index, while he was also facing mutiny by his once loyal students. Gentile's sins found him out in 1937, when the publication of Spirito's *Life as Research* (followed the next year by Calogero's *The School of Man*) opened a clear-cut rift in his school. Even before enlisting the young Garin, Gentile reacted by appealing to a younger generation of scholars (recall Cantimori's review of Spirito's book) and putting out a new edition of *A General Theory of Spirit as Pure Act*. From 1935, furthermore, he was engaged in a protracted quarrel with the newly appointed minister of education, Cesare Maria De Vecchi, whose plans for a "Fascist reclamation [*bonifica*] of culture" included tampering with Gentile's school reform and curtailing the autonomy of academic presses and universities. Reacting vehemently and publicly against De Vecchi's initiatives, Gentile was removed from his office as director of the Normale in the fall of 1936 (despite his appeal to Mussolini). He was reinstated a year later, on 29 October 1937.[38] Kristeller's emblematic investiture, we shall see, occurred between these two dates—in other words, during the lowest point in the career of his "benefactor" (as Kristeller called him). It is thus in light of the so-called 'dissolution' of the hegemony of Gentilean actualism that Kristeller's role in Italian academia is best understood, for ultimately it was the young German scholar—not just another outsider but the most foreign of them all—that Gentile tapped to channel his legacy.

With the first half of his Ficino book, parts of which were published

---

38. An account of Kristeller's involvement in some of these events can be found in Paolo Simoncelli, *Cantimori, Gentile e la Normale di Pisa: Profili e documenti* (Milan: FrancoAngeli, 1994), chap. 3.

in the *Giornale critico* upon his arrival in Italy, Kristeller secured his first emigration, but the new position he occupied on the academic scene centered on his fieldwork, the archival research that had led him to rediscover Ficino's minor works. The materials he collected make up the *Supplementum Ficinianum* (1937), an austere two-volume anthology (annotated and introduced in Latin) that was meant to supplement the flawed Basel edition of Ficino's *Opera Omnia* (1576).[39] It was at the public launch of this work, which took place under highly emblematic circumstances, that PAVLVS OSCARIVS KRISTELLER (as his name is given on the title page) was invested with the responsibility of driving Italian Renaissance scholarship into a new era. The book launch occurred during the inauguration of the humanist exhibition (the last one in a long series) of a hundred incunabula and manuscripts organized by Leo S. Olschki and his son Leonardo in Florence on 18 April 1937. It was the same event that Garin, who on that occasion drew closer to Gentile, later described as an "act of faith in the values of human culture." At the time of the event, Garin had never met Gentile; his monograph on Pico was still forthcoming (the following October), and his allegiance was still solidly with the Florentine positivism in which he was raised: "I went to the inauguration of the exhibition with him who had been my 'professor' at the university of Florence: Ludovico Limentani, who following in the footsteps of Felice Tocco had given himself to a detailed illustration of Giordano Bruno."[40]

As Garin later recalled, he met Limentani at his home, and as they walked together along the Mugnone toward the Olschkis', they amused themselves by derisively trying to anticipate Gentile's speech word for word. Garin and Limentani were quite correct in their predictions, but they later had to admit that, for once, Gentile's rhetoric had been particularly rewarding. He had evoked the famous letter Machiavelli addressed from his political exile to his friend and hoped-for patron Francesco Vettori, a text best known for its description of the edifying evenings Machiavelli spent with his cherished books: "When evening comes . . . , I am unashamed to converse with them and to question them about the motives for their actions, and they, out of their human kindness, answer me. And for four hours at a time I feel no boredom, I forget all my troubles,

---

39. Paul Oskar Kristeller, ed., *Supplementum Ficinianum: Marsilii Ficini Florentini Philosophi Platonici Opuscula Inedita et Dispersa*, 2 vols. (Florence: L. S. Olschki, 1937).
40. Eugenio Garin, "Un ricordo di Casa Olschki," in *Olschki (1886–1986): Un secolo di editoria*, 2 vols., vol. 1, ed. Cristina Tagliaferri (Florence: Leo S. Olschki, 1986), 293. For a thorough account of the events I describe here, see also "Giovanni Gentile e la casa editrice Olschki," in *Olschki*, 1:367–82.

I do not dread poverty, and I am not terrified by death. I absorb myself
into them completely."[41] To which Gentile added: "Wonderful words that
may never be reread without lively commotion. Machiavelli's spirit lives
in these words as well as, squarely, in the Renaissance, the spirit of the humanist who for four hours of his day transports himself totally among the
ancients. . . . The scholar who wishes to understand the historical significance of humanism needs to look at those four hours of the humanist."[42]
As Garin saw it, Gentile had expounded eloquently on the humanist *topos*
of books transfigured into living people and reading as a conversation leading to the blissful life that, through the commonality of ideas and ideals,
encourages brotherhood and unity among men of all times and places.

In his late years, Garin understood that, in part by force of circumstance, a rite of passage had taken place during the Olschkis' exhibition:

> The legacy of a certain culture was transmitted right then and there,
> in that room. The manuscripts by which the heritage of ancient Hel-
> lenic wisdom were entrusted to the printing press, saved from savage-
> ries [*barbarie*] and from wars, were again at hand, to be studied and
> circulated so as to reveal their most secret message just as the storm
> that would carry away many of the people reunited in that room was
> gathering in Europe. But with the aid of those texts and their doctrine,
> the very values that cannot decline without destroying humanity itself
> would be defended.[43]

Within a few years, most of the special attendees of this event were indeed "carried way": Kristeller relocated to the United States in 1939, as did
Leonardo in the same year, while Gentile was assassinated in 1944, four
years after the deaths of Limentani and Leo Olschki in their forced exiles.
Also owing to the anti-Jewish laws of 1938, moreover, the press was renamed "Bibliopolis": editions continued to carry the initials of its founder,
LSO, in the emblem of the press, thanks to an ingenious idea, attributed
to Leonardo, which had them stand for *Litteris servabitur Orbis*, or 'letters will save the world.' No wonder, then, that Garin, the sole 'survivor,'
would come to interpret the event as a turning point in his life.

As if they foresaw events to come, older authorities invested younger

41. Niccolò Machiavelli to Francesco Vettori, 10 December 1513, in *Machiavelli and His Friends: Their Personal Correspondence*, trans. James B. Atkinson and David Sices (DeKalb: Northern Illinois University Press, 1996), 264.

42. Giovanni Gentile, "Intorno al concetto dell'umanesimo," *La Bibliofilia* 39 (1937): 147.

43. Garin, "Un ricordo di Casa Olschki," in Tagliaferri, *Olschki*, 1:293.

scholars in that room with an epochal responsibility, rather, a literary and scholarly mission that was concretely rejuvenated for the modern era with a projected series of heretofore unpublished humanist texts ("Nuova collezione di testi umanistici inediti rari"), which was also announced that morning in the presence of its two directors, Gentile and Kristeller. The latter was described in the series' statement of purpose as "a young erudite, of German origin, but naturalized Italian for the love with which he studied, moving from Marsilio Ficino and his friends, the things and men of the Italian Quattrocento."[44] Kristeller's *Supplementum*, the most recent publication of the Olschkis, was displayed side by side with Renaissance incunabula and was thus presented as a model and standard for the announced series. Gentile was passing a torch to Kristeller, but it was Garin who readily took it up. In his own recollection, Kristeller stated simply that "the ceremony was well attended" and that it was then that he met Garin for the first time, "with whom I have remained in cordial friendship and companionship ever since" (*SRTL*, 4:494).[45]

How invested was Kristeller—or, more to the point, how invested could he be—in a ceremony that was (owing to Gentile's influence) formally and rhetorically couched in the aspirations of the Italians' Renaissance? The prospectus for the "Nuova collezione," which was published as an appendix to the *Supplementum*, was signed, probably not by chance, by Gentile alone, suggesting that Kristeller may have been a less naturalized Italian, at least culturally, than was advertised. From the outset, Gentile was clear: the series would be a means by which to counter the thinking of the Neothomists, who had recently attempted to "cancel or attenuate the contrast" that Risorgimento and idealist historiography had rightly posited, from Gentile's perspective, between the modern spirit ("prepared" by humanism and the Renaissance) and the spirit of the previous century. He specified: "The difference between the two ages is ever more evident and is claiming the attention of historians," who are therefore in need of a more "detailed," "profound," "concrete," and "exact" understanding of humanism. Gentile goes on to describe a "movement," that of the Quattro-

44. Giovanni Gentile, "Nuova collezione di testi umanistici a cura di Giovanni Gentile e Paolo Oskar Kristeller," in Kristeller, *Supplementum Ficinianum*, 2:380.

45. Kristeller's subdued recollection fruitfully compares with Garin's emphatic one, though he might not have made Garin's acquaintance at that time: "la nuova casa è luminosa e quieta, e molto comoda, in una zona che forse ricorderai. Venendoci m'è tornato in mente il giorno in cui, qua vicino, Gentile ti presentò come autore del *Supplementum* e curatore dei Testi umanistici. Ero presente con Limentani, anche se non ti conobbi allora. Pare, ormai, storia antica." Garin to Kristeller, 16 February 1959, cited in Hankins, "Garin and Paul Oskar Kristeller," 483.

cento, in his usual terms: as being riddled with ambiguities and relevant mostly for its inspirational qualities, a "teeming [*brulichio*] of greater and lesser men, yet all united in a single physiognomy of thought, sometimes of high ideal significance, sometimes of trite commonplaces [*di banale conio corrente*], and of vivacious polemics, more or less passionately experienced, from which, little by little, a new form of humanity emerged." The series, finally, was intended to foster a laboratory in which to "train the mind" of students of the Scuola Normale—"that is, if one really wants to educate intellects to the healthy balance between philology [*il positivo*], which endows thought with accuracy, and philosophy [*la speculazione*], by which freedom of thought is restored."[46] In advancing this commixture of positivism and idealism in the formation of the ideal scholar-philosopher for the Scuola Normale and the Italian nation, Gentile was perhaps offering a truce to Limentani.

There was little of Kristeller (at least, of the Kristeller we have come to know in the postwar period) in the plans for a series whose first volume, edited by Alessandro Perosa, was dedicated to him, its exiled director: "Paulo Oscario Kristeller sodali liberalissimo."[47] In the preface for the *Supplementum*, in which Ficino is described as the first to translate humanism's potential (for the rest of Western philosophical history) in comprehensible and enduring terms, Gentile portrays Kristeller as a humanist redivivus in the process of reexperiencing the Renaissance in his own career—reexperiencing, that is, the passage from humanism to Renaissance proper, from philology to philosophy. In fact, Kristeller, in Gentile's assessment, "is not a pure philologist who accidentally came across the problems of Ficino's writings and documents. Rather, he took his cue from the philosophy of Plotinus, which he turned into the subject of a very noteworthy study, and from the deep root of Florentine Platonism he

---

46. Gentile, "Nuova collezione di testi umanistici," in Kristeller, *Supplementum Ficinianum*, 2:379–80.

47. See Alessandro Perosa, "Leo S. Olschki e l'edizione di testi umanistici," in Tagliaferri, *Olschki*, 1:339. And yet Kristeller might have had an active role in drafting the detailed methodological requirements that circulated among the contributors (cited in *Olschki*, 1:379–80), which were inspired by the influential work of Giorgio Pasquali (1895–1952), a renowned classicist at Pisa who in those years adapted textual criticism to the exigencies of Renaissance sources. Kristeller himself, in later years, commented on the limitations of traditional methods for the study of Renaissance sources. See, for example, Paul Oskar Kristeller, "The Lachmann Method: Merits and Limitations," *Text: Transactions of the Society for Textual Scholarship* 1 (1981): 11–20. For the Italian background to these revolutions in classical scholarship in Italy, see Glenn W. Most, editor's introduction, in Sebastiano Timpanaro, *The Genesis of Lachmann's Method* (Chicago: University of Chicago Press, 2006), 1–32.

gravitated spontaneously to Marsilio Ficino, around whom he is shaping a wide and systematic monograph."[48] He thus expected Kristeller's study to present Ficino's immortality to the world and unlock for all intelligent readers the "powerful humanity" of his philosophy, which, as he had just stated in reference to Machiavelli, "unites men of all ages and all countries fraternally."[49]

Of all Gentile's principles and ideals, only the one pertaining to human fraternity overlapped with—and indeed had recently been bolstered by—Kristeller's research and concerns. Again, in the "Unity of the World" chapter of his Ficino monograph, an excerpt of which was published independently in Italian translation in the *Giornale critico*, Kristeller had attempted a definition of Ficino's notion of *humanitas* in analogy with the principles of education—established on a threefold veneration "for what is above us, for what is equal to us, and for what is beneath us"—that were articulated in a chapter of Goethe's Bildungsroman *Wilhelm Meister*. (The principles themselves, Kristeller explains, may have been inspired by Plotinus, whom Goethe read in Ficino's translation.) In expounding on Ficino's theory of universal love, Kristeller noted that *humanitas* has two meanings, for which a single word is lacking in modern languages: "the essence of man as a natural species" and "human love as a moral quality that has to do with man's relation to other men." It is to Ficino's credit that he was able to interconnect the two meanings:

> The virtue of humanity is nothing but the love of men for men, in other words, the universal love of equal for equal. . . . The more a man loves others as equals, the more he proves himself a member of the whole species, the more perfectly he expresses the essence of humanity, the more humane he is. And the more cruel and inhumane a man is, the more he removes himself from the essence and community of his species, finally arriving at a point at which he is a man in name only. (*PMF*, 113–14)[50]

The resulting fraternity, a wholly Italian, humanist, and modern achievement, was a concept that would have appealed to Gentile after having faced repeated charges of philosophical solipsism. And perhaps it was Kristel-

48. Gentile, "Nuova collezione di testi umanistici," 2:380

49. Giovanni Gentile, "Prefazione," in Kristeller, *Supplementum Ficinianum*, 1:iii–iv.

50. I cite here directly from the English translation of Kristeller's Ficino book, as there is no significant discrepancy with the Italian.

ler's intention to promote such an ideal when, in his acknowledgments in the *Supplementum*, he meted out a pardon to his two fascist mentors, Heidegger and Gentile, "who honored respectively the opening and closing phases of my studies with their advice and help."[51]

But of course these acknowledgments also sound a farewell. The *Supplementum*, for Kristeller, was playing a part in a different story, an all or mostly German one (the work had already been completed by 1934). Kristeller thanked not only Heidegger, Gentile, and Olschki but also Ludwig Bertalot ("viro doctissimo"), for his help with Italian libraries and manuscripts, and Hans Baron ("viro erudito"), who had generously shared many documents he had originally tracked down. Indeed, the correspondence between Baron and Kristeller shows that their lifelong relationship was coterminous, at least in its initial stages, with the making of the *Supplementum*.[52] At the time of their first contact, initiated in 1932 by Kristeller, the younger man by five years, Baron was the semi-established editor of an anthology of Bruni's works and, as we have seen in the previous chapter, was basically in charge of a series, directed by Goetz, on which Gentile's "Nuova collezione" may have been modeled. Kristeller introduced himself to Baron as a student engaged in a 'philosophical' work on Marsilio Ficino and needing some clarifications on matters of chronology and reception history.[53] Baron, who claimed to be at work on a massive and 'historical' book on Italian humanism, was overjoyed to initiate a conversation with a philosopher from whom he could learn more about Ficino's foundational positions in his principal works.[54]

By the second letter, following a rendezvous in Berlin in which notes and materials were exchanged, Kristeller—whose wish at this point was

---

51. Kristeller, *Supplementum Ficinianum*, 1:ii.

52. I am presently editing the vast correspondence of Baron and Kristeller for publication, which comprises more than 350 letters exchanged between 1932 and 1988. This exchange is one of a kind, for it runs uninterrupted and thus represents virtually the entire relationship between the two scholars. This is due to a specific reason: Baron's partial and increasing deafness, which prevented the telephone from being substituted for the written word. Furthermore, the correspondence reveals that the two scholars rarely met in person, due to the physical distance between them and Baron's financial difficulties. The correspondence is interestingly lopsided to the advantage of Baron, whose interiority is revealed as he confesses himself in very long letters to his more academically successful friend and colleague. It details how Baron and Kristeller came to take their first steps in Renaissance scholarship in Germany before political circumstances forced them into exile; it recounts the story of their emigration and their strategies for survival in Italy, Great Britain, and the United States; it reveals the impact of the American academy on their intellectual journeys, and their self-conscious role as lonely representatives of a methodology about to go extinct.

53. Kristeller to Baron, 11 September 1932, HBP.

54. Baron to Kristeller, 28 December 1932, POKP.

to enrich his Ficino book with an appendix of unpublished materials—got down to business:

> I would like to reach an understanding with you here, so as not to encroach upon the plan of your edition. At this time, I would suggest something like the following: 1. As concerns the texts you yourself have found and copied out, I hope you will permit me to refer to them in the philosophically pertinent portion of my work as well as in the catalog referring to them—with acknowledgment of you, naturally. 2. The texts mentioned in your notes, but not copied out, I shall presumably read myself in Florence. Should any of them prove of great interest to me, I will publish them only on the condition that you stake no claim of your own to them. 3. The texts I have found, and any I shall yet find independently of you, I should publish myself—perhaps even sooner than my own work, which will likely not appear until 1934. This publication will be merely provisional from a philological standpoint, and you will have the opportunity to take what is significant to you from it into your collection and to publish it with the text. I hope you approve of these arrangements; I will not in any case bypass you, and will keep you abreast of anything further, provided I do not thereby make a nuisance of myself.[55]

Baron was amenable, especially since he admitted to having no "energy" to work on a definitive edition and to being less of a "philologist" than Kristeller. In any case, the edition Baron had in mind was really centered on the influence of the Florentine *Burgerkreis* on later philosophy; it would include Ficino but also non-Italian humanists such as Erasmus, Lefèvre, and so on. Therefore he concluded: "I believe . . . that our works will coexist well side by side."[56]

But after a first trip to Italy, and as the material grew in his hands, Kristeller began pressing Baron to collaborate on a supplementary volume of Ficino's *Jugendschriften*; he succeeded in persuading his colleague after assuring him that the volume he had in mind—a readable reproduction of unknown sources—would not require too much work, aside from a brief research trip to Italy, perhaps. As it happened, what persuaded Baron were Germany's incipient anti-Semitic laws, which in effect brought his work on Goetz's series to a halt. Baron now expected Kristeller to prepare an

55. Kristeller to Baron, 31 December 1932, HBP.
56. Baron to Kristeller, 19 February 1933, POKP.

exit strategy for them both by means of his contacts in Italy: "Hopefully before long you will have secured something certain regarding publication opportunities, because those are the grounds without which we cannot be expected to build anything."[57]

A year later, writing from Rome, and after having received the green light from Olschki and Gentile (who is never actually mentioned by name in the correspondence), Kristeller was in a position to assure Baron. But a new problem arose—an "Existenzfrage," as Kristeller puts it—regarding the nature of their collaboration and its acknowledgment on the cover page of the *Supplementum*. Given that he had done most of the work, Kristeller hoped that Baron would not mind being labeled as "in Gemeinschaft mit" (in collaboration with) or "unter Mitarbeit" (with the assistance of).[58] Baron answered: "I, too, have given much thought to the question of the title page, for, certainly, I am in your same predicament and wish to treat the capital of our finished works, with which we build our new future, with the utmost care." But precisely because the *Supplementum* mattered to his career, Baron was uneasy with the idea of being listed as "collaborator," a title usually reserved for young students or assistants. He preferred "in Gemeinschaft mit," asking, "but how can this be best formulated in Italian?"[59]

In the meantime, Baron avowed, he had been rushing to complete his work on the "Lebensanschauung" and "Bildungsidee" of Italian humanism (a manuscript of about 500 pages), which he hoped to have ready for a possible Italian translation by the summer of 1934, Kristeller's experience having showed him that it would be hard to establish any "worthy personal relationship" until he had an Italian "opus" to lay on the table.[60] Within two months, however, after considering the question at length and redirecting his emigration aspirations to London, Baron contacted Kristeller again to resign all rights to the *Supplementum*.[61] Circumstances had changed, and their original plans—which did not compass the "definitive philological edition" that Kristeller had come to prepare while enjoying a full year of free and "systematic" work in Italy—no longer applied. Baron realized that his task, at this point, was limited to collating and transcribing his materials, purely mechanical work that would be no match for Kristeller's "Acribie." Moreover, the work of his colleague had proven that

57. Baron to Kristeller, 29 May 1933, POKP.
58. Kristeller to Baron, 29 March 1934, HBP.
59. Baron to Kristeller, 3 April 1934, POKP.
60. Baron to Kristeller, 3 April 1934, POKP.
61. Baron to Kristeller, 28 May 1934, POKP.

these minor texts, in their relationship to Ficino's major works, were in "need, in the main, of a philosophical and not historical commentary," and even in this respect Baron felt that his abilities were not even remotely comparable to those of Kristeller. Baron's "rights of priority" on the material had been superseded by the far-reaching work of Kristeller, and he was ready to bow out. On 6 June, Kristeller agreed, with gratitude as well as manifest "surprise," to take full charge.

Baron's hesitation, founded on questions of philological competence, certainly owed something to the fierce criticism that his Bruni collection had received (with dire consequences, thought Baron, for his career in Germany) from the other colleague whom Kristeller wished to thank in his acknowledgments, Bertalot.[62] What concerns us now is the fact that Baron's disappearance from the *Supplementum*'s title page was largely circumstantial. In hindsight, this would seem to be a pity, given the influence that the Olschkis' event (which Baron, we now know, had a right to attend) had in defining the relationships and conflicts that would affect the future of Renaissance scholarship: the antagonistic friendship between Garin and Kristeller, Garin's move toward Gentile, Gentile's own investment in Kristeller, and subsequently Kristeller's shift away from the ambitions of Italian academia. Clearly, the *Supplementum* bore for its authors a significance very different from the one it acquired when it was appropriated by Italian scholars as a means of reviving a moribund actualism and its historiographical ambitions. It is worth noting, for example, how Baron and Kristeller divided the labor that went into the book's production along the lines of discipline and subject matter: early Quattrocento humanism was the responsibility of the 'historian' Baron, late Quattrocento Platonism, the task of the 'philosopher' Kristeller. Needless to say that from an Italian perspective, such a division of labor was unnecessary, even inconvenient—a perspective that is visible in the rhetoric attending the presentation of the *Supplementum* as well as in Garin's concurrent appropriation for philosophy of Baron's 'civic humanism.' Meanwhile, the *Supplementum* became, too, an opportunity to secure a career in Italy, something that Kristeller went on to achieve (much to Baron's unconcealed envy) by playing along as best he could.

Strictly speaking, Kristeller's career as a Renaissance scholar began in Italy. His first publication in the field, an essay entitled "Ficino's His-

---

62. On the Bertalot affair, which, as already mentioned in the previous chapter, played a determining role in shaping the relationship between Baron and Kristeller in their later years, see Rocco Rubini, "A 'Crisis' in the Making: The Hans Baron-P. O. Kristeller Correspondence," forthcoming.

torical Position," was an Italian translation of an introductory section of his Ficino manuscript. It was published in *Civiltà moderna* (a journal directed by Ernesto Codignola, who was a longtime collaborator with Gentile on the Italian school reform of 1923), a sharp foil for *Civiltà Cattolica*, the Neothomist publication.[63] The purpose of the piece was to show how Ficino had come to reconcile Platonism, or the *ratio platonica*, with Christianity and the divine law. Ficino was the first to bestow "independent philosophical consideration" on Platonism and to endow Plato's corpus with an "authority" until then attributed only to sacred scripture. Thus Ficino came to see Plato as the "perfecter of an old tradition of 'theology,'" and, seeing no opposition, he was able to give "Christian doctrine a philosophical confirmation."[64]

Of course, the promotion of religion via philosophical means that were derived from a religiosity that was truer, older (than institutionalized religion), and, in Gentilean terms, personally experienced, could be interpreted as proof of the actualists' claims against the Neothomists; and, furthermore, Kristeller's elaboration could have been drawn from one of Gentile's speeches, the emphasis on Plato excepted:

> [Ficino] assigns to Platonic philosophy the task of furthering religion and of bringing men back to the Christian faith. Anyone who has had a philosophical education and as a result is wont to follow reason alone, can find the way to religion and to eternal salvation only through a religious philosophy, in other words, through Platonic reason (*ratio platonica*). Along with and in accord with the Christian tradition, therefore, the Platonic tradition fulfills a mission necessary to the divine scheme of world history. (*PMF*, 28)

Gentile had always presented his actualism as a "religious philosophy" of Quattrocento origins, to say nothing of the self-appointed "mission" of his philosophy to fulfill certain political and intellectual schemes in world history. Because of the journal in which it was published, then, Kristeller's piece came to serve the cause of an embattled actualism.

63. On Codignola and the fascist press, see Alessandro Piccioni, ed., *Una casa editrice tra società, cultura e scuola: La Nuova Italia, 1926–1986* (Florence: La Nuova Italia, 1986); Simona Giusti, ed., *Una casa editrice negli anni del fascismo: La Nuova Italia (1926–1943)* (Florence: Olschki, 1983); and Nicola Tranfaglia and Albertina Vittoria, eds., *Storia degli editori in italiani: Dall'unità alla fine degli anni sessanta* (Rome: Laterza, 2000).

64. Paul Oskar Kristeller, "La posizione storica di Marsilio Ficino," *Civiltà Moderna* 5 (1933): 438–45. I cite from the English translation in *PMF*.

Kristeller's awareness and acceptance of the instrumentalization of his work is confirmed by the fact that the same piece was also, in the main, a reflection on the notion of 'Renaissance' as literally a rebirth in art, religion, and philosophy. And in this context one of Kristeller's most quoted passages made its debut here:

> Ficino is evidently convinced that he is doing for Platonic philosophy what, in the opinion of his contemporaries, Giotto had already done for painting and Dante for poetry. The Platonism of the Renaissance was really conceived as a genuine renaissance of Platonism. In other words, Ficino's Platonism is not a philosophical conception that just happened to appear during the period of the Renaissance; it is, so to speak, the Renaissance become philosophical—in other words, the philosophical expression and manifestation of its leading idea. (*PMF*, 23)

The idea that a mostly literary humanism had turned into philosophy in the hands of Ficino was another pillar of idealist historiography. And in the abridged Italian version Kristeller appeared, again, to sustain the cause.

Yet the same passage took on very different connotations when it was reprinted in the freer setting of the American academy as part of the first edition of *The Philosophy of Marsilio Ficino*. In this version, Kristeller's intentions are openly polemical, as the already published portion of the chapter is preceded by speculation about the viability of the notion of 'Renaissance.' At stake in this version is Burckhardt's portrait of the epoch, but, more important, it targets those who would correct that portrait, toiling to reintroduce philosophy where Burckhardt had seen none. Kristeller singles out Wilhelm Dilthey and Cassirer, but interestingly not Gentile, whose name is omitted or, rather, replaced by that of Francesco Fiorentino (the same pioneering historian of Italian Renaissance philosophy whom Cassirer had enlisted in *The Individual and the Cosmos* to support his enthusiasm for Cusanus against Gentile's nationalist bias). More important, it is here that "humanists" as such make one of their first appearances in Kristeller's corpus and are described as "slightly amateurish in their philosophical works, but in compensation . . . inclined to give direct expression to the modern idea of the age" (*PMF*, 11). This assessment is followed by ruminations, reworked in his famous article of 1946, regarding the dearth of philosophical concerns at Italian universities. While granting the humanists some influence on Ficino's early work ("in his theory of love, his doctrine of the dignity of man, and the central position given to man with respect to the medieval emphasis on God"),

he asserted that Ficino was resolutely unattached to these purported precursors. If one took a closer look and focused on his major work, Ficino's
philosophy was humanist solely in its "literary form" and owed its content (terminology and method) to an enduring medieval Aristotelianism
(13–14).

Kristeller was fortunate in that he was perceived in Italy to be an accomplished philologist as much as a budding philosopher. And in matters
that called for sheer erudition his task was somewhat easier, though by
no means free of pitfalls. A consistent aim of Kristeller's Italian publications was to amend the work of Arnaldo Della Torre (1876–1915), whose
massive *History of the Florentine Academy* (1902) was still at the time the
standard text, albeit an obsolete and misleading one, for all things pertaining to Renaissance Platonism. Permission to tamper with such authority
was granted by Gentile himself, who in the prologue to the *Supplementum*
described Della Torre's works as "replete with youthful exuberance," "dis-
proportionate," and "unenlightened," thus marking him out for Kristeller's target practice. Again, Kristeller's predicament cannot be properly appreciated without realizing that Della Torre's magnum opus was dedicated
to—and was effectively the offspring of—the last great generation of Florentine positivists: Guido Mazzoni, Pio Rajna, Felice Tocco, and Pasquale
Villari. They were the forefathers of a school kept alive by Limentani and,
ultimately, by Garin but were traditionally disfavored and successfully
challenged by Gentile and his followers.

In "For the Biography of Marsilio Ficino," one of the last essays that he
published in Italy and, owing to the anti-Semitic laws, under a pseudonym
chosen by Codignola, "Platonicus," Kristeller argued that Della Torre had
not always been able to sift truth from myth.[65] Typical of the aura that
surrounded the legendary Florentine Platonist is the story of an eternal
lamp that the philosopher supposedly kept lit under an image of Plato.
Kristeller's goal, as it were, was to snuff out Ficino's lamp. In the essay, he
takes on and debunks many of the "legends" crowding Ficino's biography
as perpetuated by Giovanni Corsi (Ficino's first biographer) and uncriti-

---

65. In an interview, Kristeller clarified as follows: "and interestingly enough one of the
book reviews and also one article accepted by Codignola were published with pseudonyms
after I had to leave Pisa, and I got a certificate confirming that these articles are by me, which
I have among my papers, so I felt entitled to republish them under my name in a collection of
articles after the war. That's a curious little episode." In "The Reminiscences of Paul Oskar
Kristeller," typescript, Oral History Collection of Columbia University, 1983. The interviews
took place between 13 March 1981 and 25 February 1982.

cally reiterated by Della Torre, whom Kristeller accuses of flawed methodology and a certain naïveté in his use of sources (*SRTL*, 1:192).[66] Given that
Kristeller was writing four decades after Della Torre's book and drew on
a prodigious amount of new empirical evidence, his criticism (addressed
as if to a contemporary) may seem unfair or uncalled for, if not downright
arrogant. Yet something else seems to be going on here, for when we take
the methodologically sound principles advocated by Kristeller for the first
time in this essay and read them side by side with Della Torre's work, they
appear to be an almost word-for-word replication of the 'positivist' ideals
that Della Torre had put forth in the preface and introduction to his own
work—which, as he stated, was written "for the sake of truth."[67]

What did Kristeller really think? What would have been his career had
he not been forced to leave Italy just as he became established? And for
how long could he have kept up the dissimulations he was forced into because of his affiliation with the actualist camp? Gentile was not simply
a patron, someone who could be betrayed without embarrassment. It is
well known that Gentile went out of his way to advance Kristeller's tenure at the Scuola Normale, to sponsor his Italian citizenship, and, finally,
when those attempts came up empty, to intercede with Mussolini, first,
personally, and, finally and somewhat desperately, with an emotional letter pleading that some sort of exception be made for the "poor devil."[68]
As a result, Kristeller was summoned by government officials, only to be
presented with a stash of money, compensation that the scholar could not
accept in good conscience and that he immediately remitted to the Scuola
Normale, save for the amount needed to pay his way to America. If any-

66. For current scholarship on the Platonic Academy in Florence, still a topic of heated
debate, see James Hankins, "The Myth of the Platonic Academy in Florence," *Renaissance
Quarterly* 44 (1991): 429–75; Hankins, "The Invention of the Platonic Academy of Florence,"
Rinascimento 41, no. 2 (2001): 3–38. For an alternative view, see Arthur Field, "The Platonic
Academy of Florence," in *Marsilio Ficino: His Theology, His Philosophy, His Legacy*, ed.
Michael J. B. Allen and Valery Rees with Martin Davies (Leiden: E. J. Brill, 2002), 359–76. For
a critical reaction to Kristeller's interpretation of Renaissance Platonism, see Michael J. B.
Allen, "Paul Oskar Kristeller and Marsilio Ficino: E tenebris revocaverunt," in Monfasani,
Kristeller Reconsidered, 1–18; Michael J. Allen, *Plato's Third Eye: Studies in Marsilio Ficino's
Metaphysics and Its Sources* (Aldershot, UK: Variorum, 1995).
67. For Della Torre's methodological premises, see his preface and introduction to *Storia
dell'Accademia Platonica di Firenze* (Florence: G. Carnesecchi, 1902), vii–x and 1ff.
68. Simoncelli, *Cantimori, Gentile e la Normale di Pisa*, 83. Throughout the chapter, Simoncelli cites copiously from the correspondence of Gentile and Kristeller. For an exhaustive
account of exiles in Italy, see Klaus Voigt, *Zuflucht auf Widerruf: Exil in Italien (1933–1945)*,
2 vols. (Stuttgart: Klett-Cotta, 1989–93).

thing, his unavoidable second emigration to the United States—made possible by Gentile's and, especially, Delio Cantimori's intercession with Yale
professor Roland H. Bainton—spared Kristeller from a 'philosophical' and
'methodological' outing in Italy.[69] Once he was among American scholars
Kristeller could proceed to downplay the Italian Renaissance and the merits of humanism, something unthinkable in the polarized academic scene
of Italy, where any concession to the Middle Ages would add a point to the
Neothomists' scorecard. Meanwhile, the positivist or strictly philological
approach despised by Italian idealists offered a most welcome rigor in the
American scene where it was largely untested.

In exile, or at least for as long as the United States felt like exile, Kristeller struggled to keep Gentile in the picture, but that, too, was no longer
necessary after Gentile's death in 1944.[70] Yet Kristeller's time in Italy resonated for some years after, and it is not strange for us now to want to make
sense of it. If Kristeller had been able to remain in Italy or, more important, had his *The Philosophy of Marsilio Ficino* been published in Italian
as scheduled, in 1938, he would have had to confront (more directly than
he ended up doing) the other great figure in Ficino scholarship, Giuseppe
Saitta, the living scourge of Neothomist philosophy. Saitta's own *The Philosophy of Marsilio Ficino*, published in 1923, was in fact the only other
monograph on the subject and, naturally, the one Kristeller set out to
replace.

First of all, Kristeller's choice of title for the English version of his
book—Saitta's own title—seems like a direct challenge, if not an insult,
to the scholarly community that had nurtured him in Italy. Certainly this
seems to have been the opinion of Saitta, who put out a new edition of
his book in 1943 (the same year as Kristeller's book was first published in
English) with a modified title—*Marsilio Ficino and the Philosophy of Humanism*—which in itself emphasized what Kristeller had seemed to deny:
namely, the philosophical significance of humanism and its connection to
Ficino. In the preface to this second edition, however, Saitta's polemic was
still aimed, as in the first, against the Neoscholastics. By the third edition,
which appeared in 1954 immediately after Kristeller's Italian edition (and

---

69. The best account of Kristeller's emigration to the United States can be found in the
introduction, notes, and documents in John Tedeschi, *The Correspondence of Roland H. Bainton and Delio Cantimori (1932–1966): An Enduring Transatlantic Friendship between Two
Historians of Religious Toleration* (Florence: Olschki, 2002).

70. It is perhaps noteworthy that an early draft of the programmatic article that Kristeller
published in *Byzantion* in 1946 was presented at a talk on 15 December 1944.

this time it was Kristeller's turn to alter the title of his book), Saitta directed his polemic at Kristeller, though without naming him:[71]

> The fundamental principles of the first edition of this work are retained, but within them I insist on criticizing the stances of others on the philosophy of Ficino —whom they downgrade to a reproducer of old and superseded ontological and Scholastic notions, thus depriving him of any appeal and attraction. We've returned—incredibly!—to the old and haggard positivist criticism, scavenging sources and testimonies with the sad result of presenting humanism as having no originality in the realm of thought. . . . But what may appear most strange of all is that some scholars, otherwise meritorious, have appropriated for themselves themes and insights found in my work to prove the opposite of what I attempted to demonstrate. . . . But let the simpleminded philologists [filologi simpliciores] rummage again and again in the ancient documents and among the wrecks of Scholasticism to deny the originality of Ficino's philosophy—which is not just a method or an attitude or a new way of seeing things, as I tried to demonstrate before others, but contains a cluster of truths that, in the cauldron of a deeper vision of Christianity, send out rays so intense as to illuminate the future path of thought.[72]

Saitta's indictment confirms that Kristeller, definitely among the "simpleminded philologists" in his view, would have had a hard time, perhaps an impossible time trying to correct the idealist agenda without appearing to fall squarely into positivism and, if not properly into Neothomism, into some form of medievalism.

Saitta's embattled stance speaks for itself, and as Garin realized in his own confrontation with this authority, self-contained systems can never be overcome by argument. The issue then becomes one of inspiration and values. We have seen that Garin, especially the mature Garin of the postwar period, did not forsake the "fecund pathos" of Saitta's embittered ac-

---

71. Paul Oskar Kristeller, *Il pensiero filosofico di Marsilio Ficino*, 2nd ed. (Florence: Le Lettere, 1988). The Italian title of Kristeller's book reads "The philosophical thought of Marsilio Ficino," no doubt to avoid being taken for the work of Saitta, who had, however, already acted on his own initiative to avoid confusion.

72. Giuseppe Saitta, *Marsilio Ficino e la filosofia dell'Umanesimo* (Bologna: Fiammenghi e Nanni, 1954), ix–x. Interestingly, in the preface to the first edition, Saitta had asked Italians to rely no longer on the opinions of foreign scholars on the subject of the Italian Renaissance.

tualism, in and of itself innocuous once revealed for what it was. Already in 1940, Saitta was writing to Garin calling attention to what he perceived as the latter's "indulgence for the historiographical criteria" of Kristeller, who is an "esteemed philologist" but has no "philosophical penetration," and whose "trashing about among the most banal humanist and Renaissance themes" has displeased even the "pure literati" at a recent conference.[73] Saitta looked forward to meeting Garin in person to discuss his work and offer guidance, and perhaps on such an occasion he won his sympathies. It is possible that this happened, and yet it should be emphasized that Garin's resolution to establish a new era in Renaissance scholarship on a purification and improvement—not a dismissal—of the actualist heritage was less personal than generational.

Again here, and specifically in relation to the Saitta/Kristeller affair, the mediating role of Delio Cantimori is pivotal. We have met Cantimori as the author of *The Italian Heretics of the Cinquecento*, the work that thematized the 'Nicodemism' or 'honest dissimulation' on which Garin had expounded to account for the interwar generation's scholarly production. As we have seen in chapter 2, furthermore, Cantimori was also the younger scholar to whom, in 1937, Gentile entrusted a generational reply to Spirito's attempted dissolution of actualism, and he was the author, in 1955, of an influential essay calling for a "critical awareness" (*coscienza critica*) in scholars' approach to the Renaissance.[74] Cantimori, in other words, had come to occupy a role as peacemaker and as mouthpiece of generally held sentiments, a role he played especially in his coveted reviews.

Kristeller had already asked Cantimori to review his *Supplementum* in 1937; but at that time Cantimori relieved himself of the responsibility by passing it on to his dissertation advisor, Saitta.[75] In 1954, the third edition of Saitta's monograph came out "within a few weeks" (as Cantimori specifies) of the publication of the Italian edition of Kristeller's Ficino, and

---

73. Saitta to Garin, 28 July 1940, AEG.

74. Delio Cantimori, "La periodizzazione dell'età del Rinascimento," in *Studi di storia* (Turin: Einaudi, 1959), 340–65.

75. In effect Saitta provided only a brief note. See Giuseppe Saitta, review of *Supplementum Ficinianum* (Firenze: Olschki, 1937), by Paul Oskar Kristeller, *Leonardo* 7–8 (1937): 264. Years later, Saitta provided a longer and scathing review of the Italian edition of Kristeller's Ficino book, qualified as a "summula" or "gloss" of Ficino's philosophy, in which the hypothesis was ventured that Kristeller may have been influenced by Garin's exaggerated exaltation of Pico. In a reply, Garin specified that his Pico monograph, though finished in 1934, was published just as Kristeller had completed his own work. See Giuseppe Saitta, review of *Il pensiero filosofico di Marsilio Ficino* (Firenze: Sansoni, 1953), by Paul Oskar Kristeller, *Giornale critico della filosofia italiana* (1955): 114–17; and Eugenio Garin, "Postilla Ficiniana," *Giornale critico della filosofia italiana* (1955): 431–32.

Cantimori was saddled with a difficult mediating role.[76] He did it unwillingly, denouncing the bad faith of scholars—Saitta and Kristeller were not excepted—who declined discussion and took "any criticism as an excuse or as an attack"; books, he says, are nothing but human actions, and their authors should be "explicit" in their dissent rather than leaving others to do the dirty work.[77] Cantimori goes on to recall having met Kristeller for the first time in 1934 in the Berlin Staatsbibliothek, when he was approached because he was a student of Saitta. Cantimori emphasizes that despite their differences, Saitta and Kristeller are both representatives of idealist historiography, but whereas Saitta's idealism is expressed in the "immanent and subjectivist impetuousness" typical of Gentile's first disciples, Kristeller's is concealed in some form of "neopositivism." He adds that Kristeller, like any good idealist, believes in a "Western tradition of philosophy" developing from Plato to Hegel, and that this ideal is a stronger guiding force in his actual work than any single methodological principle or conclusion.

But Cantimori had hit the nail on the head when he noticed that Saitta and Kristeller were both interested in the same Ficino; for both scholars Ficino's position in the Western philosophical tradition was paramount. The perceptible difference lay in their choice of contexts: whereas Kristeller framed the Neoplatonist within the Renaissance, which Cantimori deemed an abstract periodization, Saitta placed him within the "concrete" context of "humanism" or, rather, in the context of the very concrete exchanges between humanists and intellectuals long after the so-called Renaissance. And from this perspective, which highlights Kristeller's difference with respect not just to Saitta's but to the entirety of the Italian tradition of Renaissance scholarship, from Spaventa to Garin, the two stances are indeed incommensurable. Cantimori's labored conclusions are of particular interest to us:

> We certainly have here two works of fundamental importance whose contents would merit being thoroughly reviewed. Kristeller's bibliographical exactitude, his philological and exegetical meticulousness,

---

76. In a letter dated 15 March 1947, Cantimori apologizes to Kristeller for his abandonment of the study of humanism. In expressing his deference for Kristeller, Cantimori writes: "Ma ora ho deciso di rinunciare un po' all'Umanesimo [/] e alla Riforma [/], e così mi faccio coraggio, e le scrivo. Intanto, le chiedo scusa, e spero che comprenderà le mie ragioni: per me Lei è l'umanesimo in persona, cosicché non riuscivo a distinguere il caro 'humanista' dal caro amico." Cited in Tedeschi, *Correspondence of Roland H. Bainton and Delio Cantimori*, 274–75.

77. Delio Cantimori, "Divagazioni profane su Marsilio Ficino," in *Studi di storia*, 396–97.

his precise and accurate demonstrations are admirable and often convincing. So much so that we are inclined to bridle at the enthusiasm for Ficino's "originality" and the "revolutionary" force of Ficino's thought that we tend to feel *qua* students of the Normale [students of Saitta]. Nevertheless, as we read again the new edition of Saitta's work, we cannot refrain from adhering to, and voicing our pleasure in, Saitta's energetic affirmations. We cannot avoid noticing the warmth and vigorous acumen in our old teacher's historical view. If it weren't for our faith in "close readings," we would not hesitate to affirm, paradoxically, that Saitta's Ficino is less historically true compared with that of Kristeller but certainly more alive historically or, should we say, poetically. After all, history deals with that which becomes and not that which is immutable: and such liveliness is magnificently conveyed by Saitta, albeit in an exuberant manner. And yet we cannot doubt that Kristeller's observations better correspond to reality than Saitta's appealing evocations.[78]

Cantimori's to-and-fro in this passage is impressive, and indicative of the internal struggle, typical of Italian scholars of all ages, between philology and philosophy and their reconciliation —a reconciliation that Cantimori eventually attributed to Garin, whom he once called the "new Burckhardt."[79] But between these two extremes, it appears that Saitta and/ or philosophy was ultimately the preferred choice, certainly a more congenial one to the Italians. Almost two decades after Gentile's appraisal of Kristeller as "not merely a pure philologist" but as a philosophical mind about to bloom with a monograph on Ficino that the father of actualism never got to read, Cantimori took it upon himself to bid Kristeller farewell on behalf of the entire Italian philosophical and scholarly community.[80]

FICINO, A DIAMOND IN THE ROUGH: KRISTELLER'S NEO-KANTIANISM

In his appraisal of Saitta's and Kristeller's relative merits, Cantimori also lingered on the heuristic distinction between "originality" and "indepen-

78. Cantimori, "Divagazioni profane su Marsilio Ficino," 397–98.
79. See Delio Cantimori, "Burckhardt e Garin," in *Studi di storia*, 311–14. In the same volume, see also "Valore dell'umanesimo," 379–590 (translated in *RIP*, 215–23).
80. In a letter, Kristeller courteously thanked Cantimori for his review, but interestingly he avoided touching on the prickly matters brought up by his colleague. The letter is in Tedeschi, *Correspondence of Roland H. Bainton and Delio Cantimori*, 287–88.

dence" that Kristeller drew at the beginning of his Ficino monograph in an attempt to define true philosophy. Kristeller asserted that Ficino was well known as a translator and commentator of Plato and Plotinus but that he was often undervalued as a philosopher, owing to his purported lack of "originality." Writing in the mid-twentieth century, Kristeller felt that this distinguished representative of Renaissance Platonism had fallen prey to the prejudices of those who want everything resolved *ab origine*; it was the same sentiment, he noted bitterly, that precludes making sense of philosophical "traditions" and that might have led Caliph Omar to order the destruction of the library of Alexandria. It was to justify Ficino as an object of study, then, that Kristeller felt compelled to elaborate on the origins of rigorous thinking.

Kristeller observed that from the dawn of time, men were inclined "to reflect on the nature of their being and upon the relation of their being to reality as a whole," and that "primitive man" did so through myth, poetry, aphorism, and proverb. "Prephilosophic" expressions of this kind, while presenting some awareness of history, did not "rest consciously upon any doctrinal tradition." To the contrary, "philosophy properly so-called" began when "civilized man" strove "to arrive at a logical coherence in such expressions and at a systematic interpretation of the whole of reality in its manifold aspects of content" (*PMF*, 3–4). But since "systematic perfection" is unachievable in the span of a single man's life, every philosopher necessarily builds upon past foundations. This is why, in Kristeller's final analysis, a philosophical tradition develops by a kind of intellectual selection, honing a "common fund of basic postulates," which, reconfirmed in successive eras for their intrinsic "meaning" and "significance," survive the test of time.

Philosophers can therefore be appraised according to their relative "independence" from, or "originality" with respect to, a "tradition" so conceived:

> If by independence in thought we mean an individual and unmediated approach to truth, Ficino must be considered an independent thinker— a conclusion which it remains for our study to prove. But "independence" taken in this sense must not be confused with "originality" taken in the ordinary sense, as a capacity of saying "things new and never before said." While Ficino holds his ground in any comparison with other philosophers from the standpoint of "independence," in point of "originality" he is certainly inferior to his contemporary Pico, who makes frequent boast of being "original," especially during his

earlier years. But such "originality," if we consider carefully, may be
the outward manifestation of a very superficial "independence." . . .
"[O]riginality" is one of those specious values, secondary at best, that
are either mere natural endowments or else incidental by-products of
the process of thinking. (*PMF*, 5–6)

In Ficino's thought "essential" ideas coexist with "incidental" ones, yet
his philosophy is shown to be capable of discrimination by the level of sys-
tematicity he achieves in his *Platonic Theology*. Essential ideas (and here
Kristeller again relied on the hermeneutical circle) always relate to and co-
here in a well-defined whole; in the case of Ficino, they do so in the "comprehensive view of the universe" put forth in his magnum opus. This is
not the case with Pico, an "original" but unsystematic philosopher whose
tenets—isolated, scattered, and disconnected as they invariably are—may
be "disposed" of by simple enumeration and description.

Cantimori insightfully notes that in his methodological premises
Kristeller may have been out to disavow Saitta who, from his earliest forays
into Renaissance thought—as well as in correlated attempts to carve out
a privileged place for Ficino in his promotion of an Italian philosophical
tradition—had often put particular stress on the Italians' "originality."[81] It
could be added that 'originality,' as a positive connotation of 'difference' or
'anomaly,' was a criterion that appealed not just to Saitta but to any Italian
thinker who in the wake of Spaventa turned to philosophy with the aim
of overcoming the Renaissance shame. At the same time, however, Cantimori was far less perceptive in detecting the roots of Kristeller's stance;
in amicable fashion he wanted to attribute his colleague's viewpoint to
his well-known scholarly "fastidiousness" as well as to a narrow circle
of philosophical and scholarly influences: Jaeger, Norden, Hoffmann, and
Heidegger. Cantimori was extremely well versed in German intellectual
history, and one might have expected him to pinpoint Kristeller's true
philosophical allegiances, especially since these were articulated more
fully and clearly in the Italian version of the Ficino monograph.

The English version left out some important qualifications: for example, that it is part of the very essence of philosophy, but not of art and poetry, to engage its history; that true philosophy begins when expressions
are "freed from their arbitrary particularity" and therefore employed to
"construct a realm of objectivity within thought"; and that philosophi-

---

81. Saitta's early essays, including "L'originalità della filosofia italiana" (1919), are collected in *Filosofia italiana e Umanesimo* (Venice: La Nuova Italia, 1928).

cal interpretation is established on the "quality of its object," which transcends the realm of opinion and contradictions. Moreover, in the Italian version Kristeller specified that philosophical thoughts should not be considered mere "facts," for "claims to truth" are indeed qualitatively distinguishable one from another, and the aim of philosophical analysis should be to delve far enough into philosophical argument to recover its "starting points." These are not many, even in the greatest philosophers, but only they have "the nature of concepts" and are thus unreceptive to a "psychologically oriented" analysis founded on "nonconceptual elements," such as, for example, a thinker's motives and personality:

> In order to evaluate philosophical affirmations according to their claim to truth, one will first need a canon of truth; and this could have some believing that everything depends on the arbitrariness of the interpreter. But while one may well object that subjectivity can never be completely eliminated in knowledge, the subjective element can be reduced to its utmost indispensable limits with a firm and honest orientation toward the object.[82]

"Basic postulates," "intrinsic meaning and significance," "realm of objectivity," "quality of the object," "canon of truth," "orientation toward the object," "evaluation," and so on . . . With these premises, Kristeller is clearly speaking the language of the philosophical school of Neo-Kantianism, which in its southwestern version—that is, the one developed in Freiburg and, principally, in Heidelberg by Heinrich Rickert, Kristeller's teacher—presented itself as *Wertphilosophie*, a philosophy founded on a recognition of and orientation toward transcendent values.

That Kristeller cherished Neo-Kantianism, a long-standing and varied tradition, first and foremost as a form of historicism may be inferred from numerous articles he published in the United States on the topic of historical methodology. Also in 1943, for example, Kristeller endeavored to familiarize his American readership with the degree of scientific rigor to which (philosophical) historiography could lay claim. This had been the subject of an epoch-making debate in late nineteenth-century and early twentieth-century Germany that, Kristeller lamented, had little or no resonance across the Atlantic. In this article, co-authored with Lincoln Reis, Kristeller went so far as to deny any "basic difference between the historical and scientific method," yet he argued against the assimilation by his-

82. Kristeller, *Il pensiero filosofico di Marsilio Ficino*, 6–7.

toriography of the standards of the American "social sciences." The latter, he felt, relied on generalizations that were at once too exclusive and too comprehensive for the history of culture and philosophy, which concerns itself with "specific, unique, and concrete events" and therefore naturally resists the formulation of general laws. "Universals," Kristeller specified, still had a place in historiography, but only "before" (as guiding principles) and "after" (for the sake of interpretation) the process of "fact-finding," itself made up of different stages: collection, selection, evaluation, and reconstruction.

But "interpretation," the task of the historian, has always been the dilemma of historiographical research. If too little interpretation is applied, the historian risks succumbing to sterile positivism; if it is applied too much or too fast, then the risk is one of generalization. Kristeller's response is to note that if "the world of historical events is full of different meanings," then it is important to distinguish and choose carefully between "horizontal interpretation," "which tries to understand a specific event through its relation to other events," and "vertical interpretation," "which aims at an understanding of the inherent significance of any event or group of events."[83]

Horizontal interpretation is useful for drawing causal relationships between distinct realms of culture. It is the approach preferred by the social scientists, but while it may help us understand philosophy in context, it is only by means of vertical interpretation that we can come to evaluate a distinct cultural artifact free of contradiction and hypothesis: "We do not want to understand a work of art or a philosophical idea only in so far as it is related to others, but also in so far as it has a specific meaning in itself which is accessible to our understanding and appreciation. . . . Such interpretations give the event or idea its specific physiognomy which would disappear if it were viewed only in a variety of casual relations, and we wish to say that without it history is incomplete and in a higher sense impossible."[84] Again here, as in the methodological premises he was simultaneously publishing as part of the Ficino monograph, Kristeller ventured the possibility of understanding or interpreting according to standards of "intrinsic value" or "inherent significance," suggesting, coherently, that anything in philosophy that should be valued for its "autonomy" deserves to be interpreted "vertically."

83. Paul Oskar Kristeller, "Some Remarks on the Method of History," *Journal of Philosophy* 40 (1943): 240.
84. Kristeller, "Some Remarks on the Method of History," 243–44.

Obviously, Kristeller's predicament was to define interpretation as something closer to 'evaluation' than 'opinion.' If only our guiding principles could be flexible—that is, critical and not dogmatic, "in a Kantian sense"—then vertical interpretation, founded exclusively on the object of research, could aid in formulating "valid" general questions and in perceiving even wider and more far-reaching contextualizations than the ones sought for horizontally:

> We may ask, for example, why ideas, institutions, and traditions persist, and the reason for the continuity of history in the midst of change. We may ask in what ways such channels and forms of civilization develop, and to what extent some may be permanent in so far as they correspond to primary and essential needs for men. We may inquire as to the relation between facts and values as exemplified by historical events, and how far historical facts are subject to different types of evaluation, and whether these types of evaluation are compatible with each other or whether there is a hierarchy among them.[85]

Kristeller's frequent use of "evaluation" may be misleading here. In current usage it tends to indicate discretion and appraisal on the part of the historian. But as we shall discuss shortly, and as the passage implies, "evaluation" signified in Neo-Kantian jargon something that is based less on ethical (good/bad) or ontological (true/false) grounds than on the mere recognition of "validity," itself the product, at least for Rickert (whom Kristeller is again following here), of some sort of transhistorical consensus.

It may come as a surprise that in the mid-twentieth century, and in conversation with American social scientists, Kristeller was in fact (as his footnotes confirm) tinkering with a historiographical methodology put forth by Johann Gustav Droysen (1808–84). Droysen's *Historik* (1857) and its handier abridgement (*Grundriss*; 1858), were works of paramount consequence in the development of German historicism and hermeneutics, and were still being debated when Kristeller was a student; indeed he first honed his critical skills while reading Droysen as a student of Heidegger.[86] In his groundbreaking work, intended to provide an *organon* of the historical sciences, Droysen had set out to counter the philological tradition of

---

85. Kristeller, "Some Remarks on the Method of History," 245.

86. Kristeller avers to have formed an original methodology in historiography in a report on Droysen's *Historik* submitted to Heidegger in 1926. See Paul Oskar Kristeller, "Recollections of My Life," in *The European Legacy* 1 (1996): 1866.

his own time, which he perceived as sterile *Gelehrsamkeit*, erudition.[87]
Central to this tradition was the idea of philology as a path to the objective restoration of classical antiquity, itself idealized for its normative and
prototypical exemplarity (*Vorbildlichkeit*). Against the hypostatization of
a given historical period as promoted by the contemporary study of classical antiquity (*Alterthumswissenschaft*), he advanced the possibility that
conversation with the ancients should edify us in the here and now. Thus,
Droysen (unlike Kristeller) sought to foreground the subjectivity of the
historian:

> Those who perceive the greatest task of the historian to be that of add-
> ing nothing of his own, but rather to simply have the facts speak for
> themselves, do not see that facts do not speak at all apart from the voice
> of those who have grasped and understood them. These facts absolutely
> do not simply exist as such, but, rather, they exist either as remnants in
> which we recover them as efficient causes, or as reminiscences which
> already carry within themselves, to the highest degree, those subjec-
> tive instances that one would want to prohibit to the historian.[88]

The idea that the past is mute without an intermediary is what led Droysen to articulate philosophy's circle of "fact-finding" (organization of the
material) and "interpretation" (the understanding of this material in the
larger context of one's own investigative agency). The problem was how
to gain knowledge about a subject matter intimately tied to our own self-
perception, and it was in order to solve this problem that Droysen momentously introduced the dichotomy between "understanding" (*Verstehen*),
the proper task of the historian, and "explaining" (*Erklären*), the task of
the natural scientist.

---

87. For a brief introduction to Droysen and his work, see Thomas Burger, "Droysen's
Defense of Historiography: A Note," *History and Theory* 16, no. 2 (1977): 168–73; Michael J.
Maclean, "Johann Gustav Droysen and the Development of Historical Hermeneutics," *His-
tory and Theory* 21, no. 3 (1982): 347–65; Felix Gilbert, "The New Edition of Johann Gustav
Droysen's *Historik*," *Journal of the History of Ideas* (1983): 327–36; and Ulrich Mühlack,
"Johann Gustav Droysen: 'Historik' et herméneutique," in *La naissance du paradigme her-
méneutique: Schleiermacher, Humboldt, Boeckh, Droysen*, ed. André Laks and Ada Neschke
(Lille: Presses universitaires de Lille, 1990), 359–80. For a more comprehensive contextualiza-
tion, see Robert Southard, *Droysen and the Prussian School of History* (Lexington: University
Press of Kentucky, 1995). Droysen's *Grundriss* has an English translation: *Outline of the
Principles of History (Grundriss der Historik)*, trans. E. Benjamin Andrews (New York:
H. Fertig, 1967).
88. Johann Gustav Droysen, *Historik: Die Vorlesungen von 1857*, ed. Peter Leyh (Stutt-
gart: Bad Cannstatt, 1977), 218.

Droysen thus engaged in a *Methodenstreit*, a quarrel of method, with those forms of empiricism sustained by the likes of Leopold von Ranke (1795–1886), one of the best-known exemplars, who famously called for the historian's "self-effacement" in the cause of telling "how things actually happened" (*wie es eigentlich gewesen*).[89] With his defense of subjectivity, Kristeller realized, Droysen had revivified a central debate in Western intellectual history, one whose modern form originated in Renaissance humanism:

> Ever since classical antiquity, history has been associated with grammar and rhetoric and treated as a subdivision or appendix of the liberal arts; beginning with the fifteenth century, it appeared among the *Studia humanitatis*, which survive, at least in name, in our humanities, and which gave way, among the French and Italians, to the "moral sciences." From the Renaissance we may also date the close connection between history, philology, and critical method that culminated in the effort of eighteenth- and nineteenth-century scholarship, especially in Germany, to raise history and philology to the rank of genuine sciences. This development had its repercussions among the philosophers who came to treat history as one of the major divisions of human experience and finally assigned to the historical and philological disciplines the status of separate sciences, different in subject matter and perhaps even in method from the natural sciences (*Geisteswissenschaften, Kulturwissenschaften*)—as did Dilthey and Rickert, and to some extent Cassirer. As a consequence the historical and philological disciplines have had in Germany and most other European countries a much higher standing in academic and public life, and in philosophical thought, than they seem to have at present in this country.[90]

The qualification of the humanities as "sciences" began with Italian humanism and climaxed in Germany when a debate about method among historians was institutionalized and given a wider theoretical foundation by philosophers: first of all by Wilhelm Dilthey, who in his *Introduction to the Human Sciences* (1883) developed Droysen's dichotomy (*Erklären* vs. *Verstehen*) into a full-fledged opposition between the *Geistes-* and *Natur-*

---

89. On Droysen and Ranke, see Jacques Bos, "Individuality and Interpretation in Nineteenth-Century German Historicism," in *Historical Perspectives on Erklären and Verstehen*, ed. Uljana Feest (Dordrecht: Springer Science+Business Media, 2010), 207–20.

90. Paul Oskar Kristeller, "Some Problems of Historical Knowledge," *Journal of Philosophy* 58, no. 4 (1961): 86–87.

wissenschaften, and, later, by his critics Wilhelm Windelband (1848–1915) and Windelband's student, Heinrich Rickert.

What is striking here is that what went down in history as an unresolved issue—the problem of historiographical relativism, resulting in the crisis of German historicism—was instead for Kristeller a problem that had been circumvented, if not exactly solved, by Rickert.[91] It is also interesting that Kristeller would finally choose to single out his Neo-Kantian teacher only in 1991, in a testament composed for a Festschrift in honor of Garin. In fact, it seems that for Kristeller Rickert's value philosophy was as connected and relevant to Italian concerns as to German ones:

> The combination of philosophy and philology involves grave methodological difficulties. The mainstream of rationalist philosophy from Plato to Kant rests on self-evident or a priori principles, not only on empirical facts: it rejects positivism for good philosophical reasons, and has no place in its system for history and philology. On the other hand, the methodology of the historical and philological disciplines rests on the evidence of texts and documents that is strictly empirical, and this methodology is thus at least implicitly positivistic. Thus I must admit to being inconsistent, if you wish to call it that, when I profess to be a rationalist in philosophy and a positivist in history and philology. Yet I should like to cite in support of my position those philosophers who have tried to find a place for history and philology in their systems, that is, Vico, Hegel and Dilthey, Croce, Gentile and Collingwood, but especially Rickert who attempted to construct an entire methodology of the historical disciplines, distinct from that of the natural sciences, within a basically Kantian framework.[92]

Kristeller credits Rickert specifically for enabling a compromise between rationalism and positivism, philology and philosophy—a compromise, it seems, sought unsuccessfully in the Italian tradition. More important, it was Rickert's value philosophy, more than his sporadic borrowings from

---

91. The standard work on the dissolution of German historicism is Ernst Troeltsch, *Der Historismus und seine Probleme*, vol. 3 of *Gesammelte Schriften* (Tübingen: Mohr, 1922). On the genesis of *Historismus*, see Friedrich Meinecke, *Die Entstehung des Historismus*, in *Werke*, ed. Hans Herzfeld et al., vol. 3 (Munich: Oldenbourg, 1965). For a comprehensive introduction in English to German historicism, see Frederick C. Beiser, *The German Historicist Tradition* (Oxford: Oxford University Press, 2011).

92. Paul Oskar Kristeller, "The Study of the History of Philosophy and Its Problems," in *Filosofia e cultura: Per Eugenio Garin*, ed. Michele Ciliberto and Cesare Vasoli, 2 vols. (Rome: Editori Riuniti, 1991), 1:355.

Heideggerian existentialism, that 'validated' Kristeller's stubborn downplay of 'humanism.'

It may be useful now to turn to the works by Rickert that Kristeller so admired since his early years as his student in Heidelberg: *The Limits of Concept Formation in Natural Sciences* (1896), and the shorter, handier *Science and History* (*Kulturwissenschaft und Naturwissenschaft*) (1899).[93] Both were written with the aim of reestablishing commitment "to the clarity and penetrating force of rational thought" against "the romantic excesses and insipid aestheticism" of "an exhausted and purely imitative idolization of Nietzsche" and with Dilthey's notion of the *Geisteswissenschaften* in mind, itself a flawed nomenclature.[94] Rickert maintained that "Geist" (mind, psyche) was an unsatisfactory term because, in reducing the humanities to mental phenomena, it put psychology, itself a generalizing or natural science, at the center of investigation. What was not acceptable, from Rickert's perspective, was Dilthey's suggestion that historiography be based on an analysis of history as a mode of being and experience, for this fails to draw a distinction between the "meaningful content of culture" as perceived in the mental life of single individuals and what Rickert defined as "unreal meanings."

For an elaboration of Rickert's contention we can turn to Kristeller, who in this case, too, echoed his teacher's criticism of Dilthey without qualification:

> Dilthey often confused the psychological understanding of an artist or thinker with the interpretive understanding of a work in its meaning.... [I]t seems extremely difficult to recapture the thoughts or feelings of an artist or thinker from his works, except when we are aided by biographical documents, diaries, letters, or the like. Yet this is not what we primarily want to achieve when we try to understand or interpret a work of art or a philosophical text. We rather want to understand its intellectual or artistic content as expressed in the work, the irreal meaning of it, as Rickert called it in his critique of Dilthey. We are thus

93. In what follows I cite from Heinrich Rickert, *The Limits of Concept Formation in Natural Science: A Logical Introduction to the Historical Sciences*, ed. and trans. Guy Oakes (New York: Cambridge University Press, 1986), and Heinrich Rickert, *Science and History: A Critique of Positivist Epistemology*, trans. George Reisman (New York: Van Nostrand, 1962). In what follows I also rely on Guy Oakes, *Weber and Rickert: Concept Formation in the Cultural Sciences* (Cambridge, MA: MIT Press, 1988), and, especially, Anton C. Zijderveld, *Rickert's Relevance: The Ontological Nature and Epistemological Functions of Values* (Leiden: Brill, 2006), chap. 4.

94. Rickert, *Limits of Concept Formation*, 8.

driven to overcome Dilthey's psychologism, but to accept his formula
that there is a fundamental category which we may call expression, or,
with Cassirer, symbol, and a fundamental capacity of the human mind
to give physical expression to spiritual meanings, and vice versa, to understand these meanings through their physical expressions. There is a
realm of essences with which the intellectual and cultural historian is
concerned, and I am afraid it is not reducible to sense data.[95]

Kristeller follows Rickert in understanding the humanities as a "cultural
science" (*Kulturwissenschaft*), that is, a science dealing with sensory as
well as nonsensory objects whose individualization is owing to those transhistorical (cultural) "values" or "unreal meanings" that are made to adhere to them.

Rickert had conceived of "unreal meanings" in an attempt to counter
scientists' simplistic notion of the objectivity of reality, which they were
wont to disengage wholly from subjectivity. In opposition to the special-
ized sciences, he sought to link the reality accessed through sense perception to the reality constituted by those theoretical values that guide our
cognitive activity (such as judgment) and our emotions (such as the experiences of beauty, justice, etc.). This second realm is nonempirical, and in
this sense "unreal," yet ever so close to us. In order to avoid relapsing into
Platonic dualism, Rickert suggests that the gap between the two realms
is continually bridged by means of an "evaluation act" (*Akt des Wertens*)
that imbues empirical objects, in themselves factual and of no interest to
man, with the "meaning" with which unreal values are laden and with
respect to which man is constantly "oriented." Rickert illustrates his theory through the notion of cultural "goods" (*Güter*), such as books, paintings, hoary institutions, and so forth: it is only though a man's evaluating
act that a painting, in itself a congeries of colors and lines, may come to
"mean" or "signify" a masterwork. Evaluation is thus man's natural defense against the plague of "relativism," a notion that Rickert likens to
"relationism," the inability to see and appraise things "independently" or,
in Kristeller's terms, "autonomously."

As for Kristeller's related notion of "horizontal" and "vertical" interpretations, this amounted to an elaboration of Rickert's understanding
of reality as a Heraclitean river in permanent flux and therefore in need
of discrimination between essential and inessential elements. In our approach to reality, says Rickert, we can either choose to see connections,

95. Kristeller, "Some Problems of Historical Knowledge," 98–99.

as scientists tend to do, or stress "differences," as historians ought to do in their quest for the "unique" and "unrepeatable," for only via the latter approach does the "homogeneous continuum" of reality turn into a "heterogeneous *discretum*." Cultural values, Rickert avowed, are never "real"; rather they are "valid," because they are "accepted as valid by all men" or at least by some "civilized men." Just how many men are needed to make up a validity-granting quorum is not specified by Rickert; for him what matters is the indubitable quality of one's conviction: "civilization, or culture in the highest sense, must be concerned not with the values attaching to the objects of mere desire, but with excellences which, if we reflect at all on the validity of values, we feel ourselves more or less 'obligated' to esteem and cultivate for the sake of the society in which we live or for some other concomitant reason."[96]

It would appear that in the relativistic world we have come to inhabit, the very one that Rickert (and Kristeller) wished to forestall, too much is sacrificed to the individuation of excellences or canons. This is most evident in one of Rickert's most illustrative and provocative passages:

If we compare a personality such as Goethe with any average person, and if we ignore the consideration that even the individuality of this average person means something with reference to some value or other, it follows that Goethe is related to such a person in the same way the Koh-i-noor diamond is related to a lump of coal. In other words, with reference to the *general* value, the individuality of the average person can be replaced by any object that falls under the concept of a person. The significance of Goethe, on the other hand, lies precisely in what distinguishes him from all other instances of the concept of a person. There is no general concept under which he can be subsumed. Thus the individual Goethe is an in-individual in the same sense as the individual Koh-i-noor: His distinctive status as an individual is valued by *everyone* for its individuality. As a result, we see how the relation to a general value makes it possible not only to distinguish two kinds of individuals in every reality whatsoever but also to draw this distinction in such a way that we can expect everyone to acknowledge its validity. . . . In this way, history as a science distinguishes the essential from the inessential in a *generally valid fashion* and consolidates the essential as a necessary unit.[97]

96. Rickert, *Science and History*, 22.
97. Rickert, *Limits of Concept Formation*, 89

Life compels us to choose between the valuable and the common in order to restrain, if not completely regulate, the chaos of physical process. By replacing Goethe with Ficino, we can finally grasp the very distinct philosophical grounding on which Kristeller's Renaissance scholarship was established. In Kristeller's eyes Ficino, too, was a Koh-i-noor, an excellence in the midst of relative goods and/or an island of permanence in the eternal floating of time. But the problem that besets Rickert's theory, which concerns itself only with 'excellences' without, however, explaining how thought comes to conform to norms in the concrete historical world, is even more palpable in Kristeller's application of "value theory" (*Wertlehre*) in order to draw a clear-cut distinction between philosophy and humanism in the Renaissance.

In Kristeller the "lump of coal," the "specious values" or "incidental by-products" of thought against which background Ficino's luminosity is appreciated, is none other than Pico, where Pico represents an "original" and thus, in Neo-Kantian terms, "inessential" form of thought such as humanism. It is ironic, then, that Kristeller's Renaissance scholarship, founded on Rickert's axiology, came to be viewed (admiringly) as objective and free of value judgments. Such a view can be sustained only if one follows Rickert in believing that the bias of "valuation" (*Wertung*), which always involves praise or blame, may be circumvented by means of purely theoretical reference to values (*Wertbeziehung*) that are "beyond question." Kristeller did so, thinking that there could not, or should not, be any doubt that humanism was, in the main, a frivolous intellectual movement goaded by "love of gossip," and adamant that it had "shamefully" introduced into highbrow literature those values that Kristeller, like Rickert, saw as "attaching to the objects of mere desire."[98]

In the end it should be evident how a Neo-Kantian-inflected historicism—useful as it may be in foregrounding, or rather in lifting, Ficino's thought out of its Renaissance context—naturally and willingly eschews inquiring about the context itself, that is, Quattrocento humanism. Rickert, who claimed that his system held no sway in the realm of art, religion, and practical reason, was more straightforward on this point than Kristeller. Because 'excellences' of the kind that Kristeller sought for at the beginning were of course few and far between, a great part of his career was devoted, with the *Iter Italicum* (a finding list of uncatalogued Renaissance manuscripts), to the classification and organization of the humanist

98. See Paul Oskar Kristeller, "Humanist Learning in the Italian Renaissance," *SRTL*, 2:103.

by-product of the history of thought (pure fact-finding), for true (vertical) interpretation could not be granted to lesser values.[99] In our day and age, scholars may still be inclined to agree with Rickert's impersonal "everyone" regarding Goethe's preciousness; less tenable, however, is the idea that he might have been a diamond in the rough. Kristeller's Rickertianism explains why a new generation of Renaissance scholars in the United States are no longer "content to see themselves only as minions" engaged in the never-ending task of gathering empirical evidence in support of humanism's irrelevance.[100]

We are now in a position, furthermore, to understand that Kristeller's *prise de position* concerning humanism was not personal, as is usually maintained, but 'scientifically' Neo-Kantian, and his choosing it preceded his vicissitudes as a Jewish German émigré, usually seen as the root cause of his coldness toward any form of engaged, mundane philosophy. This realization allows us, in conclusion, to review the Kristeller-Garin debate for its philosophical rather than polemical value.

CONCLUSION: RENAISSANCE SCHOLARSHIP AS PHILOSOPHICAL DISCOURSE

Insofar as Neo-Kantianism may be said to have filled the void left by the dissolution of German idealism following Hegel's death, its fate can be compared to that of Italian neo-idealism: both philosophies, after holding absolute sway in nineteenth- and early twentieth-century academia, were rapidly and systematically superseded in the interwar period by various forms of 'life philosophies' and/or 'existentialisms'—in other words, they eventually succumbed to the widely shared desire for intellectual concreteness that ensued from the trauma of World War I.[101] As is often the case, however, what in hindsight appear as clear breaks were in fact experienced as slow transitions: the change was navigated by separate generations of thinkers disjointedly rather than in linear succession.

For example, we have seen that in Italy, until World War II, the turn

99. On the *Iter Italicum*, Kristeller's major scholarly feat, see Arthur Field, "Reading and rereading Kristeller's 'finding list': Iter iterum iterumque," in Monfasani, *Kristeller Reconsidered*, chap. 5.

100. See Celenza, *Lost Italian Renaissance*, 53–54.

101. For a thorough sociological account of Neo-Kantianism in the nineteenth century, see Klaus Christian Köhnke, *The Rise of Neo-Kantianism: German Academic Philosophy between Idealism and Positivism*, trans. R. J. Hollingdale (Cambridge: Cambridge University Press, 1991).

against actualism was less radical and less unconditional as implemented by younger generations than the patricide called for by erstwhile Gentile-ans. And the differences of attitude that can be observed in, say, Garin and Spirito with respect to Gentile resemble what we see in Kristeller and Heidegger vis-à-vis their common teacher, Rickert. In the preface to his *Habilitation* thesis, *The Doctrine of Categories and Meaning in Duns Scotus* (1915), Heidegger programmatically stated that the philosophy of value "is summoned to a decisive forward movement," one that he set out to achieve through a "creative" reshaping of the problem "out of a strong, personal experience."[102] What existentialism or Heidegger disowned, then, was recouped by Kristeller; and so, much like Garin's, Kristeller's inter-pretive paradigm was founded on a conscious conservatism with respect to new philosophies, which both thinkers embraced (to differing degrees) with the proviso that time-honored values, be they Rickert's or Gentile's, not be sacrificed in the process. Unfortunately, Garin and Kristeller ap-pear to have sometimes missed or to have voluntarily eschewed the sig-nificance of their conversation—the fact that they were carrying over into Renaissance scholarship certain philosophical stances and polemics that were destined to vanish from philosophical discourse itself.

Garin and Kristeller's quarrel climaxed in the early 1950s when the second editions (or translations) of their principal works (originally com-posed in "brotherly spirit") were deployed to stake out their respective po-sitions. We have seen that around this time, with Kristeller's pieties well in mind, Garin had reaffirmed his distaste for Ficino by emphasizing this "first great courtesan philosopher's" attack against the "noble and intran-sigent" Savonarola, after he was burnt at the stake.[103] To which, in due time, Kristeller replied by recounting the affair surrounding the abduc-tion and murder of Simon of Trent. In the late fifteenth century, this boy's disappearance infamously led to a killing spree against the city's Jewish community, which was falsely accused of ritual murder. In his treatment, Kristeller, unable to resist the temptation of returning a cheap shot, took note that Johannes Hinderbach, the bishop who sentenced the Jews to death, "was applauded in prose and in verse, in Latin and in vernacular, by

102. Marion Heinz, "Philosophy and Worldview: Heidegger's Concept of Philosophy and the Baden School of Neo-Kantianism," in *Heidegger, German Idealism and Neo-Kantianism*, ed. Tom Rockmore (New York: Humanity Books, 2000), 210. See also Martin Heidegger and Heinrich Rickert, *Briefe 1912 bis 1933 und andere Dokumente* (Frankfurt am Main: Kloster-mann, 2002).

103. Eugenio Garin, "Ritratto di Marsilio Ficino," *Belfagor* 6 (1951): 289–301.

a number of humanists including Pomponio Leto and Bartolomeo Platina, whereas the only scholar who tried to defend the Jews, the papal commissioner Battista de' Giudici, Bishop of Ventimiglia, was a theologian with a Thomist background who was not devoid of humanist learning, but who wrote against Bruni and against Platina" (*STRL*, 2:73–74). In this passage Kristeller is perhaps his least professorial but his most trenchant: his original decision to side with Rickert against any form of intellectual relativism, be it Nietzscheanism or humanism, would of course seem justified in view of later historical events.

The two scholars saved their most profound, most civil confrontation for a private exchange of letters. This took place in 1953 and was occasioned by a comment Garin made in print regarding what he had perceived as his colleague's wish to deny any philosophical significance to the Renaissance.[104] Seeking to settle matters between them, Kristeller wrote:

> When you conclude from my assertions that Italian humanists were not philosophers (and I think of Poggio, Guarini, Pius II, and Filelfo, etc., but not of Ficino and Pico) and that I reject any philosophical significance of the Renaissance, you are not doing anything else but identifying humanism with the Renaissance—that is, you attribute to me a use of words that you actually follow in your own volume on humanism, and this is one of the few points on which I do not agree with you.[105]

Kristeller perhaps believed that Garin's justification of humanism qua philosophy was aimed at providing, once again, a unitary qualification of the Renaissance, for an epoch's Weltanschauung is determined by its leading philosophy. But Garin saw things quite differently:

> I am sorry if I've expressed myself equivocally in what I stated. At the first opportunity—if it occurs—I will attempt to better clarify my point of view and the reasons for my dissent, which, it seems, reside less in a historical view than in a conception of philosophy that is itself closely related to historical interpretation. In my view, it is pre-

104. For Garin's comment, see "Rassegna bibliografica: Il Rinascimento," *Giornale critico della filosofia italiana* 31 (1952): 97–105.

105. Kristeller to Garin, 21 September 1953. Cited in Rubini, "The Last Italian Philosopher: Eugenio Garin (with an Appendix of Documents)," *Intellectual History Review* 21, no. 2 (2011): 229.

cisely the new logical, linguistic, methodological, and moral-political investigations that constitute "philosophy." "Humanism" is surely to be reconnected to the "studia humanitatis," whose speculative foundations it rediscovers, but this does not limit, as you would have it, the vital nature of those positions that culminate in Vico. "Morality" does not turn into a subset of philosophy to be placed next to others, but bears the mark of a new philosophy, which is to be placed next to science in the liquidation of "theology." Nobody wants to deny that the old and ancient structures survive in Ficino, Pico, and Bruno, but their importance—whether they realized it or not—was not in this. . . . [Y]our very own distinctions plainly point not so much to the coexistence of "moral" and "speculative philosophy," but to different ways and conceptions of philosophizing. It doesn't seem of great importance, therefore, what their representatives wanted to call each other or what position they had in the university. I am not convinced that the history of thought coincides with the history of university faculties. And I cannot forget to mention the limit case represented by Vico, who is for me a supreme philosopher [*filosofo sommo*], yet a professor of rhetoric, of the "humanities," who repeatedly failed in academic contests. Or even the case of Croce.[106]

Garin seems to be saying that Kristeller's own scholarship implies that Renaissance philosophy and, more to the point, Renaissance philosophers are usefully defined in confrontation with their humanist counterparts—self-avowed representatives of a *different philosophy*. Therefore, is not 'humanism' essentially a philosophical problem? Furthermore, if only one subject of the *studia humanitatis* (i.e., moral philosophy) is nominally concerned with philosophy, does this not point to a particular emphasis on the part of humanists rather than to their philosophical irrelevance? Finally, why should the fact that Renaissance thinkers sustained older views inhibit us from emphasizing what was actually 'original' to them? These questions went largely unanswered in Kristeller's corpus, and this because, as we now know, they were not allowed in the Neo-Kantian framework that had inspired him.

At the same time, Garin's mention of Vico and Croce as "limit cases" of the humanism problem allows us to unfold a conversation that never

---

106. Garin to Kristeller, 25 September 1953. Cited in Rubini, "Last Italian Philosopher," 229.

took place.[107] Indeed, an understanding of Vico, or rather Italian Vichianism, something that Garin cultivated to perfection, is fundamental to
grasping the two scholars' divergences, as Kristeller intuited when he accused his colleague of identifying humanism with the Renaissance, and
as Cantimori almost nailed when he argued for Kristeller's, not the Italians', reliance on this epochal periodization. Unable to discern Kristeller's
Neo-Kantianism, Cantimori failed to grasp that Kristeller was out to sub-
tract Ficino from the intellectually bleak historical context represented
by Quattrocento 'humanism,' a 'humanism' that Kristeller, by seeing it
as a uniquely Renaissance phenomenon, refused to 'interpret.' However,
what Cantimori says of Saitta is all the more true of Garin: his 'humanism' might originate in the Italian Renaissance, but its qualification as
philosophy (just as in Kristeller's understanding of 'philosophy') grants it a
transhistorical contextualization. The problem is that while Platonism is
by definition perennis philosophia, humanism's immortality remains to
be proven. Could it be that Vico, Croce, and, with them, the Italian philosophical tradition are evidence of such endurance?

Because it included the British Enlightenment, Garin's framework was
more cosmopolitan than that of the idealists, yet it was his emphasis on
the unquestionably 'neohumanist' turn embodied by the philosophy of
Vico (himself an idiosyncratic representative of the Italian Enlightenment)
that allowed him to account for humanism not just as an alternative *philosophy* recurring in distinct times and places, but—and the difference
is all-important—as a more or less continuous philosophical *tradition*,
at least in Italy. That Garin's Renaissance scholarship was defined from
the outset by a latent Vichianism can be seen in his first monograph from
1937, where he was already qualifying Pico's "truer humanism" as "transcending the literary world and extending, in Vichian fashion [*vichiana-
mente*] to all the fields pertaining to human action" (*GP*, 5 and 223). Garin
first approached Vico systematically in the *History of Philosophy* that was
commissioned from him by Vallecchi in 1943, and here he depicted Vico
as reacting against the literary (rather than spiritual) understanding of
humanism in the Baroque period—an era, Garin lamented, in which the
purely aesthetical ideals of, say, an Ermolao Barbaro took over from the
genuinely philosophical ones of a Pico. He saw Vico, on the contrary, as

107. It is significant that, in his reply, Kristeller would remain silent on Croce while
"granting" Vico a great degree of "originality"—by which he means, we know now, that Vico
lacked philosophical merit.

trying to reconnect with the best Renaissance conclusions, renewing the humanist ideal of the "dignity of man" as he set out to confront the new Cartesian culture, "which was itself totally permeated with the essential values of mathematical knowledge."[108]

Garin's Vichianism grew more sophisticated, beginning with his treatment of the philosopher in his 1947 *History of Italian Philosophy*.[109] As with his Renaissance scholarship, Garin's ambition, at this point, was to reconfirm the idealist insights regarding Vico without resorting to an actualist (Gentile) or generally idealist/historicist (Croce) approach, that is, by relying exclusively on a close reading of sources. This was a difficult task, for if the Vico celebrated by Gentile and Croce was already an (Italian) heir of the (Italian) Renaissance, he was so according to the idealist view of the Renaissance, which meant the Cinquecento: an epoch of isolated heroes, martyrs in the flesh, and, spiritually, the unheeded progenitors of German philosophy, both the idealist and the historicist camps.[110] Instead, as Garin eventually specified, Vico had realized what Italian (Quattrocento) humanism could amount to philosophically, and by 'humanism' Garin meant what *he*, together with a generation of (co)existentialists, had come to understand by that term: at bottom a moral kind of *inquiry* to be practiced and advanced among men for the sake of men (and not for the sake of ahistorical and disembodied truths).

In his attempt to readapt Vico, too, to the, 'civic,' 'positive,' 'constructive,' or 'coexistential' frame of mind of the interwar generation, Garin therefore began extracting Vico from the legendary isolation into which he had been forced since the Risorgimento; he expounded on the Neapolitan culture of Vico's time, insisting that it was by no means provincial but rather a crossroads for Europe's great intellectual trends. As important (and contested) as his achievements were in promoting a contextual reading of Vico and his environs, Garin's greatest merit was to emphasize the Vichianism and thus the enduring humanism that lay at the heart of the Italian philosophical tradition of the nineteenth and early twentieth cen-

108. Eugenio Garin, *Storia della filosofia* (1945; Rome: Edizioni di Storia e Letteratura, 2011), 401–3.

109. For this assessment, see Enrico Nuzzo's vast review, published in two parts, of Garin's Vico studies, "Gli studi vichiani di Eugenio Garin," in *Bollettino del Centro di Studi Vichiani* 38, no. 1 (2008): 9–61; and Enrico Nuzzo, "Gli studi vichiani di Eugenio Garin," in *Bollettino del Centro di Studi Vichiani* 39, no. 1 (2009): 7–68.

110. Gentile's Vico scholarship, which momentously and enduringly linked the Italian philosopher to his Renaissance forefathers, is collected in *Studi Vichiani*, ed. Vito A. Bellezza (Florence: Sansoni, 1968). On the topic, see Pietro Piovani, "Il Vico di Gentile," *La cultura* 14 (1976): 214–54.

turies. In his view, Italian modern culture, from Cuoco to Spaventa and Croce, but also Gentile, was distinctively 'humanistic' owing to its civic and historicist bent. Relying on Vico as both a subject and a practitioner of Italian humanist inquiry, Garin was able to achieve an 'internalist' perspective not just on Italian philosophy but on what, in his assessment, may have been the most discernibly continuous, or unbroken, humanist tradition in the West.

What we might call the metahistorical significance that Vico, as an ideal type, held for Garin is best illustrated by his appearance in *Philosophy as Historical Knowledge*, the book in which, as we have seen in the conclusion to the previous chapter, Garin collected his theoretical essays. Here he mentions Vico in relation to the question of the "necessities and contingencies that attend the development of philosophy." Garin asks, are the "antecedents" of a given philosopher to be recovered uniquely within philosophy, or are extraphilosophical concerns—such as the juridical, philological, and historical concerns that interested Vico—also relevant? Furthermore, are the connections we seek to promote between a philosopher and his past always intrinsic to the subject studied, or are they instead motivated by our own concerns? To be sure, says Garin, these questions themselves are mostly about us and our own time.

For example, when we try to understand the influence of Galileo on Vico's formation, we do so, no doubt, because in our day and age we feel "the pressing urgency to confront the relationship between moral and natural sciences." And yet the necessary presentism of our historical questions does not reaffirm the "relativity of history"; rather it "acknowledges how man actually goes about construing the understanding he has of himself, which, according to the very nature of human consciousness, cannot but be in perennial development." For this reason,

all of Vichianism belongs to Vico's history, and a mature historiographical consciousness will not return to Vico empty-handed; rather, it will present the history of Vichian interpretations and will seize on its motivations and meaning: it will place Vico in this wider horizon which helps in comprehending how things were reprised and rethought. But just as the historian will for this reason more clearly grasp the genesis of such retrievals, he will more clearly grasp, beyond any programmatic deformation, the very question to which Vico paid heed, the range of his experiences, the value of his answers. Vico, that is, will recover his proper dimensions, his genesis, his life after death—beyond the romantic myths that turn him into a misunderstood precursor—in a participatory detachment [*distacco partecipe*], in a shared memory [*memoria consaputa*], in the "past recaptured" [*tempo ritrovato*], in the problems solved [*nessi chiariti*].[111]

The philosophical tradition, which Kristeller, following Rickert, posited as always already existing in a "common fund of basic postulates" beyond the contingencies of human life and history, is instead, in Garin's view, produced laboriously by man in his attempt to bring about an (oxymoronic more than anachronistic) encounter of past and present or, in the lexicon of Gadamerian hermeneutics, a 'fusion of horizons.' The footnote that Garin adds to the passage cited above, to Droysen's *Historik*, more closely substantiates the relevance of Garin's statement to his quarrel with Kristeller: "It is the right of the historical consideration to grasp facts in light of the significance they acquired by means of their consequences."

The idea that "effects" or "consequences" (*Folgewirkungen*) are legitimate materials of historiographical research was not the only one of Droysen's ideas that Garin elaborated through Vico. Equally important was Droysen's thematization of the "historische Frage," the historical question that motivates the scholar-philosopher's research and determines his orientation in the midst of historical records. Any research is always antedated by a question; any research is the attempt to answer such a question. There is, finally, no history without a question, asked in the present, for present or future purposes. This is what makes any historical investigation, any reading of 'any book,' as Droysen (and Croce and Garin) but not Rickert (and Kristeller) would put it, an 'interpretation.' Finally, Garin took from Droysen the idea that history is a "werdende Summe," an integrative accretion rather than a subsumption. Droysen's notion, dear to the German hermeneutical tradition, was explicated by Gadamer in *Truth and Method*:

> [Droysen's] basic viewpoint is that continuity is the essence of history, because history, unlike nature, includes the element of time. Droysen constantly quotes Aristotle's statement about the soul—that it increases within itself (epidosis eis hauto). Unlike the mere repetitiveness of nature, history is characterized by this increase within itself.

111. Eugenio Garin, *La filosofia come sapere storico: Con un saggio autobiografico* (Rome: Laterza, 1990), 73.

But this involves preservation and at the same time surpassing what is preserved. Self-knowledge embraces both. Thus history is not only an object of knowledge; self-knowledge determines its being.[112]

The dialectic of knowledge and self-knowledge within a theory of history seen as an integrative movement of the past in the present can perhaps shed some light on what Garin meant when he, elaborating on Gentile, stated that philology (i.e., humanism) is "already a philosophizing" when reading contributes to *Bildung*—the process of self-formation.

The affinity between Italian humanists and German historicists, from Droysen to Dilthey, continued: between Croce and Friedrich Meinecke, for example, who had wanted to begin his history of the rise of historicism (*Die Entstehung des Historismus*; 1936) with Vico. Yet Croce lamented that Meinecke did not go far enough, did not realize that true "precursors are only those who, within immature or adverse contexts, anticipate the thought and action that in their extension will form an epoch. . . . In this rigorous sense, in the eighteenth century historicism has but one true precursor, Giambattista Vico, whom Meinecke . . . treats accurately and diligently in a paragraph, but to whom he does not assign the lone position, the role of solitary that he deserves."[113] "Humanism" and "historicism," ventured Croce in the same context—his influential *History as Thought and Action* (1938)—are in fact mutually enlightening terms, as "historicism is the true humanism, that is, the truth of humanism," for "[i]n effect, the universal principle of humanism—that which in antiquity found its main representative in Cicero, as well as the new humanism that blossomed in Italy between the fourteenth and sixteenth centuries, or even those derived or artificially attempted thereafter—consists in a return to the past in order to find inspiration for one's own work and action."[114] Croce's statements illustrate Garin's predicament in having to simultaneously agree and disagree with his Italian predecessors. Humanism should indeed, even for Garin, be presented as a return to the past for the sake of the present, but in the process of affirming this, we should neither turn historicism into a philosophical fulfillment of Italian Renaissance humanism, nor turn Vico into an unheeded precursor.

---

112. Hans-Georg Gadamer, *Truth and Method*, ed. Joel Weinsheimer and Donald G. Marshall (London-New York: Continuum, 2006), 206.

113. Benedetto Croce, *La storia come pensiero e come azione* (Naples: Bibliopolis, 2002), 66.

114. Croce, *La storia come pensiero*, 308.

In seeking to present his 'absolute historicism' as the ultimate humanism, Croce rearticulates the vicious circle into which Gentile fell when
he sought to make his 'actualism' the true philosophical version of Renaissance humanism. Their ambitions rely on a recapitulation, on the idea
that humanism per se was no philosophy but was only turned into one in
a German detour before being perfected, once and for all, in Italy. As the
last self-conscious historian of Italian philosophy, Garin realized that the
problem, the Achilles heel of Italian thought, lay in the difficulty, the impossibility, even, of demonstrating that German idealists and hermeneu-
tists were engaged in a conversation with Renaissance humanists, or that
the German historical school had formed itself with Vico's *New Science*
as a textbook. What could not be demonstrated regarding the Germans,
however, can be demonstrated regarding the Italians, and this is why modern Italian philosophy, in the last analysis, is neither an actualism nor a
historicism, but simply a humanism. In turn, this means not that Vico
or the humanists are the precursors of something but rather that Croce
and Gentile are the heirs to a past they constantly revisited. The adhe-
sive chauvinism of nationalism, which seeks for an immovable identity,
was traded in by Garin for the affirmation of *con-geniality*, itself a never-
ending practice.

It is not that Garin rejected an association of humanism with historicism, even his own brand. To the contrary, he welcomed the comment
made by Peter Munz, the translator of his *Italian Humanism* in English,
that placed him directly in the line of the historicist school that stretched
from Dilthey to Croce (see *UI*, 3). Dilthey, in fact, had been a major source
of inspiration for the young Garin; on the advice of his teacher Limentani
he had read *Weltanschauung und Analyse des Menschen seit Renaissance
und Reformation* (1914) alongside Cassirer's *The Individual and the Cosmos*.[115] In his recollections and theoretical works, furthermore, Garin repeatedly mentions that Dilthey's long essay *Das Wesen der Philosophie*
(1907) made a lasting impression on him.[116] This work had opened his eyes
to the "plurality of philosophies" and to the difficulty yet necessity of
holding these various strands in "conversation"; it had taught him never to
"privilege monologue over dialogue" ("for who chooses just one, precludes
for himself historical research"), to eschew the "insinuation of extrinsic

115. Wilhelm Dilthey, *Weltanschauung und Analyse des Menschen seit Renaissance und
Reformation*, vol. 2 of *Gesammelte Schriften* (Leipzig: Teubner, 1914).
116. See now Wilhelm Dilthey, *Das Wesen der Philosophie*, ed. Otto Pöggeler (Hamburg:
Meiner, 1984).

value discriminations in temporal dimensions," and, finally, never to forget that "knowledge is always relative to a particular epoch and to a given cultural climate."[117] Garin and Dilthey agreed in wanting to treat philosophy *sub specie historica*. And it is their 'agreement' that we should emphasize, for Garin did not read Dilthey back into humanism; rather, Garin recovered in German historicism much of what he had independently discovered in his study of the Italian Renaissance.

These considerations, prompted by the 1953 exchange between Garin and Kristeller, allow us to focus on the relevance of their quarrel beyond the realm of Renaissance scholarship. In other words, how was it relevant to the "crisis consciousness" that informed Italian and German thinking alike in the transition between the nineteenth and twentieth centuries, a period that enabled, at a distance, the advent of the postmodern moment?[118] Their disagreement, Garin rightly perceived, could be attributed to early philosophical choices that necessarily oriented their historiographical work toward a shared corpus of writings. Specifically, they brought to their scholarship the controversy over method (*Methodenstreit*) regarding *Historismus* or *storicismo*. In following Dilthey, Garin came to admit the 'plurality' of histories and philosophies that he deemed crucial for a rehabilitation of 'humanism' and with it the entire Italian philosophical tradition. Kristeller, following Rickert, was primarily concerned with remedying the relativization of 'philosophy,' a discipline of universal appeal, certainly, but a domain in which Germans took pride of place.

This disagreement notwithstanding, the genuine philosophical value of Garin's and Kristeller's Renaissance scholarship is affirmed when we realize that in the postwar era they both held tight to the same traditions— traditions that, as they rightly predicted and feared, the mainstream would want to jettison, in thrall instead to superficial and historically dubious amalgamations. And so, ultimately, their scholarship, although it has been superseded in matters of detail, remains unmatched in its general and inspirational appeal. It provided Renaissance studies with the wherewithal to mature into a healthy and robust discipline untrammeled by extrinsic concerns. Perhaps some of the tools they employed to achieve such a secure status were beyond the Renaissance scholar's theoretical acumen or

117. Garin, *La filosofia come sapere storico*, 31ff.
118. Charles R. Bambach, *Heidegger, Dilthey, and the Crisis of Historicism* (Ithaca, NY: Cornell University, 1995), 3.

competence, but what remains to be seen—at a time when we are probing interwar and postwar legacies, both scholarly and philosophical, for suggestions of a new beginning—is whether the Renaissance problem as it was redefined by the likes of Grassi, Garin, and Kristeller, among a few others, can assist an intellectual reorientation.

Humanism before Cartesianism
(despite Heidegger)

[In the Renaissance] one advances in the way that young people do, without knowing precisely what is left behind and what is sought for, without knowing what the path really is. One is carried by a life instinct that will come to full awareness of the new and to a negation of the old at a later time. This is why all the thinkers of this age have two faces; they present us with contradictions that seem to displace the very principles of their philosophies. Those who look at only one of these two faces will no longer see the other. Some go so far as to make them the harbingers of modern thought, others push them back into medieval Scholasticism; meanwhile they owe their historical significance to the position they occupy between a philosophy that they only barely overcome and a philosophy that they only barely establish.
—Giovanni Gentile

In this study, I have sought to describe the emergence and development of a philosophical tradition whose peculiar outlook was formed in confrontation with the elusive beginnings of modernity. There is no denying that in Italy, over the course of more than a century, the 'Renaissance' was ideologized, pigeonholed, falsified, censured, misrepresented, and generally manipulated. At the same time, however, the 'humanism' of this epoch—to the extent that it was continuously tested by new intellectual exigencies—gained stature and dignity by remaining relevant. Nineteenth- and twentieth-century Italian thinkers came to see their epoch(s) as a historical recurrence of the fifteenth and sixteenth centuries, a view that we can attribute to remarkably comparable political circumstances, institutional conflicts, and intellectual aspirations, and to the shared Vichian framework that informed the intergenerational discussion of Italian philosophy. They saw the Renaissance as a foundational enterprise that was unfulfilled, and the present as offering a second chance to partake of it. To them, the repetition denoted that the Renaissance experiment was an essentially ungratifying one, and thus the defining challenge, one that was often unmet (especially by Gentile, despite what he sometimes intended), was to resist the temptation to concretize its transient suggestions.

The protagonists of the story told in this book stood outside the twentieth-century mainstream in their insistence that the fate of humankind depended on a reappraisal rather than a rejection of our modern origins. Consequently they subjected the Renaissance to analeptic revisions in light of new discoveries and concerns, while, proleptically, they saw in the epoch an anticipation of every new 'modernity' that followed in its trail, including that which in a supreme and final act of philosophical hubris the mainstream has come to call 'postmodernity.' Therefore, the 'Renaissance' that developed in Italy was both immanent and inescapable. It is interesting, given this context, that what Italians brought to the *philosophical* conversation in the mid-twentieth century was a historiographical account of Quattrocento anti-Scholasticism. Moreover, it might seem as though the concerns of the immediate postwar period, by overlapping at least nominally with 'humanism,' indicated that the time was ripe for a fruitful convergence of Italian peninsular and European continental thought. As we have seen, it was a series of contingencies, not irreparable divergences, that assured their inassimilability.

In the aftermath of the postmodern moment we have an opportunity for a new reckoning, and the notion of a fruitful convergence may hold appeal. As we now attempt to reconcile with the Western philosophical legacy (for what else is left for us to do?), we have the chance to relish, with less panic and less prejudice than in times gone by, the plurality of distinct but overlapping traditions that constitute that legacy. In the process, we have the chance to explore the possibility that we have been, for a while now, humanists (not antihumanists) of a primordially modern (not unmodern) ilk—in short, that we have been Renaissance men mediating another historical and intellectual transition. Perhaps what the Italians offered was not theoretically exciting; historiographically, however, it stood on grounds so solid that a call for a revolutionary new beginning would seem shrill by comparison. The prerogative of the philosopher—in contrast to the humanist—is to work via *ex nihilo* commencements, rather than *ab ovo* regenerations. Descartes, as we know, introduced his philosophy as a 'revolution.' As such, it was self-consciously a more abrupt rebirth than what is implied by concepts like 'renaissance' and 'reformation'—

the same (philosophical) concepts upon which nations such as Germany and Italy would be built. The fact that 'revolution' was not a universally appealing notion, politically or philosophically, became apparent as the nationalization of philosophies reached its peak. This is something that Germany and Italy, as political latecomers, bear witness to.

Indeed, revolution's lack of appeal is strikingly evident in the Italian tradition, where the recognition that there was no escaping the imprint of its past intellectual precocity, its 'Renaissance,' or more accurately, its Renaissance humanism, was triggered by the realization that neither the French Revolution, nor the long rationalist tradition that appeared to have sustained it, fit the Italian experience of modernity. As Italy began to take an alternative route, refounding itself on a second renaissance, the Risorgimento, it rediscovered itself as Vichian, that is, anti-Cartesian, before it came to accept itself, after a belabored introspection, as properly humanistic. Throughout this process Italy desperately sought an intellectual alliance with Germany. But it seems that neither Hegel nor Heidegger was as accommodating as Italians thought or hoped he might be. In hindsight, of course, Hegel could be Vichianized, but just as Italians were finally recovering from their stifling and self-defining antihumanism, Heidegger, a notable source of inspiration for such an emancipation, called for another 'revolution.' This one would be exposed in the Italian (as opposed to the French) experience of it as being profoundly Cartesian in its blithe dismissal of past achievements.

Italian thought, from Vico to Grassi and Garin, alerts us with distinctive clarity, then, to the fact that the outer boundaries of 'modern' philosophy, with Descartes at one end and Heidegger at the other, were marked by a strikingly similar antihumanistic resolve. This fact alone should have made the Renaissance a focus of postwar philosophical debate and refashioning. Instead, we have yet to see a sustained philosophical (or theoretical) engagement with Renaissance humanism, even now as we reckon with an apparently concluded cycle. And at this point we may ask ourselves again, why did Heidegger's 'provocation,' for this is what we are now ready to see it as, have such a strong appeal, strong enough to outmatch Western thought, taken as an undifferentiated mass? This time, rather than turn to French theory, we may turn to Heidegger himself for an answer. We may recall here the words with which Heidegger introduced a course on Plato, when he was still the "hidden king," an unequaled pedagogue in the eyes of his students, a philologist (albeit self-styled), and thus more of a humanist: "To appropriate a past means to come to know oneself as indebted to that past. The authentic possibility to *be* history itself resides in this, that philosophy discover it is guilty of an omission, a neglect, if it believes it can begin anew, making things easy for itself, and let itself be stirred by just any random philosopher."[1] This statement clarifies the enduring relevance of a humanist critique of 'philosophers' and their foreshortened 'histories.' Is it possible that in preferring 'revolutions' over 'rebirths' and 'reformations,' philosophers and historians of philosophy have been looking for a shortcut?

Heidegger's statement interests us not only because (with his "Letter") he would come to represent the last "random philosopher" to sweep us off our feet. It also interests us in light of the fact that, just as this second (post-*Kehre*) Heidegger exhausted his momentum, some corners of philosophy would, for lack of serviceable paradigms, rejuvenate themselves at the fount of the younger Heidegger. In fact, in recent times, the piecemeal publication of Heidegger's *Gesamtausgabe* (comprising unpublished lectures) has brought us closer to the experience of his students, and like them we have been inspired to look at the Western philosophical tradition with new eyes.[2] This trend is most visible in current Plato studies, in which the early Heidegger is employed to defend the Greek philosopher from the later Heidegger's attacks. In the process, the provisional nature of the dialogues is being rediscovered as a constitutive feature of Platonic philosophy, and Plato himself as having been "metaphysical in his own way: in a manner different from either Aristotle or Plotinus."[3]

We cannot help but notice that this new current in Plato studies, the so-called "dialogical approach," was prefigured in the early work of Gadamer and Grassi, who, although they still believed they were furthering Heidegger's intention, felt as we do now that Greek ontology was not "committed 'to a naïve and unproblematized identification of Being with presence."[4] Given that Heidegger later allowed his anti-Platonism to

1. Martin Heidegger, *Plato's* Sophist, trans. Richard Rojcewicz and André Schuwer (Bloomington: Indiana University Press, 1997), 7.

2. The publication of Heidegger's complete works began in 1975 with *Die Grundprobleme der Phänomenologie*. As reported by the editors (http://www.klostermann.de), the complete collection will include 102 volumes edited according to Heidegger's wishes (established together with F.-W. von Herrmann): that is, his lectures will be published in the order in which Heidegger wanted to make them available and without critical apparatus. Translations in other languages are based on and depend on the output of the Klostermann editions. About one third of the expected volumes are still to be published.

3. Franco Trabattoni, *Scrivere nell'anima: Verità, dialettica e persuasione in Platone* (Florence: Nuova Italia, 1994), 9.

4. Francisco J. Gonzalez, "Confronting Heidegger on Logos and Being in Plato's *Soph-ist*," in *Platon und Aristoteles, sub ratione veritatis: Festschrift für Wolfgang Wieland zum*

collapse into antihumanism, it is striking to us now that Gadamer and Grassi could, coherently and intuitively, and even preempting Heidegger in Grassi's case, reinterpret humanism on the basis of their newly rediscovered (Heideggerian) Plato.

Just how fundamental the problem of Plato was to the study of Renaissance humanism may be seen by turning to the moment of its most forceful reemergence, that is, in the late careers of Grassi and Kristeller, at a time when Renaissance studies had ostensibly been long out of touch with its interwar philosophical origins. Because Grassi and Kristeller reached dramatically opposite conclusions (far more irreconcilable than those reached by Garin and Kristeller) from similar, albeit sequentially inverted, intellectual backgrounds between Germany and Italy, their confrontation in Renaissance scholarship is an important, yet heretofore missed, opportunity: a central episode in the quarrel of rhetoric and philosophy in the latter part of the twentieth century.

While Kristeller never mentioned in print the work of his Italian colleague (although he kept up a slender correspondence with him), Grassi, who always sought to confront possible interlocutors directly, repeatedly refers to Kristeller in his late works. For example, in the first chapter of *Renaissance Humanism* (1988), Grassi surveyed for one last time the history of the "negative attitude towards the traditions of Humanism," looking at Descartes, Hegel, E. R. Curtius, Ernst Cassirer, and, last on his list, Kristeller, Werner Jaeger, and Heidegger.[5] By citing these last three names in this order, Grassi identified Kristeller as his contemporary and pointed to their common background in Germany prior to World War II, a moment when philology divided into opposing, Jaegerian and Nietzchean/Heideggerian, camps (as we are in a position to appreciate now, thanks also to Grassi's direct involvement). Upon landing in the United States and in the process of refashioning "humanism as philosophical tradition," as the subtitle of his 1946 book phrased it, into a simpler, though reductive, "rhetoric as philosophy," as his most famous work is titled, and more than half a

---

70. *Geburtstag*, ed. G. Damschen, R. Enskat, and A. G. Vigo (Göttingen: Vandenhoeck & Ruprecht, 2003), 126. See also Francisco J. Gonzalez, ed., *The Third Way: New Directions in Platonic Studies* (Lanham, MD: Rowman & Littlefield, 1995); Francisco J. Gonzalez, *Dialectic and Dialogue: Plato's Practice of Philosophical Inquiry* (Evanston, IL: Northwestern University Press, 1998); Francisco J. Gonzalez, *Plato and Heidegger: A Question of Dialogue* (University Park: Pennsylvania State University Press, 2009).

5. Ernesto Grassi, *Renaissance Humanism: Studies in Philosophy and Poetics*, trans. W. F. Veit (Binghamton, NY: Center for Medieval and Early Renaissance Studies, 1988), 2–5.

century after the publication of his first Platonic writings, Grassi felt compelled to make an important and final clarification as to what he meant by 'humanism.'[6]

Working under the impression that humanist philosophy had, through Kristeller, become identified with Marsilio Ficino's Platonism, Grassi emphasizes that the true philosophical novelty of the period was represented by that tradition which, through the preeminence of poetic and metaphoric language, allowed for existential access to Being:

> The Platonic Humanist tradition distances itself radically from these problems. It proceeds from the problem of the rational definition of being, in accord with which knowledge endeavors to attain "surety" or "certainty" by anchoring these in abstractions, as universals, in the non-historical. Everything which is revealed through the senses appears as a reflection of "ideas," of the rational concepts which constitute the eternal cause of the appearance. The meaning of words is located in the logical transcendence of what the senses reveal; so man is raised through this rational process to a vision of the eternal, to being by and for itself. Philosophical Platonism . . . will scarcely add anything new from a philosophical standpoint to this traditional schema of metaphysical thought.[7]

At the end of his career, and in direct confrontation with Kristeller, Grassi thus specifically defines his sources as the "non-Platonic" tradition of humanism, that is, the humanism that develops in the humanist dialectic of, say, Nizolius, and onward perennially in Vico and beyond, rather than being fulfilled in late Quattrocento Platonism.[8] This kind of humanism—

6. I am referring to two works often cited in the course of this study: *Verteidigung des individuellen Lebens: Studia humanitatis als philosophische Überlieferung* and *Rhetoric as Philosophy: The Humanist Tradition*.

7. Grassi, *Renaissance Humanism*, 115.

8. Grassi, *Heidegger and the Question of Renaissance Humanism: Four Studies* (Binghamton, NY: Center for Medieval and Early Renaissance Studies, 1983), 9: "The term 'Humanism' has such a broad meaning today that we have forgotten its precise historical sense. By Humanism I mean that philosophical movement which characterized thought in Italy from the second half of the fourteenth century to the final third of the fifteenth century. In my view, Ficino's translation of Plato at the end of the fifteenth century and the speculative metaphysical Platonism and Neo-Platonism which it triggered led to a break with the Humanist approach to philosophy, which was taken up later only by isolated thinkers such as Nizolius or, outside Italy, by Vives and later by Gracian in his theory of Ingenium. Finally, the Humanist controversy reached its height in the thought of Giambattista Vico, whose work provides an outline of the whole range of Humanism's implications. Hence, the Humanist

the kind whose origins he sought in the works of Bruni, Bruno, and Vico in his early career and in Coluccio Salutati, Cristoforo Landino, Giovanni Pontano, and others in the 1980s—embodies the neglected "inversion" of the "schemata of traditional metaphysics," which Kristeller, indebted to a Neo-Kantian tradition that in some quarters identified Plato with Kant and with idealism altogether, would necessarily disregard.⁹

In *Heidegger and the Question of Renaissance Humanism*, Grassi's most sustained attempt to argue against his teacher's antihumanism, Kristeller already played a prominent role. In fact, here Grassi went as far as to attribute Heidegger's misunderstanding of humanism, setting aside Burckhardt's notion of a Renaissance "individualism" and Cassirer's epistemological concerns, to Kristeller's traditional Platonism.¹⁰ And so what has recently been said of Gadamer's Platonic rhetoric is certainly true of Grassi's interpretation as well. In their readings, "Plato becomes strange to all ersatz Platonists, and the great body of the dialogues become the gravitational center of a humanist rhetoric."¹¹ By recovering in Grassi another precedent for the idea that humanism or "rhetoric as philosophy" may represent a continuous tradition, beginning with Socratic discursive contingency, we come a little closer to a rhetoric that is no longer, in the best of cases, *altera philosophia*, but *philosophia perennis* in its own right. The outcome of this reorganization, and humanism's role in it, depends on *how* we read our Plato.

Though a traditional reading of Plato and his legacy certainly did inform Kristeller's assessment of 'humanism as rhetoric' (and, thus, from his perspective, as nonphilosophy), it should be acknowledged that Grassi's evaluation of his colleague was unfair in two ways. First, if Heidegger's stance toward humanism could be attributed to a single individual, it was Grassi himself who, having drawn his teacher into a humanistic reprisal of traditional philosophy and philology in the interwar period, may be said to

---

tradition should not be discussed as a purely literary question. We must approach Humanism also from the standpoint of its philosophical significance and importance today. Otherwise, Humanist research can have no fundamental interest for us."

9. For the Neo-Kantian approach to Plato, see Paul Natorp, *Platos Ideen-Lehre: Eine Einführung in den Idealismus* (Hamburg: Felix Meiner, 2004). See also Karl-Heinz Lembeck, *Platon in Marburg: Platonrezeption und Philosophiegeschichtsphilosophie bei Cohen und Natorp* (Würzburg: Königshausen and Neumann, 1994); and Manfred Kühn, "Interpreting Kant Correctly: On the Kant of the Neo-Kantians," in *Neo-Kantianism in Contemporary Philosophy* (Bloomington: Indiana University Press, 2010), 113–31.

10. Grassi, *Heidegger and the Question of Renaissance Humanism*, 31.

11. John Arthos, "Gadamer's Rhetorical Imaginary," *Rhetoric Society Quarterly* 38 (2008): 172.

have trained Heidegger for his bout with Sartre. Grassi's obsessive finger-pointing in his late career can, perhaps, be excused as a symptom of psychic suppression. The idea that he, the staunchest defender of philosophical *studia humanitatis*, had possibly played an instrumental role in the rise of an epoch-defining antihumanism might have been too much to bear. Second—and here we can only speculate as to why—Grassi chose to give a skewed account of Kristeller's interpretation of Renaissance thought. For nowhere in *The Philosophy of Marsilio Ficino*, the work on which Grassi bases his criticism, or in numerous related writings, does Kristeller indicate that he equates humanism with Renaissance Platonism.

In his own attempt to recover the Renaissance *ratio platonica* that links Plato to Kant in the tradition of *perennis philosophia*, Kristeller characterizes Platonism not as a better or superior form of philosophy but as "the realization of an old humanistic dream" *transported* into the field of philosophy. The conclusion of one of Kristeller's most sustained studies of rhetoric and philosophy is worth citing: "I am at heart a Platonist, on the issue of rhetoric as on many, though not all, others. Rhetoric in all its forms is based on mere opinion, and therefore it should be subordinated to philosophy, that is, to all forms of valid knowledge where such knowledge is available."[12] The "golden chain" of rational metaphysics that runs from the pre-Socratics to Hegel, via Plato, Plotinus, and Ficino, is a "rock of intellectual and moral support" for Kristeller, who wishes that "this tradition will also give the same support, in the midst of future crises which can hardly be avoided, to some of our successors among the thinkers and scholars of the future."[13] Intellectual freedom, Kristeller states, returning in times of reckoning to the principles of his teacher, Rickert, is not just the right to any opinion whatsoever, but "also a voluntary submission to valid thought."[14]

12. Paul Oskar Kristeller, "Philosophy and Rhetoric from Antiquity to the Renaissance," in *Renaissance Thought and Its Sources*, ed. Michael Mooney (New York: Columbia University Press, 1979), 258.
13. Kristeller, *Marsilio Ficino and His Work after Five Hundred Years* (Florence: L. O. Olschki, 1988), 16.
14. Kristeller, "The Study of the History of Philosophy and Its Problems," in *Filosofia e cultura: Per Eugenio Garin*, ed. Michele Ciliberto and Cesare Vasoli, 2 vols. (Rome: Editori Riuniti, 1991), 1:362–63: "Another widespread tendency that is destructive of the historical method as well as of philosophy is the newly developed cult of rhetoric. . . . Its relation to philosophy varied, and the two disciplines were often rivals. . . . [T]he tendency to reduce the whole history of philosophy to rhetoric and to opinion, must be resisted. We have in philosophy as well as in the sciences and in scholarship a core of valid knowledge that is beyond mere opinion. Although we may not endorse all of Plato's critique of rhetoric, we must

If these considerations are useful for sketching the outer extremes within which the innumerable humanisms of the Renaissance scholars are contained (and they are no less numerous than philosophical humanisms), then it is likewise useful to examine the cultural backgrounds of different philosophical traditions in order to understand the fervor or, rather, the militancy with which these interpretations were maintained. And so we come to appreciate that a shared philosophy may run different courses even in neighboring countries—countries, moreover, that were politically allied toward that common disaster which lent the question of 'humanism' its urgency. While Grassi, an Italian, could recover in Nietzsche's rupture with Hegelianism an antidote to Gentilean idealism (it also seems that Grassi consciously played the part of a Nietzschean figure in Italian philosophy), Kristeller, a German, came to identify that same rupture (Kristeller seldom cites Nietzsche, but, like Rickert, does so disparagingly) as the fons et origo of the relativization of values or "rhetoric" which heralded that same disaster.[15] Once again, is it humanism or phi-

---

maintain with him that there is a clear distinction between opinion and knowledge, and that philosophical as well as scientific and scholarly knowledge have a validity that is different from, and superior to, anything that rhetoric can offer. It makes no sense for a philosopher to play up the Sophists against Plato, or to consider the acceptance of valid truths in philosophy, mathematics or the other disciplines, as a restriction of our intellectual freedom. True intellectual freedom includes not only the right to formulate and express our opinions, but also a voluntary submission to valid thought, not the freedom of ignorance and lying, of wrong reasoning and inconsistency, or even crime. The excesses of rhetoric, unlimited by any factual or rational or moral restraint, have led to the current praise of 'advocacy' and of 'commitment' to causes that are chosen for emotional, selfish or political reasons, not on the basis of careful thinking or observation. We have lately come close to the view that bad means are justified by bad ends."

15. Kristeller, "Study of the History of Philosophy," 357–58: "The Romantics, however, and their later successors, by stressing feeling and intuition as irrational (and infrarational, not suprarational) sources of knowledge, paved the way for an irresponsible kind of irrationalism which basically undermines all serious forms of philosophy and the sciences of history and philology, and especially of ethical, legal and political theory. Modern ethics has been corrupted by a pervasive aestheticism. The great artist may be a genius, but this does not free him from all rules of art and poetry, let alone, from law and morals. The tragic hero may be in conflict with his moral duties or be torn between conflicting duties, and this may have a strong emotional effect on the spectator or listener or reader of a play or a novel, but should not serve as a model for our moral conduct in real life, or as an excuse for our immoral thought or actions. The aestheticism inherent in certain forms of Romantic thought actually subverts our ethical standards which should be maintained in their autonomous validity. To consider the feelings of individual persons or of social groups as moral or legal criteria, as is done by many contemporary philosophers, opens the door to all forms of immoral and illegal conduct, including Nazism. The same is true of Nietzsche's glorification of the will to power and of his reckless critique of the Platonic and Christian traditions which has had an

losophy, Nietzsche or Hegel, Pico or Ficino, that precipitated a disaster of morality? This was an *Existenzfrage*, as inescapable for even the most pre-pared among the interwar generation of scholars and philosophers as it is preposterous for us, who are unable to relive it unless by proxy, and even then only with difficulty, despite the best goodwill.

Perhaps the contemporary Renaissance scholar of humanism, in tan-dem with philosophers who currently seek a "reading of Plato before Pla-tonism (after Heidegger)," could consider the more modest question, would a reading of humanism before Cartesianism (despite Heidegger) be equally productive in the field of Renaissance studies?[16] What this study has shown is that this question should no longer be seen as inapt. Although Heidegger never engaged, at least not overtly, with Renaissance sources, his humanism was certainly informed by the scholarly and philosophi-cal humanisms pursued by some of his students (it can be easy to forget that teacher-student relationships are two-way streets!). Even more to the point, the student of Renaissance humanism can no longer ignore the ef-fects of a protracted 'antihumanism'—notwithstanding its ties to actual historical humanism, faint or nonexistent as they are—on her field. In-deed, the Renaissance scholar bears some responsibility for allowing anti-humanism to run its course unhampered. It is not a matter of needing to give (Renaissance) 'humanism' its due, for this can be carried out in disci-plinary isolation; rather, it is that the postwar schism between philosophy and historiography had the effect of making Renaissance scholarship on humanism a *theoretical* wasteland. This same schism likewise explains why theory and its parent, Continental philosophy, are so historiographi-cally insouciant—although the latter often flaunts a solid historical self-consciousness. What Italian thought helps reveal is that this has been a self-delusion deriving from Continental thought's narrow quarrel with an-

appalling influence on much recent thought and which leads to a complete intellectual and moral anarchy. Immoral and illegal actions of all kinds have been consistently excused and left unpunished because of their alleged psychological or social causes, and valid moral ideas have been absurdly discredited because they are not consistently followed by most people. In ethical discourse, the formulation of valid general principles has been carefully avoided, and everything has been reduced to a kind of casuistry, and it is rather ironical to observe the moral positivists, in their appeals to personal and group feelings, follow unwittingly the worst excesses of Neoromanticism. . . . Much political discourse is based on ad hoc argu-ments related to the particular situation of the moment, without any regard for facts, for logic or even for consistency. Action is praised for its own sake, as opposed to thinking, whereas in fact our responsible actions should be guided and enlightened by valid rational thought."

16. Peter Warnek, "Reading Plato before Platonism (after Heidegger)," *Research in Phe-nomenology* 27, no. 1 (1997): 61–89.

alytic philosophy, a brand of thought in comparison to which everything seems historical.[17]

To illustrate the validity of this critique one need only point to the fact that the radical rethinking of 'philosophy' and its task, as pursued over the past few decades, has left our philosophical canon virtually unaltered. In part, this is because (post)modern antifoundationalism brought with it a distrust for metanarratives, as all philosophical historiography was thought to be, but then the question is even more pressing: how to rewrite the Renaissance, let alone humanism, into a history of philosophy that is no longer being written or, worse, may have been written once and for all? In truth, if collected volumes counting dozens of contributors of varying competencies have any historiographical value, then it may be said that the Renaissance scholar has been actively engaged in writing the intellectual history of the epoch. The problem, then, is whether this newly acquired knowledge, without being part of a larger whole, holds any value outside the confines of the field. It seems obvious that the rediscovery of two hundred years' worth of philosophical activity would necessitate a revisionism—as much because of what followed as for what had passed. In other words, if chronology is still relevant, a new appreciation of Renaissance philosophy or philosophies reopens issues traditionally foreclosed by philosophical historiography; it shows empirically what has up to now only been theorized: that our epistemological models have been built on judgments made by a few "random philosophers."

These considerations point to an urgency for Renaissance scholars to achieve what medievalists, who are one step ahead on this front, call "futural thinking."[18] Bemoaning the refusal of twentieth-century medieval scholars to acknowledge the role of their field in shaping the discourses of modernity, medievalists have began to explore the genealogies of the

17. Different interpretations of Continental philosophy have been offered in recent years. See Simon Critchley and William R. Schroeder, eds., *A Companion to Continental Philosophy* (Malden, MA: Blackwell, 1998), and David West, *Continental Philosophy: An Introduction* (Malden, MA: Polity, 2010). For an attempt to trace Continental philosophy back to pre-Kantian concerns (but not further back than Descartes), see William R. Schroeder, *Continental Philosophy: A Critical Introduction* (Malden, MA: Blackwell, 2005); and for Continental philosophy as practiced today, in a post-poststructuralist era, see John Mullarkey and Beth Lord, eds., *The Continuum Companion to Continental Philosophy* (New York: Continuum, 2009). On the Continental/analytic divide, particularly informative are C. G. Prado ed., *A House Divided: Comparing Analytic and Continental Philosophy* (Amherst, NY: Humanity Books, 2003), and Franca D'Agostini, *Analitici e continentali: Guida alla filosofia degli ultimo trent'anni* (Milan: Raffaello Cortina, 1997).

18. See Andrew Cole and D. Vance Smith, eds., *The Legitimacy of the Middle Ages: On the Unwritten History of Theory* (Durham: Duke University Press, 2010), 16.

postmodern and the modern in search of "'old fault lines,' for such fault lines have everything to do with the intellectual and institutional habits of segregation that continue to define contemporary regimes of periodization and disciplinarity."[19] Capitalizing on the decline of the (post)modernist hegemony, such excavation has led these scholars to recover "traces of the medieval" in the discourses of postwar France and, having found many such traces, to entertain the possibility of making a history of "theoretical medievalism." In short, if medievalists did not always produce theory, the "medieval" did; this realization may be forcing medievalists out of the self-legitimating isolation into which they were driven by the discourse of modernity, whether it was the version offered by Burckhardt, Hans Blumenberg, or even Jean-François Lyotard.

The urge to postulate a future for their studies, and to retrieve the "sense of the future" of their epoch of choice—in sum, a disciplinary self-consciousness—is what scholars of Renaissance humanism and thought seem to lack, compared with their colleagues in medieval and Plato studies. And yet it is undeniable that discourse on modernity—which, at some point, has defined itself at a distance from the Renaissance as much as from the Middle Ages—should have been a concern for Renaissance scholars, too. In the latter's defense, it should be noted that in the postwar period they have at least departed from the radical presentism that had characterized the field since its birth in the nineteenth century. And yet, after this long and fruitful interlude, they can no longer avoid the simple question: Is the study of the Renaissance still relevant to understanding present and future modernities?

It is worth noting here that prior to World War II, the intellectual's relationship to the Renaissance was generally more intimate. And yet while the rapport felt by Italians for *their* Renaissance was, as it were, *familiar*, and thus eminently quarrelsome, outside of Italy the relationship was often exceedingly reverential. The Italian Renaissance that leaped from Burckhardt's head, fully grown and armed, was an expression of awe and gratitude commonly felt, but also, for the same reason, a celebration of values and achievements that Italy, seemingly left nationless by that very same historical period, could not take for granted. We can sense a nineteenth-century Italian restlessness even in Garin's assessment of Burckhardt, whose "humanistic exigencies" to free historiography from metaphysical speculation he saw as leading paradoxically to a "total nega-

---

19. Bruce Holsinger, *The Premodern Condition: Medievalism and the Making of Theory* (Chicago: University of Chicago Press, 2005), x.

tion of human history." Burckhardt's Renaissance was a framed portrait, an ideal utopia, written from an "Archimedean point" from which vantage one could serenely contemplate historical vicissitudes. Meanwhile, actual Renaissance humanism, Garin insisted, "negated any metahistorical immobility" and wished to "condemn without appeal every attempt to escape from the world."[20] In sum, *The Civilization of the Renaissance in Italy* appeared to Garin as the last manifesto written on behalf of the Renaissance man. It amounted to an act of "propaganda" aimed at presenting the Renaissance as a self-fulfilling prophecy.

Behind Garin's scathing assessment, clearly, is the interpretive tradition inaugurated by Spaventa, a tradition that from the outset saw the Renaissance less as a period in history to be represented in Burckhardtian fashion than, in its equation of the Renaissance with its intellectual strands, ultimately with humanism, as an intellectual movement and thus con-genially accessible transhistorically.[21] The interpretation of the Renaissance as an intellectual movement is valuable, as it was noted, for making it possible not only to see some modern scholars, including many discussed in this work, as rightful "latter-day Renaissance humanists" but, and this is implied, to interpret humanism as an enduring tradition.[22] This is not a vantage point afforded by the legacy initiated by Burckhardt, and unfortunately it remained hidden to Burckhardt's interpreters as well. When, in 1948, Wallace K. Ferguson accounted for the Burckhardtian tradition, he did so in the honest belief that by uncovering the "subjective biases" attending the long interpretive tradition of the "so-called Renaissance," one could achieve "a truer conception of the Renaissance itself, the Renaissance as historical actuality."[23] But from our vantage point,

20. Eugenio Garin, "Il 'Rinascimento' del Burckhardt," in Jacob Burckhardt, *La civiltà del Rinascimento in Italia* (Florence: Sansoni, 2000), xiii.

21. This is an interpretation usually attributed to a well-known essay by E. H. Gombrich, but which in fact lies at the heart of the Italian interpretive tradition of the Renaissance. See E. H. Gombrich, "The Renaissance: Period or Movement?," in *Background to the English Renaissance: Introductory Lectures*, ed. A. G. Dickens et al. (London: Gray-Mills, 1974), 9–30. Scholars see the assimilation of the Renaissance problem, the problem of its definition, to the problem of a definition of humanism as having emerged in the postwar period, originating in the work of scholars like Kristeller and Garin. But in fact it can be attributed to these scholars' assimilation of a long-standing perspective in Italian philosophy. See James Hankins, "Renaissance Humanism and Historiography Today," in *Palgrave Advances in Renaissance Historiography*, ed. Jonathan Woolfson (New York: Palgrave Macmillan, 2005), 73.

22. On the value of this interpretive alternative, see Robert Black, "The Renaissance and Humanism: Definitions and Origins," in *Palgrave Advances in Renaissance Historiography*, 98–99.

23. Wallace K. Ferguson, *The Renaissance in Historical Thought: Five Centuries of Interpretation* (Toronto: University of Toronto Press, 2006), 388.

it seems that his book offered palliative rather than curative treatment. In the immediate postwar period, study of the Renaissance was indeed reborn to new life when a generation raised during the interwar period came to focus its attention on the philosophical relevance of Quattrocento humanism. Despite their unprecedented competence in the handling of sources, however, their 'humanism' turned out to be a notion as loaded as 'Renaissance,' and the "conflict" and "confusion" denounced by Ferguson endured.

More than half a century later, the recent 150th anniversary of the publication of Burckhardt's masterpiece has passed, largely, in silence. This may be a sign of the deliverance made possible by an achieved objectivity in the study of Renaissance sources, but also, for the same reason, a signal that detachment might not be our first priority. To the contrary, we may finally be in a position to acknowledge that in honing our professional skills perhaps we have grown dispassionate to a fault. This, at least, is the lesson to be learned from a close review of the motivations and aspirations of the scholar-philosophers on whose shoulders we stand—because of their unprecedented competence, yes, but, make no mistake, principally because of the pathos they brought to bear on the study of the sources they revealed. Their competence, we now realize, coexisted fruitfully with well-defined purposes. Indeed the stories of Baron, Kristeller, Garin—and one might add Grassi and Castelli—show the extent to which Renaissance scholarship can profit from an agenda. Their experience, especially when we consider their youthful associations rather than the sterile squabbles of their mature years, is evidence of the fact that subjective beliefs, particularly when they are shared commonly by a generation, do not always amount to deception or ulterior motives.

We may scrutinize the conclusions of the generation discussed in this work, but it would be bad faith to reproach their ethos. The values that they recovered from, or read into, the Italian Quattrocento amount to an 'interpretive' understanding of historical truth. We may recall here the words with which Kristeller bid farewell to—and simultaneously invoked the blessing of—Cassirer and Gentile at the outset of his American career: "May we too be given an equal capacity to learn!" There was no denying, for Kristeller, that these two giants had infused the Renaissance with present-day concerns, and yet he recognized that this was how they were eventually able to engage the Renaissance man on his own terms. Kristeller's appraisal applies to the generation of thinkers that followed, which includes Kristeller; likewise, his wish applies to them, and it applies to us too. In our own reappraisal, then, we should focus on their deontology, their ability to reform a profession beyond self-serving means. The fact is that they all, despite and beyond their differences, came to read the Renaissance through its humanism, and thus as a praxis to be enacted, as it had been originally (in the Renaissance), for the sake of spiritual edification. They all, furthermore, agreed that their present bore a striking resemblance, intellectually, to the Quattrocento. And finally, they showed—and this is their most enduring lesson—that to interpret the Renaissance one must reown it for the sake of some positive, present, and relevant ideal.

It is sometimes noted with regret that the transformative power and affective elements of the humanists' encounter with the past have been sidestepped in current attempts to achieve a balanced interpretation of the Renaissance.[24] These shortcomings may, perhaps, be imputed, as some are wont to do, to a reliance on Kristeller's restrictive interpretation of humanism as a specific program of studies. But it remains unclear, setting aside Kristeller, who had his own philosophical and biographical reasons for his stance, why the modern scholar must play down their achievements. What is to be lamented is not the presence of well-informed, well-argued denigrations of humanism but rather the absence, in current scholarship, of a clear motive, of a personal existential question, something that might motivate such denigration. What makes this lack of transparency all the more lamentable is that it has enabled the equally subjective Kristellerian 'antihumanism' that has reigned in some Renaissance scholarship to be sold as an uncomfortable truth about humanism and its practitioners that bad-faith scholars (that is, Italian scholars) have long wanted to keep hidden from the reading public. And it is for the sake of transparency that a dialogical encounter with humanists, as well as with one's contemporaries—teachers and colleagues—is being sought most forcefully by some scholars.[25]

Yet while some sort of dialogism would no doubt dispose us favorably toward the affective elements of humanist inquiry and, in old hermeneutical parlance, toward some sort of "fusion of our horizons," it is clear that such an approach would do little to dispel the perceived abomination of 'presentism,' anathema to the most entrenched Renaissance scholars. Nor would the impasse be resolved merely by granting humanism *philosophical* value, as some Italian scholars, detached from the larger context of Ital-

24. See Kenneth Gouwens, "Perceiving the Past: Renaissance Humanism after the 'Cognitive Turn," *American Historical Review* 103, no. 1 (1998): 55–82.

25. For the application of a Rorty-inspired dialogism to Quattrocento humanists, see Christopher S. Celenza, *The Lost Italian Renaissance: Humanists, Historians, and Latin's Legacy* (Baltimore: Johns Hopkins University Press, 2004), 69.

ian philosophy, were seen to do. Taken as a whole, the interpretation developed in Italy affords us this insight: Italian scholarship was not Whiggish, it endowed humanism with a *traditional* value. For it is only within the well-determined internalist horizon offered by culturally embedded traditions that anachronism is impossible. And this is why the current interest in tracing philosophy's lineage, culturally, linguistically, and historically, may represent a welcome turn, advantageous to Renaissance intellectual history.

It is not all that long ago that one might have asked whether Italy, Spain, or Russia—to name some countries that have attracted attention recently—had any 'philosophy' of its own. If their traditions all amounted to forms of modern humanisms—as current opinion has it—then that fact alone would have been reason to exclude them from the philosophy handbook. Perhaps the scholar of Italian philosophy is not equipped to judge whether the "Russian philosophical humanism" of an Alexander Herzen, Boris Cicherin, or Vladimir Soloviev may indeed be genealogically traced back, via the Greek patristic tradition, to the celebration of human dignity of some Italian Renaissance humanists, or whether it makes sense to anthologize together Juan Luis Vives and Miguel de Unamuno, but he can confidently claim strong affinities between the ideas of Renaissance humanists and their self-conscious representatives in modern Italian philosophy.[26]

No one, I suspect, would find it strange that a Gramsci scholar might have something significant to say about Machiavelli; it seems all the more reasonable, then, for a student of Leonardo Bruni to offer an insightful reading of Benedetto Croce, who never tired of reminding us that "all true history is contemporary history."[27] This is why it is worth exploring the Renaissance also (but not exclusively) from the *internalist* or *traditional* vantage that was formed in Italy, and to do so without the residual patriotism of late Italian scholars. This would challenge students of the Italian

26. For an interpretation of Russian philosophy as a 'humanism' with a Renaissance connection, see G. M. Hamburg and Randall A. Poole, eds., *A History of Russian Philosophy: Faith, Reason, and the Defense of Human Dignity* (Cambridge: Cambridge University Press, 2010). For Spanish philosophy, see *Other Voices: Readings in Spanish Philosophy*, ed. John R. Welch (Notre Dame, IN: University of Notre Dame Press, 2010). See also the studies published in the series "Philosophy in Spain" (Value Inquiry Book Series), and the "SUNY Series in Latin American and Iberian Thought and Culture" (SUNY Press).

27. This is in fact the epigraph chosen by the author of a recent, exhaustive, and long overdue study of Bruni's historical writings. See Gary Ianziti, *Writing History in Renaissance Italy: Leonardo Bruni and the Uses of the Past* (Cambridge, MA: Harvard University Press, 2012).

Renaissance to acquire a useful sense of 'Italian' that transcends a mere geographical determination. By realizing that she, too, is an 'Italianist' to some extent, the scholar of Italian Renaissance humanism may come to see that movement not just for its achievements, or just for its failures, but for its unexhausted potential and thus possible endurance. She may come to see the Renaissance not just as an unrealized possibility in modernity (at best), but as a realized one, albeit by approximation.[28] The Renaissance man himself, the humanist, we too often forget was given as much to conversing with the remote past as to addressing posterity. This futural dimension of Renaissance humanism is something we have for a long time now failed to appropriate, to the detriment of our understanding of their past as well as our present.

28. For a compelling interpretation of early modernity as an unrealized possibility, see Nancy S. Struever, *Rhetoric, Modality, Modernity* (Chicago: University of Chicago Press, 2009).

INDEX